Understanding Social Inequality

Second Edition

Understanding Social Inequality

Intersections of Class, Age, Gender, Ethnicity, and Race in Canada

Julie McMullin

OXFORD

UNIVERSITY PRESS

OXFORD

UNIVERSITY PRESS

8 Sampson Mews, Suite 204, Don Mills, Ontario, M3C 0H5
www.oupcanada.com

Oxford University Press is a department of the University of Oxford.
It furthers the University's objective of excellence in research, scholarship,
and education by publishing worldwide in

Oxford   New York

Auckland Cape Town Dar es Salaam Hong Kong Karachi
Kuala Lumpur Madrid Melbourne Mexico City Nairobi
New Delhi Shanghai Taipei Toronto

With offices in

Argentina Austria Brazil Chile Czech Republic France Greece
Guatemala Hungary Italy Japan Poland Portugal Singapore
South Korea Switzerland Thailand Turkey Ukraine Vietnam

Oxford is a trade mark of Oxford University Press
in the UK and in certain other countries

Published in Canada by Oxford University Press

Library and Archives Canada Cataloguing in Publication

McMullin, Julie Ann, 1965–

Understanding social inequality : intersections of class, age, gender,

ethnicity, and race in Canada / Julie McMullin. — 2nd ed.

Includes bibliographical references and index.

ISBN 978-0-19-542778-3

1. Equality—Canada—Textbooks. 2. Social classes—Canada—Textbooks.

3. Canada—Social conditions—1991– —Textbooks. I. Title.

HN110.Z9 S6 2009a   305'.0971   C2009-901306-1

Cover image: © Veer Incorporated/Stockbyte Photography

This book is printed on permanent (acid-free) paper ∞.
Printed and bound in Canada.

5 6 – 13 12

Table of Contents

Preface

When I was five years old I decided that I wanted to visit a friend who lived quite a distance away. When I asked my mother and father if I could go to Susan's house, they said no. When I asked why, they said, 'Because we said so.' At this point I became aware of the fact that I was young and that being young didn't seem fair. I remember this incident because when my parents couldn't give me a good reason for not visiting my friend, I decided to run away from home. Luckily, as I was hitch-hiking down the street with my hand open wide (my version of the one-thumb-up pose), a friendly woman picked me up and told me she'd take me home. I couldn't remember where I lived, so the woman drove me up and down many streets until we found one that I recognized as my own. When I was 16 years old, I worked as a waitress, but I was paid less per hour than my 18-year-old friend. This too seemed unfair.

When I was eight, my younger brothers and I were playing outside on a very hot day. My mother took off my brothers' shirts for relief from the heat. When I started to take off my shirt, my mother told me that girls must keep their shirts on. 'Why?' I asked. 'Because,' she said. I couldn't understand this at all; my brothers and I looked the same. I thought to myself, being a girl isn't fair.

When I went to university I discovered I was a member of the working class. My professors told me that capitalists employed workers at relatively low wages to ensure high levels of profit for themselves. They told me about the social and cultural disadvantages of being from a working-class background. Gradually my university experience began to make some sense. I couldn't figure out why my grades were only average despite my considerable effort. Part of it was that I didn't know how to play the game—that is, how to ask my professors for help, how to use a big library, how to study effectively—and no one I knew could coach me. This seemed unfair.

It wasn't until I was in my late twenties that I discovered I was white. This awareness came as I was reading Patricia Hill Collins's book, *Black Feminist Thought* (1990). Of course, at some level I knew I was white, but I wasn't fully aware of the privilege associated with the colour of my skin until then. This too seemed unfair.

Structures of inequality in Canada are organized along age, class, gender, ethnic, and racial lines. The preceding stories, as trivial as they may seem, show some of the ways in which this occurs. They show that inequality involves power, the ability of individuals or groups to impose their will, with or without resistance, on others. They show that ideology is an important dimension of inequality; that societal beliefs about what is appropriate for people to do on the basis of their sex, class, race, or age creates advantage for some and disadvantage for others. The stories show that inequality is about the distribution of material, cultural, and social resources. And they show that the meaning people attribute to sex, class, race, and age is shaped by experience. These are some of the complex issues that I will consider throughout this book.

Acknowledgements

As I wrote the first edition of this book, I often reflected upon my life as an academic and thought about how privileged I am. Part of what makes my life so privileged is that I am surrounded by wonderful colleagues, family, and friends, to whom I owe much gratitude for the help and support that they graciously give me. When I didn't know how to begin to write this book, James Teevan, Michael Gardiner, Edward Grabb, Victor Marshall, and Ingrid Connidis read my proposal and provided me with valuable feedback. To Ed I am especially grateful because he suggested that I send my proposal to Megan Mueller, then acquisitions editor for Oxford University Press. Megan liked my proposal and pursued the book project with vigour. Although Megan persuaded me to write this manuscript much more like a textbook than I had originally intended, I thank her for her welcome and very positive encouragement along the way.

In writing the first edition of this book and revising it for the second edition, I have been fortunate to work with very talented research assistants. Thanks go to Katherine Pendakis and Erin Demaiter (first edition) and to Catherine Gordon, Jennifer Silcox, and Juyan Wang (second edition) who did literature and data searches, tracked down references, and combed the Internet for stories that could be used in the boxed inserts. I am particularly indebted to Tammy Duerden Comeau, who also worked as a research assistant on both editions of the book. Tammy saved my sanity by agreeing to co-author chapters 10, 11, and 12 with me for the first edition and helped me revise them for the second. Finally, Emily Jovic deserves a very special thank you for her work on the second edition of this book. Emily's industry and resourcefulness helped to make this book what it is, and I will be forever grateful for her help.

Parts of this book have been adapted from some of my previously published work. Chapter 5 is a revised version of my article 'Diversity and the State of Sociological Aging Theory', which appeared in volume 40 of *The Gerontologist*, and bits of chapters 9 were taken from 'Social Class and Inequality', which appeared as chapter 14 in *Sociology: A Canadian Perspective*, edited by Lorne Tepperman and Jim Curtis, and published by Oxford University Press. Other parts were read by my colleagues Tracey Adams and Lorraine Davies, who took the time away from their own work to comment on mine; for that I thank them. My thanks also go to two anonymous reviewers for their helpful suggestions; to Phyllis Wilson, managing editor of Oxford University Press for answering all of my silly questions; to Freya Godard (first edition) and Stephanie Fysh (second edition) for excellent editorial suggestions; and to Sharon Sabourin (first edition) and Jennifer Silcox (second edition) for helping me compile and format my list of references.

As I was writing this book and its second edition, Ingrid Connidis, Lorraine Davies, and I shared many moments of joy, sadness, anger, and frustration owing to both our work and our personal lives. It is impossible to imagine my life without having Ingrid and Lorraine to celebrate the good times with and to lean on when the times are tough. What an honour it is to have them as friends, collaborators, and colleagues!

I am very fortunate to have a wonderful family and two very special friends who serve as an important diversion from my work. Maureen MacPherson and her daughter Claire, are very special people in my life; no more needs to be said and I thank them for that. I am grateful to my father-in-law, Peter Arnold, and step-mother-in law, Irene Say for their babysitting services. Thanks to my brothers Rick and Rob, my sisters-in-law, Louanne Provost and Kristi Adamo, and my nieces and nephews, Malcolm and Makayla, and Kysia for many fun cottage days and for their unending support. My mom and dad made many sacrifices for their children, and for that we cannot thank them enough. Whenever I have needed them they have been there for me. To them I give my love and deepest thanks.

When I was writing the first edition of this book I went to work every day between 6:30 and 7:00 a.m., shut my office door, and wrote until about noon. For the second edition, I would begin working early in the morning but often also needed to work late. For my husband, Scott Arnold, that meant caring for our daughter on his own more than any of us like. For our daughter, Emma McMullin Arnold, that meant asking why I had to work so much. Scott would say, 'Mommy is writing a book', to which Emma would reply, 'Why?' Why indeed. Emma and Scott are the loves of my life, and without them my work, and this book, would be for naught. Thank you both.

For Emma and Scott.

PART I

The first objective of Part I is to discuss and assess theories of class, age, gender, ethnicity, and race that have been used to explain inequality. Of course, it would be impossible to discuss all of the theories; instead, the first part of this book considers theories that have made influential contributions to our understanding of class, age, gender, ethnicity, and race in relation to inequality, especially in Canada. Furthermore, theories that consider the structural nature of these factors are prioritized. However, because structures do not exist outside of the individual interaction that creates them, some symbolic-interactionist perspectives are discussed. In particular, there has been some very good work done on gender and race from a symbolic-interactionist perspective and to ignore it would be remiss.

The second objective of Part I is to examine human agency and the relationship between social structure and human agency. Although most of the work on social inequality is at the macro, structural level, sociologists recognize that to understand social life better, assessments of the intersection between individual agency and social structures are required. However, there is very little agreement regarding the specific relationship between agency and structure.

The third objective of Part I is to integrate ideas from the various perspectives on class, age, gender, ethnicity, race, and human agency into a cohesive conceptual framework. The aim of this exercise is to provide an organizational tool that will enable us to explore social inequality without giving a priori emphasis to any of class, age, gender, ethnicity, or race. In doing so, we will be able to examine how structures of inequality are produced and reproduced through human agency and interaction.

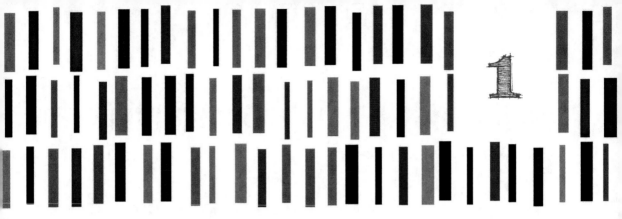

Introduction

This is a book about social inequality, and to begin it describes the life of a woman I know. Anna was born to white, English-speaking parents of British descent in 1915, just after the First World War began; she grew up on a farm in Ontario with her mother, father, and two brothers. Although it was only a small farm, Anna's father and mother worked hard and were able to provide their family with the essentials of life. Anna graduated from high school, which was unusual for a rural girl in that day, and although she had the opportunity to go on to teachers' college, as her mother had done, she decided to marry John Warner, a local man who was seven years her senior. She married well. John's family were well-to-do small business owners, and with their help, Anna and John began their marriage in the late 1930s in relative financial stability. They moved to town and had two daughters, one in 1941 and the other in 1943.

Anna was always a homemaker, and John never had a stable job. His older brother, who was married and childless, inherited their father's business and John worked for him occasionally. John also bought houses, restored them, and sold them for a profit. Money was tight in the Warner household, but no one seemed to want for anything. There was food on the table, they

had paid for the house in full when they bought it, and they had a few good clothes.

In 1970, John died suddenly in a car accident. He was 62 and Anna was 55. John's estate consisted of some savings and his house. His will stipulated that Anna could draw $200 per month from his estate until she either remarried or died, at which time the estate would be divided equally among her daughters. Suddenly, Anna was poor. Her income was well below the qualifying cut-off for social assistance, but she refused to apply for it and was too young for the old age pension. The will stipulated that she could not sell John's house. Aside from a brief stint in business college, Anna had no training, no work experience, and no marketable skill. Besides, at 55 she was unlikely to find work. Her daughter hired her to babysit her grandchildren, and for the next 10 years she made do with the clothes she already owned, shopping at yard sales and eating anything that she could buy for next to nothing in the grocery store—old bread, dinted canned food, and so on. After 10 years Anna turned 65 and began receiving old age security. Though she was still poor, she was no longer destitute. Five years later her sister-in-law, the widow of John's childless brother who had inherited the family business, died, leaving Anna one-third of her quite large estate.

Box 1.1 Measuring Poverty

Low income cut-offs (LICOs)—more commonly known as Canada's 'unofficial' poverty lines—are established by Statistics Canada using data from the Family Expenditure Survey (now known as the Survey of Household Spending). LICOs indicate the level of income at which a family may be living in 'straitened circumstances' because it spends a greater proportion of its income—20 percentage points more—on necessities of food, shelter, and clothing than does the average family of a similar size.

Separate cut-offs are determined for seven sizes of family—from unattached individuals to families of seven or more persons—and for five sizes of communities—from rural areas to urban areas with a population of 500,000+. (See table below.)

Statistics Canada does not refer to the LICOs as poverty lines, although they concede that LICOs identify 'those who are substantially worse off than the average'. And in the absence of official poverty lines, the LICOs are used by many analysts to study the economic security of Canadian families and report on important trends over time.

Statistics Canada's After-Tax Low Income Cutoffs (1992 Base) for 2006

Family Size	Community Size				
	Cities of 500,000+	100,000–499,999	30,000–99,999	Less than 30,000	Rural Areas
1	$17,568	$14,857	$14,671	$13,152	$11,492
2	$21,381	$18,082	$17,857	$16,008	$13,987
3	$26,624	$22,516	$22,236	$19,932	$17,417
4	$33,216	$28,091	$27,741	$24,867	$21,728
5	$37,823	$31,987	$31,590	$28,317	$24,742
6	$41,946	$35,474	$35,034	$31,404	$27,440
7+	$46,070	$38,962	$38,477	$34,491	$30,138

Source: National Council of Welfare (2008).

Source: Canadian Council on Social Development (2007a).

Suddenly, at 70, Anna was better off financially than she had ever been before.

A central aim of this book is to develop a conceptual framework that will help explain the ebb and flow of poverty that Anna experienced throughout her life. We often think of the conditions of inequality, such as poverty (see Box 1.1) or homelessness (see Box 1.2), as inescapable fixed states, and indeed there is ample evidence that for many this is true. However, the description of Anna's life demonstrates that for others, experiences of inequality may be more

Box 1.2 'People Who Slipped thru the Cracks'

Julia Vinograd is a street poet who lives in Berkeley, California. In her poem 'People Who Slipped thru the Cracks', Vinograd presents a conversation with a man living on the streets and trying to stay safe and sane.

People Who Slipped thru the Cracks

I talked to a man who wasn't there.
'Well, that's not exactly fair', he said,
'the cold still gets to me
and I only go invisible when the cops come
and I can't keep it up for long.
It's like holding your breath
to hold light away from your skin,
you just have to know how.
But I'm not like those imaginary people
crazies are always losing arguments with,
at least not yet.'
He sounded a little wistful.

'Would you like that?' I asked.
'Dunno', he shrugged. 'It'd be easier.
I always have to check the back of my knees
I keep leaving them behind.
Not fingerprints, they were easy.'
He held up his hand and the lines spun for me.
Like a child's whirligig in the wind.
'Imaginary people don't get cold
but they're stuck with their crazies.
I suppose I'll just go on like this
till I'm hit by a truck that didn't see me.'
He laughed, the sound low in his throat
like a beaten dog, afraid to come close enough
to a fire.
I wondered how old he'd been before
and how many other people weren't there
And no, it isn't fair.

Source: Vinograd (1997).

complex, involving multiple transitions in and out of relative states of deprivation (see Cooke 2005; L. Davies, McMullin, and Avison 2001; Leisering and Leibfried 1999). As Box 1.3 shows, 7.6 million Canadians experienced poverty for at least one year between 1997 and 2001. Yet in any given year, that number is lower. To understand inequality in this way requires a definition that considers durable patterns of advantage and disadvantage, the capacity of individuals to act toward change, and time.

Defining Social Inequality

Sociologists argue that inequality is *not* caused by innate personality flaws. People are not poor because they are lazy or because they lack motivation or ambition. They are poor because opportunities are distributed differentially in society on the basis of things such as class, age, gender, ethnicity, and race. Sociologists are interested in why social inequality exists, what factors contribute to social inequality, how and through which processes it is maintained, and what changes need to be made to create a more equal society. A unifying assumption in much of the contemporary sociological work on social inequality is that it is a social problem. Few sociologists would argue that we need higher rates of poverty; more hungry, malnourished people in the world; or more disparity in wealth between the rich and the poor. Indeed, many

Box 1.3 Persistence of Poverty

Many people and families move in and out of poverty. Some only stay in poverty for a short period of time while others experience deep and persistent poverty. For children, chronic poverty has a significant effect on both their short-term and long-term developmental outcomes.

Duration of poverty

Some 7.6 million people or 30.7 per cent of the population experienced poverty for at least one year form 1996 through 2001.

Just over 2 million people lived in poverty for only one year.
Nearly 1.5 million people lived in poverty for all six years.

Persistent poverty

Almost 400,000 children lived in poverty for all six years between 1996 and 2001.

About 13 per cent of people with less than a high school education lived in poverty for all six years. Less than two per cent of people with university degrees lived in poverty for all these six years.

Transitions in and out of poverty

The one age group that stands apart is youth aged 18 through 24. This group has a high poverty rate in any given year, but often tends to be poor for only one or two years at a time. They have the highest rate of moving into or out of poverty, almost double that of people aged 25 to 54.

Number of years in poverty[a]

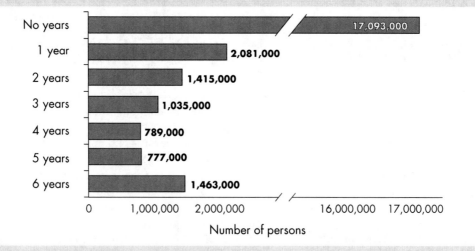

No years — 17,093,000
1 year — 2,081,000
2 years — 1,415,000
3 years — 1,035,000
4 years — 789,000
5 years — 777,000
6 years — 1,463,000

Number of persons

a Excludes persons whose status was not known in each of the six years
Source: National Council of Welfare 2006a..

sociologists search for ways in which problems of inequality can be alleviated and, in doing so, they specify policies and programs that would help to eradicate it. This line of inquiry is as old as the discipline itself, for Karl Marx and Max Weber both considered these issues (see Grabb 2007 for a detailed account).

At a very basic level, inequality is a condition or situation that is not equal. This suggests that *inequality* does not simply refer to differences among individuals but rather reflects differences that matter, differences that result in unfairness and disadvantage for some and privilege for others. In Canada, class, age, gender, race, and ethnicity are differences that matter; hair colour or texture do not. **Social inequality**, as it is usually defined, refers to relatively long-lasting differences among individuals or groups of people that have implications for individual lives, especially 'for the rights or opportunities they exercise and the rewards or privileges they enjoy' (Grabb 2007: 1; see also Pampel 1998). So, for example, compared to people from the middle and upper classes, people who are a part of the working class do not have the same educational opportunities and tend to have worse health. Women and members of racial and ethnic minority groups tend to work in bad jobs while good jobs are reserved for men and members of privileged racial and ethnic groups. And, compared to middle-aged adults, older and younger people suffer longer bouts of unemployment and earn less money. In these examples, class, gender, race, ethnicity, and age are social structures of inequality that result in outcomes that matter. These **structures of inequality** are patterns of advantage and disadvantage that are durable (Tilly 1998) but penetrable.

At an individual level, the experience of inequality refers to the meaning that is attached to unequal life conditions as well as to the things that people do to manage or penetrate the structures of inequality. These issues reflect human agency or the capacity of individuals to interpret their situation and act to change it. However, the experience of inequality is at odds with the experience of privilege by which those in positions of power act to maintain their advantage and reproduce the structures of inequality (see Box 1.4). Furthermore, the experience of inequality must be examined within the context of social time. For our purposes, *social time* refers to issues of generation and the life course. The experience of inequality in this context is understood as a dynamic process that evolves throughout one's life and is influenced by the generation in which one is born.

In short, the perspective developed in this book suggests that to understand social inequality we need a framework that integrates social structure, human agency, and social time. Hence it is important to define each of these terms carefully and to discuss the assumptions made about them in this book.

Defining Social Structure

If we acknowledge the assumptions that sociologists make about social structures in their work, we can understand better why certain research questions are asked in the first place and we can interpret research in context. **Social structure** generally refers to relatively long-lasting, patterned relationships among the elements of society (Abercrombie, Hill, and Turner 2000). Although this broad definition holds true regardless of one's sociological perspective, there is little agreement in sociology about what social structures precisely are and even less agreement about their relationship to individuals. In general, however, there are two dominant views of social structure; one has its intellectual roots in structural functionalism, the other in critical theory.

Following the work of Talcott Parsons, structural functionalists conceive of society as an all-encompassing social structure that may be decomposed into several specialized substructures. Examples of these substructures are the economic, the political, and the educational systems of society. From this point of view, the elements of social structures include social institutions (e.g., work organizations and political institutions) and patterns of social roles (Parsons 1951). Roles are the building blocks of institutions, which are, in turn, the building blocks of society (Parsons 1951; Riley 1971). Structural functionalists tend to overemphasize the degree to which individuals conform to the values and

Box 1.4 Toronto's Tent City Sealed Off, Squatters Ejected

By Wallace Immen and James Rusk

A shantytown that had become a civic embarrassment for Toronto was cleared yesterday in an operation Mayor Mel Lastman praised and poverty activists condemned.

About 100 people looked dishevelled, dazed and angry as security officials hired by the landowners, Home Depot Canada, rousted them from the camp in a rubble-strewn field near the harbour.

Some wept and others yelled in contempt as a police cordon kept them from retrieving their belongings from the makeshift shanties that had been home to some for as long as two years.

'Shame on you. You don't have the right to destroy people' s houses,' one yelled.

Mr Lastman defended the action, telling reporters that the eviction was at Home Depot's, not the city's, initiative.

'Home Depot has the same right as you or I to move trespassers from their land,' he said.

No one has claimed the collection of cobbled shelters that became known as Tent City would ever be a permanent solution to Toronto's lack of housing for the poor. There was no running water and no electricity, and the soil of the former industrial site on the shore of Lake Ontario is tainted with toxic wastes.

The camp had attracted a growing population of homeless men and women who refused to use the city's shelters, many of whom have drug and alcohol addictions or mental illness.

Home Depot Canada had warned the squatters repeatedly that they must leave the crime-plagued, litter-strewn site or be moved out.

First, security officials in flak jackets marched through openings in a chainlink fence that surrounded the site in an industrial zone on the city's eastern harbour. A large number of Toronto police stood by.

When the people and their pets had been moved out, trucks moved in carrying front-end loaders while teams went into action to install more secure chainlink fencing.

Meanwhile squads of workers wearing white coveralls and face masks used chain saws and weed whackers to clear-cut a patrol zone around the entire perimeter of the site.

Police arrested two people, including a woman who was handcuffed and held in a van during the eviction.

The eviction shocked Sam Rosen, who said he was sitting in a latrine when he heard an announcement that everyone had 10 minutes to leave the site.

'They told me if I left peacefully they would arrange food and shelter. But now there's nobody doing anything for us,' said Mr Rosen, who moved into a wooden shack in Tent City this summer after eight years of using shelters. He said he had to leave behind his clothes, pots and pans and books and was allowed to return only to get medication for his diabetes.

Those evicted were handed pink notices that resembled traffic tickets. A box checked on each said they were charged with trespassing and faced a fine of up to $2,000.

. . . . .

After the operation, advocates for the homeless held protests at City Hall and the Tent City site. A press conference Home Depot had planned was cancelled when a large angry group gathered to protest. Some of those evicted and their supporters briefly broke up a meeting of Toronto Council's planning and transportation committee, which was conducting a hearing on the new official plan.

The meeting recessed for about 10 minutes while they shouted slogans such as 'The people's homes cannot be bulldozed,' but resumed after a meeting was arranged between the protesters and the city's chief administrative officer, Shirley Hoy.

Source: Immen and Rusk (2002). Copyright © CTVglobemedia Publishing Inc. All Rights Reserved.

norms established in the social structure and the degree to which society is based on consensus (Layder 1994). Furthermore, structural functionalism de-emphasizes the possibility of conflict in society or the possibility that individual choices are constrained by the forces of social structures.

Stratification approaches to the study of inequality tend to make assumptions about social structures that are in line with structural-functionalist thought (see Grabb 2007: 98–102). According to stratification theory, individuals can be ranked hierarchically according to socially desirable characteristics such as income, education, occupation, status, or prestige. This hierarchical procedure groups individuals together in discrete categories or social strata (J. Turner 1988). Because social structures are thought to comprise patterns of social roles that are acted out by individuals, much of this work focuses on the characteristics of individuals rather than on relationships among people. This led Tilly (1998: 34) to suggest, 'Instead of reducing social behaviour to individual decision-making, social scientists urgently need to study the relational constraints within which all individual action takes place.' The idea of 'relational constraints' points to the importance of adopting a more critical view of social structures when studying inequality.

Critical approaches to studies of inequality and social structures are sometimes informed by Marxist sociology; they assume that social

relations, especially class relations, are the fundamental elements of the social structure. Of course there are many definitions of *social class*, the details of which will be discussed in chapter 2. Put simply, however, *class relations* refers to the relative rights and powers that people have in production processes (Wright 1997). The structural significance of class relations is the manner in which they produce durable and patterned systems of inequality; central to this process is the conflict embedded in class relations. According to these approaches, inequality results largely from class structures, and thus explanations of inequality are reduced to issues of economic subordination. Yet, to understand inequality better, the structures of age, gender, ethnicity, and race must also be considered.

Structures of Inequality

In studies of inequality, scholars make different assumptions about which social structures are important. Some emphasize class, social gerontologists focus on age, feminist researchers concentrate on gender relations, and still others consider race or ethnic relations as the central element of social inequality. This is not to say that there has been no overlap. Many have considered at least two of these dimensions, but few have examined each of them in relation to the others. This book begins with the assumption that researchers should consider all of these factors and that neglecting one or more of them may distort descriptions and explanations of social inequality. Consider, for example, the following discussion of age, social inequality, and social policy.

The importance of age relations in the analysis of social inequality is crucial, particularly in light of population aging. The fact that Canada's population is aging is well known. At the beginning of this century, 5 per cent of the Canadian population was aged 65 and over; by 2001, this had almost doubled, to 12.6 per cent (Beaujot, McQuillan, and Ravanera 2007). Beaujot, McQuillan, and Ravanera (2007) predict that by 2051 the proportion of the population aged 65 and over will more than double again, to 26.4 per cent. The proportion of the population aged 75 and over is growing even faster. Between 1967 and 2006, the percentage of the population in this age group had increased from 2.8 per cent to 6.3 per cent, and by 2051 it is expected to reach 14.7 per cent, more than double the 2006 figure (Beaujot, McQuillan, and Ravanera 2007). Although demographic predictions about the aging of the population vary depending on the assumptions made about future immigration, mortality rates, and fertility rates, most people agree that, barring disaster or unforeseen circumstances, the trend is real and significant.

The economic strain that an aging population may impose on Canada cannot be ignored. However, the crisis ideology that often frames political and media discussions of this topic serves to create a sense of urgency about Canada's financial problems while downplaying the economic needs of disadvantaged people. Thus, the emphasis is placed on Canada's fiscal well-being rather than on that of the over three million Canadians who are poor (Canadian Council on Social Development 2007a).

These discussions also create an environment of competition over the distribution of limited resources between younger and older adults. Although debates over generational equity have been slow to evolve in Canada (V. Marshall, Cook, and Marshall 1993), with health care and pension reform at the anterior of the political agenda, politicians started to make proposals in the 1990s that fuelled such debates. For instance, in 1994 Lloyd Axworthy, then human resources minister of Canada, suggested that a portion of the money spent on old age security should be redirected toward job retraining for young people (*The Globe and Mail*, 9 March 1994, cited in Myles and Street 1995). Indeed, poverty is an important issue among youth. In 2003, the poverty rate for families in which the major income earner was under the age of 25 was 33 per cent, and for unattached individuals that rate was 69.8 per cent (National Council of Welfare 2006b). Yet one might ask why these monies could not also be redirected toward older people who are economically disadvantaged.

Part of the problem with policy directives like the ones mentioned above is that the population is categorized into the old and the young without taking gender, class, race, ethnicity, or further age distinctions into account. Close examinations of poverty rates do not support the simple bifurcation of the population according to age. For instance, the poverty rate among people aged 55 to 64 was 15.4 per cent for men but 16.4 per cent for women. This gender difference was more pronounced among those aged 85 and over, for whom the poverty rate for women was 28.6 per cent compared to 11.7 per cent for men. Marital status also differentially affects the poverty rate for men and women 65 and older. In 2003, the poverty rate for unattached women in this age group was 40.9 per cent and for unattached men of the same age it was 31.6 per cent (National Council of Welfare 2006b).

Poverty rates vary by occupation (which is often used as a measure of social class) among those under age 65. Family heads and unattached individuals employed in managerial occupations have the lowest poverty rate, while those employed in services have the highest. The year of immigration to Canada is another important consideration. For unattached persons who arrived in Canada between 1946 and 1960, the poverty rate in 2003 was 33.0 per cent. For those who came to Canada in the 1960s, 1970s, and 1980s respectively, it was 35.5 per cent, 39.2 per cent, and 57.3 per cent. For those who arrived after 1989, the poverty rate in 2003 was 38.5 per cent. Heads of family had much lower poverty rates, ranging from 8.7 per cent if the immigration years were between 1946 and 1960 to 19.7 per cent for those who immigrated in the 1980s. Interestingly, poverty rates were similar and quite high for immigrants who arrived in Canada after 1989, regardless of whether they were unattached persons or family heads (National Council of Welfare 2006b).

These figures provide useful information about economic inequality in Canada, but they are limiting because they do not take more than two factors into account at the same time. This narrow type of analysis, which is typical of the analyses conducted by governments, is somewhat misleading because only two factors are considered at once. One of the key assumptions that the analysis in this book makes clear is that class, age, gender, ethnicity, and race must each be considered in studies of inequality. Scholars have attempted to integrate two or three of these factors with varying success. The challenge here is to give equal theoretical weight to each of these factors in order to understand social inequality. To do this I will argue that a framework must evolve that considers at least three interconnected processes of social life: production, reproduction, and distribution—processes that are central to the survival of individuals and societies. In chapter 2, I define these processes, and in chapter 7, I elaborate upon how they are structured by the power relations that are assumed to exist among class, age, gender, and ethnic and race relations.

Class, age, gender, ethnicity, and race are conceptualized here as sets of **social relations** that are characterized by power and that are fundamental structures or organizing features of social life (Calasanti 1996; Calasanti and Slevin 2006). Power relations, which are essential to Weberian approaches to inequality, are determined by the ability of individuals in social relationships to impose their will on others regardless of resistance (Weber [1922] 1978). Conceptualizing class, age, gender, ethnicity, and race as social relations characterized by power suggests that conflict is present more often than consensus in these sets of relations (McMullin and Marshall 1999: 308–9). Indeed, a relational understanding of class, age, gender, ethnicity, and race requires an emphasis on 'structured forms of power, organization, direction, and regulation that exist in modern societies and through which ruling groups maintain and reproduce their dominant positions' (Layder 1994: 159; see also D.E. Smith 1987). These structured forms of power are established and reproduced through daily experiences as individuals and groups interact with one another (Grabb 2007; McMullin 2000; D.E. Smith 1987).

These views of social structures and power fall more in line with critical approaches to social inequality than with those found in stratification theory or structural-functionalist approaches. It is generally assumed that social relations are composed of social structures and that conflict and power are fundamental characteristics of these relations. This does not mean that social relationships are in a state of constant conflict or that people engage in daily power struggles. It does suggest, however, that the possibility of conflict and power struggles in these relations is omnipresent. In chapters 2 to 5, I expand on these ideas by providing an overview of the principal theories of social class, gender, race and ethnicity, and age.

Chapter 2 considers sociological debates about the conceptualization of social class. It begins with a discussion of Karl Marx's and Max Weber's theories of social class. It then considers the elaboration and extension of these classics by leading neo-Marxist and neo-Weberian thinkers and briefly discusses stratification approaches to social class. Chapter 2 concludes with a working definition of *social class* that will be used in this book.

Chapter 3 explores the relationship between gender and social inequality. It discusses various feminist approaches to social inequality, including radical feminism and socialist feminism. In particular, this chapter considers how the combination of patriarchy and capitalism leads to gender inequality. The chapter moves on to examine the pervasiveness of gender inequality in daily life; it concludes with a discussion of the approach to gender that will be used in this book.

Chapter 4 examines conceptualizations of race and ethnicity in relation to inequality. Beginning with the contentious debate about whether the term *race* should be used at all, chapter 4 outlines and contrasts various points of view about this issue. Chapter 4 considers the relationship between the concepts of race and ethnicity, although the emphasis is more on the former than the latter. The chapter also examines some theoretical work that has considered the experience of everyday racism. It concludes with a discussion of how race and ethnicity will be conceptualized in this book.

Chapter 5 considers various approaches to the study of age relations and the conceptualization and social construction of age. This chapter discusses how age is a structure of inequality in society and considers the stratification approaches and political economy approaches to age relations in this regard. Chapter 5 concludes with a working definition of *age relations* that will be used in the conceptual framework presented in chapter 7.

Human Agency: Connecting Individuals to Social Structures

Too often, research and theory on inequality concentrate either on structure or on individuals rather than combining the two. The framework in this book highlights the importance of agency and its relationship with social structures. *Agency* expresses the idea that individuals do not passively conform to the circumstances of their lives. Rather, they are active participants in social relationships. They sometimes rebel and sometimes choose to follow the crowd, and so on. In this regard, I make two related assumptions about social life. First, 'social structures do not stand outside of the human, social behaviour that produces them, yet, they nevertheless take on properties that transcend the behaviour of those who construct it'; and second, 'while these properties of durability constrain and limit the agency of the individual they never do so completely' (McMullin and Marshall 2001: 114). In this light, although I assume that analyses of social inequality cannot be reduced to issues of individual motivation, ambition, and the like, individuals nonetheless make choices and decisions that influence their lot in life.

In chapter 6, I discuss how actors are conceptualized in this book by drawing on key works in several different theoretical traditions. In particular, I argue that we need to clarify and specify what is meant by *structuration theory* (Giddens 1984) by focusing on how individuals and structures are connected to one another. Thus, I place emphasis on how individuals negotiate real social structures, the mechanisms through which they do so, the constraints placed on individual negotiation by social structures, and how social structures gradually change or are reproduced through individual negotiations.

Lives in Time and Place

As noted above, *social time* refers to life course and generation issues. The life-course perspective allows us to examine how individuals manage social change and how their past experiences affect their ability to cope. It also considers transitions and trajectories involving school,

Low Income Rate by Heaalth Region 2001 Cencus (2000 Income)

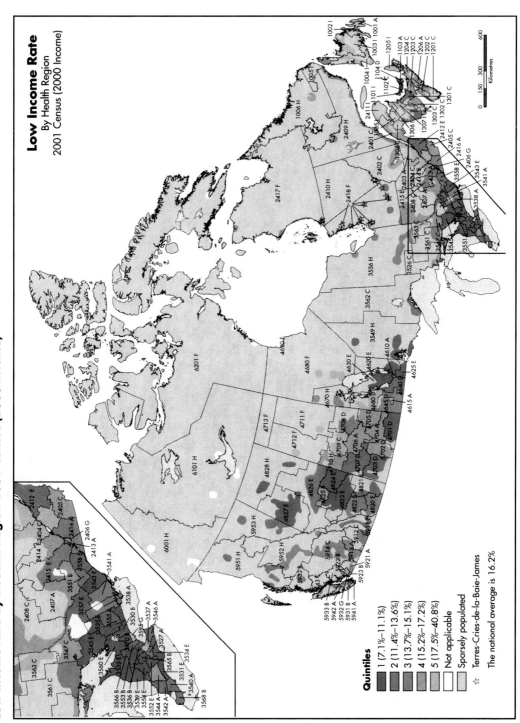

Low Income Rate
By Health Region
2001 Census (2000 Income)

Quintiles
1 (7.1%–11.1%)
2 (11.4%–13.6%)
3 (13.7%–15.1%)
4 (15.2%–17.2%)
5 (17.5%–40.8%)
Not applicable
Sparsely populated
☆ Terres-Cries-de-la-Baie-James
The national average is 16.2%

Source: Statistics Canada (2004).

work, parenthood, retraining, job exit and re-entry, and retirement, and the timing of these, all of which influence inequality. *Generation* reflects the idea that people are born into groups that have meaningful significance because of the social-political culture of a given time in a given place. For instance, individuals who were born between 1910 and 1915 were coming of age during the Depression and their lives have been similarly shaped by that experience. But the effects of the Depression were experienced differently in farming communities in southern Ontario than they were in Vancouver, Montreal, or Toronto. Although theories of social inequality have been slow to recognize the importance of spacial inequality (Lobao, Hooks, and Tickamyer 2007; Tickamyer 2000), patterns of social inequality clearly vary regionally in Canada and around the world. Figure 1.1, for instance, shows, using 2001 Census data, how low income rates vary by health region in Canada. Higher rates of low income are found in the Maritime provinces, in northern Ontario, and in central Saskatchewan than is true in most of southern Ontario and much of Alberta. This is a result of many structural and political factors that will be discussed throughout this book. For now, suffice it to say that where one is born and where one subsequently lives influences life chances and the likelihood of experiencing outcomes of social inequality.

In chapter 7, I discuss the life-course perspective and the concept of generations and integrate them into a conceptual framework of inequality that also considers the intersections between agency and structure. I revisit Anna's life and show how the conceptual framework developed in Part I of this book is a useful tool in explaining the ebbs and flows of social inequality she experienced.

The second part of this book considers empirical research on social inequality in various domains. In sociological research, studies of social inequality often consider the gap in earnings, income, and assets between advantaged and disadvantaged groups of people (Albrecht 2007; L. Casper, McLanahan, and Garfinkel 1994; Grabb 2007; Langton and Pfeffer 1994; Martin and Robinson, 2007; Morris, Bernhardt, and Handcock 1994). To restrict analyses of social inequality to economic issues is limiting because inequality encompasses all differences between people that become embedded in the social structure and that influence social relations (Grabb 2007). Hence, among the other issues that are important to consider when examining social inequality are education, health, and unpaid labour.

Chapters 8 to 12 examine the ways in which the factors considered in the conceptual framework developed in Part I influence outcomes of inequality in families (chapter 8), labour markets (chapter 9), schools (chapter 10), health (chapter 11), and states (chapter 12). These chapters show how class, age, gender, ethnicity, and race affect outcomes of inequality through the processes of production, distribution, and reproduction. Each chapter concludes with policy implications and directions for further research.

Chapter 8 examines inequality in families. In particular it considers how the processes of reproduction are organized in such a way as to assign the unpaid labour responsibility of housework and caring disproportionately to women and, when these tasks are paid for, to women in ethnic and racial minorities. The relationship between these issues and the processes of production and distribution are also explored. Finally, this chapter considers the power imbalances in families and the violence that occurs there.

Chapter 9 outlines aspects of inequality in labour markets. It considers changes in Canada's class structure, the polarization of income, and issues with respect to skill and alienation in the workplace. Each of these points, and related issues that classify jobs as good or bad, are examined. Chapter 9 also examines how the social organization of production processes and the relationship between production, distribution, and reproduction lead to inequality in various working conditions and in the intrinsic and extrinsic rewards of paid work.

Chapter 10 considers educational attainment in Canada. In particular, it examines the barriers to education and how they are influenced by social class, race, ethnicity, gender, and age. It also examines the influence that each of these factors has historically had on educational attainment, how they affect educational attainment today, and the relationship between these factors and the returns on education achieved through labour markets.

Chapter 11 considers inequality in health in Canada. It critiques current theoretical perspectives that focus too little on how health experiences are structured by class, age, gender, ethnicity, and race. It moves on to consider the relationships between class, age, gender, ethnicity, and race and each of mortality, morbidity, mental health, lifestyle behaviour, and access to and use of health care services.

The state is ubiquitous; it weaves through all aspects of our lives and determines who is a deserving recipient of state benefits. The 'deservingness' of Canadians revolves around the concept of citizenship, the central topic of chapter 12.

Chapter 12 discusses unemployment insurance, parental benefits and maternity leave, social welfare, pensions, and old age security and shows how they reproduce existing inequalities and shore up long-standing advantages for privileged groups. Chapter 12 also considers the role that the state plays in social regulation and how the law works to the advantage of some and the disadvantage of others.

Chapter 13 begins by summarizing the main points and findings of this book. Next, it discusses the ways in which research and policy would be improved by adopting an inclusive and integrated approach to inequality, such as the one outlined here. For instance, feminist scholars have long argued that much social policy, although seemingly gender-neutral, is not, and that this has harmful effects for women. I argue that the same can be said for age, ethnicity, and class and that when the four are considered together, the effects are particularly troublesome. The same is true of research. I argue that to understand social inequality, we must understand better how the bases of inequality are connected and how actors negotiate these structures in day-to-day life. Until we do so, our assessments of inequality will remain both biased and inaccurate.

||||||| |||| Questions for Critical Thought ||||| ||||||||| |||| ||||||| | |||||||||||||||| ||

1. Some people argue that social welfare recipients are lazy, that they don't want to work, and that governments should not contribute to the 'cycle of poverty' by providing these people with monetary assistance. These arguments focus on individual attributes in explanations of poverty. Discuss the alternative, structural explanation of poverty.

2. Julia Vinograd's poem 'People Who Slipped thru the Cracks' is reproduced here in Box 1.2. In this poem, Vinograd discusses the invisibility of homelessness. In contrast, the visibility of homelessness is made evident in the newspaper article that discusses the eviction of homeless squatters (see Box 1.4). From a social-structural point of view, how can homelessness be both visible and invisible?

3. What are the structural factors that contributed to the ebb and flow of poverty in Anna's life? How did agency affect the ebb and flow of poverty in Anna's life? What role does social time play in explaining Anna's relative advantages and disadvantages throughout her life?

4. Is it possible to understand and explain poverty in Canada by considering only social class? Why or why not?

5. What are the advantages and disadvantages to stratification approaches to social inequality?

Glossary

Critical approaches, critical theory Approaches to the study of social inequality that (1) assume that social relations are the essential elements of social structures; and (2) assume that social relations are characterized more by conflict than by consensus. Commentators sometimes reserve the term *critical theory* to refer to the work of scholars associated with the Frankfurt school of sociology. These theorists, however, have strong intellectual roots in Marxist and Weberian thought and were certainly not the first to think 'critically' about social life.

Social inequality The existence of advantages and disadvantages in many aspects of social life, including income, education, health, opportunities for paid work, and unpaid work responsibilities. The study of social inequality involves an examination of the factors that contribute to meaningful differences in the rights, resources, and privileges of individuals and groups of people.

Social relations Fundamental elements of the social structure. The term does not refer to interpersonal relations. Rather, social relations are structural and reflect power differences among groups of people. Examples of structured sets of social relations are class, age, gender, ethnic, and race relations.

Social structure A well-established pattern of social organization among the elements of society. Sociologists disagree over which elements of society are of most concern.

Stratification An approach to the study of social inequality that ranks individuals in a hierarchy on the basis of socially desirable characteristics such as income, status, wealth, or occupation. These approaches often draw on structural-functionalist thought and assume that social roles are the principal elements of the social structure.

Structures of inequality Durable patterns of social organization that influence social inequality.

Recommended Readings

Curtis, James E., Edward G. Grabb, and Neil L. Guppy, eds. 2003. *Social Inequality in Canada: Patterns, Problems, and Policies*. 4th edn. Scarborough, ON: Pearson Education Canada. This is *the* information source on various aspects of social inequality in Canada.

Davies, Lorraine, Julie Ann McMullin, and William R. Avison. 2001. *Social Policy, Gender Inequality and Poverty*. Ottawa: Status of Women Canada. A study that uses both qualitative and quantitative data to examine how the social policy changes in Ontario

in the mid-1990s affected poverty among women.

Leisering, Lutz, and Stephan Leibfried. 1999. *Time and Poverty in Western Welfare Studies*. Cambridge: Cambridge University Press. One of the very few books that take a life-course approach to poverty and emphasizes agency in the transitions onto and off of social assistance.

National Council of Welfare. 2000. *Poverty Profile: A Report*. Ottawa: Minister of Works and Government Services Canada. An excellent source book with lots of data on and information about poverty in Canada.

Ross, David P., Katherine J. Scott, and Peter J. Smith. 2000. *The Canadian Fact Book on Poverty*. Ottawa: Canadian Council on Social Development. This book provides a comprehensive overview of poverty in Canada.

||||||| |||| **Relevant Websites** ||||| |||| || |||| || |||| ||||| || ||||||| |||| |||||| || |||||| || |||||| ||

Make Poverty History
www.makepovertyhistory.ca
**The Make Poverty History campaign, symbolized by a white bracelet, started in the United Kingdom and aims to increase awareness of absolute poverty and pressure governments into taking action toward relief. The Canadian chapter calls for urgent and meaningful policy change in four areas: more and better foreign aid, trade justice, cancelling the debts owed by poor countries, and the elimination of child poverty in Canada.

Campaign 2000—End Child and Family Poverty in Canada
www.campaign2000.ca
**Founded in 1991, Campaign 2000 is a cross-Canada movement to eliminate child poverty in Canada. This organization aims to build awareness and support for the 1989 House of Commons resolution to end child poverty by the year 2000. Nearly a decade past the deadline, this group continues to lobby all parties in the federal and provincial governments to enhance social policies relating to child care, social housing, community services, and labour market supports.

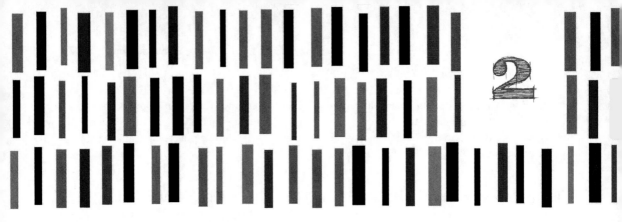

Class and Inequality

When I look back on my childhood I wonder how I survived at all. . . . People everywhere brag and whimper about the woes of their early years, but nothing can compare with the Irish version: the poverty; the shiftless loquacious alcoholic father; the pious defeated mother moaning by the fire; pompous priests; bullying schoolmasters; the English and the terrible things they did to us for eight hundred long years.

—Frank McCourt, *Angela's Ashes*

Introduction

The quotation that opens this chapter is from *Angela's Ashes* (1996), Frank McCourt's touching and funny yet disturbing memoir. Indeed, as one reads this book one wonders how Frank did survive his childhood. He did not have enough clothes to keep him warm, proper shoes for his feet, enough food, or much of a roof over his head. The neighbourhoods where he lived were decrepit and unsanitary. Frank's father was an alcoholic who couldn't hold down a job; his mother was chronically depressed and thought it improper for women to work. In reading this book one also wonders why Frank's parents didn't do something to change their lives—if only Mr McCourt had stopped drinking and held down a job, and if only Mrs McCourt had got a job instead of 'moaning by the fire'. But to blame the McCourts' poverty on an individual's alcoholism or mental health ignores the complex reality of the social structures in which the McCourts were embedded. Class, gender, and ethnic structures in Ireland during McCourt's childhood (the 1930s) were pervasive. English imperialism over Ireland produced and reproduced economic and other hardships for the Irish. Advanced education was essentially unavailable to the poor, women, and minorities. Labour laws did little to protect workers, and as a result, the conditions of the 'working man' were deplorable. And, on top of it all, because Frank's parents came of age during the Depression, paid work was hard to come by.

The conditions of Frank McCourt's childhood may be explained by his class position, which, in turn, negatively affected his family relations, education, and health. The McCourt family was in a state of constant conflict. Frank's mother and father either fought or did not speak, and the children were often ignored and neglected. Education, beyond the state-required minimum, was unattainable. The children had various health difficulties, the most severe of which culminated in the death of Frank's baby sister.

Although the effects of the McCourts' class position are evident, a more complex question is, what accounts for their lower-class position? Is it because they had no money and little food? Is it because Mr McCourt rarely had a job and when he did it was a bad one? Is it because his family had too little power or authority to impose their will on others? Is it because Mr and Mrs McCourt were poorly educated? These are among the questions that are asked by sociologists who study class.

There is considerable disagreement among sociologists over how to conceptualize social class, how many classes there are, the extent to which class conflict exists, and how classes are formed. These points of contention stem from the analysis of social class that was put forth by Karl Marx and then critiqued and expanded upon by Max Weber. Volumes have been written about these issues, and it is certainly beyond the scope of this chapter to engage in all of these debates. Instead, the ensuing discussion will focus on the question of how to conceptualize social class and will venture into other areas of debate only if they are important to the argument being presented.

Marx and Marxism

Marx: Class as a Productive Social Relation

In the *Communist Manifesto*, Marx ([1848] 1983: 203–4) wrote,

> The history of all hitherto existing society is the history of class struggles. Freeman and slave, patrician and plebeian, lord and serf, guild-master and journeyman, in a word, oppressor and oppressed. . . . Our epoch, the epoch of the bourgeoisie, possesses, however, this distinctive feature: It has simplified class antagonisms. Society as a whole is more and more splitting up into two great hostile camps, into two

great classes directly facing each other—bourgeoisie and proletariat.

In these few lines Marx emphasizes the importance of class and class conflict in his work and implies that a distinctive feature of capitalism is the division of society into two central classes. But what is left unsaid here and in much of Marx's work is a precise definition of *class*, of what distinguishes capitalists from workers, and whether the polarization of the classes assumes that the **petite bourgeoisie** and others in the middle classes will become extinct. Ambiguity around these issues has led to various interpretations of who belongs to what class, how many classes there are, and what distinguishes the middle class from the others (Poulantzas 1975; Wright 1985).

Marx began what appears to be a systematic analysis of social classes in the last chapter of volume 3 of *Capital* ([1893–4] 1956: 178–9) but wrote only a few paragraphs before the project was interrupted. In the first two paragraphs Marx writes that the three classes of modern capitalist society are the owners of **labour power**, the owners of capital, and the landowners, but he suggests that this is the pure form of class distinction. 'Intermediate and transitional strata obscure the class boundaries' even in the case of England, where the 'economic structure of modern society is indisputably the most highly and classically developed' (178). However, Marx dismisses strata distinctions as immaterial to his analysis because of the tendency of capitalism to transform labour into wage-labour, the means of production into capital, and landed property into a form that corresponds with the capitalist mode of production.

In the next paragraph of this last chapter of *Capital* ([1893–94] 1956: 178), Marx suggests that the answer to what constitutes a class can be determined by answering the question 'What constitutes wage-labourers, capitalists and landlords as the three great social classes?'

For Marx, the answer to this question does not come from examining differences in income or status. Rather, the key is the means by which people derive their income, that is, from the use of their labour power, capital, or landed property. In the concluding paragraph, Marx's analysis breaks off just as he suggests that this distinction is not complete.

On the basis of the scattered references to class throughout Marx's work, researchers generally agree that, in principle, Marx believed that society is divided into classes that are defined by their relationship to the principal means of production in society (Giddens 1971; Zeitlin 1990). Put simply, in capitalism those who own the means of the production (the **bourgeoisie**) exploit labourers (the **proletariat**), who have no choice but to sell their labour power to (i.e., to work for) the bourgeoisie in order to survive. The emphasis in Marx's work, then, is on relationships between those who appropriate the labour of others to make a profit and those who need to sell their labour power. Hence, Marx is less concerned with how resources are distributed within capitalism and instead emphasizes the relationships among people who engage in economic systems of production.

According to Giddens (1971: 37), Marx developed a dichotomous conception of two antagonistic classes; these classes 'are constituted by the relationship of groupings of individuals to the ownership of private property in the means of production.' Marx recognized that historically, class societies were more complex than this theoretical dichotomy revealed (Giddens 1971; Zeitlin 1990). He was also aware that in bourgeois society, classes were divided into strata and that there were individuals who were located at the margins of the class system, such as lumpenproletariat and a reserve army of labour (Giddens 1971).

Two themes emerge from Marx's work on social class that help us define what is meant by *class* in Marxist sociology:

1. *Social class is based in productive relations.* That is, individuals who engage in production processes have various rights and powers over the resources that are used in production processes (see also Wright 1999).
2. *Social class is conceptualized in relational terms.* Unequal access to the rights and powers associated with productive resources (which by definition is relational) is thought of as class relations (Wright 1999). Ownership of the tools that are required in production processes is a necessary but not sufficient condition for being a member of the bourgeoisie. Thus, the issue is not simply that capitalists own machines, but that they 'deploy those machines in a production process, hire owners of labor power to use them, and appropriate the profits from the use of those machines. A collector of machines is not, by virtue of owning those machines, a capitalist' (Wright 1999: 5).

The preceding discussion also shows that there is a great deal of uncertainty in Marx's work about how many classes there are (although most agree that Marx believed that as capitalism developed, society would become polarized into two central classes) and how we are to conceptualize social classes that do not fall neatly into either the capitalist or working-class categories. Indeed, these are two crucial issues for present-day Marxists.

Neo-Marxism: Issues of Exploitation, Authority, and Credentials

More than two decades ago, Alfred A. Hunter (1981: 12) observed that 'contemporary Marxism is a growing and several-headed beast which defies simple, summary description.' This observation still applies today. Some rather orthodox Marxists, who believe that Marx got it right, stray very little from his ideas and theories (Braverman 1974; Rinehart 2006). Others, while maintaining the basic premises of Marx's work, elaborate, modify, and extend his theories with the belief that social life has changed too much since Marx's time to leave his theories unchanged (Poulantzas 1975; Wright 1997). Into this latter category falls the work of Erik Olin Wright.

Although many neo-Marxists have rethought Marx's ideas of social class, I will focus on Wright's class analysis because it has arguably been the most influential neo-Marxist approach to class issues, at least in North American sociology. Shortly after completing his doctoral dissertation in 1976, Wright began his international research on class structure and class consciousness. Since that time he has written an impressive amount of work on Marxist conceptualizations of social class and has rethought his original ideas of class several times.

Exploitation is a central dimension of Wright's latest approach to class analysis. He argues that the following principles form the basis of class exploitation:

(a) The inverse interdependence principle: The material welfare of one group of people causally depends upon the material deprivations of another.

(b) The exclusion principle: The inverse interdependence in (a) depends upon the exclusion of the exploited from access to certain productive resources, usually backed by property rights.

(c) The appropriation principle: Exclusion generates material advantage to exploiters because it enables them to appropriate the labor effort of the exploited (Wright 1997: 10; Wright 1999: 11).

According to Wright, if the first of these two conditions are met, 'non-exploitative economic oppression' occurs but is not technically a situation of class exploitation per se. Exploitation exists only when all three principles are operating simultaneously.

Let's consider these principles by way of example. Consider gender and social inequality in relation to (a) and (b) above. In Canada, men's material advantage (e.g., better jobs, higher salaries) is causally dependent upon women's material deprivations. This is largely because women are excluded from having access to certain productive resources primarily due to their responsibility for caregiving within families. This idea will become clearer in chapters 3 and 9. But the point here is that this is not class exploitation but rather, in Wright's terms, 'non-exploitative economic oppression'.

According to Wright, exclusion in (b) through ownership and the appropriation of labour are conditions of class-based exploitation. Consider, for instance, the owner of an auto parts manufacturing company. This person owns the factory or the infrastructure that is required to make the auto parts—the building, the machinery, and so on. In order for this owner to make a high income, the business needs to have a significant profit margin. To make a profit (that profit being the owner's material welfare), the owner of the company must pay those who work in the firm less (material deprivation) than what they would make if the profits of the company were split equally among the workers. This is legitimized because the workers do not own the factory and have no property rights in this regard. In other words, owners take the work of those who work at their firm for their own benefit (appropriation) in order to make a profit. The result is class exploitation.

Note the relational component in each of these exploitation principles. Explicit in these statements is the idea that class exploitation involves social interaction and that this interaction is structured by sets of productive social relations that serve to bind exploiter and exploited together (Wright 1997: 12). Following Marx, Wright's conceptualization of class exploitation also highlights the presence in class relations of inherent conflict. Put simply, a profit-driven capitalist system requires that owners want workers to work longer and harder than the workers would freely choose to. Hence, class conflict results not simply over wage levels, but also over how much 'work effort' is expected (Wright 1997: 18).

Turning back to the example of the auto parts manufacturing company owner and workers, it could be that if the owner reduced his profit margins, auto parts workers could work for half a year and make the wages that they currently make. But owners want to make as much money as possible in a profit-driven capitalist system, so they require a worker to work for the entire year earning the half-year salary.

To deal with the problem of 'middle classes', Wright (1997) integrates two key concepts, authority and skill, into his ideas of exploitation. For Wright, authority involves domination and is one axis upon which employees in capitalist systems are differentiated. If owners of capital relinquish control over the production process to managers or supervisors, then people in these positions have various degrees of authority and are able to dominate their subordinates in the workplace. Furthermore, managers and supervisors earn wages that are higher than the costs of producing and reproducing their labour power. Managers and supervisors are in contradictory class locations because (1) they earn higher wages than what makes sense under the logic of capitalism, (2) they help to exploit the workers they manage, and (3) their labour is exploited by the capitalists they work for (Wright 1997: 20–1).

The second axis of class differentiation in Wright's scheme is skill. As is the case with authority, there is an emphasis here on the wage. Because certain skills or credentials are scarce resources in certain labour markets, people who possess them are able to command a wage that is higher than the costs of producing and reproducing their labour power. Furthermore, when workers have control over knowledge or skill

sets, their labour is hard to monitor or control (Wright 1997: 22–3).

In the end, Wright comes up with a class typology that is outlined in Figure 2.1. Here we see that people are cross-classified according to their relation to the means of production, their relation to scarce skills, and their relation to authority. Also included in this scheme is the number of employees. This latter classification category refers to the number of people under the authority of each particular class location. For example, managers tend to have many employees over whom they have authority and dominance, whereas non-managers have authority over no one. Owners are separated from employees in this scheme. Owners are differentiated from one another only on the basis of whether they have employees and, if so, how many. Hence, owners who have only a few employees are thought to be different from both those who have many and those who have none. Employees, on the other hand, are differentiated on the basis of skills, authority, and the number of employees 'beneath' them. Expert managers, then, have high levels of authority and high levels of skill and tend to supervise many employees. They stand in most stark contrast to non-skilled workers, who have no authority and no skill and who supervise no other employees.

In this typology, the cells do not represent classes as such; rather, they refer to class locations within the capitalist class structure. The distinction here is a subtle but important one that allows Wright to cover all his bases. Unlike an earlier version of this framework, in which he refers to the various groupings in this model as classes (Wright 1985), in his most recent work Wright makes it clear that these cells represent class locations within an overriding framework of class relations.[1] In doing this, Wright can stay true to a Marxist version of class relations in which exploitation is at the core while at the same time identifying contradictory places within class relations that individuals occupy.

Figure 2.1: Wright's Class Typology

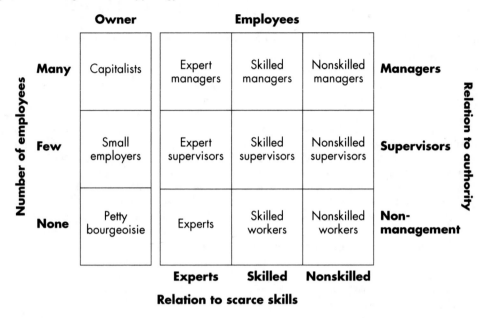

Source: Wright (1997: 25).

Again, let's turn back to the auto parts manufacturing company's owner and workers. The owner would fall in either the 'capitalists' or the 'small employers' cell of Wright's framework, while the worker could fall into any of the 'employees' categories. Auto parts manufacturing companies have many employees, and occupations range from 'expert managers' (head of the information technology department) to 'non-skilled workers' (assembly-line workers). These workers are differentiated in terms of their class location: some have more authority and control in the workplace than others. But, according to Wright, regardless of the specific cell in which an employee is located, an exploitative, class-based relation exists between that employee and the employer.

Wallace Clement and John Myles also take a Marxist approach to the study of social class. Through their work on Eric Olin Wright's Comparative Project on Class Structure and Class Consciousness, Clement and Myles (1994) developed a four-category class-classification scheme. As Table 2.1 shows, the capitalist-executive class controls both the labour power of others and the

Table 2.1 Clement and Myles's Class Typology

Command Means of Production	Command Labour Power of Others	
	Yes	**No**
Yes	Capitalist-executive	Old middle class
No	New middle class	Working class

Source: Clement and Myles (1994: 16). Reprinted by permission of McGill-Queen's University Press.

Box 2.1 Criteria for Operationalizing Class Categories in the Clement and Myles Typology

Capitalist-Executive   (A) If self-employed or has paid employees and number of permanent employees is three or more;

OR   (B-1) respondents make decisions about such things as the products or services delivered, the total number of people employed, budgets, and so forth; and are personally involved in decisions to increase or decrease the total number of people employed in the place where they work; or about policy decisions to change significantly the products, programs, or services delivered; or the policy concerning the routine pace of work or the amount of work performed in the work place as a whole; or about policy decisions to significantly change the basic methods or procedures of work used in a major part of the workplace; or deciding the overall size of the budget; or in general policy decisions abut the distribution of funds within the overall budget of the workplace;

AND   (B-2) if for any of these, the respondents make the actual decisions themselves or make the decisions as voting member of a group;

AND   (B-3) respondents are located within the organization as top, upper, or middle managers.

New Middle Class   (A) If, as an official part of their main jobs, the respondents supervise the work of other employees; and decide how fast they work, how long they work, or how much work they have to get done; or grant a pay raise or promotion to a subordinate; or prevent a subordinate from getting a pay raise or promotion because of poor work or misbehaviour; or fire or temporarily suspend a subordinate; or issue a formal warning to a subordinate;

OR   (B) if, as in B-1 above, and for any of B-1, the respondents make the actual decisions, as voting members of group. Or make the decisions subject to approval.

Old Middle Class   If self-employed and not more than two people are employed by the respondents on a permanent basis.

Working Class   If employed by someone else or work without pay and not included above.

Note: The logic of this operationalization requires that each set of requirements occur in succession, so if the requirements for capitalist-executive are met, the person is not eligible for the new middle class, and those meeting these conditions are not eligible for the old middle class and, finally, the working class.

Source: Clement and Myles (1994: 257–8). Reprinted by permission of McGill-Queen's University Press.

means of production. The 'old' middle class—the petite bourgeoisie in Marxist terminology and in Wright's classification—commands the means of production but not the labour power of others (e.g., a local butcher owns her shop and employs one or two people). The 'new' middle class controls the labour power of others but not the means of production. The advantage of this approach lies in its parsimony. It accurately explains the relations of ruling in Canada while at the same time eliminating the unnecessary and often tedious class-location distinctions of Wright's approach. Notably, however, embedded within the seeming simplicity of Clement and Myles's typology is a complex set of criteria for inclusion and exclusion in the various cells. Box 2.1 outlines these criteria.

Weber and the Neo-Weberians

Weber: Class, Power, and Distribution

Some scholars argue that Max Weber's assessment of social class is in fundamental opposition to that of Marx (Parsons 1929; J. Turner and Beeghley 1981). Others suggest that it is more likely that Weber attempted to develop Marx's thought—agreeing with some of his points, disagreeing with others, and elaborating upon his ideas in a way that corresponded to recent developments in the capitalist system (Zeitlin 1990). Indeed, some of the concepts that are central to Marx's analysis—class consciousness, class conflict, and class interest—are found in Weber's writing as well (Zeitlin 1990). Weber also agrees with Marx regarding the importance of property ownership in the assessment of class (Giddens 1971; Zeitlin 1990).

For Weber, classes are groups of people who share a common class situation. In *Economy and Society*, Weber defines *class situation* as the

> typical chances of material provision, external position, and personal destiny in life which depend on the degree and nature of the power, or lack of power, to dispose of goods or qualifications for employment and the ways in which, within a given economic order, such goods or qualifications for employment can be utilised as a source of income or revenue. ([1922] 1978: 57)

Weber argued that there are three types of classes: property classes, income classes, and social classes. A *property class* is one in which differences in property ownership determine the class situation. An *income class* is one in which 'the chances of utilising goods or services on the market determines the class situation' (Weber [1922] 1978: 57). A *social class* is a combination of the class situations created by property and income, and one where mobility between the social classes is a typical occurrence either within an individual lifetime or over successive generations.

Weber identified four main social classes: (1) the working class as a whole; (2) the petite bourgeoisie; (3) propertyless intellectuals, technicians, commercial workers, and officials who are possibly different from one another socially, depending on the cost of their training; and (4) classes privileged by property or education. Although these social-class distinctions are similar to those proposed by Marx (except in the emphasis on education and on the cost of training), Weber employs a different method in assigning groups of individuals to each class. For Weber, the emphasis is on the distribution of resources (see the definition of class situation above), whereas Marx is mainly concerned with the social relations of production.

Parties and **status groups** are other pillars of social power according to Weber. By *parties*, Weber means voluntary associations that organize for the collective pursuit of interests, such as political parties or lobbying groups. A *status group* consists of a number of individuals who share a common status situation. Although members of a particular class may not be aware of their common situation, members of a status group usually are (Giddens 1971; Grabb 2007). Classes, status groups, and parties sometimes overlap, but not always. Thus, each is analytically distinct and central to any class analysis (Weber [1922] 1978; see also Giddens 1971; Grabb 2007).

Weber's assessment of status groups and parties and the analytical importance that he attaches to these multiple bases of **power** point to the fundamental difference between his analysis of class and Marx's. According to Weber, although status groups and parties are analytically distinct from classes, they are central to class analysis (Giddens 1971; Grabb 2007). For Weber ([1922] 1978), *status situations*, although related to class situations, are distinct from them and refer to the social status, prestige, and esteem that are associated with a social position. Unlike Marx, who believed that power is held by those who own the means of production, Weber felt that certain people in high-status groups derive power by virtue of their social position rather than through economic control.

The analytical importance that Weber attaches to the concept of power is evident in the preceding discussion. Unlike Marx, who believed that power relations are structural and cannot be separated from class relations, Weber ([1922] 1978: 38) defines *power* as 'every possibility within a social relationship of imposing one's own will, even against opposition, without regard to the basis of this possibility'. Weber clarified this broad definition of power by introducing the concept of domination. Domination exists in social relationships when one person (or group) comes to expect that their orders will be followed by the other person (or group) (Weber [1922] 1978: 38–9).

Domination is a specific power relation in which 'regular patterns of inequality are established whereby the subordinate group (or individual) accepts that position in a sustained arrangement, obeying the commands of the dominant group (or individual)' (Grabb 2007: 56). Weber states that although relations of domination are usually at work in associations or in cases where an individual has an executive staff, other non-economic situations are also characteristic of relations of domination. One of the examples Weber gives is that the head of the household exercises domination over the members of the household 'even though he does not have an executive staff' (Weber [1922] 1978: 39).

Although Weber recognized that subordinate groups or persons accept domination for a host of reasons, his analysis focuses on three pure types of legitimate domination, or *authority.* *Traditional authority* is a dominating relationship based on the acceptance that those in charge should be in charge because of traditional right. Individuals might also be in dominant relationships based on *legal authority*, in which case subordinates accept the legal right of those in charge. Finally, *charismatic authority* refers to the situation in which leaders have control of others because of the leaders' appeal or charm (Weber [1922] 1978).

Three themes in Weber's concept of class separate his work from that of Marx. First, Weber's insistence that classes, class situations, parties, and status groups must all be considered if we are to understand the class structures of societies differs significantly from Marx's view. Second, and related to the first, is Weber's emphasis on power. Marx felt that power was derived from an economic base and was largely structural. Weber, on the other hand, saw power as multifaceted, derivable from many sources, and with both structural and individual dimensions. And third, rather than adopting the social-relational approach to class in Marxist sociology, Weber focuses far more on distributional issues. For Weber, people's ability to gain access to scarce resources such as income and education is central to any analysis of class. Indeed, these three central themes of Weber's work lie at the heart of its appeal.

Neo-Weberian Approaches: Frank Parkin

In the tradition of Weber, power is a central component of Frank Parkin's approach to class analysis. But Parkin takes a rather different view of power than Weber, and indeed suggests that Weber's definition is unhelpful (Parkin 1979). Instead, Parkin discusses power in relation to the idea of social closure. *Social closure*, as discussed by Weber, refers to processes through which collectivities restrict access to resources and opportunities to those inside the group. According to Parkin, classes should not be defined in relation to the means of production, but rather in relation to their modes of social closure.

Parkin argues that the classes of the bourgeoisie are formed and continue through two means of social closure, one involving property and the other involving credentials. The issue for property ownership is that the exclusionary powers of certain groups determine the basis of whether individuals own property that can be used in production processes. The legal, exclusionary property rights that come with this ownership are critical for class analysis to the extent that they have 'important consequences for the life chances and social condition of the excluded' (Parkin 1979: 53). The crucial issue in this exclusionary process of social closure is not exploitation, but whether property owners can legally exclude people from making a living. Hence, the role of the state in legitimizing social closure is central to Parkin's framework.

The second means through which social closure is invoked is *credentialism*, which is the 'inflated use of educational certificates as a means of monitoring entry to key positions in the division of labour' (Parkin 1979: 54). Credentialism allows high-status occupations to limit entrance to their ranks by making the credentials for entrance into the occupation increasingly onerous. Professional occupations thereby limit the supply of their labour, thus heightening its value and status. Credentialism also masks variations in skill among the members of a professional group and in that way protects the least skilled among them from the sanctions that might otherwise come their way (less pay, demotion, firing). As is the case with exclusion on the basis of capital ownership, the state is important in legitimizing the exclusionary practices of credentialism. States legitimize exclusionary strategies by issuing professional licences only to members of professional organizations who have achieved the credentials required by the professional organization.

Recall that Parkin argues that social classes should be defined in relation to the modes of social closure. The two central modes of closure

for Parkin are exclusion on the basis of property and exclusion on the basis of credentials. Both modes of closure use exclusionary rules to confer rights and privileges on some while denying those rights and privileges to others. Hence, according to Parkin, 'the dominant class under modern capitalism can be thought of as comprising those who possess or control productive capital and those who possess a legal monopoly of professional services' (1979: 58).

That said of the dominant classes, the question that remains is how Parkin deals with subordinate class boundaries. If exclusionary practices are power tactics that dominant classes use to maintain social closure, then, for Parkin, *usurpation strategies* are countervailing uses of power mobilized by subordinate classes to gain access to scarce resources or to achieve 'distributive justice' (1979: 75). Members of subordinate classes have no legal property rights and have limited credentials. However, subordinate classes vary in the extent to which they can activate usurpation strategies. For instance, if a group of workers is unionized, those workers have considerably more usurpation power by which to achieve distributive justice than do workers who are not unionized (Parkin 1979). The middle classes, for Parkin, consist of persons who tend not to have legal property rights but who do have certain credentials. There is also variation among semi-professionals in the power they have to encroach on the privileges of professional groups. Such power depends, in large part, upon how successful a semi-professional group has been in gaining legitimate authority in the eyes of the state and of group members' clients. Semi-professionals are not, however, completely aligned with the 'working class', for they use usurpation strategies to gain privilege and exclusionary strategies to maintain the privilege they already have. Parkin (1979) refers to this as a *dual-closure strategy*.

Several well-founded criticisms are levied against Parkin for his emphasis on the legal bases of power to the neglect of other dimensions of power (see Grabb 2007). But what is particularly problematic about Parkin's approach is his use of the term *power* to refer to the strategies that subordinate classes use for gaining access to scarce resources and privileges. This lies at the heart of Parkin's argument regarding class boundaries. Notably, Parkin sees usurpation as a mechanism of closure that is less powerful than exclusion, but does it really make sense to discuss this as an issue of power? I think not. Power is held by dominant groups in society and is structural in form. Individuals may draw on the power they have by virtue of being a member of a dominant group in order to get what they want. However, as Parkin points out, power is much more than the ability of an individual to exercise his or her will over someone else. To be sure, subordinate groups act; they struggle to get higher wages, more prestige, or more status. They mobilize themselves and lobby to do so. But do they use power in doing so? No. At best, to gain distributive justice they use mechanisms such as resistance, influence, or persuasion.

The idea that subordinate groups do not hold real power is worth pursuing here. Parkin is certainly not the only scholar who argues that subordinate groups or individuals have power (see Giddens 1979). More radical thinkers such as Wright (1997) argue that workers have power because they control their labour and can therefore use that control to struggle for their interests. Yet although it is true that, collectively, workers can generate opposition to capital because they control their labour, to suggest that they are in a position of power as a result is misplaced. Further, although it is also true that a worker could choose not to work, the alternative to working for a wage is rather bleak in contemporary capitalism. Is this then a true choice that confers power upon the labourer? Imagine this rather extreme analogy: A man is being held at gunpoint in a secluded area by another man, who is demanding that the first man hand

over his wallet. The victim in this case has two choices—he can either hand over the wallet or not. Suppose he chooses not to and is shot. The victim acted, he made a choice, and he used his agency; but did he use power in this situation? No. This analogy demonstrates that clear distinctions need to be made between power and agency, and this is true even in situations that are far less extreme.

Ironically, though, the strength of Parkin's approach lies in this criticism of his concept of power. In Parkin's model, the importance of human action, both collective and individual, is evident. Hence, his model effectively considers the intersection of individual action and social structure, and on this score it is an improvement over most theoretical and empirical accounts of social inequality.

Neo-Weberian Approaches: Edward Grabb

In Edward Grabb's work on social inequality and social class, power is of central importance. According to Grabb (2007: 211), power is the 'differential capacity to command resources, which gives rise to structured asymmetric relations of domination and subordination among social actors'. In an elaborate scheme of power, domination, and social inequality, Grabb (2007: 211) suggests that there are three means of power—control of material resources, control of people, and control of ideas—that correspond primarily with economic structures, political structures, and ideological structures respectively (see Figure 2.2). These structures of power are crossed by class and non-class bases of inequality that represent the 'human content' of power relations. Hence, like Parkin, Grabb should be commended for rightly emphasizing the dualism between structure and human agency.

Grabb defines *class* on the basis of ownership, education, and occupation. For Grabb, these factors represent a synthesis of the key concepts in class analysis discussed by other influential

Figure 2.2: Grabb's Conceptual Framework

The Major Means of Powers, Structures of Domination, and Bases for Social Inequality

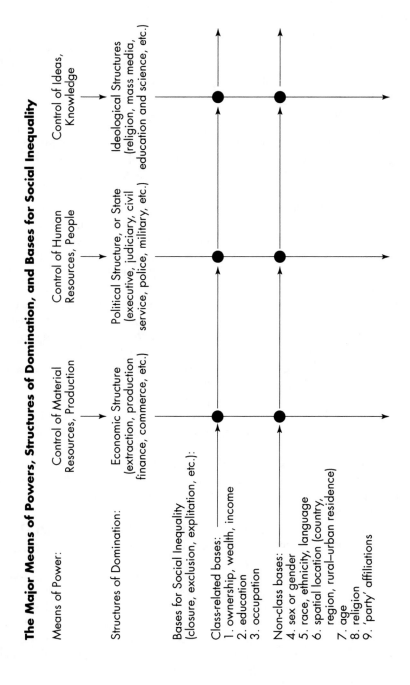

Means of Power:

| Control of Material Resources, Production | Control of Human Resources, People | Control of Ideas, Knowledge |

Structures of Domination:

Economic Structure (extraction, production finance, commerce, etc.)

Political Structure, or State (executive, judiciary, civil service, police, military, etc.)

Ideological Structures (religion, mass media, education and science, etc.)

Bases for Social Inequality (closure, exclusion, explitation, etc.):

Class-related bases:
1. ownership, wealth, income
2. education
3. occupation

Non-class bases:
4. sex or gender
5. race, ethnicity, language
6. spatial location (country, region, rural–urban residence)
7. age
8. religion
9. 'party' affiliations

Source: Grabb (2007: 212).

class analysts, such as Wright and Parkin. *Ownership* includes ownership of property but also material possessions and income. *Education* comprises credentials and knowledge. *Occupation* involves distinctions such as manual versus non-manual labour but also includes issues of skill. Grabb (2007: 214–15) suggests that although classes should not be considered in static terms because they vary over time and space (i.e., historically and across different regions and countries), there tend to be three main class categories in modern capitalist systems: an upper class, a heterogeneous central category, and a working class. Like Wright and Parkin, Grabb defines the working class as those who do not own capital, have no special skills or credentials, and sell their labour to make a living. The upper class consists mostly of the capital owners, although persons with significant political or ideological power fall into this category as well. The middle class is a diverse group that may or may not have limited ownership but that is distinguishable from the working class mostly on the basis of credentials.

According to Grabb, the means of power (economic, political, and ideological) are differentially distributed along class lines. Of course, people in the upper classes control the means of material production or the economic structure by virtue of their ownership of the means of production. The middle classes may have some economic power depending on whether their incomes are sufficient to purchase desirable consumer goods and to the extent that their occupation confers upon them a certain amount of authority or autonomy. And the working classes tend not to have economic power at all. In Grabb's scheme, class also crosses political and ideological structures of power. Hence, those in the upper class, by virtue of their capital, high levels of education, and good occupations, tend to control political and ideological institutions such as the judiciary and educational systems. Those in the working class tend not to have ideological or political power, and those in the

middle class vary in the extent to which they hold such power, again on the basis of class-related factors.

Assuming that social inequality is a multi-faceted phenomenon that involves many bases of inequality (as most researchers and theorists now acknowledge), then both Grabb's and Parkin's work represents significant conceptual contributions to understanding inequality. Why? Because the emphasis in both frameworks is on power, not class. The inherent problem with theories of inequality that begin with class is that other bases of inequality, such as gender, race, ethnicity, and age, carry less theoretical significance. Notably, in both Grabb's and Parkin's work, class takes a certain primacy, but there is nonetheless room for conceptual development in each approach across the other significant bases of social inequality.

There is one minor point in Grabb's framework that needs to be addressed: the underlying tendency in his approach toward a reification of the structures of power. According to Grabb, the organizations and collectivities that compose the power structures operate in complex ways, and 'together they largely determine the nature and extent of inequality in society, what the social bases for inequality will be and how much they will matter' (2007: 213). Thus, although Grabb discusses a 'dualistic view of power', it is unclear whether or how people act within power structures to either resist or maintain them (see chapter 6 for an in-depth discussion of agency).

Globalization and the Death of Social Class

The quite recent insurgence of globalization in sociological discourse is interesting because *globalization* is 'a new word for an old process': 'the integration of the global economy that began in earnest with the launch of the European colonial era five centuries ago' (Ellwood 2001: 12). However, the recent accelerated pace of globalization has been fuelled by rapid technological change, an unprecedented number of free trade agreements, and the powerful rise of multinational corporations; this has led to heightened concerns over the impact of globalization on nation-states and individuals (Ellwood 2001).

According to Ulrich Beck, *globalization* refers to the convergence of economic, political, cultural, and social changes emergent in the 'second modernity' (Beck 2000; Beck, Bonss, and Lau 2003). A key aspect of these changes is that boundaries that were rigid and fixed in the first modernity now prove to be malleable (Beck, Bonss, and Lau 2003). The globalization of labour is evident in, for instance, the 'social despatialization of work and production' (Beck 2000: 73). Individualization, gender revolution, underemployment, and global risks lead, within the context of globalization, to a 'new kind of society' that is organized according to the rules of a 'new kind of capitalism' and a 'new kind of economy' (Beck 1999: 2). All of this, in turn, means that risks in employment or other aspects of social life are extending their reach to groups that have previously been sheltered from them (Beck 1999).

There is some merit to Beck's argument. As Box 2.2 shows, fears over job losses in Canada

Box 2.2: Is Globalization Killing the American Middle Class?

By John Ibbitson

Alan Greenspan and Naomi Klein see things the same way.

The front half of the former chairman of the Federal Reserve Board's bestselling memoirs has been receiving plenty of attention, especially the parts in which he trashes George W. Bush's spendthrift ways. But the back half of *The Age of Turbulence* is more compelling. In its dry but lucid pages, he sounds the same alarm that social activists have been raising for years.

Mr Greenspan embraces the argument that moving manufacturing offshore to low-wage countries has depressed wages at home. The result is a worsening gap in incomes between the wealthy and the working class and increasing danger of social tensions and economic decline.

Ultimately, he believes, globalized trade is good for the planet, because living standards are steadily rising in the developing world, and equilibrium will be reached in a few decades. (This writer recalls a conference where one respectable speaker maintained that the Bush administration was spending so much on HIV-AIDS in Africa

because the business class knew that, in 50 years, it would be the only place left with cheap labour.)

But it also means that, in the US and Canada, semi-skilled workers are struggling, while the highly skilled elites on whom the entire economy now rests are making a killing.

This far, Mr Greenspan and Ms Klein, author of the recently released *The Shock Doctrine* (it blames capitalism for most of the ills of the world) walk together. But no farther.

The solution to the wage gap, Mr Greenspan asserts, is not to increase taxes on the rich and raise tariffs, as Ms Klein and her allies favour, because that would damage the economy and lead to greater long-term misery. Instead, the US needs to increase the pool of skilled workers, which would reduce demand for their services and depress their wages, even as the wages of those entering the pool increased.

But that's not happening, Mr Greenspan believes, because America's public schools are failing to properly teach math and science. No math, no skills. Simple as that.

Why are they failing? Because teachers' unions depress math teachers' salaries. Forty per cent of math teachers in American high schools did not major or minor in math while at university. That makes most of them unfit to teach math. But schools can't recruit qualified math teachers, because the unions insist that teachers be paid according to seniority rather than skill.

'Since the financial opportunities for experts in math or science outside teaching are vast, and for English literature teachers outside of teaching limited, math teachers are likely to be a cut below the average teaching professional at the same pay grade,' Mr Greenspan writes. 'Teaching math is likely to be left to those who are unable to claim the more lucrative jobs. This is far less true of English literature or history teachers.'

The solution is obvious: Allow market forces to dictate the wages of teachers. Math and science teachers will make six figures; English and history teachers will have to take weekend jobs to make ends meet. Students will get a better education, the labour pool's quality will rise, the wage gap will shrink and the expanded base of knowledge workers will stimulate growth.

But politics being politics, and unions being unions, this is unlikely to happen overnight. As a quicker fix, Mr Greenspan advocates dropping the tariff on labour.

If the market demands shoes but government bans shoe imports, shoe manufacturers get rich, but everyone has to pay more for shoes. If Microsoft needs software engineers but the federal government limits immigration, then software engineers earn fabulous salaries, but we all pay more for software, less software gets developed, and productivity and the economy suffer.

That's why immigration policies should be wide open to skilled labour. Canada's record on this is better than most, but the Americans, because of disputes over illegal Latino immigration, can't agree on immigration reform. Unless the next president is able to craft consensus, the American economy will pay the price.

Mr Greenspan's analysis reminds us that the left-right dichotomy is often futile. Smart thinking seeks to analyze problems devoid of ideological blinkers, borrowing from all parts of the political spectrum to build an analysis grounded in reality rather than dialectic.

Naomi Klein needs to read Alan Greenspan more than Alan Greenspan needs to read Naomi Klein.

and the United States as a result of globalization are reaching beyond the manufacturing sector to semi-skilled work. But, for Beck and others, the rise in global economic capitalism means that social class, which has traditionally been assessed according to national boundaries, is dead, or at least of less significance today than in the past (Beck 1992; Beck and Beck-Gernsheim 2002; see also Pakulski and Waters 1996).

Although it is true that, with increases in globalization, risk is being distributed to other classes and groups (see Beck 1992), alienation and exploitation are still organization features of capitalism and the working class is still at *heightened* risk of unemployment and poverty, pointing to the continued importance and relevance of social class (Goldthorpe 2002). Indeed, some argue that Canada and the United States are two of the most 'classist' countries in the world (see Box 2.3).

A Note on Stratification Approaches

It would be remiss to discuss social inequality without paying heed to social stratification research. Indeed, stratification approaches to

Box 2.3 The New Class Wars

By Sarah Hampson

This may feel like an intrusion upon your dearly held beliefs—which in itself is rather rude, so forgive me—but here's the truth.

Class snobbery is not an antique notion that only exists in Britain. Judgment of others, based on class, is terribly common.

And it's a two-way street—the upper-class types look down upon the lower; and the lower look askance at those who seem to hold themselves above the rest.

Conrad Black's lawyers are only too aware of the class divide as the jury deliberates in Chicago, where the former press baron is on trial for allegedly looting more than $60-million (US) from investors.

'He is different from you and me,' lawyer Edward Greenspan said of his client. 'He's a rich man.' He urged jurors not to convict Lord Black because of 'his wealth, his lifestyle or his vocabulary'.

Canada and the United States are 'two of the most classist countries in the world,' says Shirley Steinberg, a cultural theorist and associate professor at McGill University whose book, *Cutting Class: Social Class and Education*, co-authored with Joe Kincheloe, was published this year.

'Absolutely, we have class and discrimination in this country,' she says. 'But in Canada, it's harder to spot. We give it plausible deniability. You can act as though it doesn't exist. And if you deny that which exists, no one can get you on it. We who talk the loudest about what we don't have, have it.'

Canadians shouldn't feel smug about policies of multiculturalism, she notes. 'That's tokenistic, liberal drivel. Besides, who wants to be tolerated? I'd rather be liked.'

Maritimers are second-class citizens compared to central Canadians, she says by way of an example. 'They're not seen as professionals, generally. Their trades are fishing and farming and manufacturing.' (Any fan of *Trailer Park Boys*, a TV series from the Maritimes, knows class distinctions can even be fodder for comedy.)

Ethnic and even regional accents can spur discrimination, Ms Steinberg adds. Political leaders are subjected to the same silent class judgment, she points out. 'Jean Chrétien had low-class irritating mannerisms as opposed to Pierre Elliott Trudeau.'

But more insidious than its denial is the fact that the rules of snobbery continually evolve. 'Class distinction always reinvents itself,' she notes.

Acquisition of high class was pursued by the first immigrants to Canada. They did what Lewis Lapham said of early settlers in America in *Money and Class in America*. They 'assigned spiritual meaning to the texts of money'.

In Montreal, the centre of Anglo economy in the 19th century, a class rose up that was commonly referred to as 'the merchant princes'. They had a society photographer, William Notman. They had debutante balls as part of the St Andrew's Society.

In a souvenir book about the Montreal Board of Trade in 1893, the text made Anglo-Saxon commerce seem like a noble cause. 'The flag has acknowledged commerce as mistress and followed humbly in her wake,' it intoned.

Along with the railway barons, bankers and financiers, the leather-bound book documented the leaders in the trades, puffing up each man (and there were only men, of course) to render him as important as the next. 'There is no surer criterion, no more accurate judge, of the progress of a country in the higher and more artistic ranges of civilization than is afforded by the condition and expansion of her dry goods trade,' the script heralded.

But that notion seems rather quaint in modern times, when being 'in trade' is deemed a low-class pursuit. Why else did the Eatons distance themselves from, and ultimately lose, the department store that bore their name? It was beneath them to be thought of as shopkeepers.

Even the WASP card is no longer a social passport. 'I would have to say that the old Anglo brand names do not really carry any class clout,' says a Montreal native of some notable pedigree, who only spoke on condition of anonymity (as befits the rule of not talking openly about fellow members of one's socio-economic tribe).

'It is always a bit of a surprise to come across a Birks, Molson or McConnell with a continued strong presence in the Montreal milieu, business or otherwise, and so those that are "still here" are so because they have, on the whole, distinguished themselves as individuals,' he says. '. . . In North America, class is no longer gene-based.'

A sure sign that class distinctions have changed is that once-prominent families in Canada are now subject to 'reverence and nostalgia', observes Alexander Reford, a historian whose great-grandmother was Elsie Reford, the niece of Lord Mount Stephen, financier of the Canadian Pacific Railroad in the 1880s.

Mr Reford lives in Jardins de Métis on the Gaspé, where his ancestors established a summer fishing retreat. Tourists, predominantly French Canadian, flock to the area, not just for the beautiful gardens his great-grandmother started, but to soak up some Anglo history.

Mr Reford, perfectly bilingual, can often be seen in the summer months regaling his visitors with stories about the class of men who often oppressed French Canadians. 'We're a long way from the time when those merchants were routinely condemned,' he explains. 'I'm in the business of selling nostalgia.'

But if class always mutates, it has only come full circle. We're back to money: new, old or borrowed. To be snobby about snobbery is an indication, if anyone needed one, that class distinction has never been a high-minded preoccupation.

A resident of Rosedale, a Toronto neighbourhood of big trees and money that seems to grow on them, says she no longer feels at home there because of class discrimination.

'I grew up here,' she says. 'I've never lived anywhere else. But I feel uncomfortable here. I feel controlled by my neighbours, by their expectations and also by their arrogance. I feel a pressure around how the property looks and the fact that I like to do my own gardening. People look down on that. People see me out there in the garden, and they think I'm out of my mind. If you have to do it, then they figure you don't have the money to hire landscapers.'

She and her husband have decided to move to a different neighbourhood.

'There's a strange entitlement culture in Rosedale,' she says. 'You get sussed out very quickly about where you are in the pecking order. It's not good enough to just live here. It's what you do, who you know and how much money you're perceived to have.'

One new emerging social divide is the class of the philanthropists, a development linked to the status that money brings. After all, philanthropy suggests that you have so much, you don't need it all for yourself. It's a show of generosity, but also of vast wealth; a form of that ancient class practice known as *noblesse oblige*.

The recent opening gala at the newly renovated Royal Ontario Museum in Toronto was a celebration of the new class of philanthropists as much as it was of Daniel Libeskind's architectural audacity. Many of the significant donors, including Jamaican-born Michael Lee-Chin, come from the city's ethnic-minority communities.

'There may be a lot of smiles through clenched teeth at the Michael Lee-Chins of society,' observes Robert Gage, a Toronto hairdresser who watches more than what ladies should or should not do with their appearance. 'But the FOOFs [Fine Old Ontario Families] are fooling themselves if they think they still matter. They know the game is up.'

Source: Hampson (2007). Copyright © CTVglobemedia Publishing Inc. All Rights Reserved.

social inequality have been very influential, particularly in American sociology. As noted in chapter 1, stratification approaches conceptualize inequality as a hierarchal order (Davis and Moore 1945), in which individuals are grouped into strata on the basis of their income, education, occupation, prestige, or status. Inequality, then, tends to be conceptualized at the level of individual difference rather than in relational terms or on the basis of class structures (Grabb 2007: 112–13; Tilly 1998: 27–31). Traditionally, stratification approaches have assumed that the rank ordering of people into socially defined strata is a universal and functionally necessary dimension of society (Davis and Moore 1945). In other words, some ordering of people according to their worth, variously defined, is required for the smooth functioning of society. Certain positions in society are more valued than others because of the high level of skill that is attached to them. Only a few people can attain the skill required to fulfill these positions, and the appropriate training for such attainment requires significant time. People who choose to invest the time in such training deserve higher-status positions in society and the resultant rewards attached to these positions. Furthermore, there is general agreement among the members of society that such stratification systems are acceptable (Davis and Moore 1945).

Nonetheless, there are two common underlying assumptions in contemporary stratification research that set it apart from the Marxist or Weberian approaches to inequality discussed in this chapter. The first is the tendency to overemphasize the extent to which society operates on the basis of consensus. The second, related to the first, is the underemphasis in stratification research on issues of power and exploitation (see Grabb 2007 for an extensive discussion of these issues). These are the crucial problematic assumptions of stratification research that scholars have taken issue with for decades and that are highlighted by Melvin Tumin's 1953 response to

Davis and Moore's 1945 seminal article 'Some Principles of Stratification' (see Table 2.2).

The identification of problematic assumptions in stratification research has not, however, led to its demise. It remains influential in studies of inequality and informs much empirical research on the subject. Grimes (1991: 212) argues that many researchers apply stratification measures to the study of class inequality either because they remain committed to certain aspects of functionalist thought or because stratification measures are often used in large surveys. It is important to clarify that stratification researchers do not suggest they are studying class and that class researchers, although they sometimes do stratification research, make the distinction between the class and stratification. The point that Grimes makes is nonetheless an important one that stems, perhaps, from a more general observation that researchers whose primary interest lies outside of class and stratification analysis tend to confound the two approaches. This propensity is most likely a result of the significant overlap among the various social factors that are examined in these approaches. For instance, occupation, defined in various ways, tends to be at the core of research on social inequality regardless of theoretical perspective. Further, there is a general concern in all conceptual frameworks over the distribution of scarce resources such as income, education, and skill. Hence, the tendency to use stratification measures as indicators of inequality likely stems from the continued use of traditional measurements in survey research and from the fact that the indicators of social inequality are quite similar, regardless of theoretical perspective.

Conceptualizing Social Class in a Framework of Inequality

The preceding discussion highlights several issues that are central to the conceptualization of social class—power, exploitation, oppression,

Table 2.2 Some Principles of Stratification

Davis, K., and W.E. Moore. 1945. 'Some Principles of Stratification'. *American Sociological Review* 10: 242–9.	Tumin, M. 1953. 'Some Principles of Stratification: A Critical Analysis'. *American Sociological Review* 18: 378–94.
(1) Within any society, certain positions are functionally more important than others and require special skills for their operation.	(1) There is no clear understanding of what is meant by 'functionally important'; rather, judgments are usually arbitrary, based upon the dispensability and replaceability of a particular division of skills in the population.
(2) There is a limited number of individuals who have the particular talent to be trained in the skills required for the functionally more important positions.	(2) The range of talent within any society is not known within stratified systems, as there are obstacles to the exploration of available talent. This is true of societies where the opportunity to discover talent is dependent upon the resources of the parent generation. In addition, the unequal distribution of rewards of the parent generation results in the unequal distribution of motivation in the succeeding generation.
(3) A period of training is necessary for the conversion of talent into skill, during which period sacrifices are made.	(3) The two sacrifices are said to be a loss of earning power and the cost of training. However, the latter is usually assumed by parents, and the former becomes inconsequential as those with training acquire much higher wages than their untrained counterparts once they are employed.
(4) In order that an individual may be persuaded to endure these sacrifices, positions must contain inherent value in the form of privileged access to scarce rewards.	(4) There are an assortment of alternative motivational mechanisms that could be institutionalized and used effectively, such as the 'joy of work' inherent in a position.
(5) These scarce goods consist of rights and advantages attached to or built into the positions and can be organized into those things which contribute to (a) sustenance; (b) humour and diversion; (c) self-respect and ego expansion.	(5) There are alternative rewards that could be used, but Davis and Moore's analysis does not allow for this.
(6) The consequence of differential access to rewards is the differential of the prestige and esteem which various strata acquire. This, along with rights and privileges, constitutes institutionalized inequality, or social stratification.	(6) There has been no demonstration that it is unavoidable that differential prestige and esteem shall accrue to positions that command differential rewards in power and prestige.
(7) Therefore, social inequality in the amounts of scarce goods and in the amounts of prestige and esteem individuals receive is functional and inevitable.	(7) The only things that must be distributed unequally are the power and property necessary to accomplish particular tasks. If in this differential, power and property are deemed merely to correspond to the differential responsibilities, and to be resources rather than rewards, then it is not necessary that differential prestige and esteem follow.

property ownership, education, and so on. All of these approaches contribute in one way or another to the working definition of *social class* presented here. In this section I draw on approaches discussed above to develop a concept of social class that is compatible with the view that gender, age, ethnic, and race relations are equally important structural dimensions of inequality.

One way to approach our understanding of social inequality is to consider how social processes are shaped by structured sets of social relations such as class, age, gender, ethnicity, and race. Three such processes that are critical for individual and societal survival are production, distribution, and reproduction. According to Marx, *processes of production* are the ways by which raw materials are converted into useful and valuable objects (Allahar 1995). *Processes of distribution* are the ways in which material resources change hands in society (Acker 1988, 1989; Weber [1922] 1978). Distributive processes include wage, state, personal, and marital transfers (Acker 1988). *Processes of reproduction* refers to the ways in which life is maintained both daily and from one generation to the next; these processes include 'how food, clothing, and shelter are made available for immediate consumption, the ways in which the care and socialization of children are provided, the care of the infirm and elderly, and the social organization of sexuality' (Laslett and Brenner 1987: 382).[2] The mere fact of these social processes does not necessarily imply an outcome of social inequality; however, understanding the historical context and the nature of the social relations that structure these processes is fundamental to understanding and explaining social inequality (McMullin 2000).

A central problem in traditional class analysis is that it has focused far too much on production to the neglect of reproduction and, to a lesser extent, distribution. Yet class relations are social relations that extend beyond the arena of production: Marxist approaches that conceptualize social class simply as a relation of production are too restrictive. This is true, in part, because traditional class analysis excludes far too many people who are not directly linked to production processes, such as homemakers and retired individuals. Notably, scholars have tried to reconcile this problem by attributing to homemakers the social class of their husbands and by assigning a class to retired persons based on their pre-retirement status. However, none of these approaches is satisfactory because they do not capture important distributive and status differences between housewives and their husbands or between a retired auto worker and her employed counterpart (see Acker 1988; Estes 1999).

How then do we conceptualize social class in such a framework? At the outset, it is important to point out that there are many indicators of social class—occupation, education, status, wealth, ownership—all of which tell us something about class-based inequality. However, these indicators cannot fully capture the view of social class presented in this book. Instead, as I suggested above, a relational understanding of

social class is necessary. Such an understanding follows a long tradition in Marxist sociology that suggests that class is not merely an economic matter. Rather, social class manifests itself when people from various classes interact with one another. On the shop floor, employers and employees interact with one another in production processes, and it is through that interaction that social class is produced and reproduced (Reiter 1996). In schoolyards, working-class children interact with middle-class children, and their social class is realized in relation to the other (Willis 1977).

Second, material oppression is a primary organizing principle of social class in this framework. This view stands in contrast to Marxist approaches that focus on exploitation (see Wright 1997). Modifying Wright's account of 'non-exploitive economic oppression',[3] material oppression occurs if (1) the material welfare of one group of people depends upon the material deprivations of another and (2) the material deprivations of the oppressed group depends upon the exclusion of the oppressed group from access to productive resources, backed by *ownership of the means of production, occupation, or some combination of the two* (italics indicate modification to Wright's principles).

Much research and theoretical effort has been devoted to trying to establish elaborate and conclusive typologies or categorizations of social class. Although this work is valuable, I do not plan to add to that dialogue here. For the purposes of this book, I assume that, in Canada, three broad classes can be distinguished from one another on the basis of ownership of the means of production and of occupation. Of course, there will be important variation within these classes with respect to income, status, power, relative oppression, and so on.

Members of the upper class own the means for production and/or control the work process. Hence, company presidents and CEOs are part of the upper class not necessarily because they own the means of production (although most have a stake in it) but because they are ultimately in control of how work gets done. Working and middle classes are distinguished from one another largely on the basis of occupational characteristics. Working-class jobs are highly oppressive, and workers have very little control over the work process. Assembly-line workers are part of the working class because (1) the material welfare of one group (their employers) depends on the material deprivation of the workers; (2) their material deprivation depends upon their exclusion from access to productive resources (note that these first two points are the conditions of material oppression listed above); and (3) they have little say about how they do their work. Middle-class jobs may be characterized by similar levels of oppression but more control over the work process, as is the case in many middle-management positions. Alternatively, middle-class jobs may not be oppressive in the preceding sense, but individuals employed in these jobs have relatively little control over how they do their work. This is true for nurses, elementary and high school teachers, social workers, and other similar-status service occupations.

At first glance, the self-employed and professionals seem not to fall anywhere in this schema. Members of each group tend to have control over their work, and their material well-being seems not to rely on the material welfare of another group. Nonetheless, the self-employed are thought to fall into this middling category because their ability to make a living

is often contingent upon whether large global conglomerates actively seek to monopolize their markets.

It is difficult to think of professionals (e.g., physicians, professors, or lawyers) as an oppressed group, and, for the most part, they also control their work processes. How then do they fall into the middle? Professionals are not part of the upper class because their access to productive resources is restricted. Professionals tend not have the exploitive capabilities of the upper class, and productive resources are generally outside of their reach. Thus, professionals fall between the upper- and working-class groups.

One important issue missing from the preceding discussion is the effect of social class on identity formation and everyday interaction, issues that are of particular concern to scholars such as Anthony Giddens and Pierre Bourdieu. These are issues that will be discussed in chapter 6. For now, it is important to recognize that the conceptualizations of class presented here do not take into account how class identities and inequalities are produced and reproduced through daily interaction. Indeed, the view of social class presented in this chapter does not stray very far from more established structural approaches. However, as the next chapters show (see especially chapter 7), the subtle differences in the conceptualization of social class presented here merge nicely with conceptualizations of gender, ethnicity, race, and age to form an integrated and coherent framework of structural social inequality. With that in mind, I now turn to a discussion of gender relations.

Notes

1. Wright has vacillated on this issue since his earliest work. In the late 1970s he referred to these groups as *class locations*; then, in his 1985 publication *Classes*, he called them *classes*. In *Class Counts*

(1997), however, he makes it quite clear that these are class locations but not classes as such.

2. This view of reproduction is generally held by socialist feminist scholars and should

not be confused with reproduction in the Marxist sense of the term.

3. Recall that Wright argues that if appropriation of labour power does not exist, neither does exploitation. He suggests, however, that if the inverse interdependence and exclusion principles are fulfilled, 'non-exploitive economic oppression' occurs.

IIIIIIIIII Questions for Critical Thought IIIIIIIIIIIIIIIIIIIIIIIIIIIIIIIIIIIIIIIIIIIIIIIIIIIII

1. Some researchers have argued that social class is becoming insignificant to issues of inequality in contemporary Western nations. Do you agree or disagree with this view? Why?

2. How does Wright's view of social class differ from that of Karl Marx? Is Marx's approach to social class useful in present-day Canadian society? In what ways?

3. What are the chief differences between Marxist accounts and Weberian accounts of social class? Which view of social class is more helpful for understanding class-based inequality in Canada?

4. Compare and contrast Wright's view of social class with Grabb's. Which is more helpful for understanding class-based inequality in Canada?

5. What are the advantages of defining *class* in terms of material oppression as opposed to exploitation? What are the disadvantages?

IIIIIIIIII Glossary IIIIIIIIIIIIIIIIIIIIIIIIIIIIIIIIIIIIIIIIIIIIIIIIIIIIIIIIIIIIIIIIIIIIIIIIIIIIIIIIIIIII

Bourgeoisie   The class that owns the means of production; the ruling class.

Exploitation   At the heart of Marxist sociology, *exploitation* refers to the situation under capitalism in which the bourgeoisie take advantage of the proletariat. Class-based exploitation occurs when the bourgeoisie appropriate the labour effort of the proletariat to create their own material advantage.

Labour power   Marx argued that *labour* is work and *labour power* is the capacity to work. According to this view, the only 'real' power that the proletariat has under capitalism is the power to choose whether to work.

Parties   Voluntary associations, such as political parties or lobbying groups, that organize for the collective pursuit of interest. The term is common in Weberian scholarship.

Petite bourgeoisie   In Marxist sociology, those who own the products of their labour and who do not exploit the labour power of others. Members of the petite bourgeoisie are self-employed and are also referred to as the *old middle class*.

Power   In Marxist sociology, *power* is essentially a social relationship that has a material base. Those who own the means of production have the power to exploit workers through the appropriation of their labour efforts. In Weberian sociology, where the term is more broadly defined, *power* can mean an individual's or group's capacity to impose their will on others.

Proletariat   The working class, the members of which sell their labour power to the owners of the means of production in exchange for a wage.

Status groups   Organized groups comprising people who have similar social-status situations.

IIIIIIIIIIII **Recommended Reading** IIIIIIIIIIIIIIIIIIIIIIIIIIIIIIIIIIIIIIIIIIIIIIIIIIIIIIIIIIIIII

Clement, Wallace, and John Myles. 1994. *Relations of Ruling: Class and Gender in Postindustrial Societies*. Montreal: McGill-Queen's University Press. Applies Wright's conceptualization of social class in an analysis of class and gender inequality. Although it is concerned primarily with Canada, there are also comparisons with the United States, Norway, Sweden, and Finland.

Edgell, Stephen. 1993. *Class: Key Ideas*. London: Routledge. Provides an excellent overview of the key themes in class analysis.

Grabb, Edward. 2007. *Theories of Social Inequality*. 5th ed. Toronto: Thomson Nelson. An excellent overview and analysis of classical and contemporary theories of social inequality.

McCourt, Frank. 1996. *Angela's Ashes: A Memoir*. New York: Touchstone. An autobiography that tells a heart-wrenching story of what it is like to grow up poor.

Wright, Eric Olin. 1997. *Class Counts: Comparative Studies in Class Analysis*. Cambridge: Cambridge University Press. A comprehensive book that outlines Eric Olin Wright's ideas on social class.

IIIIIIIIIII **Relevant Websites** IIIIIIIIIIIIIIIIIIIIIIIIIIIIIIIIIIIIIIIIIIIIIIIIIIIIIIIIIIIIIIIII

Eric Olin Wright's home page
www.ssc.wisc.edu/~wright
**In addition to a CV and descriptions of research projects and course syllabi, this unique website offers users PDF links to Wright's books, recent articles, and unpublished versions of manuscripts and interviews. Going beyond the typical academic website, Wright's home page facilitates learning by granting users access to his work.

Canadian Centre for Policy Alternatives—
Growing Gap
www.growinggap.ca
**The GrowingGap.ca is an initiative of the Canadian Centre for Policy Alternatives' Inequality Project, a national project to increase public awareness about the alarming spread of income and wealth inequality in Canada. GrowingGap.ca is an informative website about 'the growing gap between the rich and the rest of us'. This group envisions a Canada where no one is left behind and is hopeful that this can be achieved.

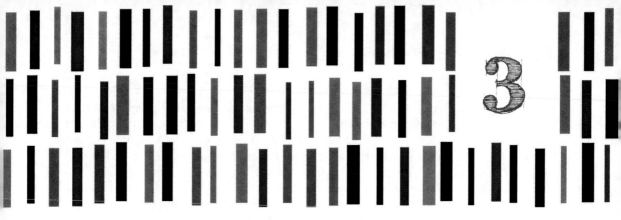

Gender and Inequality

Introduction

In 1998 I met Beth, a 64-year-old mother of seven children, who agreed to be a part of my three-generation family study. One of the things we asked the study participants was how they had managed to combine employment, domestic labour, and child care when their children were young. Beth had married when she was 18 years old and had seven children in the next eight years. Although it was not what she would have preferred, her husband John insisted that she work for pay. Beth was also responsible for all of the housework and child care when their children were young. Indeed, John, who worked the day shift in a manufacturing company, spent most of his free time with his friends at the pub.

To manage her family responsibilities in combination with her factory job, Beth worked the night shift. When she was pregnant with her seventh child, she would arrive home from work at 8:00 a.m., get the three oldest children ready for school, and spend the rest of the day caring for her two preschool-age children:

> I would come home [from the factory] and get the kids off to school and then tend to the younger kids. And do what had to be done [housework]. And the

older kids would come home for lunch. . . . I'd look after them [the two youngest children] through the day and just sleep when I could get them down together. When they got up, I got up. . . . The younger kids went to bed at 7 o'clock at night, I'd lay down from 7 to 10 before going back to work. . . . I didn't have the energy to even think that it wasn't fair.

Gender affects almost every aspect of social life and is often the basis of differential access to resources and power in Canada and in other Western societies. Usually, although not always, men as a group benefit from gender patterns. Beth's situation is somewhat extreme because she had both a large family and an absent husband. However, the fact that she was responsible for unpaid work in the home and needed to combine that responsibility with paid labour is a typical experience for women. Indeed, research on families and unpaid labour shows that women are disproportionately responsible for household labour, child care, and emotion management in families and for caring for older relatives (see chapter 8).

Beth's story also demonstrates gendered disadvantage in labour markets. In fact, industries, labour markets, occupations, and jobs are segregated on the basis of gender (see chapter 9).

Compared to women, men tend to be concentrated in industries, labour markets, occupations, and jobs that are characterized by higher salaries, more benefits, greater autonomy, and higher status. Women are sometimes subjected to discrimination and sexual harassment in their workplaces (Welsh 1999; Welsh et al. 2006), and they often encounter the 'glass ceiling', or invisible barriers to promotion, in their careers (see Krahn, Lowe, and Hughes 2007 for an overview). At the same time, when men are employed in occupations that are typically seen as female, they are often given a ride on the glass escalator and promoted early and often (Williams 1992).

Explanations of Gender-Based Inequality

Scholars disagree about how to explain gendered inequality, and they emphasize different factors in understanding the role that gender plays in individuals' lives. Unlike social class, gender relations were not generally studied before the 1970s. Although there were before that time various statements about sex differences (see, for example, Parsons 1942), these were not generally framed in relation to inequality. Research over the past few decades has evolved so that gender relations are now widely recognized as a ubiquitous pillar of inequality. Yet, as with social class, there is much disagreement in the literature over how gender should be conceptualized and what lies at the root of gender-based inequality.

Before we turn to various conceptualizations and explanations of gender-based inequality, the distinction between sex and gender must be addressed. The term *gender* was introduced in sociology as a way of avoiding biological essentialist views that were associated with the term *sex*. Essentialist perspectives reinforced beliefs that biological differences between men and women determine their disparate positions in society. *Gender*, on the other hand, was used to express the view that there is nothing innate about men or women that makes one sex more suitable for performing a particular task than another. *Gender*, then, refers to the social construction of difference that is largely organized around biological sex. This view of gender is widely held in sociology and in feminism (Nicholson 1994). Yet some feminist scholars argue that biological sex is also socially constructed (see Box 3.1).

Box 3.1 Biology as Ideology

Until the eighteenth century, Western philosophers and scientists thought that there was one sex and that women's internal genitalia were the inverse of men's external genitalia: the womb and vagina were the penis and scrotum turned inside out (Laqueur 1990). Current Western thinking sees women and men as so different physically as to sometimes seem two species. The bodies, which have been mapped inside and out for hundreds of years, have not changed. What has changed are the justifications for gender inequality. When the social position of all human beings was believed to be set by natural law or was considered God-given, biology was irrelevant; women and men of different classes all had their assigned places. When scientists began to question the divine basis of social order and replaced faith with empirical knowledge, what they saw was that women were very different from men in that they had wombs and menstruated. Such anatomical differences destined them for an entirely different social life from men.

. . . . .

Neither sex nor gender are pure categories. Combinations of incongruous genes, genitalia, and hormonal input are ignored in sex categorization, just as combinations of incongruous physiology, identity, sexuality, appearance, and behaviour are ignored in the social construction of gender statuses. Menstruation, lactation, and gestation do not demarcate women from men. Only some women are pregnant and then only some of the time; some women do not have a uterus or ovaries. Some women have stopped menstruating temporarily, others have reached menopause, and some have had hysterectomies. Some women breastfeed some of the time, but some men lactate (Jaggar 1983, 165fn). Menstruation, lactation, and gestation are individual experiences of womanhood (Levesque-Lopman 1988), but not determinants of the social category 'woman', or even 'female'. Similarly, 'men are not always sperm producers, and in fact, not all sperm producers are men. A male-to-female transsexual, prior to surgery, can be socially a woman, though still potentially (or actually) capable of spermatogenesis' (Kessler and McKenna [1978] 1985, 2).

When gender assignment is contested in sports, where the categories of competitors are rigidly divided into women and men, chromosomes are now used to determine in which category the athlete is to compete. However, an anomaly common enough to be found in several women at every major international sports competition are XY chromosomes that have not produced male anatomy or physiology because of a genetic defect. Because these women are women in every way significant for sports competition, the prestigious International Amateur Athletic Federation has urged that sex be determined by simple genital inspection (Kolata 1992). Transsexuals would pass this test, but it took a lawsuit for Renée Richards to play tournament tennis as a woman, despite his male sex chromosomes (Richards 1983). Oddly, neither basis for gender categorization—chromosomes nor genitalia—has anything to do with sports prowess (Birrell and Cole 1990).

In the Olympics, in cases of chromosomal ambiguity, women must undergo 'a battery of gynecological and physical exams to see if she is "female enough" to compete. Men are not tested' (Carlson 1991, 26). The purpose is not to categorize women and men accurately, but to make sure men don't enter women's competitions, where, it is felt, they will have the advantage of size and strength. This practice sounds fair only because it is assumed that all men are similar in size and strength and different from all women. Yet in Olympics boxing and wrestling matches, men are matched within weight classes. Some women might similarly successfully compete with some men in many sports. Women did not run in marathons until about twenty years ago. In twenty years of marathon competition, women have reduced their finish times by more than one-and-one-half hours; they are expected to run as fast as men in that race by 1998 and might catch up with men's running times in races of other lengths within the next 50 years because they are increasing their fastest speeds more rapidly than are men (Fausto-Sterling 1985, 213–18).

The reliance on only two sex and gender categories in the biological and social sciences is as epistemologically spurious as the reliance on chromosomal or genital tests to group athletes. Most research designs do not investigate whether physical skills or physical abilities are really more or less common in women and men (Epstein 1988). They start out with two social categories ('women', 'men'), assume they are biologically different ('female', 'male'), look for similarities among them and differences between them, and attribute what they have found for the social categories to sex differences (Gelman, Collman, and Maccoby 1986). These designs rarely question the categorization of their subjects into two and only two groups, even though they often find more significant within-group differences than between-group differences (Hyde 1990). The social construction perspective on sex and gender suggests that instead of starting with the two presumed dichotomies in each category—female, male; woman, man—it might be more useful in gender studies to group patterns of behaviour and only then look for identifying markers of the people likely to enact such behaviours.

References

Birrell, Susan J., and Sheryl L. Cole. 1990. 'Double Fault: Renée Richards and the Construction and Naturalization of Difference'. *Sociology of Sport Journal* 7: 1–21.

Carlson, Alison. 1991. 'When Is a Woman Not a Woman?' *Women's Sport and Fitness*, March: 24–9.

Epstein, Cynthia Fuchs. 1988. *Deceptive Distinctions: Sex, Gender and the Social Order.* New Haven, CT: Yale University Press.

Fausto-Sterling, Anne. 1985. *Myths of Gender: Biological Theories about Women and Men.* New York: Basic Books.

Gelman, Susan A., Pamela Collman, and Eleanor E. Maccoby. 1986. 'Inferring Properties from Categories versus Inferring Categories from Properties: The Case of Gender'. *Child Development* 57: 396–404.

Hyde, Janet Shibley. 1990. 'Meta-analysis and the Psychology of Gender Differences'. *Signs* 16: 55–73.

Jaggar, Alison M. 1983. *Feminist Politics and Human Nature.* Totowa, NJ: Rowman & Allanheld.

Kessler, Suzanne J., and Wendy McKenna. [1978] 1985. *Gender: An Ethnomethodological Approach.* Chicago: University of Chicago Press.

Kolata, Gina. 1992. 'Track Federation Urges End to Gene Test for Femaleness'. *New York Times*, February 12.

Laqueur, Thomas. 1990. *Making Sex: Body and Gender from the Greeks to Freud.* Cambridge, MA: Harvard University Press.

Richards, Renée, with Jack Ames. 1983. *Second Serve.* New York: Stein and Day.

Source: Lorber (2000: 568–70). Reprinted by permission of Sage Publications, Inc.

One significant point that feminist sociologists identified in their critique of sex research is that it is difficult, if not impossible, to address structural aspects of gender through empirical research. Framing their argument in a more general critique of positivist science that privileges hegemonic knowledge, feminists argued that multivariate, empirical models can take our understanding of gender only so far because the interpretation of these models tends to be reduced to individual difference (D. Smith 1987). Most sociologists now dismiss arguments that treat such differences as innate. Yet there remains a tendency to interpret these sex and gender differences as individual characteristics rather than as structural features of social life.

Structural accounts of gender inequality generally address how various social institutions such as states, families, and labour markets are 'gendered'. In other words, feminist researchers have shown that women and men have different experiences and opportunities in most institutions. For example, labour markets are structured such that women have fewer opportunities for promotion than men, which, in turn, is related to women's primary responsibility for domestic labour within families. Although studies that consider the gendered nature of social structures have advanced our understanding of gender inequality, they fall short of assessing the full nature of gender inequality because they tend not to treat gender itself as a social structure (Risman 1998). To suggest that gender is a social structure is to see gender as a central organizing feature of social life. What we do, who we are, how we interact with others, our opportunities and constraints, our advantages and disadvantages are all patterned by gender (Chafetz 1990; Lorber 1994). Patterns of gender, in turn, are made manifest through human interaction (West and Zimmerman 1987) in our productive, reproductive, and distributive activities.

In summary then, although the conceptualization of gender may at first seem straightforward—there are women and there are men—the seeming simplicity of this exercise adds to its complexity. Gender relations are historically variable, cultural, ideological, biological, sexual, political, and material (see K. Marshall 2000). Gender involves identity, power, exploitation, and oppression. The debate among feminist scholars and others about which of these matters lies at the heart of gendered inequality is long-standing and ongoing. In the sections that follow, these issues will be considered as they pertain to the processes of reproduction, production, and distribution.

Social Relations of Reproduction: Patriarchy as a System of Domination

Whereas the social relations of production are an essential element of social-class analysis, assessments of gender inequality are often grounded in the relations of social reproduction and sexuality. **Radical feminists**, for instance, generally assume that gender inequality is a function of men's control of women's reproduction and sexuality (Firestone 1971; O'Brien 1981). This produces an inherently unequal gendered power relationship that determines the sexual division of labour, is perpetuated by the nuclear family, and makes women economically dependent upon men. Hence, radical feminists suggest that gender inequality is distinct from other forms of oppression, that sex-based inequality is the original and most basic form of oppression, and that the dominance of women by men is universal (Firestone 1971; Millett 1969; O'Brien 1981).

According to Shulamith Firestone (1971), women's subordinate position in relation to men is rooted in the human *biological family*. Biological families are characterized by four universal features: (1) women's biological capacity to reproduce made them dependent on men for their survival; (2) children take a long time to become independent compared to the young of

other species; (3) bonds between mothers and children are universal, and these bonds determine the psychology of all women and children; and (4) the reproductive biological capacity of women led to the first categorical division of labour. According to Firestone (1971), these characteristics of biological families and the sexes lead to a power imbalance between men and women that needs to be overcome. She argues that if women are to be emancipated, there must be a revolution in which women gain control over their reproduction in much the same way as a working-class revolution would lead to the control of the means of production. She argues that, to free 'women from the tyranny of their reproductive biology', natural reproduction must be replaced by the use of new reproductive technologies.

In *The Politics of Reproduction*, Mary O'Brien (1981) also argues that the root of women's oppression lies in their biology, but unlike Firestone, she suggests that the reproduction process is dialectical and has changed throughout history. Men need to control reproduction because, unlike women, they are 'alienated from their seed of reproduction' through the act of sexual intercourse. To compensate for this alienation, men seek to control women through patriarchal order.

Although radical feminists differ in their explanations of how and why men have come to control reproduction, they agree that it is, in part, through this process that gendered subjectivities—defined as psyches, personalities, or levels of self-conscious awareness—are born (Firestone 1971; O'Brien 1981). Furthermore, gendered ideologies of love, sexuality, and motherhood perpetuate gender inequality by keeping women unaware of their subordinate status (Burton 1985). For instance, Firestone (1971) argues that the joy of giving birth is a patriarchal myth. Instead, she says, pregnancy is barbaric and natural childbirth is 'at best necessary and tolerable' and at worst 'like shitting a pumpkin'.

Explanations of gender inequality have benefited from radical feminist thought, in particular the importance it places on the relations of reproduction, gendered ideology, power, and control. However, radical feminist thought has been criticized on several counts. For our purposes, the most important criticism is that it treats the system of male dominance or **patriarchy** as a 'universal, trans-historical and trans-cultural phenomenon; women were everywhere oppressed by men in more or less the same ways' (Acker 1989: 235). Conceptualizing patriarchy in this way tends to reduce male oppression of women to biological essentialism and is limiting because it does not consider historical or contemporary variations in women's situations (Acker 1989; Fox 1988). Moreover, this view of patriarchy leads to assessments of men as having an 'innate desire for power' (Fox 1988: 165).

Another problem with radical feminist thought is its rather limited focus on the procreative aspect of social reproduction. Missing in these accounts is an assessment of social reproduction as a material relation that includes 'the activities and attitudes, behaviours and emotions, responsibilities and relationships directly involved in the maintenance of life on a daily basis, and intergenerationally' (Laslett and Brenner 1987: 382). Social reproduction is work, and how social reproductive labour is divided is critical to social organization. Finally, in its emphasis on social reproduction, radical feminist thought tends to neglect the relationship between gender and the processes of production.

Social Relations of Production and Reproduction: Capitalism and Patriarchy as Intersecting Systems of Domination

Socialist-feminist accounts of gender inequality consider the relations of production and reproduction in their work. Influenced by Marxism, **socialist feminism** has united the relations of production and reproduction by linking the systems of patriarchy and capitalism in an integrated theory (Young 1981). **Dual-system theorists**, for instance, suggest that patriarchy and capitalism are two distinct systems that intersect in relation to the oppression of women. Heidi Hartmann developed one of the most prominent and most debated dual-systems theories in her paper 'The Unhappy Marriage of Marxism and Feminism: Towards a More Progressive Union'. Hartmann (1981: 14) defines patriarchy as 'a set of social relations between men, which have a material base and which, though hierarchical, establish or create inter-dependence and solidarity among men that enable them to dominate women'. The material base of patriarchy, she suggests, is the control of women's labour power by men. Men control women by restricting their economic and sexual activity. Women, according to Hartmann (1981), work for men by raising their children and doing their housework. These social relations are perpetuated ideologically through the systems of patriarchy and capitalism, in part by equating male characteristics with capitalist values and female characteristics with social reproduction (Hartmann 1981: 28).

According to Hartmann (1981: 24), capitalism and patriarchy are systems with competing interests that adjust to and reinforce one another. Capitalism is not an 'all-powerful' system of inequality; rather, it is responsive and flexible to contradictions that stem from patriarchy. This is the crux of Hartmann's argument, and to illustrate this point she relies on a historical analysis of women's labour power and the development of the family wage in the nineteenth-century United States. During this time, working-class men, women, and children were working in factories; this kept the supply of labour large and wages low. Wages were based on what would be required for individual, not family, subsistence. Hence, many members in working-class families were required to work in factories for their very survival. Male workers and unions opposed women's factory work, recognizing, first, that the excess supply of labour lowered wages and, second, that if women worked for pay, there was no one left to tend to the home. According to Hartmann (1981: 21), rather than organizing the labour of women and children, a tactic that would have solved the first problem, working-class men fought for the family wage, a solution that would allow them to maintain patriarchal power in the home as well as to obtain higher wages. Hence, 'family wages may be understood as a resolution of the conflict over women's labour power which was occurring between patriarchal and capitalist interests' (Hartmann 1981: 22).

According to Hartmann, although women's labour-force participation has increased dramatically since the Second World War, this does not signify the emancipation of women, as Marxist scholars might argue. Rather, the family wage is still institutionalized in capitalism because men continue to be primarily responsible for earning a living, women remain primarily responsible for maintaining families, and women earn lower wages in labour markets than men do (Hartmann 1981: 25). Hence, Marxist analyses of women's oppression are flawed because they do not fully acknowledge the strength of patriarchy in maintaining a system of disadvantage for women.

Responding to Heidi Hartmann's article and other dual-system approaches, some feminists argue that it is a mistake to treat patriarchy and capitalism as separate systems of oppression (Young 1981). This is largely because dual-system theories tend to relegate patriarchy to one level of analysis—usually the ideological, which organizes women's unpaid work—and capitalism to another, the material, which organizes women's paid work (Hartmann 1981; Young 1981). Although Hartmann avoids this specific problem by giving patriarchy a material base, it is unclear how the analytic separation between patriarchy and capitalism can be maintained.

Others, most notably Sylvia Walby, suggest that dual-system theorizing is appropriate but that it must be further developed, conceptualizing patriarchy as a multidimensional structure.

In several publications in the late 1980s and early 1990s, Walby developed a theory of patriarchy that attempted to correct the shortcomings of the concept by defining patriarchy as 'a system of social structures and practices in which men dominate, oppress, and exploit women' (1989: 214). According to Walby (1989, 1990), considering the social-structural nature of patriarchy corrects the problems of biological essentialism and the idea that all individual men dominate all individual women.

In order to understand the structural nature of patriarchy, Walby (1989: 214) argues that it should be considered at different levels of analysis. Most abstractly, patriarchy is a system of social relations that exists alongside capitalism and racism. At the next level are six patriarchal structures: the patriarchal mode of production (household production), patriarchal relations in paid work, patriarchal states, male violence, patriarchal relations in sexuality, and patriarchal culture. Finally, in each of the patriarchal structures, patriarchal practices establish or reinforce systems of patriarchy (Walby 1989, 1990). Walby argues that these patriarchal structures are not sites of oppression but are rather defined 'in terms of the social relations in each structure' (1989: 220); these structures 'represent the most significant constellations of social relations which structure gender relations'. This statement leads to some difficulty in understanding Walby's work because she does not define what is meant by 'constellations of social relations'. Farther on in both her 1989 article and her 1990 book, *Theorizing Patriarchy*, Walby suggests there are characteristics of gender relations that are crucial in every patriarchal structure. In paid employment, these characteristics are a sex-segregated labour force, sex-based wage discrimination, and the fact that women engage in the paid labour force at lower rates than men; in household production, the domestic division of labour, reproductive capabilities, and household compositions more generally are the key features of gender relations (see Box 3.2 for an example of patriarchy in paid and unpaid labour). What remains unclear is how 'constellations of social relations' shape these features of gender relations and what these social relations are.

Nonetheless, Walby, in identifying six structures of patriarchy, addresses another of the central criticisms of the concept, namely, the tendency among those who use it to locate women's oppression in one or possibly two domains of social life (Acker 1989; Fox 1989). As shown above, radical feminists most often discuss patriarchy in relation to women's domestic responsibilities, their reproductive capacity, or

Box 3.2 Housework Doesn't Pay

Leslie Bennetts, author of *The Feminine Mistake*, talks to Kate Fillion about women's risks, assets and delusions:

Q: You've ignited a firestorm by saying it's a mistake for mothers to stay home with their kids because it renders them economically dependent on men. And yet, stay-at-home moms are blogging all over the place that it's the best decision they've ever made. Are they just deluded?

A: I found in my own interviewing something that is backed up by a lot of social science research: women do not make these decisions knowing a lot of the information they really should know in order to make informed choices. The consequences only catch up with them later, and they're blindsided by a lot of very difficult challenges that they didn't anticipate. It's later on that they say, 'Oh my God, I made such a mistake, why didn't anybody tell me this information?' So no, they're not deluded, but there is an information gap.

Q: Well, why is it a mistake to stay home with the kids?

A: It's a mistake for women to drop out of the labour force thinking that they can come back in when their kids are older, because the barriers are extraordinary. They will encounter tremendous ageism, sexism, overt discrimination against mothers, and employers are very negative about women who have been out of the labour force for any

length of time. Women also don't seem to realize that they lose nearly 40 per cent of their earning power when they take a time out as short as three years or less. But the larger question is the general risks of life: the divorce rate is 50 per cent, and the average age of widowhood in America is 55. Women are living to be in their 80s and 90s, and by the time women are 60 years old, two-thirds of them are without partners. And then there's unemployment. It's a very volatile and insecure labour market, so even if your husband's a wonderful guy and he doesn't get sick and he doesn't die, he can lose his job. When you add up all the risk factors, it becomes clear that it's not a small minority of women who are going to have these problems—the majority of women over the course of their lifetimes are going to end up on the wrong side of the odds. It just takes years for all of this to play out, and women tend to be focused very much on the moment and on immediate needs rather than considering the questions in terms of the long run.

Q: Is there anything at all to recommend staying at home?

A: Well, I wouldn't take such a high-risk gamble with my children's lives. Different people have different appetites for risk. I wouldn't go climb Mount Everest because I know that one out of the eight people who do that die. In the case of stay-at-home moms, two-thirds to three-quarters of them will probably end up having really serious challenges.

A parent's first obligation is to provide food and shelter for their children, and if a mother does not maintain the ability to do that, I would question whether she's really being a responsible parent.

Q: One of your arguments is that working moms have a fuller life, that it's a way to express your individuality and grow as a person.

A: Freud and the developmental psychologist Erik Erikson both defined work and love as the two essential components of a mature, healthy adult life, and I think for many of us, work is intellectually challenging and permits us to keep on growing and finding new challenges and new rewards in ways that are not necessarily possible if you stay home. If other people don't want those kinds of challenges, that's fine with me, I just hope that they have made a plan about what they're going to do and how they're going to support their children if something happens to [their] breadwinner. These days, it takes two incomes to provide the kind of middle-class lifestyle that one income was able to provide a generation or two ago, so families that rely on a single breadwinner are very vulnerable.

Q: I can already see the letters to the editor. Stay-at-home moms are going to write, 'But this is work.'

A: It's tons of work to run a household. I run a household, I've made a homemade dinner for my children every night for the last 18 years. But you don't get paid for it. So I'm sorry, when the rent cheque comes due, or the grocery bill has to be paid, it doesn't matter that you worked hard doing housework. You can't pay it if you don't have an income! And if you were depending on a man, and he left or just died, and you haven't thought through how you're going to provide for your kids, it doesn't matter how much housework you did. I don't understand why there's this confusion. Paid work gives you money, you need money to support your kids—what's complicated about that? If [they're] not getting paid, women end up with fewer pensions, fewer savings, and women end up in poverty at twice the rate of men. Another thing that's important to note is that four out of five of the women who end up in poverty didn't start out poor. These are people who had comfortable lives, then they lost their breadwinner, and hadn't planned for their own futures, and ended up poor.

Q: You say that a lot of women don't so much opt out of work as seize the excuse of having kids and run with it, to get away from jobs they were disillusioned with. Why do women give up so easily?

A: Girls grow up thinking on some level, even if they're not conscious of it, that you're going to meet Prince Charming and you're going to live happily forever after and he's going to take care of you. And so what you see is that when young men hit roadblocks in their careers, they figure out a way to go around them or over them. They persevere. Whereas girls just shrug and say, 'Well, I didn't really want to do this anyway, and I can go home and be supported by my husband.' This is not a viable long-term strategy for life in the 21st century. As the experts I quoted in my book put it, marriage is an economic partnership—the problem is that women assume nearly all the economic risk. So what you see for example after divorce is that women's standard of living goes down by 38 per cent and men's goes up by 26 per cent. The man's just walked out the door with the family's major asset, which is his career, his earning power. A lot of women don't know that one of the results of the equality revolution of the last 30 years is that the courts are saying to women, 'Well, you have an education, so we'll give you a couple of years of rehabilitative alimony, and then you're on your own.' And the woman is just thunderstruck, she says, 'Wait a minute, I've been out of the workforce for 18 years, I just sent out a hundred résumés and I can't get one job interview, what do you mean I'm on my own? I can't support myself!'

Q: The mothers you interviewed were really well-educated, but the stay-at-homes came off like ninnies who hadn't thought of any of this. Why not?

A: These are women who wouldn't think of having a child without baby-proofing their houses and researching which is the best stroller to buy, and yet they seem unable even to think about how they're going to pay for food and shelter if something happens to their husbands. I think there's a lot of denial around the subject of men and marriage. It's like the promise is more real than the reality, so you will talk to women who say, 'Yes, all my friends are getting divorced, but nothing bad will ever happen to me.' Well, that's just not a prudent way to be a grown-up if you have children depending on you.

Q: One of the interesting things in the blogosphere, maybe not in real life, is this idea that the 'Mommy Wars' have been harmful, that women who stay home should not judge women who work outside the home, and vice versa, that no one should be calling anyone's life choices a mistake. Why do you think it's okay?

A: It's unfair to say that I'm calling people's life choices a mistake as if this were a qualitative judgment. It's a question of facing the facts. If I had done investigative reporting and found out that there's some kind of poison in their water supply that's going to make their children sick, I think women would want to know about it, they'd probably agitate to solve the problem. And yet when it comes to questions of a family's finances, all the financial planners and investment people that I talked to said it's really difficult to get women to step up to the plate. Women will say things like, 'Oh, my husband has a life insurance policy, so if something happens to him, we'll be okay.' They haven't really sat down to do the math, and haven't thought through the fact that the husband's life insurance policy would carry the family for three or four years; if they're 40 years old, they may live for another 50 years! I'm not saying that their lives are a mistake, I'm saying that it's a mistake to depend on a man to support you. If this is your life plan, it probably won't work out.

Q: Obviously working-class women and single moms have never had the luxury of opting out of the workforce, and quite a few middle-class moms don't either

A: Many people think this is just an elite phenomenon that only is relevant to privileged women. The *Wall Street Journal* reported a couple of months ago that the new data shows this is occurring at all socio-economic levels. It becomes an aspirational model, and it's also a question of women having been brainwashed into believing this is necessary for their children to turn out well, which it's not.

Q: Do you think, and does social science show, that kids are better off in any way when their mothers stay home?

A: No. Social scientists have been studying the children of working mothers and the children of stay-at-home moms for more than 40 years, trying to prove that one group does better than the other, and they've completely failed to show any evidence to suggest that it's preferable to have stay-at-home mothers. That's not what determines whether children turn out well. When I say things like that, women then come back at me and say, 'Well, you're just saying we should all warehouse our children in substandard daycare.' Child care of all kinds has been so demonized.

Q: But the reality is it's very hard to find affordable, accessible, high-quality child care.

A: I think that's absolutely true, it's a national disgrace. This is not a women's issue, it's not a woman's problem. Fathers should be doing a lot more to be partners as parents, and the government should be doing more, and corporations should be doing more to develop family-friendly policies. But the way things are right now, it is not true that the children of working mothers do worse than the children of stay-at-home mothers.

Q: Men in your book are either dumping their wives, dying on them, or losing their jobs—it's one depressing example after another.

A: Go out there and try interviewing women about what happens to them, the stories of women's lives are harrowing. And yet we still keep on thinking these are the exceptions to the rule. They're not the exceptions to the rule. They're the norm. It does not help women or their kids to be wildly unrealistic. I'm not saying all men are scoundrels, but enough of them are, and women are shocked and surprised by the consequences often enough that I would think that you should consider it as being within the realm of possibility.

Source: Fillion (2007).

'compulsory' heterosexuality (Firestone 1971; O'Brien 1981; Rich 1980). The problem with such approaches is that they fail to acknowledge that the oppression of women occurs outside the home as well, most notably, for Walby, in paid labour, culture, and the state. Furthermore, variations in women's experiences, both historically and cross-culturally, are difficult to capture if assessments are limited to one domain. Hence, Walby (1990) suggests—and rightly so—that she rescues patriarchy from one of its essential pitfalls by considering six structures of the oppression of women.

In her work, Walby (1989, 1990, 1997) is concerned primarily with patriarchy and capitalism, although she does acknowledge that these systems vary by other dimensions as well, such as race and age. Hence, she favours a dual- or plural-system theoretical approach and conceptualizes patriarchy as a system of oppression that is separate from capitalism, racism, and ageism. In dual-system theories, the roots of patriarchy are generally thought to be located within the reproductive sphere of the family, whereas the roots of the political-economic system are located in the mode of production (Hartmann 1981). Walby (1989, 1990) argues that patriarchy infiltrates both, and that over time women's oppression and inequality have come to be based less on 'private' patriarchy and more on 'public' patriarchy. Private patriarchy is centred on the home and is distinguished by the exclusion of women from public roles and by men's appropriation of women's domestic labour. Public patriarchy, on the other hand, is centred on the economic and political spheres of social life and is characterized by the segregation of women into less powerful positions than men (Walby 1989, 1990).

Walby concludes *Theorizing Patriarchy* (1990: 243) by stating bluntly that patriarchy is an essential concept for understanding gender inequality. Interestingly enough, Walby is less inclined to use the term *patriarchy* in her 1997 book, *Gender Transformations*, favouring instead the term *gender relations*. Yet her theoretical premises have changed only slightly, and she continues to insist on a separate-system approach.

Combining the Relations of Production and Distribution

Taking issue with both dual-system theory and the concept of patriarchy, Joan Acker (1988, 2000, 2006) sets out to develop a single-system theory of social relations that places equal emphasis on gender and social class. According to Acker, this requires 'broadening class' and 'the economic' (2000: 59). She argues that one way to do this is to consider in conceptualizing class both the social relations of distribution and the social relations of production, an idea that she introduced in her 1988 article 'Class, Gender, and the Relations of Distribution'.

The relations of distribution 'are sequences of linked actions through which people share the necessities of survival' (Acker 1988: 478). According to Acker, the fact that there has always been a sexual division of labour suggests that in all known societies the relations of distribution are influenced by gender and take on a gendered meaning. Gender relations of distribution in capitalist society are rooted in history and are transformed (like the relations of production) as the means of production change.

Acker suggests that the wage, which is rooted in the relations of production, is the essential component of distribution in capitalist society. The wage has developed historically as a gendered phenomenon because women have always been paid less than men and gendered job segregation is typical. Thus, 'the wage and the work contexts within which it is earned are gendered in ways that re-create women's relative disadvantage' (Acker 1988: 483).

Personal relations, marital relations, and state relations are the gendered processes through which distribution occurs. According to Acker, *personal relations of distribution* are held together by emotional bonds, usually between blood relatives, and are dependent upon the wage. As a result of both the sex-based division of labour and the ideology of the family wage, gender serves to organize the personal relations of distribution. In its simplest form, this system requires that at least part of the male wage be distributed to women, who then redistribute it to the dependants in their families. The personal relations of distribution often extend beyond the household. In instances where economic hardships are typical, women often maintain extensive kinship networks in which survival is ensured through the allocation of resources between households. Among the economically advantaged, gender-based personal relations of distribution also occur, thereby helping to ensure the stability and reproduction of class (Acker 1988).

Marital relations are the central component of distribution for married women who do not work for pay and are thus dependent upon their husbands for their wage. According to Acker, unwaged housewives are connected to the production process through their husbands' wages. Although they share common standards of living with their husbands, they do not assume the same class, because their situations, experiences, and activities are different. Unwaged wives have little control over their economic situation, although Acker suggests that this control likely varies by the men's and women's class.

State relations of distribution are the final type of distribution arrangement that Acker considers. State relations of distribution are based on laws and governmental policies that have historically been developed in gendered ways. Policies and laws established to alleviate the financial burden of the working class when the market fails are based on gendered ideologies supporting the 'male breadwinner/dependent housewife' ideal. This renders some groups of women—those who remain unmarried, single mothers, poor

working women—particularly disadvantaged. Women are further disadvantaged by the gendered nature of entitlement regulations, because many social security programs are based on the labour-force experiences of men.

For Acker (1988: 495), the culmination of these gendered relations shapes social class. Conceptualizing class in this way allows unwaged persons to be included in the class structure. Thus, in order to fully understand the links between gender and class, divisions must be changed. One way to do this is to see class as rooted in relations of distribution (as well as in relations of production) that necessarily embed gender, both as ideology and as material inequality (Acker 1988: 496).

Besides 'broadening class and "the economic"' (Acker 2000: 57), Acker draws on the work of E.P. Thompson (1963) and Dorothy Smith (1987) to argue that class should be conceptualized as social relations that take into account the 'processes that produce contradiction, conflict, and different life experiences' (Acker 1988: 496) and that are understood from the 'standpoints of a multiplicity of women' (Acker 2000: 59). This view stands in contrast to those that argue for categorical conceptualizations of class; instead it emphasizes the things people do to manage their day-to-day lives. Furthermore, when class is understood from the standpoint of women, activities that may seem irrelevant in traditional class analysis, such as housework, become subjects worthy of analysis.

Finally, Acker (2000) argues that to understand fully the intersections between gender and class, scholars must understand that each mutually constitutes the other. In other words, the experience of being a woman or a man is fundamentally shaped by her or his social class, but class experience is also fundamentally shaped by one's gender. Acker points out that this applies to intersections between class, race, and gender as well; and, although underdeveloped in Acker's work, this mutually constitutive nature of gender, race, and class has been taken up by multicultural feminist scholars, notably Evelyn

Nakano Glenn and Patricia Hill Collins. What is missing in feminist scholarship, however, is a systematic assessment of the relationships between age relations and gender, class, ethnicity, or race (Calasanti and Slevin 2006; McMullin 1995, 2000).

'Doing Gender': Issues of Agency and Identity

Also missing in the preceding discussion is an assessment of how gender is produced and reproduced, or socially constructed, in daily interaction and of how **gendered identities** are formed. Candace West and Don Zimmerman's seminal article 'Doing Gender' (1987) deals with these issues. As Table 3.1 shows, West and Zimmerman argue that to understand gender, a distinction needs to be made between sex, sex category, and gender. *Sex* refers to the biological criteria that are widely accepted in society to signify whether one is a man or a woman. *Sex category* is defined as the 'socially required identificatory displays' that help to determine whether one is a man or a woman (see Table 3.1 for examples). *Gender* is 'the activity of managing situated conduct in light of normative conceptions of attitudes and activities appropriate for one's sex category' (West and Zimmerman 1987: 127).

According to West and Zimmerman, if we are to understand the social significance of gender, consideration needs to be given to both sex category and gender. Sex is less important, because we rarely scrutinize individuals' genitals or chromosomes. Rather, sex is assumed on the basis of sex categorization. Yet 'socially required identificatory displays' in and of themselves are not sufficient explanations of gender. Rather, we must understand that individuals 'do gender', and it is through doing gender that sex categorization is reproduced:

> Doing gender involves a complex of socially guided perceptual, interactional,

and micropolitical activities that cast particular pursuits as expressions of masculine and feminine 'natures'. . . . Gender is an emergent feature of social situations: both as an outcome of and a rationale for various social arrangements and as a means of legitimating one of the most fundamental divisions of society. (West and Zimmerman 1987: 126)

Unlike the preceding discussions, in which gender inequality is largely considered a structural issue, West and Zimmerman draw on **symbolic interactionism**, arguing that gender inequality is realized and socially constructed through our daily activities in interaction with others. It is through social interaction that we develop gendered identities (masculinity and femininity) that come to be seen as 'natural'.

Although West and Zimmerman make occasional references to social structures in their work, the relationship between gender (as an activity) and the social structure remains ambiguous. This is, in part, because they never define what they mean by 'social structure'. Early in the article they seem to suggest that gender is a social structure when they note that Agnes's situation (see Table 3.1) 'demonstrates how gender is created through interaction and at the same time structures interaction' (1987: 131) and that 'doing gender' is institutional in character (137). But in their concluding discussion of gender, power, and social change, they state that 'if we do gender appropriately, we simultaneously sustain, reproduce, and render legitimate the institutional arrangements that are based on sex category' (146). Hence, rather than gender being a structure in itself, West and Zimmerman argue (1987: 147) that

> doing gender furnishes the interactional scaffolding of social structure. . . . Gender is a powerful ideological

Table 3.1 Sex, Sex Categorization, and Gender

	Definition	Example of Agnes: A transsexual, raised as a boy who developed a female identity at age 17
Sex	Biological criteria: genitalia at birth (i.e., penis or vagina) or chromosomal typing (i.e., XX or XY).	Agnes had a penis. She thought it was a mistake and had sex reassignment surgery (several years after she developed a female identity) to correct it.
Sex Categorization	Socially required identification that determine one's membership in a sex category (i.e., style of hair or dress; mannerisms, etc.).	At age 17 Agnes began looking like a woman by dressing 'appropriately', wearing make-up, etc.
Gender	Configurations of behaviour and activities involved in 'being' a woman or man.	Agnes began acting like a woman by learning appropriate and inappropriate gendered behaviours. This behaviour was learned, in part, through interactions with her fiancé, who would comment on whether other women were acting appropriately. For instance, she learned that it was 'offensive' for a woman to sunbathe on her front lawn because 'it put her on display to other men'.

Source: West and Zimmerman (1987).

device, which produces, reproduces, and legitimates the choices and limits that are predicated on sex category. An understanding of how gender is produced in social situations will afford clarification of the interactional scaffolding of social structure and the social control processes that sustain it.

Here, doing gender seems to reflect the interactional activities that are temporarily attached to an evolving social structure based on sex category.

In short, West and Zimmerman seem to vacillate between an approach that conceptualizes gender as a social structure and one that locates it as part of what Goffman (1983) has referred to as the 'interaction order'. It is likely that West and Zimmerman intended to develop a conceptualization of gender that encompassed both structural and interactional components. However, their lack of clarity about what social structure is and about the relationship between structural and interactional orders leaves the reader rather confused about their assessment of

gender. Nonetheless, their article is one of the few conceptual papers on gender that explicitly consider agency and interaction (see McMahon 1995 for an excellent example of this approach with respect to motherhood).

Bringing It All Together

In an effort to incorporate macro and micro assessments of gender, Barbara Risman develops an instructive conceptual framework that treats gender itself as a social structure. As Figure 3.1 shows, Risman argues that to conceptualize gender as a structure in its own right, one must consider three levels of analysis. At the individual level, socialization processes and identity formation are at issue. The interactional level of analysis considers cultural, taken-for-granted expectations about behaviour, whereas the institutional level of analysis considers processes of distribution, organizational rules, and ideological discourse. For a full understanding of the structural nature of gender, Risman (1998: 26–9) argues, the relationship between all three levels of analysis must be considered: 'Gender

Figure 3.1: Risman's Structure Framework

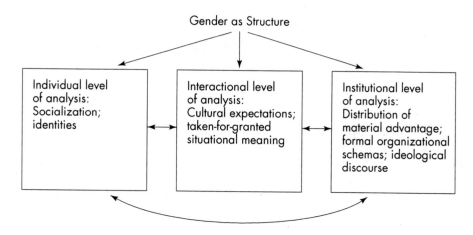

itself must be considered a structural property of society. . . . Gender is deeply embedded as a basis for stratification, differentiating opportunities, and constraints' (28). The idea that gender is a structural property of society aligns well with the conceptual development of gender presented in this book. Yet, because Risman does not discuss gender in relational terms, the gender structure seems, in her argument, rather unconnected from individual experience. This idea is developed further in the next section.

Conceptualizing Gender in a Theory of Inequality

An essential task for the present analysis is to develop gender as a concept that can be well integrated with class, ethnic, race, and age relations. Some argue that, to accomplish this, the gendered division of labour must be at the core of the analysis (Chafetz 1990; Young 1981). Indeed, my emphasis on the processes of production, reproduction, and distribution suggests that I am sympathetic to such calls. However,

it is a mistake to place the 'gendered' division of labour at the forefront of such work: the division of labour in society, in families, and at work is organized simultaneously around the structures of gender, class, race, ethnicity, and age. What we need to ask, rather, is how labour and distribution processes are racialized, gendered, class-based, and age-based (with the exception of age, see also Acker 2006). In other words, we need to know how these fundamental processes of social life are structured by the intersections of class, gender, age, race, and ethnic relations. Focusing on the practices of everyday life—on the things that people do—rather than on categories of people is important for understanding social inequality (Lorber 2006; Ray 2006).

A relational understanding of gender assumes that it is through our interactions with others that the structure of gender is realized. This view is similar to West and Zimmerman's view of gender, in its emphasis on interaction. As West and Zimmerman point out, the structure of gender is not something that acts upon people. Rather, as individuals engage in interactive processes of production, reproduction, and distribution, they reinforce and sometimes modify existing masculine and feminine identities and structures. Structure does not exist outside of the individuals who produce it. However, unlike in West and Zimmerman's view of gender as an activity, in this analysis gender as a structured social relation is conceptualized as a 'deep' social structure (Sewell 1992). Deep social structures underlie all of the activities of everyday life, and they are often invisible. In other words, a deep social structure such as gender is so pervasive in its influence that it is often 'unconscious' and reflects 'taken-for-granted mental assumptions or modes of procedure that actors normally apply without being aware that they are applying them' (Sewell 1992: 22). These taken-for-granted mental assumptions reflect the formal and informal cultural rules of behaviour (Sewell 1992) that influence the actions of women and men. It is important that assumptions about gendered behaviour are not thought to emerge from biological sex differences. Rather, these gendered structures refer to socially constructed differences that reinforce inequality on the basis of one's membership in a particular sex category (Gerson and Peiss 1985; Glenn 2000; Tilly 1998).

As is the case in most structural accounts of gender (see especially Acker's and Walby's, discussed above), a relational understanding of gender focuses on how oppression is implicated in relations among women, among men, and between women and men. Hence, like social class, oppression is an organizing feature of gender relations. For gender relations, however, material oppression is extended to include all types of oppression. Oppression occurs if (1) the welfare of one group of people depends upon the deprivations of another, and (2) the deprivations of the oppressed group depend upon the exclusion of that group from access to resources, rewards, and privileges. In this sense, gendered oppression can be both material and non-material and

it can take place in various settings, including families, labour markets, states, and the education and health systems.

Charles Tilly (1998) argues that exploitation and opportunity hoarding are two mechanisms through which categorical inequality is produced. These mechanisms are especially helpful in explaining the relationship between oppression and structured gender relations. Unlike Wright's view of exploitation (see chapter 2), Tilly's definition does not depend on the appropriation of labour but rather sees exploitation as a mechanism 'which operates when powerful, connected people command resources from which they draw significantly increased returns by coordinating the effort of outsiders whom they exclude from the full value added by that effort' (1998: 10).

Opportunity hoarding is a second mechanism through which categorical inequality is produced. Tilly (1998: 10) defines opportunity hoarding as a mechanism that 'operates when members of a categorically bounded network acquire access to a resource that is valuable, renewable, subject to monopoly, supportive of network activities, and enhanced by the network's modus operandi.'

Although these definitions are abstract, if we consider housework as a concrete example, we can see how gendered oppression is produced through exploitation and opportunity hoarding. When applied to the situation of housework, the assumption of power in Tilly's definition of exploitation suggests that men have the power and resources to have women do their housework for them. Power, in this instance, stems from many sources, including the ideological and cultural schemas that guide gendered behaviour. In twenty-first-century Western civilizations, our ideology and culture suggest that housework is, for the most part, women's work and responsibility. These ideologies combine with the material advantages that most men have over most women to create a situation in

Box 3.3 Why Married Men Earn More: A New Study Says It Solves the Puzzle

By Gene Koretz

What explains the so-called marriage premium—the fact that married men tend to earn more than single men of similar backgrounds and educations? Economists have been divided on the issue.

Some believe that married men earn more because women tend to select mates with good earnings prospects. Others credit the institution of marriage itself, arguing either that it makes men more responsible and diligent or that it boosts their productivity by freeing them from housework and allowing them to focus more on their jobs.

In a new study in the journal *Economic Inquiry*, Hyunbae Chun, of Queens College in New York, and Injae Lee, of New York University, claim to solve the puzzle. Analyzing 1999 survey data covering nearly 2,700 men, they find that married men earn an average of 12.4 per cent more per hour than never-married men, after adjusting for age, work experience, education, and other factors that may affect both wages and marriage prospects.

The two researchers find no evidence that the marriage premium reflects the better economic prospects of men who tend to get hitched. Rather, it appears related to the state of being married—and specifically to the likelihood that wives shoulder household tasks.

Chun and Lee report that the wage gap declines as wives put in more hours working outside the home. While married men whose wives aren't employed earn about 31 per cent more per hour than never-married men, for example, men married to women with a full-time job earn only 3.4 per cent more.

Thus, having a wife who devotes most of her time to raising the kids and other housework evidently pays off for dad in his work on the job. All of which implies that the marriage premium will inevitably shrink as more wives spend longer hours at outside jobs.

Source: Koretz (2001).

---

which men can exploit the unpaid labour of women. Men, then, benefit from increased returns on their material advantages by coordinating the unpaid work efforts of women, 'whom they exclude from the full value added by that effort' (Tilly 1998: 10). (See Box 3.3.)

In the case of housework, opportunity hoarding works to men's advantage in dyadic relationships in which women have more material resources. In these situations, women are still generally responsible for the housework and men tend not to labour for their wives (L. Davies and McAlpine 1998). This happens because men are members of a *categorically bounded network* (Tilly 1998) who have access to unearned resources (i.e., to traditional authority) simply by virtue of their group membership. Recent work on the important connections between hegemonic masculinities and capitalism also point to the significance of opportunity hoarding (see Box 3.4) but notably neglect the problems that older men may face within the context of hegemonic masculinities (Calasanti 2004; Calasanti and Slevin 2006).

Box 3.4 Masculinities and Capitalism

Maculinities are essential components of the on-going male project, capitalism. While white men were and are the main publicly recognized actors in the history of capitalism, these are not just any white men. They have been, for example, aggressive entrepreneurs or strong leaders of industry and finance (Collison and Hearn 1996). Some have been oppositional actors, such as self-respecting and tough workers earning a family wage, and militant labor leaders. They have been particular men whose locations within gendered and racialized social relations and practices can be partially captured by the concept of masculinity. 'Masculinity' is a contested term. As Connell (1995, 2000), Collison and Hearn (1996) and others have pointed out, it should be pluralized as 'masculinities', because in any society at any one time there are several ways of being a man. 'Being a man' involves cultural images and practices. It always implies a contrast to an unidentified femininity.

Hegemonic masculinity can be defined as the taken-for-granted, generally accepted form, attributed to leaders and other influential figures at particular historical times. Hegemonic masculinity legitimates the power of those who embody it. More than one type of hegemonic masculinity may exist simultaneously, although they may share characteristics, as do the business leader and the sports star at the present time. Adjectives describing hegemonic masculinities closely follow those describing characteristics of successful business organizations, as Rosabeth Moss Kanter (1977) pointed out in the 1970s. The successful CEO and the successful organization are aggressive, decisive, competitive, focused on winning and defeating the enemy, taking territory from others. The ideology of capitalist markets is imbued with a masculine ethos. As R.W. Connell (2000: 35) observes, 'The market is often seen as the antithesis of gender (marked by achieved versus ascribed status etc.). But the market operates

through forms of rationality that are historically masculine and involve a sharp split between instrumental reason on the one hand, emotion and human responsibility on the other' (Seidler 1989). Masculinities embedded in collective practices, are part of the context within which certain men made and still make the decisions that drive and shape the ongoing development of capitalism. We can speculate that how these men see themselves, what actions and choices they feel compelled to make and they think are legitimate, how they and the world around them define desirable masculinity, enter into that decision making (Reed 1996). Decisions made at the very top reaches of (masculine) corporate power have consequences that are experienced as inevitable economic forces or disembodied social trends. At the same time, these decisions symbolize and enact varying hegemonic masculinities (Connell 1995). However, the embeddedness of masculinity within the ideologies of business and the market may become invisible, seen as just part of the way business is done. The relatively few women who reach the highest positions probably think and act within these strictures.

References

Acker, Joan (2006) *Class Questions, Feminist Answers*. Lanham MD: Rowman & Littlefield Publishers.

Collinson, David and Jeff Hearn. 1996. Breaking the Silence: On Men, Masculinites and Managements. In *Men as Managers, Managers as Men*, ed. David L. Collinson and Jeff Hearns. London: Sage.

Connell, R.W. 1995. *Masculinities*. Berkeley: University of California Press.

———. 2000. *The Men and the Boys*. Berkeley: University of California Press.

Hearn, Jeff. 1996. 'Is Masculinity Dead? A Critique of the Concept of Masculinity/Masculinites'. Pp.

207–17 in M. Mac an Ghaill, ed., *Understanding Masculinities: Social Relations and Cultural Arenas*. Buckingham: Oxford University Press.
Kantor, Rosabeth Moss. 1977. *Men and Women of the Corporation*. New York: Basic Books.
Reed, Rosslyn. 1996. 'Entrepreneurialism and Paternalism in Australian Management: A Gender Critique of the "Self-Made" Man'. Pp. 99–122

in David L. Collison and Jeff Hearn, eds, *Men as Managers, Managers as Men*. London: Sage.
Seidler, Victor J. 1989. *Rediscovering Masculinity: Reason, Language, and Sexuality*. London: Routledge.

Source: Acker (2006:., 82–3).

According to Tilly (1998), categorical inequality is maintained through emulation and adaptation. That is, we learn from our interaction in social relations in one place, such as the family, and transpose that knowledge to another one, such as labour markets, and adapt accordingly. Continuing with the example of gendered oppression in unpaid work, the experiences of women labouring for men in the home may be transposed to other settings, thereby reinforcing and reproducing gendered oppression. Consider, for instance, a secretary getting her boss a cup of coffee or the segregation of women in undervalued nurturing-type jobs, such as nursing or elementary-school education. Both examples reproduce a structure of gender relations that privileges men at work and at home.

While the concepts of exploitation, opportunity hoarding, emulation, and adaptation account nicely for the depth of structured gender relations, they shed very little light on how the structure of gender relations has changed or on how it continues to evolve. The challenge, then, is to tie the insights gained from 'doing gender' to more structural accounts of gender relations so that social change and the significance of human agency are accounted for (see Gerson and Peiss 1985). Structure and agency will be discussed in chapter 6, but before that, the structures of race, ethnicity, and age will be examined.

Questions for Critical Thought

1. What does it mean when someone says that sex is socially constructed?
2. Discuss the 'problem with patriarchy'. How can patriarchy be reconceptualized as a useful theoretical tool?
3. Choose an activity you regularly engage in. How does that activity reflect the idea of 'doing gender'? Try to think of a social activity that is not gendered. Now, show how gender may influence that activity.
4. How was Beth's life shaped by gender? Discuss the processes of production and reproduction in this regard.
5. How does the concept of opportunity hoarding apply to gender relations? Use two examples (other than housework) to discuss your points.

IIIIIIIIIIII Glossary IIIIIIIIIIIIIIIIIIIIIIIIIIIIIIIIIIIIIIIIIIIIIIIIIIIIIIIIIIIIIIIIIIIIIIIIIIIIIIIIIIIIIIIIIIIIIIIIIIIIIIIIIIIIIIIIIIIIIIIIIIIIIIII II

Dual-system theorists   Socialist feminists who consider patriarchy and capitalism simultaneously as they interact with one another. The problem with dual-system theory is that it does not acknowledge how capitalism and patriarchy mutually constitute one another.

Gendered identities   The feelings, meanings, and subjective experiences attached to a particular gender. Such meanings are developed as we interact with others and are shaped by dominant gender ideologies.

Patriarchy   As discussed by Weber, a form of traditional authority that reflected the relations between men and the power men had over women, children, and often slaves. Feminists consider patriarchy a system of inequality in which men dominate women.

Radical feminism   A branch of feminism that places emphasis on the relations of reproduction and the disadvantages that women face as a result of how reproduction is organized in society. Traditionally, this branch of feminism tended to reduce explanations of women's inequality to their capacity to give birth.

Socialist feminism   A branch of feminism that explains gender inequality by considering simultaneously gender relations and class relations or patriarchy and capitalism.

Symbolic interactionism   A sociological approach that bases its understanding of social phenomona in daily interpersonal interactions. One important criticism of this approach is that it emphasizes individual behaviour to the neglect of social-structural issues.

IIIIIIIIIIII Recommended Reading IIIIIIIIIIIIIIIIIIIIIIIIIIIIIIIIIIIIIIIIIIIIIIIIIIIIIIIIIIIIIIIIIIIIIIIIIIIIIIIIIIIIIIIIIIIIIIIIIIIIIIIIIII

Acker, Joan. 1988. 'Class, Gender, and the Relations of Distribution'. *Signs* 13, 8: 473–97. A seminal article that tackles the complexities of integrating gender and class into a single system of inequality.

Acker, Joan. 2006. *Class Questions, Feminist Answers*. Lanham, MD: Rowman & Littlefield. In this book, Joan Acker further develops her theories on the mutual constitution of class and gender.

Fox, Bonnie J. 1988. 'Conceptualizing "Patriarchy"'. *Canadian Review of Sociology and Anthropology* 25: 163–83. This article provides a good overview of the debates in feminism about the problems with the concept of 'patriarchy'.

Marshall, Barbara L. 2000. *Configuring Gender: Explorations in Theory and Politics*. Peterborough, ON: Broadview Press. In this book, Marshall explores the concept of 'gender', how it has changed, and how it has been used politically in various contexts.

Walby, Sylvia. 1997. *Gender Transformations*. London: Routledge. Sylvia Walby is an ardent supporter of the 'patriarchy' concept. This is one of her latest and best books on how gender structures many domains of social life.

West, Candace, and Don Zimmerman, 1987. 'Doing Gender'. *Gender and Society* 1: 125–51. This is perhaps the most widely cited theoretical article on gender. Using a symbolic-interactionist perspective, it is a theoretical account of how gender is reproduced in everyday life.

||||||||||| Relevant Websites |||||||||||||||||||||||||||||||||||||||||||||||||||||||||||||||||||||||||||||||||||||||| ||

Status of Women Canada
www.swc-cfc.gc.ca
**This website is run by the government of Canada and provides much statistical information, many reports, and funding opportunities for research about women and social inequality.

United Nations Population Fund: Promoting Gender Equality
http://www.unfpa.org/gender/index.htm
**This website focuses on gender equality across the globe. It includes information on gender and development, gender and health, and gender and violence against women.

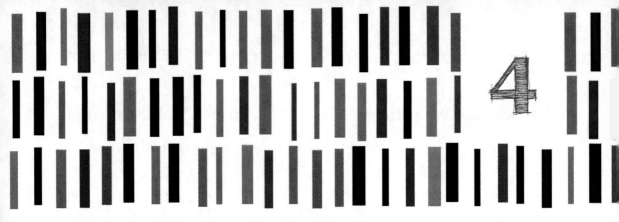

Race, Ethnicity, and Inequality

Introduction

The following quotation is from the end of an influential book by Michael Omi and Howard Winant, *Racial Formation in the United States* (1994: 158–9):

> In the US, race is present in every institution, every relationship, every individual. This is the case not only for the way society is organized—spatially, culturally, in terms of stratification, etc.—but also for our perceptions and understandings of personal experience. Thus as we watch the videotape of Rodney King being beaten, compare real estate prices in different neighbourhoods, select a radio channel to enjoy while we drive to work, size up a potential client, customer, neighbor, or teacher, stand in line at the unemployment office or carry out a thousand other normal tasks, we are compelled to think racially, to use the racial categories and meaning systems into which we have been socialized.

Although there are notable differences between the historical processes of racial formation and racism in Canada and the United States, it is nonetheless clear that racial issues of social inequality are omnipresent in Canada as well. In Canada, we need only be reminded of Darrell Night, a First Nations man who was dumped by the police on the outskirts of Saskatoon on a freezing February night in 2000, and of the numerous other instances of police brutality and racialization in justice and policing that have occurred across Canada (see Box 4.1). We need only remember how Native children were taken from their homes, placed in residential schools, and often abused in the last century. We need only remember Oka and Caledonia. As Valerie Bedassigae Pheasant's narrative in Box 4.2 shows, the experience of racism is devastating in its social and psychological consequences.

Of course, the history and extent of white privilege and racism in Canada extends beyond the First Nations/white racial dichotomy. During the early twentieth century, Chinese immigrants were required to pay an exorbitant $500 'head tax' for entry to Canada; according to one government spokesperson, this tax 'so effectually restricted the inflow from China that it ceased to be a cause for alarm' (Craig 1968, cited in Knowles 1992: 48). During the Second World War, Japanese Canadians were moved to internment camps simply because of their ancestry. Japanese Canadians have since

Box 4.1 Fact Sheet #7: Understanding the Racialization of Poverty in Ontario in Justice & Policing in 2007

How does the criminal justice system affect and impact racialized communities?

Research shows that crime and violence in communities are very closely linked to the despair and loss of hope that come from inequality and poverty.

With the growing poverty among racialized communities in Ontario, gangs and gun-related crime have also grown. Governments and law enforcement agents tend to treat racialized persons as criminals and use the justice system to punish them, rather than addressing poverty, unemployment and inequality in these communities.

Racial profiling—targeting of racialized persons by policing authorities—is all too common. For example:

- African Canadian students in Toronto are 4 times more likely to be stopped and 8 times more likely to be searched than White students in the same places.
- In a large sample of Toronto youth who had no police records, more than 50 per cent of Blacks had been searched by police in the previous two years, compared to only 8 per cent of Whites.
- A study in Kingston showed that police were 3.7 times more likely to stop Black people.

In Ontario, Black suspects are 5.5 times more likely to be killed or seriously injured from police use of force than White suspects, and they are 10 times more likely to be shot by police.

African Canadians represent over 6 per cent of the federal prison population even though they comprise only about 2 per cent of the Canadian population. In Ontario, they make up 14.0 per cent of the federal offender population but only 33.3 per cent of the provincial population.

The so-called 'war on drugs' targets racialized communities. Police focus on low-level street dealers instead of powerful druglords because it makes for high arrest records and publicity. Many dealers are poor, racialized youth with few opportunities.

Quick Notes

- Ontario's growing racialized communities face a disproportionate, ongoing, and increasing risk of being poor.
- Racialized persons refers to people of colour who are Canadian-born and to newcomer communities of colour.
- By racism, we mean both the individual attitudes and behaviours as well as the built-in ways in which social policies and societal institutions discriminate.
- Households that fall below Canada's low income cut-off (LICO) measure spend a much larger percentage of their income on basic necessities like food and shelter than the average family.
- Racialized families are from 2 to 4 times more likely than White families to fall below the LICO.
- Individual and systemic racism have clear & negative impacts on life chances for people of colour in Ontario.

A study of more than 10,000 arrest records in Toronto showed that:

- Whites arrested on drug charges were more likely than Blacks to be released at the scene.
- Blacks were twice as likely as Whites to be held overnight for a bail hearing.
- Blacks were more likely to be charged for offences that could only be detected *after* being pulled over in traffic by police.

Research in Toronto shows that White men are less likely to be stopped by police as they grow older and have higher incomes, but these factors make no difference for Black men.

Racism is the most common reason for hate crimes in Canada with 57 per cent of such crimes against Blacks and South Asians.

Everyday Lives

'I'm scared when they go out with Black friends. They're like a magnet. It's not fair that four Black kids can't walk around.'

'Just before take-off my colleague and I were called out from inside the place and asked to bring out our carry-on luggage. We were told that due to a security reason we will not be able to take this flight. After asking repeatedly for the reason, I was told that a passenger complained to the pilot that I was staring at the passenger. The pilot considered this to be security risk. . . . I wear a turban and the pilot mistook my identity for a Muslim person.'

'[After being interrogated and searched 8 out of 9 times when crossing the border], it is extremely difficult to develop a sense of loyalty to a country where each time one attempts to re-enter he is treated in such fashion.'

'When you're a young person people think you're bad, what is the point of behaving well anyway, if they are going to treat you like a criminal . . . ?'

'Where I live, which is a lower-income neighbourhood, where we are "housed"—there's no other word for it—[our] youth live in a glass bowl, in a poisoned environment, where they are continually . . . harassed and brutalized by security forces—not just the police, but by security guards also.'

'The constable assumed either my wife was a prostitute . . . or we were in Parkdale to buy drugs.'

The Canadian government recently issued a 'no fly' list of people who are thought to pose a threat to security; those on the list are banned from air travel. There is good reason to believe the list will unfairly target racial and religious minority groups.

Many racialized persons, particularly Muslim men, are targeted for searches or questioning at the Canadian border.

Toronto police are compiling a 'no walk' list, which requires racialized youth to show ID and consent to questioning and searches whenever the police approach them. Their personal details are written on a special form and kept in police files.

In the name of fighting terrorism, the Canadian government has put several Muslim men under detention for years without charges by using 'security certificates'. While the Supreme Court of Canada has rules that security certificates violate these individuals' rights, the court has allowed their detention to be in effect for at least another year.

Racialized and poor women are among the fastest growing groups in the prison population in Ontario.

Seven times more Black women than White women are sent to Ontario prisons. 1 of 3 women in prison is from a racialized group.

Source: Colour of Poverty, www.colourofpoverty.ca, accessed February 5, 2009.

---

received compensation and a formal apology from the federal government for the injustices they suffered, and class action suits arguing that the Chinese head taxes were discriminatory and racist were recognized by the Canadian government in 2006. Although these events appear to be part of a distant past, the racialized persons and their families who were affected by these events still suffer the social, economic, and health effects of the original injustice (Ujimoto 1994).

Those are some examples of the blatant racism that occurs in Canada. More subtle forms of racism and racial discrimination also exist

Box 4.2 My Mother Used to Dance

By Valerie Bedassigae Pheasant

She was graceful and light. Her movements made the room disappear. There was only her. Every shift and swirl of her warp caused the air to move so that I could see the patterns in the air. I looked at her face. It was my mother's face, but it was possessed by a spirit that I had not seen before. She kept moving, without touching the floor. She smiled and danced. Her face radiated—my mother was free.

I sat on the banister railing for what felt like an eternity watching my mother. As silently as I crept to watch, I left. I wondered why she did not dance for us. That was the first and only time I saw my mother dance with abandon. What I did see was a gradual freezing of her emotions and a treacherous walk with silence. Her metamorphosis had happened before our eyes and we were unable to stop it. Why didn't she yell at them? Why didn't she tell them—no? Where did the fire go? When was it that the dancing stopped?

The cocoon that encased my mother was woven by inside thoughts that constricted her more strongly than anything tangible in the human world. Inside thoughts reacting to outside action generated towards our family's Nativeness. Blatant racist remarks and statements by women who did not care to know us. Each word, each comment diminished her capacity to speak—she moved slower and slower.

. . . . .

I have to accompany my mother to the school for parent-teacher interviews. We go from teacher to teacher. My mother glances at the report cards and listens to the teacher pass information to her about her children. Each in succession. We are almost finished. It is time for her to see the grade three teacher. I am instructed to wait outside the door. My mother is alone. In the stillness I can hear everything that my mother hears. I am afraid to move. The voice grows loud in my ears, telling her that her son doesn't know what to do. How can he pass? He has trouble reading. The voice grows louder, trying to convince her. I hear no response. Pages are being torn out of a workbook. The voice burns in our ears. . . . 'He cheated. He could not have done this. This work will not count!' More pages being ripped. I feel the shame and the guilt. It grows quiet. A chair moves. The door opens. My mother walks out. I am waiting. I see the humiliation and the pain. My anger ignites, recedes, and begins to smoulder. My mother is exhausted. We go to the next teacher.

More pressure is put on the older children to help the younger ones with their homework. We do it because we cannot allow people to think that we are 'stupid Indians'. I detest these people I do not know. How can they make a judgement about Native people without knowing or caring to know about us?—judgements made in ignorance. I decided that someday I would tell them about things they did not want to hear, about things they were afraid to ask. I decided to talk back. There was nothing to lose. People hated us anyway.

. . . . .

Parent-teacher interviews for my daughter. I go alone. I am afraid. Each time, I am afraid. I recognize the fear—we have met before. Now I am the mother. There is no child outside the door. I will not let her come along. The meeting is between adults—both trained in the same Bingo Palace. Only this time one of us refused to be a player.

We meet. Cordial greeting. Forced pleasantries. I am asked what the problem is. Why is it that your daughter will not participate? Why does she think she can get away with this? How come she didn't finish her project on the family unit? I cut in. I willed my voice to an even tone. There are explosions in my brain. I refuse to have this woman speak to me in a condescending fashion. I inquire about my daughter's lack of participation; about the model of family structure that is being recognized and rewarded in class. Ours does not fit the mould, I explain. My words are vaporized. I ask about forms of resistance being demonstrated by other girls. None. I ask about the manner in which questions are directed at my daughter. The teacher's voice rises by several decibels. She yells, 'I am sick and tired of hearing Athena this and Athena that. She is not that special. What's all the fuss about?'

I breathe in. I stare in disbelief. I refuse to accept the blame, and feel the guilt and shame this woman, this teacher, is trying to place on me. Sparks are flying. I must remain in control. I refuse to speak. I can only stare. She stops to catch her breath. She demands to show me her proof. I move the chair and stand up. She steps back. I look at her with disgust. I start towards the door. She yells out at me, 'I am not finished yet!' I am overwhelmed by her bile. I begin to smile, the images of long ago play themselves out, and the anger subsides. The spectre of my younger self shadowed in the doorway looks on, lips upturned and eyes strong and steady. I turn and distinctly reply, 'Yes, but I am.' My smile grows. I walk out on shaky legs. Somewhere music—and my spirit starts to dance.

Tears? Yes, there are tears. I cry for my mother, myself, and my daughter. I cry because our children's spirits are still being assaulted—not educated. My tears (I am reminded) are good. They help us to heal. They return to Mother Earth. They cleanse us, help us grow.

My anger is still in me. It is mine. I earned it. I share it. It belongs to all of us, collectively. The forces of religion, education, society, the judiciary, the media, make it a real, everyday occurrence. At times I do not realize there is a difference between being happy, being angry, and being alive. I have had to make friends with anger. We are together when people continue to say—you sound so angry when you speak about the education system. Yes I am, because it continues to perpetuate inaccuracies. I am angry when Aboriginal peoples are labelled 'Indians'. I am angry when a person is devalued by the colour of their skin. Yes I am, when children are victimized. Yes I am, when I am patronized. Yes I am, when teachers continue to tell us that we were discovered out of our own savage chasm of non-sentience. Yes, I am angry when people are silenced. Yes I am, when people try to use me to justify their theories. Yes, I am angry.

Who says we can't dance? 'Whoever pays the piper, calls the tune'—well, we've paid the piper for half a millennium. It's time to call the tune. It's time to dance.

Source: Pheasant (2001). Carl E. James and Adrienne Shad, eds., *Talking About Identity: Encounters in Race, Ethnicity and Language* (Toronto: Between the Lines, 2001)

in our schools, families, labour markets, and health systems, and in the state. These issues will be discussed in the second part of this book. The purpose of this chapter is to assess several approaches to race that have been proposed in the sociological literature, as well as the relationship between ethnicity and race. The chapter will conclude with a discussion of the conceptualization of race that will be used in this book.

Thus far in this discussion I have taken as given the concept of race. Some sociologists argue that using the concept 'race' without being critical of it is misleading, analytically incorrect, and politically dangerous (Loveman 1999; Miles and Torres 2000; Satzewich 1998). They argue that if scholars use the concept of race without problematizing it, race becomes reified. Sociologists use the term **reification** to refer to processes in which abstract concepts become real. Usually, processes of reification involve a generally held acceptance of a particular concept as immutable and somehow grounded in nature. Although most sociologists now accept that the character of race varies historically and temporally and that it has no biological basis, the problem is that these are not universally held views. By using the concept 'race', it is argued, sociologists reinforce and reproduce commonly held assumptions about the 'nature' of race. Hence, scholars who see reification as a problem argue that race as a category of sociological analysis should be abandoned entirely. Debates about this issue are rampant and contentious. It is to these debates that I now turn.

Abandoning the Concept of Race

The dangers of reifying race, combined with ambiguities about the concept itself, have led some to argue that the concept should not be used at all in social-scientific analysis (Loveman 1999; Miles and Torres 2000; Satzewich 1998). Arguments of this sort emerged in the social sciences in the early twentieth century, when scholars such as Max Weber, W.E.B. Du Bois, and Franz Boas rejected biological assessments of race (Omi and Winant 1994). Ashley Montagu was perhaps the first physical anthropologist to adopt this view, in his controversial and bold book *Man's Most Dangerous Myth: A Fallacy of Race* (see Reynolds 1992). Montagu argued against the use of mainstream classifications of race that relied on biological or physiological criteria. Since then, social scientists have disputed the scientific 'evidence' that suggests that *Homo sapiens* can be neatly divided and classified into different racial categories on the basis of some physical characteristic (by phenotype, e.g., skin colour) or genetic difference (by genotype—for example, identification of a 'race' gene). Historical research outlining how the meaning of race has changed over time and place (Miles 1989) adds support to the idea that

'race' categories are fluid. Most sociologists who study race are persuaded by these arguments and view race as a **social construction** rather than a biological essence. Notably, however, there is still a tendency among physical and developmental psychologists either to endorse the existence of a biologically grounded 'race' concept or to be ambivalent about it (Reynolds 1992). Outside of academia it is generally believed that clearly demarcated 'races' do exist. The persistence of these beliefs combined with the limited academic endorsement of biological race is one of the central reasons that critics of the term call for it to be abandoned (Miles and Torres 2000; Satzewich 1998).

A second argument against the use of the concept of race reflects the complexity and ambiguity associated with the term (Small 1998). If we accept, for instance, that physical characteristics and biological differences cannot accurately classify races of people, then what can? Country of birth? Nationality? Mother tongue? Some combination of these things? Does the colour of one's skin matter at all? Further confusion arises when one considers the relationship between race and ethnicity. Is race different from ethnicity? If so, how?

Notably, scholars who condemn the use of the 'race' concept in the social sciences do not dispute that white privilege, racism, and inequality on the basis of what many refer to as 'race' exists. And, indeed, arguments that call for us to abandon race in our scholarship are meritorious. However, just as using the concept 'race' is risky business, so too is abandoning it. This is especially true in an era in which academic work is increasingly subjected to scrutiny by politicians, members of the media, and the public and in which the potential exists for a conservative misinterpretation of 'race' as insignificant (Omi and Winant 1994). In fact, others argue that because race is real in its consequences, it should not be abandoned as a category of sociological analysis (Bonilla-Silva 1997; Fleras and Elliott

2007; Omi and Winant 1994). Indeed, Omi and Winant go so far as to say that it is only

> by noticing race [that] we can begin to challenge racism, with its ever-more-absurd reduction of human experience to an essence attributed to all without regard for historical or social context. By noticing race we can challenge the state, the institutions of civil society, and ourselves as individuals to combat the legacy of inequality and injustice inherited from the past. By noticing race we can develop the political insight and mobilization necessary to make the US [and Canada] a more racially just and egalitarian society. (1994: 159)

Race is *not* rooted in biology. It is *not* a natural category of distinction. Race *is* socially constructed. And the social construction of race *does* matter. Although the use of the term *race* is unfashionable, I am convinced by Omi and Winant's argument and hence I use the term here. The challenge lies in conceptualizing race in a way that (1) does not disregard the complex social processes that lead to racialized outcomes of inequality (e.g., differences in income or occupational status) and (2) does not lead to a legitimation of the 'essence' of race by either academics or non-academics (see Miles and Torres 2000).

Conceptualizing Race/Ethnicity and Racism/Ethnicism

Although the preceding discussion has focused on race, both race and ethnicity have historically been significant structures of inequality in Canadian society (see Kalbach and Kalbach 2000). Not surprisingly, in light of some of the questions posed above, there is in the empirical literature on race and ethnicity considerable conceptual confusion between the two terms. Indeed, one cannot understand race without understanding ethnicity, and yet distinguishing between them is complex.

Ethnicity: Issues of Culture and Identity

There is a decided emphasis in ethnic studies on culture, **ideology**, and descent as determinants of ethnic group and ethnic identity. Such accounts probably stem, at least in part, from Weber's assessment of ethnicity in *Economy and Society* ([1922] 1978). For Weber, ethnicity is socially constructed because beliefs about group differences serve to exclude individuals from certain associations while including them in others. Actual group differences need not have considerable social consequences. The social consequences of group differences emerge only when people begin to believe that those differences are significant. For Weber, ethnicity is constructed around several dimensions, including differences in language, customs, religion, ancestry, and physical characteristics. Again, however, these various differences have social significance only when they serve as the basis for labelling people as members of one ethnic group or another (Weber [1922] 1978). Weber argued that the reason for this labelling is not to identify groups of people with a common ancestry or nation. Rather, it is to exclude some groups from the rights and privileges that other groups enjoy. Social exclusion is thus a crucial concept in Weberian scholarship on ethnic-based inequality.

Similarly, Allahar and Côté (1998: 72) rely on social exclusion, or what they refer to as an 'in-group/out-group dynamic', in their definition of ethnicity. In their view, ethnic-group identification and membership involve both subjective and objective assessments about whether the following characteristics apply to an individual or group:

> (a) a common history with a set of shared values and customs, language, style of dress, food, music, and other cultural attributes

Figure 4.1: Visible Minority Groups, Canada, 2001 and 2006

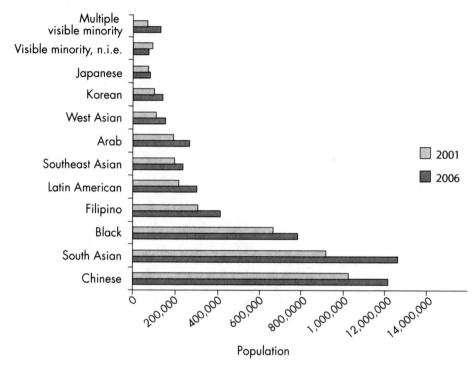

Source: Statistics Canada, 2001 Census, Statistics Canada catalogue 95F0489XCB2001001; 2006 Census, Statistics Canada catalogue 97-562-X2006010.

(b) a myth of common descent

(c) national or territorial claims to sovereignty

(d) an assumed inherited racial marker such as skin colour, hair texture, or facial features

(e) some degree of economic or occupational specialization (Allahar and Côté 1998: 72)

Using one or more of these criteria, most Canadians engage in subjective assessments about whether they belong to a particular ethnic group and to which ethnic group others belong. We often interpret each other's names and physical characteristics and ask questions such as 'Are you Italian?' 'What am I?' or assign some sort of ethnic identity (Scottish, Greek, Italian) to ourselves and others. Researchers also examine ethnicity on the basis of these self-assessments. (See Figure 4.1 and Table 4.1 for description of the racial and ethnic composition of Canada's population.)

Studies of ethnicity tend to be concerned with assimilation (the extent to which ethnic groups are integrated into communities), cultural pluralism (the extent to which ethnic groups have maintained their ethnic identity), and whether certain ethnic groups are socially disadvantaged compared to other ethnic groups (see Kalbach and Kalbach 2000; Satzewich 1998). Although all of these issues are related, the focus in this book is on the last.

Table 4.1 Top 10 Ethnic Origins, Based on Total Responses, Canada, 1996, 2001, 2006

1996			2001			2006		
	n	%		n	%		n	%
Total population	28,528,125	–	Total population	29,639,030	–	Total population	31,241,030	–
Canadian	8,806,275	30.9	Canadian	11,682,680	39.4	Canadian	10,066,292	32.2
English	6,832,095	23.9	English	5,978,875	20.2	English	6,570,015	21.0
French	5,597,845	19.6	French	4,668,410	15.8	French	4,941,210	15.8
Scottish	4,260,840	14.9	Scottish	4,157,215	14.0	Scottish	4,719,850	15.1
Irish	3,767,610	13.2	Irish	3,822,660	12.9	Irish	4,354,155	13.9
German	2,757,140	9.7	German	2,742,765	9.3	German	3,179,425	10.2
Italian	1,207,475	4.2	Italian	1,270,369	4.3	Italian	1,445,335	4.6
Chinese	1,026,475	3.6	Chinese	1,094,700	3.7	Chinese	1,346,510	4.3
North American Indian	921,585	3.2	Ukranian	1,071,055	3.6	North American Indian	1,253,615	4.0
Ukranian	916,215	3.2	North American Indian	1,000,890	3.4	Ukranian	1,209,085	3.9

Note: Table shows total responses. Because some respondents reported more than one ethnic origin, the sum is greater than the total population or 100%.
Source: Statistics Canada (2003: 45); 2006 Census, Statistics Canada catalogue 97-562-X2006006.

Notably, certain characteristics that are usually associated with 'race', such as colour of skin, are included as one component of ethnicity in Allahar and Côté's definition. Indeed, in sociological research, race is often subsumed under the broad rubric of ethnicity (Anthias 1992; Loveman 1999). For instance, Anthias (1992: 421) argues that race categories 'belong to the more encompassing category of ethnic collectivity' because 'race' is only one of many ways in which exclusion is perpetuated on the basis of one's ethos or origin (either socially constructed or real). Similarly, Loveman (1999: 895) argues against the separation of race and ethnicity as categories of analysis because she questions whether there is anything 'unique about the operation or consequences of "race"'. Omi and Winant (1994), on the other hand, argue that processes and consequences of racial formation are very different

from processes and consequences of ethnic formation. For example, the social construction of 'Native' or 'black' in Canada and the United States—rooted in processes of genocide and slavery—is very different from the ethnic formation of and **discrimination** experienced by Irish immigrants in North America in the nineteenth century. What is needed, Omi and Winant argue, is a structural approach to race that does not reduce it to issues of ethnicity.

Toward a Structural Account of Race and Racism

In the Marxist tradition, race and ethnicity 'are the masks behind which actors conceal their class position both from each other and from themselves' (McAll 1990: 70). Marxist accounts of social inequality examine the role that race and ethnicity play in maintaining class boundaries.

According to these perspectives, owners in certain manufacturing industries have traditionally hired immigrant workers at low levels of pay in order to maintain or increase their profit margins. Because these immigrant workers have little choice but to work for low wages, they are considered a threat by the established and higher-paid working class. Race and ethnicity become divisions within the working class. This process is useful for capitalism because hostilities that would normally be directed toward the owners of the means of production are now contained among the workers themselves (Miles 1989; and see also McAll 1990). As Miles (1989: 111) argues, 'racism became a relation of production because it was an ideology which shaped decisively the formation and reproduction of the relation between exploiter and exploited: it was one of those representational elements which became historically conducive to the constitution and reproduction of a system of commodity production'. The main problem with Marxist approaches to race and ethnicity is that their analysis is reduced to issues of social class; ethnicity and race do not warrant investigation in their own right (Bonilla-Silva 1997). Taking issue with approaches to race that focus on class (or ethnicity or nation), Omi and Winant (1994: 55) define race as 'a concept which signifies and symbolizes social conflicts and interests by referring to different types of human bodies'.

Racial Formation

According to Omi and Winant (1994: 55), racial formation is a 'sociohistorical process by which racial categories are created, inhabited, transformed, and destroyed'. The theory of racial formation centres on two related social phenomena: (1) historically situated racial projects and (2) the evolution of **hegemony**. Hegemony, a concept Omi and Winant borrow from the work of Antonio Gramsci, is the achievement and maintenance of rule by both political coercion

and ideological consent (Gramsci 1971). Hence, Omi and Winant emphasize the role that political structures play in racial formation, arguing that 'race is now a preeminently political phenomenon' (1994: 65) maintained through hegemonic forms of racial rule (67).

According to Gramsci (1971), hegemonic forms of rule evolve in modern societies as the force and coercion necessary for a ruling class to achieve dominance gives way to consent. Consent does not replace coercion in hegemonic forms of rule, but it takes on a more central role in modern systems of domination. Consent is achieved through the assimilation of crucial interests of subordinate groups with the interests of dominant groups, often to the disadvantage of the dominant groups themselves. It is maintained through an ideological system that is controlled by the ruling group but that subordinate groups accept as legitimate. Such ideological systems are perpetuated in practice through institutions such as the family, religion, education, and the media.

With respect to racial formation in the United States, Omi and Winant note that the use of extreme force in a racial dictatorship through African slavery and the mass murder and expulsion of First Nations peoples gave way to consent in what might now be referred to as a 'racial democracy'. Crucial to this process were efforts of the subordinate racial groups to usurp, and later embrace, the religious and philosophical ideas of their oppressors. Regarding African slaves, Omi and Winant (1994: 67) write:

> In their language, in their religion with its focus on the Exodus theme and on Jesus's tribulations, in their music with its figuring of suffering, resistance, perserverance, and transcendence, in their interrogation of a political philosophy which sought perpetually to rationalize their bondage in a supposedly 'free' society, the slaves incorporated elements of racial rule into their thought

and practice, turning them against their original bearers.

Besides hegemony, Omi and Winant argue, racial formation also relies on racial projects. *Racial projects* are processes through which 'human bodies and social structures are represented and organized' (Omi and Winant 1994: 56). They link everyday experiences with social structures. In other words, racial projects 'connect what race means in a particular discursive practice and the ways in which both social structures and everyday experiences are racially organized, based on meaning' (Omi and Winant 1994: 56). Hence, racial projects occur at both the structural level and as individuals interact with one another. Racial projects are historically situated, and, say Omi and Winant, conventional understandings of race vary accordingly. In other words, what is meant by *race*, *black*, *white*, or *Aboriginal* today is very different from what these words meant 100 years ago. And the meanings of these words are different depending on where one lives (e.g., Canada as opposed to South Africa).

Structural racial projects occur in social, political, and economic domains, and examples of structural racial projects appear in Canada's newspapers nearly daily. For instance, in 2001 the government of British Columbia attempted to resolve Native land claim disputes and other 'Native' issues by conducting a survey of its residents to assess their views on these issues. The questions were worded in such away that the answers would favour right-wing government action. Aboriginal groups and human-rights advocates argued that the questions were biased against First Nations peoples. The use of the survey by the government of British Columbia and the negative response to it by some groups are examples of politically structured racial projects. In labour markets, the failure of management or unions to take claims of racism seriously is another example of a structural racial project (see Box 4.3).

Racial projects also occur at the individual level as people interact with one another. People make assumptions about others on the basis of their race and interact with them accordingly. Box 4.4 provides many examples of interactional racial projects. In it is the story of Crystal Samms, an Aboriginal 15-year-old who recently transferred to a Toronto high school that takes pride in its diversity. One of Crystal's racial projects becomes clear early in the article when she notes, referring to Caribbean classmates, that she is 'not racist, but there's a certain race that causes trouble'. And the racial projects of others in her class emerge when Crystal recounts how she was mistaken for Hispanic and how, when she corrected this misconception, her friends stared at her blankly, not knowing how to respond.

These examples of racial projects point to the importance of distinguishing racist racial projects from non-racist racial projects. Omi and Winant argue that 'a racial project can be defined as racist if and only if it creates or reproduces structures of domination based on essentialist categories of race' (1994: 71). The BC government's survey can be defined as a racist project because it meets both of these criteria. However, mistaking Crystal for Hispanic does not contribute to creating or reproducing a structure of domination and hence it is not likely 'racist'. As Omi and Winant (1994: 71) conclude, 'to attribute merits, allocate values or resources to, and/or represent individuals or groups on the basis of racial identity should not be considered racist in and of itself'.

Paying close attention to the ways in which social structures and individual experiences intersect, Omi and Winant argue that it is through structural and interactional racial projects that race becomes 'common sense' (Omi and Winant 1994), conventional (Giddens 1993), or a deep structure (Sewell 1992). Through our experiences with racial projects, we internalize racial classification schema and make assessments

Box 4.3 Ontario's Black Jail Guards Want Probe into Workplace Racism. Complaints Taken Seriously, Minister Says, But No Inquiry Planned

By Colin Perkel

The day Anthony Weekes started working as a corrections officer in Toronto, the racist response from fellow guards stunned him.

'You mean they hired another effin' nigger?' Mr Weekes remembers one saying. 'That was my greeting on the first day of the job,' he told a news conference yesterday.

Seventeen years later, rampant and systemic racism persists, Mr Weekes and other black corrections workers say, and neither the government nor their own union has done much to stop it.

They want a public inquiry, saying it's the only way to shed light on what they describe as an ugly environment for members of visible minorities working in Ontario's prison system.

From racial slurs and Ku Klux Klan signs scribbled on prison walls to denials of promotions, the workers say they've paid a price for the colour of their skin, and a dearer price for speaking out.

'Our careers are done,' said Anthony Simon, 54, another guard who says his car was smashed after he complained.

'This is the reality of the society that we live in . . . that when we speak up for our own, when we speak up for our rights and justice, we pay the price.'

Correctional Services Minister Rob Sampson says the government takes the complaints 'quite seriously' but immediately refused a public inquiry, saying a process is in place to deal with them.

Liberal Alvin Curling says Mr Sampson has 'failed miserably'.

'Nothing has been done. People continue to be harassed and discriminated against.'

Mr Curling believes a public inquiry is required because the complaints processes aren't effective. Recommendations for the Human Rights Commission and labour board rulings have been ignored, he says.

The officers say their own union has failed them as well.

Leighton Hope, 46, who works at the Maplehurst Correctional Complex, says he filed a grievance in 1989 through the Ontario Public Service Employees Union after being denied a promotion.

His case remains unresolved more than a decade later.

'I have resigned myself that not much will change,' Mr Hope said.

OPSEU officials could not be reached for comment.

Anthony Garrick, 41, who started working at the Toronto youth detention centre in 1986, has been active on the ministry's antiracism committee and represented the union on race issues.

'It's very difficult because you're addressing the problem while being victimized,' Mr Garrick said.

The managers who are supposed to implement anti-racism policies in the workplace are among those who either overlook the racism or practise it themselves, Mr Garrick said.

For Mr Weekes, the situation at the probation office where he now works got so bad he took stress leave last August to escape the 'poisoned environment'. When his vacation and sick time expired, Mr Weekes says he was forced to return to work against his doctor's orders.

'It clearly shows there is no hope for any improvement in this ministry unless the public gets involved.'

Source: Perkel (2000). Reprinted by permission of The Canadian Press.

Box 4.4 Canada's Apartheid Part 2: Crystal's Choice: The Best of Both Worlds

By John Stackhouse

Beneath the west flight path into Toronto's international airport sits a swath of portable classrooms, unheated and dimly lit, and each one resounding with a medley of accents.

On a field that was part of an Indian village before it was plowed by British settlers, converted to subdivisions and finally jammed with apartment blocks full of new immigrants, St Francis Xavier Secondary School in central Mississauga has become the image of a new Canada.

In a Grade 9 portable, a couple of Jamaicans talk about a coming track meet and plans for a weekend party. Italian, Ecuadorean and Chinese kids join in, ignoring their math assignments as they jabber in some of the 16 languages known to the school, and then revert as easily to English.

After a while, the conversations weave through each other so much that any inflection or slang becomes indistinguishable from the next. It seems as though the students and their families have always been here.

Except for one girl. She looks a bit uncomfortable as she sheds her nylon jacket and settles at the back of the classroom, but she knows that even though she is new to the school, her people always have been here.

At 15, Crystal Samms bubbles with the pride and confusion of someone trying to find her way in a foreign land. St Francis Xavier's 1,000 students list 90 countries as their homelands, but she is the only native Canadian among them. 'When you speak of Canada, I am Canadian,' she says. 'This is my country.'

Which is why, in Grade 9, she represents the biggest emerging challenge for native Canadians. Once segregated and forgotten on remote reserves, Aboriginal people are fast becoming urban people. But in the ethnic sprawl of Toronto or Vancouver, or even Edmonton, Winnipeg, and Ottawa, they are finding a very new Canada that is not very white, not very homogenous and not very interested in their concerns.

For Crystal, there is an age-old struggle here to preserve her native identity as she grows more distant from her ancestral reserve in Southwestern Ontario. But there is also that new challenge: how to forge an identity as one minority among many.

Inside the main building at St Francis Xavier (which relies on portables to keep up with local population growth), the hallways are a river of colours and torrent of international concerns. There are posters denouncing Third World sweat shops, coffee slaves and sugar slaves, as though the school were preparing for a Naomi Klein convention. By the entrance, there are also sacks and sacks of clothes, toys, and cooking utensils, collected by students as part of a drive to help families in Zambia and Malawi.

Soon after she transferred here in September, 2000, Crystal discovered that most students hang out with kids of their own race or colour. The school is proud of its diversity, even in the face of emerging ethnic gangs. ('I'm not racist, but there's a certain race that causes trouble,' Crystal says of the Caribbean girls in her class.)

At first, many kids took her for Hispanic, with her lip gloss, long nails and dark hair slicked back into a ponytail. When she told them she was Aboriginal, most of them stared blankly, which angered her more.

Didn't the students understand, she wondered, that there is a Third World just down the highway, a place where she once lived?

'I want them to focus on our world,' Crystal says as her teacher interrupts his lesson to listen to her. 'This is our land. The Spanish people, their land is in Ecuador. The Jamaican people, their land is in Jamaica. The English, their land is London. Our land is right here and we had it taken away.'

By the time math class ends, Crystal has calmed down and turned her attention to another conversation, to find out where the weekend party will be. She also needs to collect her books and hurry to the main building to find her friend Amber. They need to talk about lunch.

While Crystal may have to shout to express her native identity, she also has to cope with the struggle of every teenager, to find herself in a world her parents do not understand. On the reserve, it might have been dictated by elders and traditional mores. But in the city, she has only herself, in an ocean of choices.

As Crystal goes in search of her best friend, she passes through the crowded school atrium, slipping by the taunts of a thuggish Hispanic gang. She hopes to find Amber at the entrance to the cafeteria, which is licensed to Harvey's, but the doorway is blocked by a group of black kids.

Crystal pushes past them too, as if she were at Square One, Mississauga's nearby shopping centrepiece. She's in a hurry, and afraid of no one.

When she was introduced at an assembly as the school's only Aboriginal student, jokers began to call her 'Running Water' and ask if she parked her canoe in the school lot. Others showed reverence.

'I wish I could be native, it's the coolest culture,' she remembers one girl saying to her. 'It's so spiritual.'

Those who knew anything about natives seemed to get their images from television, from Hollywood stereotypes and shocking nightly news clips, like the ones last year that showed children sniffing gasoline in Sheshatshui. At the time, someone asked Crystal why the Labrador gasoline sniffers did it. She said she didn't know. They weren't her kids. She said she was 'disgusted' with the media for focusing on one negative image of native life.

'I had friends come up to me and ask me, "So what's that all about?"

'I said, "How am I supposed to know?"

'"You're native."

'I said, "Because I'm native, I'm supposed to know all the answers?"

'Then an Italian friend said, "Is it like that on your reserve?"

'"Like what?"

'"I heard there's lots of drugs and drinking on reserves."

'I was disgusted. I told her to walk away. Then I said, "Oh, yeah, I heard Italians are fat and eat a lot of pasta. Is that true?"'

about our own racial identity and that of others. For Omi and Winant, then, racial projects connect social structures with individuals and are simultaneously interactional and structural.

Omi and Winant's racial-formation theory has been most strongly criticized for their use of the concept of race (Loveman 1999; Miles and Torres 2000; Satzewich 1998). As noted above, while I am sympathetic to arguments in favour of abandoning 'race', I remain convinced of the utility of studying it as a social-structural, relational, and socially constructed concept. Eduardo Bonilla-Silva's comments in defence of his use of the concept of race are telling in this regard:

As long as 'reified' blacks in the United States are still lynched by individual whites (as in the recent case in Jasper, Texas) and are 4.3 times more likely than whites to receive the death sentence; insofar as 'reified' white Brazilians are 8.5 times more likely than black Brazilians and 5 times more likely than *pardos* to receive a college education; and as long as black Puerto Ricans have little access to political, economic, and social resources, I, a 'reified' black-looking Puerto Rican, will continue to study racial structurations throughout the world. (1999: 905)

Although he agrees with Omi and Winant in their use of the concept 'race', Bonilla-Silva (1997) is critical of them for not placing enough emphasis on the structural component of race and racism.

Structural Racism

Dissatisfied with Omi and Winant's work, as well as with Marxist and ideological accounts of race and racism, Bonilla-Silva (1997) argues that a structural view of race and racism is necessary. While he recognizes that races are socially constructed, he nonetheless feels that we need to understand that the social relations that emerge through these constructions are real in their consequences. Racial classifications in particular require analysis because they limit the life chances and status of certain racial groups in relation to others.

Bonilla-Silva (1997) develops a conceptual framework of racialized social systems to understand various racial phenomena. He argues that many societies experience a process of racialization as racialized groups oppose one another at all societal levels. Such societies are racialized social systems 'in which economic, political, social, and ideological levels are partially structured by the placement of actors in racial categories or races' (Bonilla-Silva 1997: 469) where 'races' are socially constructed categories usually identified by phenotypes. The placement of actors in racial categories corresponds with a hierarchy of social relations in which 'superior races' have advantages that 'subordinate races' do not have. According to Bonilla-Silva (1997: 470), subordinate races are in positions in society that limit their access to valuable resources. These resources are both material (e.g., lower-status occupations) and ideological (e.g., superior races being considered smarter or better looking), and 'the totality of these racialized

social relations and practices constitutes the racial structure of society'. Furthermore, the dynamics of everyday life in racialized social systems 'always include[s] a racial component' (473).

Bonilla-Silva argues that in racialized social structures, races come to define their interests collectively, not individually, according to relations between racial groups. Race relations are rooted in power struggles where power is defined as a 'racial group's capacity to push for its racial interests in relation to other races' (Bonilla-Silva 1997: 470). Racial power struggles lead to racial 'strife', or what Bonilla-Silva refers to as 'racial contestation' (1997: 473). Racial contestation is the 'struggle of racial groups for systematic changes regarding their position at one or more levels', where 'levels' refers to economic, social, political, and ideological domains (473). Hence, it is through the processes of racialization and racial contestation that 'a set of social relations and practices based on racial distinctions develops at all societal levels' (474).

The crucial distinction between Bonilla-Silva's perspective and other views of race and racism is his focus on the structural nature of race relations rather than on their ideological character. In his view, although ideology plays a significant role in determining how various races are treated and viewed, the structure of race relations extends to social, political, and economic realms as well. In short, race also has a material base. Race relations are deep structures that are taken for granted and that inform individual interaction every day. Race structures everything.

Despite Bonilla-Silva's view that his approach differs significantly from Omi and Winant's, the two views seem more similar than different. It is true that Omi and Winant focus somewhat more on ideology than Bonilla-Silva, but that does not necessarily mean that their view of race and racism is not structural, as Bonilla-Silva implies. Indeed, Bonilla-Silva recognizes that ideology is one of several structural dimensions of race that need to be acknowledged. Further, by focusing on the structural nature of race and racism, Bonilla-Silva underemphasizes human agency and its relationship to structure in the process of racialization. Hence, one advantage of Omi and Winant's perspective is their conceptualization of racial projects as a link between structure and agency. However, neither of these approaches theorizes the relationship between social structure and agency fully enough for us to understand the everyday experience of racism.

Racism in Everyday Life

In her book *Understanding Everyday Racism*, Philomena Essed (1991) formulates a theory of race and racism that starts with the assumption that to understand the experience of racism, we must consider both macro and micro issues, or the relationship between structure and agency (see chapter 6 for a detailed discussion of structure and agency). On the question of race, Essed uses the term in quotation marks and refers to it as both an ideological and a social construction. Her ideas about the social construction of 'race' are similar to those of Omi and Winant and Bonilla-Silva, but her approach differs in its emphasis on race's ideological construction. According to Essed, race is an ideological construct because the 'idea of race has never existed outside of a framework of group interest . . . in which whites rank higher than non-whites' (1991: 43–4).

Essed's view of the structure of race is also very similar to those of both Omi and Winant and Bonilla-Silva. She argues, for instance, that 'racism is a system of structural inequalities and a historical process, both created and recreated through routine practices' (1991: 39). In her definition of racism, Essed uses the term *system*, which follows Anthony Giddens's use (see chapter 6) to mean the 'reproduced social relations between individuals and groups organized as regular social practices' (Essed 1991: 39). The term *social relations* does not refer to interpersonal relations between two people; rather, it is a structural term that refers to the rights, privileges, and rewards that define relationships among groups. Hence, the term *race relations* highlights the fact that access to resources and political, economic, and social rights varies among racial groups, creating systems of advantage for some and of disadvantage for others.

Essed differs from Omi and Winant and Bonilla-Silva in her emphasis on agency. She argues that, at a micro level, we must pay attention to the intentional and unintentional practices and consequences of human agency. In short, 'structures of racism do not exist external to agents— they are made by agents—but specific practices are by definition racist only when they activate existing structural racial inequalities in the system' (Essed 1991: 39).

Racism, for Essed, is at once an ideology, a structure, and a process in which power, **prejudice**, and meaning are central elements. Relying on the work of Hannah Arendt and Steven Lukes, Essed defines power as a process in which certain groups (not individuals) maintain their position of power by drawing on ideologies that suggest there are innate differences between the powerful group and others. Furthermore, power 'over other people affects them, through action or inaction, in a manner contrary to their interests, whether or not those who exercise power are aware of the success or consequences of their practices and whether or not the other party is aware of the power being exercised over him or her' (Essed 1991: 41). According to Essed, the idea that inaction is a form of power is especially important in understanding racism. Its importance is particularly evident when individuals from dominant racial groups do not speak out against racism and instead are passively tolerant of it. Say, for example, that you are a part of a privileged racial/ethnic group and that you have just been told a joke by someone who is also part of a privileged racial/ethnic group. This joke makes fun of a racial/ethnic group that is less privileged than your own. You do not find the joke funny and, indeed, feel that it is offensive. But rather than telling the person who told the joke that it is offensive, you say nothing. According to Essed, this inaction on your part reinforces the power your privileged group holds in society: you are reinforcing that power by being passively tolerant of the racism and by not speaking out against it.

According to Essed (1991: 44), racism is a process whereby structures and ideologies are produced and reproduced through prejudice and discrimination. The central components of prejudice are feelings of superiority, perceptions of intrinsic group differences, feelings of 'propriety claim' to privileges and resources, and fear or suspicion that the subordinate race may take privileges away from the dominant race. Whereas prejudice is an attitude, discrimination consists of acts of behaviour with 'intended or unintended negative or unfavourable consequences for racially or ethnically dominated groups' (Essed 1991: 45).

Finally, Essed argues that meaning is central to understanding the process of everyday racism. From this point of view, the meaning assigned to everyday events and interpersonal interaction is critical to the existence of society. Through processes of socialization, we learn to take the rules and norms of social behaviour for granted, and we attribute meaning to them accordingly. Although individuals engage in heterogeneous activities, there are underlying patterns of uniformity and acceptable modes of behaviour on which we rely in our everyday encounters with others. Hence, everyday racism is defined as a process in which '(a) socialized racist notions are integrated into meanings that make practices immediately definable and manageable, (b) practices with racist implications become in themselves familiar and repetitive, and (c) underlying racial and ethnic relations are actualized and reinforced through these routine or familiar practices in everyday situations' (Essed 1991: 52).

Essed elaborates upon her theory of everyday racism as she recounts the intensive interviews she conducted with well-educated, professional black women who live in the United States and the Netherlands. The story of Rosa N. is particularly telling. Summarizing the experiences of everyday racism she has experienced as a doctor at a hospital in the Netherlands, Rosa discusses how difficult it is to acknowledge racism in an environment where it is not supposed to be tolerated:

> I can never in my life bring up the subject of racism. That just can't be, because they'll only trip me up. If you want to say anything about racism, you've got to state your case very well. Otherwise . . . they tackle you and lay down a thousand pieces of evidence to prove the opposite, and they make you ridiculous. (Essed 1991: 155)

Hence, the subtle nature of everyday racism exists in part because people of dominant groups are reluctant to acknowledge and address their own racist behaviour.

Essed develops a theoretical framework, shown here in Figure 4.2, that outlines the structure, ideology, and process of everyday racism. Here we see that culture (at the top of the diagram) and structure (at the bottom of the diagram) serve to rationalize and legitimize racial hierarchies (centre column) that are defined by meaning ('definitions of reality' in the diagram), norms and values, and access to resources. Structure and culture influence and are influenced by processes of exclusion and subordination. Examples of exclusion include racial- and ethnic-based labour-market segmentation (see chapter 9), the banning of certain racial-minority and ethnic-minority groups from organizations such as golf clubs, not recognizing certain credentials, and ignoring racism (e.g., the earlier example of not voicing objections to a racist joke). These forms of exclusion lead to a reproduction of the dominant views of the status quo. Examples of subordination include patronizing

Figure 4.2: The Structure of Everyday Racism

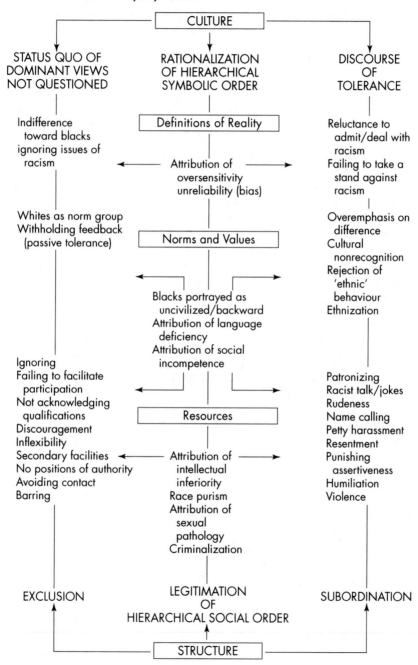

CULTURE

STATUS QUO OF
DOMINANT VIEWS
NOT QUESTIONED

RATIONALIZATION
OF HIERARCHICAL
SYMBOLIC ORDER

DISCOURSE
OF
TOLERANCE

Definitions of Reality

Indifference
toward blacks
ignoring issues of
racism

Attribution of
oversensitivity
unreliability (bias)

Reluctance to
admit/deal with
racism
Failing to take a
stand against
racism

Whites as norm group
Withholding feedback
(passive tolerance)

Norms and Values

Overemphasis on
difference
Cultural
nonrecognition
Rejection of
'ethnic'
behaviour
Ethnization

Blacks portrayed as
uncivilized/backward
Attribution of language
deficiency
Attribution of social
incompetence

Ignoring
Failing to facilitate
participation
Not acknowledging
qualifications
Discouragement
Inflexibility
Secondary facilities
No positions of authority
Avoiding contact
Barring

Resources

Attribution of
intellectual
inferiority
Race purism
Attribution of
sexual
pathology
Criminalization

Patronizing
Racist talk/jokes
Rudeness
Name calling
Petty harassment
Resentment
Punishing
assertiveness
Humiliation
Violence

EXCLUSION

LEGITIMATION
OF
HIERARCHICAL SOCIAL ORDER

SUBORDINATION

STRUCTURE

as well as other forms of racist behaviour and attitudes; subordination is influenced by tolerance, including a reluctance to take a stand against racism.

The strength of Essed's approach is its theoretical emphasis on the relationship between structure and agency and its acknowledgement of the intended and unintended consequences of human action, including the decision not to act at all. However, Essed's emphasis on ideology as the structural base on which race relations are organized is unfortunate. As Omi and Winant and Bonilla-Silva point out, race relations have historically had and continue to have a material base, characterized by exploitive labour practices. Although this oversight may be somewhat justified because of Essed's analysis of professional black women, her neglect of the material base of the social structure becomes problematic when one considers other occupational groups.

Conceptualizing Race and Ethnicity in a Theory of Inequality

If we are to understand inequality in Canada, both race and ethnicity must be addressed. Although some argue that race and racism must be given priority to fully appreciate inequality (Dei 1996), the approach taken here is that class, age, gender, ethnicity, and race must all be given equal weight. Some will be critical of such an approach and will question a white woman's right to make such claims. Though I empathize with such views, I agree with Davia Stasiulis, who says, 'No one gender, race, or class should have the monopoly on intersectional theorizing' (1999: 391).

Markers of race and ethnicity, such as skin colour, mother tongue, and country of birth, may be identified for the purpose of empirically

Table 4.2 Objective and Perceived Ethnoracial Inequality in Canada, by Ancestry

	IE income (mean $)[a]	Poverty Rate (%)[b]	Perceived Discrimination (%)	Perceived Vulnerability (%)	N
Nonvisible minorities (by ancestry)[c]					
Canadian	1,258.7	16.4	10.7	14.3	10,293
French	750.5	16.6	9.1	19.2	592
British	3,386.1	11.8	10.7	15.0	1,744
Northern and Western European	2,238.2	12.5	10.0	11.2	4,356
Russian and Eastern European	405.7	16.2	12.5	16.5	299
Other Southern European	–2,778.6	14.3[d]	14.7	16.8	2,098
Jewish	11,637.7	13.3[d]	20.0	38.7	276
Arab and West Asian	–6,058.4	29.2	18.9	21.2	125
Latin American	–7,416.6	25.1	24.2	23.8	5,893
Greek	–617.4	16.3[d]	13.6	15.6	291
Italian	1,278.0	12.2[d]	11.5	19.2	207
Portuguese	–5,832.7	12.8[d]	8.9	15.9	568
Other European	9,453.1	12.5	16.2	16.0	4,109
Total nonvisible minorities	**1,895.3**	**14.2**	**10.6**	**16.0**	**30,851**

Table 4.2 continued

	IE income (mean $)[a]	Poverty Rate (%)[b]	Perceived Discrimination (%)	Perceived Vulnerability (%)	N
Visible minorities (all ancestries)					
Chinese	–6,730.2	26.9	33.2	33.6	513
South Asian	–5,815.8	21.7	33.1	38.7	1,424
Black	–10,607.2	31.1	49.6	43.0	2,421
Filipino	–5,063.5	16.4d	35.8	48.8	653
Latin American	–10,270.3	29.3	28.6	30.0	362
Southeast Asian	–6,829.3	25.6	34.5	37.7	148
Arab and West Asian	–13,359.4	40.8	29.8	27.0	386
Korean	–17,145.0	40.8d	40.5	49.0	209
Japanese	4,079.5	n/a	42.8	34.2	1,892
Other visible minorities	–7,114.5	23.7	33.3	36.8	331
Multiple visible minorities	–4,304.2	n/a	41.5	28.7	283
Total visible minorities	**–7,686.4**	**26.6**	**35.9**	**37.3**	**8,622**
Total					39,473

a Individual-equivalent household income, relative to the census metropolitan area (CMA) mean. The individual-equivalent income adjusts household incomes for household size, and is calculated by dividing household income by the square root of household size.

b Data on poverty rates are from the 2001 Census Public Use Microdata File, 2.7 per cent sample, for people aged 15 and over, and are based on Statistics Canada's low-income cutoff. In those data, visible minorities are identified only as Black, South Asian, Chinese, and other visible minorities. In this table, 'other visible minorities' are further identified as Filipino, Latin American, Southeast Asian, Arab and West Asian, and Korean, based on ancestry.

c The origins of the groups in the 'nonvisible minorities' category include Arab, West Asian and Latin American, and these also appear in the 'visible minorities' group. Those who are considered in the 'nonvisible minorities' category described themselves as White in the visible minority question. Those who did not identify any ancestry or visible minority group or did not report household income or perceived inequality were excluded.

d Data exclude Maritime provinces.

Source: Statistics Canada (2003) in Reitz and Banerjee (2007: 5).

analyzing various outcomes of inequality. Such markers do not tell us much about the historical processes of racial and ethnic formation (Omi and Winant 1994) or about the everyday experiences of racism (Essed 1991); nevertheless, they are important for descriptive assessments of various outcomes of inequality, such as income, poverty, and perceived discrimination and vulnerability. Indeed, as Table 4.2 shows, such markers indicate that 'visible minorities' have lower incomes and higher poverty rates and that they perceive more discrimination against them and more vulnerability than do non-visible minorities. Hence, in Part II of this book, such markers will be used as indicators of race and ethnicity, although it will be noted simultaneously that race and ethnicity are social and ideological constructions that cannot be fully understood by being reduced to variables.

The challenge that remains is to conceptualize race and ethnicity within the theoretical framework of inequality that has slowly been evolving in this book. Recall that the processes of production, reproduction, and distribution are at the core of such a framework. Race and ethnicity, like gender and class, are consequential to these processes (Acker 2000). For instance, racial and ethnic minority groups face discrimination in production processes, and their positions within production processes are often less autonomous and more alienated than those held by members of dominant groups (Das Gupta 1996). Dominant racial and ethnic groups have exploited and continue to exploit the reproductive labour of subordinate racial groups (Glenn 1992), and processes of reproduction vary considerably among racial groups (Collins 1990). Processes of distribution are also structured by racial and ethnic relations, as is evident in 'racially and ethnically neutral' state unemployment insurance policies that model entitlement on the typical employment patterns of white middle-class men.

As was the case with gender and class, a relational understanding of race and ethnicity that focuses on how oppression is implicated in relations among various racial and ethnic minority groups is necessary for this framework. Although the theories discussed in this chapter do not elaborate upon issues of racial and ethnic oppression, they all mention its importance. Recall that oppression occurs if (1) the welfare of one group of people depends on the deprivations of another and (2) the deprivations of the oppressed group depend upon the exclusion of the oppressed group from access to resources, rewards, and privileges. Racial and ethnic oppression, like gender and class, is both material and non-material and can take place in various settings. Exploitation, opportunity hoarding, emulation, and adaptation, as Tilly (1998) discusses them and as they are discussed in relation to gender in chapter 3, are also important

considerations in assessments of race and ethnic relations.

Clearly, ideology is a central concept in assessments of race relations, and although I have discussed ideology in relation to class and gender, I have yet to provide a working definition of the term. This is, in part, because it is used in many diverse ways, making it an elusive concept in sociological theory. At a very basic level, *ideology* refers to the ideas, attitudes and beliefs, and norms and values that are held by members of a particular social group. With respect to race and ethnicity, ideology encompasses, for instance, ideas of racial and ethnic inferiority and attitudes toward inclusion or segregation. In theories of inequality, ideology is important to the extent that ideology serves to reproduce the rewards and privileges of certain groups in relation to others. Hence, when ideology is used to legitimize the inferior position of members of racial and ethnic minority groups in social hierarchies, it becomes a central issue in studies of inequality. Indeed, recall from chapter 2 that Grabb (2007) considers the control of ideas to be one of three constituent elements of power (the other two are control of material resources and control of people).

The difficulty with integrating the concept of ideology into a theory of inequality is the relative emphasis that it is given in the framework of inequality. In Marxism, it is often thought that ideology stems from the economic relations of production and that dominant belief systems exist only to serve the interests of capitalists and of capitalism more broadly. On the other hand, radical feminists, as well as some of the theorists discussed in this chapter, tend to think of ideology as systems of ideas (e.g., patriarchy and racism) in their own right that have little to do with the relations of production. Neither of these approaches is sufficient for a theoretical framework of inequality that assesses the intersection of class, age, gender, ethnicity, and race. Hence, for the purpose of the theoretical framework presented in this book, I view ideology as systems of ideas and beliefs (sexism, racism, ageism, individualism, elitism, and so on) that are dialectically intertwined with one another and with the structures of gender, class, age, race, and ethnicity. Hence, as Omi and Winant put it, 'ideological beliefs have structural consequences and social structures give rise to beliefs' (1994: 74).

IIIIIIIIII Questions for Critical Thought IIIIIIIIIIIIIIIIIIIIIIIIIIIIIIIIIIIIIIIIIIIIIIIIIIIII

1. What are the advantages and disadvantages of using the concept of race in sociological research? In light of these advantages and disadvantages, construct an argument in favour of one approach or the other.
2. Discuss a racialized project that you've read about in the news or heard about on radio or television. Is this racial project racist?
3. Assume that two people who had equal qualifications apply for a job. One of these people is black, the other white, and all else is equal. The place of employment has an equal-opportunity hiring policy and the black person is hired. According to Omni and Winant, is this a racial project? Is this racist? Why or why not?
4. Choose an activity in which you regularly engage. How does that activity reflect the idea of 'doing race'? Try to think of a social activity that is not racialized. Now, try to show how race or ethnicity may influence that activity.
5. Compare and contrast the concept of race with the concept of ethnicity.

IIIIIIIIII Glossary IIIIIIIIIIIIIIIIIIIIIIIIIIIIIIIIIIIIIIIIIIIIIIIIIIIIIIIIIIIIIIIIIIIIIIIIIIIIIIIIIIIIIIIIII

Discrimination   Prejudicial treatment of a person or group. Although related to prejudice, *discrimination* refers to behaviour rather than to subjective feelings. Discrimination results when individuals or groups carry through with their prejudice and preclude members of other groups from gaining access to resources, rewards, or privileges.

Hegemony   The dominance of one group over another. *Hegemony* expresses the idea that dominance is achieved and maintained through both ideological and coercive processes.

Ideology   Generally held beliefs, ideas, attitudes, or opinions about social life that significantly influence human behaviour. These ideas are not viewed simply as a product of thought but are based on economic and social realities. Some argue that people who hold power in society actively construct a dominant ideology that will allow them to maintain their control (see also *Hegemony*).

Prejudice   Feelings of superiority that often result from beliefs in intrinsic differences between racially classified groups.

Reification   Social processes through which social phenomena or characteristics become naturalized and thereby considered immutable.

Social construction   The process through which meaning is attributed to social rather than to biological or genetic factors. Closely connected to ideas associated with reification. Although much sociological work is socially constructive, the social construction of sex and race are more controversial.

IIIIIIIIIII **Recommended Reading** IIIIIIIIIIIIIIIIIIIIIIIIIIIIIIIIIIIIIIIIIIIIIIIIIIIIIIIIIIIIIIIII

Bonilla-Silva, Eduardo. 1997. 'Rethinking Racism: Toward a Structural Interpretation'. *American Sociological Review* 62: 465–80. This controversial theoretical article acknowledges race as a socially constructed category and works toward developing a structural conceptualization of race with respect to inequality.

Essed, Philomena. 1991. *Understanding Everyday Racism: An Interdisciplinary Theory*. Newbury Park, CA: Sage. This research monograph is based on a qualitative study of black women. The quotations and analyses in this book provide valuable insight into the experience of racism.

Fleras, Augie, and Jean Leonard Elliott. 2007. *Unequal Relations: An Introduction to Race, Ethnic, and Aboriginal Dynamics in Canada*. Toronto: Pearson, Prentice Hall. This comprehensive text covers the politics of race, racism, immigration, and multiculturalism and also includes excellent website links and film suggestions relevant to these issues.

Kalbach, Madeline A., and Warren E. Kalbach, eds. 2000. *Perspectives on Ethnicity in Canada*. Toronto: Harcourt Canada. Topics in this collection of articles on race and ethnicity in Canada include ethnic identification, ethnic diversity, and intersections of gender, race, and ethnicity.

Omi, Michael, and Howard Winant. 1994. *Racial Formation in the United States from the 1960s to the 1990s*. 2nd edn. New York: Routledge. This is a very influential book on the formation of race in the United States. The authors argue in favour of using race as an analytic concept.

Satzewich, Vic, ed. 1998. *Racism and Social Inequality in Canada*. Toronto: Thompson Educational. This comprehensive collection of articles on racism in Canada covers both theoretical and empirical issues and includes discussions of education, immigration, and justice.

IIIIIIIIIII **Relevant Websites** IIIIIIIIIIIIIIIIIIIIIIIIIIIIIIIIIIIIIIIIIIIIIIIIIIIIIIIIIIIIIIIIIIII

Canadian Heritage
www.pch.gc.ca
**A federal government website with links to official pages for anti-racism, multiculturalism, diversity, and official languages.

Colour of Poverty
www.colourofpoverty.ca
**This website is sponsored by the Department of Canadian Heritage and contains useful facts about racialized poverty in Canada.

National Anti-Racism Council of Canada
www.narcc.ca
**This is a national community organization that works to eliminate racism in Canada.

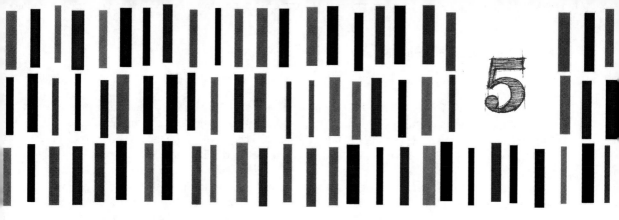

Age and Inequality

Privacy is a privilege not granted to the aged or the young. Sometimes very young children can look at the old, and a look passes between them, conspiratorial, sly and knowing. It's because neither are human to the middling ones, those in their prime, as they say, like beef.

—Margaret Laurence, *The Stone Angel*

Introduction

In the short quotation from *The Stone Angel* that prefaces this chapter, Hagar Shipley, the 90-year-old protagonist of Margaret Laurence's novel, laments that her son and daughter-in-law have not complied with her request to put a lock on her bedroom door. In doing so, she astutely recognizes several issues that will be discussed in this chapter. First, Hagar recognizes that certain privileges in society are distributed on the basis of age. Second, she notes that age distinctions are made between the old, the middle-aged, and the young. And third, she observes a connection between the young and the old because of their relationships to the more privileged 'middling ones'.

Margaret Laurence's choice of the word 'middling' to refer to those who are neither young nor old is interesting. At first one is struck by how much the word 'middling' sounds like 'meddling'—interfering in other people's lives. The *Oxford English Dictionary* illustrates this use of the word with the following quotation: 'A meddling government, a government which tells them what to read, and say, and eat, and drink, and wear.' This meddling government bears a striking similarity to Hagar's perceptions of the roles her son and especially her daughter-in-law play in her life. Second—and, in the context of the above quotation, ironically—the word *middling* may refer to 'a person who or a thing which is mediocre or second-rate' (OED). Hence, Laurence may also use the phrase 'middling ones' to express Hager's contempt for those who, because of their age, occupy a more privileged position in society than she does.

The privileges that are distributed on the basis of age relations extend far beyond that of privacy. In Canada in the early twenty-first century, very rarely are young children or teenagers afforded higher levels of status and power than middle-aged adults. Regardless of maturity, dexterity, or intellectual ability, teenagers who live in North America must reach a certain chronological age before they can legally drive a car, vote, or drink alcohol. Wage scales are established for teenagers not on the basis of what they do, but by their chronological age. Hence, a 17-year-old working at the same job as a 20-year-old can legally be paid less for doing the same work. All of this suggests that the status and power of younger people in North America lags far behind that of middle-aged or older persons.

Yet, as Hagar Shipley knew, this age-based assessment of status and power is far too simple because it does not account for the decline in status and power older adults experience. How does this happen? In North American culture there is a cult of youth that favours young over old and that suggests that to be young is to be vibrant, beautiful, and happy whereas to be old is to be tired, unattractive, and grim (see Box 5.1). These cultural views do little to take away from the status and power of middle-aged people. They are, however, especially detrimental for older adults because, combined with the loss of youthful appeal and the resultant difficulties with self-image and self-esteem (Hurd Clarke

Box 5.1 Ageism and Old Bodies

Power relations result in some groups being more likely to become 'dependent' than others. However, this is not the only source of ageism, of designating someone as 'old' and 'other'. Another critical source of ageism is physical appearance, and this too varies by the intersection of social locations.

Bodies serve as markers of age. Gray hair, wrinkles, brown spots—each of these denotes 'old'. Yet if we think about it, these traits are not universally judged to signify someone is old. Not all gray-haired people are seen to be old, nor are all who exhibit wrinkles. Most of us have heard of the 'double standard' of aging, by which we usually mean that women are seen to be old at an earlier age than men. Recent attitude polls confirm that the gray hair and wrinkles a woman experiences mark her as old sooner. Why is this the case? How and why ageism based on physical appearance occurs is very much related to power relations. We begin with a focus on gender to make this clearer.

Why would people see an old woman wearing a miniskirt as deviant? Part of the reaction, and the rationale for regarding women as old earlier in their lives, arises from the fact that their value is based on their attractiveness to men and their reproductive abilities. Thus the old woman in the miniskirt is deviant for appearing sexual beyond her fertile years. By contrast, men's attractiveness stems from other sources not as quickly diminished. Indeed, sometimes age enhances men's attractiveness, especially if they are associated with public achievements, money, and power. Women even 'age' more quickly than men in the workplace, where they do deal with money, power, and public achievement. This is particularly true if they are engaged in jobs where 'attractiveness' matters— such as jobs dealing with the public or working for (predominantly white) male supervisors. For instance, when airline attendants in this country were almost exclusively women, their unions fought the airlines on a number of occasions where women were removed from their jobs because they were seen as 'too old' (in other words, no longer attractive). However, as we have noted, such issues are shaped differently in different societies. Thus, for example, we find that in Finland youthfulness and attractiveness are not as important for women as they are in the United States.

Having said this, however, we must note that the preceding scenario is too simplistic. What women are we talking about? Do physical signs of aging result in ageism for all women in similar ways? If we accept the fact that people see employed women as old sooner than men, and that this hinges at least in some part on their attractiveness to White men, we must question what this means for the aging of Black women, for example, in the labour force. Are they sexualized in the same way as White women, earlier or later in life? How about women who live openly as lesbians? Or working-class women?

Class plays an important role in another way as well. As was apparent in our discussion of dependence, class—through economic resources—can play a critical role in denying or providing resources that allow the old to choose the ways in which they will manage growing old. To the extent that outward signs of aging can be forestalled by such physical transformations as facelifts, the well-to-do enjoy an obvious advantage. 'Remaking' aging bodies is expensive and time consuming and, hence, beyond the reach of the working-class or poor. At the same time, which women do the remaking, and how, tells us about racial and ethnic relations. Not all women feel the 'need' to hide gray hair or diminish wrinkles.

Although earlier studies on gay men suggested that the influence of age on one's appearance is critical, and even more so or earlier than among heterosexual men, more recent research has failed to corroborate this assertion. Adam's recent study suggests that age preferences of homosexual men are as similar to and as complex as those among heterosexual men. Similarly, despite assertions that lesbians' changes in appearance with age appear to be more 'acceptable', old lesbians still report feeling like outcasts and age still plays a role in the organization of gay and lesbian communities.

References

Adams, Barry D. 2000. 'Age Preferences among Gay and Bisexual Men'. *GLQ: A Journal of Lesbian and Gay Studies* 6, no. 3: 413–33.

Source: Calasanti and Slevin (2001: 24–5).
Reprinted by permission of AltaMira Press, a division of Rowman & Littlefield Publishers, Inc.

2001; McMullin and Cairney 2004), these adults lose the power and status associated with middle-aged activities, such as working for pay and raising families (see Calasanti and Slevin 2001).

Explanations of Age-Based Inequality

Age is the fifth dimension of inequality considered in this book, and it may well be the most understudied of the five. This is curious in light of the fact that the Canadian population is aging and that changes to the population age structure have led to considerable discussion of the challenges facing public pension schemes such as the Canada Pension Plan. As Table 5.1 shows, in 2006, 13.7 per cent of Canada's population was aged 65 and over (an increase over 13.0 per cent in 2001), while 24.4 per cent was aged 19 and younger. This figure represents a more than 10 per cent increase in the number of people aged 65 and over since 1996 and a 1.5 per cent decrease in the number of persons aged 19 and under since 2001. Yet while there are obvious challenges that will result from the aging of populations, if we place too much emphasis on older adults and on the elderly, we are liable to ignore the difficulties that face younger adults and to fuel intergenerational equity debates. Indeed, age relations are important in assessments of inequality regardless of chronological age.

Age Stratification Theory

The development of a formal statement of age stratification theory was foreshadowed in the late 1950s and early 1960s by Leonard Cain and Bernice Neugarten (V. Marshall 1995), but it was Matilda White Riley and her colleagues who were responsible for the formalization and subsequent elaborations of the theory. The basic premises of age stratification theory have

Table 5.1 Age Distribution, Canada, Provinces, and Territories, 2001 and 2006, as Percentages of Total Population

	2001			2006		
	0–19	20–64	65+	0–19	20–64	65+
Canada	25.9	61.1	13.0	24.4	61.9	13.7
Newfoundland and Labrador	25.0	62.7	12.3	22.2	63.9	13.9
Prince Edward Island	27.3	59.0	13.7	25.0	60.2	14.9
Nova Scotia	25.0	61.1	13.9	22.8	62.1	15.1
New Brunswick	24.8	61.7	13.6	22.7	62.5	14.7
Quebec	24.2	62.5	13.3	22.9	62.8	14.3
Ontario	26.3	60.8	12.9	25.0	61.4	13.6
Manitoba	28.1	58.0	14.0	26.9	59.0	14.1
Saskatchewan	29.2	55.8	15.1	27.1	57.5	15.4
Alberta	28.3	61.4	10.4	26.4	62.8	10.7
British Columbia	25.0	61.4	13.6	23.2	62.2	14.6
Yukon Territory	29.0	64.9	6.0	26.3	66.2	7.5
Northwest Territories	35.0	60.7	4.4	32.5	62.7	4.8
Nunavut	46.5	51.2	2.2	44.7	52.6	2.7

Note: Figures may not add up to 100.0 per cent because of rounding error.

Source: Statistics Canada 2001; Statistics Canada, 2006 Census of Population, Statistics Canada catalogue no. 97-551-XCB2006012.

changed little since its conception, although recent statements of this approach, now referred to as the **aging and society paradigm**, are perhaps clearer and more succinct (Riley, Foner, and Waring 1988; Riley and Riley 1994b).

Riley and her colleagues conceptualized age as both a process and a structure. At the structural level, similar-aged individuals form strata that may be defined on the basis of either chronological age or biological, psychological, or social stages of development (Riley, Johnson, and Foner 1972: 6). **Age strata** differ from one another in size and composition as well as in the relative contributions that each makes to society. Age is also established in the social structure as a 'criterion for entering or relinquishing certain roles' (Riley, Johnson, and Foner 1972: 7), and thus it is used as a marker by which age-appropriate behaviour is gauged.

Riley uses the concept of structure without providing a concise definition of the term (Dowd 1987). Functionalist leanings are, however, clearly present in her discussions of social structures. Elements of the social structure are viewed either as social institutions (families, schools, work organizations, and nations; see Riley 1994; Riley and Riley 1994a, 1994b) or as patterns of social roles (Riley, Johnson, and Foner 1972). People (population structure) and roles (role structure) are differentiated by an age structure (Riley, Johnson, and Foner 1972: 6), the elements of which are age strata, age-related acts, age structure of roles, and age-related expectations and sanctions.

The fundamental processes in age stratification theory (Riley, Johnson, and Foner 1972) are cohort flow, individual aging, allocation, and socialization. Figure 5.1 documents how these

Figure 5.1: Processes Related to Structural Elements: Age Stratification Perspective

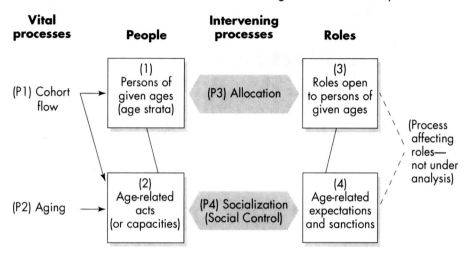

Source: Riley, Johnson, and Foner. (1972: 9). © 1972 Russell Sage Foundation, 112 East 64th Street, New York, NY 10021. Reprinted with permission.

processes influence the age-related social structures discussed above. In describing this figure, Riley and colleagues suggested that cohort flow is the 'essential process underlying the changing size and composition of the age strata [and] consists of the formation of successive cohorts, their modification through migration and the gradual reduction and eventual dissolution of each cohort through the death of individual members' (Riley, Johnson, and Foner 1972: 8).

The aging process is conceptualized as a **biopsychosocial process** (Riley 1994), thus capturing psychological and biological development as well as the experience of entering and exiting social roles (Riley, Johnson, and Foner 1972). According to this theory, the aging process influences the structure of age-related acts or capacities (see Figure 5.1). Allocation and socialization are the processes that intervene between the social structures relating to people (persons of given ages or age strata and age-related acts or capacities) and those relating to roles (roles open to persons of given ages and age-related expectations and sanctions). **Allocation** is the process by which individuals are continually assigned and reassigned to particular roles; **socialization** is the process of teaching individuals how to perform new life-course roles (Riley, Johnson, and Foner 1972).

To disentangle issues related to aging from those related to cohort succession, Riley and colleagues (1972) developed another conceptual scheme, one that incorporates time. Figure 5.2 presents this scheme and shows that as cohorts age, they move through time and through age strata (represented by the vertical lines). Thus, differences in age strata reflect a culmination of the effects of individual aging as well as different patterns of cohort composition (Riley, Johnson, and Foner 1972: 11).

The difference between the earlier and later models and theory that Riley developed lies more in clarity than in content. The first model (Figure 5.1) is now considered a synchronic view of the paradigm, while the second model (Figure 5.2) expands the first by enveloping it in

Figure 5.2: Processes of Cohort Formation and Aging Showing Selected Cohorts over Time: Age Stratification Perspective

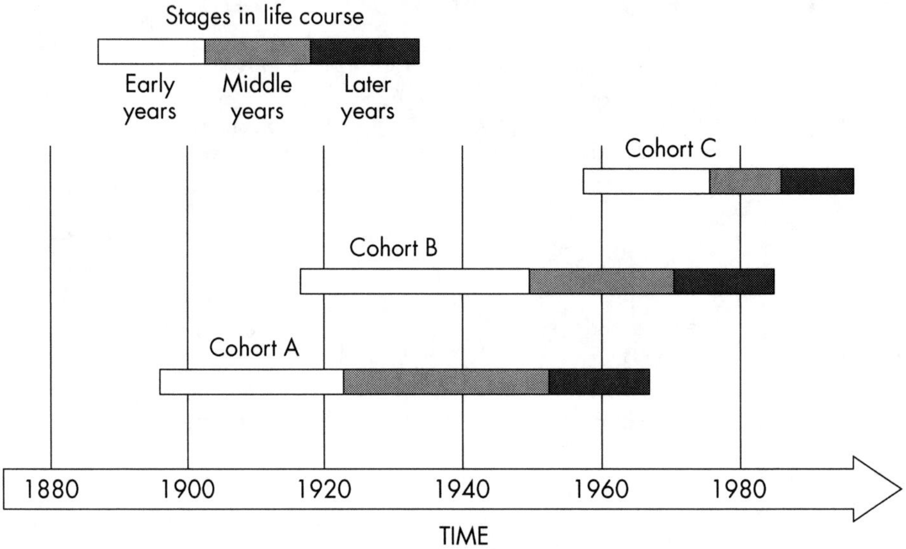

Source: Riley, Johnson, and Foner. (1972: 10). © 1972 Russell Sage Foundation, 112 East 64th Street, New York, NY 10021. Reprinted with permission.

social values and the physical environment. The second model is now considered to represent a **diachronic** view of the paradigm. The conceptual clarity of this model is greatly improved; it is reproduced here in Figure 5.3. The vertical axis represents aging, which is conceptualized as changes in individual lives and in the age criteria for entering and leaving roles. The horizontal axis represents time or history and refers to political, economic, and cultural changes in society over time. The letters A, B, and C, representing **cohorts**, are placed on the diagonal to show the simultaneous processes of cohort flow and aging. The vertical bars represent the people and associated roles that constitute age-related structures, such as families, schools, and work organizations. Finally, the cross-sections show 'how many people who are at different stages of their lives and involved in different social roles and institutions, are organized roughly in socially

recognized age divisions or strata' (Riley, Foner, and Waring 1988: 244). The addition of age-related structures and the clarity of this model make it different from its predecessors. It does not, however, represent a significant change in the perspective itself: its components and their specification are the same.

Nonetheless, subtle changes in the terminology used to describe the theory came with the elaboration of the model, not least of these changes the change of name to 'aging and society paradigm'. In the mid- to late 1980s, the word *dynamism* appeared in association with it, encompassing both process and change (Riley 1988). Riley described the evolution of the paradigm when she noted that the 'distinction between people and roles led us to focus directly on the central theme of the paradigm: the two dynamisms—changes in lives and in structures' (Riley 1994: 438). Each dynamism is a distinct

Figure 5.3: The Age-Stratification System: A Schematic View

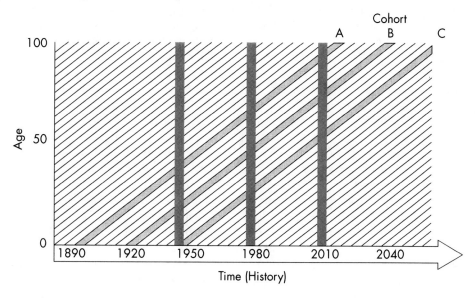

Source: Riley, Foner, and Wang (1988: 245). Copyright © 1998. Reprinted by permission of Sage Publications, Inc.

and separate process, they are interdependent, and both are asynchronous (different in timing) (Riley, Foner, and Waring 1988; Riley and Riley 1994b); as a result, they produce a **structural lag**, as human lives change faster than the social structure (Riley and Riley 1994b).

The models that make up age stratification theory were primarily established to organize a large body of data and to dispel several fallacies that were common in the aging literature before 1972 (some of which persist today). The *life-course fallacy* is the assumption that cross-sectional age differences capture the process of aging. *Cohort centrism* is the error of assuming that other cohorts age in the same way as one's own. *Age reification* treats chronological age as *the* life-course variable and does not take into account other factors that influence aging. Finally, *reifying historical time* places emphasis on historical change rather than drawing attention to the particular aspects of change that are central to an understanding of variations in age

structures or processes (Riley, Foner, and Waring 1988: 248).

By recognizing these misinterpretations, the aging and society paradigm seeks to explain the processes that underlie the movement of age cohorts through time and through age-related social structures. Exploring the asynchrony between individual and structural change, it attempts to resolve issues of conflict related to this structural lag. The theory also strives to understand the interdependence between age cohorts, social structures, and individual aging processes (Bengtson, Parrott, and Burgess 1994).

Age Strata

In age stratification research, the age system of inequality is generally conceptualized in terms of the differences between older, middle-aged, and younger age strata. Although there is some recognition that inequalities arise as age strata are constructed and reformulated through the changes in society and age-related processes (Riley, Foner, and Waring 1988: 268), age tends to be treated in static rather than dynamic terms. Thus, the processes and changes that are captured in the diachronic view of age stratification theory (see Figure 5.3) are generally absent in assessments of social inequality. Instead, there is a tendency to start with the assumption that age strata, with clearly defined roles and consequential rewards and expectations, exist and that they constitute a system of age-based inequality (Foner 1974, 1986; Riley, Foner, and Waring 1988; Riley, Johnson, and Foner 1972). Hence, these theories of inequality are generally framed within the **synchronic** model of age stratification theory (see Figure 5.2) and focus on the process of allocation and on the structure of roles and age-related expectations and sanctions.

Literature on the cultural meanings that individuals attribute to age casts doubt on the assumption that there are clearly defined age norms for different age strata. For instance, Neugarten, Moore, and Lowe (1965) showed long ago that the importance individuals assign to age norms in determining appropriate behaviour is a function of the age of the respondent (see also Elder and Rockwell 1976; Fallo-Mitchell and Ryff 1982). Compared to younger and middle-aged respondents, older adults tend to hold stronger convictions about age norms. Compared to older women, younger women prefer later ages for the onset of family events and earlier ages for educational and occupational events (Fallo-Mitchell and Ryff 1982). Assumptions about widely held age norms are also tenuous in the face of anthropological evidence showing that there are variations in the meanings attributed to age both within a given society and cross-culturally (Fry 1976, 1980, 1985, 1986). For instance, when Christine Fry (1976) asked a group of American adults to sort pictures that depicted people in different life situations into as many age categories as they deemed necessary, the respondents created between 2 and 15

age categories and used more than 100 different terms to describe them. The average number of age categories chosen was between 5 and 6, depending on other variables such as gender or marital status. Indeed, some argue that boundaries between culturally specified age categories are becoming increasingly blurred as active lifestyles, related consumer products, and the promotion of never-ending sex through medicalization (e.g., Viagra) are being marketed to aging baby boomers (Katz and Marshall 2003; B. Marshall and Katz 2002).

The preceding findings suggest that there are problems with the underlying assumptions about age strata as used in the age stratification approach. Nonetheless, the usefulness of this conceptualization comes from the idea that age distinctions are fundamental in our society and that they influence patterns of resource distribution for youth, the 'middling ones', and the old.

Cohorts

The process of cohort flow is considered in age stratification discussions of inequality. In fact, Riley (1985: 386) goes so far as to suggest that age may predominate over other bases of inequality,[1] largely because cohort differences in education have strengthened the age stratification system. Here, the concept of cohort flow is discussed within the confines of the synchronic model. Historical, time-related issues—such as the experience of the Depression or of the Second World War—are left unmentioned, even though their influences on an individual's life chances have been demonstrated (Easterlin 1987; Elder 1985).

The relative neglect of temporal issues in this approach suggests that the conceptualization of cohort in age stratification theory may be problematic. Riley defines a cohort according to the definition Norman Ryder (1965) proposed in his seminal article 'The Cohort as a Concept in the Study of Social Change'. For Ryder (1965:

845), a *cohort* is an aggregate of individuals who experienced the same event within the same time interval; birth cohorts are only a special case of this more general definition. Notably, Ryder's conceptualization allows for individuals to be grouped according to any significant event. In practice, however, birth tends to be the event that is assigned the greatest significance. Thus, Riley views cohorts as aggregates of individuals who are born in the same time interval.

However, conceptualizing cohorts in arbitrarily defined single- or five-year age categories reifies chronological age as the basis of inequality and ignores more subjective dimensions of age that may be relevant (V. Marshall 1983; Passuth and Bengtson 1988). By assuming that one-year or five-year age cohorts take on meaningful significance, this approach masks qualitative differences in personal experience that are related to age (V. Marshall 1983).

Age Stratification Theory and Inequality

Age stratification theory has been applied to a large gamut of substantive research, including inequality in labour markets and families. According to age stratification theory, paid employment and family membership are considered socially valued roles because they function to maintain order in society. Older and younger age strata are relatively disadvantaged because they tend not to take part in the productive roles that are highly valued in modern society. Labour-force entries and exits are allocated by age, both directly through labour laws and indirectly by educational criteria, for job entry, and by perceived age-related performance abilities, for job exit. There are also age differences in the kinds of jobs people hold and in the age distribution of the work force (see Chapter 9 for details). Younger workers are disproportionately employed in 'bad jobs' that are poorly paid and have few benefits (see Box 5.2 for a description of the job ghettoization of youth). Age-related

roles and expectations for labour-force participation lead to different rewards according to age, as well. Thus, compared to labour-force participants, retired workers and young people tend to be less powerful and are economically disadvantaged (see Box 5.3 for a narrative on the experience of inequality in later life). In labour markets, middle-aged and, sometimes, older workers assume more power and tend to make more money than younger workers, especially in well-established firms (Foner 1986; Foner and Schwab 1981; Riley, Foner, and Waring 1988; Riley, Johnson, and Foner 1972). However, when older workers lose their jobs, they are unemployed longer than younger workers (McMullin and Marshall 2001) and experience age discrimination in their search for employment (McMullin and Berger 2006).

Age stratification discussions of the family have concentrated on the age-graded nature of the family, its changing structure, its functions, and the roles and norms associated with different types of membership in families (Foner 1986). Inequality in families is generally assessed through economic differences and power imbalances between parents and their younger children. In families of procreation, parents have more power and economic control than their children because they assume the socializing and caregiving roles. In some of the worst cases, power imbalances in families cause children to run away from home, quit school, and live on the streets. The emphasis in discussions of later-life families is on whether older parents are neglected by their adult children (Riley, Foner, and Waring 1988). Although these discussions tend not to be framed within the context of power, an imbalance is implied in which the power shifts from parents to children.

In summary, age stratification researchers believe that people and roles are differentiated by an age structure, the elements of which are cohorts, age strata, age-related acts, age structure of roles, and age-related expectations and sanctions (Riley

Box 5.2 Job Ghettoization

By James E. Côté and Anton L. Allahar

Studies show that on average young workers are not only paid less, and participate in the workforce less, but they are becoming less well-represented in all job categories, except consumer services. Indeed, it is in the subordinate service occupations that their cheap labour is most in demand. During the 1980s, the proportion of jobs held by young workers (16 to 24) that were in the service sector rose from 69.7 per cent to 75.8 per cent, while in the goods sector it dropped from 30.3 per cent to 24.2 per cent (Betcherman and Morissette, 1994). The two most common service sector jobs held in 1989 were retail trade (22.7 per cent), and accommodation and food (13.7 per cent). These authors note 'the substantial absolute decline of youth employment in the goods sector and in public administration, health, social services, and education' and they conclude that for 'earlier generations of young people, these industries typically offered good entry-level opportunities' (1994, p. 3). When broken down by gender, over 84 per cent of females aged 15 to 19 worked in the service sector, compared with about 60 per cent of their male counterparts (Statistics Canada, 1994, p. 21). These trends did not reverse in the 1990s.

From a critical perspective, this reorganization of the labour force, and the redistribution of wealth that has followed, was not merely the result of certain isolated individuals feathering their own nests, or the nests of their age-mates. Indeed, many of the policy adjustments undertaken by the Canadian government have made it a key mediator between the interests of adult-controlled Capital and youth wage-labour. One key policy pertains to the setting of minimum levels. In the mid-1970s, minimum wage would have put one about 40 per cent *above* the office poverty line; it now puts one 30 per cent *below* that line (see Schlosser, 2001, for comparable figures from the United States). Moreover, two thirds of minimum wage earners are under 24 years of age (Hess, 1991). In this example, government policies endorsed by the Canadian electorate have clearly contributed to age-based discrimination, with the interests of adult élite of professionals, managers, and owners, as previously discussed, clearly getting preference over youth wage-labour interests. Few people seem to be aware of the role that the State has played in mediating the interests of this élite in this regard, and many of those who are aware seem to see nothing wrong with it. Had young people taken part in this decision-making process, it is doubtful that things would have worked out this way for young workers.

References

Betcherman, G., and Morissette, R. 1994. *Recent Youth Labour Market Experiences in Canada.* Analytical Studies Branch Research Paper Series 63. Ottawa: Statistics Canada.

Hess, M. 1991. 'Sinful Wages'. *Perception* (Canadian Council on Social Development) 15, 3: 29–32.

Schlosser, Eric. 2001. *Fast Food Nation: The Dark Side of the All-American Meal.* New York: Perennial.

Statistics Canada. 1994. 'Working Teens'. *Canadian Social Trends*, Winter: 18–22.

Source: Côté and Allahar (2006: 54).

1994; Riley, Johnson, and Foner 1972). Although this approach has made the theory accessible to large audiences of gerontologists (Dowd 1987), it has led to an oversimplification of the inequalities

Box 5.3 A Window Full of Sky

By Anzia Yezierska

A few blocks away from the roominghouse where I live is an old people's home. 'Isle of the Dead', I used to call it. But one day, after a severe attack of neuritis, I took a taxi to that house of doom from which I had fled with uncontrollable aversion for years. Cripples in wheelchairs and old men and women on benches stared into vacancy—joyless and griefless, dead to rapture and despair. With averted eyes I swept past these old people, sunning themselves like the timbers of some unmourned shipwreck.

The hallman pointed out a door marked 'Miss Adcock, Admissions'. I rapped impatiently. Almost as though someone had been waiting, the door opened, and there was Miss Adcock trimly tailored with not a hair out of place. Just looking at her made me conscious of my shabbiness, my unbrushed hair escaping from under my crumpled hat, the frayed elbows of my old coat. She pulled out a chair near her desk. Even her posture made me acutely aware of my bent old age.

The conflict, days and nights, whether to seek admission to the home or die alone in my room, choked speech. A thin thread of saliva ran down from the corner of my mouth. I tried to wipe it away with my fingers. Miss Adcock handed me a Kleenex with a smile that helped me start talking.

'I've been old for a long, long time,' I began, 'but I never felt old before. I think I've come to the end of myself.'

'How old are you?'

'Old enough to come here.'

'When were you born?'

'It's such a long time ago. I don't remember dates.'

Miss Adcock looked at me without speaking. After a short pause she resumed her probing.

'Where do you live?'

'I live in a roominghouse. Can anyone be more alone than a roomer in a roominghouse?' I tried to look into her eyes, but she looked through me and somehow above me.

'How do you support yourself?'

'I have a hundred dollars a month, in Social Security.'

'You know our minimum rate is $280 a month.'

'I've been paying taxes all my life. I understood that my Social Security would be enough to get me in here. . . .'

'It can be processed through Welfare.'

I stood up, insulted and injured: 'Welfare is charity. Why surrender self-respect to end up on charity?'

'Welfare is government assistance, and government assistance is not charity,' Miss Adcock calmly replied. 'I would like to explain this more fully when I have more time. But right now I have another appointment. May I come to see you tomorrow?'

I looked at Miss Adcock and it seemed to me that her offer to visit me was the handclasp of a friend. I was hungry for hope. Hope even made me forget my neuritis. I dismissed the thought of a taxi back to the roominghouse. I now had courage to attempt hobbling back with the aid of my cane. I had to pause to get my breath and rest on the stoops here and there, but in a way hope had cured me.

The prospect of Miss Adcock's visit gave me the strength to clean my room. Twenty years ago, when I began to feel the pinch of forced retirement, I had found this top-floor room. It was in need of paint and plumbing repairs. But the afternoon sun that flooded the room and the view across the wide expanse of tenement roofs to the Hudson and the Palisades beyond made me blind to the dirty walls and dilapidated furniture. Year after year the landlord had refused to make any repairs, and so the room grew dingier and more than ever in need of paint.

During my illness I had been too depressed to look at the view. But now I returned to it as one turns back to cherished music or poetry. The sky above the river, my nourishment in solitude, filled the room with such a great sense of space and light that my spirits soared in anticipation of sharing it with Miss Adcock.

When Miss Adcock walked into my room, she exclaimed: 'What a nice place you have!' She made me feel that she saw something special in my room that no one else had ever seen. She walked to the window. 'What a wonderful view you have here. I wonder if it will be hard for you to adjust to group living—eating, sleeping, and always being with others.'

'I can no longer function alone,' I told her. 'At my age people need people. I know I have a lot to learn, but I am still capable of learning. And I feel the Home is what I need.'

As if to dispel my anxiety, she said, 'If you feel you can adjust to living with others, then of course the Home is the place for you. We must complete your application and arrange for a medical examination as soon as possible. By the way, wouldn't you like to see the room we have available right now? There are many applicants waiting for it.'

'I don't have to see the room,' I said in a rush.

She pressed my hand and was gone.

About two weeks later, Miss Adcock telephoned that I had passed the medical examination and the psychiatrist's interview. 'And now,' she said, 'all that is necessary is to establish your eligibility for Welfare.'

'Oh, thank you,' I mumbled, unable to conceal my fright. 'But what do you mean by eligibility? I thought I was eligible. Didn't you say . . . ?'

In her calm voice, she interrupted: 'We have our own Welfare man. He comes to the Home every day. I'll send him to see you next Monday morning. As soon as I can receive his report, we can go ahead.'

The Welfare man arrived at the appointed time.

'I'm Mr Rader,' he announced. 'I am here to find out a few things to complete your application for the Home.' The light seemed to go out of the room as he took possession of the chair. He was a thin little man, but puffed up, it seemed to me, with his power to give or withhold 'eligibility'. He put his attaché case reverently on the table, opened it, and spread out one closely printed sheet. 'Everything you say,' he cautioned, 'will of course be checked by the authorities.' He had two fountain pens in his breast pocket, one red and one black. He selected the black one. 'How long have you lived here?'

'Twenty years.'

'Show me the receipts.' He leaned back in his chair and looked around the room with prying eyes. He watched me ruffling through my papers.

'I must have last month's receipt somewhere. But I don't bother with receipts. I pay the rent . . . they know me,' I stammered. I saw him make rapid, decisive notations on his form.

'What are your assets?' he continued.

My lips moved but no words came out.

'Have you any stocks or bonds? Any insurance? Do you have any valuable jewelry?'

I tried to laugh away my panic. 'If I had valuable jewelry, would I apply to get into the Home?'

'What are your savings? Let me see your bankbook.' I stopped looking for the rent receipts and ransacked the top of my bureau. I handed him my bankbook. 'Is that all your savings?' he asked. 'Have you any more tucked away somewhere?' He looked intently at me. 'This is only for the last few years. You must have had a bank account before this.'

'I don't remember.'

'You don't remember?'

Guilt and confusion made me feel like a doddering idiot. 'I never remember where I put my glasses. And when I go to the store, I have to write a list or I forget what I came to buy.'

'Have you any family or friends who can help you?' He glanced at his watch, wound it a little, and lit a cigarette, puffing impatiently. 'Have you any professional diplomas? Do you go to a church or a synagogue?'

I saw him making quick notes of my answers. His eyes took in every corner of the room and fixed on the telephone. He tapped it accusingly.

'That's quite an expense, isn't it?'

'I know it's a luxury,' I said, 'but for me it's a necessity.'

He leaned forward. 'You say you have no friends and no relatives. Who pays for it? Can you afford it?'

'I use some of my savings to pay for it. But I have to have it.'

'Why do you have to have it?'

'I do have a few friends,' I said impulsively, 'but I'm terribly economical. Usually my friends call me.'

I could feel my heart pounding. My 'eligibility', my last stand for shelter, was at stake. It was a fight for life.

'Mr Rader,' I demanded, 'haven't people on Social Security a burial allowance of $250? I don't want a funeral. I have already donated my body to a hospital for research. I claim the right to use that $250 while I am alive. The telephone keeps me alive.'

He stood up and stared out the window; then he turned to me, his forehead wrinkling: 'I never handled a case like this before. I'll have to consult my superiors.'

He wrote hastily for a few minutes, then closed the attaché case. 'Please don't phone me. The decision rests in the hands of my superiors.'

When the door closed, there was neither thought nor feeling left in me. How could Miss Adcock have sent this unseeing, unfeeling creature? But why blame Miss Adcock? Was she responsible for Welfare? She had given me all she had to give.

To calm the waiting time, I decided to visit the Home. The woman in charge took great pride in showing me the spacious reception hall, used on social occasions for the residents. But the room I was to live in was a narrow coffin, with a little light coming from a small window.

'I do not merely sleep in my room,' I blurted out. 'I have to live in it. How could I live without my things?'

She smiled and told me, 'We have plenty of storage room in the house, and I'll assign space for all your things in one of the closets.'

'In one of the closets! What earthly good will they do me there?'

I suddenly realized that it would be hopeless to go on. Perhaps the coffin-like room and the darkness were part of the preparation I needed.

Back in my own place, the sky burst in upon me from the window and I was reminded of a long-forgotten passage in *War and Peace*. Napoleon, walking through the battlefield, sees a dying soldier and, holding up the flag of France, declaims: 'Do you know, my noble hero, that you have given your life for your country?'

'Please! Please!' the soldier cries. 'You are blotting out the sky.'

that are associated with age. Age strata, with their related roles, expectations, and sanctions, are assumed and are considered necessary to the functioning of society. Hence, this approach neglects the conflict that occurs when normative—in this case, age-based—roles are violated.

The Political Economy of Aging

Between the late 1960s and the early 1980s, social gerontologists and youth theorists began to critique the normative and highly individualistic theories that neglected the importance of social class (V. Marshall and Tindale 1978; Tindale and Marshall 1980; Rowntree and Rowntree 1968). Responding to these critiques and to calls for a more radical and critical approach, several scholars from different countries began to assess age from a political-economy perspective: old age in one body of literature (Estes 1979; Estes, Swan, and Gerard 1982; Guillemard 1982, 1983; Myles 1980, 1981, 1984; Phillipson 1982;

Townsend 1981; Walker 1981) and youth in another (Côté and Allahar 1994, 2006; Rowntree and Rowntree 1968).

Political-economy theorists seek to explain the relative situation of older and younger individuals by examining the relationship between the economic, political, and ideological structures that these systems of domination construct and reconstruct. Rather than explaining the problems that older and younger people face as a result of their inability to adjust to retirement or aging or because of a lack of experience among young job seekers, political economists attribute their problems to structural characteristics of the state and the economy and to inequalities in the distribution and allocation of resources and opportunities that these institutions create (Côté and Allahar 1994, 2006; Myles 1989; Phillipson 1982; Walker 1981).

The following are among the topics political-economy scholars have examined in relation to old age and youth:

1. How social policy has structured dependency and limited opportunities in old age and in youth (Côté and Allahar 1994; Phillipson 1982; Townsend 1981; Walker 1981).

2. How the commodification of the needs of older adults benefits capital and creates an 'aging enterprise' (Estes 1979, 1991).

3. How old age and youth are dependent on the division of labour in society as well as on the distribution and allocation of resources. Related to this is how the institution of retirement creates a 'social death' that serves to define old age (Guillemard 1982, 1983) and how limited job opportunities and other structural factors have created a situation of 'arrested adulthood' among youth (Côté 2000).

4. The contradiction between the principles of democratic citizenship and the principles governing the capitalist system of allocation (Côté and Allahar 2006; Myles 1989).

To a greater or lesser extent, these studies consider the socially constructed nature of age and dependency; the influence of ideology in this construction; the influence of state, capital, and labour relations on the construction of age and age relations; and the effects of social policy for the elderly and youth. Although it is beyond the scope of this chapter to discuss the specifics of each of these arguments, it is important to consider the role of the state in political-economy research.

Although the state comprises many institutions (such as those concerned with education, criminal justice, and health care), research focusing on old age from a political-economy perspective generally equates the state with the governing bodies responsible for policies related to social welfare. *Social welfare* in studies of aging most often refers to social security and health benefits (Estes, Linkins, and Binney 1996). The importance of the state in this research stems from the power the state has over resource allocation and distribution because of its relations with capital and labour and its ultimate responsibility for the survival of the economic system (Estes, Linkins, and Binney 1996; Myles 1989, 1995). From the political-economy perspective, the state is thought to represent the interests of the most powerful members of society, and the existing social order is thought to be the result of power struggles in which the state participates (Estes 1991; Estes, Linkins, and Binney 1996). Rather than using consensus models, in which the state is considered a 'neutral entity, operating in the universal interests of all members of society' (Estes 1991: 22), political-economy scholars generally believe either that the state acts to maintain its own bureaucratic control (Offe and Ronge 1982, cited in Estes 1991) or that power struggles within the state represent class struggles (Myles 1989).

Similarly, and as Côté and Allahar discuss (2006), in studies of youth, the political-economy approach posits that the state serves the

interests of capitalism by creating and reinforcing education and labour-market systems in
which youth become dependent and alienated.
According to this view, youth are, for instance,
encouraged to gain further education not only
because it is in their best interests but because it
serves the interests of the capitalist economy. In
an environment where jobs are scarce, keeping
people out of the labour market is seen as a good
thing. Youth are then put into a kind of holding
pattern in which they are circling through poorly
paid jobs and various educational systems, waiting until they can land a decent job and properly
come of age.

Important advances in the study of social
inequality and aging have come from the political-economy analysis of state policies regarding retirement and pensions. For instance,
Myles (1980, 1984, 1989) shows that income
inequality in older age is a function both of the
overall levels of inequality in a society and of
the way pension systems alter or reproduce that
inequality. Although inequalities in pre-retirement years persist after retirement, an understanding of income inequalities among older
people and between the old and the young requires an analysis of public-pension structures.
Traditionally, public pensions have been based
either on pre-retirement incomes or on the idea
of a national minimum benefit. In the first instance, pensions perpetuate class-, gender-,
and ethnicity-based inequalities in older age by
graduating pension incomes according to pre-
retirement income. In the second instance, income equality among older people is achieved
because the same sum of money is paid to everyone (this is known as *flat-benefit structure*;
see Myles 1980, 1984, 1989).

Most Western capitalist nations have pension structures that combine flat and graduated
schemes (Myles 1980). In Canada, for instance,
the Canada Pension Plan/Quebec Pension Plan
(C/QPP) represents a graduated scheme in which
employees and employers pay into the plan

according to the employee's pre-retirement income. However, these plans have an upper contribution limit that renders the pension scheme
graduated at the bottom and flat on top (Myles
1980). Old Age Security (OAS) is a Canadian
pension scheme that traditionally guaranteed a
flat, per month benefit to all people aged 65 and
over. There are also several provincial and federal programs that, based on income tests, provide
income supplements to low-income pensioners.

The interplay of the C/QPP and OAS highlights
a contradiction in modern, liberal-democratic
states between the rights attached to the ownership of property and the rights afforded to persons in their capacity as citizens (Myles 1984,
1989). According to Myles (1989), the strategies
used by different countries to come to terms
with this contradiction determine the relative
pension benefits of older people and are a re-
flection of class struggles within the state. Thus,
Myles suggests that the quality and quantity of
pension benefits are largely a function of the political mobilization of the working class and the
election of working-class parties.

This brief summary of Myles's work illustrates
the power the state has in determining the economic status of older adults. Few researchers who study aging would dispute this point,
although there is some disagreement among
political economists over the precise conceptualization of the state (see Estes 1991; Estes,
Linkins, and Binney 1996) and over the relative
emphasis that should be placed on state relations (Myles 1989) as opposed to the relations
of production (Guillemard 1982, 1983) in assessments of inequality. Most would also agree
that old age and aging are socially constructed,
in part, through these and other state policies.

Crucial to the political-economy perspective
is the concept of social class. It is in discussions of social class that the Marxian influence
in this perspective is most evident. Like Marx
(1969; Marx and Engels [1848] 1970), political-
economy researchers emphasize the relations of

production in their conceptualization of social class, specifically the relations between those who own the means of production and those who do not (Guillemard 1982, 1983; Myles 1980, 1984, 1989; Phillipson 1982; Townsend 1981; Walker 1981). Thus, according to Guillemard (1982: 228), 'the traditional Marxist definition, which analyzes the class structure of the capitalist mode of production by basically contrasting the two antagonistic classes—capitalist and proletarian—must be upheld.'

The emphasis on the relations of production in the political-economy approach is paradoxical in the study of old age because most older people are no longer directly engaged in socially defined productive relations (Dowd 1980; Estes 1991; Estes, Swan, and Gerard 1982). One strategy of political economists to deal with this paradox is to use a life-course framework to assess the class relations of older adults according to their pre-retirement social class (Guillemard 1982, 1983; Phillipson 1982; Walker 1981). Aware of life-course processes, these political economists believe that power relations and resources in later life are shaped by people's earlier location within the social structure or by their class position. Missing in these accounts, however, is an analysis of the relationship between age relations and class relations as they structure inequality in later life. As others point out (Kohli 1988; Myles 1980), the economic and social locations of older people result not only from class inequalities in early life but also from unique processes that are structured by age relations.

Estes deals with the contradiction between the Marxist emphasis on productive labour and assessing the social location of older people by turning to a more Weberian view of class. Drawing on Ehrenreich and Ehrenreich (1979: 11), she suggests that a social class is 'characterized by a coherent social and cultural existence; members of a class share a common life style, educational background, kinship networks, consumption patterns, work habits, and beliefs' (Estes 1991: 25). This definition of social class, Estes argues (1991; Estes, Swan, and Gerard 1982), is analytically appropriate for older people because it does not necessarily reflect productive relations and can capture the dynamics involved with aging and social inequality.

Another way of dealing with this paradox is to assume that more than one structure of domination influences social inequality. Myles (1989), who employs this approach, argues that inequality in older age is shaped by two structures of domination in Western capitalist societies. One is based on the productive relations by which power is given to those who control economic resources. The other is based in the polity, where power is maintained by those who control political resources. The interplay between these power sources determines, both in principle and in practice (these do not often converge), the value of old age pensions, and hence structures economic inequality in later life.

According to Myles (1989), negotiations between the polity and the economy over old-age benefits are framed in contradictions because the principles of democratic politics are inconsistent with the principles of a capitalist economy. Public pension systems represent the compromise between these sets of principles that have been negotiated in the political arena. Thus, Myles argues that income inequality in old age is structured by the state rather than being controlled by the market's invisible hand. However, a critical factor determining the extent of pension entitlements is the political mobilization of the working class (defined in Marxist terms), for Myles believes that power struggles within the state are essentially class conflicts.

The Social Construction of Old Age and Youth

Theorists who study age from a political-economy perspective tend to conceptualize age in terms of **age groups**. From this perspective, Western capitalist societies are thought to be organized on the basis of whether one is old, middle-aged, or young. Political economists are, however, critical of these divisions: they question how a particular chronological age becomes the marker by which one is defined as old or young and how the polity and the economy legitimize old age and prolonged youth by defining them as a problem and then by developing solutions to deal with the problem (Côté and Allahar 2006; Estes 1979; Guillemard 1982, 1983; Myles 1989; Phillipson 1982; Walker 1981). *Adolescence*, for instance, is a relatively new term for a period of life that didn't exist until quite recently; the prolongation of youth has more to do with a lack of the opportunities typically available for adults than it does with chronological age (Côté 2000; Côté and Allahar 1994). And, some are now advocating that the terms *teenager* and *adolescent* and the corresponding lack of legal rights and citizenship privileges be eliminated entirely.

Estes describes an 'aging enterprise' that comprises 'programs, organizations, bureaucracies, interest groups, trade associations, providers, industries, and professionals that serve the aged in one capacity or another' (1979: 2). The interests of those who constitute the aging enterprise are realized by making the elderly dependent upon the services they offer. In this way, the aged are processed and treated as a commodity (Estes 1979; Estes, Swan, and Gerard 1982). The social construction of old age is especially fuelled by the medical profession, which has transformed aged bodies into sick bodies (Katz 1996). Further, this 'socially constructed problem, and the remedies invoked on the policy level, are related, first, to the capacity of strategically located interests and classes to define the problem and to press their views into public consciousness and law and, second, to the objective facts of the situation' (Estes, Linkins, and Binney 1996: 349).

The crisis ideology perpetuated by the state and the media regarding social welfare and the aging of the population is another example of how old age becomes socially constructed as a problem (Gee 2000b). The message put across is that with the increasing number of seniors will come a financial burden too large for Canada to bear (the emphasis is usually on the baby-boom generation reaching old age). However, as Myles (1980, 1995) and others have demonstrated, although the structure of state spending, ownership, and control will probably change, it is unlikely that population aging will 'break the national bank'.

The political-economy approach has advanced the state of theorizing gerontological and youth studies over the last 20 years by examining issues relating to age through a critical lens. Nonetheless, the conceptualization of age by political economists is problematic on several counts. First, although this approach places emphasis on the structural characteristics that frame the aging experience, youth, and older age, age relations themselves are often considered secondary to issues of social class. Second, political economists have been critical, and rightly so, of research that seeks to explain age by 'naturalizing' the biological conditions of aging or by providing essentialist kinds of explanations for problems associated with youth (Côté and Allahar 2006). As a result, the tendency in this school of thought has been to understate the significance of the biological aging process. Rather than examining the subtle institutional procedures that discriminate on the basis of age (Charness, Dykstra, and Philips 1995), understating biological aging has the effect of rendering the aging process insignificant. Third, the emphasis in this approach on social structure leads to a neglect of human agency. This serves to depict older people and youth as powerless and exploited without paying attention to the meaning older adults and youth attribute to their experiences and to the strategies that they might use in dealing with some of their difficulties.

Conceptualizing Age in a Theory of Inequality

The way in which age is conceptualized depends a lot on what it is that people want to study. Age strata, biopsychosocial processes, cohorts, and age groups are the four views of age that emerge from the theories discussed above. Age-strata and stratification research stems from the economic stratification research that was discussed in chapter 2 and that for similar reasons is discarded here. More useful in studies of inequality are conceptualizations of age that consider biopsychosocial processes, cohorts, and age groups. The importance of biopsychosocial processes and cohorts is discussed in greater detail in the conceptual framework presented in chapter 7. For now, we must consider how age groups are viewed in this approach.

The idea from the political-economy approach that Western societies are loosely organized or structured according to socially constructed age groups is correct as long as we emphasize the social construction of age and recognize that the chronological ages associated with such groupings depend on the specific social context. There are old workers, middle-aged workers, and young workers, and there are old family members, middle-aged family members, and young family members; the chronological ages associated with age groups at work are different from the chronological ages associated with age groups in families.

According to the political-economy perspective, age groups structure social life in large part because an age structure serves the interests of the dominant social classes (Côté and Allahar 2006; Estes 1999; Myles 1989). Power does not seem to be derived from relations between age groups but rather from relations between classes. Yet to understand age and inequality better, age relations must be conceptualized as oppressive relations in their own right. What then are age relations, and what distinguishes age relations from age groups?

In this book I argue that age is a relational and structural basis of inequality in Canada. On the one hand it is relational because people define their various positions in society according to their membership in a particular age group as it relates to other age groups. It is relational in a second sense as well, because various rights and privileges are assigned on the basis of age-group location.

A relational understanding of age requires an emphasis on forms of oppression and power that are structured on the basis of membership in age groups. Recall that oppression occurs if (1) the welfare of one group of people depends upon the deprivation of another and (2) the deprivation of the oppressed group depends upon the exclusion of the oppressed group from access to resources, rewards, and privileges. In this sense, age-based oppression, like gender-, race-, and ethnicity-based oppression, can be both material and non-material, and it can take place in various settings, including families, labour markets, states, and the education and health systems. An obvious example of age-based oppression for older adults is mandatory retirement, which still exists in some provinces in Canada; for younger adults, it is the fact that the minimum wage varies with age.

Besides the economic power differences that result from material oppression, ideological power also varies on the basis of age (Calasanti and Slevin 2001; Côté and Allahar 2006). Recall that the dominant ideology in North American culture favours youth and suggests that to be young is to be vibrant, beautiful, and happy whereas to be old is to be tired, unattractive, and grim. At the same time, people are judged on the basis of whether they act their age, look their age, and are aging well. Yet there is no linear relationship between age and ideological power, for while it is considered a great compliment to be told you look young if you are old and mature if you are young, an older woman who wears a miniskirt may be scolded for not acting her age (see Calasanti and Slevin 2001) and a mature young man may be criticized for not being one of the boys.

|||||||||| **Note** ||||||||||||||||||||||||||||||||||||||||||||||||||||||||||||||||||||||||||||||||||||||||||||||

1. Notably, Riley may be overstating the significance of age here. In contrast, Neugarten (1970; Neugarten and Hagestad 1976) has argued that the potential exists for an age-irrelevant society because the cohorts that are currently becoming old are like the young in terms of health, educational attainment, income security, and social values.

|||||||||| **Questions for Critical Thought** ||||||||||||||||||||||||||||||||||||||||||||||||||||||||||||

1. Discuss the social construction of age in the following domains: work, sport, and health. How old does one have to be to be considered old in each of those domains? What factors influence the social construction of age in each domain?
2. Many provinces in Canada require their employees to retire at age 65. Yet the human rights codes in these same provinces state that it is unlawful to discriminate on the basis of age. Using what you have learned about the social construction of age, answer the following question: Is mandatory retirement discriminatory?
3. Age strata, age groups, and cohorts are related but distinct categories of analysis.

Compare and contrast each of these terms in relation to the chronological age markers that are used to demarcate categories within these concepts.
4. Increasingly, consumer products are being developed for older adults. Using a political-economy perspective, apply the 'aging enterprise' concept to critically assess this marketing strategy.
5. Drawing on what you know about class, age, gender, ethnicity, and race, discuss why there has been less research on age structures of inequality than on class, gender, ethnicity, and race.

|||||||||| **Glossary** ||||||||||||||||||||||||||||||||||||||||||||||||||||||||||||||||||||||||||||||||||||||

Aging and society paradigm   A modified and more dynamic version of Matilda White Riley's original approach. Known formally as the *age stratification perspective*.

Age group   In Canada, adults are often categorized as being old, middle-aged, or young. These are social constructions of age categories that are referred to as 'age groups'.

Age strata   Recognizing that all societies are organized on the basis of age and the associated rites of passage, *age strata* and related terms such as *age set* refer to the stratification of societies along these lines. The assumption is that there are specific sets of roles and responsibilities attached to membership in a particular age stratum and that status varies accordingly.

Allocation   Processes through which individuals are assigned and reassigned to social roles.

Biopsychosocial process   The intersections of social, psychological, and biological factors that contribute to processes of aging and development.

Cohorts   Aggregates of individuals who are born in the same time interval.

Diachronic   Changing, in reference to states.

Socialization   Processes through which individuals learn how to engage in appropriate social roles. This involves learning and conforming to normative rules of behaviour.

Structural lag The gap between the activities individuals engage in and the ability of structures to adapt to people's behaviour. Recall that in age stratification theory, *structures* refers to institutions. The idea of structural lag is that institutional arrangements need to be modified to catch up with behaviour. For example, although women's rates of labour-force participation are higher than they ever have been, institutional family and work arrangements have not kept up with these changes. As a result, women (and some men) find it difficult to balance work and family responsibilities.

Synchronic Static, in reference to states.

Recommended Reading

Calasanti, Toni M., and Kathleen E.Slevin. 2001. *Gender, Social Inequalities, and Aging*. Walnut Creek, CA: Altamira Press. An excellent book that examines the intersections between age and gender as they frame social inequality throughout life and especially in old age. A particularly useful part of this book is its discussion of the body, which is rare in assessments of inequality.

Côté, James E., and Anton L. Allahar. 2006. *Critical Youth Studies: A Canadian Focus*. Toronto: Pearson Prentice Hall. This book provides a very good overview of issues related to youth, such as education, work, and financial independence. It takes a critical approach and draws on evidence from several disciplines to support its theses.

Estes, C.L. 1999. 'The New Political Economy of Aging: Introduction and Critique'. Chapter 1 in M. Minkler and C. Estes, eds, *Critical Gerontology*. Amityville, NY: Baywood. In this article, Estes elaborates upon her previous work by including gender in her critical assessment of aging and later life.

Katz, Stephen. 1996. *Disciplining Old Age: The Formation of Gerontological Knowledge*. Charlottesville: University Press of Virginia. A theoretically rich account of the 'social, political, organization, and epistemological conditions' that made the study of aging and old age possible.

Myles, John F. 1984. *The Political Economy of Public Pensions*. Boston: Little Brown. A classic Marxist account of how the state and economy intersect in creating situations of relative advantage and disadvantage in later life.

Riley, Matilda White, Anne Foner, and Joan Waring. 1988. 'Sociology of Age'. Pp. 243–90 in N.J. Smelser, ed., *Handbook of Sociology*. Newbury Park, CA: Sage. One of the most comprehensive accounts of how age is conceptualized from a sociological perspective.

Relevant Websites

Youth Canada
www.youth.gc.ca
**This is a portal for government programs relating to youth (Service Canada) as well as information on education, employment, travel, and community events.

MySafeWork.com
http://mysafework.com
**This site is one focus of the charitable foundation Our Youth at Work, which advocates for health, safety, and wellness in the workplace with a focus on young workers.

CARP
http://carp.ca
**Although CARP (formerly the Canadian Association of Retired Persons) is a membership organization, you can check this site out for the latest issues facing older Canadians.

AARP
http://www.aarp.org
**Search AARP (formerly the American Association for Retired Persons) for research and you will find over 600 links to various publications regarding older adults.

Actors and Agency

Introduction

As the preceding chapters show, sociological theories of inequality usually highlight social structures as key explanatory mechanisms of advantage and disadvantage in social life. In chapter 2, for instance, we saw how Frank McCourt's childhood poverty may be understood on the basis of his social class rather than through individual characteristics of his father or mother. Chapter 3 showed how the structure of gender can explain the various hardships that women such as Beth experience. Chapter 4 showed how racial projects structure the everyday experiences of individuals such as Crystal Samms, and chapter 5 outlined how age structures Hagar Shipley's experiences with her family in Margaret Laurence's novel. The preceding chapters also illustrate how structures of class, age, gender, ethnicity, and race constrain the choices of individuals who are disadvantaged as a result of these structures: individuals are poor, for example, not because they are stupid, unambitious, or lazy, but because they have had limited opportunities to be anything other than poor. However, if we were to take these structural explanations to the extreme, there would be no room in society for the **social mobility** demonstrated by Frank McCourt.

Studies of social mobility are common in sociology. Some of this work characterizes particular countries on the basis of how much opportunity each has for social mobility. Studies of intergenerational mobility examine parents' characteristics and assess the likelihood that children will attain higher-status occupations or higher levels of education than their parents. According to this research, children are constrained by their parents' education and occupation but in some countries there is more opportunity for ambitious and able children to do better than their parents. In explaining Frank McCourt's situation, then, social mobility researchers might argue that McCourt's ambition and ability led him to move to a country that offered more opportunity than his homeland and that as a result he was able to live a better life than his parents. But there is a tension in sociology, between structural and individual explanations of inequality. How do we explain the lives of those of McCourt's peers who did not do as well as he? The logic in social-mobility studies suggests that these children were less ambitious and less able to succeed than McCourt was. Although I do not dismiss the importance of ambition and ability in one's life, such explanations oversimplify the processes through which individuals either challenge or comply with the structural circumstances of their lives.

Unlike proponents of theories that emphasize the social structure over and above the actor, I do not start with the assumption that structure ultimately determines individual action. Individuals are not passive objects who conform to structural forces in their day-to-day lives. Nor do I start with the assumption that individuals act freely in a world that is untouched by structural pressures. Indeed, the range of options available to individuals varies, and these options are constrained by a host of structural factors, including gender, class, ethnicity, race, and age. The theories of inequality presented in the preceding chapters vary in the extent to which they put emphasis on individuals, social structures, or some combination of the two. Indeed, we see glimpses of actors in even the most structural of these theories. As Marx suggested, 'men make their own history.' Yet Marx focused not so much on the human action that was required in doing this as on the idea that while people make their own history, 'they do not make it just as they please; they do not make it under circumstances chosen by themselves, but under circumstances directly encountered, given, and transmitted from the past.' The tradition of all the dead generations weighs like a nightmare on the brain of the living' (Marx [1852] 1963: 15). The task ahead here is to develop an approach to inequality that considers the intersections between social structures and individual actors. Before considering such intersections, however, I consider what is meant by *actors* and **action** in sociology.

Actors and Human Action

When sociologists discuss actors and **social action**, they are examining social life at the level of the individual. Most of the sociological insight we have regarding individuals comes from the symbolic-interactionist tradition. **Symbolic interactionism** is, however, a diverse field of inquiry, and action is only one small component of it. Although in the symbolic-interactionist tradition, action is related to other individual-level concepts, such as self, identity, and meaning, it must not be confused with them.

The sociological understanding of actors and action stems, in large part, from the work of Max Weber. In Weber's conceptions of social life and social theory, unlike those of Marx, actors and action were central. Indeed, according to Weber ([1922] 1978), the objective of sociology is to interpret social action through causal explanations. Put simply, actors or agents are individuals who take part in action that is meaningful or intentional. Most of us, then, are actors in the sociological sense, most of the time.

Weber ([1922] 1978) distinguished between action and social action. He considered action to be meaningful human behaviour from the point of view of the actor or actors involved. Action can be internal behaviour, as when individuals justify or rationalize spending money on something that they don't really need. Action can also be external behaviour, including decisions to either act or not. Thus, action is implied both in sending flowers to someone on their birthday and in deciding not to send them. Weber also suggests that *action* can refer to the act of having something done to you. For instance, your receiving or not receiving flowers from someone on your birthday is action because this act is subjectively meaningful to you.

Whereas action is behaviour that is individually meaningful, social action according to Weber refers to action that is meaningful only in relation to another person's behaviour. To explain this point, Weber ([1922] 1978: 23) discusses two cyclists who collide with each other. The fact that the cyclists collide is not social action but merely an event. Social action involves the negotiation that transpires after this event, whether it be a fight, an argument, or a peaceful resolution. Notably, and as with action, social action also includes deciding not to act or being acted upon.

Weber ([1922]1978: 24–6) distinguishes four **ideal types** of action and social action: traditional, affectual, instrumental (*zweckrational*), and rational (*wertrational*). *Traditional action* refers to actions that take place because they are habitual and have taken place in the past; *affectual actions* are the things people do to display emotion. The latter two types of action can be categorized as *rational action* and were of most concern to Weber. *Zweckrational*, or *instrumental*, *action*, refers to appropriate actions in which individuals engage while deciding how they can attain something and whether it is worth attaining. It also refers to meaningful assessments about what is required to achieve this goal. For example, if a woman decides—by carefully assessing what she is required to do, what she may have to give up, what the consequences of these actions is likely to be, and whether attaining a law degree is worthwhile—that she wants to go to law school, she is acting rationally in the *zweckrational* sense. *Wertrational*, or *value-rational*, *action* refers to action performed to attain a goal rather than the means through which the goal must be attained. The actor does not compare different means to an end or evaluate the consequences of the action but rather acts out of conviction. A mother who is committed to breastfeeding her premature baby and does so against her doctor's orders and without regard for the possible consequences of disregarding the status quo is acting in the *wertrational* sense.

Drawing on Weber, Talcott Parsons (1951) developed a theory of social action in which motivation and values determine action. Parsons believed that people are naturally capable of making choices and that they behave rationally to attain goals. Action is constrained by social systems, but it also conveys the idea that actors make conscious decisions to attain goals (Parsons 1949). Values and motives determine the type of action individuals engage in. Parsons identified three types of action: instrumental, expressive, and moral. *Instrumental action*, which is similar to the rational action of Weber's framework, refers to action that allows people to achieve a particular goal efficiently. *Expressive action*, which is similar to Weber's affective action, is that which people do to attain emotional satisfaction. *Moral action*, which is not found in Weber's framework, is behaviour that is concerned with standards of right and wrong (Parsons 1951: 45–51).

Whereas Weber acknowledged that an individual's behaviour could consist of more than one type of action simultaneously, Jürgen Habermas (1984) makes this point central to his theory of action. According to Habermas, there are different kinds of action, and what distinguishes them from one another has nothing to do with the act itself but rather with how agents are oriented to the act. The task for theory is to determine the various ways in which individuals may be compelled to act. In this vein, Habermas identifies five kinds of action: instrumental, strategic, normatively regulated, dramaturgical, and communicative (Habermas 1984: 273–337). Individuals engage in *instrumental* and *strategic action* when they are striving for success in the physical world (instrumental action) or for success that takes the social context into account (strategic action; for both, see Habermas 1984: 285–6). *Normatively regulated action* occurs when individuals take norms into account before acting. An individual who is concerned about how he or she appears to others and who acts accordingly is acting *dramaturgically*. Finally, *communicative action* aligns with needs for mutual understanding; the term refers to actions people engage in to make themselves understood (Habermas 1984: 333–4).

To illustrate Habermas's views on action, let us consider the act of sitting down in a chair. We cannot classify this act as normatively regulated, instrumental, or dramaturgical unless we know what prompted the individual to sit down. The kind of action that this act reflects depends on whether it was in response to being tired or a reaction to someone saying, 'Please sit down.'

When an employee enters an employer's office and chooses to stand until asked to sit down, the behaviour is normatively regulated action and probably involves some component of dramaturgical action. If the employee chooses to remain standing after the invitation to sit down, he or she is probably acting strategically as well.

Several key ideas from the work of Parsons, Weber, and Habermas have informed most sociological views on actors and action. First, part of being human is the capacity to make intentional choices. Second, action is not simply the act of doing, but also both the act of not doing and having something done to you. Third, there is a rational component to action: people calculate the potential rewards and sanctions of their actions and behave accordingly. Fourth, there is also a non-rational component to action: people act in traditional, normative, and affectual ways without rationalizing their behaviour. Fifth, any particular act may represent more than one kind or type of action. And sixth, people act within a social structure that constrains and orients action. This last point has been most contentious among sociologists and has led many to use the term *agency* in their work.

Agency

In an effort to avoid overly deterministic views of social life in which actors are like puppets being manipulated and constrained by social structures, scholars began using the term *agency*. In contrast to Parsons's theory of action, which emphasizes structure over and above action, the term *agency* stresses the idea that structures are composed of individuals who engage with social structure and can initiate structural change (Barnes 2000: 45–9). It is on this point that the similarities in theories of agency end. Indeed, there is little theoretical consensus over what *agency* means (Barnes 2000: 49) and whether or how it is different from the concept of action. In this section I will discuss two central views of agency, one put forth by Anthony Giddens and a second developed by Margaret Archer in reaction to Giddens.

Since the mid-1970s, Anthony Giddens has been arguing for a conceptualization of social structure that is inextricably bound to human action, and it is arguably through his work that *agency* has become a fashionable term in sociology. In developing his theory, Giddens, claiming that agency and structure 'presuppose one another' (1979: 53), develops a theory of structuration that involves 'the duality of structure which relates to the fundamentally recursive character of social life, and expresses the mutual dependence of structure and agency. By the duality of structure I mean that the structural properties of social systems are both the medium and the outcome of the practices that constitute those systems' (Giddens 1979: 69).

As Figure 6.1 shows, for Giddens, *agency* refers to a continuous flow of conduct by an actor or the activities of an agent and captures the ideas of progress, intentionality, and responsibility in the actions of human beings. Another central feature of agency is the capacity of actors to have acted differently, either by doing something else or by not acting at all. Involved in action are issues relating to its purposive or intentional processes, its human accountability, its unintended consequences, and the unacknowledged conditions under which it takes place.

Clearly, there are many similarities between Giddens's view of agency and the views of action espoused by Weber, Parsons, and Habermas. Indeed, Giddens uses the terms *agency* and *action*, *agent* and *actor* interchangeably in his structuration theory; this has led Margaret Archer to be critical of his work and to theorize the distinctions between the two.

Unlike Giddens, who views structure and agency as part of the same thing, Archer favours analytic dualism in her approach to sociology. In other words, she believes that structure is analytically distinct and temporally separate

Figure 6.1: Action and Agency in Giddens's Framework

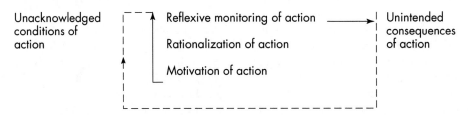

Source: Cassell (1993: 92).

from agency yet 'intimately intertwined' with it (1995: 65–75). And, for Archer (1995: 252–3), agency and structure must be separated if we are to understand the processes through which both are transformed over time. This is the crux of Archer's response to Giddens, and it is a point that I return to below. For now, I will focus on Archer's conception of agency, keeping in mind that she makes a distinction between agency and social structure.

According to Archer (1995: 248–9), there is a fundamental difference between action and agency and between human beings, social actors, and social agents. Archer (2000: 261) defines *agents* as 'collectivities sharing the same life-chances' and suggests that all persons are agents because all persons occupy a position in relation to the distribution of resources in society. Hence, agents are not individuals but rather groups of individuals who have in common their privilege or disadvantage in society. When Archer refers to an *agent*, she is referring not to an individual, but rather to a single group of people who share the same life chances. People are born into predetermined structures and are hence 'involuntarily situated beings' (Archer 2000: 262). Thus, according to Archer (2000: 262), 'humanity enters society through the maternity ward doors and we immediately acquire the properties of Primary Agents through belonging to particular collectivities and sharing their privileges or lack of them—as males/

females; blacks/whites; foreigner/indigenous; middle class/working class.'

Social agency, then, refers to relations or interactions between groups and can affect social change and stability. It is 'reflective, purposive, promotive, and innovative' (Archer 1995: 249) and it often operates under 'unacknowledged conditions of situated action [that] lie beyond the ken of time-and-space-bound agents' (Archer 1995: 250). Finally, 'courses of action are produced through the reflexive deliberations of subjects who subjectively determine their practical projects in relation to their objective circumstances' (Archer 2007: 17).

According to Archer (1995, 2000), time links agents with actors and agency with action because we are born agents and grow into mature actors. Individuals have no choice about their agent status or over what social collectivity they are born into. One is either male or female, white or black, middle-class or working-class, and so on. Choice is, however, implied in Archer's view of social actors. Social actors are 'role incumbents' (Archer 2000: 283). Action, which seems to be synonymous with choice in Archer's view, is exercised as individuals decide which roles they will take and which they will reject. Agents vary, however, in the options and opportunities that are available to them, and therefore action is conditioned by agency.

This rather confusing view of agents and agency is Archer's critical response to approaches to inequality that view categorical distinctions (between, for instance, women and men or blacks and whites) as individual characteristics. It is also a critical response to Giddens, who, in Archer's view, does not allow in his theory for collective action. According to Archer, by conceptualizing agents as collectivities and actors as role incumbents, we eliminate both problems.

Intersections of Agency and Structure

As the preceding discussion shows, there is little agreement in sociology over what is meant by *agency* and *action*. Indeed, the two concepts are often used to mean the same thing. For the time being, then, let us think of the terms *agency* and *action* as interchangeable and as referring to the capacity of humans to make choices and to behave in meaningful, thoughtful ways. That being said, the next issue to consider is the relationship between agency and structure. Approaches to this topic fall into two broad camps. In the first, 'integrated' camp, scholars consider structure and agency to be part of the same thing. In the second, 'analytic dualism' camp, scholars treat structure and agency as separate yet related features of social life.

Integrated Approaches

One of the best-known integrated approaches was described by Peter Berger and Thomas Luckmann in their book *The Social Construction of Reality* (1967). Berger and Luckmann approach the relationship between structure and action in dialectic terms. According to Berger and Luckmann (1967: 18), reality is socially constructed through three dialectical processes in which 'subjective meanings become objective facticities'. The first of these processes is *externalization*. In this process individuals create their social worlds through their own actions. Social order is the result of past human activity, and the reproduction of this social order is only possible

through this action. The second process, *objectivation*, involves the views that individuals share about social reality. In this process individuals come to understand that everyday life is ordered and prearranged. The third process is called *internalization*. In this stage social order is legitimized and reinforced. Elements of socialization are apparent in internalization as individuals learn what is expected of them and behave accordingly. When individuals engage in this process by conforming to the existing social order, they are also reproducing that social order. Reification of the social order occurs when individuals forget that human activity created the social order in the first place.

In Berger and Luckmann's (1967) approach to social life, individuals are treated as active participants. Individuals are able to evaluate the social structure and respond critically to it. However, it is assumed that individuals are on a level playing field in their ability to oppose any aspect of the social order. Furthermore, although this approach recognizes that many actors feel their choices are limited, the responsibility for perceptions of limited choice lies in the hands of the individual. If individuals perceive that they have no choice, the dialectical processes that create and recreate the social structure disappear and the actor is only acted upon. This analysis underemphasizes the fact that it is in the interests of some individuals or groups to maintain the existing social order and to limit the choices available to others. Hence, by assuming that individuals are on a level playing field and by locating limited choice within the realm of individual responsibility, this approach neglects to consider power relations as fundamental elements in social life and in an explanation of inequality.

Perhaps the best-known integrated approach is Anthony Giddens's structuration theory. According to Giddens, structure is composed of rules and resources that are organized as properties of social systems. Rules are the norms and practices of a society, and resources are bound to power relations. In fact, resources are the bases of power that make up the structures of domination. Social systems are systems of social interaction that reproduce relations between actors or collectivities and have structural properties. The theory of structuration seeks to explain 'the ways in which that [social] system, via the application of generative rules and resources, and in the context of unintended outcomes, is produced and reproduced in interaction' (Giddens 1979: 66).

According to Giddens, structure is involved in the production of action, but structure is not thought to place limits on action. Giddens (1979: 71) suggests that 'rules and resources are drawn upon by actors in the production of interaction but are thereby also reconstituted through such interaction. Structure is thus the mode in which the relation between moment and totality expresses itself in social reproduction'. (See Box 6.1 for a conversation with Anthony Giddens on structuration theory.) Accordingly, the assumption that structure is involved in the production of action stands in opposition to the view that structure places limits on action. However, one might argue that to adhere to the assumption that structure is involved in the production of action

is not to oppose the view that structure places limits on action; the distinction is more subtle, and it lies more in language than in philosophy.

In fact, Giddens's discussion of power points to the distinction, not the opposition, between a structure that produces action and one that confines it. Giddens rejects views of power that treat it as a phenomenon of intended action. He also rejects views of power that locate it within the social structure as a medium by which group interests are realized. According to Giddens, Lukes comes closest to the correct consideration of power. Lukes (1974) suggests that

> a person or party who wields power could have acted otherwise, and the person or party over whom power is wielded, the concept implies, would have acted otherwise if power had not been exercised. In speaking thus, one assumes that, although the agents operate within structurally determined limits, they none the less have a certain relative autonomy and could have acted differently. (Cited in Giddens 1979: 91)

Box 6.1 Conversations with Anthony Giddens: Interview Three: Structuration Theory

Christopher Pierson *The relationship between agency and structure and, paralleling that, between voluntarism and determinism is amongst the most ubiquitous and difficult issues in all social theory. In a number of texts in the late 1970s and early 1980s, culminating in the publication of* The Constitution of Society *in 1984, you developed your own distinctive resolution of this issue under the rubric of the theory of structuration. Perhaps I could begin by asking how you understand the*

traditional problem of structure and agency in social theory.

Anthony Giddens It isn't a 'traditional problem', at least expressed in these terms. In the past it was usually seen as a dualism between individual and society, or the actor and the social system. Thinking about this traditional question of the relationship between the individual and society lay at the origin of the idea of structuration. I felt these were all unelaborated notions. People would speak of the individual as though it was obvious what 'the individual' was and quite often the same was true of 'society'. I wanted to break them down and give them more substance. The term 'structuration' I originally borrowed from French—I don't think it was used in English before I appropriated it. I wanted to place an emphasis on the active flow of social life. We should see social life not just as 'society' out there or just the product of 'the individual' here, but as a series of ongoing activities and practices that people carry on, which at the same time reproduce larger institutions. That was the original thought and from there I tried to elaborate each of the key terms, precisely by speaking of 'agency' and 'structure'. I put the idea of recurrent social practices at the core of what social sciences are about, rather than either starting with 'the individual' or starting with 'society'.

The Constitution of Society is not necessarily the easiest book. Could you give some indication, in fairly straightforward terms, of how the theory of structuration resolves the dualism between structure and agency?

This depends on two things really. The first is rethinking the notion of structure. I wanted to get away from the characteristic Anglo-Saxon way of conceptualizing structure, where structure is some given form, even a visible form of some sort. But I also sought to get away from the idea that agency is just contained within the individual. I wanted to see it as more of a flow of people's actions and to connect it with attributes of self-consciousness. Within certain limits, speaking a language shows us something about what the relationship between them might be. In other words, language has structure, language has form, but it isn't visible and it is only 'there' in so far as it actually forms part of what people do in their day-to-day use of it. That is what I call the recursive quality of language. I didn't claim that society 'is like a language', as the structuralists used to say; but language gives us

key clues as to how recursiveness happens. 'Society' can be understood as a complex of recurrent practices which form institutions. Those practices depend upon the habits and forms of life which individuals adopt. Individuals don't just 'use' these in their activity but these life practices constitute what that activity is.

You talk in some places about structural effects and these being a better way of describing the impact of structure. Are 'structural effects' simply a euphemism for some kind of structure which is observable or has some existence other than through these perceived effects?

The structural properties of societies and social systems are real properties, but at the same time they have no physical existence. They are real properties in the sense in which they depend upon the routine qualities of people's actions and they can be very fixed or 'hard'. I don't want to discard the Durkheimian point that society is a structured phenomenon and that the structural properties of a group or a society have effects upon the way people act, feel, and think. But when we look at what those structures are, they are obviously not like the physical qualities of the external world. They depend upon regularities of social reproduction. Language has this incredibly fixed form. You can't go against even the most apparently minute rules of the English language without getting very strong reactions from other speakers. But at the same time, language doesn't exist anywhere, or it only exists in its instantiations in writing or speaking. Much the same thing is true for social life in general. That is, society only has form and that form only has effects on people in so far as structure is produced and reproduced in what people do. This to me applies right through from the most trivial glance you might give someone to the most globalized of systems.

Source: Giddens and Pierson (1998).

However, Giddens (1979: 91) argues that by suggesting that structure places limits on agency, this approach is 'unable satisfactorily to deal with structure as implicated in power relations and power relations as implicated in structure'. This problem can be alleviated only 'if the resources which the existence of domination implies and the exercise of power draws upon are seen to be at the same time structural components of social systems. The exercise of power is not a type of act; rather, power is instantiated in action, as a regular and routine phenomenon.' For Giddens, it is important to consider the dialectic between action and structure in discussions of power: 'Resources are the media whereby transformative capacity is employed as power in the routine course of social interaction; but they are at the same time structural elements of social systems as systems, reconstituted through their utilisation in social interaction' (1979: 92). Thus, the subtle difference between the view that structure limits action and that structure produces action lies in Giddens's dialectical assumption that one mutually creates the other.

Arguably, a more accurate view of social life lies within the combination of these two approaches. Structure produces action, but the particular action that is produced lies within the realms of structure itself. Only under exceptional circumstances does human agency push structural barriers to the extent that structure itself is changed. Yet agents have a certain relative autonomy and could have acted differently even though they operate within structurally determined limits. This view of social life challenges integrated approaches to social structure by considering agency and structure as distinct yet related social phenomena, as do theorists in the analytic-dualism camp.

Analytic Dualism

Scholars who favour analytic dualism suggest that integrated approaches are problematic because they conflate issues of structure and agency (Archer 1995, 2000; Layder 1994). Analytic dualists argue that agency and structure are distinguishable yet related features of social life (Archer 1995: 65). The task of sociologists, according to analytic dualists, is to examine how structure and agency are related and to analyze the processes and mechanisms that bind them together.

Although Erving Goffman was much more concerned with the interactional order than with the structural order, in his undelivered presidential address to the American Sociological Association, published after his death, he discusses the relationship between the two. In this paper, Goffman (1983) argued that there are social membranes that act like filters to determine which structural influences are let through and whether they are transformed in the process. The relationship between structure and agency, he claims, is fluid or 'loosely coupled' (Goffman 1983), and the membranes that connect them will vary depending on the empirical and historical reality that encompasses them. One example Goffman (1983: 11) mentions is 'precedence through a door'. Door-opening rituals are situated within the interaction order, and 'at best they are likely to have only loosely coupled relations to anything by way of social structures that might be associated with them' (11). Indeed, Marilyn Frye (1983) quite convincingly discusses the practice of men opening doors for women as an expression of women's structural oppression in relation to men. But we know from our experiences that this 'act' is only loosely coupled with structural realities. There are men who hold doors open for painfully long periods of time for women who are 10 yards away from the door. Yet women also hold doors open for men and some men do not hold doors open for women. A membrane is at work here such that 'social structures don't "determine" culturally standard displays [but] merely help select from the available repertoire of them' (Goffman

1983: 11). Although Goffman does not explain precisely how these membranes work, he does point us to the mutual and reciprocal constuitive processes between the structural and interactional orders.

In a similar vein, Pierre Bourdieu (1977) argues that structure and agency are linked through habitus. *Habitus* refers to relatively stable sets of attitudes and beliefs that social actors hold and that reflect their social circumstances, such as their class background, gender ethnicity, or race. They are 'generative principles of distinct and distinctive practices' (Bourdieu 1998: 8) that influence the behaviour of individuals as well as their preferences and choices. Habitus is the mechanism through which the structural circumstances of individual lives play out in the actions of individuals—what and how they eat, what activities they engage in, and how they are engaged in them. Individuals can act only on the basis of what they know, and past experience crucially influences action. Members of different classes or different ethnic or racial groups eat and play differently not because of innate differences between them, but because their habitus informs their behaviour and distinctions get reproduced. Distinctions in behaviour between groups take on a certain value status, and here we see a striking similarity to Goffman's idea of loose coupling. Acts tend to be judged by members of society as good or bad, distinguished or vulgar, and so on. But the very same act can be perceived in many ways depending on the structural circumstances of the actor and of the perceiver. Box 6.2 shows that decisions about what clothes to wear, how to speak, and how to act vary according to race and class structures. It also shows how actors attempt to change these social structures through their actions, sometimes resulting in the loss of a job. In sum, habitus is embodied in individuals as links between social structural circumstances and actions while they simultaneously serve to distinguish between groups of people (Bourdieu 1998).

A central problem in Bourdieu's work on structure and agency is that social change seems unlikely (Sewell 1992). Habitus influences behaviour but in a unidirectional way; it tends to constrain individual actions because people can only act on the basis of what they know and within the limits of their social-structural constraints. This is, in part, because Bourdieu does not engage in a discussion of time, an issue which is at the heart of Margaret Archer's theory of structure and agency.

The problem of structure and agency is a 'vexatious fact of society' according to Archer; neither society nor social interaction can be discussed in isolation from the other, and yet there are properties of both that transcend the other (Archer 1995, 2000). In fact, Archer takes issue with theorists in the integrated tradition, and much of her work serves as a useful critique of these perspectives. Archer elaborates upon her critique by developing a theory that relies on the notions of **morphogenesis** and **morphostasis**. The former means the processes that 'elaborate or change a system's given form, state, or structure' (Archer 1995: 166). The latter means 'processes in complex system-environmental exchanges which tend to preserve or maintain a system's given form, organization or state'. Put simply, Archer is referring here to the transformation and reproduction of social systems or to the processes through which social systems change or remain the same. Hence, unlike Goffman's and Bourdieu's views, one advantage of Archer's theory is that it explicitly considers social change.

According to Archer (1995: 193), problems with both practical theorizing and **realist social ontology** can be overcome by creating bridges between the two. To accomplish this, Archer conceives of three related morphogenetic/static cycles that refer to structures, cultures, and agency (see Figure 6.2). Regarding the structural and cultural morphogenetic/static cycles, at time one (t_1), individuals are faced with structural and

Box 6.2 Black and Not-So-Beautiful Stereotypes

By Vanessa E. Jones

To counteract racial perceptions, black men have had to act differently in workplaces. A new generation is trying to change those rules.

On Fridays, staff at Boston Architectural College have the option to dress casually. But when Michael James, a director of human resources and diversity at the school, donned denim shorts one recent Friday, his clothing elicited a few comments.

One person wasn't used to seeing Mr James dressed so informally, someone else asked him, 'What happened?' and another supportively told him to 'fight the fight'.

The interest in Mr James's attire wasn't based on a pitched battle about what comprises casual dress. He believes the comments reflected the fact that he is a black man who decided to dress down at the office. 'Even when we have casual Fridays,' he says, 'I'm expected to wear a suit and tie.'

Like many other black men, Mr James, 36, says unspoken rules limit how they interact in predominantly white workplaces. In some cases, they must dress more formally than their co-workers, speak softly, or generally comport themselves in non-aggressive ways to counteract American stereotypes that paint black men as unintelligent, violent, and dangerous. These biases are based on long-held beliefs about black masculinity and sexuality that grew out of the United States' history of slavery and segregation.

In the past, black men had no choice but to succumb to white society's fears and present themselves deferentially. But today a new generation of black men is bringing attention to and trying to change these implied rules of conduct.

Last month, in an interview on HBO's *Real Sports With Bryant Gumbel*, Philadelphia Eagles quarterback Donovan McNabb talked about how black quarterbacks have to work harder than white ones to prove their worth. He said even when he plays well in a game, critics will say of

him: 'We would have scored more points if he would have done this.'

Isaiah Washington, who uttered a homophobic slur on the set of the television drama *Grey's Anatomy*, has spoken bluntly about the predicament of being a black man in the corporate world. After it was announced last spring that his contract was not renewed, he told *Newsweek*: 'I had a person in human resources tell me after this thing played out that "some people" were afraid of me around the studio. I asked her why, because I'm a 6-foot-1, black man with dark skin and who doesn't go around saying "Yessah, massa sir" and "No sir, massa" to everyone? It's nuts when your presence alone can just scare people . . .'

Although some have criticized Mr Washington for using race to excuse his alleged homophobia, his statement shows just how outspoken some black men have become about inequities in the workplace. It's usually black men with the wealth, fame, or social class to withstand the negative consequences of speaking out about such issues who discuss it.

Those who are dependent on corporations for job security learn to deal with this issue by approaching it with a different mindset.

'You can't simply see it as somehow an erosion of who you are,' says Mark Anthony Neal, a professor at Duke University and author of last year's non-fiction work about black masculinity and sexuality, *New Black Man*, 'that you're inauthentic because you're "acting white". It's simply a strategy that needs to be employed in order for you to be successful in your career and in your life.'

As an allocation analyst at TJX Companies Inc. in Framingham, Mass., for three years, starting in 2000, Wynndell Bishop says he made a conscious decision to speak with a softer voice and present himself in an non-aggressive manner. 'I would say 60 per cent of the division I was in was young, white women between the ages of 21 and 28,' says Mr Bishop, 28, who received his MBA from Boston College in May. 'A lot of those women, to my knowledge, didn't have a lot of interaction with black folks other than what they saw on TV.'

Mr James makes accommodations because of his 6-foot-2 height, which, he says, has made people view him as 'threatening and menacing even though I'm the most peaceful person out there'. He shies away from making declarative statements at work, to prevent himself from appearing too aggressive. 'I say: "What are your thoughts about it?" rather than demanding they do certain things,' James says. 'I put it out there in a fashion that they feel they have a choice.'

The adjustments black men make in how they handle themselves often depend on the sex and class of the people with whom they work. When Mr Bishop later held a management job at Gillette Co.'s factory in Andover, Mass., with a predominantly white group of male blue-collar workers, he says he felt a lot more comfortable.

Although Asian Americans, Latinos, and men of other ethnic groups also face stereotyping in the workplace, they don't experience the problems that black men do, Prof. Neal and others say. Although Asians look physically different from whites, Asian Americans are stereotyped as unthreatening. Unless they're dark-skinned, speak in their native language, or have an accent, Latino men don't stand out.

Black men do.

'If we're sitting in a room of a hundred,' Mr Bishop says, 'and there's all different white heritages in the room, no one's going to necessarily know the Jewish person is Jewish, but everyone will know that I'm black.'

Mr James finds the persistent negative stereotyping that accompanies having brown skin baffling. 'It's like we have our priorities in the wrong place,' he says. 'My success shouldn't be dependent on how I look or how well I can replicate what you're comfortable with. It should be about what I bring to the table and how I help the organization advance in its goals and objectives.'

Mr James made a conscious effort to adapt to the corporate world after a series of bad experiences. Finding mentors to guide him through the process helped, he says.

His boss at Boston Architectural College is Theodore Landsmark, a prominent figure in the 1970s, when tensions arose over busing in Boston, who shares the wisdom he's gathered over the years.

'I've been terminated from [a] job,' says Mr James, who didn't want to specify which company, 'because I've taken on the top leaders based on ethical principles. At the end of the day I realized that you can win the battle yet lose the war . . .

'You could be the world's best advocate for the right thing, but you would not be as effective sitting on the outside of the door looking in than you are sitting on the inside influencing the change, even if it's not going at the rate you would like to have it go at.'

Source: Jones (2007).

cultural conditioning. Between times two (t_2) and three (t_3), social interaction transpires. The result, at time four (t_4), is structural and cultural elaboration. In the morphogenesis of agency, t_1 is characterized by the socio-cultural conditioning of groups. Recall that, in Archer's view, agents are groups of people born in similar structural and cultural circumstances. Between t_2 and t_3, group interaction occurs; it is at t_4 that there is group elaboration. All of these cycles intersect because they have as a common thread social interaction, which is the middle component in each of them.

One important component of Archer's theory is her distinction between corporate agents and primary agents. Corporate agents are more able than primary agents to affect social change because they are born into structural circumstances

Figure 6.2: Archer's Morphogenesis of Structure and Culture

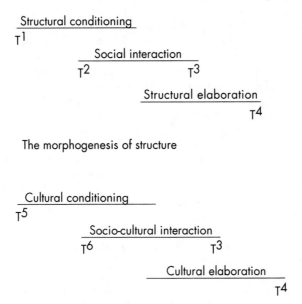

The morphogenesis of structure

Source: Archer (1995: 193). Reprinted by permission of Cambridge University Press.

that better enable them to do affect change. In Archer's words, 'corporate agents maintain/re-model the socio-cultural system and its institutional parts: primary agents work within it and them' (1995: 265). Social change occurs when the lives of primary and corporate agents are altered by the other group; it is 'the resultant of aggregate effects produced by primary agents in conjunction with emergent properties generated by corporate agents and thus does not approximate to what anyone wants' (1995: 265). In other words, for social change to take place, agents with different amounts of power and resources must enter into a state of conflict; change occurs to resolve the conflict. A double morphogenesis is possible whereby 'agency leads to structural and cultural elaboration, but is itself elaborated in the process' (Archer 2000: 258). It is important to note that in Archer's view, agents are not actors. Social actors only embrace sets of social roles, and inasmuch as Archer is concerned with

large-scale social change, social actors then have very little influence.

For the purpose of research on inequality, Archer's work is dense, complex, and overly complicated. It is unclear, for instance, why Archer feels the need to distinguish agents from actors on the basis of what social circumstances individuals are born to. Individuals are born into lives that vary on continua of advantage and disadvantage. This has much more to do with structure than with agency. Indeed, referring to groups of people who share similar life circumstances as agents who vary in terms of whether they can initiate social change serves only to conflate structures and agency. Ironically, this is the very problem Archer was trying to avoid in her work.

Nonetheless, it is clear from Archer's work (and from Goffman's and Bourdieu's) that there are advantages to analytic dualism. Primary among these is that analytic dualism allows us to study properties of structures and individuals that do not transcend one another. Empirically, this is a very useful strategy. And to the extent that sociologists are concerned with the practicalities of social inequality as much as with abstractions of it, such approaches are worthwhile. However, unlike integrated approaches, these theories usually end up favouring either structure (Archer and Bourdieu) or agency (Goffman). What is required then is a perspective that bridges integrated and analytic dualism approaches, a framework that gives equal theoretical weight to structure and agency while at the same time noting their distinctiveness.

A View in the Middle

William Sewell's (1992) account of structure and agency, which straddles the integrated and analytic-dualist positions, represents the best statement on the relationship between structure and agency. Notably, Sewell wants to retain Giddens's idea of the duality of structure, and he rethinks certain categories that are central to Giddens's structuration theory in this light. Simultaneously, he relies quite heavily on Bourdieu's notion of habitus, specifies nicely what is meant by *agency* and *structure*, and discusses how the two are linked. Hence, his theory is best described as lying somewhere between analytic dualism and integrated approaches.

To begin, Sewell (1992; see also Sewell 2005) takes Giddens to task for the idea that structures are virtual and composed of rules and resources. To do so, he first explains what he means by *rules*. In line with Giddens, Sewell suggests that rules are things that people draw on when they engage in social interaction. They are the taken-for-granted informal schemas that guide individual action. This, of course, stands in opposition to a more common definition of *rules* as being formally stated regulations, such as laws, about how one should behave. To resolve the possible confusion about these two very different views

of rules, Sewell suggests using the term *schemas* to refer to 'generalizable procedures' that apply to a variety of social interactions. Schemas are generalizable in the sense that individuals draw on them in various contexts. Some examples of schemas are etiquette, aesthetic norms, or the assumptions about how people should act on the basis of categorical distinctions such as 'female' and 'male'. Such 'recipes' for behaviour can be applied to both old and new situations, and it is because of their transposability that they may be understood as virtual. Hence, schemas are virtual because they are generalizable and cannot be specifically located in any particular social interaction or in any particular place and time. In other words, they exist but they cannot be empirically specified.

Resources, for Sewell, are of two types, human (Giddens's *authorization*) and non-human (Giddens's *allocation*). Human resources are things such as physical strength, emotional commitments, and knowledge; non-human resources are animate or inanimate objects; and both can be deployed in power relations. Unlike Giddens, Sewell argues that whereas schemas are virtual, resources are actual. Here lies a contradiction between Giddens and Sewell that Sewell must reconcile before moving on. If structures are virtual, then they cannot be composed of both schemas and resources as Sewell has defined them. To solve this conundrum, Sewell argues that we should think of resources as the effect of schemas and of schemas as the effect of resources. This is similar to Bourdieu's idea of habitus, whereby a dialectic process occurs such that structures are formed through the mutual constitution of schemas and resources.

Having defined *structure*, Sewell goes on to describe how agents intersect with social structures, thereby potentially changing them. According to Sewell (1992: 20), 'to be an agent means to be capable of exerting some degree of control over the social relations in which one is integrated, which in turn implies the ability to transform those social relations to some degree.' Sewell conceptualizes agency as the human capacity to be intentional, creative, and ambitious, but he suggests that people develop different levels of this capacity depending on the structural circumstances they are faced with.

Because societies are characterized by a 'multiplicity of structures' that intersect one another—for example, the class, age, gender, ethnicity, and race structures that are discussed in this book—social actors are required to draw on a range of schemas and resources in their social interactions with others. This creative capacity allows for the possibility that actors may transpose the schemas that they draw upon from one structure to another. Furthermore, because of the intersection and multiplicity of structures, individuals may attribute different meanings and interpretations to resources and schemas. The various meanings that may be attached to one structure or another by different actors depending on the array of schemas and resources at their disposal signify the possibility of social change.

Finally, according to Sewell (1992: 18), there is a certain 'unpredictability of resource accumulation' that allows for the transformation of social structures. Because social actors attribute different meanings to structures, have the creative capacity to transpose schema from one to another, and are located across a wide array of structural positions, 'the resource consequences of the enactment of cultural schemas is never entirely predictable' (Sewell 1992: 18). What Sewell seems to be referring to here is the unintended consequences of one's actions: 'If the enactment of schemas creates unpredictable quantities and qualities of resources, and if the reproduction of schemas depends on their continuing validation by resources, this implies that schemas will in fact be differentially validated when they are put into action and therefore will potentially be subject to modification' (Sewell 1992: 18). Thus, according to Sewell, if the unintended consequences of one's actions affect one's resources, then structural change is likely to occur (see also Archer 1995, 2000).

In short, although Sewell suggests that his approach modifies and expands on Giddens's idea of the duality of structure, he veers away from the heart of this approach by discussing the intersections of structure and agency rather than their presuppositions. In other words, he discusses the unique characteristics of agency, agents, and structures in a way that Giddens does not, while at the same time recognizing their influences on one another. Furthermore, his approach avoids the problems with Bourdieu's tendency toward structural determinism and Archer's view that agents are only collectivities that share similar structural backgrounds. Although I quibble with some of the specifics of Sewell's approach to structure and agency (more on that in the next chapter), it is, in my mind, the best statement on the topic.

This chapter has examined various sociological meanings of *action* and *agency* as well as theoretical views on the links between agency and structure. In the next chapter, a conceptual framework is developed that specifies how the concepts introduced in the preceding chapters come together. Also clarified in the next chapter is the relationship between structure and agency. In particular, several mechanisms are introduced that link structure and agency in relation to social inequality.

|||||||||||| Questions for Critical Thought |||||||||||||||||||||||||||||||||||||||||||||||||||||||||||

1. Critically assess the views of action put forth by Weber, Parsons, and Habermas. Evaluate

an action that you do every day according to each of these perspectives.

2. Consider the decision that you made to attend university. What role did structure play in that decision? What role did agency play? Which theory of structure and agency best explains your decision-making process?

3. Compare and contrast the theories of structure and agency put forth by Giddens and Sewell. Why is Sewell's theory more applicable than Giddens's structuration theory to the study of social inequality?

4. Does Sewell's theory improve upon the work of Berger and Luckman? If so, how? If not, why not?

5. In chapter 3, housework and child care were discussed in relation to the oppression, exploitation, and opportunity hoarding that characterize the structure of gender relations. Continue that discussion by evaluating how Goffman's idea of membranes relates to the negotiation of child care and housework in families.

‖‖‖‖‖ Glossary ‖‖

Action   Meaningful human behaviour from the point of view of the actor or actors involved.

Ideal types   Theoretical abstractions of a particular social phenomenon. Observations that are exaggerated and used as a methodological tool to provide insight into the observed phenomena and for assessing variations from the abstraction. Introduced by Weber.

Morphogenesis   Processes that elaborate or transform an existing system or structure.

Morphostasis   Processes that work at maintaining a system's organizational structure.

Realist social ontology   Philosophical assumptions about the realism of unobservable social phenomena. *Realism* is the idea that abstract ideas are real in their consequences. Social structures, for instance, are not directly observable but their social influence is real. *Ontology* refers to the philosophical beliefs about the nature or essence of being.

Social action   According to Weber, action that is meaningful only in relation to another person's behaviour.

Social mobility   The process of moving between status positions in society. Studies of social mobility sometimes examine country variations in opportunities for occupational or educational mobility. Other social mobility studies examine intergenerational mobility and whether children have surpassed the occupational status or educational attainment of their parents.

Symbolic interactionism   An approach to sociological study that situates analysis within interaction. People evaluate and define themselves on the basis of how they think others view them. We imagine ourselves in other social roles, and through role playing we learn appropriate and inappropriate forms of behaviour.

‖‖‖‖‖ Recommended Reading ‖‖‖‖‖‖‖‖‖‖‖‖‖‖‖‖‖‖‖‖‖‖‖‖‖‖‖‖‖‖‖‖‖

Bourdieu, Pierre. 1998. *Practical Reason: On the Theory of Action*. Stanford, CA: Stanford University Press. A collection of Bourdieu's lectures that covers his key ideas, including that of habitus.

Giddens, Anthony. 1984. *The Constitution of Society: Outline of the Theory of Structuration*. Berkeley: University of California Press. This book develops Giddens's seminal work on structuration theory.

Goffman, Erving. 1983. 'The Interaction Order'. *American Sociological Review* 48, February: 1–17. This is Goffman's presidential address to the American Sociological Association, published shortly after his death. Notwithstanding the title, this paper considers the relationship between the interaction order and social structures.

Layder, Derek. 1994. *Understanding Social Theory*. Thousand Oaks, CA: Sage. This book focuses on the agency/structure dualism in sociology. It covers theorists ranging from Dorothy Smith to Michel Foucault.

Sewell, William H.J., Jr. 1992. 'A Theory of Structure: Duality, Agency, and Transformation'. *American Journal of Sociology* 98: 1–29. In this excellent, clearly written article on agency and structure, Sewell draws heavily on Giddens and Bourdeau to develop his own ideas about the production and reproduction of social life.

IIIIIIIIIII **Relevant Websites** IIIIIIIIIIIIIIIIIIIIIIIIIIIIIIIIIIIIIIIIIIIIIIIIIIIIIIIIIIIIIIIIIIIIIII

Margaret Archer on Reflexivity
http://video.google.co.uk/videoplay?docid=915
6562982538374872
**A video of Margaret Archer speaking on reflexivity at the launch of the *Critical Realism Dictionary*.

Theory.org.uk
www.theory.org.uk
**This site of 'social theory for fans of popular culture' is also the parent site for social-theorist trading cards, including of Giddens, Goffman, and Foucault. The site contains media and identity resources and links as well as a link to order Giddens and Foucault action figures.

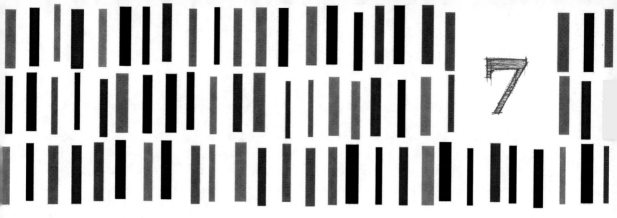

Actors and CAGE(s)

Introduction

The preceding chapters have outlined many of the elements of inequality that are included in the conceptual framework developed in this chapter, which brings these elements together in a coherent whole. As a first step, however, it is important to acknowledge the general assumptions that guide this approach. These assumptions are informed by several branches of critical theory and are summarized by Connidis and McMullin (2002: 559) as follows:

1. The social structure of Western nations is comprised of interlocking sets of social relations that privilege certain groups of people over others. Key sets of social relations include those that are based on class, gender, age, race, and ethnicity (Acker 1988; Collins 1990; Glenn 1992; McMullin 2000; Tilly 1998).

2. Individuals, though constrained to varying degrees by the social structure, attempt to exert control over their lives. They act with agency (Dannefer 1984; Habermas 1987; Lukes 1974; V. Marshall 1995; Weber [1922] 1978).

3. Social life is negotiated through interaction. It is constituted by and constitutive of interaction (Berger and Luckman 1967; Dannefer 1984; Giddens 1979; V. Marshall 1995).

4. Society is more accurately characterized as based on conflicting interests than on consensus. Different placement in the social structure creates conflicting interests and investments in the status quo (Marx [1848] 1983). There is an essential conflict or tension between the constraints placed on individuals by social structure and the desire of individuals to act with agency (Habermas 1987). Such an approach recognizes that conflicts are not episodic and unpredictable but rather are patterned features of relationships (D. Morgan 1985).

Although theoretical assumptions influence all sociological work, they are often left unacknowledged. Yet to understand theoretical frameworks, the assumptions that guide them must be recognized. These assumptions are listed for readers to keep in mind as they consider the conceptual framework developed here. To develop the framework, this chapter begins by revisiting the life of Anna (the woman discussed in chapter 1). It then discusses social time and the life-course perspective and in doing so introduces the concept of the **substantive birth cohort**.

Next, the concepts discussed in earlier chapters are integrated into the framework throughout this chapter. Finally, this conceptual framework is used to analyze Anna's life.

Figure 7.1 depicts Anna's life graphically. As shown on the far left of the figure, and as mentioned in chapter 1, Anna was born to white, English-speaking parents of British descent in 1915, during the First World War. She grew up on a farm in Ontario with her mother, father, and two brothers. Although it was only a small farm, Anna's father and mother worked hard and were able to provide their family with life's essentials. The arrow at the bottom of Figure 7.1 maps out the timing of some life events and transitions that Anna experienced. Anna graduated from high school, an unusual achievement for rural girls in that day; and although she had the opportunity to go on to teachers' college, as her mother had done before her, she decided to marry John Warner, a local man seven years her senior. She married well. John's family were well-to-do farmers, and with their help, Anna and John began their marriage in the late 1930s in relative financial stability. John and Anna moved to town and had two daughters, one in 1941 and the other in 1943.

Located in the centre of Figure 7.1 are the central activities in which Anna engaged to maintain her life and the life of her family. Anna was always a homemaker, and John never had a stable job. His older brother, who was married and childless, inherited their father's farm, and John worked for him occasionally. John also bought houses, restored them, and sold them for a profit. Money was tight in the Warner household, but no one seemed to want for anything. There was food on the table, John had paid for the house in full when he bought it, and the family had a few good clothes.

John died suddenly in 1970, when he was 62 and Anna was 55. His estate comprised some savings and his house. He had stipulated in his will that Anna could draw $200 per month from his estate until she either remarried or died, at which time the estate would be divided equally between her daughters. Suddenly, Anna was poor. Though her income was well below the qualifying cut-off for social security, she refused to apply for it and was too young to receive Old Age Security. The will stipulated that she could not sell the house. Other than a brief stint in business college, Anna had no training, no work experience, and no marketable skill. Besides, at 55 she was unlikely to find work. Her daughter hired her to babysit her grandchildren and for the next 10 years she made do with the clothes she already owned, shopping at yard sales and eating anything she could buy for next to nothing in the grocery store—old bread, food in dinted cans, and so on. After 10 years Anna turned 65 and began receiving the old age pension. She was still poor but no longer destitute. Five years later Anna's sister-in-law, the wife of John's childless brother who inherited the family business, died and left Anna one-third of her quite large estate. Suddenly, at age 70, Anna was better off financially than she had ever been before.

In chapter 1, I noted that a central aim of this book is to develop an understanding of inequality that can help us explain the ebb and flow of poverty that Anna experienced. In the preceding chapters, class, age, gender, ethnicity, and race have been considered mostly as static structures that constrain opportunity. Yet, as was noted in chapter 1, social inequality as it is experienced by individuals is dynamic, and to understand it we need to take social time into account.

Social Time

Structural accounts of gender and of race and ethnicity rarely take social time into account. This is partly because gender, race, and ethnicity are usually considered to be ascribed and static individual characteristics. Yet historical sociology shows us the importance of the

Figure 7.1: Anna's Life

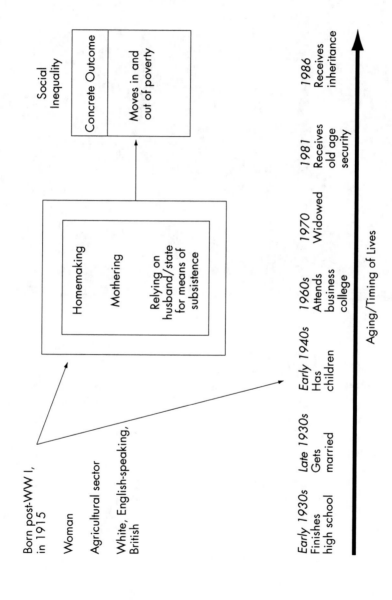

Figure 7.2: Anonymous, *The Stairway of Life*, c. 1640.

The Stairway of Life, c. 1640

social context to variations in gender, racial, and ethnic inequality (Adams 2000; Laslett and Brenner 1987). Moreover, the individual experiences of gender, racial, and ethnic inequality may vary throughout one's life. Social time is, however, considered in studies of social mobility (see chapter 6) that examine whether social class changes across generations. It is also considered in studies of aging that assess the biopsychosocial processes associated with the passage of time. Indeed, Anna's life shows that to understand the structural inequalities faced by individuals throughout their lives, we must address the intersection of individual and historical time. The life-course approach, as outlined by Glenn Elder (1974, 1995), provides useful insight into how issues of time might be considered in an integrated framework.

The Life-Course Perspective

The life-course idea, that people progress through life by taking on different roles and statuses at various ages, is not new. Among the earliest depictions of the life course is the seventeenth-century anonymous Dutch painting entitled *The Stairway of Life* (see Figure 7.2). In this picture we see a boy who ascends in his life until he reaches a peak at age 50 and then descends thereafter until his death at age 100. The various roles and statuses this boy takes on are conveyed through his clothes, the objects he holds, and his posture on each step of the stairway. For centuries, until recently, Europeans were given, as gifts to mark life transitions such as birth or marriage, stairways made in various media, which they would hang on the walls in their homes (Dekkers 2000).

The life-course perspective develops the ideas represented by *The Stairway of Life* and theoretically guides research in problem identification and formulation (Elder 1995; Elder and O'Rand 1995). In particular, it has 'made time, context, and process more salient dimensions of theory and analysis' (Elder 1995: 104). Life-course research conceptualizes social time by recognizing and attempting to understand (1) that individuals begin the dynamic and contextual aging process at birth; (2) that historical time, period, and cohort influence the aging process; (3) that aging is a biopsychosocial process related to and shaped by social contexts, cultural meanings, and social-structural locations; and (4) that age-related life transitions and trajectories are heterogeneous and are marked by sequences of events and social transitions (Bengtson, Parrott, and Burgess 1994; Elder 1995; Elder and O'Rand 1995; Hagestad 1990; Hagestad and Neugarten 1985; Passuth and Bengtson 1988). Furthermore, in the European tradition, life-course researchers emphasize the influence of the state and social policy in structuring individuals' life courses (Heinz 2001; Marshall and Mueller 2002).

According to Elder (1994, 1995), two of the central principles of the life-course paradigm are the **timing of lives** and **lives in time and place**. Issues related to the timing of lives include historical time, the social timing of transitions across the life course, the synchrony (or asynchrony) of individual careers, and one's life stage at the point of social change (Elder 1995). Thus, 'social timing refers to the incidence, duration, and sequence of roles; and to related age expectations and beliefs' (Elder 1995: 114). Hence, for instance, the era in which people are born (i.e., historical time) influences the average age at which they get married for the first time (social timing of the transition to marriage), which in turn influences the age at which it is socially appropriate for individuals to marry for the first time. For instance, during times of economic recessions and depressions, the average age of first marriage tends to be higher than during times of economic prosperity.

The 'lives in time and place' principle refers to the effect of contextual change caused by a particular historical event on individual life trajectories, noting that historical changes do not uniformly occur in different places. This is conceptually distinct from other life-course work that either studies birth cohorts in their relevant historical context (as in age-stratification theory—see chapter 5) or examines individual life courses as they are framed and constrained by a social system (see Mayer and Muller 1986). Instead, Elder's research starts with the properties of social change and then moves to an assessment of how this change affects individual life trajectories (Elder 1995), taking into account the age of individuals at the time of the historical event that led to social change. For example, Elder (1974, 1995) suggests that research on the effects of the Depression (with its resultant social changes), once traced through individuals and families, shows that children of the Depression developed individual characteristics such as a 'sense of industry and responsibility from the required helpfulness experience of needy households' (Elder 1995: 110).

Figure 7.3, which depicts my conceptual framework, illustrates the influence of the life-course perspective (Elder 1995) in my work. The 'lives in time and place' principle is located on the far left of the diagram under the umbrella term **substantive birth cohort**. Substantive birth cohorts also represent the geographic location (place), generation, gender, ethnicity, race, and class positions in which people are born through no choice of their own. This concept takes social time into account, which Margaret Archer (see also chapter 6) alludes to when she says, 'We are all born into a structural and cultural context which, far from being of our own making, is the unintended resultant of past interaction among the long dead' (1995: 253). The social structures and experiences of gender,

Figure 7.3: The Coalescence of Class, Age, Gender, and Ethnicity

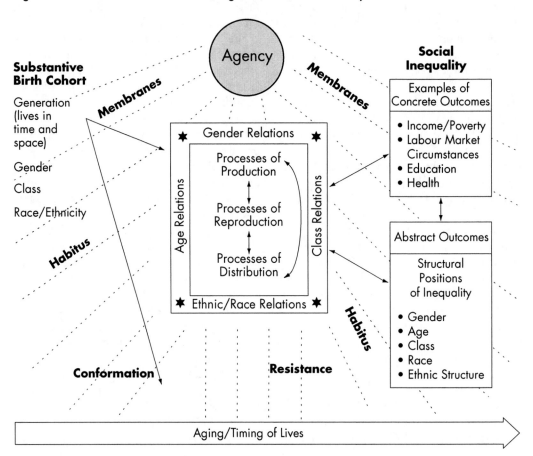

ethnicity, race, and class have been discussed in previous chapters, but it is their relationship to the 'generation' concept and to the ideas of social time that requires introduction here.

The term **generation**, as used here, is similar to the 'lives in time and place' concept in Elder's life-course perspective. *Generation* is used in various ways in the literature. Some scholars use it to refer to age-based locations within families. Hence, four-generation families are those comprising great-grandparents, grandparents, parents, and grandchildren. Others, however, use the concept of generation to mean time-specific

social locations that are similar to social-class locations and that might give rise to group conflict and consciousness (Mannheim [1928] 1952; V. Marshall 1983). It is the latter understanding of generation that I use here.

In his classic article 'The Problem of Generations', Karl Mannheim ([1928] 1952) generalized Marx's conception of class to demonstrate the sociological significance of generations. Mannheim criticized previous assessments of generations, arguing that those assessments relied too much on chronological age or on the biological fact that generations reproduce themselves. Hence, past treatments of genera-tions neglected the true sociological importance of generational relations. According to Mann-heim, although it is true that the sociological phenomenon of generations is based on the bio-logical rhythm of birth and death, 'were it not for the existence of social interaction between human beings—were there no definable social structure, no history based on a particular sort of continuity, then generations would not exist as a social location phenomenon' (Mannheim [1928] 1952: 290–1).

Thus, Mannheim believes that a generation represents a unique type of social location based on the dynamic interplay between being born in a particular year in a particular place and the socio-political events that occur while a birth cohort comes of age. Generational location is an objective fact similar to that of class position. Hence, all individuals, whether they acknow-ledge it or not, belong to a particular genera-tional location within a given society.

According to this view of generations, the im-portance of generation lies not in the fact that one is born in a particular year, but in the socio-logical relevance of being born at a particular historical time in a given society. It reveals that belonging to the same generation

> endow[s] the individuals sharings in them with a common location in the social and historical process, and thereby limit[s] them to a specific range of potential experience, predispos-ing them for a certain characteristic mode of thought and experience, and a characteristic type of historically rel-evant action. Any given location, then, excludes a large number of possible modes of thought, experience, feeling, and action, and restricts the range of self-expression open to the individual to certain circumscribed possibilities. (Mannheim [1928] 1952: 291)

The significance of substantive birth cohorts may be illustrated with a simple example. The life choices available to a white English woman born into a working-class family in 1920 are not the same as those available to a white English woman born into a working-class family in 1965. For the first woman the likelihood of finding work in the manufacturing sector (particularly because she was probably looking for work during the Second World War) is much greater than it is for the second woman, who is likely to find work in the service sector. The Second World War, while significantly influencing the first woman's life, will only indirectly influence the second woman's life. Likewise, the second woman will be influenced by the women's movement in a much different way than the first. Furthermore, the locale in which these women are born (urban versus rural; Maritime versus central regions in Canada) will influence their life experiences and opportunities (Lobao, Hooks, and Tickamyer 2007). Not only are the relations of production, reproduction, and distribution different, but the way those relations are shaped by gender, age, and racial, and eth-nic processes is considerably different as well. In turn, all of these processes influence and are in-fluenced by the timing of lives.

The 'timing of lives' concept and aging are di-mensions of social time (which are represented along the bottom of Figure 7.3), and both are influenced by substantive birth cohorts. The 'timing of lives' concept mirrors the life-course perspective's conceptualization of it (see above). Thus, the substantive birth cohort into which one is born shapes the incidence, timing, dur-ation, and sequencing of various life-course events and transitions such as marriage, parent-hood, and retirement. For instance, people who were born in the generation that came of age during the Depression were more likely to delay marriage than was the generation that followed them, in part because of the macro-economic situation in which members of each generation were required to make decisions.

The process of aging, which is also shown along the bottom of Figure 7.3, is the final dimension of social time that is considered in this framework. *Aging* refers to the experiences that come with the passage of time, as well as to the biopsychosocial processes that alter one's body and physical capabilities. The substantive birth cohort into which one is born influences aging processes to the extent that physical decline can be reduced by certain social habits that have changed over time, such as eating, smoking, and exercising. Such processes are also influenced by the generation, gender, ethnicity, race, and class in which one is born, as is evident from the different life expectancies of these various groups at birth.

Social Processes

Located in the centre of Figure 7.3 are the interrelated processes of production, reproduction, and distribution. These three processes constitute the organization and nature of the activities that are required for the survival of individuals and species. Recall from chapter 2 that *processes of production* are the ways by which raw materials are converted into useful and valuable objects; *processes of distribution* are the ways in which material resources change hands in society (Acker 1988, 1999, 2006; Weber [1922] 1978); *distributive processes* include wage, state, personal, and marital transfers (Acker 1988); and *processes of reproduction* are the ways in which life is maintained both daily and intergenerationally (Laslett and Brenner 1987). Social processes of production, reproduction, and distribution are interrelated. People who have indirect relationships with a particular social process tend to be more directly involved with another. A retired worker, for instance, has no direct relationship to production processes but is indirectly linked to them through the distributive processes by which he or she receives a company pension. A divorced father may not have a direct relationship with the processes of

reproduction but may be linked to those processes through the distribution of money to his children and former wife.

Processes of production, distribution, and reproduction become sociologically significant when we recognize that they are carried out by individuals in interaction with other individuals. In other words, it is the social relations of production, distribution, and reproduction that are of primary concern to sociologists. In the literature on social inequality, researchers generally emphasize one set of social relations as it relates to a specific social process. For example, social class relations are often seen as the root of inequality in production processes, and indeed the terms *social class relations* and *relations of production* are often used interchangeably. Similarly, gender relations are most often considered at the heart of inequality in processes of reproduction. However, there is ample evidence to suggest that the rewards, privileges, and resources associated with one's relationship to the processes of production, distribution, and reproduction are affected by a complex interplay of class, age, gender, ethnic, and race relations. Class, for instance, does not account for all of the power differentials that occur as a result of production processes (Acker 2006). Hence, it is unacceptable to suggest, as Wright (1997) does, that gender-based worker exploitation is simply a specific kind of class relation; this privileges class in the analysis of inequality and ignores the uniqueness of other forms of disadvantage. What is needed is a theoretical shift in which the relations of production will assume not only class relations but gender, ethnic, racial, and age relations as well.

Social Structure

The existence of the social processes discussed above does not necessarily imply an outcome of social inequality. Rather, understanding how these processes are structured is of fundamental importance to understanding and explaining social inequality (McMullin 2000). Figure 7.3 shows that class, age, gender, race, and ethnic relations frame the interrelated processes of production, reproduction, and distribution. Here, the connections (indicated by the stars in Figure 7.3) of class, age, gender, race, and ethnic relations with the power and rewards associated with one's position within these structures shape the ways in which production, reproduction, and distribution are organized.

As noted in the previous chapters, class, age, gender, and ethnicity or race are conceptualized as sets of social relations characterized by power that are fundamental structures or organizing features of all aspects of social life (Calasanti and Slevin 2006), including the processes of production, distribution, and reproduction (Ng 1993). Embedded in these social relations (or structures) are the taken-for-granted informal schemas (see Sewell 1992 and chapter 6) that guide individual action (e.g., ideas about appropriate behaviour) and various human resources (e.g., physical strength and knowledge) and non-human resources (e.g., money and property). Structures of class, age, gender, ethnicity, and race are formed through the mutual constitution of such schemas and resources (see Sewell 1992 and chapter 6).

Although the processes of class, race, ethnic, age, and gender formation are unique, several interrelated theoretical constructs have been identified in preceding chapters that apply, in varying degrees, to all of them: oppression (see chapters 2 through 5), power (see especially chapter 2), exploitation, and opportunity hoarding (chapter 3 and Tilly 1998). Recall that oppression occurs if (1) the welfare of one group of people depends upon the deprivation of another and (2) the deprivation of the oppressed group depends upon the exclusion of the oppressed group from access to resources, rewards, and privileges. As we have seen in the preceding chapters, in contemporary Canadian society both conditions of oppression apply to class, age, gender, race, and ethnic relations.

Oppressive relations are produced and reproduced through power. Power results from the control that certain groups have over economic, political, and ideological resources (Grabb 2007). It is through these systems of control that certain groups exclude others from gaining access to resources, rewards, and privileges. Thus, certain groups are deprived relative to others through mechanisms of power. Notably, there is a recursive relationship between power and oppression that is actualized in class, age, gender, ethnic, and race relations and through which patterns of inequality are produced and reproduced.

This recursive relationship is fostered through two mechanisms of control. First, exploitation produces oppressive relations when individuals and groups control resources (economic, political, ideological) and use those resources to their advantage by mobilizing others' efforts for their own gain (Tilly 1998). Second, oppressive relations are produced and reproduced through the mechanism of opportunity hoarding. Here, members of a particular group obtain a valuable resource that reinforces the group's privilege and status. The group then acts in ways that will ensure the maintenance of their monopoly over that resource (Tilly 1998).

When the disadvantage of certain groups depends on the advantage of others, the oppression that results is relational. It is in this sense that class, age, gender, ethnic, and race relations were discussed above. Relationality takes on a second meaning when it is positioned within a structure and agency framework. Here, a relational understanding of class, age, gender, ethnic, and race relations takes into account the meaning that is attributed to these categories of inequality based on relative positioning within social hierarchies (Glenn 2000; Stasiulis 1999). Meaning is derived through the assessment of difference, by which 'oppositional categories require the suppression of variability within each category and the exaggeration of differences between categories' (Glenn 2000: 10). Hence, even though men and women are physiologically more similar than different (Lorber 1994), small differences are exaggerated and problematized. Men appear genderless, and the inequalities that women face are assigned meanings that are derived from these differences (Glenn 2000).

The graphical depiction of class, age, gender, ethnicity, and race relations surrounding the processes of production, reproduction, and distribution resembles a picture in its frame. This representation illustrates that these structured sets of social relations are not thought to be causally linked, in any linear sense, to the processes of production, distribution, and reproduction. Rather, they mediate these processes and cannot be separated from them. This approach allows for considerable latitude in assessing both the independent and combined effects of these sets of relations on the processes of inequality. This suggests, following Wright's (1997) discussion of the connections between gender and class, that some of what is consequential about each of these sets of relations occurs independently of the other sets of relations, and yet an assessment of inequality would be incomplete without also considering intersecting influences.

However, this does not imply that one can pick and choose among the components of the framework that one deems worthy of study. Rather, the issue of coalescence in this approach suggests that inaccurate assessments of social inequality will result from such strategies. Although one can examine both the independent and interlocking effects of the components of this, the processes and sets of relations contained within it must be considered as a whole if we wish to understand the nature of social inequality. To examine one component without the other will present a distorted picture of social reality. It will also miss the fact that social life is mutually constituted by gender, class, race, age, and ethnicity (Glenn 2000). Thus, the coalescence represented in this approach might be visualized as a colourful and tightly woven fabric; the threads may be discernable from one another, but the removal of any one of them distorts the overall pattern.

Interestingly, the first letters of class, age, gender, and ethnicity or race form the word CAGE. There is a lot of imagery that comes to mind when one hears the word CAGE, and much of it is relevant to studies of inequality. I use this acronym to depict images of the social-structural constraints that individuals and groups often face. However, to make too much use of this metaphor would diminish the significance of individual agency in systems of inequality and in everyday life.

Agency and Structure: Actors and CAGE(s)

In the coalescence framework in Figure 7.3, agency flows throughout the diagram in a way that represents its omnipresence in social life. Recall that agency is the ability to exert some control over the social relations in which one is enmeshed (Sewell 1992). Agency includes decisions to act and not to act, and discussions of agency and structure must take into account both the intended and unintended consequences of one's action or non-action. The location of agency at the top of the diagram does not imply that it has a superior status to social structure. Rather, it is meant to capture the idea that agency runs through social structures and that 'social structure does not stand outside of the human, social behaviour that produces it yet, it nevertheless take on properties that transcend the behaviour of those who construct it' (McMullin and Marshall 1999: 309)

As argued in chapter 6, this approach favours analytic dualism over enmeshed accounts of the relationship between structure and agency. Recall that analytic dualism suggests that there is something unique about agency and about social structure, even though the two are intricately connected.

Notably, the theories presented in chapter 6 were not established primarily as explanations of social inequality but were concerned with explaining the relationship between structure and agency in relation to social change. Although social change is a central topic in the study of inequality, it is not the subject of this book. However, the organizational and conceptual framework developed here will help us to understand social inequality as it exists in Canada in the early part of the twenty-first century. A remaining challenge is to explain the mechanisms that link structure and agency in relation to inequality.

Habitus (Bourdieu 1977) and membranes (Goffman 1983) represent two linking mechanisms that apply generally to daily interactions. Recall that habitus is the cumulative embodied experiences that are shaped by structural realities. Individuals rely on their habitus in their daily interaction with others. Recall also that membranes are meant to represent Goffman's idea of the loose coupling of social orders. According to Goffman, membranes determine which aspects of the social structure influence an individual's behaviour and which do not. Both habitus and membranes work simultaneously in everyday life as individuals negotiate the social-structural realities of their lives.

Two other mechanisms, conformation and resistance, pertain more specifically to inequality. **Conformation** refers to the processes through which individuals comply with and accept the various schema and resources that structure society. Conformation captures Sewell's (1992) idea of transposability (see chapter 6) and Tilly's (1998) notions of adaptation and emulation. Thus, schemas are learned in one setting and used in others, thereby reinforcing the social structure itself. **Resistance** is the processes through which individuals reject and act against established social structures. Resistance can be subtle (a wife ignoring her standards of cleanliness so that her husband will continue to clean the bathroom) or blatant (protesting discrimination on Parliament Hill), and it can be chronic (being an ongoing and active member of the Grey Panthers) or acute (taking part in one activist march). Although conformation and resistance are set up here as antitheses of one another, no one ever completely conforms or resists. Rather, a complexity of resistance and conformation emerges as individuals negotiate their interests within the various domains of social life. Conformation and resistance are acted out by individuals, but the choice to conform or resist as well as the specific strategies one uses in these processes are influenced by the structured sets of social relations described above. Furthermore, tensions, contradictions, and paradoxes result from the complexities of resistance and conformation. Individuals then act to negotiate the ambivalence created by these tensions, contradictions, and paradoxes in everyday life (see Connidis and McMullin 2002).

Structure, Agency, and Anna's Life

The discussions of social time and place, social processes, structure, and agency presented above are necessarily abstract. To demonstrate how they work in real life we turn back to Anna's life and superimpose Figure 7.1 (Anna's life) onto Figure 7.3 (the coalescence framework), the result of which is depicted in Figure 7.4.

The substantive birth cohort in which Anna was born structurally affected her life chances. Even though women's rights and opportunities were expanding during the early twentieth century, women who were born during this time were still not encouraged to be economically self-sufficient, especially if they lived in rural areas as Anna did. Instead, they were expected to marry a man who would be able to provide for them and their families. English common law, by which property was passed on to the eldest son, was still well established in practice in Canada. Hence, Anna, by virtue of the fact

Figure 7.4: The Coalescence of Class, Age, Gender, Ethnicity, and Race in Anna's Life

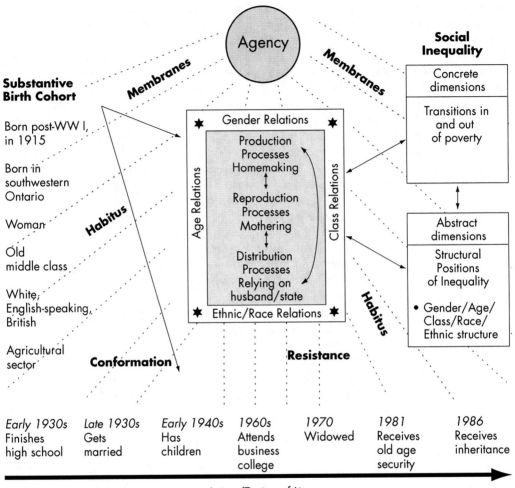

that she had been born a girl, had little hope of inheriting any property from her family. The fact that Anna's family worked in agriculture meant that there was little money to spare and that all family members needed to work on the farm and in the home in order to make ends meet. Anna helped her mother with household chores, gathering eggs, gardening, and making meals for her family and the boarders they took in.

Like many other farmers of British descent, Anna's mother and father embraced white, middle-class ideologies of family and work: a woman's place was in the home and good men provided for their families. Anna's parents also embraced the middle-class idea that their children should pursue post-secondary education. For Anna, these two sets of ideals created a tension. Why go to teachers' college if it is not needed to be a wife and a mother? A complexity of resistance and conformation emerged in Anna's life when she was caught between the structure of gender, which suggested that she didn't need post-secondary education in order to fulfill her social role, and middle-class ideals that encouraged higher education. Anna resolved this complexity by completing high school but marrying instead of going on to teachers' college. This complexity was negotiated not only through Anna's actions and the meaning that she attributed to the structures of class and gender, but also by her parents' actions and their understanding of white, middle-class values. Anna did not regret this resolution but rather interpreted it as a 'proper' course of events.

Anna became a full-time homemaker and mother who relied for her means of subsistence on the money her husband distributed to her (see centre of Figure 7.4). Indeed, her life progressed in a typical fashion after she completed high school. She was married in her mid-20s, which was considered 'on time' for women who were coming of age during the Depression. Anna and John had two children shortly after they married. Their daughters were born 'on time', and it was typical for people who came of age during the Depression to have only two children.

The ways in which the processes of distribution, production, and reproduction were organized in Anna's life are a direct result of the gender, age, ethnic, and class relations in which she was enmeshed. Anna and her family of procreation were no longer farmers. John occasionally worked for his older brother in the family business but earned his living mostly by buying and selling property. They had little money, but John did own the house in which his family lived. The Warners tried very hard to achieve the white, middle-class standards that were typical of the times, especially regarding education, the appropriate gendered division of labour in the family, and religious morality. The fact that Anna chose not to rely on social assistance after the death of her husband is linked to the pressures that she felt to continue to maintain these standards. Paid work may have been an option for her, but the structures of gender and age stood in her way.

Clearly, the choices Anna made during young adulthood and through the middle years of her life fall much more toward the conformation end of the conformation–resistance continuum than toward the resistance end. But these choices must also be seen in light of the habitus that Anna developed through her early experiences—a habitus that was shaped by rigid gendered expectations, middle-class ideals of work and family, and the hardships many faced during the Depression. Anna would probably not view the choices she made as choices at all but rather just as 'the way things were meant to be'. Hence, for Anna, the membranes that linked social structure and agency during this time were very thin; structural constraints were adhered to, not challenged.

Given the circumstances and habitus of Anna's life, it is difficult to make sense of her decision to go to business college. One possible explanation, however, is linked to her daughters' decisions to pursue post-secondary education (one attended business college and the other went to teachers' college). Perhaps she decided that if her daughters could further their education, she could too, especially since her daughters now needed less of her time. That the decisions and circumstances of others in our social networks influence our choices and life circumstances is an important consideration. This idea is captured by the term *linked lives* (see Elder 1995). Indeed, there are several times at which the circumstances and choices of people close to Anna affected her life and the ebb and flow of her poverty. Her husband decided to invest his wealth rather than leaving it to her, so when he died, she became poor. Her brother and sister-in-law did not have children, both died, and, at a time quite late in her life, Anna became rich.

Social Inequality

Recall from chapter 1 that *social inequality* refers to relatively long-lasting differences between individuals or groups of people, and that these differences have considerable implications for individual lives, especially 'for the rights or opportunities they exercise and the rewards or privileges they enjoy' (Grabb 2007: 1; see also Pampel 1998). Thus, social inequality has both abstract and concrete dimensions. Rights and opportunities are shaped by one's position in structured social hierarchies. As Figure 7.3 shows, the interplay between agency and structure organizes the processes of production, reproduction, and distribution, the combination of which leads to abstract outcomes of inequality. These abstract outcomes are the structural hierarchy of inequality in which categorical differences between sexes, races, ethnic groups, age groups, and classes are reinforced and, in some cases, modified. There is a reciprocal relationship between objectively defined structural positions of inequality and the organization of the processes of production, reproduction, and distribution: the two mutually constitute one another.

The second dimension of social inequality is more concrete, representing the advantages and disadvantages experienced by members of society. Hence, the ways in which the processes of production, reproduction, and distribution are organized shape, in Anna's case, transitions in and out of poverty. More broadly, the organization of production, reproduction, and distribution influences the rewards, privileges, and resources that are accrued in various social domains, such as families, labour markets, states, education, and health. These issues are discussed in Part II of this book.

‖‖‖‖‖‖‖ Questions for Critical Thought ‖‖‖‖ ‖‖‖‖‖‖‖ ‖‖‖ ‖‖‖‖‖ ‖ ‖‖‖‖‖‖ ‖‖‖‖‖‖ ‖‖‖‖ ‖

Map the life course of either your mother or your father on the conceptual framework presented in the coalescence framework in Figure 7.3, and consider their paid- and unpaid-labour circumstances.

1. What structural conditions influenced these circumstances in your mother's or father's life?
2. Did your mother or father act with agency in determining these circumstances? What are the choices she or he made that influenced paid and unpaid labour? Were these truly choices?
3. What role did your mother's or father's substantive birth cohort play in influencing her or his paid- and unpaid-labour circumstances?
4. What role has aging and the timing of lives played in your mother's or father's paid- and unpaid-labour circumstances?
5. What other factors influenced your mother's or father's paid- and unpaid-labour circumstances? Where do they fit in the framework (i.e., structure, agency, linking mechanism)?

‖‖‖‖‖‖‖ Glossary ‖‖‖‖‖ ‖ ‖‖‖‖‖ ‖‖‖‖‖‖‖ ‖‖‖ ‖‖ ‖‖‖‖‖ ‖ ‖‖‖‖ ‖‖‖‖‖‖ ‖‖‖ ‖‖ ‖‖‖‖ ‖ ‖‖‖‖ ‖‖‖‖‖‖ ‖‖‖ ‖

Conformation   The processes through which individuals comply with and accept the various schemas and resources that structure society.

Generation   The subjectively meaningful cohort into which one is born. This concept is similar to the 'lives in time and place' concept in Elder's life-course perspective but reflects

Mannheim's ideas involving the sociological relevance of being born at a particular historical time in a given society.

Lives in time and place The effects of contextual change, caused by a particular historical event, on individual life trajectories.

Resistance The processes through which individuals reject and act against established social structures.

Substantive birth cohort An umbrella term that includes the ideas captured by 'lives in time and place' while also representing the generation, gender, ethnicity, race, and class positions into which people are born through no choice of their own.

Timing of lives An umbrella concept that captures issues relating to social time, the timing of significant transitions (e.g., transition to parenthood), historical time, and the duration and sequencing of life events.

Recommended Reading

Elder, Glenn H., Jr. 1974. *Children of the Great Depression: Social Change in Life Experience.* Chicago: University of Chicago Press. A classic study of how substantive cohorts and historical time influence inequality and other life experiences.

Elder, Glenn H., Jr, and Angela M. O'Rand. 1995. 'Adult Lives in a Changing Society'. Pp. 452–75 in K. Cook, G. Fine, and J.S. House, eds, *Sociological Perspectives on Social Psychology.* New York: Allyn and Bacon. A clearly written article that lays the foundations of Elder's life-course perspective.

Laslett, Barbara, and Johanna Brenner. 1987. 'Gender and Social Reproduction: Historical Perspectives'. *Annual Review of Sociology* 15: 381–404. Perhaps the best historical account of the processes of reproduction and the social construction of gender and gender relations.

Mannheim, Karl. [1928] 1952. 'The Problem of Generations'. In Karl Mannheim, *Essays on the Sociology of Knowledge*, edited by P. Kecskemeti. London: Routledge and Kegan Paul. In this essay, Mannheim applies Marxist theories of social class to the study of 'generations'.

Tilly, Charles. 1998. *Durable Inequality.* Berkeley: University of California Press. A comprehensive account of categorical inequality. In this book, Tilly argues that some categories of inequality have more depth than others depending on how and whether various mechanisms, such as opportunity hoarding, are implemented by the dominant group.

PART II

Part II reviews the Canadian literature on social inequality in five domains of social life: families and domestic labour, paid work, health, education, and states. The conceptual framework presented in Part I is used as an organizational tool for presenting the information in Part II. Although efforts were made to find literature that considered the intersections of class, age, gender, ethnicity, and race, few if any studies have examined all of these factors simultaneously. And even fewer have explicitly considered the links between structure, agency, and social time and place. As a result, the goals of Part II are modest. It provides a partial picture of various outcomes of inequality as they play out in families, paid work, health, education, and the state in Canada.

Each chapter in Part II begins with an example or case study. Through these examples, the ideas presented in the conceptual framework are most easily observed. Next, an overview of the literature on each domain of social inequality is presented. This will enable the reader to gain an understanding of the structure of social inequality in Canada.

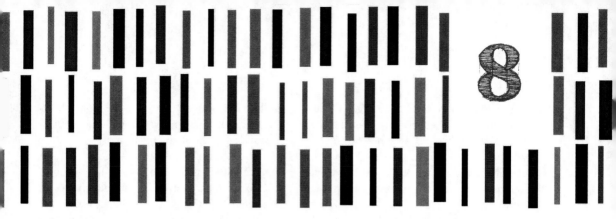

CAGE(s), Families, and Domestic Labour, and the Processes of Reproduction

Introduction

In 1998 and 1999, I worked on a project that involved collecting life-history interviews with 60 low-income mothers (see L. Davies, McMullin, and Avison 2001). Part of this research examined the extent to which mothers' family responsibilities influenced their poverty. Using life-history analyses, we found that the processes through which women became mothers influenced their experiences of poverty. Mothers faced barriers in continuing their education and in securing gainful employment (see chapter 10). One of the most significant barriers for these mothers was finding suitable and affordable child care, but there were also ideological barriers. One of the mothers in our study told us that she quit high school after she became pregnant because of the attitudes of the teachers and principal. In fact, the principal told her she could not take her physical education class because he feared that someone from the board of education would come to the school and see a 'big fat blimp running around the gym' (L. Davies, McMullin, and Avison 2001: 63).

Beginning in early childhood, beliefs about motherhood and family are instilled in us. For some of the study participants, these beliefs acted as barriers to education and employment. One mother had this to say: 'Girls were raised to

think they had to grow up and get married and I thought that was the be-all and end-all and the only way that I was ever going to be independent was to be married. It didn't even enter my mind to think well I could go to school and get a job and I don't have to be married.' And another said, 'I wasn't getting a lot of support or encouragement at home [regarding her schooling]. In fact, I was basically told by my parents that it wasn't as important for me to succeed as it was for my brothers.' These ideological beliefs about families and women's roles within them were best summarized by the comments of a third study participant:

> I had two or three [career] goals, lawyer, nurse, airline stewardess, but my parents said don't go into that, just get a job, get married, and you know you're going to get married and you're going to have a husband that looks after all that. Like you're so wrapped up in what you want but you're going to get married and you're going to have kids, so there's no sense even setting a goal like that, just do well in school and get yourself a job. . . . So that's what I did.

Such traditional belief systems 'place girls on trajectories of low income because they often emphasize the importance of marriage and family at the expense of economic self-sufficiency' (L. Davies, McMullin, and Avison 2001: 63).

Traditional family belief systems, combined with family violence or insidious poverty, made life especially difficult for some of the mothers in our study. In these cases, physical or sexual abuse, neglect, or parental alcoholism in their families of origin often led them to leave home when they were young teenagers. In one study participant's case, the mother helped her daughter leave home when she was 14 so that Mary could escape her mother's abusive partner. Unable to support Mary for very long outside of the home, Mary's mother encouraged her to become pregnant so that she could collect social assistance and mother's allowance. Mary did as her mother said, had a baby when she was 15 years old, and continues to struggle with poverty.

Among the low-income mothers in this study, 87 per cent had received social assistance at least once in their lives, but 60 per cent of these women were not receiving social assistance at the time of the interviews. This allowed us to assess the pathways through which women move from social assistance to economic self-sufficiency. For the mothers in this study, the most common pathway off welfare was a marriage or common-law relationship with an employed man (L. Davies, McMullin, and Avison 2001: 72).

The preceding discussion points to the importance of the intersections between the processes of production, distribution, and reproduction in systems of inequality that were discussed in Part I of this book. It shows that women provide for families and children and that the ideologies that shape this care (reproduction) limit their opportunities for education and paid work (production). As a result, distributive processes vary accordingly, with women often relying on spouses or the state for their means of subsistence (see the coalescence framework, Figure 7.3, page 128). Furthermore, the findings from the poverty study discussed above suggest that

families are one of the principal domains in which the processes of reproduction, distribution, and production are organized.

Over the last several decades there has been considerable debate among academics and policy makers regarding the status of families in Canada and the United States. Some commentators argue that contemporary families are in a state of crisis. The American sociologist David Popenoe (1993, 2005) argues that the family is in a state of decline. According to Popenoe, families do not provide functions such as procreation, socialization, caring, economic support, and sexual regulation as effectively as they once did. He argues that families have lost their social power and control over their members, in part because they are smaller and less stable, and do not last as long as they used to. In a move toward individualism, American families are less willing to invest time, money, and energy in family life.

For Popenoe, who uses statistics about American families from the 1960s until the 1990s to support his claims, the most significant trends since the 1960s have been the following: (1) considerable fertility decline; (2) 'marital role erosion', with more women working for pay and fewer taking full responsibility for the care of their children; (3) increases in divorce rates, stepfamilies, and lone-parent families; and (4) increases in singlehood and non-family living. As a result of these trends, Popenoe concludes that families are in a state of decline. Family members are less bound to one another because women are more economically self-sufficient than they used to be. Families are less willing and able to carry out their traditional functions (see above), and they have transferred their power to other institutions such as schools and states. According to Popenoe, families are also in a state of decline because family values are eroding. Family identification, loyalty, mutual assistance, and concern for the perpetuation of family have given way to values of self-fulfilment and egalitarianism. The consequences of such decline are alarming to Popenoe because the family is the most fundamental unit of society and 'breaking up the nucleus of anything is a serious matter' (Popenoe 1993: 539). He considers the most serious consequence of family decline to be that fewer children are living in nuclear families, and he believes that children cannot become successful adults without proper socialization within families (Popenoe 2005).

The American trends that Popenoe uses in support of his argument are indisputable and are similar to trends in Canada (see K. Johnson, Lero, and Rooney 2001: 17–19). In 1961, the **fertility rate** in Canada was 3.85; by 2005, it had fallen to 1.54. More Canadian women and mothers are working for pay now than ever

before (see chapter 9). Canadian divorce rates are higher now than they were 30 years ago, and there are fewer nuclear families than in the past. Higher proportions of Canadians are remaining single or living in non-traditional families, such as same-sex unions (Gee 2000a), and more men are heading single-parent families (see Box 8.1). Common-law unions continue to rise, and although they are typically associated with a younger demographic, common-law relationships among those aged 60 to 64 increased by 77 per cent between 2001 and 2006 (Agrell 2007). However, Popenoe's interpretation of these trends may be criticized on at least two counts. First, because he uses a very conservative and limited conceptualization of 'family', he underestimates how central families remain for many people in

---

Box 8.1 The Canadian Family Is Slowly Being Reshaped; More Men Heading Up Single-Parent Households; Same-Sex and Common-Law Unions on Rise: Census

By Francine Kopun

Sean Slaven cannot imagine his life without the routine of picking up his 11-year-old son Brendan after school, monitoring his homework, making his favourite meal of Indian butter chicken, and then playing ball or watching the season finale of *Canadian Idol* together.

Slaven, 42, is the male head of a single-parent family—one of a growing number of men in Canada who care for their children half or more than half of the time. He shares custody of his son with his former wife, and Brendan is with him as much as 65 per cent of the time. Slaven wouldn't want it any other way.

'If you're an access parent you're a visitor in that child's life. You're always trying to do things that are fun, fun, fun—you don't get involved with their school, you don't get involved with their lives.

They're strangers to you,' says Slaven, a self-employed sales professional in Burlington.

According to 2006 census data released yesterday, lone-parent families headed by men increased 14.6 per cent during the five years prior to 2006; lone-parent families headed by women increased 6.3 per cent.

In fact, the Canadian family is slowly being reshaped: Marriage continues to lose ground to common-law relationships, same-sex unions are on the rise and families without children have become more common than families with children as the population ages and fertility rates decline.

'Family has always been a dynamic institution,' said Alan Mirabelli, executive associate of the Vanier Institute for the Family. 'If you ask people what their ideal of family is, they'll simply describe the family they grew up in, but family goes back 3,000 years. It transforms itself.'

The 2006 census enumerated nearly 9 million families in Canada. Married couples constituted the largest group at 68.6 per cent, but their proportion has been steadily decreasing for 20 years. The proportion of common-law families, meanwhile, has been growing in leaps and bounds. In 1986, they accounted for 7.2 per cent of all census families. Now they account for 15.5 per cent.

Of the 33 census management areas in Canada (population of at least 100,000) Toronto has the second-highest percentage of married couple families at 75.3 per cent. (Abbotsford, B.C., has the highest at 76.2 per cent.) Toronto has the lowest percentage of common-law families at 7.8 per cent.

'It may be that immigrant families are more likely to be married than to live common-law, and certainly the high immigrant population in Toronto may be a contributing factor,' said Pamela White, director of the demography division at Statistics Canada.

Christine van Cauwenberghe, a financial planning expert with Investors Group, says many people in common-law relationships often don't realize the implications of their union. They may find that in some ways they are as legally bound to each other as married couples, but there are important exceptions: in Ontario, for example, married and common-law couples are treated differently when it comes to the division of family property and inheritances.

Nationally, the number of same-sex couples grew 32.6 per cent between 2001 and 2006, to 45,300 couples. Of these about 7,500 or 16.5 per cent, were married. A little more than half of the couples were men (53.7 per cent).

The trend to lone-parent families may have stabilized, according to the data. The proportion of lone-parent families in 2006 was 15.9 per cent, up just .2 per cent from 2001.

Although the majority of lone-parent families in 2006 were headed by women (80.1 per cent), the number of lone-father families rose dramatically over the five years preceding the census.

One explanation is that fewer mothers are granted sole custody following a divorce. In 1980, mothers got custody 78.2 per cent of the time. By 2003, the figure had dropped to 47.7 per cent, with joint custody awarded in 43.8 per cent of cases, according to the census report.

'There is certainly much more shared custody, especially when you're talking about couples in the 35–45 age range, because more women in that age range have careers that are very demanding,' said Nicola Savin, a Toronto family law lawyer with 20 years of experience.

'I'm delighted to see this, absolutely delighted, because I was one of those dads,' said Danny Guspie, executive director of Fathers' Resources International. 'It tells me that finally society is starting to catch up with itself. As our judiciary begins to age, younger people are coming in with more well-suited family ideas, rather than gender-based family ideas.'

In a way the increase in single-parent households led by men is not surprising, says the Vanier Institute's Mirabelli. With more dual-income families, the decision about who gets custody is shaped to a certain extent by the job demands of both parents. He said it could also be that older children are choosing dad as opposed to mom and dads are now willing to honour that choice.

Michael Kaufman, 56, a former single dad who shared custody of his son between the ages of 9 and 16 with his former spouse, says he believes the arrangement allowed him to share more quality time with his son.

'I think quality comes out of quantity,' said Kaufman, an educator and independent consultant on gender issues. 'Those moments happen when you're shopping together or washing the dishes or making a meal or working in the garden or building something. If you're spending time together, if you're doing things together, those conversations will happen, those wonderful moments will happen.'

Source: Kopun (2007).

contemporary American and Canadian societies. Second, he ignores the fact that 'the family' is a primary site of oppression of and violence against women, children, and the elderly.

Defining Families

Popenoe defines *family* as 'a group in which people typically live together in a household and function as a cooperative unit, particularly though the sharing of economic resources in the pursuit of domestic activities' (2005: 20). On the surface there is nothing particularly troubling about that definition. Yet, because he argues that there are fewer families today than in the past and is critical of lone-parent families, his ideal 'group of people' is narrowly defined. Although it is true that the number of **nuclear families** has declined over the years, the majority of Canadians live together with 'a group of people'. According to the 2006 census, 89 per cent of Canadians lived in a household with two or more people. However, only 72 per cent of these are considered 'families' according to the census definition. The Canadian census definition of *family* is

> a married couple and the children, if any, of either or both spouses; a couple living common law and the children, if any, of either or both partners; or, a lone parent of any marital status with at least one child living in the same dwelling and that child or those children. All members of a particular census family live in the same dwelling. A couple may be of opposite or same sex. Children may be children by birth, marriage or adoption regardless of their age or marital status as long as they live in the dwelling and do not have their own spouse or child living in the dwelling.
>
> Grandchildren living with their grandparents but with no parents present also constitute a census family. (www.statcan.ca/english/concepts/definitions/cen-family.htm 2/15/2008)

Hence, siblings who live together, parents who live with their divorced child and his or her children, and same-sex partners who live together are not families according to the census definition. Indeed, the term *family* is typically a middle-class construct that reproduces white privilege and ideology and neglects racialized families (Dua 1999), older families (Connidis 2009), and working-class families (Gardiner-Barber 2003). Historically, white, middle-class men and women took an especially active role in promoting such ideologies. So too did the Canadian state, which has continued to reproduce white, middle-class views of family through discriminatory immigration and family-welfare policies (see Das Gupta 1995; Mandell and Duffy 2005; chapter 12). Here we see the importance of ideology, as it was discussed in Part I, for understanding social inequality.

Useful and inclusive definitions of families have been elusive in the family-sociology literature. Table 8.1 shows how the definitions of family have evolved. The restrictions in Murdock's definition are obvious, but they resemble the definitions of family proposed by some vocal conservative organizations in Canada, such as Focus on the Family. Margrit Eichler's discussion of family, which is in reaction to Murdock's and other conservative definitions, concentrates on who constitutes families. Unlike the other definitions, that of the Vanier Institute of the Family concentrates more on what families do (points 1–6) than on who comprises them (e.g., two or more people who are 'bound together by ties of mutual consent, birth and/or adoption or placement'). Finally, Fox and Luxton focus exclusively on what families do, equating family with the relations of social reproduction as they are defined in this book (see chapter 3). Hence, a family comprises anyone who is involved in the

Table 8.1 Definitions of Family

George Murdock. 1949. *Social Structure*. New York: MacMillan, p. 1.

'. . . a social group characterized by a common residence, economic cooperation and reproduction [including adults of both sexes, at least two of whom maintain a socially approved sexual relationship] and one or more children, own or adopted, of the sexually cohabiting adults.'

Margrit Eichler. 1988. *Families in Canada Today*. Toronto: Gage, p. 4.

'. . . a family is a social group which may or may not include adults of both sexes (i.e., lone-parent families), may or may not include one or more children (i.e., childless couples), who may or may not have been born in wedlock (i.e., adopted children or children by one adult partner of a previous union). The relationship of the adults may or may not have its origin in marriage (i.e., common-law couples), they may or may not share a common residence (i.e., commuting couples). The adults may or may not cohabit sexually, and the relationship may or may not involve such socially patterned feelings as love, attraction, piety and awe.'

Vanier Institute. 2008. www.vifamily.ca/about/definition.html.

'. . . any combination of two or more persons who are bound together over time by ties of mutual consent, birth and/or adoption or placement and who, together, assume responsibilities for variant combinations of some of the following:

- Physical maintenance and care of group members
- Addition of new members through procreation or adoption
- Socialization of children
- Social control of members
- Production, consumption, distribution of goods and services, and
- Affective nurturance—love'

Statistics Canada. 2008. 'Concept: Census Family'. http://www.statcan.gc.ca/concepts/definitions/cfamily-rfamille-eng.htm.

'. . . a married couple and the children, if any, of either or both spouses; a couple living common law and the children, if any, of either or both partners; or, a lone parent of any marital status with at least one child living in the same dwelling and that child or those children. All members of a particular census family live in the same dwelling. A couple may be of opposite or same sex. Children may be children by birth, marriage or adoption regardless of their age or marital status as long as they live in the dwelling and do not have their own spouse or child living in the dwelling.

'Grandchildren living with their grandparents but with no parents present also constitute a census family.'

Bonnie Fox and Meg Luxton. 2001. 'Conceptualizing Family', p. 26.

The study of family involves 'the maintenance of life on a daily and generational basis'. Families are 'the social relationships that people create to care for children and other dependants daily and to ensure that the needs of the adults responsible for these dependants also are met'.

processes of reproduction, which are contained in the centre of the coalescence framework that was presented in chapter 7. The obvious advantage to this definition is that it includes those who have traditionally been excluded in definitions of family. Fox and Luxton (2001) argue that in all social systems there is a relationship between the processes of production and

reproduction. Before industrialization, both productive and reproductive work were organized in the household. These processes were separated by the development of industrial capitalism as more and more men were required to work for a wage so that their families could make ends meet. Processes of reproduction were privatized in a way that they had not been in the past, and the division of labour between men and women became increasingly stringent (Fox and Luxton 2001). Also during this time, ideologies evolved that reinforced the relegation of women to domestic duties and of men's responsibilities for paid labour (Cott 2001; Margolis 2001; May 1993). As the findings from the poverty study discussed above show, these ideologies still exist. The next section of this chapter considers how reproductive processes of care and housework are organized in Canada in ways that create and recreate systems of advantage and disadvantage for various groups of people.

Domestic Labour

There are three main elements of domestic labour, which in turn are all part of the reproductive processes discussed in Part I of this book. These are (1) maintaining the household; (2) caring for adults and children; and (3) the processes involved in consumption or making ends meet (Luxton and Corman 2001). Cleaning, cooking, gardening, shovelling snow, and mowing lawns are examples of the activities required to maintain a household (Luxton 1980). Caring includes both 'caring about' and 'caring for' others. Hence, *caring* refers to 'feelings of affection and responsibility combined with actions that provide responsively for an individual's personal needs or well-being' (Cancian and Oliker 2000: 2). Economic support for caring comes through the processes of distribution (see the coalescence framework, Figure 7.3) in the form of wages, social assistance, retirement pensions, or some combination of these distributive mechanisms. Individuals and families use the money gained through these distributive mechanisms to purchase clothes, food, shelter, and other necessities of life. Low-income families, which usually do not have enough money to buy these things, often use creative and strategic methods to make ends meet.

In Canada, domestic labour is usually organized in families and households, and most research on domestic labour has used the household as the unit of analysis (but see Worts 2005 for an excellent study on the transcendence of domestic labour across households in a co-operative housing community). Yet for the 11 per cent of Canadians who live alone (and probably for many others), the processes of domestic labour transcend household boundaries. This is particularly true for people aged 65 and over, who are more likely to live alone as a result of widowhood, and for younger people, who are more likely to be childless and unmarried. Members of other households or paid workers often help older people with household maintenance, while the labour of caring for and about them is often (but not always) undertaken by close relatives (Connidis and McMullin 1994). Although research tends not to consider how domestic labour is organized among younger, unmarried, and childless Canadians, we can speculate that they either purchase these services or do it on their own. Their care is likely provided by close family ties, with friends also being instrumental in providing support. However, because most of the research on domestic labour has used the household as the unit of analysis, this chapter must do the same.

Gender is an important structural determinant of who does what for whom in families, regardless of age (Connidis 2009). As Figure 8.1 shows, women aged 25 to 54 spend an average of almost two more hours per day doing unpaid work than do same-aged men (see also Beaujot and Andersen 2007). The average amount of time per day men spend engaged in unpaid labour increased between 1986 and 2005 by half an hour, whereas the amount of time women spent engaged in unpaid work declined by half an hour (see Figure 8.1). Women tend to take primary responsibility for meal preparation, washing dishes, and cleaning, men for household maintenance (Beaujot 2000). Of course, making meals, cleaning dishes, and general housecleaning are done every day, whereas

Figure 8.1: Time Spent on Paid and Unpaid Work, Men and Women, 1986 and 2005

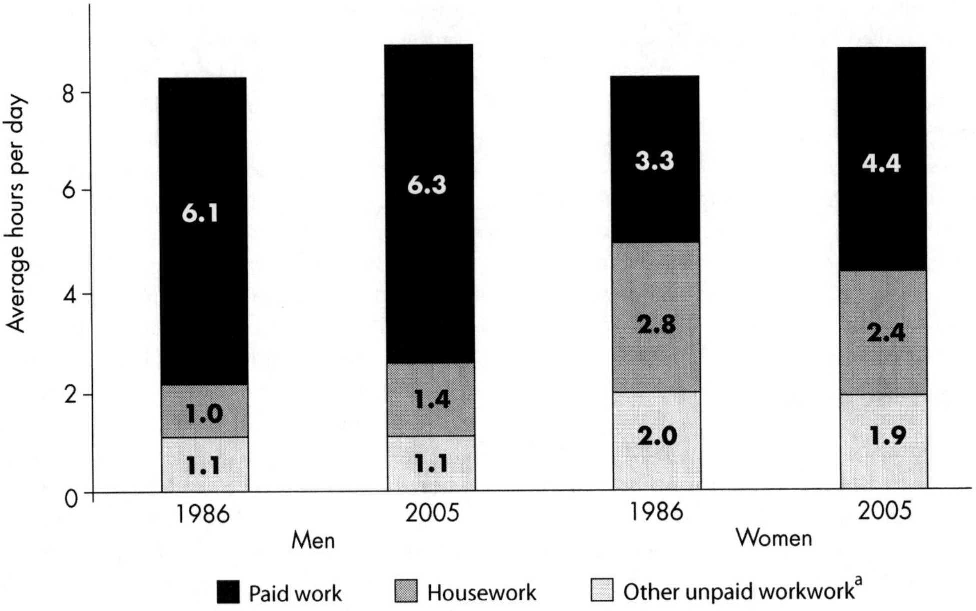

a Primary child care and shopping for goods and services.
Source: K. Marshall (2006).

household maintenance is done much more sporadically. Hence, it is no surprise that compared to men, women spend more time doing housework (Gazso-Windle and McMullin 2003; K. Marshall 1993a, 1993b). This overall pattern in the gendered division of labour in the home intensifies when couples have children, and it remains more or less the same as couples age (McDaniel 2005). But when husbands and wives retire, husbands increase the number of masculine tasks that they perform (Askam 1995).

The amount of household work men and women do seems to vary according to employment and parental status (K. Marshall 2006). For instance, the amount of housework husbands and wives do increases with the number of hours their partners spend engaged in paid labour (Gazso-Windle and McMullin 2003) and

when children live in the home (K. Marshall 2006). The more hours women work for pay, the fewer hours they spend doing household labour (Luxton and Corman 2001). Among younger and middle-aged men, married fathers do twice as much unpaid work (includes child care and volunteer work) as unmarried, childless men and one and a half times as much unpaid work as married, childless men. Similarly, married mothers do twice as much unpaid work as childless women regardless of marital status. Women who are employed full-time do less unpaid labour than do those who are either not employed or work part-time, regardless of how many children they have living at home. Furthermore, compared with all families, higher proportions of men in two-earner families do half or more of the main household tasks (e.g., cooking and cleaning) and take primary responsibility for them (Beaujot 2000).

Caring within families transcends household boundaries more than housework does. Many of us care about our mothers, fathers, grandchildren, brothers, sisters, aunts, uncles, and so on, even if we do not live with them. Grandparents often care for their grandchildren when parents need help with child care. Similarly, aunts and uncles sometimes care for their siblings' children. Children sometimes care for their older parents, especially if they are ill and unable to care for themselves. Husbands and wives often care for one another and, with increasing age and illness, are often required to provide much more physical care for one another.

The obligations that family members have to care for and about one another are structured by class, age, gender, ethnicity, and race. This is the idea conveyed in the central part of the coalescence framework (Figure 7.3). These obligations are contained within the processes of reproduction and are framed (or structured) by class, age, gender, ethnic, and race relations. The extent and nature of family care one provides will vary depending on how one is situated within these social structures (Finch 1989). Among the many caring relationships within families, the most widely studied is the relationship between younger parents, especially mothers, and their young children. One of the most consistent findings in the family-sociology literature is that women are primarily responsible for child care and that, compared to men, they spend more time providing care (Rapoport and Lebourdais 2006). This is still the case even though many more women are working in the paid labour force now than in the past (see chapter 9). However, the nature of how and by whom children are cared for has evolved over the past few generations. Compared to past generations of children, more pre-school-aged children are being cared for by babysitters and licensed care facilities. This is, in large part, because labour-force participation by women has increased substantially. As a result, mothers and fathers make child-care arrangements with one another, with child-care providers, with their employers, and with other family members more than in past generations.

Although fathers have increased the number of hours that they spend with children over recent decades, this has not led to an overall decline in the amount of time mothers spend with their children. In two-parent families, this is probably because, compared with mothers, when fathers spend time with their children it is more often in the context of family activities in which their wives or partners are also involved (Rapoport and LeBourdais 2006)

Parenting and the care involved do not end when children leave home, but the nature of the care relationship changes significantly. Yet, with a few notable exceptions (see Connidis 2009; Eichler and Albanese 2007), family studies rarely consider either how processes of caring evolve throughout the life course or the experiences of caring and parenting in mid-life. Unlike the mainstream family literature, the gerontology literature has paid some attention to issues of lifelong parenting. Early research on mid-life families, for instance, identified a stage in life after children left home that was named the **empty nest**. It was thought that because women in their middle years disengage from their active parenting role, these women would experience the 'empty nest syndrome' and have various social and psychological problems as a result. Later research, however, found that in fact many women enjoyed their lives after their children had left (Black and Hill 1984). More recently the term **cluttered nest** has surfaced to refer to families whose children, after having left home and living elsewhere for a period, return to live with their parents (Mitchell 2000; Mitchell and Gee 1996). Research has shown that parents provide more support to these children, both financially and with respect to domestic services, than they receive from the children (Mitchell 2000).

When we consider the links between pro-cesses of production and reproduction, it is im-portant to note that most working-age mothers work for pay and most mothers in the labour force work full-time (K. Johnson, Lero, and Rooney 2001). Yet the labour-force participation rate among working-age mothers is still much lower than it is for working-age fathers. Barring unemployment or disability, almost all working-age fathers work for pay and almost all fathers in the labour force work full-time. Indeed, com-pared to fathers, mothers are more likely to have discontinuous paid-work histories and to have more tenuous attachments to the labour market, largely because of their family responsibilities. A substantial number of younger mothers forgo a wage to stay at home and raise their children, making them economically dependent on either their partners or the state. Women who work for pay take primary responsibility for the care of their children by making arrangements for child care and taking time off from work when the chil-dren are ill or when child care is unavailable (see K. Johnson, Lero, and Rooney 2001). This, how-ever, places women at a labour-market disadvan-tage because very few workplaces offer child care or dependant care for their employees (Ranson 2005, and see Box 8.2). Because domestic labour is undervalued in Canada, such patterns of paid and unpaid labour result in long-term financial

Box 8.2 Balancing Work and Family: Firms Still Struggling with How to Help Workers Who Care for Others

By Elizabeth Church

A new study by the Conference Board of Canada has some good news and some not-so-good news if you're struggling to keep your head above wa-ter when it comes to balancing work and family.

As you race to pick up the kids or hurry home to make dinner for an aging relative, you'll be happy to learn that compared with 10 years ago, more companies understand how your situation may be increasing your stress level and hurting your morale.

Better still, the board says, the majority of em-ployers feel they have a role to play in helping you achieve some kind of balance on the home and work front.

But if you are expecting help from your employ-er with child care or support for an elderly relative, chances are you are going to be disappointed.

'Organizations do realize they have a role to play. I just think a lot of them are still struggling with what that role is and how to make it work within the organization,' says Kimberley Bach-mann, author of the study *Work-Life Balance, Are Employers Listening?*

While the report finds generally the answer is yes, it says that in some areas such as child care and dependent care benefits, most organizations have a long way to go.

The finding is based on a survey of 220 pub-lic- and private-sector organizations, in which they were asked about the benefits offered to non-union staff. The research, conducted in 1999, replicates in many areas work that was done a decade earli-er by the board, providing a look at how attitudes and practices have changed during that time.

The report finds a broad and growing accep-tance among employers for programs such as flexible scheduling (88 per cent offer it, compared with 49 per cent in 1989), job sharing (52 per cent, up from 19 per cent) and telecommuting (50 per cent, up from 11 per cent).

More employers also offer workers a compressed workweek option (48 per cent, up from 28 per cent) and some form of part-time work arrangement with a variety of benefit options.

But when it comes to child care and dependant care benefits, companies offering programs are still in the minority. According to the study, only 15 per cent of organizations have a day care on site or near their offices. That's up from 5 per cent a decade ago. Four per cent have before-school or after-school programs, up from 1 per cent.

Ten per cent of companies offer employees emergency care for elderly relatives or elder care case management services.

About half the organizations that do not offer any of these benefits say they have never even considered it, about the same number as in 1989.

The largest increase is in referral services for obtaining help. About one-third of companies offer these for elder care, child care, and care of relatives with disabilities. That's up from 10 per cent or less in these categories a decade ago. Ms Bachmann explains that such services have become part of many organization's employee assistance programs. But she adds that with the country's aging population, she expects to see growth in this area.

'A lot of these programs haven't taken off as much as we would have liked to see, especially in the area of elder care,' she says. 'That's an area that employers are going to have to move on quickly.'

As well, while most companies are now on the record as offering programs such as flexible scheduling, the study finds that the use of many alternative work arrangements are often left to the discretion of management.

Front-line managers, Ms Bachmann says, may be faced with a balancing act of their own. With pressure from superiors to improve performance and produce results, they may be reluctant to accommodate employees who want to cut back hours or work in a way that does not fit the status quo.

'They are getting squeezed from both sides,' she says.

The study found only one-third of companies offered education to managers on work-life balance issues; 27 per cent encourage them to share experiences in this area; and less than one-quarter recognize and reward supportive managers.

'That's key because [middle managers] are the ones who have to implement policy,' Ms Bachmann says. 'A lot of work has to be done in terms of how the organization is run and how management works out people issues.'

disadvantages for women in relation to men—lower pay, fewer promotional opportunities, and smaller pensions (see chapter 9).

Because gender so deeply structures our taken-for-granted assumptions (see the discussion of Sewell's work in chapter 6) about who does what in families and homes, there is little opportunity for individual men to take on the role of full-time domestic worker and men are often unable to experience the sometimes fulfilling and gratifying aspects of caring for children. For instance, the proportion of stay-at-home dads among two-parent families is very low (K. Johnson, Lero, and Rooney 2001: 19) and men are even less likely than women to get support from employers when they request alternative work arrangements. Although men are now more likely to take a paid or unpaid leave from employment following the birth of a child than was true in the past (55 per cent in 2006, compared with 38 per cent in 2001), they are still much less likely than women (55 per cent versus 90 per cent) to take such a leave (Statistics Canada 2007e).

Questions regarding what it means to be a mother or a father in a time when fathers are taking more responsibility for parenting have gained considerable research attention of late (Doucet 2006; Fox 2009; Ranson, forthcoming). The discussion in Box 8.3 suggests that men may also have a different parenting style than women. Andrea Doucet, for instance, discusses in her book *Do Men Mother?* the experiences of 118 fathers who are the primary caregivers of their children: some stay-at-home dads and others single fathers.

Mothering, according to Doucet, comprises emotional, community, and moral responsibility. In the emotional realm, the fathers in Doucet's study care for and nurture their children in ways that are quite similar to what we would expect of mothers, although there is sometimes a greater emphasis on playfulness and practicality (see Box 8.3). These fathers developed community ties and networks that facilitated their parenting and provided avenues for their children's extra-curricular activities, but here too the emphasis

Box 8.3 Raise Kids Like a Man: A Stay-at-Home Dad Rewrites the Rules of Fatherhood

By Brian Fortner

On his first day of kindergarten, my son woke at 5 a.m. He got dressed in 10 minutes, skipped breakfast, shouldered his backpack, and was out the door before sunup. I called him back inside, and for 3 hours tried to contain his excitement. 'It's not time yet,' I told him at least a dozen times, as he paced and fidgeted.

Shortly after 8 a.m., we walked outside again. Soon a pair of blinking yellow lights crested the hill up the road, and the bus came to a halt a few feet from my son's nose. When the door folded open, an older man in black driving gloves smiled. 'Good morning,' he said heartily. My son looked at him, looked at me, and turned and ran.

I don't watch Jon Stewart anymore, because I live with the two funniest people I know: my 5-year-old son and 3-year-old daughter. Sadly, my wife misses most of it. She works. I stay home with the kids.

I never thought I'd be a stay-at-home dad. My plan was similar to yours, I'll bet: Have as much fun as possible as I worked my way up the corporate ladder, then commit to a great woman when the time was right. We'd have kids, and she'd stay home to raise them. Not because I believed that's

women's work—I'm no caveman. I just figured she'd want to. But when my wife got pregnant, I did the manly thing by volunteering to do the womanly thing. It just made sense. She loved her job; I hated mine. And she earned a lot more than I did.

Childbearing may be excruciating, but it's a sprint. Child rearing is more like a marathon—a slow, dull pain that can sap your energy and accelerate your aging. I knew I'd have to pace myself. So I made it my goal to find ways to suppress the pain. That led to the following rules. Institute them at your house, whether or not you stay home with the kids, and you'll ease your stride for the long haul.

Rule #1
There's no crying. At all. Period.

Okay, there's some crying. But very little, in spells of 20 seconds or less.

Babies cry because they need something, typically food or warmth. Just give it to them. Toddlers cry because they are confused, sad, bored, or simply fond of hearing themselves cry. Interestingly enough, sometimes they're all these things at once. Shove a lollipop in their mouths. Four- and 5-year-olds cry because they are hurt. A cartoon Band-Aid should fix that, even if there's no blood.

No matter the age, you can stop most crying by redirecting the kid's attention. It's like calling a fake punt on fourth and long in your own end: totally unexpected. A few months ago, my daughter was chasing the cat with the extension tube from the vacuum cleaner. She took a turn too wide and ran face-first into a wall. She started welling and whimpering, so what did I do? I asked her to vacuum the hallway. Worked like a charm.

Rule #2
Tackle the daily chores as a team.

Kids love to do laundry. Who knew? Not Dr Spock.

When my kids were small, the wash was fairly easy work. Baby clothes are all the same. And even if you ruin them, they cost only a few bucks to replace. But as the kids got older, the stacks of clothes became unmanageable. One day, I assume because I wasn't paying enough attention to him, my son asked if he could help. Jackpot!

Now he loads the washer and dryer for me and folds all his own clothes. He takes particular care with his underwear, to ensure that, once folded, Batman is staring right back at him.

Important note: Kids bore pretty easily. Change it up by folding only the blue shirts first, or all the playclothes. Or my favorite: See how many pairs of socks can be stacked on the cat before it moves.

Rule #3
Don't race to their rescue.

One day not long ago, right after breakfast, I asked my daughter to go to her room and get dressed. She didn't emerge for an hour. I could hear her struggling with her panties, confounded by the fact that they were inside out.

But I didn't go to her room to see what was up, as most parents would. I spent that hour reading the newspaper, paying bills online, watching *Squawk Box*, and performing superglue surgery on several broken toys. She finally emerged,

naked from the waist down, handed me her panties, and said, 'These ain't right.'

Rule #4
Shop for the family but not your wife.

My wife's shopping list reads like a self-help manifesto. Last time she asked me to 'just pick up' something, she scribbled '2 pairs L'eggs Sheer Energy, size B, nude, reinforced toe'. I suspected, correctly, that these were panty hose, but just try locating this specific pair at Target or Wal-Mart. It can't be done by anyone with a Y chromosome.

The panty-hose rack is an aisle long. There are dozens of colors and three different sizes: A, B, and Q. What logic. And the difference between Sheer Energy and regular energy is a question for a physics professor. My wife wanted nude, presumably so her legs would look bare. But why not suntan? She's always spraying on that fake tanning stuff. Plus, I have suntan right here in my hand. No dice. Back to the store for nude.

Over the years, I've had a version of this experience with tampons, maxi pads, panty liners, mascara, eyeliner, foundation, moisturizer, toenail polish, styling gel, and bras. So I don't shop for her anymore. A man has to draw the line somewhere, although, if I'm being honest, I will make an exception for bras. Besides, shopping for her violates one of my most important rules . . .

Rule #5
Don't spend more than 15 minutes in any store.

Like most kids, mine thought of the grocery store as a giant toy store for the palate. We'd spend half an hour looking at every cereal box with a Disney character on the front. I couldn't take it, which is why I invented this rule.

Here's how it works: Before we leave for the supermarket, I make a shopping list. I ask my kids to do the same. They write slowly, so their lists are short. If it's not written down, we're not buying it. That's the deal. The kids usually forget their lists, so this exercise doesn't add a whole lot of time or cost.

At the store, I load both kids into the front of a race-car cart. I do enjoy flying up and down the aisles while my kids yell, 'Faster, Daddy, faster!' I doubt many moms have experienced how those carts handle at speed.

My kids love speed shopping. Our record is $71 worth of groceries in 11 minutes. But I know I can beat that—we had to backtrack for peanut butter.

Rule #6
Be buddies with your kids.

A lot of so-called parenting experts with newspaper columns will tell you this is a bad idea. Well, let me tell you: Listening to anyone with a newspaper column about parenting is a bad idea. As long as you know when to be the adult, it's okay to be a kid yourself sometimes.

Truth is, I conceived of this rule out of necessity. When I agreed to become the primary caregiver of my children, I imagined women flocking to me at the playground. 'You stay at home? Really? How . . . intriguing,' a hot blonde mom might say as our kids took turns on the big red slide. I'd fend off the hot mamas' advances and eventually meet their husbands. Then we'd all hang out on weekends. This hasn't happened. The women mostly say hello, then ignore me.

So, essentially, I've given up all the male bonding in my life. But I still go to the barbershop, watch football, and drink beer on weekends. It's just that my kids are my company. My son knows all the NFL teams with animal names. He likes to tease my wife by telling her the Chicago Bluebirds are playing the Miami Wildcats. She doesn't have a clue.

My son and I play basketball regularly, and we have backyard water battles with the neighbor kids. I take my daughter fishing; she loves watching the worms squirm. Sometimes we dig holes in the yard just for the heck of it.

I really don't miss hanging with the guys at the office anymore. How could I? I have an inflatable soccer stadium in my backyard.

Rule #7
Don't become Mr Mom.

Men can still be men in a woman's profession. I am my kids' father. I am nothing like their mother. When my son was an infant, I learned to change his diaper in less than 10 seconds. My wife, on the other hand, turned every diaper change into an event—a chance to bond with him. Let me tell you: This eventually pisses a baby off.

Had my wife decided to stay home, my daughter most certainly wouldn't have learned to appreciate a good deal on a miter saw or know that the best time to get an oil change is midday during the week, after a nap. Or that cars even need oil. My son would have been strapped into his stroller at the park, not sitting on my shoulders atop a mountain we climbed together.

As for me, I wouldn't have gotten preferential treatment at the quick lube, jiffy mart, dry cleaner, outdoor-sporting-goods retailer, or home-improvement store had my kids not been with me, causing a commotion. I would have been stuck in a cubicle, maybe just like you, YouTube-ing *Daily Show* clips.

Women have a few-thousand-year lead on us in the child-care game. But we men don't have to follow in their footsteps. We can develop our own strategies and apply our unique problem-solving skills to the situations kids throw at us.

Which brings me back to my son's first day of kindergarten. After he took off running, my wife would have chased him down, wiped his tears, and mothered him onto the bus. I did nothing. The moms at the bus stop stared at me, horrified.

But it was the right thing to do. After he ran about 20 feet, my son stopped and looked back. He saw the neighbor kids filing on. He slowly made his way back and, without a word, climbed aboard. I was so proud. I took my daughter's hand, and we went out for breakfast.

In 2 years, when my daughter boards that bus, I will relinquish my stay-at-home-dad badge. I will just be a dad. That will be a sad, sad day.

Source: Fortner (2007).

was on sport and activity. And in the realm of moral responsibility, or the ideology around the 'shoulds and oughts of parenting' (Doucet 2006: 209), there are so many structural and ideological expectations about what fathers and mothers are supposed to do that it is extremely difficult for men to mother. Fathers are meant to be earners, mothers are meant to be carers, and because these views are so deeply structured in society, fathers who care are viewed suspiciously and with concern (Doucet 2006).

Notably, the fact that many men are not afforded the opportunity to look after their children should not be interpreted as structural inequality. Recall from Part I that *social inequality* refers to unequal access to resources and privileges in society. Domestic labour is not yet considered a valuable resource or privilege in the same way that paid work is. Hence, the restrictions the gender structure places on men's involvement in housework and child care do not create disadvantage for men in the same way that restricted access to paid work does for women.

Research on caregiving has also considered the difficulties facing adult children, usually daughters, in caring for elderly parents (Aronson 1992). Much of this research emphasizes the stress of combining paid work with care of or support for older parents. Early work in this regard noted that this stress was particularly acute for women because they formed a **sandwich generation** that had to combine work, caring for older parents, and childcare. Although subsequent research showed that the proportion of women who are 'sandwiched' is actually quite small (Martin-Matthews 2000; Rosenthal, Matthews, and Marshall 1989), the proportion of employees who care for older family members and have children living at home rose from 9.5 per cent in the late 1980s to about 15 per cent in the late 1990s (MacBride-King and Bachmann 1999). As is the case with parents' child care, research shows that children who provide support and care to older parents often make alternative

work arrangements to facilitate their supportive role. And, compared to sons, daughters are more likely to make such arrangements (see Connidis 2009 for an overview).

Along with gender, indicators of social class also influence housework and family care. Although women do more housework and provide more care than do men regardless of social class, if we use income as a proxy of class, we note that income influences the amount of housework, meal preparation, and child care that Canadians do. On average, high-income Canadians (those with a household income of more than $80,000 a year) do 20 minutes less housework, 12 minutes less meal preparation, and 12 minutes less child care per day than low-income Canadians (household income of less than $30,000 a year) (C. Williams 2002). Working-class women often turn to their mothers for help with babysitting and housework (McMullin 2002). Although frequently viewed within the context of the love grandmothers feel for both children and grandchildren, we should not lose sight of the labour that is involved. This 'labour of love' is grounded in a strong gendered ideology that limits the responsibility fathers and grandfathers have in care of children and grandchildren (Fox 2001). Alternatively, middle- and upper-class women often pay other women for child care and housework. This process reproduces white and middle-class privilege because middle-class white women usually hire working-class, racialized, and immigrant women to do this work (Arat-Koc 2001; Glenn 1992).

Both class and gender structure the division of housework and child care among black Canadian families. Black women tend to be responsible for most of the housework, and among the working class, they take responsibility for making ends meet (Calliste 2001). In addition, compared to white women, black women do disproportionately more housework and child care. This is because black families are more likely than white families to be working-class and because there are three times as many female, lone-parent families among black Canadians as among all other ethnic groups (Calliste 2001).

Intersectional research on families (i.e., research that simultaneously considers class, gender, ethnicity, and race) has been less concerned with the division of domestic labour in families than with how the institution of the nuclear family has reproduced white privilege in Canada. As an institution, the nuclear family has served to promote the morality of the white middle-class and the colonialization and nation-building projects of the state. As Enakshi Dua (2005: 120) points out,

> White women were racially gendered as mothers of the nation whose participation in the nuclear family was crucial for the (re)production of the nation. In contrast, women of colour were racially gendered as posing a triple threat to the racialized nation as they could not reproduce a white population, allowed for the possibility of interracial sexuality, and challenged, by their presence within the nation state, the very racialized moral order that the nuclear family was to protect.

Such research has also been critical of feminist research on families for concentrating too narrowly on the family experiences of white women. Rather than being oppressive, families, for racialized women, are often seen as a place where they can escape from the oppression they experience in paid work, and they have striven to live in nuclear families, a privilege often denied them (see Dua 1999 for an overview). Further, government policies on immigration (e.g., family sponsorship), pensions, unemployment, and so forth shape ethnic family patterns and experiences because they are framed along hegemonic white, middle-class lines (Albanese 2005).

The transformation of wages into food and other necessities of life is another dimension of domestic labour. Although the work of making ends meet has received relatively little research attention in Canada, Meg Luxton's stands out as exceptional. Luxton's study of domestic labour, which spans three decades, examines the processes of domestic labour in white working-class families in Flin Flon, Manitoba (Luxton 1980), and Hamilton, Ontario (Luxton and Corman 2001). According to Luxton and Corman (2001: 172), transforming wages into the necessities of life involves 'allocating the available income to the various needs and choices of household members, from paying the mortgage and buying groceries to purchasing luxury goods and services'. Luxton and Corman (2001) find that the shopping involved in making ends meet is done mostly by women in families, but that the paying of bills is evenly divided between men and women. Both studies showed that shopping for the supplies necessary to run a household without breaking one's budget required considerable skill (see also Luxton and Corman 2001). This involved searching for the best deals, clipping coupons, being frugal if money is tight because of layoffs or unemployment, and coming up with creative ways to make a dollar go farther.

Even though the responsibility for making ends meet usually falls to women, Luxton and Corman's research (2001) shows that it is often men who control the money in the household. Because wages are the legal property of the person who earns them, there are no guarantees that the wage will be redistributed among the members of a family. Hence, most wives are economically dependent upon their husbands because they either do not work for pay or earn significantly less than their spouse.

Unfortunately, there is no Canadian research that assesses the work of making ends meet in middle- and upper-class families or in ethnic- and racial-minority-group families, on whether this process varies across the life course, or on whether this process transcends household boundaries. Indeed, our understanding of domestic labour in Canada is limited by a focus on households and by our typical understandings about what is meant by 'household work'. This and other limitations regarding the conceptualization of household work led Eichler and Albanese to redefine household work as the 'the sum of all physical, mental, emotional and spiritual tasks that are performed for one's own or someone else's household and that maintain the daily life of those one has responsibility for' (2007: 248). Adopting this kind of definition in studies on domestic labour (although I would change the word 'responsibility' to 'care') would take us a long way in our understanding of who does what for whom in Canadian families.

Violence in Families

According to the World Health Organization (2007), violence is 'the intentional use of physical force or power, threatened or actual, against oneself, another person, or against a group or community, that either results in or has a high likelihood of resulting in injury, death, psychological harm, maldevelopment, or deprivation'. Gender and age structure the likelihood of experiencing violence at the hand of an intimate partner or parent. Hence, women, children, and the elderly are at heightened risk of experiencing violence within families (Krug et al. 2002).

Although the violence men experience is most often perpetrated by strangers, the most common form of violence against women is intimate partner violence (Krug et al. 2002; Statistics Canada 2002b). *Intimate partner violence* (IPV) refers to intentional, controlling, and systematic behaviour in intimate relationships that causes physical, sexual, or psychological harm (Krug et al. 2002; Middlesex-London Health Unit 2000; Tjaden and Thoennes 2000). Power and control are central dimensions of IPV. Figure 8.2 identifies many of the tactics that (mostly) men use to maintain power and control in intimate

relationships. These tactics include physical, sexual, and emotional abuse; isolation; economic deprivation; intimidation; and the use of social status to reinforce power and control within an intimate partnership. All of this makes immigrant women who have become 'mail-order brides' particularly vulnerable to IPV. As pointed out in Box 8.4, with increased globalization and the international proliferation of Internet use, this is an issue that requires serious consideration so that brides know their rights.

IPV is a serious public health issue. Even considering only abuse of women, IPV is estimated to cost Canadians millions of dollars annually (Greaves, Hankivsky, and Kingston-Riechers 1995). Data from the 1993 Violence Against Women Survey show that 29 per cent of Canadian ever-married women aged 18 and older have experienced some type of violence at the hand of an intimate partner at some point in their lives (H. Johnson 1996; H. Johnson and Sacco 1995). As Figure 8.3 shows, the severity of IPV ranges from threats of violence or having something thrown at you to being pushed, shoved, or slapped to sexual assault. As Figure 8.3 also shows, more women than men experience serious violence such as sexual assault. For many women, the experience of IPV led them to fear for their lives (Statistics Canada 2002b).

Similar proportions of Canadian men (6 per cent) and women (7 per cent) report that they experienced some form of IPV in the five years preceding the 2004 General Social Survey of Canada (Statistics Canada 2005a). Although these figures indicate that more research needs to be done on intimate violence against men, they may also be misleading because they do not take into account who instigated the violence and whether it was an act of self-defence. Furthermore, the violence inflicted on women is more severe than that inflicted on men. Compared with male victims, female victims are more likely to have been beaten, choked, or threatened with a gun or knife (Statistics Canada 2005a).

Figure 8.2: Battering in Intimate Relationships 'Power and Control Wheel'

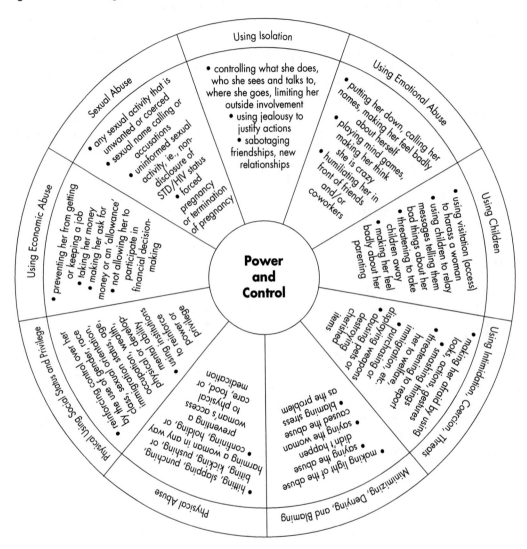

Source: Originally developed by the Domestic Abuse Intervention Project, Duluth, MN, further adapted by the London Battered Women's Advocacy Centre, London.

Twice the proportion of women victims (44 per cent) were injured as a result of spousal violence than men victims (19 per cent). And although the number of spousal homicides is declining, four times as many wives as husbands are killed each year in Canada (Statistics Canada 2007c).

Age, socio-economic status, ethnicity, and race influence the likelihood of IPV. The rate of

Box 8.4 Mail-Order Bride Industry Rife with Abuse, Study Says

By Jeremy Hainsworth

Nika thought her future was bright when she came to Canada from the Philippines as a bride to the owner of a booming taxi business.

She was following in the footsteps of her sister, Nela, who had herself immigrated as a mail-order bride and was living comfortably with her husband and two young children.

But soon after Nika arrived thanks to the sponsorship of her husband, Tom, things began to fall apart. For one, she learned she was his fifth wife.

He beat her, restricted her right to use the phone, stopped sending money to her family and even controlled her diet. Nika fled to a transition house after a month.

A new study by Simon Fraser University's Jen Marchbank says the scenario is not unique. Mail-order brides coming to Canada have little knowledge of their rights and face exploitation at the hands of unscrupulous husbands. And the business in Canada is thriving, thanks in part to the Internet.

Many of the problems such women face in Canada come as a result of changes to this country's marriage laws as they relate to immigrants. 'Unlike many U.S. states, the industry is unregulated in Canada,' Dr Marchbank said. 'In this country, there are no specific rules to control agencies, which work transnationally, and no specific provisions to ensure that brides know their rights.'

Recent changes in Canadian marriage law regarding common-law spouses could also have implications.

The Immigration and Refugee Protection Act changed the definition of a spouse in 2001 so that certain common-law marriages are recognized under the family section of immigration rules.

Under those rules, a woman can come to Canada as a common-law spouse without being married elsewhere. That, however, puts a women at the mercy of her husband. Should the relationship fail, she could be deported.

'Before, for anyone to enter Canada, they had to be married overseas prior to coming to Canada and their marriage had to be a marriage that would be recognized under Canadian law,' Dr Marchbank said.

The situation has caught the attention of Canada's Green Party, which has been busy expanding the depth of its platform beyond environmental issues. The Greens are calling for changes to the laws permitting mail-order brides. Party Leader Elizabeth May says the situation is akin to 'human trafficking'.

There are no good statistics on how many mail-order brides there are in Canada, Dr Marchbank said. Most arrive through the family section of federal immigration policy.

It's estimated there could be as many as 10,000 Internet sites worldwide offering mail-order brides. One such site listed 128 countries.

'It is a commodification of women,' Dr Marchbank said.

But, she added, 'these women are making choices. They are not just victims. Many of these women are making choices about their lives. They may be making very restrictive choices compared to women in the West, but they are making choices.'

Source: Hainsworth (2006).

spousal violence is higher among those aged 15 to 24 than among other age groups (Statistics Canada 2005a). Wives are more likely to be abused when they live in poor families than in middle- or high-income families. They are also more likely to be abused if their partners have

Figure 8.3: Family Violence in Canada: A Statistical Profile

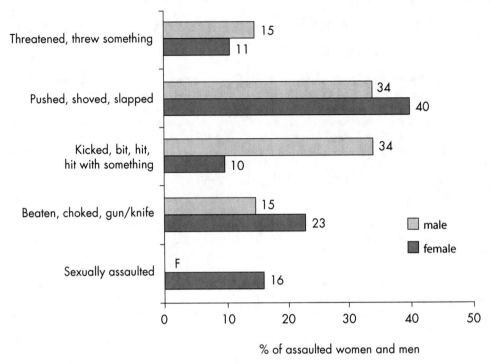

% of assaulted women and men

F: too unreliable to be published

Source: Statistics Canada (2005a).

not graduated from high school or are unemployed (H. Johnson 1996). The rate of spousal sexual and physical abuse is three times as high among Aboriginal people as among non-Aboriginal people (Statistics Canada 2005b). Taken together, these findings suggest that women who are involved with men who have relatively little power on the basis of their age, class, race, or ethnicity are more likely to experience IPV (L. Davies, Ford-Gilboe, and Hammerton 2008). Some commentators argue that men make up for their lack of power in the public sphere by dominating in the private sphere and that this occasionally results in IPV (see H. Johnson 1996 for an overview of the explanations of IPV).

Power imbalances on the basis of age make children vulnerable to abuse in families. Unfortunately, there are no data available on the prevalence of child abuse in Canada. Instead, researchers have relied on a combination of police records and reports of child welfare agencies to assess the extent of child abuse. There is little doubt that this approach underestimates the extent of child abuse and neglect in Canada, especially within families. To assess these shortfalls, the Canadian Incidence Study of Reported Child Abuse and Neglect (CIS) was conducted in 1998. This study examined the cases 'reported to, and investigated by, child welfare services during a three month period, from October to December

1998' (Statistics Canada 2001c: 4). Of course, focusing on 'reported and investigated cases' still misses the less severe instances of child abuse and maltreatment that may remain hidden within families. Furthermore, violence in families that is defined as 'punishment' is not reported as abuse. Although Canadians disagree about whether corporal punishment such as spanking should be defined as abuse, the fact that it is unacceptable to spank adults if they misbehave says a lot about power relations between adults and children (see Box 8.5).

Box 8.5 Spanking and Disciplining Children: What You Should Know about Section 43 of the Criminal Code

Spanking is a form of physical discipline known as corporal punishment. Parents and experts alike often hold different opinions on whether spanking is an appropriate way to control a child who is misbehaving. The purpose of this pamphlet is to review recent Court decisions on the use of physical discipline towards children by parents and guardians. It provides general information on the topic and discusses Section 43 of the *Criminal Code of Canada*. It should only be used as an information resource as it does not contain a complete statement of the law in the area and laws change from time to time. Anyone needing specific advice on his or her own legal position should consult a lawyer.

Is spanking children against the law?

The law assumes that spanking a child to 'correct' the child's behavior is not against the law as long as the force used is reasonable. Section 43 of the *Criminal Code of Canada* provides a defence for parents, parent substitutes and teachers who used corporal punishment to discipline a child in their care and who have been charged with physically assaulting that child. This section of the *Criminal Code* is often referred to as 'the spanking provision'.

---

43. Every schoolteacher, parent or person standing in the place of a parent is justified in using force by way of correction toward a pupil or child, as the case may be, who is under his care, if the force does not exceed what is reasonable under the circumstances. **Criminal Code of Canada**

Does that mean it's all right to use physical discipline with children?

Not necessarily. There is often a fine line between spanking a child and physical abuse of a child. If the force used slips into abusive, harmful or degrading conduct, it could result in a criminal charge or trigger a child protection investigation. There have been cases when parents or teachers have been charged with assault for spanking a child or using other forms of physical punishment. Over the past several years, many provinces have enacted legislation to prohibit the use of corporal punishment of students by teachers.

Has Section 43 of the *Criminal Code* been challenged in court?

Yes, the Canadian Foundation for Children, Youth and the Law challenged the constitutionality of Section 43 in an Ontario Court. In July 2000, the Court upheld Section 43 and the judge dismissed the application. The Foundation appealed to the Ontario Court of Appeal and in September 2001 the Court again upheld the constitutionality of Section 43. The case was then appealed to the Supreme Court of Canada, which is the highest level of court in Canada. The Supreme Court sets the standards that all other courts in the country must follow.

On January 9, 2004, the Supreme Court of Canada announced its decision in the case of *Canadian Foundation for Children, Youth and the Law v. Canada (Attorney General)*. The Court was not deciding on whether corporal punishment is good or bad. They were deciding whether Section 43 of the *Criminal*

Code violates Section 7 of the *Canadian Charter of Rights and Freedoms*. This section deals with security of the person. The Court decided that it did not violate the *Charter*. However, to ensure the best interests of the child, the Supreme Court ruling set boundaries on the use of force to discipline children.

What 'boundaries' did the Supreme Court set for physically disciplining children?

The Supreme Court of Canada stated that:

The force used must be intended to educate or correct the child;

The force used must be to restrain, control or express disapproval of the actual behaviour;

The child must be capable of benefiting from the discipline. In other words, factors such a child's age and disability will influence the child's ability to learn from the use of force;

The force used must be 'reasonable under the circumstances' and not offend society's view of decency.

What is considered reasonable force?

Since 'reasonable under the circumstances' is a broad term, the Supreme Court created a definition in relation to child discipline. The Court interpreted reasonable force as 'minor corrective force' which is short-lived and not harmful. The Court also set limits on what would be considered reasonable force. This means that Courts have an objective test to apply when deciding whether the use of force is reasonable. As well, expert advice and social consensus on the reasonable use of corporal punishment reduces the risk that courts will make arbitrary or subjective decisions.

What limits did the Court set on reasonable force?

The Court determined that the following is not reasonable:

Hitting a child under two years of age. It is wrong and harmful because spanking has no value with very young children and can destroy a child's sense of security and self-esteem.

Children under two do not have the cognitive ability to understand why someone is spanking them.

Corporal punishment of teenagers. It is not helpful and is potentially harmful to use force on teenagers because it achieves only short-term obedience and may alienate the youth and promote aggressive or other anti-social behaviour.

Using objects to discipline a child such as belts, rulers, etc. This is potentially harmful both physically and emotionally.

Slaps or blows to the head.

Degrading or inhumane treatment.

Corporal punishment which causes injury—(causing harm is child abuse).

In referring to teachers, the Court said that:

'Teachers may reasonably apply force to remove a child from a classroom or secure compliance with instructions, but not merely as corporal punishment.'

Since the force must be corrective, this rules out conduct stemming from the caregiver's frustration, loss of temper or abusive personality.

. . . . .

This pamphlet is intended to provide general information. Persons wanting to know more about corporal punishment may wish to look at What's Wrong with Spanking—Positive Parenting Tip Sheet (http://www.phac-aspc.gc.ca/dca-dea/publications/spanking_e.html), published by Health Canada, 2004. This short pamphlet gives some tips on how to effectively discipline children without spanking.

As well, you may wish to read the case. A copy of this judgment, *Canadian Foundation for Children, Youth and the Law v. Canada (Attorney General)*, is available online at: http://scc.lexum.umontreal.ca/en/2004/2004scc4/2004scc4.html.

Source: Public Legal Education and Information Service of New Brunswick (PLEIS-NB), February 2007, www.legal-info-legale.nb.ca.

Nonetheless, data from the CIS provide more information about child abuse and neglect in Canada than was previously available. These data suggest that there were an estimated 135,573 child maltreatment investigations in Canada in 1998. Of these investigations, 45 per cent were substantiated by child welfare workers, 22 per cent were suspicious but unsubstantiated, and in 33 per cent of the cases the investigation revealed that the child was not maltreated. Most of the substantiated cases involved neglect (40 per cent). Physical abuse accounted for 31 per cent of the substantiated cases, sexual abuse for 10 per cent, and emotional maltreatment for 19 per cent (Statistics Canada 2001c). In 1998 there were, in Canada, 5,958,537 children between the ages of 0 and 14 years (Statistics Canada 2001a). Hence, approximately 0.4 per cent of Canadian children were physically or sexually abused to the point that child welfare agencies intervened. Another 0.4 per cent were neglected, and 0.2 per cent suffered emotional maltreatment. According to these data, girls and boys were equally likely to experience maltreatment in families. Boys were more likely than girls to have been physically abused, and girls were more likely than boys to have been sexually abused in families, a finding that is substantiated by 2003 police record data (Statistics Canada 2005b). Older boys and girls are more likely to experience abuse than are younger girls and boys. Among girls the likelihood of sexual assault is highest among those aged 4–7 and 12–15 (Statistics Canada 2001c). Higher incidents of abuse and neglect are found in families that are more likely to be at risk of poverty (e.g., lone-mother families) (Statistics Canada 2001c), and a direct relationship between poverty and child abuse has been found in other countries around the world (Krug et al. 2002).

The above data take into account only those cases of child abuse that are reported to child welfare agencies, yet the most severe cases of child abuse are usually handled by police. Police records from 2000 show that 23 per cent of victims of physical and sexual assault were children or young people, a figure that corresponds with the percentage of children and young people in the population of Canada at the time. Data from 2003 separated out physical and sexual assault and found that 21 per cent of the victims of physical assault and 61 per cent of the victims of sexual assault were children and youth under 18; children and youth represented 21 per cent of the Canadian population in 2003. The 2000 data showed that the majority of child and youth victims of crime were assaulted by strangers or acquaintances rather than relatives. Family members were the perpetrators in 23 per cent of the cases, and, of these family-member perpetrators, parents were most likely to be the abusers. However, there was some variation on the basis of age. Children aged 5 and under were more likely to be assaulted by relatives, whereas children 6 and older were more likely to be assaulted by someone who was not related to them. In the case of homicide, infants were more likely to be killed by their mothers, and older children and young people by their fathers. With the exception of homicide, the risk of abuse increased with age (Statistics Canada 2002b).

Data taken from police records in 2005 suggest that very little has changed with respect to the physical and sexual abuse of children within families. Overall, the rates of sexual and physical assaults against children and youth committed by non-family members remained higher than the rate committed by family members (1.5 times higher for sexual assault and 2.6 times higher for physical assault), although the gap has narrowed (from 2 times and 3.6 times higher in 1998) (Statistics Canada 2007c).

Elder abuse is defined as an intentional or unintentional act of commission or neglect. It may be physical, psychological, financial, or material (Krug et al. 2002; McDonald et al. 1991; Podnieks 1992). Data from the 1999 General Social

Survey (GSS) show that physical or sexual abuse perpetrated by a spouse, adult child, or caregiver over the last five years was reported by only 1 per cent of non-institutionalized Canadians aged 65 and older. Although these numbers are too small to allow for subsequent analyses, this 1 per cent figure may represent wife abuse 'grown old' (L.R. Phillips 1986: 212).

Police records on violent crime show that adults aged 65 and older experience lower rates of violent crime that do those under 65. However, the rate of violence against older adults increased by 20 per cent between 1998 and 2005. Although overall rates of violence against seniors are higher for men than for women, older women are more likely to be subjected to violence at the hand of a family member than are older men. Those accused of family violence against seniors are more likely to be children of the abused indivual, followed by a spouse and then other relatives. Yet gender differences emerge here. Among older women, those accused of family violence are more likely to be spouses of the victims, whereas for older men, the accused are more likely to be children of the victims (Statistics Canada 2007c).

Because of the structural intersections between age and gender, Aronson, Thornewell, and Williams (1995) argue that it is important to consider 'wife assault in old age' as distinct from either wife assault or elder abuse, and they document the story of Eve, a woman who, at age 75, left an abusive relationship (see Box 8.6). Indeed, there are continuing debates in the literature about whether elder abuse is a problem unique to old age or whether it represents a continuation of lifelong family violence (McDonald and Wigdor 1995).

At an individual level, victims of familial abuse have limited agency to deal with violence because of the excessive control and power that husbands, parents, or adult children have over them (L. Davies, Ford-Gilboe, and Hammerton 2008). Nonetheless, agency among the victims of family violence is revealed in the strategies that they use to curtail it or escape from it. In violent families, wives, children, and the elderly pay attention to the things that trigger acts of violence from the abuser and actively seek ways in which they can avoid such things. Wives sometimes flee abusive relationships, often taking their children with them, and teenagers sometimes run away from home. Yet gender, age, race, ethnicity, and class structure the processes of production, reproduction, and distribution in limiting the options that are available to victims of abuse and severely restrict their ability to leave abusive families (see coalescence framework, Figure 7.3). Besides differences in physical strength, women, children, and the elderly are often financially and otherwise dependent on family members.

Box 8.6 Eve's Story

At the time that Eve participated in this project, she was 79 and living in a retirement home. She had left her husband four years earlier, at 75, after being married for almost 50 years. A year after her marriage in 1940, she give birth to a son, whom she described with great fondness and pride. Her husband went overseas with the Canadian forces in 1942 and, by the time he returned, she had accumulated enough money from her own earnings and her 'soldier's pay' to buy a house. She described how, after that, her husband's actions increasingly isolated and silenced her; for example, he bought all the groceries and clothes for the household, she seldom went out and he would not let her talk with company so that, eventually, their friends stopped visiting. When their son left home and moved to the west coast, her husband's mental, emotional and physical abuse escalated:

If he had to pass by me, like in the hallway, he would move as far away from me as possible in order to avoid touching me. He couldn't stand to be near me. He began to slap and choke me. I don't remember the times in hospital. You don't, you know. I was told that I had received shock treatments. I can't recall how long or how many times I was on the psychiatric ward, but I think it went on for years.

The worst part was the women. Young girls— he paid them . . . I couldn't do anything about it. In our bedroom we had twin beds. One night he brought a woman into bed with him while I was sleeping in the next one and I woke up . . .

I think it was during my second last hospitalization my psychiatrist drew me out—they can do that, get you to talk about things. He asked me if there was anywhere else I could go for a few months when I left the hospital. I think he knew something was wrong. I did go to my sister's for a couple of weeks but then I had to go back home. Things were worse then than ever.

The last time I came home from the hospital, my doctor ordered home care and a VON for me. The VON nurse came every day to bathe and dress me. She looked after my personal needs on a daily basis. Frank did not want this. He said we didn't need the nurse or the home care worker. The nurse and I would find him listening outside the bathroom door. She noticed that he never let me speak when he was around. She said she wouldn't put up with that and that I shouldn't have to either. I told her this was normal for Frank. She got to know what was happening.

It wasn't long before the VON and I planned my escape. She helped me pack my bag and she made arrangements with the local women's shelter. I couldn't bring myself to leave that night but the next morning I called a cab and left . . .

I didn't mind it at the shelter, but they told me that it was too noisy for me to have all the kids around and I was moved to another shelter. There, I was given clothes and a worker from a family agency visited me. She was just wonderful. I don't know what I would have ever done without her. I had no help from my family you know. My sisters, nobody believed me—they all believed Frank. I was still really not well and don't remember much about that time. My worker really helped me. It was she that found this retirement home for me and helped me through the adjustment period. I've been here four years now.

Ever since I've been here I have never again 'gone mental' or been hospitalized. I am on my own and, for the most part, look after my own affairs. It isn't easy because I never had to do these things before—banking, taxes, government pensions—all those details. Do you know, I had never been to a grocery store? Now I go to the mall and marvel at all the food . . .

As you know, I've been concerned that I'm not the best woman to talk about this because I had my own money. Most women don't, and the women in the shelters with children had nowhere to go. It was terrible for them. After a long and difficult court process, I have money to live on but it dwindles every year. It worries me because it's so expensive to live here and my bank account is going down all the time. It's a scary feeling.

The thing that really makes me mad is that Frank is living in my house. I try not to think about it. I paid for that home and he lived there rent-free all those years because of me. All the gifts and possessions I accumulated over fifty years are still there. I had to fight even to get my clothes.

Source: Aronson, Thornewell, and Williams (1995: 79–80)

This structured dependence, combined with ideologies regarding familial love, make it difficult to leave abusive families (L. Davies, Ford-Gilboe, and Hammerton 2008). For instance, only 43 per cent of abused wives leave their husbands, and three-quarters of those who leave return. Among those who return, a third do so 'for the sake of their children', one-quarter want 'to give the relationship another chance', 17 per cent feel that their partner will change, and 9 per cent lack the money or housing to live on their own (Rodgers 1994).[1] Although there is no survey evidence that indicates that violence resumes after women return to their partners, the systemic nature of family violence, combined with qualitative data that demonstrate recurring abuse (L. Davies, McMullin, and Avison 2001), suggests that this is likely. Hence, romanticized ideals of family may perpetuate family violence even among women who have once left the abusive situation. Further, remaining separated from a partner does not guarantee the end of IPV (L. Davies, Ford-Gilboe, and Hammerton 2008). Husbands sometimes find their estranged wives and continue to threaten and abuse them, and sometimes even murder them (D.K. Anderson and Saunders 2003; Statistics Canada 2001g).

Compared to individual agency, collective action has been a much more effective means of dealing with family violence. Indeed, the recognition throughout the 1970s and 1980s of the abuse of women, children, and elderly people as serious social problems was a direct result of the collective lobbying of feminist and other activist groups, such as the National Advisory Council on Aging. Through these efforts community services have been put in place, especially for women and children, that help victims of family abuse leave abusive relationships and otherwise cope.

Sexuality

Sexuality is a central dimension of the social relations of reproduction. Sexuality has different meanings in different situations. 'In some ways it is an expression of human need, of pleasure, and of the social togetherness of lovers. In other ways it is an oppressive and repressive relationship which grinds the tenderness and love out of people, leaving behind the frustration, bitterness, and violence' (Luxton 1980: 55).

Indeed, some argue that heterosexuality itself is a repressive patriarchal institution. For instance, in a seminal article, Adrienne Rich (1980) argued that heterosexuality is not natural but is a mechanism through which men maintain their powerful and privileged status in society. To truly have control over one's sexuality, Rich argues, one needs to be able to choose heterosexuality freely. Yet in contemporary Western societies heterosexuality is not questioned but is taken for granted. According to Rich, the organization of productive relations in capitalism reinforces **compulsory heterosexuality** because (1) women's success at work is often tied to their degree of femininity (which implies acting in an overtly heterosexual manner); (2) women often endure sexual harassment to keep their jobs; and (3) women are economically dependent upon men because they earn less (see also the discussion of the link between processes of production and reproduction in the coalescence framework, Figure 7.3).

In Canada, sexuality is often organized in families and is structured by class, age, gender, ethnicity, and race. Indeed, colonized peoples in North America have had to endure centuries of sexual regulation and abuse by Europeans (Stasiulis 1999). Heterosexual teenage sex, especially for girls, is subjected to excessive moral regulation, and in most nursing homes elderly residents are not permitted to have sexual relations.

Processes of production, reproduction, and distribution are evident in the rules of exchange that frame the dating experience for both teenagers and adults. Even though there has been movement toward more equality in dating, boys and men (who are often older than their dating partners) tend to pay for meals, movies, and other forms of entertainment in exchange for kissing, petting, and intercourse. We do not often think about dating in these terms because our assumptions about love and family suggest that this behaviour is both traditional and normal (Luxton 1980). Yet if a woman does not submit to a man's advances after he has paid for the date, she is at risk of 'losing' him (Luxton 1980) or, in more extreme cases, she is at risk of sexual abuse. Although determining the prevalence of sexual abuse among dating couples ('date rape') is fraught with methodological difficulties, Canadian data from the late 1990s suggest that 28 per cent of women attending college and university were sexually abused within the past year (DeKeseredy and Schwartz 1998). The fact that, on average, men earn more than women (see chapter 9), also reinforces the idea that men 'should' pay for entertainment on dates and links inequality in processes of production to sexuality. Indeed, because women are at a disadvantage in the labour market, they are more likely than men to consider the earning potential of their dating partners in making decisions about marriage (Coltrane 2000).

One of the functions that marriage continues to play in Canadian society is the regulation of sexual relations. This remains true regardless of Popenoe's claim that this function is eroding. Indeed, monogamy within marriage is the expectation in Canada. Although most Canadians report that they have never had an extramarital affair, the proportion of men who report such affairs is higher than it is for women. This suggests that there is a power imbalance in the control that men and women have over each other's sexuality within marriage. The fact that men often believe that marriage gives them the right to have sex with their wives on demand and that sex should revolve around a man's pleasures and needs is evidence of this gendered power imbalance in families (Luxton 1980). At the extreme, this gendered power imbalance leads to

sexual assault. According to 2004 Canadian GSS data, 16 per cent of women have experienced sexual assault at the hand of a spouse (Statistics Canada 2005a). Wives often feel obligated to fulfill the sexual desires of their husbands either because they fear the physical and emotional response or because they are afraid of losing their husbands to other women. Although the feelings of love and attachment that wives have toward their husbands are related to these fears, such fears are also augmented by the economic insecurity wives face. If their husbands leave, many wives would have economic difficulties. This is because wives are primarily responsible for domestic labour and consequently are connected only tenuously to the labour market (see chapter 9). Hence, sexual relations between husbands and wives are at some level economic relations as well (Luxton 1980).

Even though men control women's sexuality both inside and outside of marriage, the regulation of pregnancy and childbirth is usually the woman's responsibility. Furthermore, the consequences of poorly timed pregnancies severely affect women's economic well-being but not men's. Teenage girls who get pregnant reduce the risk of a lifetime of financial struggle if they marry the father of their child. Yet even if a marriage does take place, there is no guarantee that it will last. Furthermore, among women who work for pay and who get pregnant when they are older, careful timing is often also required so that they get the most out of public and private maternity-leave benefits. If, for instance, a woman who is working for pay gets pregnant before she has been employed with a company for six months, she is most often ineligible for either company or government benefits. In such instances, a woman would not even be guaranteed her job if she took a leave. Of course, men tend not to have to deal with these issues, but with recent changes to parental leave policies in Canada this might change (see chapter 12).

Explaining Inequality in Families

The preceding discussion shows that families are sites of considerable conflict and inequality. Because so many people view families in romanticized ways as places in which love and harmony abound, less emphasis was placed on this topic here. And there is little doubt that many families provide comfort, love, and nurturing for its members; for racialized women, families may also act as protection from oppression in paid work and other social institutions. Moreover, in some families the division of labour is organized in relatively equal ways (Ranson, forthcoming; Risman 1998). Hence, explanations of inequality within families must consider simultaneously both the harmony and conflict that characterizes family life.

Many of the models that have been put forth to explain inequality within families have focused on inequities in the division of household labour and child care. For instance, some researchers have focused on power imbalances within marriage to explain the unequal division of unpaid labour in families (Carrier and Davies 1999). In this literature, marital power is often conceptualized as the relative resources (e.g., income or education) that husbands and wives have within a marriage. For example, one might hypothesize that the more income or education a wife has compared to her husband, the less household work and care she will perform. This hypothesis is generally supported: couples who have relatively equal levels of resources tend to have a more equitable division of household labour than those whose resources are less equal (Gazso-Windle and McMullin 2003; Kamo 1988). Other models have analyzed the views that partners hold about gender equality and correlated these views with the relative time that husbands and wives spend doing household labour. Still other models focus on time availability. A serious problem with all of these models is that the researchers who use them tend not to contextualize them within the

structures of gender, class, ethnicity, race, and age. As a result, these analyses tend to place too much emphasis on individual differences to the neglect of social structure. Furthermore, such research usually avoids discussions of the struggle and conflict that often take place as families try to struggle through the work of maintaining households and caring for children.

More fruitful approaches to studies of inequality within families would take both structure and agency into account and recognize that through these structures families are often oppressive institutions. In this regard, Ingrid Connidis and I (Connidis and McMullin 2002) have worked to develop a structural concept of sociological ambivalence that characterizes family ties. Our summary of ambivalence is worth repeating here:

> Ambivalence is created by the contradictions and paradoxes that are imbedded in sets of structured social relations (e.g., class, age, race, ethnicity, gender) through which opportunities, rights, and privileges are differentially distributed. Individuals experience ambivalence when social structural arrangements collide with their attempts to exercise agency when negotiating relationships, including those with family members. Managing ambivalence in daily life shapes the very social structures that produce ambivalence in the first place. (Connidis and McMullin 2002: 565)

To explain what is meant by 'ambivalence', I will use a personal example. Gender, class, and race structure my experiences at paid work and as a mother. As a professor of sociology in a department and university that have traditionally been very conservative, there are rigid expectations about what makes a 'good' scholar, and these expectations are classed, gendered, and racialized in the ways that one would expect. One must be articulate, show little emotion, work long hours, and so on. These expectations often clash with the gendered, classed, and racialized expectations of me, particularly of me as a mother. This clash results in a structurally based ambivalence that I must negotiate and try to resolve within my family and at work, which requires me to actively renegotiate the expectations of me as a mother and as a professor.

Beyond Statistics: Agency and Experience within Families

The preceding sections illustrate structured patterns of inequality that persist in Canadian families. Within these structures, individuals negotiate their lives and, in the process, conform or resist these structures of dominance (see chapters 6 and 7). In doing so, individuals are active in the production and reproduction of these social structures. Although concentrating primarily on white middle-class mothers, Bonnie Fox (2001, 2009) has explored how parenthood in heterosexual families socially constructs gender. This study shows that new mothers actively negotiate child care and housework with their partners, but that because mothers must take responsibility for their children and become more dependent upon their partners when they do so, fathers have more 'bargaining' power in the negotiations that take place. Using Janet Finch's (1989) terminology, partners and fathers have 'legitimate excuses' for not looking after the children. A particularly telling finding from this study is that structures of gender inequality in the division of housework are reproduced through these negotiations. New mothers feel that their partners should be involved in the care of their children and have 'prioritized daddy's time with the baby' while they do the housework. As a result, 'one product of women's agency in drawing men into active fathering may be a more conventional division of housework' (Fox 2001: 385).

Within the context of class, gender, age, ethnic, and racial structures, even the most structurally disadvantaged individuals make choices about how they should best live their lives. Looking from the outside in, and without hearing the stories, these choices often seem irrational to those who have never experienced extreme disadvantage. Box 8.7 presents an excerpt from the life-history narratives in the poverty study that introduced this chapter. Pam grew up in a white, poor family with a physically abusive stepfather and a mother who drank. Poverty combined with gender- and age-based power relations forced Pam onto the streets when she was 14. Pam used various survival strategies and made choices within the context of debilitating structures of age, gender, and class to get off the streets. Although she only had a grade 8 education when she left home, when we talked with her, she was 26 years old, was a married mother of two children, had nearly finished high school, was earning a living as a part-time apartment-building superintendent, and was learning a trade. Notably, Pam makes sense of her life by contrasting her life and what she has made of it with her observations of her neighbours' problems. Throughout her teenage years, her mother tried to enforce middle-class family and gender values upon her and she resisted. Yet now she struggles to maintain a happy family life with an unfaithful husband so that her children will have what she didn't and so that she does not 'become a statistic'.

Conclusions

Although Popenoe and other neo-conservative commentators interpret changes in women's lives and families negatively, those interested in eradicating inequality view them positively. Indeed, Anthony Giddens (2002: 65), in speaking about the relationship between families and globalization goes so far as to suggest that

> the persistence of the traditional family—or aspects of it—in many parts of the world is more worrisome than its decline. For what are the most important

Box 8.7 Pam's Family Experiences

From what I remember from about seven, seven up, I don't remember a lot of traumatized stuff. A lot of abuse obviously. Strict, upper hand, you don't talk back, kids are supposed to be seen not heard. There's a lot of violence, 14 years she [Pam's mother] put up with abuse and stuck it. People say you can leave but it's not as easy as said.

I left home at fourteen, moved here, lived on the streets. Ate out of the garbage bins. I don't know, there was lots of abuse. There was alcohol in my family, left and right. Drugs and, see, my brother he was, started young, he was about eleven when he started drugs. My mom acknowledged it but she was so messed up she really, you know, she didn't do nothing about it. It was rough.

My dad was always in jail so to speak, and she met this guy. This guy was very stiff, upper hand, you know you don't talk back, you do as I say. He used to make us, as kids you know when you run down the stairs and that and you creak the stairs or something, he would think we were banging. So we would have to go up and down the stairs 150 times or more. And if we made one creak, we would have to start all over again. Well to this day I can't walk up stairs properly. Like I can't walk flat, always on the tippy toes. You know, just something like that. There was like dishes, he used to make us do dishes real young. And as kids you don't worry about every little spot on them, and if we had one we had to do them all over again. And we'd do them like five or six times, yeah, in a day. There was little things here and there that he would make us do. School, I wasn't good in school because I was, I had other problems to worry about. You know, more or less taking care of my mom when she was all drunk, and cleaning up the house and doing whatever.

We used to get hung out, we lived in a two storey house, he'd hang us upside down by our feet out the window. A lot of physical abuse. Later on the down the road, when my mom finally did leave this guy, there were two men that raped and

molested me, and I told her. She was like, no they wouldn't do that kind of thing, right. So that's when I said that's it, I've had enough. And my brother was the only one who believed me. I just left it.

I lived in the park for the longest time. I cleaned up from the water fountains there. I cleaned up the best I could. Just carried a back pack with me. At night we would have to watch. I met a couple of friends in the park and they would watch for police because at that time they would come through the park and see if anybody was sleeping on the benches and that's where we slept. Then if my friends seen them or whatever, wake me up and we'd just sit there and talk, and then go back to sleep. So it was really rough, I looked like a bag of crap. Not the proper hygiene of it all, I was fairly clean considering some of them, they were really gross. Towards the end of the night we'd just go, like there was a doughnut shop downtown at the time, and we used to go into their dumpsters and get their doughnuts and whatever garbage there was there to eat. We'd go to the Salvation Army, we'd get one meal there, so we'd do that.

And I didn't even panhandle or nothing, so whatever I could get, and it was hard. I did that for about six months and I couldn't take it no more. I was just on the verge of committing suicide and everything. It was all going downhill. I heard about this place that would help so I went there. And they weren't going to take me because I was fifteen and they don't usually, they need a consent and all this. And I explained to them there is no consent, there has never been a consent. I've been my own person for a long time. And I've been feeding myself for a while. Ok the food might have been in the cupboards or whatever, but I'd be making it. So they took that into consideration.

I hated it because people would steal what little stuff I had, and there was like fights. And they would say there is different walks of life and you're going to face that. I didn't agree with that 100 per cent, I said I understand there's different people with different problems, but leave my stuff alone that's all I want. I don't got much. Eventually I got privileges to get my own room, private room. So I enjoyed that. I stayed there for the longest time, I stayed about eight months there. So I was happy about that and when I did finally say ok, I'm out of here, I got my own apartment downtown.

And then I met my husband, well boyfriend at the time. We lived together and stuff like that, my mom was not good about that. First time I ever got a welfare cheque, and it was cool, because I saved money. I didn't really spend nothing because I wasn't in a spending mode, I just wanted to save everything I could get. So every time I'd get my welfare cheque I'd go out and hang around the café, doughnut café and stuff like that, and my mom would say well you can't do that. Well why can't I? I pay my own rent, it's my place. I'm still your mother and you can't do this and you can't do that, I'm going to send you to a girls' home. She used to threaten me with that all the time. And I just lost it, you want to send me, go for it, try it, see what happens. You're not going to get anywhere, they're going to laugh at you because I'm out on my own. You got nothing to do with me. She hated it, we fought for a while there too.

I wouldn't even tell her, because I didn't want to tell her that, my husband now, was living with me. She knew, I knew she knew because she'd seen men's stuff here and there. I just said no, it's just my friend's stuff or whatever. But she knew and I didn't want to hurt her feelings or whatever, you know.

Eventually we, me and my husband, we moved to a bigger place, it wasn't much bigger but it was bigger. We ended up being superintendents cleaning out the garbage. We had to deal with the clientele there so to speak, it was rough. There was a lot of drugs going through there. I didn't like it because I wanted to get away from that situation.

We finally made it. I was sixteen when we moved again over top of a bar and there are nice places there, really, really nice places. I ended up being a superintendent there for like five buildings. They hummed and hawed about it too because I'm sixteen being a superintendent, not mature. Well they later on realized that it was a good decision because I got rid of a lot of the drug addicts that were in there. It was hard to deal with because you kind of sleep not knowing if they would break into your apartment and do something to you because you phoned the police on them. So we had lots of difficulties with that but eventually it panned out into a nice place to live.

And then I ended up getting pregnant with my daughter, because we were doing that for a while and I was eighteen when I got pregnant. And I decided to leave [my job]. I gave the landlord proper notice and whatnot and said I can't be bringing my daughter up here in a downtown area, over top of a bar, no. There's no play land or anything for them. He kind of understood but he was disappointed because I had been there for so long. And then we moved over here, like that was a two bedroom, this is a three, and we've been here ever since. Its been not bad, I don't want stay here long because there's so to speak, people call them 'lifers' here. Been here 20, 26 years. I've been here six and when I do move its going to be to a house. I'll stay a long time, length of time you need and I'll never come back again. This is public housing, eh, so and there's different walks of life here. They don't like the fact that my husband works, because a lot of them are on mother's allowance or welfare.

Source: Davies, McMullin, and Avison, unpublished research data.

forces promoting democracy and economic development in poorer countries? Well, precisely the equality and education of women. And what must be changed to make this possible? Most importantly, the traditional family.

Yet, as Bonnie Fox points out (2001: 388), and as this chapter shows, irrespective of the positive changes that have occurred for women in families, 'the division of household work and responsibility in heterosexual couples has stubbornly resisted significant change. This absence of change suggests that gender divisions in intimate relations are deeply embedded in social structures.' Added to this is the persistence of physical and sexual violence against women, children, and older adults in families. Clearly, although power imbalances may make families 'a haven in a heartless world'[2] for men, for many women, children, and older adults the structure and experience of families may be characterized as much by ambivalence and conflict as by love and harmony.

Compared to gender and age, there has been very little Canadian research on race and ethnic inequality in families and unpaid work. The work of Tania Das Gupta, Enakshi Dua, and Agnes Calliste stand out as exceptions in this regard. Much of this work concerns the role of the state in family formation and the discrimination that racial and ethnic minority groups face in living in family forms that they choose. As these scholars have noted, more work is needed on the experiences of women and men racialized in families and on the social organization of racialized families.

|||||||||| Notes |||||||||||||||||||||||||||||||||||||||||||||||||||||||||||||||||||||||||||| ||

1. Twenty per cent of these women listed other reasons for returning to their husbands. In this survey, women were asked to report the main reason for returning to their husbands, and only one response was allowed. As a result, the data likely underestimate the role that financial dependence plays in women's decisions to return to their husbands.

2. This is the title of a famous sociological book on families written by Christopher Lasch in 1977.

|||||||||| Questions for Critical Thought |||||||||||||||||||||||||||||||||||||||||||||||||| ||

1. Statistics show that the total number of paid and unpaid hours of work that men and women do are similar. Some use these data to argue that there is an even split in the work that men and women do—in other words, that when it comes to 'work', the family situations for men and women are equal. Using the material presented in this chapter, develop an argument that would counter this claim.

2. Families are often described as a 'haven in a heartless world'. Use the information in this chapter to refute this claim.

3. Write a brief account of your family life when you were a child. Did your family situation seem to mirror the dominant family ideologies of the time? How did gender, age, ethnicity, race, and class structure your experience within your family?

4. Imagine your life 15 years from now. What do you think is the ideal life for someone of that age? How is this ideal influenced by family ideology? How is this ideal structured by gender, class, age, ethnicity, and race?

5. Write down the decisions that Pam made in her life. How were those decisions informed by ideas about what makes a good family? How were those decisions influenced by intersections of class, age, gender, ethnicity, and race?

IIIIIIIIIIII Glossary IIIIIIIIIIIIIIIIIIIIIIIIIIIIIIIIIIIIIIIIIIIIIIIIIIIIIIIIIIIIIIIIIIIIIIIIIIIIIIIIIIIIIIII

Cluttered nest The situation facing parents when children return to live with them after the parents have experienced an 'empty nest' phase.

Compulsory heterosexuality The lack of free dom women have to decide whether they will be heterosexual or homosexual. The phrase also refers to the pressures that confront lesbians when they are forced to act as if they were heterosexual or risk facing discriminatory actions.

Empty nest The life stage in which all children have left their parents' home.

Fertility rate The average number of children born to women of childbearing age.

Nuclear family A family consisting of a husband and wife who live together with their biological or adopted children.

Sandwich generation The generation in which adult children, usually daughters, are 'caught' between caring for their young children and their elderly parents.

IIIIIIIIIII Recommended Reading IIIIIIIIIIIIIIIIIIIIIIIIIIIIIIIIIIIIIIIIIIIIIIIIIIIIIIIIIIIIIIIIIIIIIII

Dua, Enakshi. 1999. 'Beyond Diversity: Exploring the Ways in Which the Discourse of Race Has Shaped the Institution of the Nuclear Family'. In E. Dua and A. Robertson, eds, *Scratching the Surface: Canadian Anti-Racist, Feminist Thought*. Toronto: Women's Press. An excellent article that examines how the institution of the nuclear family has been reinforced through racist state rhetoric and policy.

Fox, Bonnie J., ed. 2001. *Family Patterns, Gender Relations*. 2nd edn. Toronto: Oxford University Press. An excellent collection of essays on how family life is gendered and how family relations and gender relations have changed over time.

Johnson, Holly. 1996. *Dangerous Domains: Violence against Women in Canada*. Toronto: Nelson. Relying heavily on Statistics Canada data, this book provides a comprehensive account of violence against women in Canada.

Luxton, Meg, and June Corman. 2001. *Getting By in Hard Times: Gendered Labour at Home and on the Job*. Toronto: University of Toronto Press. A case study of steelworkers in Hamilton. It examines how these working-class people negotiate the demands of paid and unpaid work.

Lynn, Marion, ed. 2003. *Voices: Essays on Canadian Families*. 2nd edn. Scarborough, ON: Nelson. A collection of essays on family diversity and experiences.

IIIIIIIIIII Relevant Websites IIIIIIIIIIIIIIIIIIIIIIIIIIIIIIIIIIIIIIIIIIIIIIIIIIIIIIIIIIIIIIIIIIIIIIIIIIIIIII

The White Ribbon Campaign
www.whiteribbon.ca
**This website provides information and educational tools regarding violence against women. The White Ribbon Campaign is an organization of men who are 'working to end men's violence against women'.

Canadian Council on Social Development—Families: A Canadian Profile
www.ccsd.ca/factsheets/family
**This webpage is the place to go to for accessible statistics on Canadian families. Graphs and distribution tables for family types, lone-parent families, marriages and divorces, child-care

spaces, mothers in the paid labour force, and costs of raising children are presented. 'Families' is just one of the areas covered on the Stats & Facts online service of the Canadian Council on Social Development. Other areas include demographics, health, education, economic security, and the labour market.

Vanier Institute of the Family
www.vifamily.ca
**Established in 1965 under the patronage of Their Excellencies Governor-General Georges P. Vanier and Madame Pauline Vanier, the Vanier Institute of the Family is dedicated to promoting the well-being of Canadian families. The group aims to create awareness of and to provide leadership on the importance and strengths of families in Canada and the challenges they face in their structural, demographic, economic, cultural, and social diversity.

Long-Term Health Effects of Woman Abuse Research Consortium
http://www.women-health.ca/publications.htm
**In this group, Canadian researchers are brought together by the following goals: to understand the patterns of mental and physical health of women who have left abusive partners, to understand how health is shaped by the conditions of their everyday lives, and to shape the development of services that support women to manage health and social problems they face after leaving. This site lists the various research projects relating to these goals and provides contact information for the investigators and collaborators

CAGE(s) and Paid Work

Introduction

In the mid-1990s I analyzed focus group data, industry data, key informant interviews, and archival data from the Montreal garment industry. This research confirmed what other research has shown—jobs in the garment industry are bad and garment work is hard (Das Gupta 1995). Managers and owners exploit workers in a quest to maximize productivity and profits, and there is always pressure to produce more. Managers control their workers by restricting the opportunities of those who sign grievances and by eliminating or moving 'problem' workers to different departments or jobs (McMullin and Marshall 2001).

In the quest for maximum productivity and profits, bosses may also try to limit the contact that employees have with one another and to supervise their work very closely. As Isabella, one of the focus-group participants put it,

> The boss was never far away from us. He was there all day long, you couldn't speak too loudly because you soon saw him coming over. Ah yes and he would say, 'That's enough.' He was there early in the morning and he stayed with us at all times, all day. If he wanted to shock me, it would be in the morning when

I arrived. You had to do a repair, he brought it to you then from the minute you set foot in the office he kept you there and gave you an earful. He ruined my day from the start when he started to tell me off—[when he started to tell me] that I worked badly. (McMullin 1996: 195–6)

Although the exact words that were exchanged between Isabella and her boss in this confrontation are not discussed in detail, the excerpt illustrates how bosses attempt to control their employees by limiting their conversations with other workers and by criticizing their ability to do their job well. All of the above point to how social class shapes the production processes in garment work and how individual owners act as agents in using their power to exploit workers.

The practice of hiring the least expensive workforce in order to maximize profits has a long history in the garment industry. As a result, women and immigrant workers are disproportionately represented in the industry; in the garment industry, women and immigrant workers are paid less. At the industrial level, 82 per cent of the workers in the ladies' clothing industry in Quebec are women. Jobs within the industry are also segregated along gender lines; for instance, women make up between 88 per cent and 96 per cent of the three lowest-paid occupations in the garment industry. Ethnic groups are segregated in particular shops, with higher wages being paid in shops where most of the workers are French Canadian (McMullin 1996; McMullin and Marshall 2001).

One method that employers in the garment industry use to reduce labour expenses is to replace older workers who have been with a company for many years with younger, less expensive workers. Even though union regulations and Quebec law forbid the dismissal of workers on the basis of age, owners circumvent these rules and eliminate older workers by closing their factories and then reopening them later under different names. Bankruptcy laws allow employers to close their plants, thereby terminating their debt and decreasing their labour expenses by eliminating the older workforce and the union. Several months later, many of these companies open up under different names with younger and non-unionized employees. According to Gerald Roy, the Canadian Director of the International Ladies' Garment Workers' Union, companies go out of business, move on, and open a new firm in another location all within three or four months. The disgrace that once attached to bankruptcy has dissipated, states Roy, and now firms have 'hot shot' lawyers who tell them exactly how to go out of business; how to not pay their debts to the employees, landlords, machinery rental agencies, and banks; and how and when to open up another shop. Canadian bankruptcy legislation has not been changed to discourage such practices. Roy highlights the seriousness of this problem:

It is too easy to open and close a company in the apparel industry. What is deploring is that the workers are always at the end of the process. They lose conditions of work, they lose their paycheque, they lose vacation pay, they lose their health benefits, they lose their pension benefits, they lose and

lose and they are getting older. They are getting fed up, but they would like to go and work some place else maybe, but they do not have the opportunity because there are no jobs. (McMullin and Marshall 2001: 119)

Thus, neo-conservative state policies regarding bankruptcy favour the rights of capital over labour and serve to override legislation and union rules regarding the dismissal of older workers. José, a 53-year-old garment worker, described how difficult such practices are for older workers: 'You've been working for 25 years, with all your heart, all your soul. You gave up your health and you fall face to face with nothing . . . we lost part of our early retirement [pension contributions], we lost everything. . . . They [the company] changed the name, they changed the company but it is still there' (McMullin and Marshall 2001: 120)

The preceding discussion shows how production processes are structured by class, age, gender, and ethnicity in a working-class industry. Within these structures of inequality, owners, managers, and workers act with agency in their daily negotiations with one another. For instance, even though garment workers' choices within production processes are constrained by the structures of class, gender, ethnicity, and age relations, garment workers make informed and strategic decisions about their work and retirement within these constraints (McMullin and Marshall 1999).

Class, gender, and racism (see chapter 4) intersect in processes of professionalization as well. Tracey Adams (2000), for instance, argues that dentistry emerged in Ontario during the early part of the 1900s as a profession that was structured as white, middle-class, and male. Students of dentistry were active in this process, as was evident from the opinion pieces submitted to student newspapers, the extracurricular activities they engaged in, their style of dress, and the ways in which some confirmed and others resisted the racial structures of their historical epoch, depending on whether they refused to treat black patients (Adams 2000).

The production processes described above in relation to garment work highlight three broad issues that may be used to classify jobs as relatively good or bad. First, the physical environments of workplaces vary considerably. People employed in good jobs experience relative comfort at work and a low risk of workplace injuries or illness. Bad jobs, on the other hand, often have physical environments that are uncomfortable and dangerous or unhealthy. Second, jobs vary in the intrinsic rewards that are derived from them. Unlike bad jobs, good jobs tend to be intrinsically rewarding because they are challenging and are characterized by high levels of **autonomy** and low levels of alienation. Third, extrinsic rewards, such as high pay, good benefits, job security, and promotion opportunities, are associated with good jobs (Krahn, Lowe, and Hughes 2007; Rinehart 2006).

Within Canada's economic system of advanced **capitalism** there is a wide continuum of good and bad jobs. The ideology of capitalism suggests that good jobs and bad jobs are distributed on the basis of individual merit. Good jobs are reserved for highly educated and skilled workers whose contributions to economic activities are considered more valuable than the contributions that others make. With this logic, inequality in the outcomes of paid work seems justified. However, many sociologists are critical of this point of view and instead recognize that if productive processes were organized differently, the inequality associated with paid work might be reduced or eliminated (Rinehart 2006). At the most fundamental level this would require the abolition of capitalism as the predominant mode of production in industrialized societies such as Canada.

In its purest form, capitalism is an economic system that organizes processes of production according to the following characteristics: (1) private ownership and control of the means of production by relatively few people; (2) continuous growth, such that owners of capital continually strive to increase their profits; (3) exploitation, such that owners of capital profit at the expense of workers; (4) labour-wage exchanges, such that workers act as free agents in selling their labour power to capitalists in exchange for a wage; and (5) commodity exchange that takes place in free markets, subject to supply and demand, which in turn regulates economic activity (Abercrombie, Hill, and Turner 2000; Krahn, Lowe, and Hughes 2007; Rinehart 2006).

Karl Marx was among the first to recognize that capitalism is also a *social* system, in which production processes are organized according to the social relations of production. Owners, managers, and workers have various rights, privileges, power, and resources relative to one another. Unequal access to the rights and powers associated with productive resources shapes the social relations of production. According to the coalescence framework discussed in chapter 7, in capitalist systems class, age, gender, and ethnic relations, which are characterized by oppression, power, exploitation, and opportunity hoarding, constitute the social relations of production. The social and economic organization of the processes of production results in a continuum of good and bad jobs.

Marx also argued that as capitalism evolved there would be a proliferation of bad jobs that would result from an increasing polarization of workers into two central classes, the proletariat and the bourgeoisie. This polarization would involve at least three things: (1) a reduction in the proportion of small business owners and hence a shrinking of the old middle class; (2) increasing proportions of income going to the owners of large businesses and a reduction in the earnings of middle-class workers; and (3) continued deskilling of work and corresponding increases in the **alienation** of workers (Conley 1999). Each of these points and related issues that classify jobs as good or bad are considered in the sections below. Specifically, this chapter examines how the social organization of production processes and the relationship between production, distribution, and reproduction lead to inequality in the intrinsic and extrinsic rewards of paid work.

Canada's Class and Occupational Structure

In Canada, as in other Western industrialized countries, the processes of production are organized by class and occupation. Clement and Myles (1994) provide what is perhaps the most comprehensive assessment of the Canadian class structure. As chapter 2 shows, they define social class through a modified, more simplified version of Wright's conceptualization, in which there are four classes. The capitalist-executive class controls both the labour power of others and the means of production. The old middle class—the 'petite bourgeoisie' in Marxist terminology—commands the means of production but not the labour power of others. The 'new middle' class controls the labour power of others but not the means of production. And, finally, the working class commands neither the labour power of others nor the means of production (see Table 2.1, page 23).

According to this definition of social class, a slight majority of employed Canadians in the early 1980s formed the working class (57.6 per cent). Almost 25 per cent formed the new middle class, 11.3 per cent the old middle class, and 6.2 per cent were considered part of the capitalist-executive class (Clement and Myles 1994: 19). Since the early 1900s the proportion of Canada's class structure comprising small business owners declined considerably (Clement and Myles 1994). Between the 1930s and the early 1970s, for instance, the proportion of the workforce comprising small business owners has declined from approximately 25 per cent to between 10

and 12 per cent (Conley 1999). Much of this decline occurred in agriculture, where advances in farm technology made the business of small farming unprofitable (Clement and Myles 1994; Conley 1999).

Nonetheless, for much of the twentieth century it appeared as if Marx's prediction regarding the shrinking middle class was right. Since the mid-1970s, however, this trend has reversed. Indeed, the most significant change in the class structure over the past 20 to 30 years has been the increase in the proportion of the class structure that is held by the old middle class. Clement and Myles (1994) report that non-agricultural self-employment increased from 5.8 per cent in 1975 to 7.4 per cent in 1990. When self-employed owners of incorporated businesses are included, the old middle class made up 14 per cent of the total labour force and 9 per cent of the non-agricultural labour force in the early 1980s. By 2008, 15 per cent of the total labour force was self-employed in both incorporated and unincorporated businesses (Statistics Canada 2008d). More than 60 per cent of self-employed business owners do not hire paid help (Statistics Canada 2006a) and the majority have fewer than three employees (Clement and Myles 1994). Information regarding self-employed business owners is difficult to find, but a recent report by Industry Canada notes that 55 per cent of 'employer businesses' employ fewer than five people (Industry Canada 2009: Table 3).

Reactions to recent increases in the proportion of employed Canadians in the old middle class have been mixed. On the one hand, some hail these changes as positive. According to this school of thought, small business owners are free of the control of large capitalist enterprises and as a result have more autonomy and other intrinsic rewards associated with their work. Their work is less alienating and this is a positive development of post-industrial capitalism. Others have argued that, far from being a positive occurrence, the rise of small business owners is the result of globalization (see Box 9.1) and workplace restructuring whereby workers lose their jobs and are forced to earn a living without some of the extrinsic rewards (e.g., pensions and benefits) of employment in large companies (see Clement and Myles 1994 for an overview of these views). This suggests that the conditions under which one becomes a small business owner are important considerations in discussions of the social implications of higher proportions of workers belonging to the 'old' middle class. Notably, the old middle class is still made up of a relatively small proportion of employed

workers. Workers in the new middle class and the working class encompass the overwhelming majority in the Canadian class structure (82.5 per cent according to Clement and Myles).

One of the most significant social trends of the twentieth century was the dramatic increase in female labour-force participation rates. Although the percentage of women who entered the labour force increased throughout that century, particularly dramatic increases began after 1961. As Figure 9.1 shows, the labour-force participation rates of Canadian women between the ages of 15 and 55 have increased

Box 9.1 Globalization and Paid Work in Canada

Globalization is a multifaceted process in which economic, political, social, and technological transformations have eroded national borders in significant ways (Giddens 2002). One of the most significant ways in which globalization has affected Canadians has been in the gradual reduction in government restrictions on trade and imports. Various trade agreements reflecting the move toward globalization were put into effect during the 1980s and 1990s, including the General Agreement on Tariffs and Trade (GATT), which resulted in a new international body known as the World Trade Organization (WTO); the Free Trade Agreement (FTA), signed in early 1989, which governed trade with the United States and was signed in early 1989 (Leach and Winson 1995); and the North American Free Trade Agreement (NAFTA), which came into effect on 1 January 1994, superseding the FTA. These trade agreements, in particular NAFTA, have facilitated economic growth by allowing Canadian companies to restructure their operations and move their production processes to Mexico or the United States. Because the cost of labour is lower in Mexico and some US states, NAFTA has enabled Canadian companies to increase their profitability.

This process of economic globalization has had devastating consequences for many working-class Canadians and particularly for women (Barndt 2002), racialized men and especially women (Ng 2002), and older workers (Winson and Leach 2002). Manufacturing jobs have been lost, unionized shops have been eliminated, full-time work has been replaced with part-time work, and income has been increasingly polarized (Winston and Leach 2002). In some cases, workers have been forced to make dramatic concessions, such as accepting pay cuts and shorter vacations, in order to keep production jobs in Canada. An example is described below. Notably, the global economic circumstances that began in the fall of 2008 meant that many workers were not even given choices and simply lost their jobs.

A Painful Time for Canada's Industrial Sector

By David Crane

The Canadian economy looks healthier than its American counterpart right now. But don't get too comfortable with that. There are signs that Canada—and especially its industrial heartland of Ontario and Quebec—faces some wrenching changes.

What's happening in the auto industry, with plant shutdowns and loss of jobs, is just one example. Much of the manufacturing sector is under pressure, and this will spill over into business services such as finance, trucking, construction and wholesale trade.

This past week, analysts at both Merrill Lynch Canada and the Bank of Montreal warned that Canada's current account surplus was about to disappear. The current account is the best measure of Canada's overall performance in the global economy each year. It includes our trade in goods and services, the interest and dividends Canadians earn abroad or pay out to foreigners and Canadian tourism abroad and tourism spending in Canada.

David Wolf of Merrill Lynch suggests that Canada's current account deficit could swing from a projected surplus of $12 billion last year to a deficit of $20 billion this year and $36 billion in 2009, ending Canada's many years of surpluses.

While, as he says, 'this is not a disaster', since financial markets can handle this massive shift, it is nonetheless troubling because it is mainly the result of Canada's deteriorating merchandise trade surplus.

Canada managed a trade surplus this past year largely because of the high price it got for oil exports. Reflecting our higher dollar and the slowing US economy, our overall exports to the US fell 10.8 per cent last year, while our automotive exports fell almost 26 per cent.

In a separate report, Derek Burleton of TD Economics warned of a continuing decline for Canadian manufacturing. Since 2002, about 17 per cent of Ontario factory jobs and 20 per cent of Quebec factory jobs have disappeared. This amounts to a loss of 320,000 factory jobs in the two provinces so far, with more to come.

Canada is not unique in this regard, as the US, Europe and Japan have also seen manufacturing job losses. If Ontario and Quebec had the same share of workers in manufacturing as these other key economies, they would lose another 370,000 jobs over the next five years, Burleton said.

Why is this job shock hitting Canada now? One explanation is that for much of the past decade, our low dollar helped shield Canadian manufacturers from the need to restructure, raise productivity, participate in global value chains and become global traders, not just exporters to the US. While productivity in US manufacturing was rising by up to 4 per cent a year this decade, it has been rising just 1 per cent a year in Canada.

Now, as Burleton points out, manufacturers are being forced to make tough adjustments other countries have been making for some time and this will cause much pain and upheaval.

Moreover, just at the time that they need to invest in advanced production technologies, improve research and development spending and become more innovative, they are also facing intense cost pressures, not only because of China but also the United States.

The announcement this past week by General Motors in the US, for example, that it was offering buyouts to 74,000 unionized employees, reflects the fact that under its new union contract it can replace workers taking early retirement with new workers whose pay and benefits will be much lower, with a saving of nearly $50 an hour in pay and benefits per worker. This puts pressure on Canada in the competition for new investment.

All of this underlines the massive changes under way in the global economy. Unfortunately for our manufacturers and their workers, we have a federal government that seems indifferent to their problems, apparently operating on the dubious assumption that Canada is an energy superpower so we don't need to worry.

This will be a costly mistake for our country.

Source: Crane (2008).

Figure 9.1: Female Labour-Force Participation Rates by Age

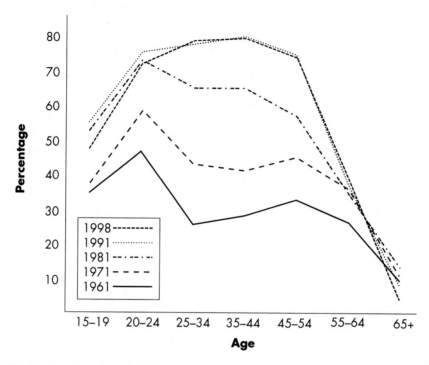

Source: 1961–71: *Census* (June figures); 1981–91: Statistics Canada, *The Labour Force Annual Averages* (71–001; 71–220). Reproduced in Phillips and Phillips (2000: 80).

quite significantly since 1961. In 1961 fewer than 30 per cent of women between the ages of 25 and 34 worked for pay. By 1998 that figure was close to 80 per cent, and for all women, the labour-force participation rate in 1998 was about 58 per cent (see Phillips and Phillips 2000 for a detailed discussion). In 2007, 82 per cent of women between the ages of 25 and 34 worked for pay, as did 63 per cent of all women (Statistics Canada 2008e). But women did not enter the labour force on an equal footing with men. Rather, their social-class positions, as well as the occupations and industries they worked in, were structured by gender.

Canada's class structure is gendered. This means that production processes are shaped by both class relations and gender relations

(Hartmann 1981). As a result, the class structure in Canada takes a different form for women and men. Clement and Myles (1994: 129) find that although women constituted 45 per cent of the Canadian labour force in the early 1980s, only 16 per cent of those were part of the executive class. Women were also underrepresented in the new middle class (41 per cent) and overrepresented in the working class (49 per cent). Finally, women were underrepresented in all occupations that involved decision-making and authority, regardless of whether they work full- or part-time.

Regarding the old middle class, the number of self-employed women has almost tripled since 1976, women still only represent about one-third of all business owners (Statistics Canada

2006a: 46). Yet in 2005, 11 per cent of employed women were self-employed compared to 20 per cent of employed men (Statistics Canada 2006a: 46). Most of the gains in self-employment that women have made in relation to men have been as 'own account' workers, that is, those who do not have any employees. In 2003, for instance, 41 per cent of self-employed men had employees on the payroll compared with only 27 per cent of women (Statistics Canada 2006a; see also Hughes 1999). Hence, although the gains that women have made in self-employment could signify improvements in women's class positions, we must be cautious about such an interpretation because the nature of work among self-employed women is different from that of men. For instance, own-account, self-employed women are more likely than men to be in this employment situation because of their caregiving responsibilities (Vosko 2007). Further, self-employed women have lower average incomes than self-employed men ($29,000 versus $42,100 in 2003; Statistics Canada 2006a).

Women who work for pay are concentrated in particular occupations and industries. In 1961 women made up 27.3 per cent of the labour force, and they were overrepresented in clerical occupations (61.5 per cent), sales (40.3 per cent), services (50.0 per cent), and professional occupations that include teachers, nurses, and social workers (43.2 per cent). Women were underrepresented in managerial occupations (10.3 per cent) and primary-sector, blue-collar jobs (19.8 per cent). By 2004, women were still underrepresented in managerial jobs (36.6 per cent versus 46.8 per cent overall representation) and primary-sector jobs (19.4 per cent), as well as trades, transport, and equipment (7.0 per cent). They remained concentrated in business, finance, and administration (71.1 per cent), health (80.7 per cent), social sciences and government services (68.2 percent), and sales and service (56.7 per cent) occupations (Krahn, Lowe, and Hughes 2007). Compared to men's jobs, women's jobs are more highly concentrated in health care and social assistance, services producing, and educational service industrial sectors of the economy. Men's jobs, on the other hand, are more highly concentrated in the goods-producing and manufacturing sectors (Statistics Canada 2002a).

The coalescence framework presented in chapter 7 suggests that production processes are organized not only according to class and gender relations but by ethnic and race relations as well. Historically, members of British and Jewish English-speaking groups have dominated the professional, managerial, and elite occupations and have been employed in **primary labour markets** (Krahn, Lowe, and Hughes 2007; Nakhaie 1995; Porter 1965). Although this dominance has declined, ethnicity still influences class and occupational structures even when education, age, and place of birth are taken into account (Nakhaie 1995).

In general, ethnic and racial minority groups (with the exception of those from a Jewish background) are underrepresented among the upper and middle classes and overrepresented in the working class (Nakhaie 1995, 1997). Although members of visible minority groups are at least as well educated as other Canadians, they are also underrepresented in professional and managerial occupational groups (Adams and Welsh 2008). For instance, although racialized groups constitute about 12.6 per cent of the Canadian population, only 8.2 per cent are senior managers and only 2.0 per cent of senior managers are women from racialized groups (Adams and Welsh 2008). With the exception of people of Arab and Chinese descent, non-white men and women are overrepresented in working-class jobs (Isajiw 1999; Kelly 2002), and racialized women are overrepresented among domestic workers in Canada (Arat-Koc 1995).

Data on the relationship between self-employment and ethnicity or race are rather scarce. However, using 1989 Canadian Social Survey data, Nakhaie (1995) shows that, among men, those from German and Jewish backgrounds are much more likely to be a part of the old middle class while men of French or Italian origin are more likely to be a part of the working class. Finally, Jewish male immigrants are much more likely to be a part of the bourgeoisie than are those from any other ethnic group. Among women and compared to men, higher proportions of each ethnic group are part of the working class. As was the case among the men, women of German and Jewish backgrounds are more likely to be a part of the old middle class and those who have either French or Italian backgrounds are more likely to be a part of the working class. Li (2001a) shows that immigrants often rely on self-employment to supplement their labour-market income and that immigrants with higher educational attainment are more likely to engage in self-employment. Li also shows that immigrants from Asia, Latin America, and Africa are least likely to engage in self-employment.

Along with class, gender, ethnicity, and race, age also structures paid work. Younger workers are disproportionately less well represented among the self-employed (Adams and Welsh 2008: 283). Labour-force participation rates for young adults (ages 15–24) rose throughout the 1970s and 1980s and then declined during the 1990s. In 2004, 67 per cent of young adults were working for pay (Krahn, Lowe, and Hughes 2007: 54). Young workers tend to be segregated in low-paid, often part-time, service-sector jobs (Allahar and Côté 1998; Krahn, Lowe, and Hughes 2007) even though they have educational attainment rates that are higher than those of previous cohorts (Lowe 2000).

Older workers are overrepresented among the self-employed (Adams and Welsh 2008: 283). The labour-force participation rate for men aged 55–64 declined throughout the 1970s and 1980s from a high of 76 per cent in 1976 to a low of 58 per cent in 1995. By 2007 that rate had climbed back to 67 per cent. The labour-force participation rate for same-aged women, on the other hand, steadily increased from 32 per cent in 1976 to 53 per cent in 2007 (Marshall and Ferrao 2007). For women, the rate is a result of overall trends toward retirement before the age of 65 as well as the contrary trend of increased overall female labour-force participation. Further, statistics on women's retirement are complicated by whether women define themselves through their husband's status or whether they consider that they 'retired' 30 years ago when they left the labour market to raise their children (Connidis 1982; Street and Connidis 2001).

The class and occupational position of older workers depends a great deal on the class and occupational positions they have held throughout their working lives. Using life-course research, some scholars have examined the cumulative advantage/disadvantage hypothesis as it pertains to inequality in paid work. According to this hypothesis, the heterogeneity between groups of people increases over time. For the purpose of this discussion, the **cumulative advantage/ disadvantage hypothesis** argues that individuals are born with specific class, gender, and racial or ethnic characteristics that provide them with a certain amount of advantage or disadvantage. Initially, there may be little separation between the haves and the have-nots on the basis of these distinctions. However, as time passes, the separation between the advantaged and disadvantaged grows and age groups become increasingly heterogeneous (Dannefer and Sell 1988). This occurs because the economic and social value attached to productive work depends on one's gender, race or ethnicity, class, and age (O'Rand 1996a, 1996b).

Younger and older workers are more likely to be employed in non-standard work. Non-standard employment includes part-time work, holding multiple jobs, temporary work, and own-account self-employment (Krahn, Lowe, and Hughes 2007: 88). In 2002, non-standard work accounted for one-third of all employment, an increase of about 5 per cent from 1989 (Krahn, Lowe, and Hughes 2007). In 2005, more than two in five younger workers (aged 15–24) and more than one in five older workers (aged 55–64) worked part-time. The latter figure is comparable to the part-time labour-force participation rate among middle-aged women (aged 25–54) but lower than that of middle-aged men—only 4.8 per cent. Younger workers are much more likely to be employed as temporary workers than are those in other age groups (Statistics Canada 2006a).

For women, rates of part-time and other non-standard employment tend to be higher than for men, regardless of age. The difference is greatest in the middle years (ages 35–54) (Krahn and Lowe 1998: 84), probably because of family responsibilities. This suggests that the specific nature of non-standard work probably varies throughout the life courses of men and women. Young workers (under the age of 15) are likely to engage in part-time work while they attend school. For older workers, non-standard work could be a choice they have made so that they can retire gradually; some older workers may engage in non-standard employment because they have lost their jobs and are having difficulties finding new ones (see the section on unemployment below).

To understand how age relations influence production processes, we need a life-course approach that documents the age composition of the occupation and class structures with longitudinal data. Unfortunately, this kind of labour market research has not yet been done in North America. Nonetheless, in 1995 Gordon Betcherman and Norman Leckie used 1991 census data to document the age structure of employment in industries and occupations. They showed that the age structures of industries and occupations may be classified in one of five ways: (1) uniform age distribution (age occupational/industrial distribution is the same as it is in the population as a whole); (2) youth overrepresented; (3)

'prime age' groups overrepresented; (4) older workers overrepresented; (5) 'prime age' groups underrepresented.

One of the most notable findings from Betcherman and Leckie's (1995) research is that only two industries (construction and wholesale trade) and no occupational groups had a uniform age distribution. Furthermore, young workers and, to a lesser extent, older workers were concentrated in 'bad job' industrial sectors and prime-age workers were concentrated in 'good job' sectors. Regarding industry, Betcherman and Leckie showed that in 1991 older workers were overrepresented in the resource sector (e.g., agriculture and fishing); parts of the manufacturing sector (e.g., clothing and primary textile); the transportation, communication, and utilities sector; and some parts of retail services (e.g., general retail and furniture and appliances). Young workers were overrepresented in all parts of retail trade, accommodation, food and beverage services, and other services. Prime-age workers were overrepresented in some parts of the manufacturing sector; the finance, insurance, and real estate sector; and the business services sector. Regarding occupation, Betcherman and Leckie found that prime-aged workers were overrepresented in most professional and technical occupations, managerial occupations, production occupations, crafts, and trades. Younger workers were overrepresented in clerical, sales, and service occupations, whereas older workers were overrepresented in some service occupations and resource-sector occupations.

Recent discussions about the 'new economy' point to the importance of social time in assessments of inequality in paid work. Tied to globalization (see Box 9.1) and the proliferation of information technology, the organization of work in new, knowledge-based economies is quite different from the organization of work in older industrial economies. Work in the new economy is characterized by greater individualism, job insecurity, risk, and instability. Hence, compared to workers in the industrial economy, workers in new economies are much less likely to be employed in the same job for life, and this has implications for how the life courses of individuals are organized (V. Marshall et al. 2001). There is increased pressure on workers to manage their own careers and to engage in lifelong learning to keep pace with technological changes. Workplaces are being restructured, and firms are recruiting employees with more knowledge-based skills (Adams and McQuillan 2000) and placing more emphasis on flexible and non-standard employment.

In summary, this section shows how classes and occupations are organized according to gender, ethnicity, race, age, and social time. Why does this matter? Because within advanced global capitalism, the intrinsic and extrinsic privileges and rewards that are attached to class position and occupations are different. Hence, the likelihood of being employed in a good job or a bad job—or, for that matter, employed at all—depends not only on one's class, but also on gender, ethnicity, race, and age. The next three sections of this chapter consider three outcomes of inequality—unemployment, levels of income and poverty, and degree of alienation and skill—that are tied to production processes.

Unemployment

Job security has traditionally been one of the most important extrinsic rewards that employment can offer. Individuals who are employed in the primary sector and in unionized occupations have high levels of job security, whereas those who are employed in the secondary sector and in non-unionized environments have low levels of job security. Of course, unions and collective-bargaining processes are gendered and racialized and have served the interests of older, white men at the expense of others (Creese 1996, 1999). Although labour laws exist in Canada to make it illegal to fire employees wrongfully, the extent to which these laws are upheld is questionable, especially for people in jobs that are unstable in the first place.

People who lose their jobs are more liable to experience poverty, homelessness, and distress (Adams and Welsh 2008; Avison, Wade, and Thorpe 1996). In Canada, the rates and duration of unemployment vary on the basis of region, industry, occupation, age, gender, and race. As the map of Canada in Figure 9.2 shows, unemployment rates in the Atlantic provinces are higher than those in the rest of Canada. This pattern is largely a result of the extent to which a particular region is economically diverse. In the Atlantic provinces, for instance, the heavy reliance on the fishing industry makes for high unemployment. Notably, these data were compiled before the global economic crisis of late 2008 and 2009. The decline in the manufacturing sector has hit Ontario quite hard and unemployment rates are on the rise as a result. This points to the connection between unemployment and each of occupation and industry. In industries such as manufacturing and construction where there are higher concentrations of working-class jobs, unemployment and layoffs are more likely. Although professional and highly skilled occupations are not as well protected from unemployment as they once were, unemployment is still less likely in professional and highly skilled occupations (Krahn, Hughes, and Lowe, 2007).

Although men and women have historically had quite different unemployment rates, their relative disadvantage with unemployment varied until the mid-1980s, when some convergence occurred. During the 1950s and until about 1966, women had lower rates of unemployment than men. From 1966 until about 1990, unemployment rates for men were lower than or similar to the rates for women. Such trends defy simple explanation, but they probably have a lot to do with the types of jobs women were employed in during the 1950s and 1960s as well as with the social stigma that was attached to unemployment

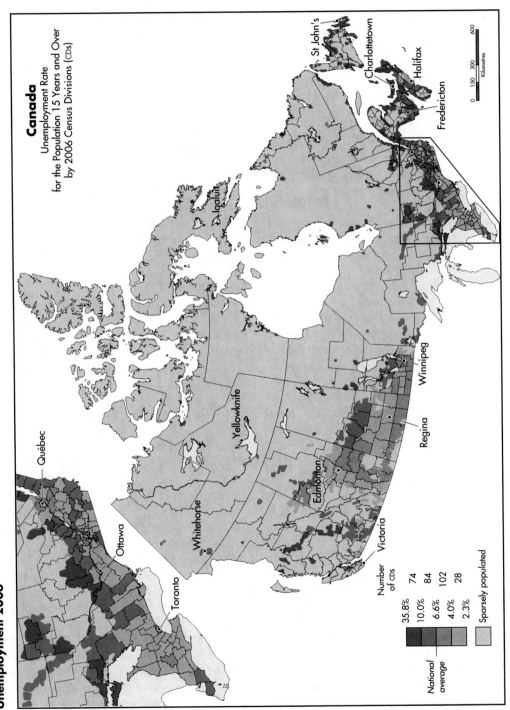

Unemployment 2006

Canada

Unemployment Rate
for the Population 15 Years and Over
by 2006 Census Divisions (CDs)

St John's
Charlottetown
Halifax
Fredericton
Iqaluit
Winnipeg
Regina
Edmonton
Victoria
Yellowknife
Whitehorse
Québec
Ottawa
Toronto

	Number of CDs
35.8%	74
10.0%	84
6.6%	102
4.0%	28
2.3%	
Sparsely populated	

National average

0   150   300   600
Kilometres

Source: 2006 Census of Canda. Produced by the Geography Division, Statistics Canada 2008.

during that time. During the 1950s and 1960s, women were usually employed in teaching and service positions, sectors that have always had lower rates of unemployment than blue-collar areas of employment (Krahn, Lowe, and Hughes 2007). Also, some women who were unemployed during this period may not have defined themselves as such but rather as housewives, because of the social acceptability of the latter status. Regardless of why there was such divergence in the unemployment rates for men and women, the important point is that there has been convergence in these rates since 1990. It should be noted, however, that women and other groups more likely to have non-standard work patterns may be undercounted in official unemployment statistics (Pulkingham 1998).

Unemployment rates and employment success vary with ethnicity and race (Reitz 2007). Members of ethnic and visible minority groups and recent immigrants have relatively high levels of unemployment. The labour-force data reported in Box 9.2 show that the unemployment rate in 2006 for those born in Canada was 4.9 per cent (for both men and women). Among recent immigrants, the unemployment rate was nearly double, at 11.5 per cent. For recent immigrant men, the unemployment rate was 10.3 per cent, and for comparable women, it was 13 per cent. Region seems to matter in this regard, with Quebec and Ontario having higher unemployment rates for recent immigrants than Manitoba and Alberta. Census data from 2006 show an unemployment rate of 6.2 per cent for those who did not identify as a visible minority and an unemployment rate of 8.6 per cent for those who did (Statistics Canada 2008f). Among the Aboriginal population in Canada, unemployment is endemic. The rate of unemployment for Aboriginals living on reserves was 37.7 per cent in 2001 (Statistics Canada 2006a: 97). In 1996 almost one in four (24 per cent) of Aboriginal labour-force participants was unemployed, and the rate was even higher for young Aboriginal workers (32 per cent) and for Aboriginal men (35 per cent).

Finally, unemployment varies with the age of workers. In Box 9.3, Gaile McGregor provides a detailed assessment of this situation in Canada. In particular, she notes that in the 1990s the unemployment rate increased more dramatically for older workers (those aged 55–64) than for members of any other age group. Moreover,

Box 9.2 Immigrant Unemployment Most Acute in Quebec

By Tavia Grant

Newcomers are facing severe challenges finding work in Quebec, while they tend to gain employment much more easily in Manitoba and Alberta, a national study showed yesterday.

Immigrants throughout Canada struggle for work in the first decade after they arrive, especially in the first five years. But nowhere is the problem more acute than in Quebec, where they experience 'substantially' higher unemployment rates than Canadian-born people—regardless of how long they've been in the country, Statistics Canada said.

Statscan used immigration figures gathered last year from its labour-force survey to analyze the immigrant labour market, focusing on people from the ages of 25 to 54. The resulting study paints a contrasting picture of how immigrants fare from province to province.

Most immigrants who've lived in Canada for a decade or longer find jobs at the same rate as Canadian-born people as they become more integrated.

In Quebec, however, even established immigrants—those who have lived in Canada for 10 years or more—can't seem to find work. Their unemployment rate in the province was 9.2 per cent last year, compared with 6.3 per cent for Quebec at large.

Linguistic challenges may be one reason.

'There may be a greater linguistic mismatch, the French language skills to Quebec versus the English language skills to the rest of Canada,' said Morton Weinfeld, chairman of Canadian Ethnic Studies at McGill University in Montreal. He believes 'there is still a large number [of immigrants] to Quebec that speak either English or neither language . . . that fact alone could explain the weaker economic integration'.

Other reasons may be that many immigrants tend to attend school or stay home to take care of their families, the study suggested.

'Another factor that could explain higher unemployment rates among immigrants in Quebec could be related to the countries of birth of immigrants living in Quebec compared to other provinces,' the study states, adding that the topic will be discussed in a future report.

On the flipside, the jobless rate for established immigrants in Atlantic Canada was just 4.1 per cent—less than half the region's 8.9-per-cent rate.

By last year, most of Canada's immigrants came from Asia, particularly India and China. About a fifth of Canada's population is born outside the country, one of the highest proportions in the world.

Immigrants will take on an even greater importance in the years ahead as Canada copes with an aging population and looming labour shortages. If current rates continue, immigration could account for virtually all net labour-force growth by 2011, the report states.

First-generation immigrants may have growing pains in integrating into the Canadian work force, but the problem eases with the second generation, Dr Weinfeld pointed out.

'The real proof of the immigration and integration process is ultimately going to be with the children of immigrants, how they will be faring,' he said. 'Take a stroll through the campuses of Canada's major universities and research centres and institutes, particularly in the sciences and in commerce. See who's enrolled and who's graduating. Enough said.'

Over all, newcomers are much more likely to have a university education than Canadian-born residents, Statscan reported. Thirty-six per cent of working-age immigrants had at least a bachelor's degree, while among those born in Canada, the proportion was just 22 per cent.

The report also shows stark gender differences.

'Labour market outcomes were better for immigrant men than their female counterparts, and . . . young immigrant women in particular have struggled,' the analysts wrote.

Regardless of how long they'd been in Canada, immigrant women had higher unemployment rates than both immigrant men and Canadian-born women.

The unemployment rate for women who've been here for five years or less was 13 per cent last year, higher than 10.3 per cent among men in the same group and 4.6 per cent among Canadian-born women.

Immigrants are more likely to work in factories, professional and technical services and accommodation and food services.

Immigrants who've been in Canada for less than 10 years, meanwhile, have tough times establishing themselves here. Very recent arrivals have a jobless rate of 11.5 per cent, more than double the Canadian average of 4.9 per cent.

The need to adjust to a new life in Canada, earn credential recognition and be retrained are some reasons for the gap. Immigrants themselves say the most serious difficulties in entering the work force are a lack of Canadian experience, lack of recognition of their credentials and language barriers, Statscan says, citing a 2003 study.

Immigrants tend to find work fastest in Alberta, where a strong economy has created labour shortages, and Manitoba, which has a program that matches skilled workers to employment before they land.

Integration is so successful in Manitoba that even recent immigrants had higher employment rates than Canadian-born people in other provinces.

Ontario is still the largest provincial destination for immigrants, with British Columbia in second spot.

Among cities, Toronto, Vancouver and Montreal are home to most immigrants. In terms of jobs, newcomers tend to fare better in Toronto and Vancouver than in Montreal.

Unemployment Rates: Share of Immigrants in Population Aged 25–54, 2006

	Born in Canada	Immigrants Less Than 5 Years	Immigrants 5–10 Years
Nfld., Labrador, NB, PEI, NS (Atlantic)	8.9	*	*
Sask.	3.7	*	*
Que.	6.3	17.8	13.4
Man.	3.2	6.8	*
Alta.	2.6	5.8	4.7
BC	3.7	9.5	5.1
Ont.	4.4	11.0	7.0
Canada	4.9	11.5	7.3

*Data unreliable/unavailable
Source: Labour Force Survey.

between 1976 and 1998 the increase in unemployment rates for older workers was 30 per cent and 50 per cent for 55- to 59-year-olds and 60- to 64-year-olds respectively. However, older workers fared quite well compared to younger workers (aged 15–24), whose unemployment rate—higher to begin with—doubled during the same period (Krahn and Lowe 1998). In 1996, youth unemployment stood at about 12.6 per cent, whereas the unemployment rate for adults aged 55–64 was only 7 per cent, somewhat lower than the unemployment rate for the population as a whole. And by 2005 the youth unemployment rate had hardly changed (12.4 per cent) whereas the unemployment rate for those aged 55 and over had dropped to 5.1 per cent (Statistics Canada 2006a).

However, we must be cautious in interpreting these statistics. Indeed, it is highly likely that biases in definitions of 'unemployment' lead to an underestimation of the problem of unemployment among older people. Compared to younger workers, older workers are unemployed for longer periods of time (Statistics Canada 2004b), and ageist stereotypes often work against older workers in finding employment (McMullin and Berger, 2006). As McGregor points out, only 67 per cent of men and 45 per cent of women between the ages of 55 and 59 and 41 per cent of men and 22 per cent of women between the ages of 60 and 64 were employed in 1996. This—combined with overall increases in unemployment rates for older workers, the difficulty distinguishing between involuntary and voluntary retirement, and the rise in non-standard employment among this group—suggests that many older workers are having increasing difficulty in finding work.

Box 9.3 (Un)Employment in Later Life

It has become a commonplace that work has been transformed over the last decade. What is not so widely recognized is that the down side of this transformation has been disproportionately felt by older workers. Women continue to suffer more from discrimination, but men have been most impacted by recent structural changes. On the low end, they are overrepresented in the traditional primary and secondary industries which have been hardest hit by a changing global economy. On the high end, they are overrepresented in the mid-to-upper management levels which have been decimated by restructuring. The low average education of both genders, moreover, is a particular disadvantage given the increased premium on skills.

Older workers have also been disproportionately affected by the recent enormous burgeoning of contingent forms of work. (Almost 75 per cent of the jobs added to the economy in the nineties were non-standard types.) Between 1976 and 1998, the number of older workers in part-time jobs increased by more than 70 per cent, roughly one and one half times the rate of increase for all ages. Although some of this is a matter of choice, 15 to 20 per cent of the change in mode of participation is estimated to be involuntary. In 1993, 41 per cent of employed men and 27 per cent of employed women 45–69 who were working part-time would have preferred otherwise. The likelihood of self-employment also increases with age. Again some of this is elective, especially among better educated males. For the swelling number of women and blue-collar workers in the category, however, the shift is more likely to reflect a lack of viable alternatives. For involuntary contingent workers, the penalties may be considerable. The vast majority of jobs in this class are characterized by short tenure, irregular hours, low pay, no benefits, and a great deal of uncertainty.

If employment has changed for older workers in recent years, the unemployment picture has changed even more so. Members of this cohort used to be protected by their experience and seniority. In the late 1970s, only about 5 per cent of employed individuals 55–64 experienced a permanent layoff, the lowest proportion of any age group. By the mid-nineties, however, the risk of a permanent layoff among older workers had risen by two full percentage points, putting it above the risk for prime-aged individuals. How did this happen? Some of it may be attributed to restructuring, particularly the tendency to leaner, meaner workplaces. The big difference between the recession of the early eighties and the recession of the early nineties was that many of the jobs lost in the later period never came back. Some of it may be attributed to the cohort disadvantages mentioned previously. Whatever the causes, the result was that the unemployment rate increased more for older workers over the nineties than for any other age group. In 1994, the percentage of unemployed in the 55–64 category jumped by 2.1 per cent, compared with an increase of 1.3 per cent for 15- to 24-year-olds and 1.7 per cent–1.8 per cent for all other cohorts. From a broader vantage, between 1976 and 1998, the relative unemployment rates of workers aged 55 to 59 increased by 50 per cent, that of those aged 60–64 by 30. But even this underrepresents the problem. Increases notwithstanding, compared with, say, 15- to 24-year-olds, strictly on the numbers older workers still seem to be doing fairly well. If one looks at those who are 'not working' rather than limiting one's purview to those who are technically unemployed, though, the figures swell enormously. In 1996, employment rates for Canadian men 55–9 and 60–4 were only 67 per cent and 41 per cent respectively. Comparable figures for women were 45 per cent and 22 per cent.

At the same time as the likelihood of unemployment has been increasing for older workers, the likelihood of re-employment has been plummeting. While the rising job risk factors are not to be sneezed at, the real problem for the cohort is that the duration of unemployment increases with age. Duration for men 45+ rose from 18 weeks in 1976 to 32 in 1985 to 35 in 1994, compared with 17 weeks for men 15–24. Duration for women has traditionally been lower than for men, but has been increasing at a faster rate. According to one government report, between 1984–6 and 1994–6 women's average jobless spells lengthened from 3.7 to 4.1 months, an increase of over 10 per cent. Duration rates for all older workers rose by 67 per cent between 1976 and 1998, compared with a 47 per cent increase for all ages. In 1998, the incidence of long-term unemployment among older workers was twice that in the labour market as a whole. In 1993, approximately 25 per cent of men and 17 per cent of women 45+ who were unemployed had been so for more than a year. This compares with 16 per cent of unemployed men and 12 per cent of unemployed women aged 15–24. To put these data in perspective, it is important to realize that high duration means more than simply a prolongation of misery. Studies show that the longer a person is jobless, the lower the probability that s/he will find work at all. More than a statistical artifact, this effect—called 'scarring'—has been related to the depreciation of human capital over the jobless spell and the stigmatization of the long-term unemployed in the eyes of employers.

Source: McGregor (2001: 5–11).

Income and Poverty

The wage-exchange relationship is a crucial process of distribution in capitalism (see the centre of the coalescence framework, Figure 7.3, page 128) and one that is intimately linked to production processes. Workers exchange their labour power for a wage that equals less than the market value of what they produce. The **surplus value** that is created in this exchange produces a profit for the owners of capital. As a result, there is a strong correlation between social class and income. Working-class jobs pay less than middle-class jobs, and owners of capital tend to have higher incomes than others (Krahn, Lowe, and Hughes 2007). For instance, in 2000, average annual earnings in Canada for dentists ($108,034), lawyers ($94,731), and managers ($61,412 in 2004) were much higher than were the average annual earnings for cashiers ($10,051), hotel clerks ($15,937), and hairstylists ($17,390) (Krahn, Lowe, and Hughes 2007: 109). These earnings stand in stark contrast to the incomes of the chief executive officers (CEOs) of large companies. In 2004, the average compensation package for the CEOs of 160 Canadian companies listed on the Toronto Stock Exchange was $5.5 million (Krahn, Lowe, and Hughes 2007: 111). However, a strong correlation between social class and income does not mean that it is a perfect correlation.

There are certain jobs that, on the basis of the above definitions of social class, would be considered working-class jobs even though they command a relatively high wage. For example, traditionally, assembly-line workers in any of the 'big three' auto-manufacturing plants, although part of the working class, were paid a relatively good wage and had good benefits because they were members of a relatively strong union. However, as Box 9.4 shows, with the rise in globalization, steep economic recessions, free trade agreements, and the like, such well-paid working-class jobs seem to be on the decline.

From the income figures listed above we can see clearly that owners of capital and executives have much higher incomes than workers. The question that remains is whether there has been an increasing polarization of income over time. One way to answer this question is to divide

Box 9.4 Manufacturing Slump Deepens: Auto Sector May Merely Be Canary in Mine to Troubled Economy in Ontario

By Nicolas Van Praet

Last spring, a local labour leader with the Canadian Auto Workers union had an impromptu meeting with Stephen Harper, the Prime Minister, at a Royal Canadian Legion branch in Kitchener-Waterloo, Ont.

Mr Harper, the union official says, told him that unemployed manufacturing workers in the area, more than 8,000 of whom have lost their jobs in the past two years, should look to Alberta to find employment.

Whether you agree with that advice or not, this past week laid bare the plain reality for Ontario and its main industry, car-making: A worsening slowdown in the US economy is smacking Canada's most populous province hard. And a loonie still flying level with the US dollar will force a shakeout in its industrial base the likes of which it has perhaps never seen.

'My most significant worry is with respect to my home province,' Jim Flaherty, the Minister of Finance, told reporters in Toronto yesterday, insisting the country as a whole will weather the storm swelling up in the United States. 'There's a danger Ontario's economy will slow down more dramatically than elsewhere in Canada.'

The latest evidence of that came just moments earlier, when Statistics Canada reported the country's manufacturing sales tanked in December to their lowest level in three years, largely due to a 25 per cent collapse in auto shipments.

About 85 per cent of passenger vehicles and parts built in Canada are sent to the United States and auto plants here experienced longer-than-normal shutdowns around Christmas to retool and adjust their inventories.

Manufacturing sales dropped 3.4 per cent to $48.6-billion for the month, the biggest decline since August, 2003, when a widespread electrical blackout and its fallout hurt Ontario's industrial output, Statistics Canada said. Overall manufacturing activity nationwide has decreased in four of the past five months.

'Things are getting ugly for Canadian manufacturers,' said Douglas Porter, deputy chief economist for BMO Capital Markets. 'This is a very weak report, providing a crystal clear view of where the US slowdown is really biting into Canadian activity.'

Most provinces will see slower growth this year than last, but Ontario and Quebec will face the brunt of the weakness as higher energy costs, a strong Canadian dollar, and a likely US recession drag GDP growth there below 1 per cent, Mr Porter predicted.

'Challenges facing the Canadian manufacturing sector are likely to get even more intense as pressure increases from the sagging US economy,' said Dina Cover, economist at TD Bank Financial Group. 'The slowdown in the North American auto industry in particular will hit Ontario hard.'

The Statistics Canada numbers capped a sobering week for the auto sector. On Tuesday, General Motors Corp., Canada's biggest exporter by sales, said the strength of the loonie against the US dollar ripped $300US-million from its bottom line last year as the cost of doing business in Canada went up. On Thursday, Statistics Canada said that Canada's 2007 auto-trade balance swung to its worst deficit since 1979, proof the industry is shrinking fast and needs help, CAW said.

Ontario's job market, which shed 55,000 manufacturing positions last year, is now losing lustre compared to the rest of Canada, BMO said yesterday. The jobless rate, at 6.3 per cent, crossed above the national average for the first time on record in 2007. And it should weaken further this year, the bank said.

Ontario's economic growth has been the most correlated of all provinces to the United States since the early 1980s, according to BMO. And what's happening further south is being closely watched from Windsor to Timmins.

New vehicle sales in the United States this year are expected to bottom to lows not seen in a decade as Americans spend less. Detroit's automakers and their suppliers have announced job cuts in Canada in recent weeks as they adjust to demand. They have promised further capacity cuts if the market worsens.

But it's not only the auto industry being hurt. Manufacturers of nonmetallic mineral products, including companies that make cement, concrete and glass, reported a 12.4 per cent decline in sales in December, to $1.1-billion, evidence the slowdown in the US construction sector is hitting home.

The housing slump contributed to widespread decreases in wood-product deliveries. Sales fell 8.3 per cent to $1.9-billion in December, the lowest level in almost 12 years.

'No matter where you look now, the negative forces are gathering against the US consumer,' BMO senior economist Michael Gregory said in a note. 'Deflating home prices, tightening credit conditions, falling equity prices, rising food prices, escalating energy costs, and, perhaps most profoundly, weakening job growth.' Average job growth in the United States during the past seven months has slowed to a pace that, looking back at history, heralded the past six recessions, he said.

If fewer new jobs means fewer new cars and new homes, Ontario's real pain may have just begun.

Source: Van Praet (2008).

Canadians into equal groups (either deciles or quintiles) on the basis of their income, calculate the proportion of the total income in Canada that each group receives, and then examine whether that proportion has changed. In 1999, 45.3 per cent of all before-tax income was concentrated in the top quintile of the Canadian population, 24.3 per cent in the fourth quintile, 16.1 per cent in the third (middle) quintile, 10 per cent in the second quintile, and only 4.4 per cent in the lowest quintile. Between 1951 and 1999, there was a 3-percentage-point shift from the second and third quintiles to the two highest quintiles, while the proportion of income concentrated in the lowest quintile remained relatively stable. Moreover, between 1981 and 1999, the second, third, and fourth quintiles lost 3.6 per cent of their before-tax income—a total of $15 billion—to the upper quintile (Urmetzer and Guppy 2004: 78). By 2003, families in the highest income quintile earned, on average, $12.90 of before-tax earnings for every $1.00 earned by families in the lowest-income quintile. Between

1996 and 2002, the gap in after-tax income grew by 23 per cent between the richest and poorest families in Canada and then remained stable between 2002 and 2003, at $96,600 (Statistics Canada 2005c). All told, these figures support the idea that there is increasing polarization of income in Canada.

It should be noted that the proportion of total before-tax income that is concentrated in the lowest quintile has remained relatively stable since 1951. What these figures do not tell us is that this stability has been maintained largely through government transfers such as tax credits, social assistance, and unemployment insurance. Indeed, for low-income families, the proportion of their total income that comes from labour-market earnings has declined since the 1970s (Picot and Myles 1995; Statistics Canada 2005c). Hence, income polarization is not as serious as it could be because government policies ensure more equitable income distributions in Canada (Ross, Shillington, and Lochhead 1994). But how equitable is a system in which

Table 9.1: Earnings of Women Employed Full-Time, Full-Year, in Dollars and as a Percentage of Those of Men, by Province, 2001

	Women	Men	Women's Earnings as a Percentage of Those of Men
Newfoundland and Labrador	$26,391	$41,059	64.3
Prince Edward Island	$27,444	$31,806	86.3
Nova Scotia	$28,822	$40,155	71.8
New Brunswick	$28,668	$39,702	72.2
Quebec	$34,973	$44,917	77.9
Ontario	$38,212	$54,223	70.5
Manitoba	$30,579	$38,669	79.1
Saskatchewan	$30,157	$41,548	72.6
Alberta	$33,618	$53,319	63.1
British Columbia	$34,095	$48,025	71.0
Canada	$35,258	$49,250	71.6

Source: Statistics Canada, 'Status of Women, Canada', http://www.swc-cfc.gc.ca/pubs/women_men_2003/women_men_2003_8_e.html, accessed 2008.

the lowest quintile receives only 4.6 per cent of all before-tax income? And how equitable is a system in which the $15 billion gain made in the upper quintile during the 1980s and 1990s is equivalent to the amount of money it would take to eliminate poverty in Canada (Osberg 1992, cited in Urmetzer and Guppy 2004)?

Historically, women's wages have been less than men's wages. In 1931 the average wage for employed women in Canada was 60 per cent that of an employed man's average wage. By 1997, women, on average, earned 63.8 per cent of the average employed man's salary (Phillips and Phillips 2000). Obviously, some of the variation between women's and men's incomes exists because more women (27.7 per cent) than men (10.2 per cent) work part-time (Beaujot 2000, using 1996 data). Yet even among full-year, full-time workers, women earned only about 71.6 per cent as much as men in 2001 (Statistics Canada 2003b). Interesting variations across provinces are evident in Table 9.1, with fully employed women earning only 63.1 per cent of men in Alberta compared with 86 per cent in Prince Edward Island.

One reason women earn less than men is that they are disproportionately employed in low-paid occupations and industries and in occupations and industries that are considered to require little **skill**. But even in the 10 most highly paid occupations—occupations that are disproportionately held by men—women earn less than their male counterparts. For instance, as Table 9.2 shows, women make up 24.1 per cent of the total employment among judges and earn an average of 90.2 per cent of what their male counterparts do. Among senior managers in the goods-producing industrial sector, women account for 11.6 per cent of the total employment and earn an average of only 62.2 per cent of the average male salary.

Wages are also linked to gendered processes of reproduction. Among full-time, full-year workers, parental status influences the personal incomes of both men and women but in different ways. Looking at Figure 9.3, we see that

Table 9.2 Ten Highest-Paid Occupations by Sex, 2000

	Women as % of Total Employment	Female/Male Income Ratio
Judges	24.1	90.2
Physicians—specialists	30.8	61.2
Physicians—general practitioners	30.8	72.5
Senior Managers—financial, communications carriers, other business services	21.5	63.9
Dentists	23.0	63.7
Lawyers and Quebec notaries	31.0	67.4
Senior Managers—goods production, utilities, transportation, and construction	11.6	62.2
Information systems and data processing managers	25.1	83.5
Senior Managers—trade, broadcasting, other services, n.e.c.	17.8	61.9
School principals and administrators of elementary and secondary education	45.5	90.7

Source: Adapted from Krahn, Lowe, and Hughes (2007: 192), Statistics Canada data.

younger mothers with children at home have lower incomes than other women or than fathers who have children at home. The difference between the groups of women is greatest between the ages of 25 and 44. On the other hand, when compared to the average income of men without children at home, the income of fathers with children at home is higher regardless of age. If we compare fathers and mothers who have children at home, the income difference increases in each age group and is greatest among 45- to 54-year-olds (a $19,793 difference) and 55- to 64-year-olds (a $21,001 difference). Hence, the responsibilities women have for raising children seem to have a long-lasting effect on income inequality (McMullin and Ballantyne 1995). This extends into old age, in part because lifelong pension contributions among women tend to be lower than among men.

Wages and income also vary with ethnicity and race (see Beaujot and Kerr 2003). Table 9.3 outlines the average incomes of various ethnic groups in Canada in 2000. The Jewish ethnic group has the highest average income ($42,668), followed by those of Scottish ethnicity. Of particular note is the concentration of 'visible minority' groups below the national income average and the fact that Aboriginal people have the lowest average incomes ($15,753). Indeed, on average, workers of colour earn 16.3 per cent less than all other workers. Among men, workers of colour earn 17 per cent less than all other workers. The difference is smaller for women, with workers of colour earning 12 per cent less than all other workers (A. Jackson 2002). And the income disadvantages for racialized persons remain when education and other social variables are taken into account (Lian and Matthews 1998). As is the case for women, occupational and industrial segregation of particular ethnic and visible minority groups accounts for much of the ethnic and racial variation in income.

Much of the research on the relationship between income and ethnic and racial minority groups has focused on poverty. If individuals

Figure 9.3: Earnings of Persons Working Full-Time,a by Family Characteristics, 2000

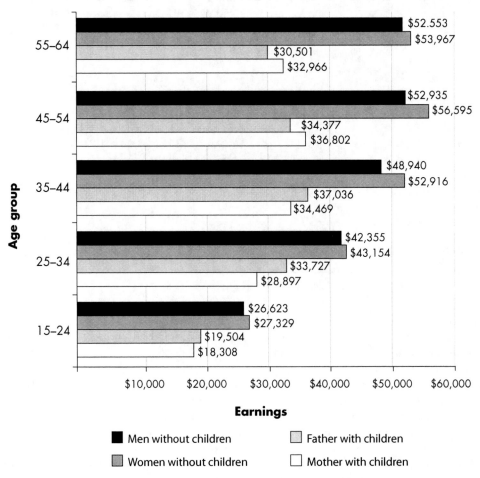

a Women and men in marriages or common-law unions, or lone parent;
full-time: working for 49–52 weeks

a Women and men in marriages or common-law unions, or lone parent; full-time: working for 49–52 weeks
Source: Statistics Canada, 2001 Census, public use data.

have tenuous ties to labour markets or if they are employed in bad jobs, poverty often results. Poverty is a serious social problem in Canada. The National Council of Welfare (2006) reports that although poverty rates declined between 1996 and 2001 there was still a higher poverty rate in 2001 (15.5 per cent) than there was in 1989 (14 per cent). Approximately 16 per cent of Canadians were poor in 2003; poverty rates are about 12 per cent for families and about 38 per cent for unattached individuals.

As a group, Aboriginal people in Canada suffer extreme financial deprivation and hardship and have higher rates of poverty (43.4 per cent)

Table 9.3 Average Total Income[a] of Single Ethnic Groups,[b] Canada, 2000

	Average Total Income ($)		Average Total Income ($)
Scottish	34,194	Portuguese	25,270
Other British	34,116	East and Southeast Asian	25,216
Irish	33,293	Greek	25,021
English	31,484	Provincial origins[c]	24,209
Dutch/Netherlands	31,364	East Indian	24,155
Northern European	30,931	Southern European	23,916
Western European	30,589	Jamaican	23,433
Ukrainian	29,915	Caribbean	22,791
Italian	29,906	Filipino	22,524
Other European	29,796	Chinese	22,265
Other single origins	29,778	Lebanese	22,067
German	29,351	Vietnamese	21,700
French	28,970	Arab	20,790
Eastern European	28,628	West Asian	19,125
Hungarian/Magyar	28,590	Latin, Central, and South American	18,833
Polish	28,547	African	18,699
Balkan	27,379	South Asian	18,022
National average	**27,418**	Korean	16,728
Canadian	25,596	Aboriginal	15,753

a Total income includes income from all sources.
b Individuals who reported only one ethnicity.
c Individuals who list a province (such as Quebec) as their ethnicity.
Source: Statistics Canada, 2001 Census, Public Use Microdata File, Individuals File (2.7 per cent sample).

Table 9.4 Comparison of Conditions in Best-Off Aboriginal Communities and Poorest Non-Aboriginal Regions

	Best-Off Aboriginal Communities	Worst-Off Non-Aboriginal Regions
With less than Grade 9[a]	12%	20%
Employed	58%	57%
Number of persons per room	0.7	0.6
Average annual income	$18,200	$18,900
Speaking Aboriginal language at home	2%	n/a
Under 18 years	36%	25%

a As percentage of population aged 20 to 64.
Source: Statistics Canada, 1996 Census of Population. Reproduced in R. Armstrong (1999: 17). Catalogue 11-008.

than non-Aboriginal people in Canada (19.3 per cent) (Ross, Scott, and Smith 2000). According to one study, 54 per cent of Aboriginal Canadians earned less than $10,000 per year, compared to 35 per cent of all Canadians (R. Armstrong 1999). Table 9.4 shows that the 'best-off' First Nations communities in Canada are more disadvantaged than the 'worst-off' non-Aboriginal areas and demonstrates that the most advantaged First Nations communities are still significantly disadvantaged when compared to the least advantaged non-Aboriginal communities (R. Armstrong 1999: 17).

Racialized persons are more likely to live in poverty and to have a longer duration of poverty than other Canadians (A. Jackson 2002). Compared to the total Canadian population (29.5 per cent), higher proportions of visible minority immigrants (42.5 per cent) and Aboriginal persons living off reserves (49.4 per cent) lived in poverty for at least one year between 1993 and 1998. Furthermore, members of visible minority groups and Aboriginal persons are more liable to be poor for two years or more (A. Jackson 2002; Ross, Scott, and Smith 2000).

There are significant regional variations in poverty rates in Canada. In 2003, British Columbia had the highest poverty rate (20.1 per cent), followed by Newfoundland and Labrador (17.3 per cent) and Manitoba (16.9 per cent). Prince Edward Island had the lowest poverty rate (11.8 per cent). Provincial variations in poverty rates are a result of regional differences in economic structures, provincial inconsistencies in government policies regarding social welfare transfers, and differential access to other social and economic resources (National Council of Welfare 2006).

Poverty rates also vary on the basis of gender, age, education, and labour-force attachment. For instance, in 2003 the poverty rate for single-parent mothers was 48.9 per cent, more than four times the poverty rate of all families. Unattached women under the age of 65 are more likely to be

poor than are their male counterparts (42.8 per cent versus 34.4 per cent respectively) as are unattached women who are 65 and over (40.9 per cent compared to 31.6 per cent). Compared to all Canadians (16 per cent), children are somewhat more likely to be poor (17.6 per cent). Gainful employment significantly reduces poverty rates among both unattached individuals and families; yet the poverty rate, which was 6.2 per cent for families with two earners, was higher for families with one earner, at 25.2 per cent. Finally, families in which the major earner is a woman are more likely to be living in poverty than are families in which the major earner is a man. This is true even when education level is held constant (National Council of Welfare 2006). Evidence also suggests that single mothers, older adults (especially women), young people (ages 15–24), children (especially under age 6), and those with less than a high school education experienced durations of poverty that lasted two years or more (Ross, Scott, and Smith 2000).

The fact that rates of poverty are higher and that poverty lasts longer among young people, children, and older adults suggests that there is a significant relationship between income and age. Table 9.5 shows the average 'real' earnings for men and women of 'working age' in 1998, along with the percentage change in real earnings between 1993 and 1998. For both men and women, average earnings were larger in each successive age group until they peaked in the 45–54 age group. Although the average income difference for men between the ages of 45 and 54 compared with men between the ages of 55 and 64 ($13,543) was about $2,793 more than it is for same-aged women ($10,750), the proportional decline was greater for women (40.8 per cent) than for men (13.2 per cent). Average earnings are lowest among the 17–24 age group, largely as a result of voluntary part-time work and minimum-wage legislation that allows employers to pay teenagers under the age of 18 less than those over the age of 18. Beyond the

Table 9.5 Earnings, 1998, and 1993–98 Percentage Change in Real Annual Earnings by Sex and Age

Age	Men		Women	
	Earnings, 1998	Change, 1993–1998	Earnings, 1998	Change, 1993–1998
17–24	$9,790	14.0%	$7,134	–3.2%
25–34	$29,203	32.5%	$17,768	12.7%
35–44	$36,868	28.8%	$20,241	11.9%
45–54	$38,281	19.2%	$19,969	5.3%
55–64	$24,738	–13.2%	$9,219	–40.8%

Source: Statistics Canada, Survey of Consumer Finances, 1998.

youngest and oldest age groups, women and men made gains in average real earnings since 1993 but the gains for women were proportionally smaller than the gains for men.

In the 25–54 age group, younger men earned on average 76 per cent (ages 25–34) and 96 per cent (ages 35–44) of the average income of men aged 45–54. For women, the experience gradient is not as large. Younger women, on average, earned 89 per cent (ages 25–34) and 101 per cent (ages 35–44) of the average income among older women (ages 45–54).

Although not shown in Table 9.5, average incomes of both men and women aged 65 and over are lower than they are for working-age Canadians, largely because of retirement. In 2005, adults aged 65 and over had average incomes of about $30,000. This compares with an average income of about $38,299 for persons in the 25–34 and 55–64 age groups and with an average income of $44,795 among those aged 35–54 (Statistics Canada 2006 Census tables: Presence of Income (9), Age Groups (5A) and Sex (3) for the Population 15 Years and Over of Canada, Provinces, Territories, Census Metropolitan Areas and Census Agglomerations 2005—20 per cent sample data). In the United States, the risk of experiencing poverty in later life is greatest for racialized women, unmarried women, and racialized men (Hardy and Hazelrigg 1995). Although research on the intersection of race and age is limited in Canada, evidence regarding the income disadvantages and poverty faced by older Aboriginal Canadians (Gyimah, White, and Maxim 2004) suggests that similar racial and age trends exist in Canada as well.

Alienation and Skill

Recall that Marx's third prediction with respect to the polarization of classes was that as capitalism developed, jobs would become increasingly deskilled and alienated. Indeed, skill and alienation are both characteristics of paid work that vary with social class. Generally, working-class jobs are characterized by low levels of skill required to do the job and often by corresponding high levels of alienation, whereas jobs held by those in the new middle class and the old middle class tend to require more skill and to be more intrinsically rewarding. Therefore, for Marx's prediction to be supported, we must see evidence that middle-class jobs have become increasingly deskilled.

In 1974, Harry Braverman wrote his classic book *Labor and Monopoly Capitalism*. Taking issue with those who argued that rising white-collar employment was a positive effect of post-industrialism that resulted in an increasingly large middle class, Braverman convincingly argued that most white-collar jobs (e.g., clerical and retail jobs) should be considered working class, not middle class. White-collar jobs, Braverman argued, were increasingly being deskilled and organized according to scientific management techniques that eliminated most of the control and autonomy that workers may have previously had over their work. Advances in new technologies contributed to this process by giving managers sophisticated tools with which they could monitor their employees' work. Before computerized cash registers, for example, cashiers needed to know how to make change. Now cash registers tell the cashier how much change to give the customer. Furthermore, cash registers can now monitor the speed of keystrokes and the number of customers a cashier serves per minute. Managers use this information to evaluate their employees' job performance. Hence, new technology has been used both to deskill the work process and to monitor and control it.

One year before Braverman published his book, Daniel Bell published what was to become an influential text on post-industrial society, *The Coming of Post-industrial Society*. Unlike Braverman, who argued that occupations were becoming increasingly deskilled, Bell (1973) looked to the future and argued that knowledge, and hence skill, would become a highly valued commodity in post-industrial society. Knowledge would be a basis of power much as the ownership of property had traditionally been, and knowledge workers would form a significant class (both in number and in power) in their own right. Bell argued that as the proportion of knowledge workers grew, the historical trend toward the polarization of society into two central classes—the bourgeoisie and the proletariat—would lose speed.

In the 30 years since Bell and Braverman published their books, debates have ensued over which thesis better explains the relationship between skill and class structure in post-industrial society. Although such debates are far from resolved, Clement and Myles are worth quoting at length on the issue:

We face either a postindustrial Nirvana of knowledge where everyone will be a brain surgeon, artist, or philosopher (Bell) or, alternatively, a post-industrial Hades where we shall be doomed to labour mindlessly in the service of capital (Braverman). When drawn in these terms, the historical debate is now no debate at all. Bell is the clear winner. Although much less than a knowledge revolution the net result of the shift to services has been to increase the requirements for people to think on the job. (Clement and Myles 1994: 72)

Furthermore, Clement and Myles point out that the growth in the services sector has brought both skilled and unskilled jobs, but they underscore the fact that, at least in Canada and the United States, unskilled service jobs are often entry jobs for new and younger workers rather than a basis for working-class formation. This—combined with the fact that these service jobs are now often exit jobs for older workers who have been displaced, discouraged, restructured, or forced to retire early—suggests that age may play a more significant role in labour-market inequality in the years to come. It is no coincidence that during the market restructuring of the 1980s and 1990s we began to see older workers greeting us in department stores or serving us in fast-food chains. As one older worker who lost his job as a computer programmer put it, 'I can't find work. But, I'm not destitute yet so I don't need to sell running shoes and make 1/8 of the salary I was making before—like my friend is doing' (personal correspondence, January 2003).

In short, although the conditions of work in contemporary Canadian capitalism are far from ideal, the proletarianization of the labour force as predicted by Braverman has not occurred, even though skilled jobs are concentrated in the new middle and executive classes (Clement and Myles 1994). However, most of the literature on the deskilling debate has focused on class. More work must be done to consider whether and how jobs that are usually held by women or by members of racial and ethnic-minority groups have been disproportionately deskilled. This requires critically examining the concept of skill itself and recognizing that gendered and racialized perceptions of skill have been driving these debates. Furthermore, when jobs are the unit of analysis (as is the case in this literature), important information regarding the 'skill mobility' of individuals over their life courses is missed.

Explaining Inequality in Paid Work

The preceding discussion shows that class, age, gender, race, and ethnicity structure the outcomes of inequality derived from paid work. And yet we know very little about how all of these structures work together in producing and reproducing market-based inequality. This points to the complexities associated with considering simultaneously all of these intersecting structures in analyses of paid work.

Labour-market segmentation perspectives help to explain many of the relative disadvantages that women, visible minorities, immigrants, ethnic minorities, and younger and older employees experience in paid work. According to these perspectives, good and bad jobs are located in different labour markets, the processes through which people get these jobs are different, there is little movement between these labour markets, and segregation within labour markets occurs on the basis of gender, race, ethnicity, and age. Bad jobs tend to be located in secondary labour markets and good jobs in primary labour markets.

The dual-economy perspective is one of many models of labour-market segmentation. It posits that there are a core sector and a periphery sector in the economy. The core sector comprises large companies that face little competition for their product. These firms 'exert considerable control over suppliers and markets and are also able to manipulate their political environment' (Krahn, Lowe, and Hughes 2007: 134). Examples of such companies are banks, telecommunication companies, automobile manufacturers, and airlines. The periphery sector of the economy, on the other hand, is dominated by smaller firms that are highly competitive with one another, are less profitable than firms in the core sector, have less political and economic power, and have lower rates of unionization. Examples of such companies are small manufacturing companies, retail outlets, and small hospitality firms. Jobs in this sector tend not to require as much skill or education as those in the core sector (Krahn, Lowe, and Hughes 2007: 135–6). According to this perspective, the reason women, people of colour, immigrants, ethnic minorities, and younger and older employees encounter labour-market disadvantages is that they are segregated in the periphery sector of the economy.

Unlike labour-market segmentation theories, which emphasize the structure of labour markets in explaining inequality, human-capital explanations of labour-market-based inequality suggest that individuals are sorted into good jobs and bad jobs on the basis of individual skill, education, and experience. Hence, those who invest more in these things will reap greater labour-market rewards, especially higher incomes. We cannot dismiss human-capital explanations, for better education does lead to better jobs and better incomes regardless of gender, age (if we consider only prime working ages), ethnicity, and race. And yet a crucial theoretical difficulty with human-capital explanations of labour-market-based inequality is that they assume that there is free and open competition for good jobs and that everyone is on a level playing field when it comes to their ability to invest in or use their education. However, research shows that racialized persons have lower returns on educational investments and that racism exists in labour markets (Kazemipur and Halli 2001; Li 2001b; Li and Dong 2007; Nakhaie 2006). A crucial methodological difficulty with human-capital approaches is that the complex multi-variate models used in assessing labour-market outcomes control for many variables but do not explain structural disadvantage.

The problem with human-capital explanations is that they often conclude that one factor accounts for more of (to give one example) the variation in income than another factor, all else being equal. The results of these models may suggest that a given bivariate relationship—between, for example, ethnicity and income—can be explained away by human-capital variables such as education, language, and experience. This then leads to the conclusion that human-capital variables account for differences in income and that ethnicity does not. Of course, what is missing in such conclusions is the fact that there are structural barriers that preclude certain ethnic and visible minority groups from attaining the human capital required for high incomes. All else is *not* equal, and adequate explanations of inequality must take that into account.

Structural barriers to good jobs and good wages feed on the logic of capitalism and its related assumptions about productive work, and they negatively affect labour-market outcomes for the working class, women, older and younger workers, particular ethnic groups, visible minorities, and Aboriginal people. As a result, all else is not equal for persons over the age of 65, who could be excluded from 'productive' life as a result of mandatory retirement. All else is not equal for 16-year-olds, who earn less than 18-year-olds doing the same job because of age-based minimum wages. All else is not equal for racialized persons, who face discrimination and racism in paid work and, before that, sub-standard education. And all else is not equal for women. Indeed, a second assumption under capitalism (and in human-capital theory) is that productivity increases with experience and that

workers with more experience should therefore be paid higher wages. Yet experience is defined narrowly, and the skills and experience that are learned in 'non-productive' activities, such as raising children, are not considered transferable to the realm of paid work. Furthermore, as Gillian Ranson's (2003) work on engineers shows, the combination of gender-minority status and lack of seniority makes it difficult for young women to challenge masculinist work cultures and career paths. Such difficulties are especially problematic in light of the fact that among computer professionals, women earn significantly less than men (Dryburgh 2000; see also Gunderson, Jacobs, and Vaillancourt 2005: 110).

The organization of production processes does not stand in isolation from the organization of distributive and reproductive processes. For instance, some argue that because women 'choose' to work part-time, only data that compare income differences between full-year, full-time male and female employees should be considered. Yet for many women part-time work is involuntary and for others the choice to work part-time is conditioned by the ways in which class and gender relations structure the intersecting processes of production and reproduction.

Indeed, 'choice' is a complex word in sociology. Some women choose not to work for pay because they believe that it is better for their children to have one parent at home when they are young. The one parent who stays at home is usually a mother, in part because mothers are most often employed in jobs that pay less than fathers. Furthermore, this is often an easy choice for women because the jobs that they are employed in tend not to be 'good' jobs. From a particular family's point of view, this 'choice' makes sense. Yet the choice is structured by gendered labour markets that pay women less and that employ them in jobs that are more alienating and less autonomous than the jobs that are more often held by men. Of course, this argument does not hold up well for working-class families. Indeed, family 'choices' are structured by both the nature of jobs held by mothers and fathers within families and by gendered ideologies that suggest that women are better caregivers than men.

The most obvious link between distributive and productive processes is through the wage (see 'Income and Poverty' earlier in this chapter). For people who have tenuous relationships to labour markets or earn very little, state-based mechanisms of distribution help to alleviate some of the financial strain such individuals face. Welfare policy, employment insurance, maternity and parental leave, old age security, and publicly managed pension schemes are examples of state-based forms of distribution. These policies will be discussed in greater detail in chapter 12.

Beyond Statistics: Agency and Experience in Paid Work

It is clear that gender, class, age, ethnicity, and race are structural barriers to securing good, well-paid employment in Canada. But how do the choices that people make intersect with these structures in creating systems of advantage and disadvantage? How do women, the working class, older and younger workers, and racialized people experience the 'isms' that infiltrate paid work? Helen Ralston's (1996) study of immigrant women in Atlantic Canada demonstrates how racialized women experience the double-edged sword of diminished labour-market returns on their education combined with public re-employment policies that are not targeted to those who have university educations. In the words of one of Ralston's (1996: 87) informants,

> If you want to go to a programme in Manpower and Immigration, if you have a degree they are not even going to look at you. They say you have a degree. But you take that degree and go for a job and they say, 'Oh, we don't

know this degree. We won't hire you.' They won't say it in so many words, but that's the implication. So I think you lose on both ends.

Once employed, subtle and overt racism, sexism, and ageism are often experienced at work (Das Gupta 2002; McMullin and Marshall 2001).

Within the structures of class, age, gender, race, and ethnicity, people make choices about the paid work that they will do. In making these choices people often conform to structural expectations about what kind of work they should do. Women work as nurses; men work as engineers. When people resist social structures and make choices of paid work that goes against the grain, they are often required to conform to established structures and to the middle-class white male way of life. This process is illustrated through Luis M. Aguiar's choices and experiences and the difficulties he faced in becoming a professor of sociology at Okanagan University College in Kelowna, British Columbia (see Box 9.5).

Conclusion

As noted in the introduction to this chapter, some sociologists argue that the elimination of capitalism and a reorganization of work is needed in order to reduce or eliminate the 'tyranny of work' (Rinehart 2006). Although theoretically and philosophically this argument makes sense, the practicalities of revolutionizing capitalism in such a way are elusive. Nonetheless, within capitalism there are ways in which work could be organized that would make the experience of it better for many. On the basis of the discussion in this chapter, obvious places to start are eliminating systemic, statistical, and other forms of discrimination; increasing wages; and reorganizing work so that it is more meaningful and autonomous. Although such changes would not require the elimination of capitalism, they would require a radical shift in logic and a commitment on the

Box 9.5 Building an Academic Career

The concept of 'career' is a central part of academic life. People build their careers, change their careers, and sometimes destroy their careers by some scandal or dishonest undertaking. In addition, people participate in shaping (or not) the careers of others. Most students know the importance of a career and the need to train for it. In graduate schools students spend most of their time 'building' their careers. They take courses with specific outlines and deadlines and receive official grades that are recorded in their files in the department and the school of graduate studies. They teach courses under the supervision of faculty members, write scholarship applications with the support of a faculty member, and undergo a long period of mentoring and disciplining within the department and faculty. With many students in a department at the same time, it behooves each of them to make him/herself visible. Visibility counts when it comes to all the intangibles available in a university—for example, excellent letters of recommendation, invitations to conferences and special events and to publish, and, in some case, offers of course directorships.

But career has a class component that is often ignored. It is a foreign concept to working-class students of immigrant backgrounds. For me, the cultural capital that would communicate the importance of career was never part of my upbringing. As I grew up, my parents spoke of jobs—how to find and keep them. My father would usually go to the *canto* and wait there to be approached by a landowner, or his helping hand, to discuss the work, wages, and period of employment. '*O canto*' was the visual expression of the labour market where we lived: in a specific area of the town men advertised their willingness to work (simply by being there), and employers sought out labour power to hire. According to my father and my brother (who experienced it as a teenager for a couple of years), they had to get to the *canto* at the break of dawn in order to be able, just possibly, to select which employer to leave with. Sometimes they were lucky and were employed by the same landowners for consecutive weeks. In such cases the family was assured a steady income. More commonly, however, the men had to make daily trips to the *canto* in search of work.

I believe my father or mother never did mention the concept of career to me. The foreign nature of this concept was compounded in the new country as Portuguese immigrants joined the secondary labour market. In Montreal my father got work as a dishwasher, first at Dorval Airport and later in the Meridien Hotel, with no mention of a 'career'. It was not until I was in university that I learned that *careira* was the Portuguese equivalent.

This lack of awareness of the culture of academia was itself compounded by the relationships developed in graduate school. At York University, experiences of being the 'other', in terms of both class and ethnicity, persisted even though I had already survived McMaster University. Indeed, my class, ethnic position, and lack of knowledge about academia exacerbated my sense of dislocation. As a result I withdrew from the department, rarely communicating with anyone other than my course colleagues. I particularly disliked the pretentious relationships developed between students and some faculty members. Often I was uncomfortable with many of my classmates and their class origins and the gap between our experiences.

York University did have other students with immigrant origins, but they tended to be from bourgeois backgrounds and possessed the cultural (as well as social and financial) capital and class arrogance to persevere and do well in graduate school despite experiences of racism (Tomic and Trumper 1992). Some graduate classes were painful and intimidating. I sat through them witnessing which student would next seek to upstage the one who had just spoken. Here too, the immigrant working-class student is at a disadvantage because not everyone is equally prepared to participate in the discussion. This format silences many working-class students of immigrant background, but rarely is this recognized by bourgeois students and faculty members, who have grown up with the cultural capital of academia and thus fail to recognize its construction and reproduction via institutional and individual practices.

For these reasons I never felt at ease or secure in my sense of belonging to the sociology department at York University. In retrospect, I can see it was my self-imposed peripheralization within the department and the university that allowed me to succeed. I created my own space outside the department and most other university activities. In so doing I was able to distance myself from the climate of the department and at the same time carry on with my work at my own pace, and according to my own perception of what university education should be.

The Imposter Syndrome—Disarming the Black Student

Most working-class students in graduate training or academic posts worry about feelings of dislocation regarding their academic and cultural milieu. Their uneasiness stems from the foreignness of the culture, climate, and milieu within which they study and work. These feelings are frequently captured in the concept of the 'imposter syndrome'. That is, having no prior inside knowledge of academia, and navigating their way in uncharted waters, working-class students and academics of immigrant origin fear being 'discovered'. They fear being exposed as outsiders in a privileged and exclusive milieu in which they are not quite sure of the rules and practices of belonging.

I have not escaped this syndrome, and I often ask myself why and how I have gotten here. That question is usually followed by another set of queries. Given that I am in the university, does it mean that the system (of mobility, and merit, for instance) works? Am I an example of the system 'working for anybody'? Can one discredit a system that has benefited a working-class student from an immigrant background, enabled someone with no family history of higher education to climb to the highest level of formal education? Other important feelings also emerge to take over my psyche. I experience numerous bouts of confidence and wonder when I will finally be denounced as an imposter and revealed to be incompetent and incapable of thinking in a scholarly fashion. These feelings repeat themselves perpetually, as does the need to 'prove' over and over that I belong in academia.

Reference

Tomic, Patricia, and Ricardo Trumper. 1992. 'Canada and the Streaming of Immigrants: A Personal Account of the Chilean Case.' In Vic Satzewich, ed., *Deconstructing a Nation: Immigration, Multiculturalism and Racism in '90s Canada*. Halifax, NS: Fernwood Publishing and Social Research Unit, Department of Sociology, University of Saskatchewan.

Source: Aguiar (2001: 187–9). Carl E. James and Adrienne Shodd, eds., *Talking About Identity: Encounters In Race, Ethnicity, and Language* (Toronto: Between the Lines, 2001)

part of members of business communities, governments, and individuals to redistribute wealth and to place less emphasis on capital growth. As it stands, if a company makes a $9-billion profit in one year and an $8-billion profit the next, it suffers on the stock market. Managers are then often forced to restructure and eliminate workers so that they can show not profitability, but *increased* profitability. To eradicate inequality, this logic must change.

Recall Marx's prediction about polarization. He argued that with advanced capitalism, work would be increasingly deskilled, the middle class would shrink, and there would be an increasing polarization of the distribution of income and poverty. This chapter has shown that, on the one hand, overall increases in the skill levels associated with many jobs and recent increases in the number of self-employed small business owners suggests that the polarization thesis is incorrect. On the other hand, huge inequities in the distribution of income in Canada cannot be ignored. Furthermore, regardless of where one comes down on the debate about overall class polarization, the fact is that compared to middle-class jobs, working-class jobs are characterized by lower levels of income and other benefits, lower levels of **autonomy** and control in the work process, poorer working conditions, lower levels of skill, and greater alienation. This chapter has also shown that discussions of polarization are incomplete unless they also consider how gender, age, ethnicity, and race influence outcomes of inequality related to paid work.

IIIIIIIIIII Questions for Critical Thought IIIIIIIIIIIIIIIIIIIIIIIIIIIIIIIIIIIIIIIIIIIIIIIIIIII II

1. Consider your ideal job or the job you would like to have after you graduate. Is it a good job or a bad job? Why or why not?
2. Consider your first job. What were the advantages of having that job? What were the disadvantages of having that job? How were the advantages and disadvantages of that job related to themes discussed in this chapter? How could the job have been restructured to make it better?
3. This chapter argued that paid-work outcomes are mutually shaped by processes of production and distribution. Discuss this in relation to income disadvantages older persons face in retirement.
4. Explain labour-market-based inequality using a human-capital framework. Critique that approach, paying attention to the structures of class, age, gender, ethnicity, and race.
5. Discuss the relationship between technology and skill. Will Marx's prediction about deskilling be realized in the years to come? How do gender, ethnicity, race, and age relations influence the 'deskilling' argument?

IIIIIIIIIII Glossary IIIIIIIIIIIIIIIIIIIIIIIIIIIIIIIIIIIIIIIIIIIIIIIIIIIIIIIIIIIIIIIIIIIIIIIIIIIIIIIII II

Alienation   Marx identified four dimensions of alienation. First, workers are separated from the products of their labour. If people work on a product without knowing its purpose, they are alienated from their product. Second, workers are separated from their labour process: they have little autonomy over how their work is done. Third, because to labour is part of the essence of being human, if workers are alienated from the products and processes of their labour, they are also alienated from themselves. In other words, workers are unable to derive a meaningful existence from their work. The fourth dimension of alienation is the separation of workers from each other. This happens because work processes are set up in such a way as to minimize interaction among workers and second that capitalism establishes inherently antagonistic relationships across classes (see Rinehart 2006: 11–13).

Autonomy   The ability of workers to make their own decisions about how to do the work, how fast to do it, and what needs to be done. It refers to the control that workers have over their work processes.

Capitalism   The economic and social organization of production processes in modern industrialized countries.

Cumulative advantage/disadvantage hypothesis   The idea that social and economic advantage and disadvantage cumulate over time. The basic premise of this hypothesis may be captured by the following colloquialism: 'The rich get richer and the poor get poorer.'

Primary labour markets   A pool of good jobs that are characterized by high pay, good benefits, and job security.

Skill   In the sociological literature, the combination of job complexity and autonomy.

Surplus value   The value of surplus product that results when workers labour for more hours than would be required for them to achieve their means of subsistence. In capitalist systems of production, workers labour for themselves and for the owners of the means of production. If workers owned the product they produced and were able to sell it, they would need to work for fewer hours than they currently do in order to make the same wage. The excess time that they work and the surplus product that results from it (surplus value) is appropriated by owners.

||||||||||| **Recommended Reading** ||||||||||||||||||||||||||||||||||||||||||||||||||||||||||||||

Adams, Tracey, and Sandy Welsh. 2008. *The Organization and Experience of Work*. Toronto: Thomson Nelson. This book provides the most comprehensive detail on each of class, age, gender, and ethnicity/race in relation to paid work and is particularly good in relation to its treatment of age.

Hughes, Karen D. 1999. *Gender and Self-Employment in Canada: Assessing Trends and Policy Implications*. CPRN Study W104. Changing Relationships Series. Ottawa: Renouf. One of the few comprehensive studies of self-employment in Canada. Although the emphasis is on gender, readers who are interested in all aspects of self-employment would do well to read this paper.

Krahn, Harvey J., Graham S. Lowe, and Karen D. Hughes. 2007. *Work, Industry & Canadian Society*. 5th edn. Toronto: Thomson Nelson. A comprehensive text on paid work in Canada. Covering a wide range of topics, including class, age, race, ethnicity, and gender, it is essential reading for students interested in paid work and inequality.

Luxton, Meg, and June Corman. 2001. *Getting By in Hard Times: Gendered Labour at Home and on the Job*. Toronto: University of Toronto Press. This excellent book is a case study of steelworkers in Hamilton, Ontario. It examines how capital restructuring is gendered and classed and how class, gender, and race mutually constitute one another through paid and unpaid labour.

Rinehart, James W. 2006. *The Tyranny of Work: Alienation and the Labour Process*. 5th edn. Toronto: Harcourt Brace. A Marxist account of paid work in Canada that concentrates mainly on social class.

‖‖‖‖‖‖‖ Relevant Websites ‖‖‖

Human Resources and Social Development
Canada
http://www.hrsdc.gc.ca/eng/home.shtml
**A federal government site for issues relating to
work and the life course.

Hire Immigrants
http://www.hireimmigrants.ca/index.php
**This advocacy site out of Toronto identifies
challenges and opportunities for businesses to
utilize the talents of skilled immigrants.

MySafeWork.com
http://www.mysafework.com
**Run by charitable foundation OYAW (Our
Youth at Work), the site presents workplace
health and wellness issues with a focus on young
workers.

Service Canada—Youth Employment Strategy
Programs
http://www1.servicecanada.gc.ca/en/epb/yi/yep/
newprog/yesprograms.shtml
**A federal government site for helping young
people who face barriers to employment.

Service Canada—Labour Market Information
http://www.labourmarketinformation.ca/
and
Service Canada—Training, Career and
Workplace Information
http://www.jobsetc.ca/
**More federal government sites for work-relat-
ed issues.

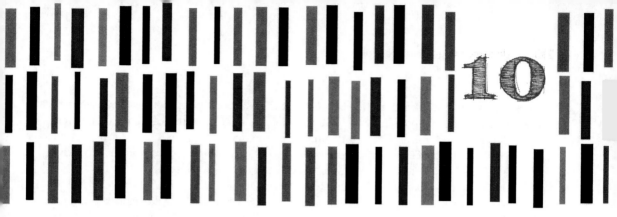

CAGE(s) and Education

by Tammy Duerden Comeau and Julie McMullin

Introduction

In 1998 the Ontario government began mandatory testing of students in grades 3, 6, and 9. These tests are thought to evaluate students' abilities in reading, writing, and mathematics. They were established to make schools and school boards accountable for the quality of education that they provide and to identify areas that need improving. The testing is done by an office called the Educational Quality and Accountability Office (EQAO). Every year, test scores are published for each school and individual students are given their scores so that they, their parents, and their teachers are aware of how they are doing and how they can improve (Bacigalupo 2003).

Ten years later, controversy over the measurement and use of these scores continues. Although EQAO and school-board officials stress that these scores should not be used to rank schools, the variation among the schools in their aggregate test scores makes that temptation hard to resist. Indeed, two conservative Canadian think tanks are in disagreement over how to rank schools and, specifically, over whether and how socio-economic factors should be accounted for in these rankings (Long 2007: C1). Using different methods from the Fraser Institute, the C.D. Howe Institute argues that 40 per cent of the variation in school test scores is related to socio-economic factors, and accounts for this in its calculations. Regardless of the statistical methods used, a number of educational administrators caution against the use of a single score to evaluate a school and have called such practices 'demoralizing' for schools and students (Long 2007: C1). Yet parents with economic means do appear to take these test scores into account, and in some cases move to areas where they believe schools are academically stronger (Alcoba 2008). Ironically, these movements may then exacerbate inequities between schools. Of course, these reports are not a systematic analysis of the relationship between socio-economic status (SES) and education. Nevertheless, a large body of literature does show that people of lower-SES backgrounds tend not to be as highly educated as those from higher-SES backgrounds. It also suggests that 'universally' accessible education in Canada may vary considerably in its quality.

The pursuit of higher education is often viewed as an accessible and practical avenue for obtaining upward mobility. In a society that strongly promotes an individualistic ethos of success and failure, education is seen as an opportunity for the talented and motivated individual to move up the social ladder. Canadians would prefer not to believe that the educational system is also a place where societal inequalities are reproduced and where privileged groups solidify and maintain their advantages (B. Curtis, Livingstone, and Smaller 1992; Lehman 2007a). This is not to deny that higher education tends to result in better life opportunities. Usually, highly educated people are employed in well-paid jobs (Chung 2006; D. Little 1995) with relatively high degrees of autonomy and authority (Butlin and Oderkirk 1997). However, the chances of attaining higher education and, more specifically, of obtaining a lucrative degree that will result in substantial labour-market returns are significantly affected by one's class (S. Davies and Guppy 2006; Frenette 2007; Knighton and Mirza 2002), race or ethnicity (Li 2000; Mata 1997; McMullen 2005), gender (S. Davies, Mosher, and O'Grady 1996; Frenette and Zeman 2007; Thiessen and Nickerson 1999), and age (Kapsalis, Morissette, and Picot 1999). The historical period in which we live also significantly shapes our chances for a higher education (Clark 2001). In 2006, for example, 11 per cent of adults aged 25–34 did not have a high school diploma, compared with 23 per cent of adults aged 55–64 (Statistics Canada 2008c: 10). At the beginning of the twenty-first century, societal demands for an educated workforce have made a high school education almost a compulsory requirement for sustained labour-force participation, which marks a significant change from the popular educational expectations and aspirations of previous generations (Bowlby and McMullen 2002; Clark 2001; S. Davies and Guppy 2007).

The chances of obtaining a post-secondary education also differ by province (Krahn and Taylor 2007). Place, or the location or region where we live, matters for educational attainment and opportunities. For example, of the provinces, Newfoundland and Labrador has the lowest proportion of adults aged 25–64 with a university degree (14 per cent) and the highest proportion with less than a high school diploma (26 per cent) (Statistics Canada 2008c:

26). It is important to note that migration and mobility also affect the educational attainment of residents—in Alberta, 22 per cent of adults aged 25–64 have a university degree; however, Alberta also had the largest net inflow of post-secondary graduates from other provinces (Statistics Canada 2008c). Provincial educational policies also help to shape opportunities and educational trajectories. In some provinces, the courses taken early on in high school can determine educational and occupational directions for years to come. The **streaming** of high school students into different educational pathways has been found to often disadvantage or close off career options for students whose parents have lower educational attainment (Krahn and Taylor 2007). Figure 10.1 illustrates this pattern by showing how students whose parents have one or two post-secondary degrees are more likely to have their post-secondary options open in grade 10. Interestingly, there are differences between provinces. For example, 86 per cent of grade 10 students in Saskatchewan whose parents have no degrees still have their post-secondary options open, compared to 52 per cent of their counterparts in Alberta (Krahn and Taylor 2007).

Pierre Bourdieu's work on the concepts of social and cultural capital has taken a prominent place in explaining the persistent inequalities (particularly in regard to social class) reproduced in educational systems (Wotherspoon 2004). According to Bourdieu, parents with more educational resources have richer reserves of cultural capital. **Cultural capital**, which is derived mostly from education, reflects middle- and upper-class values, attitudes, and beliefs that people hold about various aspects of social life. If education and related activities, such as reading, discussing politics, and learning about the world and music, are valued in a family and by its members, high levels of educational attainment are more likely. Working-class families tend not to expose their children to these activities to the extent that middle- and upper-class

Figure 10.1: Proportion of Grade 10 Students with Post-secondary Options Open, by Parents' Education, in Four Provinces, 2000

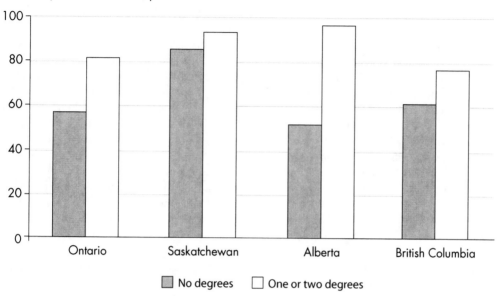

Source: Statistics Canada, 2000 Youth in Transition Survey; cited in Krahn and Taylor (2007).

families do. Therefore, these children are often less prepared and less familiar with the knowledge that is taken for granted and drawn upon in the classroom.

The related concept of **social capital** concerns the information and social connections that are available to individuals. For example, the possession of knowledge about the workings of the educational system, such as a familiarity with the meanings of terms such as **special education**, is vital to successfully navigating through that system. The future implications of decisions made now about course offerings and topics of study may also be unfamiliar to those with little experience in the educational system.

A quick look at the history of education in Canada makes it clear that achieving societal equality (even equality on the basis of 'merit') was not an overriding goal of the educational system at the outset (B. Curtis, Livingstone, and Smaller 1992; Wotherspoon 2004). Early educational aims for the Canadian masses included the desire to create agreeable and obedient workers and a contented working class (Baldus and Kassam 1996; B. Curtis, Livingstone, and Smaller 1992). Baldus and Kassam (1996), analyzing the predominant values found in nineteenth-century Ontario schoolbooks, found strong prescriptive statements and moral lessons that recommend accepting one's lot in life and embracing social inequality. This is illustrated in the following excerpt from a nineteenth-century reader:

> Our present lot, my parents say,
> Is better for us, in every way,
> Than one of our own choice could be.
> . . .
> So now I am a little child,
> Then let me try to be content;
> My duty let me strive to do,

And with a thankful heart and true,
Accept the blessings heaven has sent.
(quoted in Baldus and Kassam
1996: 338)

Children were not encouraged to strive beyond their social roots, and the virtues of leading a simple and hard-working life were extolled in poems and fables (Baldus and Kassam 1996). Historically, then, educational curricula and policies have accepted, rather than challenged, societal inequalities (B. Curtis, Livingstone, and Smaller 1992; Wotherspoon 2004).

Ng (1993) shows how the early educational aims of Canadian missionaries were structured by racist, sexist, and class-based ideologies. Aboriginal men and women were taught different skills in order to reproduce European gendered societal patterns. Only the men were taught how to farm, and the women were schooled in 'domestic' duties. The goal was to produce a new and subordinate working class that would benefit the colonizers. A strong theme of Aboriginal inferiority was woven through religious and educational teachings (Ng 1993). The delivery of these educational imperatives was later refined and developed in all-encompassing institutional forms (Guppy and Davies 1998; Wotherspoon 2004).

The residential school system to which Aboriginals in Canada were subjected in the nineteenth and twentieth centuries provides a graphic illustration of the extent to which racism and class ideologies can direct 'educational' programs (Nicholas 2001; Wotherspoon 2004). Aboriginal children were cut off from their families and taught to be ashamed of their cultural heritage (Nicholas 2001). Indeed, according to Schissel and Wotherspoon (2003: 43), 'the expressed intent of residential school policy was to destroy a culture and rebuild Indian children as active participants in the industrial economy, if not remove them as impediments to economic development'. Generations of Aboriginal people are still paying the price for the humiliating, alienating, and abusive experiences endured in residential schools (Jaine 1993; see also Box 10.1). Indeed, the last residential school did not close until the 1980s (Nicholas 2001).

This chapter examines the barriers to educational attainment in Canada. In particular, it considers the historical influence of social class, race, ethnicity, gender, and age in educational

Box 10.1 Graphic List of Abuse to Settle Claims: Complex System of Determining Payment Seen as Necessary to Manage Huge Numbers of Complaints by Former Residential-School Students

By Katherine O'Neill

It's a scorecard ranking unspeakable acts.

From sodomy to severe beatings causing disfigurement to persistent fondling—the list is graphic and disturbingly thorough.

It's all part of a complicated compensation system that a court-ordered independent program is now using to settle serious sexual- and physical-abuse claims by former residential-school students.

The majority are aboriginal. All were either children or teenagers when they were assaulted, often by the adults paid and trusted to look after or teach them.

The closed-door private hearings, which began late last year in locations across the country, are expected to process about 12,500 claimants by 2013. The more abuse a person can prove, along with providing supporting evidence of subsequent harm, such as a forced abortion, substance-abuse problems or lost income, the higher the rate of financial compensation that person is entitled to from the federal government.

The maximum amount is $245,000. However, if a person can prove income loss, the final amount can be increased to up to $430,000.

Peter Harris, a Vancouver-based lawyer who helped the federal government, aboriginal leaders, churches and others draw up the compensation rules for the new Independent Assessment Process, acknowledges they are painfully detailed and could upset victims.

'It troubles some people and it troubles me,' he said. 'But because of the huge number of claims, it's a manageable way to approach the issue and try to get some level of standardization.'

Mr Harris's law firm has been representing former residential-school students since the 1990s. He said before this program, victims either had to go to court or apply for a hearing from the federally run Alternative Dispute Resolution program.

The dispute resolution program was similar to the new program, but was voluntary and not binding and didn't have as many categories of abuse for claimants to choose from.

The new program, which is independent and supervised by nine provincial and territorial courts, is also expected to give out larger settlements.

The Independent Assessment Process is part of a larger historic $4-billion residential-schools settlement agreement that came into effect last fall. The settlement, which was negotiated by the federal government, aboriginal groups, churches and lawyers representing former students, included a lump-sum payment for all surviving former residential students, approximately 80,000 people. The average payment is about $28,000.

Former students had the right to opt out. Only 348 did, which gives them the right to settle abuse claims or other grievances through the courts.

Most of the schools were church-run, but supported financially by the Canadian government from the 1870s to the 1970s.

Angus Cockney, a 51-year-old Inuvialuit artist and businessman, is not impressed with the settlement, arguing former residential-school students like him have been largely shafted.

'Look at someone like Maher Arar. He got millions from the government. I'd argue he got it easy compared to many residential students,' he said. 'Why I should be treated less? Look at my case. Look at all of our cases.'

In 2007, Mr Arar, a Canadian engineer who had been illegally sent to Syria where he says he was tortured after the RCMP wrongly labelled him an Islamic extremist, was given a compensation package worth more than $10-million.

Even still, Mr Cockney is applying for a hearing. 'I've been silent for 35, 40 years; I can't suppress it any longer,' said the divorced father of two who now lives in Canmore, Alta.

He was born in a camp east of Tuktoyaktuk, a small community located 350 kilometres north of the Arctic Circle.

In 1961, when he was five, he remembers a float plane landing at their outpost camp on the Arctic Ocean, and people 'abducting' him from his parents. He was flown to Grollier Hall, a Catholic-run residential school in Inuvik, along with his brother Rex, who was seven, and his sister Regina, who was six.

They were all given numbers. He was 248.

The next 12 years were largely a nightmare of constant physical, sexual and mental abuse for Mr Cockney. 'These people were supposed to exemplify love, but instead they taught us to hate,' he said.

For years, Mr Cockney, who became an accomplished cross-country skiing athlete and North Pole adventurer, never admitted to anyone what had happened to him at Grollier Hall.

But in the late 1990s, after four male former school employees were convicted of sex crimes, the memories began flooding back.

He said many of his ex-classmates also struggled through the years, dozens either killing themselves or turning to drugs or alcohol to suppress the pain of the abuse and loss of language and culture.

To this day, he has still not spoken about his own horrific experience with his ex-wife, children or siblings. 'It's the native way. It's not the right way,' he admitted. Instead, Mr Cockney has often used art to express himself, and in 1999, even created a haunting sculpture called *Remembering*.

Abuse claimants are allowed to pick where their hearings are conducted, and Mr Cockney either wants his to be held in Inuvik or the spot east of Tuktoyaktuk where he was stolen from his parents.

An adjudicator conducts the hearing, which has a standard of proof similar to a civil proceeding. Only a handful of people are allowed to sit in, including the claimant, a health support worker and a representative from the Canadian government.

Mr Cockney said the compensation grid is a necessary evil, but he's concerned it doesn't go far enough because it doesn't include categories such as the effects of being abducted and the trauma resulting from the lack of an official government apology.

During this process, he also wants to find answers about his family, including what happened to his parents, Annie and Stanley, and three younger siblings. When he was eight, he was told they all died in a fire, but he has never been able to find burial markers for his siblings.

Daniel Ish, chief adjudicator of the Independent Assessment Process, is hopeful these hearings will help former residential students heal.

He said while it's a complex program, it's a 'gentler' alternative to going to court, which can be quite expensive, time-consuming and adversarial.

Mr Ish acknowledged adjudicators will face many challenges, including assessing claims where so much time has passed since the alleged abuse took place. 'But they aren't insurmountable. . . . You don't shy away because of the challenges.'

Complex Compensation Rules

A court-ordered independent program is using the following compensation system to help settle serious sexual- and physical-abuse claims by former residential-school students. The maximum amount of compensation for abuse is $245,000. However, if a person can prove income loss, the final amount can be increased to up to $430,000.

The following list outlines the approximate range of compensation allowed for the abuse described.

$54,000–$85,000
- Repeated, persistent incidents of anal or vaginal intercourse
- Repeated, persistent incidents of anal/vaginal penetration with an object

$40,000–$55,000
- One or more incidents of anal or vaginal intercourse
- Repeated, persistent incidents of oral intercourse
- One or more incidents of anal/vaginal penetration with an object

$25,000–$45,000
- One or more incidents of oral intercourse
- One or more incidents of digital anal/vaginal penetration
- One or more incidents of attempted anal/vaginal penetration (excluding attempted digital penetration)
- Repeated, persistent incidents of masturbation

$11,000–$24,000
- One or more physical assaults causing a physical injury that led to or should have led to hospitalization or serious medical treatment by a physician; permanent or demonstrated long-term physical injury, impairment or disfigurement; loss of consciousness; broken bones; or a serious but temporary incapacitation such that bed rest or infirmary care of several days duration was required. Examples include severe beating, whipping and second-degree burning
- One or more incidents of simulated intercourse
- One or more incidents of masturbation
- Repeated, persistent fondling under clothing

$7,500–$10,000
- One or more incidents of fondling or kissing
- Nude photographs taken of the claimant
- The act of an adult employee or other adult lawfully on the premises exposing themselves
- Any touching of a student, including touching with an object, by an adult employee or other adult lawfully on the premises which exceeds recognized parental contact and violates the sexual integrity of the student

$7,500–$24,000
- Being singled out for physical abuse by an adult employee or other adult lawfully on the premises which was grossly excessive in duration and frequency and which caused psychological consequential harms
- Any other wrongful act committed by an adult employee or other adult lawfully on the premises which is proven to have caused psychological consequential harms

Aggravating factors
The following could increase the amount of compensation by up to 15 per cent:
- Verbal abuse
- Racist acts
- Threats
- Intimidation/inability to complain; oppression
- Humiliation; degradation
- Sexual abuse accompanied by violence
- Age of the victim or abuse of a particularly vulnerable child
- Failure to provide care or emotional support following abuse requiring such care
- Witnessing another student being subjected to an act set out in the above list
- Use of religious doctrine, paraphernalia or authority during, or in order to facilitate, the abuse
- Being abused by an adult who had built a particular relationship of trust and caring with the victim (betrayal)

Source: Indian Residential Schools Settlement Agreement

attainment; how they currently affect educational attainment; and the relationship between these factors and the educational returns achieved through labour markets.

Focusing on Class: Historical Notes and Existing Patterns

The class position of our family of origin has a significant impact on our educational prospects and consequent life trajectory (Bowlby and McMullen 2002; Frenette 2007; Knighton and Mirza 2002). The effect of class on the educational attainment of Canadians has been described by Guppy and Davies (1998: 59) as a particularly 'enduring' feature of inequality. The education achieved by our parents and the kind of work that they perform have an undeniable influence

on our early school experiences and on our level of educational attainment (Bowlby and McMullen 2002; B. Curtis, Livingstone, and Smaller 1992; S. Davies and Guppy 2007; Nakhaie and Curtis 1998). Indeed, 'streaming', or filtering, occurs before some children ever enter a school building (B. Curtis, Livingstone, and Smaller 1992). Parents with enough money can choose to send their children to elite private schools, where students are groomed to attend the top universities. Within public schools, students have been classified and 'sorted' into various academic avenues or 'streams' in which some children are relegated to learning 'basic skills' and others are academically challenged and channelled to go on to higher learning (B. Curtis, Livingstone, and Smaller 1992).

Curtis and his colleagues (B. Curtis, Livingstone, and Smaller 1992), who have examined the practice of streaming in Ontario schools, have shown that the allocation of students to various ability levels in both elementary and secondary schools is not free of class bias. In other words, children from lower-class and lower-middle-class backgrounds were found to be much more likely to end up in special education or remedial programs at the elementary-school level and in basic streams or vocational schools at the secondary-school level (B. Curtis., Livingstone, and Smaller 1992). These authors cite studies from the 1970s and 1980s that show that children from families on social assistance were '60 times more likely' to be in special- or remedial-education programs than children from the families of professional workers (B. Curtis , Livingstone, and Smaller 1992: 59). Being in special or remedial education in elementary school tended to be a permanent placement, which led to a 'basic' stream in an academic high school or a vocational school. Students who attended these vocational schools were predominately of working-class or ethnic or racial minority backgrounds. These students faced fairly dismal job prospects, as they were not eligible for university or most college programs, and even those who achieved a vocational certificate from their high school were not actually qualified to enter many trade apprenticeship programs (B. Curtis, Livingstone, and Smaller 1992).

Some may argue that these statistics are outdated and that streaming is no longer a predominant teaching practice in the educational system. However, more recent studies indicate that children from higher socio-economic backgrounds continue to enjoy significant advantages in elementary and secondary schools (Bohatyretz and Lipps 1999; Lipps and Frank 1997; Pinto 2006). Bohatyretz and Lipps (1999) found that children from low socio-economic backgrounds were disproportionately represented in special-education programs. In addition, those children who received special education for 'problems at home' had parents with the lowest education

levels (Bohatyretz and Lipps 1999). Results from the National Longitudinal Survey of Children and Youth 1994–5 showed that children from the highest socio-economic backgrounds were significantly less likely to be receiving remedial education (5 per cent) than those from the lowest socio-economic backgrounds (17 per cent) (Lipps and Frank 1997). Children from the highest socio-economic backgrounds were also significantly more likely to be enrolled in some form of a gifted educational program (9 per cent) than children from the lowest socio-economic backgrounds (5 per cent) (Lipps and Frank 1997: 54). Children from privileged socio-economic backgrounds were also ranked considerably higher in academic ability assessments by their teachers (Lipps and Frank 1997). In fact, Lipps and Frank (1997: 54) found that students with the highest socio-economic status were 'two to three times as likely' to be ranked among the best in the class by their teachers in reading, writing, and math. Parental expectations and impressions of their children's ability have also been shown to affect educational trajectories. Figure 10.2 shows the proportion of children ranked as 'very well' by the person most knowledgable, or PMK (often the parent), of the child's academic ability in terms of math, reading, and composition. This figure demonstrates a general increase in 'very well' rankings as the socio-economic status of the child increases, especially when comparing the academic evaluations of the lowest- and highest-SES children (represented here on a scale of 1 to 9). Here we see that in most cases parents with higher SES are more likely to rank their children highly in terms of academic ability.

At the secondary level, Lehmann's (2007a) study of 105 youth in apprenticeship and academic educational tracks in Germany and Canada provides a strong illustration of the role of habitus and cultural capital in shaping educational pathways. As Lehmann points out, Bourdieu's concepts of cultural capital and habitus help in conceptualizing how agency and

Figure 10.2: PMK Evaluation of Academic Performance by Socio-economic Status (SES)

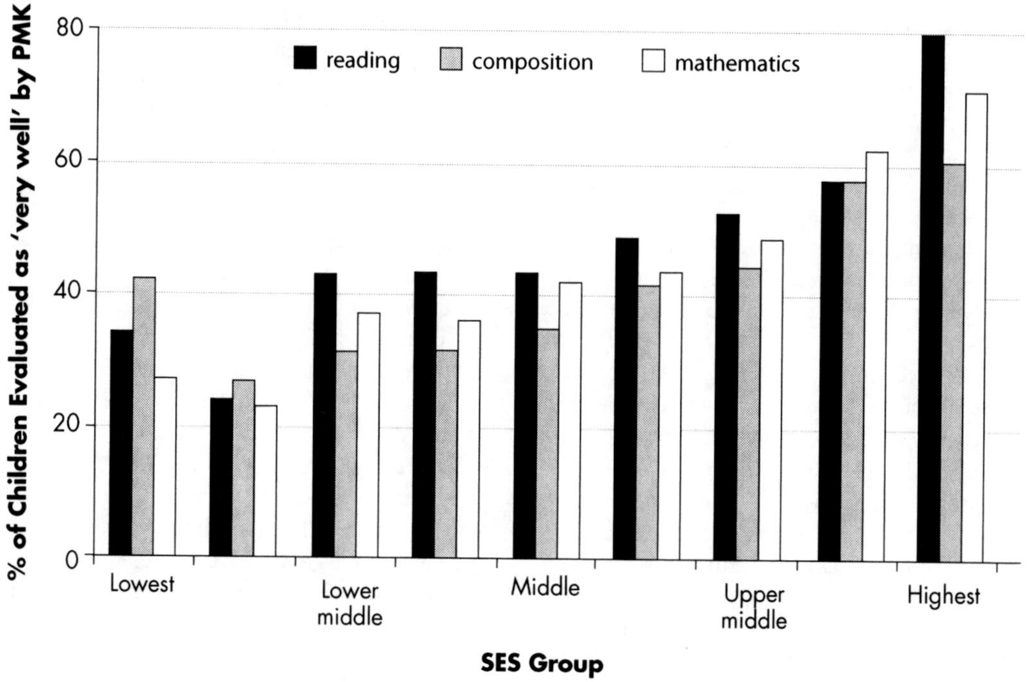

Notes: PMK: person most knowledgeable (typically a parent or guardian); SES group is composite measure comprising family income, parents' occupation, and parents' education.

Source: National Longitudinal Survey of Children and Youth, 1998–99, public use data.

human action are shaped and constrained by structure in complex ways. Educational choices that students make in selecting which 'stream' or educational pathway to take are not random but structured, in part, by what is comfortable, familiar, and perceived as attainable. Cultural capital is one way in which to encompass and assess practices and knowledge that can affect performance and preferences in school such as 'reading books versus reading magazines' (Lehmann 2007a: 84). In his measure of cultural capital for students in both countries, Lehmann (2007a: 85) found that those who scored highly on this measure were more likely to be in an academic track (61 per cent) than those in apprenticeships (39 per cent).

In Canada, parental educational background and parents' educational expectations for their children continue to exert a strong influence on whether youth attend university, and according to Frenette (2007), only 12 per cent of the gap between the attendance of high-income and low-income youth is directly attributable to finances. Indeed, the importance of cultural and social dispositions or 'fit' is a compelling component of some students' narratives of their educational trajectories. Lehmann (2007b) found that those students from working-class backgrounds who left university tended to feel alienated in certain post-secondary academic environments and that this was a factor in their departure. Thus, the patterns of educational advantage and disadvantage by class discussed by Curtis, Livingstone, and Smaller (1992) do not appear to have substantially dissipated over time.

Educational Attainment

The class background of students (including parental education, income, and occupation) exerts a significant influence on their chances of obtaining a high school diploma and for obtaining a post-secondary education (S. Davies and Guppy 2006; Frenette 2007; Knighton and Mirza 2002; Zeman 2007). Labour markets increasingly require post-secondary education of some form for sustainable employment. According to the Canadian Council on Learning (2007: 8), 'in the decade leading up to 2015, nearly 70 per cent of the projected 1.7 million new jobs in Canada are expected to be in management or in occupations usually requiring post-secondary qualification.' In this environment, prospects for people who do not have a high school diploma are not promising (Bowlby and McMullen 2005). Indeed, over the past 15 years, those who left high school without a diploma have experienced unemployment rates three times higher than those of university-degree holders (CCL 2007: 8).

Since the early 1990s, the high school dropout rate has decreased quite dramatically, from 17 per cent to 9 per cent by 2006–7 (CCL 2008a: 16). Still, some youth are more likely to drop out than others. Data on family income show that 11.7 per cent of youth from families in the lowest income quartile dropped out of high school by age 19 compared with 3.6 per cent of youth in the highest income quartile (Zeman 2007). Parental education is important: 25 per cent of youth whose parents did not complete high school also dropped out compared with only 7 per cent of youth who had at least one parent with a post-secondary degree (Hango and de Broucker 2007: 29). In addition, youth living in large cities were much less likely to drop out of high school (8.8 per cent) than those in small towns (15 per cent) and rural areas (16.8 per cent) (CCL 2008a: 17). As Figure 10.3 shows, nearly one-quarter of youth in rural Alberta dropped out of high school in 2005–6.

In their detailed study of high school dropouts and graduates, Bowlby and McMullen (2002) found that the mothers of high school graduates were more likely to work in government, health, social science, management, business, finance, art, or culture and recreation, whereas the mothers of students who dropped out were more concentrated in sales/service and manufacturing/trade occupations. Similarly, the fathers of dropouts were more likely to be employed in trades and manufacturing occupations, while the fathers of graduates were more often in management, finance, and the sciences (Bowlby and McMullen 2002). These findings suggest that it is not just family finances and income that are affecting high school completion rates but that the mechanisms of social and cultural capital in the form of the valuation of education and exposure to educationally enhancing experiences are also having an influence. According to Finnie, Lascelles, and Sweetman (2005), each year of parental post-secondary education increases the likelihood that youth will attend university by as much as 5 percentage points. More highly educated parents and those who have been 'successful' and accomplished in the educational system are more easily able to pass down the excitement of learning and to expect a certain level of education on the part of their offspring (S. Davies and Guppy 2006). The completion of high school is a necessary step for entrance to most types of post-secondary education, and it is here that the influence of income is seen more vividly.

More than one-third of youth who have not yet attended post-secondary education report that financial barriers have prevented them (Berger, Motte, and Parkin 2007: 44). Post-secondary education, particularly university education, is becoming more and more expensive

Figure 10.3: Dropout Rate in Urban and Non-urban Areas, by Region, 2002–3 to 2005–6 (percentages)

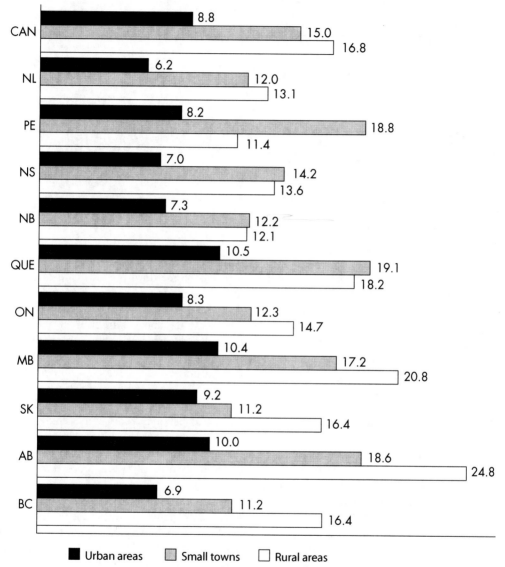

Note: Data are based on a four-year average for the academic years 2002–3 to 2005–6.

Source: Calculations of HRSDC based on special data request from Statistics Canada, Labour Force Survey, 2006.

(CCL 2007; Finnie 2002). The Canadian Council on Learning (2007: 86) notes that the cost of tuition increased 44 per cent from 1995–6 to 2005–6. Indeed, these increases have exceeded the annual inflation rate in Canada. There is a clear relationship between family income levels

Table 10.1 Post-secondary Participation by Household Income, Parental Education, Canada, 2001

	University Participation Rate (%)	College Participation Rate (%)	Total Participation Rate (%)
Before-Tax Parental Income Range			
Less than $25,000	20	29	49
$25,001–$50,000	23	37	60
$50,001–$75,000	25	38	63
$75,001–$100,000	38	38	76
More than $100,000	46	32	77
Highest Level of Parental Education			
University	50	32	81
Post-secondary certificate or diploma	28	40	68
High school or less	17	36	53

Source: Drolet (2005: 30).

and the chance or likelihood of continuing to post-secondary and particularly university education. Frenette (2007: 7) found a marked income gradient in university participation based on parental income level: 50 per cent of 19-year-old youth in the top income quartile attend university compared with 31 per cent of those in the bottom income quartile, controlling for family size.

The influence of family socio-economic status on university enrolment is outlined in Table 10.1. While 20 per cent of youth from families earning less than $25,000 attend university, more than double that, 46 per cent, of youth from families with incomes more than $100,000 attend (Berger, Motte, and Parkin 2007). Here we see that the differences in university attendance by family income are much more pronounced as compared to college attendance. Part of this difference may be attributed to doubts about the value of return on university education given the cost (Berger, Motte, and Parkin 2007).

In spite of the extension of student aid, many lower-income families are debt averse, and in fact student loan repayments can be long lasting,

with nearly one-third of students defaulting in the first three years of repayment and another third continuing to pay off loans 10 years later (Berger, Motte, and Parkin 2007: 89). Finances are a clear factor in the ability to save for and afford educational goals. For instance, families with earnings under $30,000 a year have a 24 per cent participation rate in the Registered Education Savings Plan (RESP), compared to a 56 per cent participation rate for families who earn over $70,000 a year (Berger, Motte, and Parkin 2007: 51). University student debt loads more than doubled between 1990 and 2006, from an average of $11,636 to an average of $24,047 (CCL 2007: 88). While in 1995 a substantial minority of students graduated with debt (45 per cent), in 2006 the majority of graduates had debt (59 per cent) (CCL 2007: 88). The amount of debt incurred by those graduating from college has also increased, with nearly one-third (29 per cent) of college graduates in 2006 having more than $15,000 in debt (CCL 2007; see also Box 10.2).

Still, past research and more recent reports suggest that parental education is even more influential in whether and how youth participate

Box 10.2 The Average Student: SWF, 22, Some Debt, Seeks Degree, Job

By Sandy Farran

Who

The typical undergraduate university student is female, 22 years old, and single. She has been in post-secondary education for nearly three years, is enrolled in a social sciences program, and has a grade average between a B and B+. She spends approximately 15 hours per week in class or labs, and another 17 hours studying. She lives off-campus, either with her parents or renting accommodation. She comes from a large urban centre in Ontario or Quebec and is studying outside her hometown, but in her home province. More likely than not, she is either working part-time or looking for work to help offset the cost of her education. This is probably a good idea, since the average student with debt reports owing more than $20,000 at graduation.

How Much

Last September, Canadian undergraduate students faced the smallest increase in tuition fees in more than a decade. Undergraduate students paid an average of $4,214 for the 2005–2006 academic year, up from $4,140 the year before. This is almost triple the average of $1,464 in 1990–1991. The highest fees are in Nova Scotia, where average tuition is $6,281. At $7,760, Acadia has the highest tuition in the country. Quebec universities charge the lowest tuition; it's been frozen at $1,668 since the late 1990s. But out-of-province students in Quebec pay roughly the national average. In addition, all universities charge ancillary fees: they range from $281 at St Thomas to $1,297 at McGill.

Debt

Just over half (51 per cent) of all undergraduate students have some debt. The most common source is student loans, which 33 per cent of all students report using. Other common sources of debt are loans from parents or family (18 per cent) and loans from banks (16 per cent). On average, student debt is over $16,000.

Income

Nearly 46 per cent of Canadian university students come from high-income families. That's nearly double the level of attendance of those from low-income families. The United States has an even greater percentage of children of high-income earners at university (63 per cent)—and a lower level of low-income enrolment (15 per cent in the U.S. vs 24 per cent here). Canadians who went to university make 77 per cent more than those with only high school or less. Nevertheless, parents' education levels seems to be a more important factor than family income in determining whether one goes to university or college.

Scholarships and Work

Increasingly, students are turning to a variety of other resources to avoid going into debt. Almost one-third (31 per cent) received a scholarship. (University scholarships and bursaries surpassed $900 million in 2004–2005, a six-fold increase since 1990.) Roughly 53 per cent of students work while studying; the majority (44 per cent) work off-campus. Another 14 per cent are looking for work. In the academic year 2003–2004, almost 54,000 students were enrolled in co-op programs at universities. And 36 per cent of students volunteer, either on- or off-campus.

How Many

There were more than 806,000 full-time university students in Canada in 2005. That's an increase of nearly 150,000 over the past four years due to a rise in the population of Canadians aged 18 to 24, Ontario's double cohort, and an increase in international students, whose numbers doubled to 80,000 over the past 10 years. The average age is 22, little changed since the 1960s. Females outnumber males, accounting for 59 per cent of all undergraduates. Women also represent more than 50 per cent of graduate students. Female enrolment lags behind that of males in a few fields of study, such as the physical sciences and engineering, but in most disciplines women are now the majority.

Where

The geographical distribution of Canadian university students does not differ significantly from that of the population as a whole; most live and study in the Quebec City–Windsor corridor (40 per cent), British Columbia (19 per cent) or Alberta (12 per cent). Almost half of Canadian university students come from cities with at least 100,000 people. One student in seven comes from a community of less than 5,000 or lives on a farm. Approximately 69 per cent attend just 20 institutions, 14 of which are in Ontario and Quebec. With nearly 70,000 full- and part-time students, the University of Toronto is Canada's largest university, followed by the Université de Montreal and York University.

Degrees Awarded

In 2004, Canadian universities awarded 150,000 bachelor's degrees, 30,000 master's degrees, and close to 4,000 doctoral degrees. Between 1996 and 2004, the number of bachelor's degrees rose by roughly 17 per cent. Women again outnumbered men at graduation ceremonies, receiving 60 per cent of bachelor's degrees. Degrees awarded increased in nearly every field, with the biggest jumps in visual and performing arts and communications technology.

Visible Minorities

The 2001 census showed that approximately 16 per cent of Canada's student-aged population are visible minorities, with Ontario having the highest level, at 22 per cent. And in 2003, 27 per cent of university applicants in that province identified themselves as visible minorities. University participation patterns largely reflect the population. There are, however, two major exceptions: Chinese-Canadian youth are overrepresented among university students and under-represented among college students, while the reverse is true among black Canadians. And black university applicants are disproportionately (66 per cent) female.

Aboriginal Students

Although post-secondary participation rates for Aboriginal youth lag behind the rest of the population, the number of Aboriginal students at post-secondary institutions has risen sharply over the last 40 years. In the mid-1960s, approximately 200 First Nations students were enrolled in colleges and universities. By 2000, the number had climbed to more than 27,000. The average Aboriginal student is older than the rest of the population—age 25.8—and almost 72 per cent are female. In addition, roughly half are either married or in a long-term relationship, and 30 per cent have children.

Source: Farran (2006). Material reprinted with the express permission of the Calgary Herald Group Inc. a Canwest Partnership.

in post-secondary education (CCL 2007; S. Davies and Guppie 2006; Frenette 2007; Knighton and Mirza 2002). These differences are evident in Figure 10.3, which shows that half of students who have at least one university-educated parent also went to university compared to only 17 per cent of youth whose parents' highest level of education is high school or less. In fact, among those youth aged 18 to 24 whose parents' highest educational level is high school, more than half (53 per cent) do not attend a post-secondary educational institution at all compared with

Table 10.2: Probability of Having a University Degree in 2003, by Sex, Age Group, and Highest Level of Father's Education

	Highest level of father's education			
	Less than high school graduation	High school graduate	At least some post-secondary	(Weighted) Sample size
Women				
Aged 30–39	.20	.26	.47	1,449
Aged 40–49	.19	.26	.44	1,587
Aged 50–59	.18	.29	.42	1,139
Aged 60+	.11	.24	.29	1,290
Men				
Aged 30–39	.17	.29	.42	1,454
Aged 40–49	.14	.28	.45	1,565
Aged 50–59	.23	.41	.49	1,129
Aged 60+	.16	.34	.40	1,086

Note: Includes only Canadian-born; sample weighted to represent Canadian population.
Source: Davies and Guppy (2006: 100).

a post-secondary attendance rate of 81 per cent for same-aged youth with a university-educated parent (CCL 2007: 76). Although most Canadian students (60 per cent) engage in post-secondary education of some sort, higher levels of parental income and higher levels of parental education mean higher post-secondary participation rates (CCL 2007). As Finnie and his colleagues (2005: 22) note, 'family background appears to have an enduring effect on the determination of who goes on to post-secondary participation, even among what appear to be equally qualified, and perhaps evenequally motivated young people.' Table 10.2 illustrates the enduring nature of these relationships by showing how little these odds have changed over time.

As Davies and Guppy (2006: 100) point out, those individuals whose fathers had at least some post-secondary education are more than twice as likely to have a university degree themselves compared with those whose fathers have less than a high school diploma, and these ratios have changed little over time. Davies and Guppy conclude that educational opportunity has not extended its reach in more recent generations.

The aspirations of students are significantly affected by the aspirations their parents have for them (Looker and Lowe 2001), and the aspirations of those students from more privileged socio-economic backgrounds are usually higher than those from less privileged backgrounds. The benefits of social capital in terms of the depth of information available about post-secondary options and the consequences of early academic decisions thus play a role in the advantages accrued for those from higher-SES backgrounds (CPRN 2002).

Educational Returns in the Labour Market

The decisions to attend university as opposed to college, which university or college, what program of study, and whether to pursue graduate studies have consequences for students' future earnings potential (Betts, Ferrall, and Finnie 2007; Butlin 2001; S. Davies and Guppy 2006; Guppy and Davies 1998). For example, in the examination by Guppy and Davies (1998) of 1990 earnings by field of study chosen for a bachelor's degree, some fields of study had definite earning advantages over others. Those who enrolled in programs such as engineering, law, and medicine reaped higher earnings than the average BA graduate, and those with more general degrees (e.g., in the humanities and social sciences) earned less than the average BA graduate (Guppy and Davies 1998). In a more recent study by Betts, Ferrall, and Finnie (2007), earnings five years after graduation differed by as much as 60 per cent between fields of undergraduate study. The authors conclude that 'what you study' and 'where you study' have a large bearing on postgraduate earnings (Betts, Ferrall, and Finnie 2007).

The choice of what type of post-secondary or university program to enroll in depends on adequate information; however, it also increasingly depends on finances. This is particularly true in professional programs, which tend to have the highest labour-market returns. Interestingly, although there has been a large push for Canadian youth to move into apprenticeships and trades, a recent study of educational investments show that returns 'remain stubbornly low' (Boothby and Drewes 2006: 17). Issues of financing have especially been the case in Ontario, where fees for professional programs rose as much as 241 per cent (for medicine) and 315 per cent (for dentistry) from the mid-1990s to the early 2000s (Frenette 2005). In the wake of these increases, enrolment levels rose among youth whose parents had a graduate or professional degree as well as among youth whose parents had no post-secondary education (Frenette 2005). Frenette (2005) states that while access for disadvantaged students opened up through

bursaries and scholarships, those students in the middle (whose parents had some post-secondary qualification) saw their enrolment levels in professional programs drop dramatically.

Parental education also has a significant effect on whether or not students who achieve a bachelor's degree continue on to graduate studies (Butlin 2001). Students whose parents had a high school diploma or less were much less likely to enrol in master's or doctoral programs than students with university-educated parents (Butlin 2001). The advantage for those students whose parents had obtained a master's or doctoral degree was particularly pronounced, for these bachelor-degree recipients were three times more likely to pursue master's or doctoral programs than were bachelor's-degree recipients whose parents had only a high school education (Butlin 2001: 28). Higher levels of education tends to lead to more authoritative and higher-paying jobs (Butlin 2001; Butlin and Oderkirk 1997). Butlin (2001: 28) notes that recipients of master's degrees could expect to earn $9,000 a year more than those with only the bachelor's degree. Therefore, those students who come from more highly educated families maintain their advantage throughout university and into the labour market.

Focusing on Race/Ethnicity: Historical Notes and Existing Patterns

Issues of class and race or ethnicity are closely bound together, and many of the educational disadvantages and difficulties faced by racial and ethnic minorities stem from long-standing economic exploitation and disadvantage (as in the case of Aboriginal Canadians) and from the financial and social struggle of emigrating to a new country (Ali and Grabb, 1998; Bernhard and Freire 1999; S. Davies and Guppy 2006). In spite of these barriers, visible minorities in Canada tend to be more highly educated than the general population; they are more likely to have a high school diploma and more likely to be university-educated (S. Davies and Guppy 2006: 118; Taylor and Krahn 2005). Currently, higher levels of education among visible minorities are due to the high levels of education required to gain entrance to Canada through immigration policy: more than half (51 per cent) of immigrants who came to Canada between 2001 and 2006 had university degrees compared to only 20 per cent of Canadian-born persons and 28 per cent of immigrants prior to 2001 (Statistics Canada 2008c: 6). Indeed, minority groups in Canada have historically faced barriers and educational obstacles based on their perceived ethnic and racial background. Individuals from racial and ethnic minority groups have experienced exclusions and racism in Canadian classrooms (Carr and Klassen 1996; Kelly 2002; Knight 1997; Dei 1993, 2006). This is illustrated by the history of classroom segregation and eventual 'separate' schooling for black students in Canada West in the nineteenth century, instituted in spite of vigorous protests by black parents (Knight 1997). In Upper Canada, the Common School Act of 1859 provided black students with schools that were distinctly 'separate' from the institutions attended by white children (Knight 1997). By the twentieth century, these schools no longer existed, though the act remained on the books until 1964. These issues continue today as the Toronto District School Board opens a school for black students that some call 'segregated' and others call 'Afrocentric' (see Box 10.3).

These sentiments of exclusion and difference are echoed in the history of educational programs directed at Aboriginals in Canada (Wotherspoon 2004). The residential schools for Aboriginal children that operated from the late nineteenth century until the 1980s effectively stripped these children of their families and their culture (S. Davies and Guppy 2006; Guppy and Davies 1998). This was entirely intentional. Guppy and Davies (1998: 180) note that 'a deliberate and concerted effort was made to remove thousands of Aboriginal children from their families and communities and immerse them in European traditions, thereby assimilating or "Canadianizing" large portions of the Aboriginal population.' These programs have had a devastating and lasting impact on Aboriginal populations (Guppy and Davies 1998). Only very recently (11 June 2008) has the Canadian government formally apologized to Aboriginal communities for its role in creating and administering these residential schools.

Davies and Guppy (2006: 120) point out that the relationship between visible minority status and educational achievement is complex and highly influenced by Canada's changing immigration policy, by its history of colonization, and by socio-economic factors. The high education levels of more recent immigrants are becoming evident in the high educational aspirations and attainments of their children (Krahn and Taylor 2007; Taylor and Krahn 2005). In addition, recent data on reading, vocabulary, and mathematics test scores of the children of immigrant and non-immigrant parents show a convergence over time. In other words, immigrant children whose parents' mother tongue is not English or French catch up to their peers in academic performance (Guppy and Davies 2006). Yet some visible minority groups continue to encounter exclusion and barriers in Canadian educational settings. Bernhard and Freire (1999) give an example of the way in which elementary schools fail students from minority backgrounds. They specifically look at the school experiences of the children of recent Latin American immigrants to Canada and the way in which these parents and teachers interact and communicate (Bernhard and Freire 1999). A primary aim was to find out how the school system could serve these families better and how these parents could be more effective advocates for their children. In spite of the high educational aspirations and valuation

Box 10.3 Afrocentric Schools Not about Segregation, Advocates Argue

By James Bradshaw

Teaching different students the same way will not make them equal, teachers and parents who led the charge to create an Afrocentric alternative school in Toronto said yesterday.

Advocates including the original proposal's co-authors, Donna Harrow and Angela Wilson, gathered at Queen's Park to refute criticism of the plan and claims by Premier Dalton McGuinty and Education Minister Kathleen Wynne that the school would create a harmful racial divide among students.

The group argued the school is not about segregation, but rather about being able to choose a nurturing and inclusive environment for disengaged students.

'A curriculum that assumes sameness or colour-blindness does not necessarily lead to equality,' said Grace-Edward Galabuzi, an associate professor at Ryerson University. 'Equal treatment does not mean same treatment.

'There's a recognition by the board that different children benefit from varied curricula, varied learning styles, varied pedagogical approaches,' he added.

Mr Galabuzi was responding in part to comments Mr McGuinty made Wednesday reiterating his belief that students learn best in an integrated and multicultural environment.

'We believe it's a matter of principle, that the single most important thing we can do for our kids is bring them together so they have an opportunity to come to know one another, to understand one another and to learn together and grow together,' Mr McGuinty said. 'We think that's the foundation for a caring, cohesive society.'

Mr McGuinty has said he would prefer to include more Afrocentric elements in the Ontario curriculum, where they would reach all students.

Louis March, communications officer for the African Canadian Heritage Association, countered that 'there is an illusion of inclusion' in Toronto public schools, a phrase he heard from a teacher that he thinks highlights the flaw in Mr McGuinty's philosophy.

He said it is erroneous to suggest that a student's mere presence at a school means they are being included in its educational processes.

Ms Wilson agreed with Mr Galabuzi's emphasis on differing student needs, arguing Toronto's system of 36 alternative schools recognizes the need for choice in children's education.

'Education is not one-size-fits-all, and therefore broadening choices for children who learn differently is really what education is all about,' she said.

Ms Harrow also dismissed Mr McGuinty's concerns as retrograde thinking.

'This notion of segregation is kind of old,' she said. 'We really need to move on to the positive, pro-active ways in which we help a group of students who are not doing well within our system.'

of education found in these Latin American families, the authors found a general pattern of academic underperformance for these children and parental alienation and confusion in the parents' relations with educational personnel (Bernhard and Freire 1999). One of their main findings was that many parents did not understand much of the vocabulary used by the teachers.

For instance, teachers' practice of using 'positive' and complimentary descriptors when describing difficulties with a child's progress was seen by parents to indicate a good performance. In addition, educational terms like 'special education' and 'reading clinics' were not fully understood by or explained to parents. Parents expected a more compassionate and personal approach from their children's teachers and were disappointed with the impersonal and all-business attitude on the part of Canadian teachers (Bernhard and Freire 1999). These findings illustrate that even when parents have high educational goals for their children and want to facilitate their child's education, the structures of the institution itself (e.g., institutional jargon) can pose significant barriers to a positive academic experience and effective parental involvement.

Educational Attainment

Although there is a significant body of research on the educational attainment of Aboriginal people in Canada, much more information is needed on the effect that race or ethnicity and place of birth have on educational attainment (Looker and Lowe 2001). The diversity among groups designated 'visible and ethnic minorities' and the factors of nativity, the period of immigration, and the changing effect of immigration policy make these investigations complex (S. Davies and Guppy 2006). Again, the high educational attainments required by current immigration regulations and the younger age of many immigrants compared to the general population may artificially inflate the educational levels of ethnic and racial minority groups and thus underestimate the barriers encountered in the Canadian educational system (Guppy and Davies 1998). Nonetheless, a number of studies contend that class is a more important predictor than race and ethnicity of educational attainment (Ali and Grabb 1998; S. Davies and Guppy 2006; Guppy and Davies 1998).

In fact, visible-minority youth are slightly *more* likely than other youth to have their post-secondary options open in Grade 10 (Taylor and Krahn 2007), and the aspirations of visible-minority immigrant youth for university are also higher than those of other youth (Taylor and Krahn 2005). Indeed, in the latest results from the Youth in Transition Survey, 62 per cent of visible-minority youth aged 24 to 26 had attended university compared to 49 per cent of same-age youth who were not a member of a visible minority (Shaienks and Gluszynski 2007: 9). Davies and Guppy (2006: 118) highlight Frenette's (2005) data that show that in terms of educational attainment, visible minorities as a group are not collectively disadvantaged when compared to non-visible minorities. In terms of university-degree attainment, 29.6 per cent of those aged between 25 and 34 with visible minority status had a university degree in 2001 compared to 23.7 per cent of same-aged whites (S. Davies and Guppy 2006: 118). Of those who reported Asian visible minority status, fully 41 per cent had a university degree. While university degrees are more common among visible-minority adults than among other adults, the educational attainments of racial and ethnic minorities are extremely variable (S. Davies and Guppy 2006).

Table 10.3 illustrates the diversity in educational attainment among men in Canada by ethnic group. In this table, the age comparison accounts partially for potential differences between foreign-born and Canadian-born individuals. Note that while less than 5 per cent of Aboriginal men aged 25–44 have a university degree, nearly half of same-aged Chinese men do and close to 60 per cent of Korean men (Census of Canada 2001). At the same time, less than 20 per cent of black men aged 25–44 have a university degree, little different from the percentage of those aged 65 and older (13 per cent). In earlier studies, Guppy and Davies argued that the diversity of levels of educational attainment among

Table 10.3 Percentage of Men with a University Degree, by Ethnic Origin and Age Group, 2001

	25–44			65+		
	Population	% with university degree	Rank	Population	% with university degree	Rank
Chinese	160,965	47.3	2	46,500	15.0	9
South Asian	154,320	35.6	6	26,925	20.4	5
Black	96,140	19.4	9	12,855	13.3	12
Filipino	41,565	32.7	7	6,485	24.3	3
Latin American	39,455	19.4	9	2,770	14.3	10
Southeast Asian	36,100	16.7	11	4,015	13.8	11
Arab	39,085	43.1	3	4,030	20.2	6
West Asian	21,370	38.0	5	2,500	39.6	1
Korean	14,885	57.4	1	2,020	37.1	2
Japanese	9,425	42.3	4	4,555	14.5	9
Visible minority, n.i.e.[a]	16,690	18.2	10	2,625	15.6	7
Multiple visible minorities[b]	10,160	30.9	8	1,395	21.1	4
Aboriginal	138,680	4.4	12	18,145	2.3	13
Total	**778,840**	**29.1**	**–**	**134,820**	**15.6**	**–**

a Includes respondents who reported a write-in response classified as a visible minority (e.g., 'Polynesian' or 'Guyanese').

b Includes respondents who reported more than one visible minority group by checking two or more mark-in circles (e.g., 'Black' and 'South Asian').

Source: 2001 Census.

ethnic and racial minorities means that specific groups (e.g., Aboriginal people and blacks) face systemic obstacles in the process of educational attainment that not all racial and ethnic minority groups encounter (Guppy and Davies 1998; Simmons and Plaza 1998).

Aboriginal people in Canada have encountered numerous barriers in the educational system (CCL 2007; CPRN 2002; S. Davies and Guppy 2006; Mata 1997). Though the educational attainment of Aboriginal people in Canada is improving, 8 per cent of Aboriginal people aged 25–64 had a university degree in 2006, which is a large gap considering that 23 per cent of same-aged non-Aboriginal Canadians have a university degree (Statistics Canada 2008c). Some of

the obstacles faced in the process of obtaining a post-secondary education reported by on-reserve Aboriginal Canadians are as follows: '53 per cent have inadequate funding, 46 per cent have poor academic preparation, 28 per cent do not feel welcome on campus, 20 per cent consider post-secondary education unnecessary' (CCL 2007: 76). This combination of factors echoes many of those identified in Frenette's study (2005) on the gap in university participation between low-income and high-income youth. Box 10.4 highlights aspects of these structural barriers and the difficulties in gaining access to post-secondary and university education, particularly for those whose parents did not go to university and are therefore 'first-generation'.

Box 10.4 Bridging the Access Gap: It Starts with First-Generation Students

By Judith Maxwell

It's called the access gap and it's been getting wider.

According to the Canada Millennium Scholarship Foundation, 81 per cent of 18 to 24 year olds whose parents have university degrees participate in postsecondary education, compared to 53 per cent for young people whose parents did not go past high school. About 40 per cent of 20 year olds showed no sign of attending a college, vocational or university program in 2003.

There are at least three reasons to encourage these young people to become the first generation in their family to complete a postsecondary program. Most job creation in future decades will require a degree or diploma; Canada is already facing selected labour shortages; and, just when we need them most, the number of 18 to 24 year olds will begin to decline after 2011, as a result of the baby bust of the 1990s.

The young people facing the access gap come from low-income families—many are aboriginal or children of recent immigrants. For these families, the average $16,800 annual cost for a full-time university program is intimidating.

But the first barrier they face is not financial, it's attitudinal. In a Statistics Canada study ('Why Are Youth from Lower-income Families Less Likely to Attend University?'), Mark Frenette found that barriers related to academic ability, high school quality and parental influence account for 84 per cent of the access gap.

'First-generation youth are less likely to plan for higher education, to be convinced of its benefits or to have above-average high school grades,' adds the Canada Millennium Scholarship Foundation in the third edition of 'The Price of Knowledge'.

How, then, do we influence the attitudes of these young people? The best way to start is to help them become successful high school students.

The Pathways to Education project in Toronto's Regent Park shows that low ambition and low marks are a social blight that can be overcome. With the help of mentors and tutors from Grade 9 on, and the promise of a $4,000 bursary on graduation, dropout rates for Regent Park students have fallen from 56 per cent to about 10 per cent; teen pregnancies have plummeted, and so have crime rates. After graduation, college and university enrolment almost doubled, and 85 per cent of those enrolled were first-generation students.

These students show how important motivation and self-confidence are to education outcomes. And their success has provoked provincial departments of education to begin talking about early intervention.

Manitoba may be the first province to address the access gap at its roots. In his recent budget speech, Greg Selinger, Minister of Finance, promised to increase the number of students able to successfully pursue postsecondary education by improving high school graduation rates, with a special focus on under-represented groups.

Other provinces, including British Columbia, Alberta and Nova Scotia, are trying to build awareness of postsecondary options. 'Our single biggest concern', said one student aid administrator, 'is to reach the students who are not predisposed to postsecondary education. We have to reach them early on—Grade 10 or earlier. We need to talk about the value of higher education first. Opportunities for financing will come later.'

If governments do take an active role in supporting young adolescents at risk of dropping out, they will certainly need the help of community organizations like the Regent Park Community Health Centre, which spearheaded the Pathways project.

The next challenge will be to include support for first-generation students in the complex web of student financial aid, which currently costs governments $6.4-billion a year. That system strongly favours students from middle- and high-income families.

The outcry about excessive student debt burdens in the 1990s led to two major changes in student aid. The first was a dramatic increase in tax credits and other forms of tax relief.

These tax savings (which cost governments $2.6-billion) cover between one-third and one-half of tuition, depending on the province. But, because of the way tax credits work, the benefits go mainly to students and families with middle and higher incomes.

The second was an effort to curb the amount of debt a student could accumulate by offering grants and debt remission schemes. The combined cost of loans, grants and debt remission amounts to $3.8-billion a year.

The good news about grants is that students who receive them have a higher probability of completing their programs.

The bad news is that they do not serve the needs of low-income students because they are debt averse. In most cases, you have to take on a loan to qualify for a grant.

The main option for first-generation students is the 'access bursaries' provided by the Canada Millennium Scholarship Foundation and the federal government. The bursaries will be replaced in 2009 by the $350-million Canada Student Grant announced in the federal budget. But it will certainly take more than $350-million to narrow the access gap.

The key is to help young adolescents become keen students. Once first-generation students graduate, there is a high probability that their children will enroll in higher education, too.

By the numbers

81
Percentage of 18 to 24 year olds whose parents have university degrees who participate in post-secondary education.

53
Percentage of young people whose parents did not go past high school who participate in post-secondary education.

40
Percentage of 20 year olds who showed no sign of attending a college, vocational or university program in 2003.

$6.4-billion
Cost per year to governments for student financial aid.

Source: Maxwell (2008). Reprinted by permission of the author.

The educational system has failed Aboriginal students, and, consequently, Aboriginal Canadians have much lower levels of educational attainment than the non-Aboriginal population, though their levels of educational attainment are growing (Statistics Canada 2008c). According to 2006 statistics, 34 per cent of Aboriginal adults aged 25–64 had not completed high school, compared with 15 per cent of same-aged adults in Canada (Statistics Canada 2008c).

Nonetheless, Aboriginal students are increasingly engaged in post-secondary education, with 44 per cent having some post-secondary certification in 2006 (Statistics Canada 2008c: 19). For those Aboriginal students who do engage in post-secondary education, the attrition rate is extremely high (CPRN 2002). Indeed, these attrition rates may not be surprising given that 59 per cent of on-reserve First Nations youth report not engaging in post-secondary education because of the 'need to support family' (Berger, Motte, and Parkin 2007: 59). In Mata's (1997) investigation of the process of socio-economic and educational 'transmission' in Canada, Aboriginal sons and daughters experienced distinct disadvantages when compared to other ethnic and racial minority groups. While the parents in many other ethnic and racial groups were able to successfully 'transmit' their level of education to their children, in the case of highly educated Aboriginal parents, there was little success in passing on attained educational levels (Mata 1997). The only other group to face such systemic and enduring obstacles to educational attainment in Mata's study were foreign-born minority daughters.

Educational Returns in the Labour Market

The high educational attainment of many visible minority groups and the educational mobility experienced by some ethnic minority groups in a society that discriminates on the basis of race and ethnicity is a testament to the power of individual agents. Unfortunately, as is shown in chapter 9, the true impact of racial and ethnic privilege are more starkly evident in the workings of the labour market (Hum and Simpson 2007; Li 2001b; Li, Gervaise, and Duval 2006; Mata 1997; Tran 2004). Hum and Simpson (2007: 104) found that black men in Canada, whether immigrant or native-born, experience a 22 per cent wage penalty in the labour market. They further note, 'the evidence is clear that economic disadvantage for blacks in Canada stems from unique structural features of Canadian society and economy, and it is hard to resist the suggestion that racial discrimination is an important factor' (Hum and Simpson 2007: 106).

Indeed, higher education is no guarantee of occupational and socio-economic mobility (Mata 1997). All educational credentials are not valued equally, and a number of studies have shown that visible minorities encounter systemic devaluation of their educational credentials, especially when they happen to be among Canada's more highly educated recent immigrants (Li et al. 2006; Samuel and Basavarajappa 2006). Visible-minority professionals who emigrate to Canada have been found to experience downward mobility compared to their occupational positions in their country of origin (Basran and Zong 1998). Samuel and Basavarajappa (2006: 250) report that for recent immigrants (of whom 70 per cent are visible minorities), the unemployment rate for adults aged 25–44 is twice that of the same-aged Canadian-born population. Kelly (2002) notes that there are significant levels of underemployment among highly educated visible minorities and that despite their higher educational attainment, they are less likely to obtain employment in professional or managerial occupations when compared to the non-visible-minority population.

In addition, Samuel and Basavarajappa (2006: 257) note that among the Canadian born, although 'visible minority men and women had higher proportions with university degrees . . . their shares in the top income quintiles were less than those of the non-visible minority counterparts, indicating that their earnings were not commensurate with their educational attainments'. Visible-minority immigrants who are not educated in Canada also face significant barriers in obtaining jobs and earnings on par with their education (Li 2000b). In fact, Picot, Hou, and Coulombe (2008: 416) found that recent immigrants entering under the 'skilled economic' classification are more likely to become poor in Canada than those entering as 'family class'.

Li (2001b) specifically analyzes the labour-market returns that visible-minority immigrants and non-visible-minority immigrants can expect in comparison with native-born Canadians. Gender and race or ethnicity were found to have significant effects on the extent to which immigrants encountered underemployment and weak labour-market returns. Visible-minority immigrants (both men and women) were penalized much more harshly in the labour market for their foreign credentials than white immigrants. Visible-minority immigrant women with foreign degrees were the most disadvantaged in the labour market. For example, white immigrant women with a foreign degree earned an average of $30,770 annually, while visible-minority immigrant women with a foreign degree earned the least of any group, at $26,797 (Li 2001b: 32). Li and his colleagues (2006: 9) found that recent immigrants are also twice as likely to be overqualified for their jobs and twice as likely to remain in positions for which they were overqualified. These findings illustrate that the achievement of credentials and educational mobility cannot in and of themselves overcome systemic discrimination for disadvantaged groups.

Focusing on Gender: Historical Notes and Existing Patterns

Historically, women have had to fight for their right to be educated, and educational policies have tended to emphasize women's wifely and motherly roles in processes of reproduction (Ng 1993; Wollstonecraft 1792). Yet, in Canada, women's access to education and enrolments at the elementary and secondary levels have been equivalent to men's for some time (S. Davies and Guppy 2006; Wotherspoon 2004). In fact, the educational level of women has surpassed men's since the mid-1980s, except at the doctoral level (Butlin 2001; CCL 2007; Wotherspoon 2004). Although alienation and **silencing** in the classroom are still a concern for girls and women, and women continue to be underrepresented in post-secondary technical, mathematical, and engineering programs, the gender-equity issue that is gaining attention in the elementary- and secondary-school systems has been the relative 'underperformance' of boys in comparison to girls (CPRN 2002; Looker and Lowe 2001; McMullen 2004; Wotherspoon 2004).

However, lumping all boys together as 'at risk' may confuse the issue, because it is more specifically boys from families with low socio-economic status, Aboriginal boys, boys from some visible minority ethnic groups, and boys for whom English is a second language who are systemically disadvantaged in the educational system (CPRN 2002: 15). This argument is supported by the research of Thiessen and Nickerson (1999: 14), who found that the mathematical and problem-solving abilities of boys are much 'more variable' than the abilities of girls, and thus there are more boys scoring above and below average. As with race and ethnicity, where some ethnic minority groups attain very high levels of education and others are at a substantial disadvantage, within the 'variable' gender there are significant differences in academic performance and post-secondary participation rates among groups of boys (CPRN 2002). These findings speak to the complexity of identities and to the enmeshment of the social relations of class, age, gender, and race and ethnicity, particularly when it comes to social privilege and disadvantage.

Still, a number of studies illustrate that boys constitute the majority of students 'at risk' of educational difficulties (Bohatyretz and Lipps 1999; Bussière, Knighton, and Pennock 2007; CPRN 2002; McMullen 2004; Sokal et al. 2005; Statistics Canada 2008c). Unfortunately, most of these studies do not give us more specific information about the class or race/ethnicity of boys and girls in a synthesized way (i.e., where data are separately tabulated for these factors). Recent work by Thomas (2006: 48) showed that 'readiness to learn' at age five differed between boys and girls, with girls exhibiting stronger communication skills and abilities in symbol use, as well as better independence, self-control, and attention.

Similar to Thomas (2006), earlier studies found that when children were rated by their teachers for various behavioural traits, boys were perceived to be more physically aggressive and more hyperactive and inattentive than girls

(Julien and Ertl 1999). In contrast, girls exhibited better work habits and more **pro-social behaviour**, or altruistic behaviour, although they were also perceived to exhibit more indirect aggressive behaviour. Of note, however, was that there were no perceived gender differences in anxiety and emotional disorders, and when all behavioural scores were compared, no substantial behavioural differences were found (Julien and Ertl 1999). Overall, these findings provide few answers as to why boys encounter disadvantages in the educational process. Guppy and Davies (1998) have suggested that, historically, many men have not required educational credentials to obtain well-paying, stable jobs, whereas the fields of teaching, nursing, and clerical work, in which the majority of women found employment, have required an education. Therefore, this disparity in academic attainment may partially stem from lower educational aspirations on the part of boys and their families as a result of mistaken beliefs about the current demands of the labour market. Young men do tend to have somewhat lower academic aspirations than young women (Looker and Lowe 2001).

Educational 'role modelling' from our parents appears to be an important factor. Indeed, Frenette and Zeman's (2007) study found that parental expectations were more important than peer influences in education attainment; however, Frenette and Zeman found that the most critical factors in explaining the differences between boys' and girls' educational attainment were those relating to academic performance. The authors suggest that gender differences in early school performance and study habits may explain much of the differential in later educational trajectories. For example, 70 per cent of young women had parents who expected them to complete a university degree, compared to 60 per cent of young men (Frenette and Zeman 2007). Figure 10.4 shows the percentage of boys and girls rated 'very well' by the person most knowledgeable of their work (typically a parent) in various

academic subjects and overall. In this figure, we see that compared to boys, girls are rated 'very well' more often in all areas, and significantly so in writing, reading, and overall ability.

Nancy Mandell (CPRN 2002) outlines several arguments that have been proffered to explain the lower educational performance of boys. These range from an incompatibility between boys' 'inherent nature' and classroom imperatives, to a female-biased curriculum, to class and race or ethnic discrimination in the school system (CPRN 2002: 15–16). Mandell concludes that while these factors likely play a role, in order to understand boys' underachievement in school, we have to stop viewing this a problem of boys versus girls. This may be difficult to do with the data at hand; in the future more complex and detailed information about students and their families will be required.

Educational Attainment

The gendered trends of educational performance that are evident in elementary school appear to continue into secondary school (Bowlby and McMullen 2002; Frenette and Zeman 2007). Thiessen and Nickerson (1999) found that in the teen years, girls showed stronger academic performance than boys in almost all subjects. Although after the age of 16 boys do score higher on problem solving, these differences are significantly smaller than the language and reading advantage shown by girls (Thiessen and Nickerson 1999). Bussière, Knighton, and Pennock (2007) report the recent OECD's Programme for International Student Assessment (PISA) results which show that while 15-year-old Canadian boys had a 14-point advantage in mathematics, girls were 33 points ahead in reading. Likewise, Frenette and Zeman (2007) report that at age 15, approximately one-third (32 per cent) of boys have overall marks of 80 per cent or higher, compared with 46 per cent of same-aged girls. Thiessen and Nickerson (1999) partially

Figure 10.4: PMK Evaluation of Academic Performance by Gender

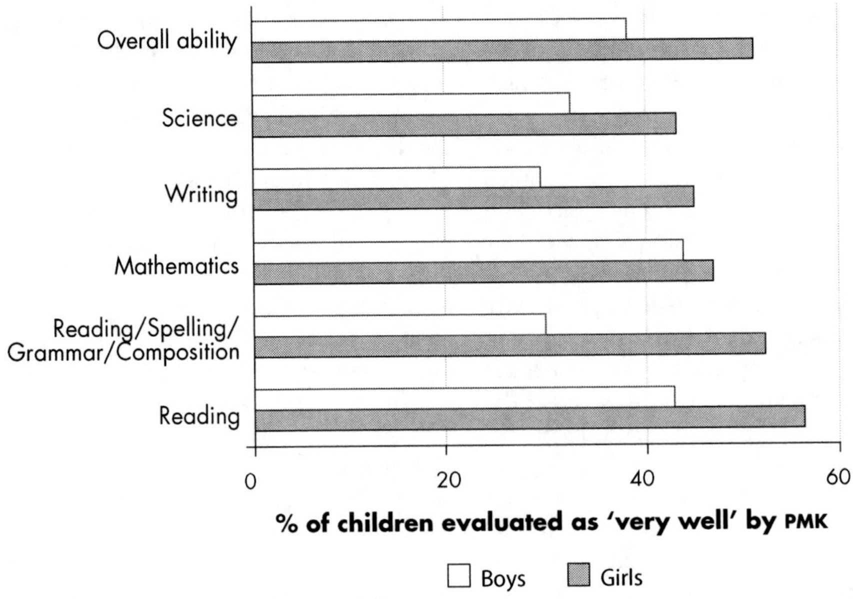

Notes: PMK = person most knowledgeable (typically a parent or guardian)
Source: National Longitudinal Survey of Children and Youth, 1998–99, public use data.

attribute differences such as these to boys' great-er disengagement and dissatisfaction with the school environment. Their conclusions remain consistent with more recent research (McMullen 2004; Statistics Canada 2008c). Young men continue to be significantly less likely than young women to complete high school (Bowlby and McMullen 2002; CCL 2008a; Looker and Lowe 2001). In 2006–7, 11 per cent of young men dropped out of high school in comparison to 7 per cent of young women (CCL 2008: 16). According to the latest Youth in Transition Survey, young men cited a desire to work and dissat-isfaction with school as their main reasons for dropping out of high school (CCL 2008).

As Figure 10.5 shows, dropout rates also vary significantly by province. Here we see that in Quebec in 2003 the male high school dropout rate is 14.4 per cent for 19-year-olds compared

with only 6 per cent for males in British Colum-bia. The ratio of male to female dropouts also shows some substantial variations by province; the least gender difference was in Saskatch-ewan, where dropout rates are nearly the same. Although dropout rates have declined in the Maritimes, there are some substantial differences evident in the rates for males and females. For example, in New Brunswick 8 per cent of males leave high school compared to only 3 per cent of females. Indeed, in Alberta and Quebec, twice as many males leave in comparison with their female counterparts (Zeman 2007).

Clearly, academic performance in high school and high school completion are significant determinants of whether students go on to post-secondary education. The academic 'under-performance' of young men in high school and their higher rate of high school non-completion

Figure 10.5: High School Status at Age 19, by Gender and Province, 2003

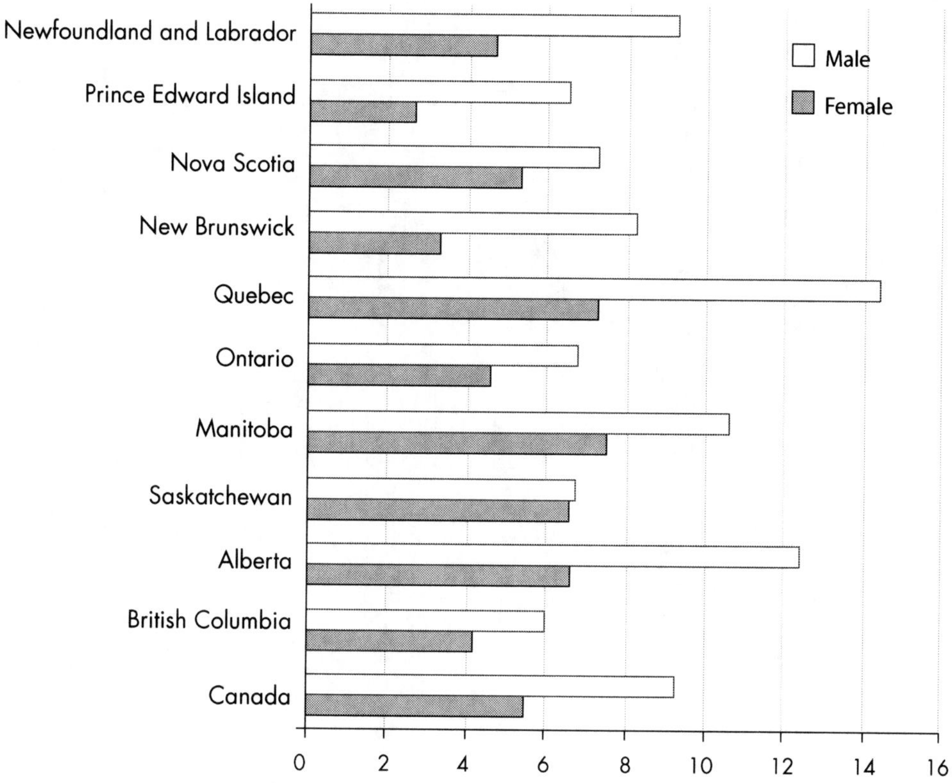

Source: Zeman (2007).

put them at a disadvantage in the pursuit of post-secondary education (Bowlby and McMullen 2002; CCL 2007; Thiessen and Nickerson 1999). According to many studies, young men are underrepresented among post-secondary graduates and participants (with the exception of doctoral studies) (Bowlby and McMullen 2002; CCL 2007; Frenette and Zeman 2007; Looker and Lowe 2001). The latest figures show that women make up 58 per cent of students in bachelor's-degree programs and that their graduation completion rates of undergraduate programs are 61 per cent compared to 39 per cent for men (CCL 2007: 77). In 2006, 33 per cent of women aged 25–34 had a university degree compared with one-quarter

(25 per cent) of same-aged men (Statistics Canada 2008c). This represents a substantial change in the gendered composition of post-secondary students in a relatively short time. For example, in 1972–3 women made up 43 per cent of university undergraduates, whereas in 1992–3 they constituted 53 per cent of undergraduates, and women's representation in higher educational levels continues to increase (Thiessen and Nickerson 1999: 27). Indeed, in 2003, among 19-year-olds, nearly 40 per cent (38.8 per cent) of girls had attended university, compared with one-quarter (25.6 per cent) of same-aged boys (Frenette and Zeman 2007). Still, change has tended to be slower in terms of the fields of

Figure 10.6: Gender Distribution of Post-secondary Students in Science and Engineering Fields, 2005–6

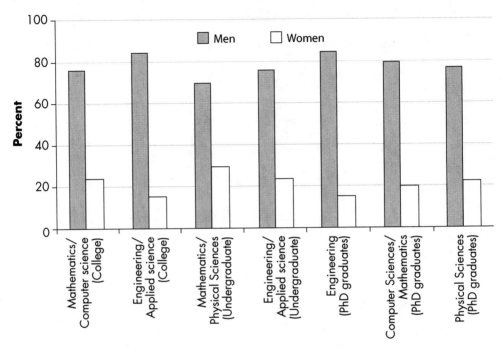

Source: Statistics Canada (2005d, 2006f), cited in CCL (2007).

university study pursued by men and women and in the number of women in full-time doctoral studies (Butlin 2001; S. Davies and Guppy 2006; Looker and Lowe 2001), though women now constitute 45 per cent of doctoral candidates (CCL 2007: 77).

Despite the fact that almost equal numbers of men and women graduate from university in Canada, the educational tracks that girls and boys and men and women take in high school and university vary markedly. As a result of socialization, the toys that girls and boys play with, and different levels of encouragement for girls and boys, few girls claim to be good at math or science—even with progressive educational programs that try to eliminate gendered messages, and regardless of girls' objective test scores. In university, these early trends translate

into fewer women enrolling in engineering, science, or math programs. Although there have been significant improvements in the number of women who enter law and medical programs, women tend to pursue the lower-status streams within these programs by specializing in family law or family medicine. Men are discouraged from entering streams of education that are associated with women, such as nursing; but once in these programs, men are often viewed with greater esteem by their peers and professors (C.L. Williams 1995).

Research suggests that the university studies pursued by young men and women continue to adhere to these traditional gendered ideologies, with women largely concentrated in education, health, and the humanities and men in mathematics and engineering (CCL 2007; Looker and

Figure 10.7: Gender Distribution of Post-secondary Students in Education and Health Fields, 2005–6

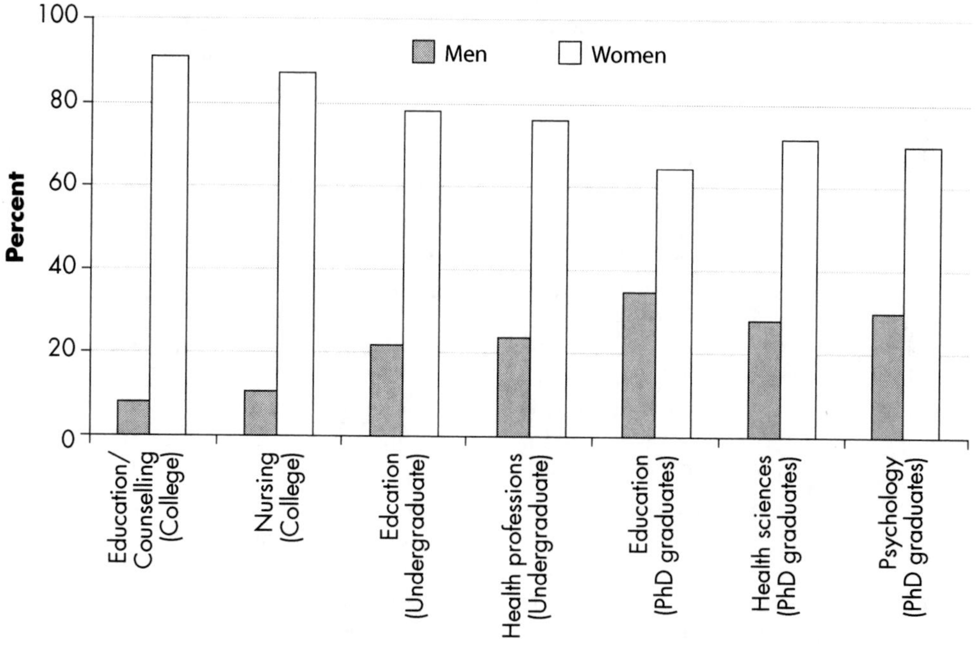

Source: Statistics Canada (2005d, 2006f), cited in CCL (2007).

Lowe 2001). As Figures 10.6 and 10.7 show, women remain clustered in education and health fields, with men dominating in engineering, mathematics, and science. The continued underrepresentation of women in these fields of study is somewhat perplexing, especially given the generally equivalent levels of mathematical performance that are emerging between young men and women. And among women who do choose the non-traditional route of the maths and sciences, attrition rates tend to be high. Erwin and Maurutto (1998) examined the experiences of university women enrolled in science programs and found that the women most likely to leave the program were those who had to engage in significant hours of part-time work, many of them black working-class students. The underrepresentation of women in these

well-paying scientific and technical fields and in doctoral studies further disadvantages women in the labour market—where women have tended to need much higher educational levels in order to earn wages comparable to those of men (S. Davies and Guppy 2006; Thiessen and Nickerson 1999).

Educational Returns in the Labour Market

In spite of being more highly educated than men, women continue to earn fewer returns on their **educational investments** than men (S. Davies and Guppy 2006; Frenette and Coulombe 2007; Frenette and Zeman 2007). Indeed, women's earnings remain lower than men's at all levels of education and in spite of women's growing educational attainment (Frenette and Coulombe

2007; Statistics Canada 2006a). Overall, little has changed in terms of the gap between men and women's earnings, and in fact, in the 1990s the earnings gap between university-educated men and women increased (Frenette and Coulombe 2007). In 2001, women aged 25 to 29 earned 18 per cent less than same-aged men (CCL 2007) and in 2003, data for full-year, full-time employment show that at all educational levels women generally earned 71 per cent of what men earned (Statistics Canada 2006a: 139). Thiessen and Nickerson (1999) suggest that **occupational segregation** and child-care responsibilities help to account for women's lower monetary returns for their educational attainment. However, it is not only monetarily that women are disadvantaged in the labour market (Butlin and Oderkirk 1997).

Although educational attainment usually leads to greater control and authority in the workplace, women were found by Butlin and Oderkirk (1997) to be far less likely than men to obtain significant amounts of autonomy and authority in their workplace even when education and other factors were controlled for. Men were more than twice as likely as women to achieve a top management post, and among male and female supervisors, men had significantly more decision-making power in their supervisory position. These patterns persist: although women in managerial positions increased to 37 per cent by 2004 (from 30 per cent in 1987), in fact women's share of managerial positions had dropped since 1996 (Statistics Canada 2006a: 113). Butlin and Oderkirk (1997) attribute these disparities largely to the concentration of women in occupations that differ in marked ways from those of men. The underrepresentation of women in the fields of engineering and the technical sciences and the concentration of women in the educational fields of teaching and nursing have a significant influence on labour-market returns and career trajectories. In the past two decades, women's representation in engineering and natural science occupations has remained virtually unchanged, from 20 per cent in 1987 to 21 per cent in 2004 (Statistics Canada 2006a: 113). Gendered discrimination in the labour market appears to be a contributing factor to the difficulty that women encounter in converting their educational credentials into monetary and other labour-market rewards (Butlin and Oderkirk 1997).

Focusing on Age and Life Course

Historical Trends in Canadian Educational Attainment

The times in which we live have a profound effect on our educational opportunities (S. Davies and Guppy 2006; Wanner 1999). Consequently, there are substantial differences in the educational attainment levels of different age cohorts in Canada (S. Davies and Guppy 2006). Younger Canadians tend to be more highly educated than older Canadians (Clark 2001; Wanner 1999). For example, in 1951, approximately 2 per cent of the Canadian population 15 years of age and older possessed a university degree, but by 1996 that number had risen to approximately 12 per cent (Clark 2001: 23). In 2006, 23 per cent of Canadians aged 25–64 had a university degree (Statistics Canada 2008—see Figure 10.8). Davies and Guppy (2006) point out that before the 1950s, very few Canadians went on to university and those who did were from a distinctly elite upper class. An even greater generational contrast is evident in the percentage of Canadians with less than a grade 9 education. In 1951, over 50 per cent of Canadians 15 years of age and older had less than a grade 9 education; in 1996, about 11 per cent did (Clark 2001: 23); and by 2001 that figure had fallen to approximately 5 per cent (S. Davies and Guppy 2006). By the mid-twentieth century, 'schooling' at the elementary and secondary levels had become an expected rite of passage for Canadian children; at the beginning

Figure 10.8: Proportion of the Population Aged 25 to 64 by Level of Educational Attainment and Age Groups, Canada, 2006

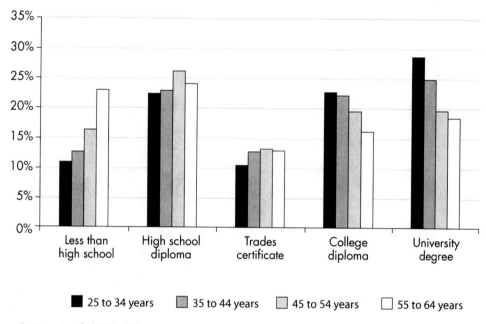

Source: Statistics Canada (2008c: 10).

of the twentieth century and before, school had played only a fleeting and sporadic role in many children's lives (Clark 2001).

The post-war baby boom and the subsequent expansion of the educational system produced some dramatic changes in the educational attainment levels of Canadians (Clark 2001; Wanner 1999). Clark (2001: 19) notes that in 1901, most children were not regularly in the classroom: only 4 out of 10 children attended elementary and secondary school daily. Even later in the century, many children began school much later than they do now (Clark 2001). In 1921, 48 per cent of 6-year-olds and 17 per cent of 7-year-olds did not attend school (Clark 2001: 19).

Figure 10.9 gives an indication of some of the significant shifts in school attendance over the course of the twentieth century. Here we see the percentage of Canadians between the ages of 15 and 24 who were attending school in selected years over the course of the twentieth century. This figure illustrates the strong differences between school attendance in the early part of the century and the current educational experience of Canadians. In 1941, fewer than half of 16-year-olds attended school, whereas in 1996, approximately 85 per cent attended (Clark 2001: 20). The school attendance rates of 20- to 24-year-olds gives an indication of the differences in post-secondary participation. Post-secondary participation rates in 1911 and 1941 were extremely small for this group, whereas in 1996 close to 50 per cent of 20- to 24-year-olds were attending school (Clark 2001: 20). These changes have continued to evolve.

Figure 10.9

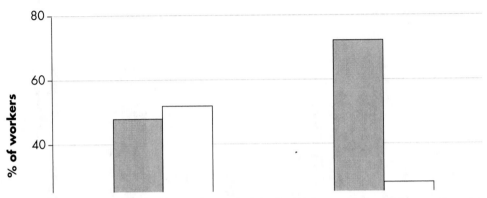

Source: Adapted from Li, Gervais, and Duval (2006: 9). Data: Statistics Canada, Survey of Labour and Income Dynamics, 1993 to 2001.

The historical shifts in educational directives from a focus on issues of citizenship and comportment to a concern with vocational skills and the accumulation of credentials has meant a substantially different educational experience for Canadians of different age groups (Bruno-Jofre and Henley 2000; Osborne 2000; Wotherspoon 2004). Over the course of the century, some groups have also experienced marked gains in their educational attainment as barriers and social norms have undergone change (S. Davies and Guppy 2006; Wanner 1999). For instance, whereas women constituted only 17 per cent of university students in 1920, today they make up the majority of those enrolled in university (CCL 2007; Clark 2001; Frenette and Zeman 2007).

Wanner (1999) specifically examines the changes in educational opportunity for Canadians throughout the twentieth century, in order to ascertain the effects of the **baby-boom expansion** on the educational opportunities of historically disadvantaged groups (e.g., women, those with a first language other than English, and those from a low socio-economic background). According to Wanner (1999), educational expansion has benefited some groups more than others. Analyzing age cohorts over time, he finds that the educational disadvantages experienced earlier in the century by women and those having English as a second language have largely been eliminated, except when it comes to graduate degrees, where men still have an advantage over women. In contrast, the educational disadvantage of coming from a lower socio-economic background has remained a stubborn feature of the educational landscape (Wanner 1999). In spite of the vast expansion in education, socio-economic background continues to operate as a most powerful predictor of educational attainment (CCL 2007; Frenette 2007; Wanner 1999). The growing importance and the length of education in the lives of Canadians in the form of adult training and educational programs means that the educational disadvantage faced by those from lower socio-economic backgrounds promises to have stronger lifelong economic ramifications than in the past (Clark 2001; Livingstone 2001).

Adult Education and the Changing Face of Education

The profile of students and of those seeking further education has changed from the stereotypical image of the young, supposedly carefree individual (Sales, Drolet, and Bonneau 2001). The imperatives of a changing labour market, along with credential inflation, have meant that a number of older adults are engaged in education and training programs (Livingstone 2001; Statistics Canada 2001f). However, recent analysis of results from the 2003 Adult Literacy and Life Skills Survey show some disturbing trends in Canada (Rubenson, Desjardins, and Yoon 2007). There has been no increase in the participation of Canadian adults in education courses between 1994 and 2003—in fact, Canadian participation rates lag behind those of the United States, Norway, and Switzerland (Rubenson et al. 2007). This is in spite of the fact that some workers see significant gains when they return to post-secondary education (Zhang and Palameta 2006). Among young men and women who return to school and get a post-secondary qualification, wages increase 8 per cent and 11 per cent respectively (Zhang and Palameta 2006: 20). The same types of gains are not evident for older workers who obtain a qualification and then switch employers; however, those who remain with their employers see a 13 per cent increase in wages (among men) and a 7 per cent increase (among women) (Palameta and Zhang 2006: 9).

Some workers have more difficulties than others in the pursuit of adult education and training. Older workers have lower adult education participation rates, with 9.9 per cent of men aged 35–59 participating compared to 19 per cent of men aged 17–34 (Palameta and Zhang 2006). Among adults aged 45–54, only 3.4 per cent attended a post-secondary education program in 2002 (Meyers and de Broucker 2006: 35). Only 8.2 per cent of men with less than a high school diploma participate in formal adult education, compared with 14 per cent who have a bachelor's degree or more (Palameta and Zhang 2006). Indeed, vulnerable groups in Canada—including those with low literacy levels, those with low socio-economic status, older adults,

and less educated adults—are least likely to engage in adult education (Rubenson et al. 2007). In other words, prior levels of educational attainment predict the participation rates of adult learners. As a result, well-educated adults are more likely to maintain and enhance their educational advantage in the workplace.

More immediately connected with the workplace, more than half (51.7 per cent) of Canadians who had an undergraduate degree participated in job-related formal training in 2002 compared with 17.9 per cent of those with high school or less (CCL 2007: 82). Researchers suggest that contrary to their purpose, adult education and training may actually 'amplify rather than attenuate social inequalities in labour market outcomes' (Rubenson et al. 2007: 38). Among those with less than a high school education and who would have liked to participate in adult education but did not, the top reasons for not going back to school are cost and family responsibilities (Meyers and de Broucker 2006). Much more support is also needed for low-literacy learners in Canada: only 1 in 10 Canadians with low literacy skills receive government support for education and training compared with 1 in 5 in Norway (Rubenson et al. 2007).

Although more adult learners are attending post-secondary institutions now than was true in the past, the age profile at universities is getting younger as more and more youth are enrolling (Meyers and de Broucker 2006). Older learners tend to face more challenges in returning to school. Sales and his colleagues (2001) analyzed the academic routes taken by a sample of university students in Quebec and found predominately non-linear and interrupted paths in the effort to obtain a university degree. These academic disruptions were primarily attributable to financial difficulties, which forced students to leave their studies and seek out means of financing their education. The students most vulnerable to these lengthened academic pathways were those from lower socio-economic backgrounds, master's students without scholarships, and older students (Sales et al. 2001).

These findings illustrate the effects of tuition hikes and loan policies on the educational experience of Canadians (Looker and Lowe 2001). In the span of a decade (1991–2001), the price of an undergraduate arts degree went up by 126 per cent, and students borrowed more in order to finance their education (Finnie 2002; Looker and Lowe 2001: 5). In Ontario and Nova Scotia, tuition costs increased 58 per cent from 1995–6 to 2005–6 (CCL 2007: 87). Older students typically have to rely on different types of financing than younger students and their expenses are generally higher (Meyers and de Broucker 2006). For example, 83 per cent of students aged 20 to 21 receive financial support from parents, compared to only 38 per cent of those aged 26 and older (Meyers and de Broucker 2006: 41). Researchers have argued that Canadian students' heavy and growing debt loads place a particular burden on the present generation of students and their families and that this may be particularly so for older students, who must borrow more heavily from outside sources (CPRN 2002; Meyers and de Broucker 2006; Plager and Chen 1999). The grant system once in place has been largely replaced by loans, and a number of graduates have difficulty repaying them (Plager and Chen 1999). One researcher poses the question, 'Why we find it acceptable that some young people, purely by an "accident of birth", are burdened by student loan debts of $20,000–30,000?' (CPRN 2002: 23). The rising cost of education is making debt an increasing reality for the present generation of post-secondary graduates.

Educational Returns in the Labour Market

There have been some changes in the labour market returns that Canadians can expect from their educational investments (Kapsalis, Morisette, and Picot 1999; Wanner 2001). Some researchers have found that younger workers in Canada experienced a drop in real wages in comparison to older age groups (S. Davies, Mosher, and O'Grady 1996; Kapsalis, Morisette, and Picot 1999). These relative declines in labour-market returns have affected men more dramatically than women (Kapsalis, Morisette, and Picot 1999; Wanner 2001). Before 1960, university graduates with a bachelor's degree, particularly male graduates, could expect much higher labour-market returns on their degree than later graduates could (Wanner 2001). Graduates with a high school diploma in the first half of the twentieth century could also expect better monetary returns in the labour market than those in the latter half of the century (Wanner 2001). However, graduate and advanced degrees brought reliable returns for men and women over the course of the century, with men maintaining their labour-market advantage within this group (Wanner 2001). Wanner (2001) suggests that the drop in the value of undergraduate degrees stems from a lowered demand for them in the labour market and not from credentialism per se, since the returns on advanced degrees have remained relatively high. In fact, Finnie (2000) argues that the concern about poor labour-market returns for younger Canadians may be overblown. He found that earnings among graduates are only moderately lower than in previous years; however, his comparison is limited to graduates in the 1980s and 1990s. More recent data on earnings and education show that at virtually all levels, higher educational attainment is coupled with higher income (CCL 2007), though it is important to note that 25 per cent of Canadians with a university degree earn less than those with a high school diploma (CCL 2007) and that the earnings of young less-educated men rose more rapidly than those of other groups between 2000 and 2005 (a rise that came in the wake of previous declines and stagnation) (Chung 2006). In fact, concern over the issue of overqualification in Canada has been growing (Li et al. 2006). The

Figure 10.10: Overqualification among Recent Immigrants and Canadian-Born Workers

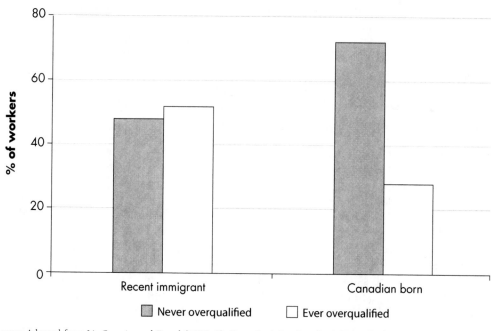

Source: Adapted from Li, Gervais, and Duval (2006: 9). Data: Statistics Canada, Survey of Labour and Income Dynamics, 1993 to 2001.

number of university-educated workers who are overqualified for their jobs is on the rise, having gone up by one-third between 1993 and 2001 (Li et al. 2006). In 2001, 19 per cent of university-educated workers were overqualified for their jobs, and while younger workers were more prone to be overqualified for their jobs, once older workers were overqualified, they were more likely than younger workers to stay overqualified (Li et al. 2006).

Among the groups most prone to be overqualified for their job was immigrant workers. Figure 10.10 shows the extent to which overqualification occurs for recent immigrants compared to Canadian-born workers. Immigrants are twice as likely to work in jobs that they are overqualified for, and twice as likely to stay overqualified for the maximum length of time measured (Li et al. 2006: 9).

In an earlier study, by Frenette (2000), respondents with master's degrees experienced high percentages of overqualification, from 48 per cent to 72 per cent across three age cohorts (Frenette 2000: 10). Even so, those with a master's degree maintained a wage advantage over those with a bachelor's degree. Frenette (2000) suggests that overqualified master's candidates are often hired for jobs that require only a bachelor's degree. This phenomenon may play a role in the lesser economic returns enjoyed by bachelor's-degree graduates in comparison to previous age cohorts.

The educational requirements of the labour market will probably continue to increase, and education continues to serve as an important control on access to monetary rewards and occupational autonomy (Butlin and Oderkirk 1997; Frenette 2000). Although some groups encounter more difficulty than others in reaping commensurable economic gains for their educational investment, the investment in education is now, more than ever, a vital requirement in the competition for jobs and occupational advancement in a global economy (CCL 2007; CPRN 2002).

Beyond the Statistics: Agency and Experience in Education

Although the preceding discussion provides a statistical overview of education in Canada, it does little to show how education is experienced or what choices people make about their education. Furthermore, because statistics rely on averages and typical experiences, variation from the average and the processes involved in varying from the norm are hidden. For instance, although women are educated at similar or somewhat higher levels than men, Judith Blackwell (1998) points out women enrolled in universities sometimes experience difficulties because of overt sexism in the classroom, which is often reinforced in other aspects of university life. White privilege is perpetuated in educational institutions (Bedard 2000; Schick 2001), with racialized students feeling that their success depends on their ability to act as if they were white (Aguiar

2001). Indeed, racism runs rampant in Canadian educational institutions: racialized students are taunted and ridiculed by students and discouraged by teachers (Codjoe 2001). Henry Codjoe (2001) describes how the different experience of racism affected students in Alberta. For a minority of students, racism made them strive to be the best students so that they could be labelled exceptional. For most, however, racism was a barrier to success in education. As Kwame, one of Codjoe's (2001: 351) informants put it,

> To this day, it [racism] still affects me. It was a big hindrance. I dropped out twice as a direct result of that and other stuff like problems in high school with security guards and principals, and when one black person does something the whole black population in the school gets to go to the principal's office and stuff like that. You get fed up and want to quit.

Whether one quits school or goes back to school after quitting is influenced not only by the structures of class, gender, age, ethnicity, and race, but by human agency. Box 10.5 describes how agency intersects with the structural difficulties of being a young single mother when one is pursuing an

Box 10.5 Refusing Mediocrity: Barriers to Higher Education for Sole-Support Parents

By Sharon G. Sabourin

No choices made in life are without their consequences, including the decision to have a child. The following is a story of the decisions I made, and the consequences that have happened since then.

No one expected that this small-town girl from Northern Ontario who was identified as being intellectually gifted in grade four and raised devoutly religious would end up begging for money to feed her and her baby before the end of her second decade. Then again, no one dreams of growing up to someday becoming a single mother either. But the reality is, it happens, and the only thing that matters afterward is how we honour the gift of becoming a mother. Let me tell you my story:

A high school dropout and expectant mother by eighteen, I often wondered if there would ever come a day when I would make my child proud to call me 'mom'. Cultural norms voiced by several people close to me led me to believe that the only penance that could be paid to free my son from bastardom would be to marry his father before the baby's birth. So, that is what I did. However, there were no guests, no cake, no rings, and certainly no gifts to commemorate the occasion. Without so much as whisper of celebration, the ceremony ended with me heading home by myself in a symbolic black dress, and the groom off to work for his afternoon shift in a food processing plant. Soon afterward, our beautiful and healthy 8-and-a-half-pound baby boy, Talon, was born . . . in wedlock.

Family grew closer as it often does with the commencement of a successive generation, but Talon's father found responsibilities surrounding parenting and family life too difficult to handle. The only thing that I had ever wanted to become was a good wife to a man that loved me and appreciated me, and I knew inside my heart that I would only ever marry once. It was my motherly duty to ensure that my marriage worked. It was a very long time, and a difficult road to realizing there is much more dignity and honour in leaving an abusive relationship, than there is in staying in one, only to be miserable for the sake of society's approval of 'intact' families.

Details that need not be mentioned here were involved and my tumultuous marriage soon began to dissolve and ultimately ended with police involvement. I was left with a newborn baby to care for, and not a glimmer of hope of becoming the confident, well-respected member of society that had been prescribed as my destiny from such a young age. The maternity-leave income that I was collecting from my job as a bartender was not enough to pay the bills, and not long after, I received an eviction notice leaving me desperate to find a home for me and my 3 month old baby. I had not completed high school, had no job, no vehicle and nowhere to go except to the local Social Service Agency. Once inside the office, I looked down at my baby

sitting contentedly in his car seat, and said to myself, 'Someday I'll make you proud of me.'

Those next few days passed so slowly and numbly. I remember waking up in early morning hours to nurse a crying baby. As I sat in the dark, half lucid, I began wondering what purpose my life had. Was I only a vessel of sustenance for my baby? Whatever the purpose, my days passed by minute by minute. I would get up and diaper and dress my baby. I would put him in his car seat on the floor of the bathroom so I could shower myself. I would put on my clothes and shoes and take him outside for fresh air. I would get hungry, and wonder what I could afford to buy to eat. His babbling would fill the dead and quiet air of our world. His rattle would fall out of reach, and I'd pick it up and return it to him. His innocence and apathy for what shame I felt was condolence for my soul.

During those few weeks of complete confusion, I remember walking Talon in his stroller during midday, and seeing other young mothers playing with their children at the park. I remember looking on them with disapproval, while precluding myself from that judgment. I remember wondering if their babies had fathers who were involved, or if they were collecting welfare. I wondered what their stories were. I daresay it was the fallacy of pride, but something made me feel that I was not like them, like those girls who went and got knocked up by some Joe who treated them like garbage and left them to care for their kids while they went off and found new fresh meat to taint. The truth was, I wasn't any different, I was just in denial.

So there I was. Soon to be homeless, penniless, and staring down at the responsibility of caring for an entire human life. Who was this kid anyway? I mean, he didn't look like me, and he certainly wasn't much fun. I felt a tremendous amount of guilt for thinking these things that 'no self-respecting mother' would dare think. I had no idea what to do but cry, and cry I did. I cried because I felt like a failure, I cried because I felt incapable of caring for myself let alone a baby. I felt sad that I had given up my dreams for the love of a man who abandoned me and made me feel helpless. But the most heart-wrenching pain was that of seeing the disappointment in my parents' faces. They didn't understand why I did the things I did, but what was worse, neither did I.

. . . . .

By far, the hardest part of beginning my education was walking into my very first class the first day of college. I was terrified that I wouldn't fit in, and not surprisingly—I didn't. But not for the reasons I thought. I didn't fit in because I was a girl on a mission, I wasn't just putting in time. I knew exactly what I wanted, whereas most people in my class were there to try and figure that out. To my surprise, instead of being condemned, most students and teachers in my classes were impressed that I was a mother! One of the strangest things I've learned about being a student is that we're all afraid at first that we won't fit in. But, it never takes long to find that everyone else feels the same way, and then friendships develop from that shared fear of rejection, becoming instead a shared feeling of camaraderie among fellow students.

I was soon in the swing of things as a college student. Juggling classes, homework, part-time work, and breastfeeding were just some of the things that were priorities for my first year of post-secondary studies. Determined to make something of myself, I took extra courses during the regular semester, and attended summer classes every summer. The following year my grades were high enough to be accepted to the University of Western Ontario's Bachelor of Health Sciences program.

. . . . .

I knew that the cost of daycare was going to be too much for me to afford, so I applied for a city subsidy. After 3 months of paperwork shuffling, and city council meetings, I finally qualified for a subsidy from the city for the periods of time that I spent in school. It was mandatory that I provide the city with a schedule from the University for each term, outlining exactly what times I was in class, as the city will not pay a subsidy for the hours not spent in class. This meant, that when I needed to study, go to the library, or meet with other students to discuss a group project, I would be charged full price for Talon's daycare. Despite this, I knew that I would still have to work in order to help pay for schooling, so I applied to the work-study program at Western. The work-study program paid $8.50 per hour. The cheapest hourly rate I could find for daycare was $5/hr. This meant, that in essence, I was working for $3.50 an hour, almost half of the minimum wage. Well, $3.50 is better than nothing, so I began working. It was a sacrifice that paid off when I discovered my passion for academic research.

While working and continuing my studies first year, I had received some poor grades on essay style assignments, and so I decided that I should get some help with my writing skills. The Student Development Centre has an Effective Writing Program; a free service for students to offer constructive criticism on their writing skills. But, children are not welcome to attend these sessions, and I simply couldn't afford to take any extra time off work during the day to go while Talon was in daycare, so I didn't get any help with my writing.

During my first week at Western, I learned that for chemistry class, there would be an 8 o'clock lab every other week, and on the weeks there wasn't labs, there would be quizzes. Waking up at 6 a.m., I had an hour to shower, breakfast, and dress both Talon and I, 45 minutes to drive into London, 15 minutes to drop Talon off at the daycare, park the car and get onto campus and to my class by 8 a.m. This wouldn't be so bad, except that I was up until 2 in the morning the night before, because the only time I could do the preparatory lab report for the next day was after Talon was asleep. Running on four hours sleep, I made it to my first lab. I was exhausted, and didn't perform the experiment properly. There wasn't time before my next class to redo it, and so I failed my first lab.

Two weeks later, Talon is sick. He had been exposed to many new viruses at the daycare centre that he wasn't yet immune to. Public Health stipulates that if a child is sick, he/she is not permitted to go to daycare. The University Chemistry Department states that if a student misses three or more labs, they are not permitted to continue in the course. The University Policies stipulate, that if a student misses a lab/test/exam they are required to provide medical documentation. But, it doesn't matter if students had to stay home because their child was sick, that doesn't count as a valid excuse. I distinctly recall one morning while conducting one of my chemistry experiments, feeling such intense pressure that I began having visual distortions and ended up having a full-fledged migraine headache. My professor was quite empathetic and helped me find somewhere to lie down until the pain abated. Twice more, Talon was sick on lab days, and I was forced to drop out of the class. I began to feel like I might not make it.

Source: Sabourin (2003). Reprinted by permission of the author.

education in Canada: Sharon G. Sabourin describes the 'choices' that she made in dropping out of school, marrying and having a baby, leaving her husband, and returning to school. These choices illustrate how conformity and resistance (see chapter 7) link structure and agency as Ms Sabourin navigates through life as a young mother.

Conclusion

The research presented in this chapter shows that a serious obstacle to high levels of education is social class; gender, race, and ethnicity seem to matter less. Yet what is also clear from this chapter is that much more Canadian research on educational attainment needs to be done to explore how class, age, gender, ethnicity, and race simultaneously shape educational pathways. Some of the research discussed above shows how class intersects with each of age, gender, ethnicity, and race, but rarely does research explicitly consider the complexities of all these factors. But the barriers to education probably vary in enigmatic ways. Consider a middle-aged black mother who just lost her job after the factory she was working in closed down and went south. She needs to work to help support her family, but she has few marketable skills. She would like to go to school to upgrade her skills, but colleges, universities, and the like are organized with the life-course stage of a 20-year-old in mind. This hypothetical case illustrates the complex relationships among class, age, gender, ethnicity, and race as they pertain to education and potential barriers to education. It also highlights the links between education, skill, and globalized labour markets.

Policy makers are quick to point out that Canada needs to be innovative in an era of globalized markets and heightened competitiveness. Yet the traditional education system in Canada lacks the creativity that is needed to break down the barriers to lifelong learning. Although there has been some movement toward distance learning and Internet-based courses, these innovations have been slow to evolve. This is at least partly due to the overly elitist, class-based attitudes among educators in our schools of higher learning, who suggest that traditional methods of learning are superior to others.

The fact that boys are falling behind in elementary and high school also requires immediate policy attention. Again, it is not enough to examine the differences between boys and girls in this regard. The family experiences of class, gender, race, and ethnicity must also be considered. Do boys and girls employ social and cultural capital in the same way? Or do masculinities (as they vary by age, class, race, and ethnicity) influence whether and how social and cultural capital is used to one's advantage (CPRN 2002)? Obviously, the agency of parents and children is important here. Once we have insight into these and similar questions, Canadians will be in a better position to devise policy that will help to make education more readily accessible and useful to all.

||||||||| Questions for Critical Thought ||||||||||||||||||||||||||||||||||||||||||||||||||

1. Why does an identical level of educational achievement not guarantee equivalent labour-market returns? What implications does this have for agency?

2. What do you think will happen to the Canadian population's educational attainment levels over the twenty-first century? What effect, if any, will tuition increases have on access to post-secondary education? What effect, if any, will educational debts have on future generations?

3. What processes do you think are responsible for the educational underperformance of boys? How does this phenomenon illustrate the enmeshment of the CAGE social relations? What can be done to improve the educational experience and attainment levels of vulnerable populations?

4. Discuss how social and cultural capital operate to advantage and disadvantage groups in the Canadian educational system.

5. What factors went into your own educational choices and opportunities? Do you think that your educational attainment and aspirations have been affected by the social relations of CAGE? If so, in what way?

||||||||| Glossary ||||||||||||||||||||||||||||||||||||||||||||||||||||||||||||||||||||||||

Baby-boom expansion   The growth in the educational sector in response to the high fertility rate following the Second World War.

Cultural capital   Bourdieu's concept of the collective dispositions, likes, dislikes, and typical recreational pursuits of the privileged classes in a given society. These activities (reading the newspaper, going to museums, golfing, and so on) are transmitted from one generation to the next through family socialization in a middle- to upper-middle-class milieu. Children from these families achieve higher levels of cultural capital and are therefore at an advantage in the educational process, where many of their activities and world views are taken for granted and are expected forms of knowledge.

Educational investment   The monetary and occupational labour-market rewards that groups can expect as a result of their level of educational attainment, their field of study, and their demographic profile (age, race or ethnicity, gender, and class).

Occupational segregation   The division of the labour force in such a way that men and women usually perform quite different tasks in their work. Men and women are generally sorted into occupations that are separate and distinct from each other (e.g., construction, transportation, and engineering traditionally employ men, while clerical work, nursing, and child care are traditionally done by women). This separation exists both in the type of work that men and women do and in the career and occupational ladders within an occupational field (e.g., within education, women tend to teach younger children while men tend to teach older children and teenagers and are more often principals and administrators). These labour divisions also operate along ethnic and racial lines, and they tend to result in occupational advantages for the dominate social group.

Pro social behaviour   Socially altruistic behaviour, including that which results in the inclusion of other children or that involves listening to and showing concern, comfort, or compassion to classmates.

Silencing   The practice among some students of remaining silent or not participating in response to a classroom experience that is exclusionary and does not validate their lived experience.

Social capital Bourdieu's concept of the social networks and informational resources from which individuals are able to draw upon in their daily lives. The possession of large amounts of social capital presumes high reserves of economic and cultural capital, as it is through monied, educational, and prestige connections that valuable social networking is accomplished.

Special education A form of educational delivery designed to address educational deficiencies and/or difficulties (e.g., social or behavioural problems, difficulty learning to read). This program may be offered directly in the classroom or it may involve separate classroom or teacher time for the student.

Streaming The educational practice of grouping and teaching children according to different levels of ability, either informally in a classroom or more formally within secondary educational programs (e.g., basic or advanced pathways).

⁌⁌⁌⁌⁌⁌⁌ Recommended Reading ⁌⁌⁌⁌⁌⁌⁌⁌⁌

Berger, Joseph, Anne Motte, and Andrew Parkin. 2007. *The Price of Knowledge: Access and Student Finance in Canada*. 3rd edn. Montreal: Canada Millennium Scholarship Foundation. An excellent resource on access to post-secondary study in Canada and how finances currently affect educational attainment.

Canadian Council on Learning. 2007. *Postsecondary Education in Canada: Strategies for Success, Report on Learning in Canada 2007*. Ottawa: CCL. A comprehensive report on the state of post-secondary education in Canada with current information on access to education for vulnerable groups.

Canadian Education Statistics Council. 2007. *Education Indicators in Canada: Report of the Pan-Canadian Education Indicators Program, 2007*. Ottawa: Statistics Canada and the Council of Ministers of Education, Canada (CMEC). The Pan-Canadian Education Indicators Program is a joint venture of Statistics Canada and the Council of Ministers of Education, Canada (CMEC). This document, aimed at policy makers, practitioners, and the general public, contains various statistical measures on education in Canada with the goal of monitoring the performance of education systems across jurisdictions and over time.

Davies, Scott, and Neil Guppy. 2006. *The Schooled Society: An Introduction to the Sociology of Education*. Don Mills, ON: Oxford University Press. This book draws on sociological research and popular accounts to examine contemporary debates about schooling and the intersections between society, education, and the labour market within a Canadian context. The authors explore the notion of a 'schooled society' in which education has become a central institution and document core themes of inequality in the context of education.

Lehmann, Wolfgang. 2007. *Choosing to Labour? School–Work Transitions and Social Class*. Montreal: McGill-Queen's University Press. This book provides an in-depth comparative analysis of how social class affects educational trajectories and labour-market pathways.

Wotherspoon, Terry. 2004. *The Sociology of Education in Canada: Critical Perspectives*. 2nd edn. Don Mills, ON: Oxford University Press. This book outlines the main sociological perspectives that have been used to explain educational inequalities and takes a critical approach to the analysis of education in Canada.

‖‖‖‖‖‖‖ Relevant Websites ‖‖‖‖‖‖‖‖‖‖‖‖‖‖‖‖‖‖‖‖‖‖‖‖‖‖‖‖‖‖‖‖‖‖‖‖‖

Canadian Council on Learning
www.ccl-cca.ca
**This site has comprehensive reports on many aspects of learning, including adult education, literacy, and post-secondary education in Canada.

Council of Ministers of Education, Canada
www.cmec.ca
**This site has current educational indicators and a wealth of information about education in Canada.

Canadian Education Association
www.cea-ace.ca
**The CEA aims to build better links between research, policy, and practice to advance under-standing of critical issues in education and learning. The site has information on the CEA's projects, events, and publications.

Canadian Federation of Students
www.cfs-fcee.ca
**The Canadian Federation of Students and the Canadian Federation of Students-Services were formed in 1981 to provide students with an effective and united voice, provincially and nationally, in order to ensure that students' rights and concerns are fully represented. This site shows how students' lives are affected by provincial and national policies.

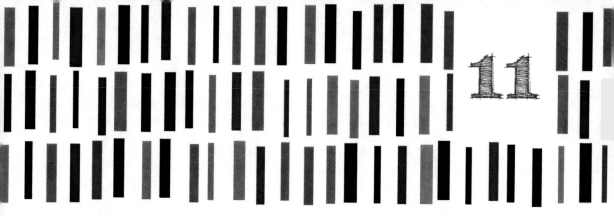

CAGE(s) and Health

by Tammy Duerden Comeau and Julie Ann McMullin

Introduction

Audre Lorde, who was born in 1934, is well known for her work as a poet and equal-rights activist. Lorde was a black woman, a feminist, and a lesbian who grew up in Harlem in the 1930s and 1940s and came of age during the 1950s. The daughter of recent Grenadian immigrants, she was raised in a working-class household. The substantive cohort in which she was born profoundly shaped her experiences in the processes of production, reproduction, and distribution—experiences that, in turn, had negative consequences for her health.

Unlike generations of black women who were born before her, Lorde did have some opportunities for paid work. This was true in part because of the progress made by equal-rights movements in the United States and in part because of the prosperous economic times that New York was experiencing in the 1950s. Yet her structural positioning as a young, working-class black woman profoundly shaped her employment options. In her search for work, Lorde's employment agency told her, 'There's not too much choice of jobs around here for Coloured people, and especially not for Negro girls. . . . [M]ost of our unskilled peoples find some sort of work in the "hardware" factories on the other side of town' (Lorde 1982:

125). Lorde chose not to tell the employment service that she could type. In her refusal to type she acted with agency and, in doing so, knew that she would have to work either in a factory or as a maid. Although some would no doubt question this decision, Lorde chose (at the time) to reserve her typing for the self-expression and creativity of her own writing.

Lorde found work in a factory. Her youth meant that the alternative 'option' of being a maid was not possible, for, as the employment agency told her, their clients 'usually like[d] older women' (Lorde 1982: 125). Lorde's factory wages were somewhat better than they would have been had she been employed as a domestic worker, but the working conditions were deplorable. The following quotation from Lorde's book *Zami: A New Spelling of My Name* (1982: 125–6) documents her harrowing experience of working at Keystone Electronics, a plant that processed the quartz crystals used in radar equipment and radios:

> It was dirty work. . . . The air was heavy and acrid with the sickly fumes of carbon tetrachloride used to clean the crystals. Entering the plant after 8:00 a.m. was like entering Dante's Inferno. It was offensive to every sense, too cold and too

hot, gritty, noisy, ugly, sticky, stinking, and dangerous. . . . Nobody mentioned that carbon tet destroys the liver and causes cancer of the kidneys. Nobody mentioned that the X-ray machines, when used unshielded, delivered doses of constant low radiation far in excess of what was considered safe even in those days. Keystone Electronics hired Black women and didn't fire them after three weeks. We even got to join the union.

Every worker in the Keystone factory was either black or Puerto Rican except for the foreman and forewoman. Jobs were segregated by sex on the basis of traditional gendered ideologies, with the men cutting the crystals and doing the 'heavy' work and the women X-raying and washing the crystals.

Before she got the job at Keystone, Lorde had worked nights as a nurse's aide and had gone to school part-time. She was a part of the working poor and was not eligible for social assistance. As an unmarried woman, she did not have access to a 'family' wage distributed through an employed husband.[1] Making ends meet was a challenge, and yet Lorde redistributed her wages by providing financial support to a number of men and women who regularly 'crashed' at her apartment. Since she could not afford nutritious food, Lorde's meals consisted of canned soup, sardines, and occasionally the treat of chicken-foot stew. Cooking was not easy, as there was no hot water (or heat) in the apartment and the kitchen was mired in years of filth and neglect from previous renters.

Regarding the processes of reproduction, high expectations of caregiving and nurturing placed upon women of colour have been well documented (Collins 2000; Glenn 1992). Lorde was unexceptional in this regard. She nurtured, fed, and sheltered her friends with what little she had, often to the detriment of her own well-being. Lorde failed the summer-school courses in

trigonometry and German that she was taking. She attributed her failure to her own capabilities and not to friends' mounting demands on her time and money. When she eventually left New York City to find work in Stamford, Connecticut (at Keystone Electronics), she escaped many of the emotional and financial demands in her life only to encounter a physically toxic environment.

Our bodies are potent signifiers of the degree to which we experience inequality throughout our lives. Audre Lorde's exposure to toxic and dangerous working conditions was not a random event; black working-class women were deliberately hired for jobs no one else wanted. Some evidence suggests that this trend continues today and that black workers may be exposed to more serious toxic contaminants than white workers (Briggs et al. 2003; Krieger et al. 1993: 88). The long-term health effects of exposure to workplace toxins, especially increased risks of cancer, have been well documented (Aragones, Pollan, and Gustavsson 2002; Fincham et al. 2000; Mao et al. 2000; Pichora and Payne 2007; Pollan and Gustavsson 1999; Richardson et al. 2007). Audre Lorde developed breast cancer in the late 1970s and died, at the age of 58, in 1992.

Although Audre Lorde's health experience centred on her blatant exposure to workplace pathogens and toxic substances, health inequalities can manifest themselves in more insidious ways. Indeed, the World Health Organization (2002) defines *health* broadly as 'a state of complete physical, mental, and social well-being and not merely the absence of disease or infirmity'. The fact that Lorde's wages were too low to provide her with nutritious meals or a suitable environment for their preparation probably took its toll on her physical, mental, and social health. Furthermore, the struggle to combine emotional and financial nurturing with long working hours in deplorable conditions has been shown to negatively influence all aspects of 'health'.

Lorde's life history demonstrates that to understand inequities in health that result from the intersection of CAGEs and agency is a complex task. Yet empirical research has rarely considered these issues simultaneously. With this in mind, in the next sections we review the literature on health inequality in an effort to weave a complex tapestry of the social determinants of health in Canada.

Inequality in Health: Some Current Perspectives and Critiques

Health researchers and epidemiologists have long struggled to discover why there are inequalities in health (Anderson and Armstead 1995; Herd, Goesling, and House 2007; House 2001; Link and Phelan 2000; Phelan et al. 2004), and explanations for inequality in the study of health and illness have gone through numerous paradigm shifts (Adler and Rehkopf 2008; House 2001). In his review of the literature, House (2001) documents the overwhelming emphasis in the mid-twentieth century on a purely biomedical approach to health and illness. Inequalities in health were analyzed and examined largely through the biology of the individual and the workings of the medical system. An individual's behaviour in the form of 'lifestyle' choices (e.g., smoking, alcoholism, obesity, and physical exercise) was also believed to have a significant impact on health (House 2001: 127). Although studies that focused on individual biology, the failings of medical systems, and lifestyle choices added to our understanding of health inequality, none of these studies explained it adequately. Rather, researchers began to recognize that factors such as socio-economic status played a significant role in health experiences and that smoking, exercise, immoderate eating, and so forth accounted only moderately (10 to 20 per cent) for socio-economic inequalities in health (House 2001: 134).

In the 1960s, psychosocial factors came to the forefront of health research and social epidemiologists began to emphasize the effects of 'stress' on the physiology of the body (House 2001: 128). This led to a recognition that health is influenced by a large number of psychosocial factors, including social support, stress, and psychological or personality dispositions (House 2001: 130). Problematic, however, was the fact that these **psychosocial risk factors** had been identified in the absence of an integrating theory; hence, much of the inequality in health remains unexplained (House 2001).

House (2001) draws on Link and Phelan's research (2000) to argue that if we are to understand health inequality, we need an integrated theory revolving around macro-social factors as the **fundamental causes** of disease risk. House (2001: 125) suggests that investigators should concentrate on factors such as socio-economic status and race or ethnicity because these characteristics 'shape individual exposure to and experience of virtually all known psychosocial, as well as many environmental and biomedical risk factors, and these risk factors help to explain the size and persistence of social disparities in health'. House's framework is outlined in Figure 11.1. This figure shows that broader societal factors such as race, ethnicity, gender, and socio-economic status are integral to health outcomes and psychosocial risk factors. Because there are complex relationships between these factors, an emphasis on psychosocial aspects alone ignores the influence that social inequities have on health. If the analytic lens is shifted to the effects of race, ethnicity, and socio-economic status on psychosocial risk factors and health outcomes, a fuller picture of health inequality emerges.

Although House's conceptual framework includes class, ethnicity, and gender, his inclusion is additive rather than interactive. A close look at Figure 11.1 reveals that gender and race or ethnicity are not considered to be related and that both race or ethnicity and gender are thought to be mediated by socio-economic status in their relation to health outcomes. Age and the

Figure 11.1: A Conceptual Framework for Understanding Social Inequalities in Health and Aging

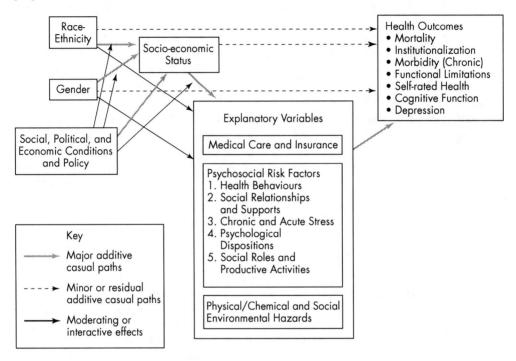

Source: House (2001). Reprinted by permission of the American Sociological Association and the author.

influence of social time are not explicitly accounted for, and the explanatory variables (e.g., social supports and social roles) are thought to be only 'minorly' affected by gender and ethnicity. Hence, this conceptualization continues to treat gender, race, ethnicity, and socio-economic status as variables that can in some way be viewed as separate from one another.

The epidemiological literature abounds in studies that document the impact on health of the variables of class or socio-economic status (Adler and Rehkopf 2008; Humphries and van Doorslaer 2000; Marmot 2005; van Doorslaer, Masseria, and Koolman 2006;), age (Menec, Lix, and MacWilliam 2005; Parker and Thorslund 2007), sex (Denton, Prus, and Walters 2004;

Rieker and Bird 2005; Trovato and Lalu 2007), and race or ethnicity (D. Williams 2005; D. Williams and Collins 2004) on health, both singly and in various combinations (Cooper 2002; Cruz, Natividad, and Saito 2007; Huguet, Kaplan, and Feeny 2008; O'Loughlin 1999; Prus and Gee 2003). There is no doubt that health is shaped and moulded by these social relations, and many of the studies listed here point out the deficiencies and difficulties inherent in treating social relations as variables. While epidemiologic research is taking note of these elements and critiques, these variables continue most often to signify differences located in 'biological' bodies rather than to indicate interrelated social patterns (Frohlich and Potvin 2008; Hatch and

Dohrenwend 2007; Inhorn and Whittle 2001; Krieger 2003; Krieger et al. 1993; Shim 2002). Given the prominent tendency of health research to treat class, age, gender, and ethnic or race relations as separate variables, the following discussion must do the same.

Mortality, Morbidity, and Mental Health

Social Class and SES

The privileged in society are those who possess more resources in the form of income, education, and social connections and who enjoy better physical and mental health and longer lives than those members of society who experience want and deprivation (Health Disparities Task Group 2005; Humphries and van Doorslaer 2000; Mao et al. 2001; Marmot 2005, 2007). Health education and awareness, access to prevention, and the capacity to avoid risk factors (e.g., toxic neighbourhoods)—all of which are resources held by members of the middle and upper classes—contribute to health advantage (Link and Phelan 2000; Phelan and Link 2005; Phelan et al. 2004). The latest figures on Canadian health-adjusted life expectancy (a measure that takes current health conditions into account) show that income makes a difference (Health Canada 2006; see Figure 11.2). Canadian women in the highest-income group have a health-adjusted life expectancy that is 3.2 years higher than that of women in the lowest-income group. Canadian men in the highest-income group boast nearly 5 more years (4.7) of life expectancy than those men in the lowest-income group (Health Canada 2006: 30–1). People in low-income groups face more constraints on their abilities to 'look after their health', and inequitable social conditions in workplaces, neighbourhoods, and regions significantly affect health throughout the life course (Krieger 2007; L. Roos et al. 2004; Safaei 2007; Wight et al. 2008).

Beyond the simple yet strong relationships among individual income, education, occupation, and each of life expectancy and health, there has been a growing focus on these factors in relation to geographic regions or studies of health and place (Bernard et al. 2007; CIHI 2006a, 2006b; Duranceau and McCall 2007; Gilmore 2004). Life-expectancy rates vary across regions of Canada, with those born in the territories (Yukon, the Northwest Territories, and Nunavut) having a life expectancy nearly 4 years (age 76.3) below the Canadian average (age 80.3) (Statistics Canada 2008b). Still, there are further differences between specific populations in the territories. Although the average life-expectancy rate increased for Canadians on the whole between 1991 and 2001, an analysis of life expectancy for the majority of the Inuit population in Canada showed no increase during this time, and life expectancy of Inuit at birth averaged 68 years (R. Wilkins et al. 2008). This marks nearly a 12-year difference in life expectancy between Inuit inhabitants and non-Inuit. Infant mortality in Nunavut was nearly double Canada's national average in 2005, with 10.0 deaths per 1,000 live births compared with the national average of 5.4 per 1,000 (Statistics Canada 2008b). Health disparities in the average length of life one can expect also vary significantly across cities in Canada. For example, in Vancouver life expectancy at birth is 81.1 years, while in Greater Sudbury it is only 76.7 years (CIHI 2006b: 13). There are mortality differences as well between rural and urban regions, with generally higher mortality rates due to injuries and various occupational hazards, particularly for men in rural areas (CIHI 2006a). Health patterns across regional Census Metropolitan Areas show that CMAs in Atlantic Canada each have life expectancies below the Canadian national average (Gilmore 2004). Within Ontario, CMAs show variation between the north and the south, with northern Ontario CMAs showing lower life-expectancy rates (Gilmore 2004).

Figure 11.2: Probability of Survival to Age 75 by Neighbourhood Income Quintile, Urban Canada, 1996

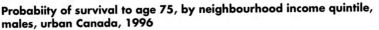

Probabiity of survival to age 75, by neighbourhood income quintile, males, urban Canada, 1996

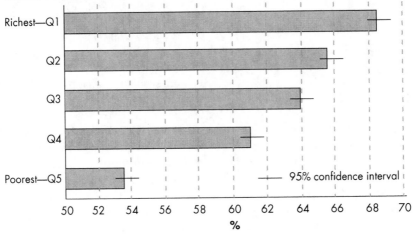

Probabiity of survival to age 75, by neighbourhood income quintile, females, urban Canada, 1996

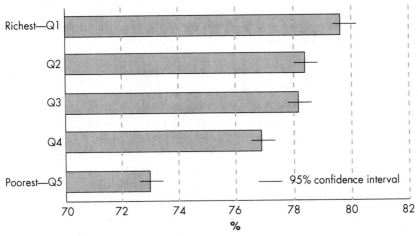

Source: Wilkins, Berthelot, and Ng. (2002).

Data source: Canadian Mortality Data Base and supplemental address files; special tabulations of census population data. Available at: http://www.statcan.ca/english/freepub/82-003/SIE/82-003-SIE2002007.pdf.

The study of low-income or disadvantaged regions and neighbourhoods contextualizes health experiences by highlighting health risks that are beyond the control of people who often have no means of moving to another area (CIHI 2006a, 2006b; Newbold 1998; Safaei 2007; D. Williams and Collins 1995). The presence of manufacturing and industry creates jobs; however, the risk of toxins and pollutions from these sources may also create health risks (Jerrett et al. 2005; Premji et al. 2007). The experience of residents in Sarnia, Ontario, shows how residents exposure to toxins may affect the very makeup of the population and create health consequences far into the future (see Box 11.1). Indeed, residents of low-income areas within the same city face many more health challenges and risks (Gilmore 2004; Latham and Moffat 2007).

Research on mortality and morbidity shows that health status is correlated with income level (Kim et al. 2008; Raphael 2007; L. Roos et al. 2004; N. Ross 2004; Safaei 2007; Wilkinson and Pickett 2007) and, further, that health status in some contexts deteriorates with incremental declines in income (Gupta and Ross 2007; Marmot 2006). Indeed, investigations of the socio-economic gradient have shown that in places where incomes are more variable, death rates are higher (Marmot 2005, 2007; Wheeler 2007; Wilkinson and Pickett 2006). Compared with findings in the United States, national socio-economic gradients in health are less evident in Canada; yet significant relationships between health and income exist both across and within Canadian cities and neighbourhoods (Wheeler 2007). Montreal ranks higher than other major Canadian cities (Ottawa, Toronto, Winnipeg, Calgary, and Vancouver) in unemployment rate (10 per cent) and poverty index (177) and lower on almost every health indicator (Health Canada 2002). Within regions, the extent of the health disparities between high- and low-income populations is stark indeed. In Saskatoon, infant-mortality rates for those born in low-income

||||||||||||||||||||||||||||||||||||||||||||||||||||||||||||||||||

Box 11.1 Sarnia's Emissions Affecting Health, Study Says

By Martin Mittelstaedt

Sarnia is fabled as Canada's chemical valley because of its many petroleum plants, but a new study says the community's industrial prosperity has a dark side: The area is the most polluted in Ontario when it comes to smokestack emissions.

The study, by Ecojustice Canada, an environmental group, also makes the controversial assertion that pollution is so severe in the city and a nearby Native reserve that the health of the 130,000 people living in the area is being harmed due to exposure to such harmful substances as mercury, dioxins and volatile organic compounds.

'The toll these emissions are taking is dramatic and there is growing evidence that the health of the residents of Sarnia and Aamjiwnaang First Nation and the local environment has been severely compromised,' says the study, a copy of which has been obtained by The Globe and Mail.

According to the study, which is being released today, the cluster of plants in and around the Southwestern Ontario city released more dangerous chemicals into the air in 2005 than all the industries in Manitoba or New Brunswick or Saskatchewan, based on federal pollution data.

Among the worrisome health developments it cited were an excessive rate of girls' births compared to boys for native women living on the reserve near the chemical plants; a toll of asbestos-related diseases among Sarnia workers, considered one of the highest in the world; and an incidence of leukemia among women aged 25 to 44 in the county that is double the provincial rate.

'We're exposing the human population, on almost like a huge clinical trial, to these very high levels of toxic substances,' said Jim Brophy, director of Sarnia's Occupational Health Clinic for Ontario Workers, which in recent years has treated hundreds of workers for medical problems related to dangerous chemical exposures.

The clinic, along with several community groups, has been lobbying to have the health of area residents studied to see what effects pollution might be having, but Mr Brophy said no level of government has been willing to commit funding for such a review.

An association representing major chemical companies in the area, the Sarnia-Lambton Environmental Association, declined to comment yesterday on the adverse health claims until the study is publicly released.

Elaine MacDonald, one of the study's authors and senior scientist at Ecojustice, said Sarnia's plants, which represent about 40 per cent of the country's chemical manufacturing, are often located near housing, without much of a buffer zone to separate residents from industry. Ministry of Environment spokesman John Steele said the province plans to place more air-monitoring equipment in the area, and in 2005 it tightened pollution standards.

. . . . .

How They Stack Up

Industrial air pollution releases by Ontario cities and selected provinces, 2005.

City	Pollutants (tonnes)
Sarnia	5,669
Sudbury	4,574
Hamilton	3,334
Toronto	2,829
Oshawa	1,939
Windsor	1,308
Kitchener	1,229
Thunder Bay	1,201

Prov., Terr.	Pollutants (tonnes)
Man.	3,966
NB	3,519
Sask.	3,177
NS	2,998
Nfld	1,061
NWT	210
PEI	72
Nun.	33

Source: Ecojustice Canada based on Environment Canada NPRI 2005 Data and pollutionwatch.org.

Source: Mittelstaedt (2007). Copyright © CTVglobemedia Publishing Inc. All Rights Reserved.

communities are more than five times higher than those of middle-income communities (Canadian Population Health Initiative 2007). Researchers also found that low-income populations were 16 times more likely to attempt suicide than high-income populations (Canadian Population Health Initiative 2007: 13).

Indeed, research assessing income and health status has repeatedly shown linkages between high SES levels and better health status (Auger et al. 2004; Gupta and Ross 2007). Recent research has shown that the length of time individuals spend in either economic advantage or disadvantage may influence health trajectories over the life course (Buckley et al. 2006; Willson, Shuey, and Elder 2007). Using US longitudinal data and measures of income, education, and wealth, Willson and her colleagues (2007) found that the duration of time for which respondents experienced economic advantage or disadvantage made a difference: extended SES disadvantage was related to stronger declines in health, and long-term SES advantage was linked to slower health declines over time. There is considerable debate among health researchers about whether the relationship between health and SES is causal or a result of selectivity. At issue is whether low income, education, and bad jobs result in poor health and an increased risk of death or whether those with poor and declining health consequently experience lower income and education levels (Phelan and Link 2005; Wolfson et al. 1993). No doubt both of these explanations account for some of the SES variation in health. Nonetheless, compelling evidence for the causality argument is evident in work by Phelan and her colleagues (Phelan et al. 2004; Phelan and Link 2005). They argue that higher socio-economic status enables individuals to marshal greater flexible resources in protecting their health (e.g., by moving to healthier neighbourhoods), and they found significantly stronger relationships between preventable causes of mortality and SES compared with less preventable forms of mortality (Phelan et al. 2004). In this way, the authors suggest, those individuals with higher SES are able to better avoid health risks from known causes of disease. In contrast, this relationship is less pronounced for diseases that are less preventable and/or less curable. This means that rather than ill health primarily influencing SES level, the relationship between SES and health is one where SES enables individuals to better avoid and predict health risks (Phelan and Link 2005; Phelan et al. 2004).

At the same time, those who struggle with existing health conditions often do face difficulty in securing stable employment and income (McMullin and Shuey 2006; C. Williams 2006). Although employers in Canada are required to accommodate workers with disabilities, stigma, misconceptions, and stereotypes have resulted

in unmet needs for many Canadians (McMullin and Shuey 2006). The tendency to regard disability in older age groups as part of the 'natural aging' process is particularly worrisome and may result in older workers' being prematurely excluded from productive employment (McMullin and Shuey 2006). Clearly, this exclusion would also negatively affect their income level and socio-economic status.

Despite evidence of a SES gradient, conditions of poverty and the associated problems of poor health cannot be ignored (Health Disparities Task Group 2005; Trovato 2001). In Canada, those who are poor face many challenges in maintaining their health over time (see Box 11.2). Less than half of Canadians in the lowest income quintile (47 per cent) report excellent or very good health compared with nearly three-quarters (73 per cent) of Canadians in the highest income quintile (Health Disparities Task Group 2005: 1). The experience of poverty has an indelible and unmistakable effect on the condition and health of the body (Adair 2001). As Adair (2001: 451) points out, 'poor children are often marked with bodily signs that cannot be forgotten or erased', and reflecting on her own experience, she says, 'In spite of my mother's heroic efforts, at an early age my brothers and sisters and I were stooped, bore scars that never healed properly, and limped with feet mangled by ill-fitting, used Salvation Army shoes' (2001: 456). Adair grew up in the United States, and many might argue that in Canada universal health care modifies or ameliorates many of the relationships between class and health. However, Crompton (2000: 16) finds in her retrospective of 100 years of health in Canada that even after 40 years of universal health care, low-income earners have higher rates of morbidity and lower life expectancies than those with higher incomes. These patterns continue to hold true (Health Canada 2006: 31).

The 'poor' are, however, not a homogenous group, and attempts to treat them as such may

Box 11.2 Poverty Takes Huge Toll on Health

By Gary Bloch

It is time to open a new front in the war on poverty.

The Canadian health-care system has devoted sizable energy and resources to reducing risks to our health over the past couple of decades. This effort has included large campaigns targeted at smoking, obesity and exercise.

Amazingly, we have largely ignored the one risk that surpasses all of these in its potential to cause ill health and its cost to our health system—poverty.

As a family physician, I see the health effects of poverty on a daily basis. One of my patients, 'Sally', is a 37-year-old single woman working at a full-time minimum wage job in Toronto that provides her with $1,280 a month (and no benefits), $450 below the Statistics Canada poverty line.

She is currently healthy, but studies have shown that her poverty places her at a 300 per cent higher risk of developing diabetes and a 200 per cent higher risk of having a major episode of depression. Her risk of developing heart disease is about the same as if she had high blood pressure or was a smoker (both conditions into which we have pumped millions of health-care dollars for prevention). Her life expectancy is 1½ years shorter, and her risk of dying from a chronic disease is 16 per cent higher per year than the average Canadian.

These are the kinds of numbers that usually make doctors, nurses, public health planners and health ministers jump into action. But we typically see poverty as a moral and political issue, not as a health risk.

While moral and political issues are easily dismissed as partisan and only of benefit to 'special interest groups', health is seen as a universal right and a fundamental social responsibility, worthy of significant social expenditure. The shift from a moral to a health perspective has taken place with smoking and is in the process with obesity. The next great preventive health frontier needs to be poverty.

Our failure to tackle poverty as a major health risk has resulted in unfortunate consequences income inequality is growing; child poverty rates are unchanged over two decades despite huge amounts of government and NGO lip service; and people living on welfare have to make do with cheques that force them into food bank lines and too often out of their homes. This neglect will only result in a worsening of the health consequences of poverty.

The cost to our health system of treating the illnesses caused by poverty is huge. Combined with the broader costs caused by disability—in lost productivity, support time from caregivers and the burden on our disability assistance system—there is strong economic incentive for immediate and drastic action from all sectors, with health planners and providers at the forefront.

But what is the health sector's role in tackling poverty? At the public policy level, we can research and comment on the health consequences of decisions that have an impact on poverty. We can speak out as health professionals about the need to increase welfare rates, build more low-cost housing, raise the minimum wage and other initiatives that will decrease the health consequences of poverty.

In our individual practices, we can support our patients in their attempts to combat the health impacts of poverty. We can act as advocates for them within the social services bureaucracy, support their efforts to obtain health-related social assistance benefits for which they are eligible and provide them with resources to facilitate access to food, housing or income supports.

We can put our resources into keeping people healthy or into treating the health problems that arise after poverty has taken its toll. When it came to tackling smoking, health advocates cut through the wall of issues put up by naysayers and focused on the simple answer. To address the health consequences of smoking, people must not smoke. The cure is just as simple for poverty. To address the health consequences of poverty, people must not be poor. It is time for health providers to lend their

powerful voices and skills to the next great battle in achieving health for all in Canada—the fight to end poverty.

Source: Bloch (2007).

mask important health risks (Adler and Rehkopf 2008; Health Disparities Task Group 2005). Everyone's 'chances' of being poor are not equal, and one's marital status (Avison and Davies 2005; Curtis and Pennock 2006), gender (Spitzer 2005), age (Bailis, Chipperfield, and Helagson 2008; Prus 2007), and race and ethnicity (Quan et al. 2007; Shuey and Willson 2008) are all integrally bound up with one's class and socio-economic status. Krieger (2007) notes that these distinctions and social factors are critically important to take into account in biomedical research. She states that the failure to recognize social determinants of health such as poverty, race, and gender has resulted in less effective and sometimes harmful treatment and research paths. Krieger (2007: 661) argues that by failing to take into account socio-economic status, research findings advocating hormone treatment to combat cardiovascular risk inadvertently caused a significant jump in breast cancer cases:

> Recommendations for hormone therapy effectively asked these women to increase their short-term and not inconsiderable risk of cancer, with the hope of decreasing their long-term risk of cardiovascular disease. The tradeoff has been costly. Studies conducted between 2002 and 2005 in the United States, United Kingdom, Australia, and Norway suggest that hormone therapy accounts for somewhere between 10 and 25 per cent of observed breast cancer cases. In the United Kingdom, this has

been estimated to translate to an extra 20,000 breast cancers among women ages 50–64 in the past decade alone.

By ignoring the impact of the social determinants of health such as the protective effect of socio-economic status, generalized recommendations from biomedical research may increase health risks. Findings such as these illustrate that biomedical research and data collection must be conducted in more complete and complex ways that acknowledge and account for socio-economic status and other social determinants of health (Krieger 2007; Krieger et al. 1999: 525).

The prevalence of mental illness also varies according to social advantage: 'The poor, the young, ethnic minorities, and blacks have higher rates of mental illness than the well-to-do, older persons, ethnic majorities, and whites' (Simon 2000: 72; Simon 2007). Data from the Canadian Community Health Survey show that 18.0 per cent of respondents in the lowest income quintile reported their mental health as 'fair' or 'poor' compared to only 3.9 per cent of respondents in the highest income quintile (Public Health Agency of Canada 2006: 10; see Figure 11.3).

Accounts of the relationships between social factors, environmental context, and mental health have focused on stress-process and vulnerability explanatory models (Simon 2000). Researchers working within the stress-process paradigm argue that the experience of stress in various forms affects physical and mental health (Avison and Gotlib 1994; H. Turner and Turner

Figure 11.3: Mental Health Perceived as Fair or Poor among Adults Aged 15+, by Household Income, Canada, 2002

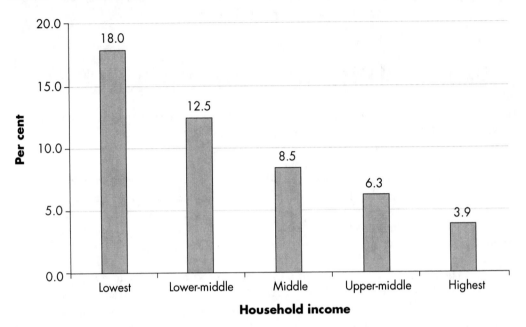

Source: Public Health Agency of Canada (2006: 10).
Data: Statistics Canada, Canadian Community Health Survey, 2002, Mental Health and Well-Being Cycle 1.2.

2005). But although stress affects physical health, much of the stress-process research has concentrated on the effects of stress on mental health (Lantz et al. 2005; Pearlin et al. 2005; Simon 2007). McLeod and Lively (2007: 277–8) note two main streams in current stress research: one examines the extent to which different societal groups (e.g., varying by income, race/ethnicity, age, or gender) are exposed to chronic strains and stressful events and, in doing so, documents the effect of inequality on population mental health; the other focuses more on individual perceptions of stress and the resources or buffers at hand for maintaining mental health.

Currently, there is some debate over the relative importance of the 'neo-material' or structural aspects prone to influence mental health (e.g., substandard housing, environmental toxins,

access to health care) and the psychosocial aspects (e.g., perceptions of inequality, health behaviours, cognitive processes) in explaining the persistent associations between socio-economic disadvantage and health (Muntaner, Borrell, and Chung 2007). Adler (2006: 848) notes that researchers pursuing the psychosocial aspects of health inequality still acknowledge the effect of structural inequality on these factors and states that the two approaches are best viewed as 'complementary'. There is general agreement that people with less power in society are more exposed to ongoing life stresses and strains and often have fewer resources and social supports to help them cope (Pearlin et al. 2005; Simon 2000, 2007; Turner and Avison 2003; Turner and Lloyd 1999). Pearlin and his colleagues (2005: 206) state this eloquently:

Salient among the circumstances linking status and health, we submit, is the differential exposure to serious stressors, both those built into the warp and woof of social and economic life and those that are eventful. We refer to the dogged hardships, demands, conflicts, and frustrations that may be instrumental in structuring people's experiences across time and to events that may disrupt the continuities of their lives.

The development of psychosocial resources, such as mastery, self-esteem, and the perception of control over one's environment, is hindered for those who encounter ongoing structural barriers and disadvantages (McLeod and Shanahan 1996; Turner and Lloyd 1999; Turner and Turner 2005). The experience of childhood poverty manifests itself in higher rates of depression and antisocial behaviour throughout the life course (George 2007; McLeod and Shanahan 1996). In their systematic review of the literature, Lemstra and his colleagues (2008) found that youth aged 10–15 from lower socio-economic backgrounds were more than twice as likely (2.49 times) to suffer from depression or anxiety disorders. Psychiatric disorders, including depressed moods, anxiety, and drug and alcohol problems, are generally more prevalent among those from disadvantaged class backgrounds—those with fewer financial assets (Muntaner, Borrell, and Chung 2007; Muntaner et al. 1998). Patten and Juby (2008) note that depression is both debilitating and prevalent in Canada with over one million Canadians experiencing a major depressive episode each year, making it as common as heart disease. In fact, the lowest-income earners in Canada are much more at risk of depression (Patten and Juby 2008). Using a national probability sample from the Canadian Community Health Survey of 56,428 adults living in 25 Census Metropolitan Areas, Matheson, Moineddin, and Glazier (2008) found that neighbourhoods with high chronic

stressors in the form of material deprivation and residential instability are associated with depression. Indeed, the nature of physical surroundings appears to be an important factor in mental health. Even the development of schizophrenia—a psychiatric condition that is believed to have a strong genetic component—is linked to early work experience of 'noisome' occupational conditions (such as noise, temperature extremes and fluctuations, hazards, and fumes), suggesting that **class-linked stress** may be a predisposing factor for the disease (Link et al. 1986: 242). Recent data snapshots of homelessness in Canada have found a much higher incidence of schizophrenia in this population as well, though the causal pathways remain uncertain (CIHI 2007).

Race and Ethnicity

In Canada, death rates and the incidence and prevalence of physical disease and mental health show variance across measures of race and ethnicity (Dunn and Dyck 2000; Kobayashi, Prus, and Lin 2008; Kopec et al. 2001; Ng et al. 2005; Trovato 2001). Aboriginal peoples in Canada face many health challenges, and their rating on a variety of health status measures is worse than those of non-Aboriginals (CIHI 2004). Table 11.1 shows comparative data for Aboriginal peoples non-Aboriginals, and Aboriginal groups in Canada for a variety of health conditions (CIHI 2004: 83). Although Aboriginal peoples are often collectively grouped, it's important to note that there are differences between peoples, such as the rate of tuberculosis, for which the rate among Inuit is 92.0 per 100,000/year compared with a rate of 30 among First Nations groups and 1.3 among non-Aboriginals in Canada. As noted, the prevalence of a number of chronic conditions is higher in Aboriginal populations, and particularly among First Nations groups. For example, 22 per cent of First Nations men have high blood pressure compared with 8 per cent of non-Aboriginal men in Canada. In a

Table 11.1 Selected Health Conditions: Chronic and Infectious Diseases in Aboriginal and Non-Aboriginal Canadians

	All Aboriginal Peoples (Non-reserve)	Non-Aboriginal Canadians	First Nations On-Reserve and Off-Reserve Status Indians	Inuit (Nunavut)	Métis and Non-Status Indian
Chronic diseases prevalence rates (%)					
Diabetes	9	3 (M)/3 (F)	11 (M)/17 (F)	2	6
Arthritis and rheumatism	26	16	18 (M)/25 (F)	9	20
Heart problems	7	4 (M)/4 (F)	13 (M)/11 (F)	5	7
High blood pressure	15	8 (M)/11 (F)	22 (M)/26 (F)	8	13
Infectious diseases (rate per 100,000/yr)					
Tuberculosis	21	1.3	30	92	5.6

Note: Shaded cells indicate age adjustment; all other data are non-age adjusted. Note that many of these comparisons ideally require age adjustment for true compatibility, since the age structures of the Aboriginal and non-Aboriginal populations are different. Data for doing this, however, are not consistently available.

Source: Adapted from Canadian Institute for Health Information (2004: 83).

Canadian study of cardiovascular disease, Aboriginal people were found to be much more likely to have the disease than those of European ancestry (18.5 per cent compared to 7.6 per cent) (Anand et al. 2001). Indeed, there are differences in the primary causes of morality between Aboriginal and non-Aboriginal people in Canada: for Aboriginal people, the leading cause of death is from injury, while injuries sit as the fourth leading cause of death in Canada for other groups (Allard, Wilkins, and Berthelot 2004). Although the Aboriginal population is substantially younger than non-Aboriginals in Canada (median age of 27 compared to 40), even when controlling for age, there are significantly more injuries among Aboriginal people (Statistics Canada 2008a; Tjepkema 2005).

Again, these health challenges should be viewed in light of the social, cultural, and economic oppression against which Aboriginal groups in Canada have struggled (CIHI 2004). Table 11.2 illustrates the employment, income, and education status of Aboriginal groups compared with non-Aboriginal groups in Canada showing the socio-economic challenges these groups face.

Given these conditions and our knowledge of the relationships between socio-economic status and health, it is not surprising that Aboriginal peoples have higher mortality rates than the non-Aboriginal population (CIHI 2004: 81), though it is important to note that compared to Aboriginal peoples in the United States and New Zealand, those living in Canada are particularly disadvantaged in terms of mortality rates (Trovato 2001). For Status Indians, life expectancy is approximately five to seven years shorter than for the general population in Canada (CIHI 2004; Tjepkema 2002) and infant mortality rates are generally twice as high—and are triple among Inuit (CIHI 2004: 81).

The high mortality and morbidity rates of Aboriginal populations in Canada are accompanied by high rates of poorer mental health (Beaujot and Kerr 2003; MacMillan et al. 2003).

Table 11.2 Education, Work Status, and Income of Aboriginal and Non-Aboriginal Canadians, Ages 15 and Over

	Aboriginal Peoples	Non-Aboriginal Canadians	First Nations[a]	Inuit[b]	Métis[b]
Highest degree, certificate or diploma (%)					
No degree, certificate, or diploma	52	33	55	66	46
High school graduation certificate	18	23	17	11	20
Trades or college graduation (or univ. cert. below bachelor's)	25	29	24	21	28
Bachelor's degree	4.4	16	4.1	1.9	5.3
Work status (%)					
Unemployment rate	19	7	22	22	14
Worked full-year, full-time	26	37	23	23	31
Income (%)					
Low income in 2000	34	16	40	24	28

a Based on the 2001 Census where 'North American Indian' was the response category; responses that identified with multiple Aboriginal groups are not included.

b Responses that identified with multiple Aboriginal groups are not included.

Source: Adapted from Canadian Institute for Health Information (2004: 85).

Depression rates are generally higher among Aboriginal populations in Canada, with as many as 12 per cent of off-reserve First Nations people reporting a major depression in 2001, compared with 7 per cent of all Canadians (Public Health Agency of Canada 2006: 164). Notably, homicide and suicide are prominent causes of death for Aboriginal Canadians, particularly for adults, but even for teens and young children (Public Health Agency of Canada 2006; Trovato 2001). Suicide rates are significantly higher, at double the national average among First Nations populations and as much as 6 to 11 times among Inuit (Public Health Agency of Canada 2006: 166). A recent report notes that the deaths due to suicide are so high that nearly one-third (27 per cent) of all deaths since 1999 among Inuit are from suicide (Public Health Agency of Canada

2006: 166). Paradoxically, only 3.1 per cent of Inuit had a major depression in 2001, leaving researchers to speculate that mental health measures may be invalid and/or that depression may manifest itself among Inuit in alternative ways (Public Health Agency of Canada 2006: 164). Isolation, poverty, racism, and post-colonial legacies of abuse continue to affect the health of Aboriginal peoples. In spite of these challenges, the majority of First Nations respondents living on-reserve reported being in balance with their physical (71 per cent), emotional (71 per cent), and mental health (75 per cent) 'most of the time' in the Regional Health Survey carried out in 2002–3 (Public Health Agency of Canada 2006: 164).

Different patterns of health and illness are evident in the study of immigrant populations in Canada, as the study of health and ethnicity is complicated by immigration screening procedures (Newbold 2005; Ng et al. 2005). Immigrants to Canada are selected partly on the basis of health, and research has shown that the 'healthy-immigrant effect' plays a significant role in studies of health and ethnicity. In other words, immigrant populations, particularly those from non-European countries, exhibit better health and live longer than Canadian-born populations (Ali, McDermott, and Gravel 2004). This is partly because immigration to Canada is dependent upon an applicant's good health. However, the healthy-immigrant effect starts to dissipate after 10 years in Canada (Dunn and Dyck 2000; Halli and Anchan 2005; Ng et al. 2005). Although it is difficult to explain, some researchers have attributed the diminishing health advantage of immigrant populations to lifestyle factors such as diet and physical activity (Chen, Ng, and Wilkins 1996; Ng et al. 2005) and to social isolation and lack of access to health care (Newbold 2005; Oxman-Martinez, Abdool, and Loiselle-Leonard 2000). Using data from the Canadian Community Health Survey (2000–1), Kobayashi, Prus, and Lin (2008) found that visible minority groups in Canada rated higher on health measures compared with non-visible-minority and Aboriginal peoples. In contrast to prior studies, these authors found that Canadian-born South Asians and Chinese had better health than their foreign-born counterparts (at least within the first decade of immigration), though the authors note that 'the health advantages of the Chinese and South Asians, regardless of immigrant status, are explained away by differences in social structural and lifestyle environments' (Kobayashi, Prus, and Lin 2008: 140). Their findings underscore the need to examine social determinants in health research.

Racism and discrimination are important factors to consider when examining the relationships between ethnicity and health (Kobayashi, Prus, and Lin 2008; Kreiger et al. 2005; Noh,

Kaspar, and Wrickrama 2007; D. Williams 2005). Karlsen and Nazroo (2002: 15) document the effect that experiences of racism have on the health status of ethnic minorities in Britain. They found a substantial correlation between reporting fair or poor health and having experienced an instance of racial harassment: 'Those who reported having experienced racially-motivated verbal abuse were 60 per cent more likely to report having fair or poor health compared with those who said they had experienced no racial harassment.' Although immigrants and visible minorities in Canada have rated higher on mental health measures than non-immigrants and non-visible minorities (Public Health Agency of Canada 2006: 34; Patten and Juby 2008), racism and racial harassment constitute a potential risk for psychological distress and depression, as well as for other morbidities (Kreiger 2003; Noh, Kaspar, and Wrickrama 2007; Noh et al. 1999; Whitbeck et al. 2001). A Canadian study involving 647 Southeast Asian immigrants showed that depression is higher for those who had experienced racial discrimination (Noh et al. 1999). Noh and his colleagues (1999) found that depression was moderated by a forbearing coping style that was characterized by acceptance and avoidance. In a more recent study using data from the Korean Mental Health Study in Toronto, Noh, Kaspar, and Wrickrama (2007) again found associations between racial discrimination and mental health. The perception of overt discrimination was associated with a decline in positive affect or mood, while the perception of subtle discrimination was associated with depressive symptoms that were strongly mediated by subjects' appraisals of the situation. According to the authors, ambiguity and uncertainty in deciphering subtle discrimination may result in considerable stress (Noh, Kaspar, and Wrickrama 2007). It is important to note that ethnic identity may also work as a protective factor in mental health. Indeed, Wu and his colleagues (2003) suggest that the superior mental health of East Asian, Southeast Asian, Chinese, and South Asian Canadians compared to English Canadians may be explained in part by the presence of a strong, positive ethnic identity that bolsters belonging and esteem for group members.

Gender

One persistent puzzle in the study of mortality rates has been women's mortality advantage over men. Women in industrialized countries tend to live longer than men of the same racial, ethnic, and SES backgrounds, though in Canada this gap is narrowing (Trovato and Lalu 2007). In 2005, Canadian women could expect to live 4.7 years longer than Canadian men, and women in general have been found to have a longer life expectancy at all ages (Statistics Canada 2008b: 7). In Canada, the leading causes of death for men and women continue to be cardiovascular disease and cancer; and although more men continue to die from both, this disadvantage is closing, particularly with regard to cardiovascular disease (Statistics Canada 2007d).

Throughout the life course, men are more likely to die than women, although this difference peaks in early and middle adulthood, owing to the strong influence of external causes on men's death rate (Statistics Canada 2007b). Cancer accounts for more potential years of life lost for women, while accidents typically account for a greater number of potential years of life lost for men (DesMeules, Manuel, and Cho 2003: 17). Age-standardized mortality rates from 2004 show a male mortality rate of 710 per 100,000 and a female mortality rate of 466 per 100,000. Although most of the causes of death are similar for men and women, suicide is a notable exception. Men's suicide rates are higher in every age group than women's, and the overall suicide rate for men is 17.3 compared to 5.4 for women in 2004 (Statistics Canada 2007a). Compared with other age and gender groups, men aged 85 to 89

have the highest overall suicide rate, at 26.8 per 100,000. Although gender differences in health behaviour and the impact of gendered identities have been suggested as possible explanations for differences in rates and causes of mortality, the mortality advantage of women over men has not yet been well explained (Ballantyne 1999; McDonough et al. 1999; Rieker and Bird 2005).

Interestingly, measures of societal gender inequity are associated with mortality and morbidity, even after socio-economic deprivation is taken into account (Kawachi et al. 1999). For example, an examination of levels of gender inequality in all 50 American states has shown that in states where women's status (measured by political participation, economic autonomy, employment, earnings, and reproductive rights) is higher, both women *and* men had lower mortality rates. However, when black women and white women were analyzed separately, only one significant correlation is found for black women (that of women in elected office), suggesting that the measures of inequality used in the study may not reflect the experiences of black women (Kawachi et al. 1999).

Historically, women have experienced a higher degree of morbidity than men (Dean 1992; Verbrugge 1989). In Canada, nearly three-quarters (74 per cent) of women aged 15 and older reported having a chronic health condition, compared with 64 per cent of men (private household dwellers) (Statistics Canada 2006b: 54). Although Canadian women's life expectancy at birth (82 years) is longer than men's (78 years), women have more disability during their lifetime (Statistics Canada 2007f, 2008b). In Canada, women generally have higher disability rates than men, and these differences increase over the life course, with women over the age of 75 having a disability rate of 57.8 per cent and their male counterparts 54.0 per cent (Statistics Canada 2007f). Women are also more likely to experience pain and limitations of mobility and agility. For almost all chronic health conditions

Figure 11.4: Health-Adjusted Life Expectancy (HALE) and Life Expectancy at Birth, by Gender, 2001 (Years)

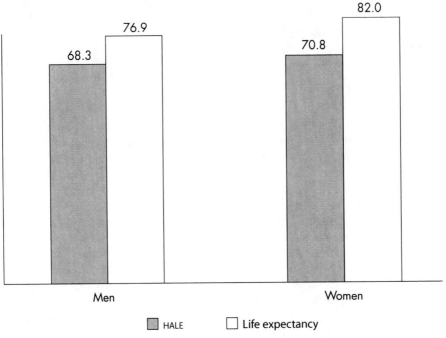

Source: Statistics Canada (2006b).

(except diabetes), women are more often afflicted than men; that is particularly the case for arthritis and rheumatism (Statistics Canada 2001e).

As Figure 11.4 shows with 2001 statistics, the gap in life expectancy measures narrows between men and women when quality of life is taken into account: women have a Health Adjusted Life Expectancy, or HALE (HALE is a relatively new measure using the Health Utility Index, taking into account quality of life or the years lived in full health), of 70.8, compared with 68.3 for men.

The long-standing finding that women have more illness than men has come under fire because so much morbidity research relies on self-reported health measures (Hunt and Annandale 1999; Macintyre, Ford, and Hunt 1999; Walters, McDonough, and Strohschein 2002). Hence, some believe that women's higher reported

morbidity rates are due to women 'overreporting' their symptoms. Yet, in a comparison of men and women's reporting on chronic illness, Macintyre and her colleagues (1999) found no gender differences in the initial reporting of a condition. Arber and Cooper (1999: 61), who examined data from over 14,000 men and women over the age of 59, found that older women did experience more functional impairments than older men but considered themselves healthier than men who were less impaired.

Historically, women were thought to suffer worse mental health than men; much of the research in this regard concentrated on depression (Simon 2000; Walters 1993). More recently, research has shown that men and women experience similar levels of mental illness but that it manifests itself in different ways in men and women (Simon 2000). Hence, the previous belief in a gendered imbalance in the prevalence of mental illness has now been offset with the inclusion of certain behaviours more common to men as indicators of psychological distress, such as alcohol consumption and drug use (Menaghan 1990; Simon 2000). These patterns are evident in Canadian data that look at the prevalence of any mood or anxiety disorder along with substance dependence. When substance dependence is included in mental health measures, the differences between men and women are slight, with 11.7 per cent of women and 10.2 per cent of men meeting the criteria for diagnosis in the past 12 months (Public Health Agency of Canada 2006: 31). The susceptibilities to various types of mental illness vary, with women being 1.5 times more likely to meet the criteria for an anxiety or mood disorder and men being 2.6 times more likely to meet the criteria for substance dependence (Public Health Agency of Canada 2006: 32). McDonough and Walters (2001) outline the hypotheses generated from the stress literature that attempt to explain this imbalance. One explanation, called the **differential exposure hypothesis**, argues that women are subject to more stressors than men on account of their heavier domestic and caring responsibilities. The other explanation, the **differential vulnerability hypothesis**, argues that women are more affected by stressors than men on account of a 'generalized female disadvantage in social roles and coping resources' (McDonough and Walters 2001: 549). McDonough and Walters (2001), who tested both hypotheses with data from the Canadian National Health Population Survey for 1994, found higher distress scores and morbidity among women. However, while women were generally exposed to more stressors than men (specifically, chronic stress and life events), this exposure accounted only for the gender differences in distress (McDonough and Walters 2001). In addition, the differential vulnerability hypothesis did not explain any of the gendered

variance in the results. The authors suggest that their results are due to the complexity in the relationship between gender and health and the inadequacy of the data to reflect this variability. They point to the impact of age on health and note that their study could not take this into account.

In a more recent study by Denton, Prus, and Walters (2004), the complexity of these relationships is further underscored, as they found that structural, behavioural, and psychosocial factors manifested differently for men and women and tended to hold different outcomes for health. Overall, structural and psychosocial factors appeared to better predict women's health outcomes than men's, with chronic stress emerging as an important health predictor. Again, women experience stress, anxiety, and depression differently depending on their socio-economic status, ethnicity, family relationships and structure, and labour-market participation (Walters 1993). Avison, Ali, and Walters (2007) found that differential exposure (rather than vulnerability) to stress explained nearly all of the elevated psychological distress experienced by single mothers compared to married mothers in both cross-sectional and longitudinal analyses. Studies such as these highlight the importance of daily pressures in women's mental health and the necessity to examine the differences in women's lives in relation to their mental health.

Age and Social Time

The length of time one can expect to live and the diseases one is likely to die from have varied considerably over time, partly because of historical variation in the social factors that influence health. For instance, education level is a strong predictor of health status, and whereas more than 50 per cent of Canadians had less than a grade 9 education in 1951, this rate had dropped to approximately 12 per cent by 1996 (Clark 2000: 7). In 2006, only 15 per cent of

Canadians had less than a high school education (Statistics Canada 2008c). Furthermore, the life expectancy and the overall health of Canadians increased over the twentieth century (Crompton 2000). Whereas an infant born in the 1920s could expect to live only 59 years, an infant born in 2005 could expect to live about 80 years (Crompton 2000; Statistics Canada 2008b). This improvement is largely attributable to public health programs, sanitation, and immunization (Crompton 2000). Sadly, the distribution of these amenities remains inequitable. For example, infants born in the territories have a life expectancy of roughly 76, and the average age of death in Nunavut was about 48 years compared to just over 74 years for Canada (Statistics Canada 2008b).

Nonetheless, in an era of globalization and 'reform' of health care delivery and service, people born today will most likely experience different health care services and delivery than those born before them. They will also be exposed to different and less well understood viruses and in some cases to the resurgence of viruses once stamped out. Indeed, since the 1970s more than 30 new disease-causing agents have been identified, including HIV and the Ebola virus (Lee and Patel 2003). Canadian events in the early 2000s point to the link between economic globalization and the international spread of disease. Four examples stand out. In 2002 the first human cases of West Nile virus (which is carried by mosquitoes) were identified in Ontario. In the early spring of 2003, major cities in the world, including Toronto, were 'combating' a new disease called SARS (severe acute respiratory syndrome). In May 2003 a cow infected with mad cow disease was discovered in Alberta, and in February 2004 avian influenza, or 'bird flu', was identified in southern British Columbia.

The global health implications of mad cow disease are worth considering in some detail. In 1986, mad cow disease, or BSE (bovine spongiform encephalopathy), was first found in a cow in the United Kingdom. It spread quickly among cattle in Britain, but the effect of BSE on humans who had eaten infected beef was unclear. Nonetheless, by the early 1990s, 15 countries, including Canada, had banned British beef imports, causing a devastating economic blow to the cattle industry in Britain. Concern over the economic impact of these bans led Britain's Ministry of Agriculture, Fisheries, and Food to minimize the potential human health risks of consuming tainted beef. However, in 1996 BSE was linked to 10 human cases of a new form of Creutzfeldt-Jakob disease (CJD), a disease of the brain that is usually fatal in less than one year. This new form of the disease (vCJD) differed from CJD because it affected young people rather than old people and because the duration of the illness from onset to death was shorter. By July 2002, there were 115 confirmed cases of vCJD in the UK and the disease seems to be spreading more rapidly despite radical measures to control it (Lee and Patel 2003). On 21 May 2003, the headline on the front page of the *Globe and Mail* read 'Mad-Cow Hits Canada Hard'. After more than a decade of being free of mad cow disease (there had been only one previous case of the disease in Canada), 'the discovery of mad-cow disease in Alberta walloped the country's multibillion-dollar cattle industry yesterday as the United States banned imports of Canadian beef and producers braced for fallout at home from frightened consumers' (*Globe and Mail*, 21 May 2003). At the time, Canadian politicians reacted to the mad cow crisis by eating beef, in order to show that Canadian beef was safe; however, long-term economic effects were not averted. The link between health, globalization, and free trade and the lasting ramifications for the Canadian beef industry are shown in Box 11.3.

Causes of mortality differ over the life course not only because of the aging of the body but also because of changes in socio-economic status, lifestyles, environmental stressors, life events, and surrounding social supports (House

Box 11.3 US Border set to Reopen to Older Canadian Cattle

By Jennifer Graham

After more than four years of restricted trade following a mad-cow disease scare and an estimated loss of more than $1.7-billion, Canadian producers are looking forward to today's reopening of the US border to older live Canadian cattle and their meat products.

The move comes after the US Department of Agriculture ruled that the risk of bovine spongiform encephalopathy (BSE) in Canadian cattle is 'negligible'.

'The border opening is going to be tremendous for all purebred breeders and all breeds because the US has been a fairly substantial marketplace for us,' said Helge By, of By Livestock, who co-manages the Regina Bull Sale.

The border slammed shut when BSE was found in an Alberta cow in May 2003, costing Canadian producers about $426-million a year. Canadian cattle under 30 months of age, deemed to be at less risk for BSE, have been allowed into the United States since July 2005. But older Canadian cattle and beef cuts from those animals had remained barred.

The trade rule to be implemented today allows the import of meat from all older animals and any live cattle born after March 1999, when a feed ban aimed at stopping the spread of BSE came into effect in Canada.

Brad Wildeman, vice-president of the Canadian Cattlemen's Association, was taking a 'cautiously optimistic' approach to the border reopening.

'It's going to take some time, I think, before the market channels get reopened,' said Mr Wildeman.

'There's more regulations to get them [into the United States] and so there's going to be a little more work to [get] them into those markets. We're not expecting a flood of cattle heading down there because of this.'

The big winners, he said, will be breeders, the genetics industry and those who ship meat to the United States. In the United States, the National Cattlemen's Beef Association has supported resuming trade.

But the rules and reopening don't please everyone. 'I don't feel that Canada has their feed ban in place yet the way that it should be,' said Allen Lund, a long-time rancher in Selfridge, ND.

Mr Lund is also a member of R-CALF USA (the Ranchers-Cattlemen Action Legal Fund, United Stockgrowers of America) which is seeking an injunction to prevent the US Department of Agriculture from moving forward with the over-30-months rule. The group argues that resuming trade increases the risk of infecting US cattle.

'I don't think we're on the same playing field as far as BSE risk goes,' said Mr Lund. 'I've seen it documented where Canada is 26 more times likely to have a cow test positive for BSE than the United States is.'

There have been 10 mad-cow cases recorded in Canada and three in the United States.

Mr Lund said that US producers fear what might happen if a case is imported from Canada into the United States.

He's also concerned that the border reopening comes at the peak marketing time for US cull cattle.

'We sold ours this week and normally we would have held onto them, put a little weight onto them,' Mr Lund said. 'But we kind of got spooked at what's going to happen with this older cattle coming in from Canada, if it's going to put a glut on the market.'

Source: J. Graham (2007).

et al. 1994; Hunt 2002; Mustard et al. 1997; Statistics Canada 2007d; K. Wilkins 2006). For example, Wilkins (2006) found that high levels of psychological distress were a strong predictor of death for women over the age of 65. This is especially worrisome given that, on average, the level of social support available to Canadians over the age of 65 is quite low (Statistics Canada 2001e: 30). The influence of persistent poverty, fluctuations in socio-economic status, marital status, and changing conceptualizations of race, ethnicity, and gendered meanings over the life course all contribute to health status, and all have changed historically.

Studies that ignore historical context and social time may present an inaccurate picture of health risks and outcomes. For example, in 1926 Canadians aged 5–64 accounted for more than half of deaths (54 per cent), whereas in 2002 this group accounted for only 21 per cent of deaths (K. Wilkins 2006). Studies show that health in later life may also depend on cumulative experiences and exposures over the life course (Hunt 2002; Willson, Shuey, and Elder 2007). Income and education are protective of health (Buckley et al. 2006; K. Wilkins 2006). For example, in a study of Canadian Mortality Database data and of data from the National Population Health Survey over an eight-year period, Canadians aged 65 and older who did not graduate from high school were more likely to die than those who had graduated from high school (K. Wilkins 2006). Other childhood experiences and exposures, such as poverty and domestic violence, also influence adult health (Chen 2004; Lundberg 1997; Raphael 2006).

Rates of sickness tend to increase as people age physiologically. Many seniors, for instance, suffer from chronic pain. Long-term limitations on mental or physical activity are also prominent among those aged 65 and older. However, these limitations are often not permanent: 60 per cent of those aged 65 and older who reported a limitation in 1994/5 were free of it by

1998/9 (Statistics Canada 2001e: 29). In 2003, only a minority of seniors (6 per cent of men and 7 per cent of women) living in private households needed assistance in their daily living activities (Gilmour and Park 2006). Although the majority of seniors (81 per cent) report at least one chronic health condition (the most common being arthritis/rheumatism) (Gilmour and Park 2006), over a third of seniors rank their health high, with 37 per cent rating their health as 'excellent' or 'very good' (Turcotte and Schellenberg 2007). Interestingly, the majority of seniors (58 per cent) aged 65–74 who are university graduates rated their health as 'excellent' or 'very good' compared to 48 per cent of 25- to 64-year-olds who did not graduate from high school (Turcotte and Schellenberg 2006: 46).

Socio-economic status has a significant influence on morbidity as we age, and a number of studies have charted the ways in which health inequities differ over the life course and at older ages (Cairney and Arnold 1996; O'Rand and Hamil-Luker 2005; Prus 2007; Willson et al. 2007). The impact of socio-economic status on health over the life course is substantial, and the cumulative effects of poverty and economic hardship have been shown to imprint health over time (Willson et al. 2007). Analyzing data from the US Panel Study of Income Dynamics, Willson and her colleagues found that socio-economic status yielded cumulative effects on health status over time, where those with higher SES saw less dramatic declines in health over time. In addition, their longitudinal data analysis found evidence of bias in the sample population over time, in that those with lower socio-economic status die prematurely. Their data suggest that those individuals most disadvantaged are not present in studies of older-aged individuals and that this bias must therefore be taken into account when interpreting data on mortality, life course, and economic advantage/disadvantage. Peek and Coward (2000) also found that age, education, and poverty status were the most predictive for disability in older age, with low educational status and the experience of poverty indicating a greater risk for developing multiple disabilities.

Mental health varies considerably over the life course. Recently, researchers have been paying more attention to the mental health of adolescents because the emergence of disorders at this time of life is a risk factor for the development of adult mental-health disorders (Gore et al. 2007; Whitbeck et al. 2001; Wight, Botticello, and Aneshensel 2006). In Canada, nearly half of adults (47 per cent) aged 45–64 who have a mental illness report that they were less than 25 years old when their mental illness began (Public Health Agency of Canada 2006: 34). Indeed, of all age groups, young adults aged 15–24 in Canada have the highest annual prevalence of mood, anxiety, or substance-use disorder (Public Health Agency of Canada 2006). Social determinants are linked with the mental well-being of children, as 46 per cent of children in Canada whose family affluence score is low report low emotional well-being compared to 24 per cent of children whose family affluence score is high (Public Health Agency of Canada 2008: 135). Socio-economic and environmental factors in the mental health of children and youth are significant. Aneshensel and Sucoff (1996) investigated whether neighbourhood racial or ethnic segregation and socio-economic stratification were associated with the mental health of adolescents. Neighbourhoods with a lower socio-economic status were perceived by study participants as the most hazardous and threatening. In neighbourhoods that were perceived as the most hazardous or dangerous, symptoms of depression, anxiety disorders, oppositional defiant disorders, and conduct disorders were more common. These neighbourhood factors were more strongly associated with symptoms of mental health than was family socio-economic status. Gender significantly influenced the type of mental disorder, with girls more commonly

exhibiting depression and anxiety disorders and boys more commonly exhibiting conduct and oppositional defiant disorders. A protective effect for depression was found in neighbourhoods with high levels of social cohesion, measured as communities where people knew one another (Aneshensel and Sucoff 1996). These findings suggest that studies of mental health must consider the milieu in which people live their lives (Aneshensel and Sucoff 1996).

Mental health and well-being are increasingly being conceptualized as cumulative effects, with experiences across the life course, particularly early experiences, shaping and determining later health outcomes (Lynch, Kaplan, and Salonen 1997; McLeod and Shanahan 1996; Raphael 2007; Wadsworth 1997). For example, Metcalfe and his colleagues (2005) found that childhood socio-economic status was associated with the incidence of stroke in adulthood. Miech and Shanahan (2000) found that low levels of education predicted higher levels of depression and that this relationship intensified with age. Education levels, age, and income mutually influence each other, as our age and our cohort influence our chances of obtaining education. In addition, our income is influenced by our age, as well as by our sex. Social time is also important, as Canadian policy changes have demonstrated. While more than half (57 per cent) of unattached women aged 65 and older were classified as low income in 1980, this number dropped to 19 per cent in 2003 largely on account of changes in distributive processes (Statistics Canada, 2006b: 144). Age also influences the extent to which we are exposed to the stressors of work and family demands, the extent to which social support is available (Shields 2004; Statistics Canada 2001e), and levels of self-esteem (McMullin and Cairney 2004). Women experience higher levels of personal stress than men at every age, but men and women aged 65 and older experience significantly less stress than younger adults. However, younger men and women experience more social support than do men and women aged 65 and older (Statistics Canada 2001e: 22). Using the National Population Health Survey, McMullin and Cairney (2004) showed that in their early teens, boys and girls, regardless of family income, have similar levels of self-esteem. However, at each successive age, girls have lower levels of self-esteem than boys do. Once people reach their mid-40s, income levels begin to significantly affect self-esteem. From middle age on, income groups diverge in their levels of self-esteem, such that men and women from the lowest-income groups have the least self-esteem. Although the level of depression in elderly men is quite low, their high rates of suicide suggest that underdiagnosis of psychological distress and disorders may be a problem, for researchers have suggested that as many as '90 per cent of people who commit suicide are suffering from depression or another mental illness, or a substance abuse disorder, which could potentially be diagnosed' (Langlois and Morrison 2001: 17).

Understanding Inequality in Health

Agency and Lifestyle Behaviour

The decisions people make about whether to smoke, how much to drink, how much physical activity to get, whether to engage in risky activities, and whether to take part in preventive health actions are all embraced under the rubric of 'lifestyle behaviour'. These factors were once thought to account for much of the inequality that manifested itself in mortality and morbidity (House 2001; Robertson 1998). Indeed, in spite of existing research on the social and environmental determinants of health, much Canadian statistical data focuses on individual behaviour in terms of health outcomes and recommendations of how health can be improved (Raphael 2004, 2007). As Raphael (2007: 10) points out, a concentration on health behaviours such as smoking

and weight deflects the focus from structural factors even though 'behavioural risk factors are rather weak predictors of health status as compared to socio-economic and demographic measures of which income is a major component'. Still, this is not to deny that agency, even when heavily constrained, plays a role in health.

Lower socio-economic status has been associated with less healthy behaviours (Pomerleau et al. 1997). Canadians in the highest income groups are more likely to be physically active, to take vitamins, and to eat fruits and vegetables than are those with lower family incomes (Power 2005; Statistics Canada 2001i)—though recent data have shown that nearly 25 per cent of Canadians in the highest income groups get 35 per cent of their dietary intake from fat compared to 15 per cent of those in the lowest income groups (Garriguet 2006). Clearly, rising obesity rates and the associations between income and weight are not explained by diet alone. Canadians living in low-income and impoverished neighbourhoods face significant challenges in obtaining fruits and vegetables and healthy foods (Grenon, Butler, and Adams 2007; Latham and Moffat 2007). Grenon, Butler, and Adams (2007) discuss how 'built environment' can affect health behaviours in terms of the accessibility and availability of food and space in which to exercise in neighbourhoods and cities. They characterize those areas where there is limited access or choice of supermarkets along with high social deprivation as 'food deserts'. Challenges in terms of obtaining healthy food in deprived neighbourhoods may account in part for the greater rate of childhood obesity in low-income neighbourhoods. Oliver and Hayes (2008) found that those children in the poorest neighbourhoods gained the greatest amount of weight over an eight-year period. In their longitudinal analysis of data from the Canadian National Survey of Children and Youth, they found that it was the negative effect of poverty (rather than the protective effect of higher income) that accounted for weight increases over time. Again, the importance of recognizing the structural context of health behaviours is shown here.

Smoking is on the decline in Canada, with 21.6 per cent of Canadians smoking in 2005 compared to 29 per cent 10 years earlier (Shields 2007). Smoking accounts for much preventable illness and death; in fact, nearly 45,000 deaths in 1996 were attributed to smoking-related illness (e.g., cancer, heart disease, and stroke) (Shields and Tremblay 2002: 3); and although smoking is decreasing among Canadians, according to a more recent study, 16.6 per cent of all deaths in Canada are attributable to smoking (21.0 per cent for men and 12.2 per cent for women) (Baliunas et al. 2007: 154). Besides the direct health effects of smoking, there are also confounding effects because smokers also tend to eat fewer fruits and vegetables and more fatty foods than non-smokers (Palaniappan et al. 2001). Nonetheless, when the number of cigarettes smoked is controlled for, the ill effects of smoking are greater among those from lower socio-economic groups than among those of higher socio-economic status (Mao et al. 2001: 7).

Among Aboriginal populations in Canada, high rates of smoking, obesity, and alcohol consumption have been documented (Anand et al. 2001; CIHI 2004; Rosenberg and Martel 1998). These health risks are probably due to the poverty and discrimination experienced by Aboriginal people throughout their lives (Lynch, Kaplan, and Salonen 1997; Whitbeck et al. 2001). In an American study, Chae and his colleagues (2008) found that racial discrimination and unfair treatment were risk factors for smoking among Asian Americans. The marked influence of environment on health behaviour is also evident among immigrants. Healthful behaviour tends to be more common among immigrants than among Canadian-born residents, although over time, non-European immigrants are more likely to report a decline in health (Chen, Wilkins, and Ng 1996; Ng et al. 2005). Physical activity also

tends to be less common among immigrants regardless of their length of time in the country (Gilmour 2007). Again the factors of structural elements and built environments should be considered when assessing whether and how people are physically active (Grenon, Butler, and Adams 2007). Smoking rates also vary significantly by ethnic group in Canada, with Asian and southern European Canadians being the least likely to smoke (Millar 1992). Immigrants tend to be significantly less likely to smoke than the Canadian-born (Chen, Wilkins, and Ng 1996; Millar 1992; Ng et al. 2005). Data from previous years show that whereas three-quarters of recent non-European immigrants had never smoked, only 34 per cent of the Canadian-born population had never smoked (Chen, Wilkins, and Ng 1996: 41). However, after 10 years in Canada, the number of non-European immigrants who have never smoked dropped to 61.7 per cent, and among recent European immigrants this number dropped after 10 years from 55.7 per cent to 37.6 per cent (Chen, Wilkins, and Ng 1996: 43). Generally, researchers believe that immigrants adopt less healthful behaviours as they adapt over time; however, little is known about the mechanisms and pathways of these changes (Halli and Anchan 2005).

Men and women exhibit significantly different kinds of health behaviour even within the same socio-economic groups (Statistics Canada 2001c, 2001i, 2006b). Although men are more likely to be physically active than women (Statistics Canada 2001i: 14), the fact that women are less likely than men to engage in binge drinking (2001i: 14), to smoke (2001b: 45), or to be overweight (2001h: 24) contributes to the higher risk of premature death from heart diseases among men (2001c). Men engage in riskier activities than women and are more likely to die as a result of suicide and motor vehicle accidents (Statistics Canada 2001b: 45). Men are also less likely than women to visit a physician and more likely than women to have emergency-room visits (Kazanjian, Morettin, and Cho 2003), while women tend to survive longer than men with the same chronic conditions (e.g., heart disease, lung cancer) (Rieker and Bird 2000, 2005).

Lifestyle behaviour varies significantly over the life course. Smoking is much less common among seniors, 12 per cent of whom are daily smokers compared with 20 per cent of those aged 20–54, and physical activity levels appear to drop substantially after the age of 19 (Statistics Canada 2006c). Other kinds of behaviour, such as eating fruit and vegetables, have been found to increase with age: seniors report eating more fruits and vegetables than those aged 18–64 (Shields and Martel 2006). Aging and generational ideologies have an effect on the health behaviour that people engage in or ignore (Gillis and Hirdes 1996; Spitzer 2005). Graham, Carver, and Brett (1995: 769) found that women aged 65 and older drink less alcohol, smoke less, and use illicit drugs less than any other age-gender group. These trends have continued: in 2003 only 3 per cent of women aged 64–75 were heavy drinkers compared with 11 per cent of women aged 25–54 (Turcotte and Schellenberg 2007). Researchers have noted that changing attitudes toward women's drinking and smoking may result in an increased risk for future age cohorts (Graham, Carver, and Brett 1995).

Alcohol consumption has been found to vary by gender, ethnicity, and changing social roles over the life course (F.W. Johnson et al. 1998). In their American study, F.W. Johnson and his colleagues (1998) found that whites drink more alcohol over the course of their lives than blacks or Hispanics; however, blacks and Hispanics drink more in later life per occasion than do whites. Men were found to drink more than women, and people who had many children or were regular churchgoers were found to drink less (F.W. Johnson et al. 1998). Recent Canadian data show that alcohol and illicit drug use are highest in young adulthood, with 60 per cent of

20- to 24-year-olds reporting heavy alcohol or illicit drug use in the past year compared with 16 per cent of those aged 55 and older (Tjepkema 2004).

Although lifestyle choices highlight the agency that people have in their lives, the simplicity of classifying behaviour as either healthful or unhealthful masks the complexity of social relations and related ideologies that mediate and constrain the lifestyle choices that people make in their daily lives. For example, the increase in the number of young women smokers in the late 1990s has been thought to stem from changes in gender ideologies (Hunt 2002).

Health Care Access and Utilization

Access to health care, even within the 'equal-access' Canadian system, varies on the basis of class, gender, ethnicity, race, and age. Poverty, for example, can impede access to health care in concrete ways. Roos and Mustard (1997) found that although prenatal visits made for the firstborn child were not significantly different for women from the lowest and the highest income groups, the number of visits decreased for women from the lower income groups with the second birth and on; it is not hard to imagine the difficulties in arranging child care, coping with children on public transportation, and other problems that would make it more difficult for the low-income mother who has several children to keep appointments than for a woman with greater socio-economic support (N. Roos and Mustard 1997: 105). Spitzer (2005) points out that current early-discharge policies for newborns have increased the hospital readmission rate for low-income families.

Reported unmet health care needs are correlated with household income: people in low-income households are 10 times more likely to report unmet health care needs than are people in middle- to high-income households (Chen and Hou 2002). Of particular concern for low-income households are the expense of drugs and transportation difficulties (Chen and Hou 2002). Curtis and MacMinn (2008) found significant inequities in the Canadian health care system in terms of initial contact with medical care and accessing specialist services. In their study of health care utilization patterns from 1978 to 2003, they found a trend toward more outpatient care for higher-SES groups over time; and until first physician contact had been made, higher-SES groups were more likely to visit a physician than were lower-SES groups. Although some aspects of health care (e.g., preventive care) are underused by low-income Canadians, other health services, such as hospital admissions (Glazier et al. 2000; Nabalamba and Millar 2007), are used by them more often. Higher rates of morbidity in lower-income neighbourhoods are thought to explain the higher levels of hospital utilization (Glazier et al. 2000). A recent Canadian study of hospitalization rates for ambulatory care sensitive conditions (ACSC) or chronic conditions considered manageable through appropriate primary care (e.g., various heart conditions, diabetes, asthma, chronic obstructive pulminary disease, epilepsy, and hypertension) found significant differences in hospitalizations by neighbourhood income levels (CIHI 2008). Indeed, the hospitalization rate for these conditions for those in the lowest income quintile was more than twice that for those in the highest income quintile (see Figure 11.5). As Curtis and MacMinn (2008) point out, the higher rate of hospitalizations for those with lower SES may well indicate gaps in primary care and access. Although the majority of Canadians do have regular medical doctors (in 2005, 17 per cent of Canadians reported not having a regular doctor; Asanin and Wilson 2008), there is geographic variation in the likelihood of having a doctor.

The map in Figure 11.6 shows that in more northern regions, access to a regular medical doctor is significantly less likely. Interestingly, in spite of the well-publicized physician shortage

in many areas of Ontario, residents in Ontario health regions are significantly more likely to have a regular medical doctor. Yet simply having a regular doctor does not guarantee access and care, as 60 per cent of Ontarians report that they cannot see their doctor within two days of becoming ill and 42 per cent report that they do not spend enough time with their doctor. In addition, only 10 per cent of Ontario doctors are taking new patients (Ontario Health Quality Council 2008). The difficulty to getting to see their physician (even among those who have one) may be exacerbated for low-income families with limited transportation options and flexibility in their jobs.

Paradoxically, even though people from lower-income and poorer neighbourhoods use hospitals more often than people from higher-income neighbourhoods, they undergo less surgery (N. Roos and Mustard 1997). Roos and Mustard (1997) argue that this is due to the underuse of specialist services by lower-income individuals, possibly owing to better access and a stronger communicative relationship on the part of individuals from higher socio-economic status. Specialists and surgeons offer more treatment to people with higher socio-economic status (N. Roos and Mustard 1997), perhaps as a result of referral decisions from a treating physician. Using data from the 2005 Canadian Community Health Survey, Nabalamba and Millar (2007) found that specialist visits were significantly less likely for those living in low-income households, visible minorities, Aboriginal people, and those over the age of 75.

These gaps in care may impact mortality. Cancer survival rates vary by community income (Boyd et al. 1999), and access to preventive treatments is a crucial factor in the cancer survival advantage that low-income Canadians have over low-income Americans (Gorey et al. 2000). Singh and his colleagues (2004) found that Ontario patients with higher SES were more likely to receive screening for colorectal cancer. The

Figure 11.5 Overall Age-Standardized Ambulatory Care Sensitive Condition (ACSC) Hospitalization under Age 75 by Income Quintile, Outside Quebec, 2006–7

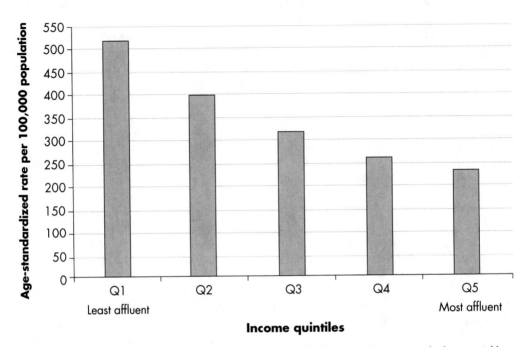

Note: Data from Quebec were not available for 2006–7 at the time of publication. Q1 represents the lowest neighbour-hood income quintile and Q5 represents the highest. Population by income quintile was projected from Canadian census definitions.

Source: Statistics Canada and the Canadian Institute for Health Information (2008: 25).

Data Source: Discharge Abstract Database, Canadian Institute for Health Information.

time it takes to wait for diagnostic tests and other procedures constitutes another barrier to quality care and is the number one health care barrier reported by First Nations adults living on-reserve (33 per cent) (Health Canada 2006: 43).

Access to health care is also determined by the extent to which people feel comfortable making use of the available resources (Benoit and Carroll 2001; Newbold 1998; Oxman-Martinez, Abdool, and Loiselle-Leonard 2000). Benoit and Carroll (2001), who interviewed urban Aboriginal women from Vancouver, found that the most important public health issues were those of access and availability of health care.

Aboriginal women underuse preventive health care services, and their access to prenatal care is limited. Accessibility meant encountering 'a non-judgmental, encouraging, informal environment . . . [which included] a more central service focus on Aboriginal women's health concerns' (Benoit and Carroll 2001: 6). Newbold (1998) also notes that Aboriginal Canadians living on reserves have very little access to physicians and hospitals; in the territories only 31 per cent of off-reserve Aboriginals reported having a regular doctor compared with 67 per cent of non-Aboriginals in the region (Tjepkema 2002: 10). Geographic isolation plays a large role in

Figure 11.6: Regular Medical Doctor by Health Region, 2005

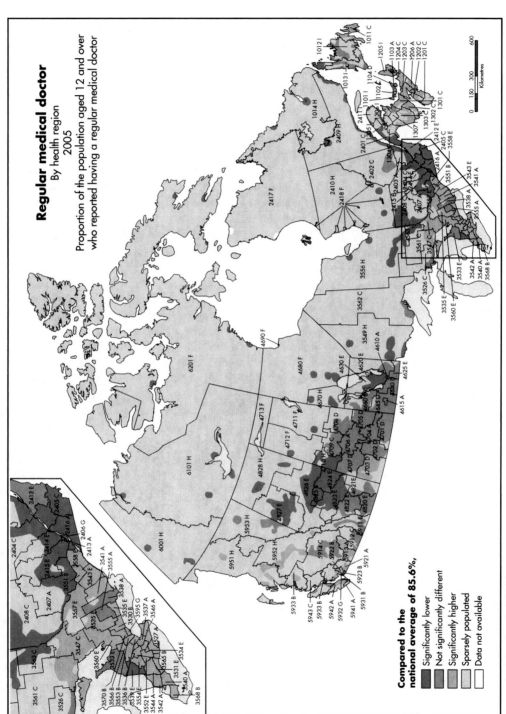

Regular medical doctor
By health region
2005
Proportion of the population aged 12 and over
who reported having a regular medical doctor

**Compared to the
national average of 85.6%,**

Significantly lower
Not significantly different
Significantly higher
Sparsely populated
Data not available

Source: Statistics Canada (2006c).

the difficulty of obtaining health services; however, education and greater self-governance over community issues are viewed by health care professionals as more vital to addressing health needs (Newbold 1998).

Immigrant status does not appear to lead to difference in physician visits. In fact, for both Canadian-born and immigrant populations with low incomes, the number of physician contacts is higher than among similar high-income Canadians (Chen, Wilkins, and Ng 1996), though Quan and his colleagues (2006) found that cancer screening and hospital services were less utilized by visible minorities. In a recent study by Wu, Penning, and Schimmele (2005), unmet health care needs were not more likely among immigrants; however, among those who reported unmet needs, immigrants were more likely to report that the care would not be adequate, that there were language barriers, and that they were not sure where to access health care. A focus group study with immigrants in Mississauga, Ontario, found that the three main issues for accessibility were geographic, socio-cultural, and economic (Asanin and Wilson 2008).

In fact, the actions and decisions of health care providers have been shown to be influenced by the racial or ethnic backgrounds of their patients (Dunlop, Coyte, and McIsaac 2000; Krieger et al. 1993; N. Roos and Mustard 1997). In their review of instances of racial discrimination in health care, Krieger and her colleagues (1993) discuss several studies that document preferential treatment regimes for white patients. Geiger (2001: 1699) notes that 'disparaging racial stereotyping, not clinical data, was predictive of refusal to recommend bypass surgery for many African-American patients in one large series of cases'. These findings suggest that once a person is in the medical system, the services that are made available to them vary on the basis of race.

Although physicians are trained to be 'neutral' and to shed or ignore their own socio-demographic characteristics and those of their patients,

studies indicate that in practice this is not done (Beagan 2000: 1253; van Ryn and Burke 2000). African American patients and patients from lower-income groups are perceived in a variety of more negative ways than white patients and patients from higher-income groups. Furthermore, physicians believe that African American and low-income patients are less compliant and less intelligent, and physicians felt less 'affiliated' with patients from minority backgrounds (van Ryn and Burke 2000). These perceptions affect the health care that racial or ethnic minorities and people of lower socio-economic status are likely to obtain (van Ryn et al. 2006). Patients sense and respond to the perceptions of the physician, so that 'when patients perceive that physicians like them, care about them, and are interested in them as a person, they are likely to volunteer more information and be more active in the encounter, more satisfied, and more compliant with medical regimens' (van Ryn and Burke 2000: 823). Patients are less likely to ask questions and be active health care consumers when they are aware of hostility or negativity on the part of their physician; and furthermore, disadvantaged groups believe that self-presentation is particularly important in the medical treatment they receive (Malat, van Ryn, and Purcell 2006; van Ryn and Burke 2000).

In fact, being an active consumer of health care may be more vital than ever. Provincial differences between what types of medicines are available and whether they are funded by the government is giving rise to new inequities in the treatment of disease and increased requirements for patients to self-advocate (see Box 11.4)

Wente's article (Box 11.4) shows the degree to which 'place' can influence the health care and treatment options available in Canada. Agency also plays a role in that the Raks were extremely active in their quest to obtain the best treatment and medical care—yet this agency is clearly constrained by structural factors: access to the Internet and the time and resources necessary

Box 11.4 Cancer Care at the Grocer's

By Margaret Wente

Every two weeks, Terry and Marj Rak go to the local Safeway to buy Terry's cancer medication. It's called Avastin, and it costs $3,000 a dose. They have taken out a loan to pay the bills. 'We get air miles at Safeway,' says Marj. 'We always order it on days when we can get the bonus miles.' Then they go to a hospital, where the medication is infused intravenously.

Avastin is a new biological treatment for people who have late-stage colorectal cancer. By dramatically shrinking tumours, it can extend lives for a few months, and sometimes for far longer. Avastin is now standard treatment in most Western countries, and was approved in Canada more than a year ago. But not all provinces will pay for it. B.C. and Newfoundland do; Saskatchewan and Ontario have refused, because they say the cost outweighs the benefits. Terry Rak, 65, lives in Saskatchewan.

'This is the home of medicare,' says his wife. 'Our province says they'll look after everyone, but the reality is, when something costs money, they deny us coverage.'

In Ontario, the government is still deciding whether it will allow cancer patients to buy Avastin privately. (It will also charge them several hundred dollars extra to administer it, something Saskatchewan does for free.) That would be an embarrassingly clear-cut example of two-tier health care. But the alternative—forcing people to buy it in the US—is even worse.

'It's crazy,' says Wendy Mundell, who was diagnosed in January. 'Why will they pay for some drugs but not for others?' Ms Mundell, who lives near Toronto, has been scrounging her Avastin supply from several sources. Her local hospital has started a fundraising drive to help her pay for it.

Medications such as Avastin are a crucial part of health care's future—high-tech, very specialized, extremely costly to develop, and potentially highly effective. Ms Mundell is only 41, and her results so far have been excellent. With luck, she could live for years. But good news for her is a nightmare for the system. Who will pay for these new wonder drugs, and how?

Colorectal cancer doesn't have the high profile of breast cancer, but it kills more people. After lung cancer, it's the second-biggest cancer killer for both men and women. When Ms Mundell was diagnosed, nobody mentioned Avastin to her. She found out about it on the Internet. When she brought it up with her oncologist, he acknowledged that it was a good drug and that she should be on it. 'But we don't know how to get it, so we don't really like to talk about it,' she remembers he said.

'Should doctors tell their patients about everything that's available, or only what they can get in their jurisdiction?' asks Barry Stein, president of the Colorectal Cancer Association of Canada. 'That's a moral dilemma for those who can't obtain these things and have to settle for what's second best.' There are other moral dilemmas. 'How would you like to be in a chemo suite and the person next to you is getting it and you aren't?' And there's another tier, too—the tier of people who have employment health plans, which may pick up 80 per cent of the costs.

Terry Rak does not have an employment health plan. He owns a bowling centre. He was diagnosed in June of 2003 after undergoing a colonoscopy across the border in Great Falls, Mont., because the wait was too long in Saskatchewan. He got surgery right away in Saskatchewan, but the cancer came back in his lungs a year later. (In a now-familiar story, he and his wife did their own research on his medical options.) After the province refused to fund Avastin, the Raks circulated a petition, wrote to every MLA, and held a demonstration in front of the Legislature.

Mr Rak had his first infusion of Avastin in March. His lesions have been decreasing in density, and his last CAT scan showed that everything is stable. According to his doctor, the treatments are doing the job. There are 80 to 100 other people in the province who are clinically eligible for Avastin, and thousands more in Ontario. 'Some people can't afford it,' says Marj Rak. 'I feel sick for them.'

The Raks are running low on money, too. But at least they're collecting lots and lots of air miles.

to carry out a petition and to travel extensively contributed to gaining life saving treatment in the case of the Raks. Many Canadians would be challenged to gather the same type of resources in order to gain the treatment that they needed. The Raks' experiences illustrate the extent to which some Canadians must go in order to gain the treatment and care that they need. In spite of the fact that Canada has a public health system, access to health care is not purely equitable, and power, knowledge, and economic and social resources can influence access to health care.

The extent to which health care is used is strongly related to gender, with women using many more health preventive and health care services than men do (Statistics Canada 2001i, 2001d, 2006b). Although some of this use is explained by visits for reproductive and prenatal care (Statistics Canada 2001i), women's greater use of health care has been documented independently of these types of visits (Green and Pope 1999; Kazanjian, Morettin, and Cho 2003). Men are much less likely to visit physicians or consult a specialist (Statistics Canada 2006b). Unlike relationships between health care access and each of class and race or ethnicity, however, explanations for the underuse of health care services by men emphasize masculine ideologies that promote unhealthy, risk-taking behaviour (Courtenay 2000; Mahalik, Burns, and Syzdek 2007; Statistics Canada 2001i, 2001b, 2001d; Trovato and Lalu 1995).

In an insightful study, Courtenay (2000), who examines the relationships between concept-

ualizations of masculinity and their consequences for men's health, suggests that different health care utilization rates for men and women are manifestations of the gender structure. According to Courtenay (2000), masculine imperatives to be 'strong' and self-sufficient inhibit men from attending to their health and encourage the medical establishment to underanalyze the effect of gendered beliefs on men's health behaviour. He argues that the attributes of 'masculinity' are in contradiction to healthy behaviour, and that the way in which these attributes manifest themselves is shaped by class and ethnicity. For example, men from different social classes may take risks in varying ways: 'Demonstrating masculinities with fearless, high-risk behaviours may entail skydiving for an upper-class man, mountain climbing for a middle-class man, racing hot rods for a working-class man and street fighting for a poor urban man' (Courtenay 2000: 1390).

According to the constructs of masculinity, health-conscious behaviour fails to connote a 'strong' persona and is considered to be 'feminine' (Courtenay 2000). This is an instance where gender structures work against both men and women. On the one hand, physicians provide less information to men than women and spend less time with men, and this may jeopardize men's health (Courtenay 2000). On the other hand, the fact that physicians spend more time with women may also be the reason for the overmedicalization and pathologization of women's bodies. Hence, although women's use of the medical system is thought to be due to their greater tendency to be ill and their overuse of health services, men's utilization of health care is considered a sign that they are healthier than women. According to Courtenay (2000: 1395), the broader societal view of women as 'overusers' of medical services and of men as 'naturally' healthy should be reversed:

> Given that women are unquestionably less susceptible to serious illness and live longer than men, it would seem that women should provide the standard against which men's health and men's health behaviour are measured. . . . If this were the case, we would be compelled instead to confront . . . men's underutilization of health care.

The actions and decisions of health care providers are influenced by the gender and age of patients. The medical establishment has played a critical role in defining and enforcing gendered behaviour norms on women (Lorber 1997; Mitchinson 1991; Offman and Kleinplatz 2004). Women's bodies have been viewed as problematic, and natural processes (e.g., menstruation) have been considered to be illnesses in need of medical treatment (Lorber 1997). The construction of 'premenstrual syndrome' as a disease is a telling example of how societal imperatives are translated into medical problems. Lorber (1997: 60) argues that 'stereotypically, women suffering from PMS are said to be cranky, irritable, angry, violent and out of control. . . . These characteristics assume some kind of comparison—with the same woman at other times of the month or with the way women are supposed to be.' She notes that there are no control groups in this research, either with men or with women cross-culturally or by ethnicity (Lorber 1997). When women voice dissatisfaction or anger about their life circumstances, physicians have tended to see the problem as an internal one requiring a medical solution (e.g., psychotropic drugs) rather than as

a symptom of societal inequality requiring a societal solution. For example, medical responses to menopause have typically involved medication such as hormone replacement therapy as opposed to challenging society's negative and stereotypical views of women aging (Calasanti and Slevin 2001, 2006; Morris and Symonds 2004). Box 11.5 shows how **medicalization** can in fact lead to illness and increased risks of disease.

Sadly, the overmonitoring of women's bodies seems to pertain largely to conditions that are believed to be 'female'. Some conditions that are common in women are undertreated or ignored despite women's greater contact with the medical profession. Adams and her colleagues (2008) found that physicians (regardless of their gender) are more likely to consider age-related conditions when diagnosing men for coronary heart disease. They note that attention to age in diagnosing men 'may, in part, reflect the historical male bias in medical knowledge, arising out of women's under-representation in CHD-related medical research' (Adams et al. 2008: 10). These biases have been well documented by McKinlay (1996) in his review of the underdetection of coronary heart disease in women. He notes that gender has been a primary determinant in treatment decisions on the part of physicians:

> When confronted with exactly the same presenting symptoms, vital signs, and test results depicted in a professionally acted colour videotaped patient-doctor encounter, 192 randomly sampled male internists were much less likely to arrive at a cardiac diagnosis in younger women, treat women medically, believe treatment was necessary or, for the younger women especially, to make health education and lifestyle change recommendation. (McKinlay 1996: 17)

Similarly, when older adults present physicians with their symptoms, physicians sometimes

Box 11.5 Mad? No, But They Deserve to Be; Post-menopausal Women Show Drop in Diseases after Giving Up HRT

By Judy Gerstel

We're mad as hell and we're not going to take it any more.

The last part, at least, is true.

Most women past menopause aren't going to take hormone replacement drugs any more.

They realize any superficial benefits of HRT—estrogen combined with progestin—are outweighed by the increased risk of breast cancer, heart disease, stroke, blood clots, ovarian cancer and dementia.

In the five years since the Women's Health Initiative (WHI) suddenly called a halt to its landmark HRT study in the summer of 2002 because it was too risky to continue, a stream of research has confirmed the havoc the drugs can wreak.

Starting that same summer, the use of hormone replacement therapy plummeted.

But what happened the very next year was unpredictable, unprecedented and stunning: a plunge in breast cancer rates—significantly, cancers fuelled by estrogen in women over 50.

'The largest single drop in breast cancer incidence within a single year I am aware of,' declared Dr Peter Ravdin, a biostatistics professor and researcher at M.D. Anderson Cancer Center in Texas, after results were announced at the San Antonio Breast Cancer Symposium last December.

'Hormones are the most logical explanation,' University of California professor Karla Kerlikowske told reporters when her study, the latest to link the abandonment of HRT with the drop in breast cancer, appeared this summer in the *Journal of the National Cancer Institute*.

US researchers say 14,000 cases of breast cancer were prevented in 2003, compared to 2002, after millions of women dumped their HRT.

Canadian estimates range from about 600 to 700 fewer cases of breast cancer in 2003 than in 2002 because of the drop in HRT.

'The WHI findings have probably prevented tens of thousands of strokes, heart attacks, blood clots, and breast cancers in the US population alone,' Dr Jacques Roussow, National Heart, Lung, and Blood Institute project officer of the WHI, has said. In April, the respected Million Women Study in the UK reported in the *Lancet* that HRT was responsible for 1,000 deaths from ovarian cancer between 1991 and 2005.

So the question is not whether HRT after menopause can fuel breast cancer and other illnesses (it can), not whether it's a dangerous drug that should be used only sparingly when absolutely necessary (it is), not whether abandoning HRT prevents life-threatening illness and death (it does).

The question isn't even why, during all these years of running for the cure and raising money for research and 'awareness,' and wearing and promoting pink, women have at the very same time been swallowing HRT propaganda and pills that were causing breast cancer.

The question is, Why aren't we mad as hell?

'It's a very good question,' says Kathleen O'Grady, with the Winnipeg-based national Women's Health Network. 'With Vioxx, there was a huge outcry and court cases right away. It's not clear why the same hasn't happened with HRT.'

British Columbia family physician Dr Warren Bell agrees there's been a disconnect between women taking an activist role in fighting breast cancer while ingesting hormones that fuel it—and then giving up hormones but not getting angry about the way the drugs were prescribed and promoted, without evidence of their safety.

'Older women are still the generation conditioned and socialized to be compliant and not to ask questions and not to get angry at the imposition of something that was inappropriate,' he says. 'And there's still a belief in the probity and scientific acumen of physicians. The combination is one that is very hard to subvert.'

(Women also know their anger is not well tolerated. For example, in his blog, medpundit.blogspot.com, a physician referred to a 2002 column I wrote post-WHI about the dangers of HRT, as 'a hormonal hissy fit'.)

Breast cancer activist Sharon Batt thinks 'women should be really angry' but 'most of the reports in the media have reported it as a finding that wasn't that clear cut. And maybe people don't understand the statistics well enough to recognize what an enormous finding this is.'

Other observers believe much of the confusion has been perpetrated by what Dr Deborah Grady, head of the Women's Health Clinical Research Center, at the University of California, calls 'the hormone-industrial complex'—Big Pharma and the constellation of businesses that feed off them.

'The industry is probably doing its best to ensure that it's considered a grey area,' says BC physician Bell. He likens the obfuscation to the tobacco industry's initial strategy. 'Create an impression of uncertainty and lack of unanimity. It's a lesson learned by the corporate sector across the board.

'If you want to keep on selling a product, actively foment the illusion of a lack of consensus.'

Dr Adriane Fugh-Berman, a professor at Washington's Georgetown University School of Medicine, and principal investigator of a project to educate physicians about the influence that pharmaceutical companies have on prescribing, published a paper last year in *Perspectives in Biology and Medicines* titled 'Gynecologists and Estrogen'.

'It is mysterious why gynecologists seem to be so much more susceptible to drug company influence,' she told the *Guardian*. 'About 10 to 20 years ago, HRT was really promoted as a panacea like snake oil, it cured and prevents everything—dementia, incontinence, wrinkles. It made you look better and feel better.

'But whenever you see something promoted as a panacea, it is a fake.'

Yet far from being mad as hell about the promotion and widespread prescribing of HRT and choosing to not take it, some women still cling to their panacea and damn the consequences.

'They were very angry at the WHI for bursting their balloon,' says American author and women's health activist Barbara Seaman. 'There was a refusal to really accept it for a while. A lot of women are very devoted to their products.'

Seaman, who warned against the use of hormones in the late '60s, has described 'the medical establishment's reckless prescription of estrogen' as 'the greatest experiment ever performed on women.'

She is especially scornful about some earlier observational studies, including one by US healthcare provider Kaiser Permanente, suggesting that HRT protected women from memory loss.

Sought after in the US by lawyers representing women who are suing drug companies, Seaman says it's very difficult to prove HRT is responsible for any particular case of breast cancer, although she believes women who have been taking HRT and have suffered strokes may have a better case.

Sadly, the confluence of genuine hope, greed and vanity has cost the lives of millions of women.

But very little anger.

Source: Gerstel (2007).

dismiss these symptoms as signs of old age and not as indicators of illness or disease.

Visits to physicians are common among those aged 65 and older, with 86.8 per cent of male seniors and 89.2 per cent of female seniors reporting they had visited a general practitioner in the last year (Rotermann 2006: 35). The gender imbalances in the use of health care services, with women having significantly more physician visits and hospitalization stays, largely disappears among Canadians aged 65 and older. This shows the impact of child-bearing and re-productive concerns on health care utilization for women in early and middle adulthood (Chen and Hou 2002). Women are more likely than men to receive home care (17.6 per cent com-pared to 11.7 per cent for men), and home care use rises over time with 42 per cent of seniors aged 85 and older receiving home care compared with 8 per cent of those aged 65–75 (Rotermann 2006). Unmet health care needs in the form of accessibility and acceptability are more common for people under the age of 45 (Chen and Hou 2002). Therefore, older age as such does not ap-pear to impede access to health care in Canada (Turcotte and Schellenberg 2007).

In fact, the process of aging has led to a num-ber of interventions that medicalize this natural process (Dinnerstein and Weitz 1998; Krieger et al. 1993; K. Morgan 1998). The medicalization of menopause and the advent of hormone replace-ment therapy epitomize the quest to freeze wom-en in a youthful mode (Lorber 1997). Vertinsky (1998: 90) notes that 'menopausal women are prime targets of medical experts, pharmaceutical companies and the media who bombard women with the message that hormones are required to cope with the "death of their ovaries"'. Moreover, cosmetic surgery is becoming more of an impera-tive than a choice for many women in response to society's valorization of youth (Hurd Clarke, Repta, and Griffin 2007; Goodman 1996). His-torically, women's bodies and functions have been medicalized, though scholars have noted the increasing tendency to medicalize men's ag-ing bodies (e.g. erectile dysfunction, andropause) (Conrad 2007; B. Marshall and Katz 2006).

CAGE(s) and the Processes of Production, Reproduction, and Distribution

Clearly, different lifestyle choices (reflecting agency) and limited access to health care do not fully explain health inequality in Canada. To understand better why some Canadians are healthier than others, we must consider struc-tural interpretations of the intersections among class, age, gender, ethnicity, and race alongside lifestyle and access factors. For instance, varia-tions in levels of physical activity illustrate how class, age, gender, ethnicity, and race structure health behaviour. Gendered ideologies inhibit women from engaging in physical-fitness activi-ties, and despite attempts to increase women's involvement in sport and exercise, fewer women than men are physically active in all age groups (Gilmour 2007; Vertinsky 1998). As Vertinsky (1998: 82) says, 'Healthy exercise is closely en-twined with the social and economic status of women, disempowering stereotypes of the fe-male body, and the issue of control over wom-en's bodies.' Vertinsky (1998) has identified four structural factors that contribute to the limited physical activity of women: (1) the authoritative role played by medical discourse in discouraging strenuous exercise for both younger and older women; (2) the impact of media and beauty stan-dards that see physical fitness only as a means to reach unattainable standards, along with the perception that women are naturally weaker and less physically able; (3) ageist assumptions about the physical abilities of older women, along with the reliance on drug therapies; and (4) racial and ethnic bias in accounts of physical activity, with young, white women idealized in sport. Further, women's positioning within the processes of production, reproduction, and dis-tribution means that women of various ages and racial and ethnic backgrounds tend not to have as much money or time to spend on physical activity as men do. This suggests that ideological structures combine with material structures to influence lifestyle 'choices'.

The ways in which processes of production, reproduction, and distribution are organized contribute to health inequalities. The nature of the productive labour that people perform may involve exposures to toxins, a lack of control over the work process, and discriminatory or oppressive treatment, all of which make an imprint on the physical and mental health of bodies. Similarly, individuals with higher degrees of control in productive processes and positive work experiences likely enjoy better health.

Of course, our place in the productive realm and the related health consequences are not randomly assigned but are strongly influenced by our class, age, gender, and race or ethnicity (Jackson and Williams 2006; Tomiak, Gentleman, and Jette 1997; Walters et al. 1996). Even when men and women share the same occupation in paid work, they often experience differing work realities, which manifest themselves in differing health consequences (Messing 1997, 1998). For example, Messing says, in her review of the literature on women's occupational health (1997: 3), 'Women and men with the same job titles can have very different exposures—male cleaners mop and female cleaners dust.' Furthermore, women's occupational illnesses are likely underrepresented because waitresses, supermarket clerks, and cleaners (female-dominated jobs) are understudied in the occupational literature (Messing 1997). Although employment is associated with better overall health for women (Elstad 1995; Rose et al. 2004; Walters, McDonough, and Strohschein 2002), some researchers have observed that the combination of caregiving and paid employment can take a toll (Dean 1992; Pavalko and Woodbury 2000), suggesting that processes of production and reproduction must be considered simultaneously. Indeed, the increased likelihood for women to be in precarious and less stable forms of employment constitutes yet another health risk stemming from production processes (Menendez et al. 2007).

Similarly, the organization of reproductive processes leads to variations in health. Social ties and contacts are not always health protective and may in fact be stressful. Thus, to the extent that women's primary responsibility for reproductive

processes engages them in vast social networks, there may be a 'cost of caring' that produces poor health effects. Moreover, marriage is health protective for many men, but the effect of marriage for women on health is more complex: 'Marriage may at once improve economic and social support opportunities, while diminishing control over paid and unpaid work—potentially increasing as well as compromising the health status of women' (Ballantyne 1999: 27).

Unpaid work includes domestic work in the form of meal preparation, cleaning, clothing care, repairs and maintenance, child care, adult care, financial management, shopping, transportation, and volunteer work (C. Jackson 1996). Among dual-earner families, women continue to spend more time in housework and domestic labour, with 90 per cent of women doing housework daily compared to 74 per cent of men (K. Marshall 2006). In spite of the importance of domestic work for women's health, Walters and her colleagues (Walters, McDonough, and Strohschein 2002: 687) note the 'striking omission' that the 1994 Canadian National Population Health Survey still contains no information on the domestic conditions in the home. Dean (1992) argues that a more equitable division of caregiving and child-raising in the family would benefit both men and women's health.

According to Katherine Marshall (2006), women, especially those balancing long work hours and child care, are more 'time-stressed' than men in similar circumstances. Walters (2003) points out that examining the social context in which lives are lived is critical in disentangling how gender, race, class, and health are intertwined. Walters and her colleagues (1996) look at the health of 2,285 male and female registered nurses in Ontario through a proportional random sample and compare their health in relation to paid work, unpaid work, and social support; they found that unpaid work substantially affected health, particularly for women. Women were much more affected by caregiver burden and time constraints and had to contend with 'having to divide themselves up in pieces and juggle things' (Walters et al. 1996: 1633). Walters and her colleagues view this as indicative of the burden of the 'double day' for women who must contend with additional responsibilities in the home. Among men in the sample, the only significant unpaid-work variable was 'disliking housework'. The occupational concerns of 'overload' and 'hazard exposure' were relevant to both male and female nurses, and the authors did not find discrimination or harassment in the workplace to be significant. However, male nurses were much more likely than their female counterparts to be concerned with issues of sexual harassment (Walters et al. 1996). This may indicate the importance of context and the experience of being in the minority in a male- or female-dominated profession.

The preceding discussion of the processes of production, distribution, and reproduction illustrates the tendency in the health literature to treat race, ethnicity, gender, social class, and age as separate entities. Yet the intersections of race and ethnicity, gender, class, and age influence health in a particular historical context and over time (Kreiger et al. 1993). The confusion and contradictions in the study of gendered patterns of morbidity discussed in the preceding sections attest to the need for integrating class, ethnicity, and age into these investigations (Ballantyne 1999; Cooper 2002; Curtis and Lawson 2000; Matthews, Manor, and Power 1999). For instance, some research has shown that in early adulthood, few socio-economic health inequalities are found for men and women. However, over time the impact of reproductive processes and the 'cost of caring' appear to have greater health consequences for women, while occupational concerns seem to have greater health consequences for men (Matthews, Manor, and Power 1999). Yet, as Walters (2003) notes, gender relations are complex, changing, and bound up with other social relations such that using an

indicator of sex or gender in research is unlikely to capture the complexity of health effects over time. Instead, the social determinants of health and the nature in which vulnerability and advantage cluster within social relations to affect health pathways and outcomes are important to research and assess (Raphael 2006, 2007).

The health status and length of life of Aboriginal people can often be attributed to poverty and geographic isolation (CIHI 2004; Public Health Agency of Canada 2006; Trovato 2001: 81), adding further support to the idea that multiple bases of inequality must be considered simultaneously if we are to understand disparities in health. Housing has been shown to be a key determinant of health (Bryant 2004; Raphael 2007) and yet there is an intensifying housing crisis in Canada, where as many as 47 per cent of Aboriginal lone parents are in need of core housing (Campaign 2000 2007). Indeed, research in the United States has revealed substantial racial differences in health that can be largely attributed to socio-economic factors (Anderson and Armstead 1995; Jackson and Williams 2006; Leclere, Rogers, and Peters 1997); however, even within socio-economic groups there are disadvantages stemming from the effects of discrimination. Anderson and Armstead (1995: 217) have found that poor whites and poor blacks in the United States experience different levels of deprivations and therefore are exposed to different health risks. Shuey and Willson (2008) also found that health disadvantages and differential outcomes between black and white Americans remained even after accounting for socioeconomic status. The **hypersegregation** or 'housing discrimination that blacks face at every level of socioeconomic status but especially at the low end . . . may partially explain the disparity in health outcomes between poor blacks and poor whites' (Anderson and Armstead 1995: 217). This hypersegregation means that more poor blacks live in more impoverished neighbourhoods than do poor whites (Anderson and Armstead 1995), and this leads to increased health risks, as these neighbourhoods are more often used as toxic waste dump sites (Jackson and Williams 2006; Krieger et al. 1993; Maher 1998). In fact, mortality rates are higher for black Americans at nearly every SES level (Anderson and Armstead 1995; Shuey and Willson 2008). Krieger and her colleagues (1993: 87) suggest that these disparities may be due to the fact that socio-economic class is experienced differently by blacks and whites: they point to studies which show that the 'economic return for the same level of education is lower for blacks than whites (and also for women than men within each racial group).' In Canada, the clustering of diverse groups of immigrants and visible minorities in neighbourhoods that are impoverished and transient has been shown to negatively affect the mental health of visible-minority youth (Abada, Hou, and Ram 2007). Scholars in Canada suggest that there is a need for further research on racism, health, and the effects of social exclusion (Abada, Hou, and Ram 2007; Galabuzi 2004). In summary, although we know much about how gender, class, age, ethnicity, and race influence health separately, the mutual structural coalescence of class, age, gender, race, and ethnicity found in only a handful of studies suggests that this issue should be further explored in health research (Krieger et al. 1993; Mullings and Schulz 2006).

Conclusion

Our experience of health is located squarely in the body, and this embodiment permeates every aspect of our lives. Health is not a haphazard phenomenon. As Audre Lorde's life history and the various sections of this chapter demonstrate, our experiences and opportunities within productive, reproductive, and distributive processes, as they are shaped by structural CAGES, influence our physical and mental health. Our class, age, gender, ethnicity, and race may work to constrain or facilitate our experiences in the processes of production, reproduction, and distribution. These processes, in turn, significantly shape both the degree of health we enjoy over the life course and the very length of our lives. Of course, biology, genetics, and physiological aging processes also play a part in determining health outcomes. So, too, does agency. People often make informed and conscious decisions about their health. They decide whether to exercise or whether a symptom warrants a visit to the physician, or they decide what type of treatment is best suited for them, including something as simple as deciding whether they need to take a pill for a headache. The extent to which people are informed or financially able to seek a physician's advice or to take a pill are, however, also influenced by structural CAGE(s).

Yet health research rarely considers how the structures of class, age, gender, ethnicity, and race mutually constitute inequality in health outcomes. Furthermore, the focus in the health literature on individual causes of disease outcomes precludes adequate consideration of how the processes of reproduction, distribution, and production as they are structured by class, age, gender, ethnicity, and race influence health. Even in the literature on occupational health, which is located squarely in production processes, the emphasis is on occupations that are more commonly held by men rather than women. We are still learning about the health effects of waitressing or of being a secretary or a teacher (Messing 1998). And, with the possible exception of mental health, we know very little about how gendered processes of reproduction influence inequality in health. We also know very little about how the processes of distribution within families influence health. In poor families, for instance, do mothers or fathers go without medicine so that they can afford to buy it for their children? When parents sacrifice good nutrition so that their children can eat well, does their health suffer?

Health care is a social-policy issue that the majority of Canadians are passionate about. In the fall of 2002, Roy Romanow, a former NDP premier of Saskatchewan, was commissioned by the federal government to write a report on the health care system in Canada. Romanow talked with Canadians from across the country and examined the provincial health care systems to assess what changes and improvements were needed. One strong message he received from Canadians was that we valued our publicly funded health care system and that most of us wanted to keep it. Romanow recommended that the federal government direct more money to health services and that reform of health services required investment in three areas: home care, primary patient care, and 'catastrophic' drug care, such as the treatment necessary for people with HIV/AIDS. Although these recommendations are commendable, basic health care services are also in need of more funding because they deteriorated significantly throughout the 1990s. Furthermore, equal access to health care, although recommended in the Romanow report, has taken a back seat to other issues, such as those listed above. Whether disadvantaged groups of Canadians will be better able to access health care services through current reforms remains to be seen.

IIIIIIIIII Note IIIIIIIIIIIIIIIIIIIIIIIIIIIIIIIIIIIIIIIIIIIIIIIIIIIIIIIIIIIIIIIIIIIIIIIIIIIIIIIII

1. Lorde was married for eight years in the 1960s.

IIIIIIIIII Questions for Critical Thought IIIIIIIIIIIIIIIIIIIIIIIIIIIIIIIIIIIIIIIIIIIIIIIIIIIIII

1. In what ways could an individual's psycho-social resources (mastery, self-esteem, social support, and so on) be shaped by his or her class, age, gender, race, and ethnicity?
2. How can we explain persistent health inequality in spite of a system of 'universal health care access' in Canada?
3. How do class, age, gender, and ethnicity or race contribute to the development of a healthy or unhealthy lifestyle?
4. Describe how societal ideologies of gender, race, ethnicity, age, and class affect patterns of health care utilization and delivery.
5. In what ways does the historical period in which we live influence our health? What do you think the major health problems will be in the future?

IIIIIIIIII Glossary IIIIIIIIIIIIIIIIIIIIIIIIIIIIIIIIIIIIIIIIIIIIIIIIIIIIIIIIIIIIIIIIIIIIIIIIIIIIIIIIIIII

Class-linked stress Stress exposures that are largely dependent on social status. For example, working-class and lower-income individuals are more frequently employed in physically stressful jobs (e.g., where there are extreme temperatures, high noise levels, shift work, or noxious fumes, or where the worker has to work at an assembly-line pace).

Differential exposure hypothesis The argument that women experience more morbidity because they are exposed to more chronic and daily stressors in their lives.

Differential vulnerability hypothesis The argument that women experience more morbidity because their caregiving role makes them more susceptible to emotional stress; this may also involve vulnerabilities due to women's internalized coping styles when dealing with stress.

Fundamental causes explanations Link and Phelan's sociologically informed theory of the reasons for the strong associations between social factors and disease. Link and Phelan (2000: 40) recommend a focus on macro factors like 'access to knowledge, money, power, prestige, and social connections' and the ways in which these factors can influence the exposure to health risks and preventive measures in order to explain long-time associations between inequality and health. As new risk factors and new technologies are discovered, those people in society with better resources and connections are more able to benefit from new knowledge and avoid health risks.

Hypersegregation The situation in which disproportionate numbers of minority-group members are located in impoverished, dangerous, and environmentally polluted neighbourhoods. Poor African Americans more often live in extremely disadvantaged neighbourhoods than do poor non-Hispanic whites.

Medicalization The defining of a natural biological event or progression as a form of illness requiring medical intervention and treatment. (For example, menopause has been treated with hormone replacement therapy.)

Psychosocial risk factors A system of exposures, resources, and situational variables believed to have an impact on health; they include mastery or sense of control, self-esteem, ease or availability of social supports, negative life events, and daily exposure to stress or exposure to traumatic events.

IIIIIIIIIII **Recommended Reading** IIIIIIIIIIIIIIIIIIIIIIIIIIIIIIIIIIIIIIIIIIIIIIIIIIIIIIIIIII

Courtenay, Will H. 2000. 'Constructions of Masculinity and Their Influence on Men's Well-Being: A Theory of Gender and Health'. *Social Science and Medicine* 50, 10: 1385–401. The author examines how socially constructed forms of masculinity (shaped by ethnicity, social class, sexuality, and so on) influence men's health behaviour and men's consequent health risks.

House, James S. 2001. 'Understanding Social Factors and Inequalities in Health: 20th Century Progress and 21st Century Prospects'. *Journal of Health and Social Behavior* 43 (June): 125–42. An important article that chronicles the main ways in which health inequalities have been explained and outlines the current state of research with future directions.

Inhorn, Marcia C., and K. Lisa Whittle. 2001. 'Feminism Meets the "New" Epidemiologies: Toward an Appraisal of Antifeminist Biases in Epidemiological Research on Women's Health'. *Social Science and Medicine* 53, 5: 553–67. The authors examine gender biases in current epidemiologic approaches to women's health research (e.g., biological essentialism) and suggest more feminist-friendly research directions.

Krieger, N., D.L. Rowley, A.A. Herman, B. Avery, and M.T. Phillips. 1993. 'Racism, Sexism, and Social Class: Implications for Studies of Health, Disease, and Well-Being'. *American Journal of Preventive Medicine* 9, 6: 82–122. The authors provide a comprehensive critical review of US epidemiologic literature, including detailed recommendations on how to overcome racism, sexism, and class biases in future health studies.

Link, Bruce G., and Jo Phelan. 1995. 'Social Conditions as Fundamental Causes of Disease'. *Journal of Health and Social Behavior* 35: 80–94. An important article in which the authors argue that health policy and research must shift from the focus on individual risk factors to more fundamental causes of disease (e.g., SES).

Lynch, J.W., G.A. Kaplan, and J.T. Salonen. 1997. 'Why Do Poor People Behave Poorly? Variation in Adult Health Behaviours and Psychosocial Characteristics by Stages of the Socioeconomic Lifecourse'. *Social Science and Medicine* 44, 6: 809–19. A population-based study of Finnish men that found that socio-economic conditions in childhood were significantly associated with adult health behaviours. This life-course approach illustrates how health or 'lifestyle' behaviour is influenced by socio-structural factors.

Raphael, Dennis. 2004. *Social Determinants of Health: Canadian Perspectives*. Toronto: Canadian Scholars' Press. An outstanding work on the social determinants of health in Canada, including the effects of food security, housing, education, and income along with a large section on the impact of social policy.

Raphael, Dennis. 2007. *Poverty and Policy in Canada: Implications for Health and Quality of Life*. Toronto: Canadian Scholars' Press. An excellent interdisciplinary text that examines the devastating and long-lasting health effects of poverty in this country and what can be done about it.

Simon, Robin. 2000. 'The Importance of Culture in Sociological Theory and Research on Stress and Mental Health: A Missing Link?' Chapter 5 in Chloe E. Bird, Peter Conrad, and Allen M. Fremont, eds, *Handbook of Medical Sociology*, 5th edn. Englewood Cliffs, NJ: Prentice-Hall. This chapter outlines the three main approaches to explaining the relationship between stress and mental health; it argues that cultural context (norms, values, and so on) and meanings deserve a more prominent place in sociological theories of stress and mental health.

Wadsworth, M.E.J. 1997. 'Health Inequalities in the Life Course Perspective'. *Social Science and Medicine* 44, 6: 859–69. The author outlines the value of a life-history approach to research by explaining how social factors (particularly those associated with poverty) may affect an individual's health trajectory. For example, nutrition in childhood may influence adult blood pressure levels, height, and so on.

IIIIIIIIIIIII **Relevant Websites** IIIIIIIIIIIIIIIIIIIIIIIIIIIIIIIIIIIIIIIIIIIIIIIIIIIIIIIIIIIIIIIIIIII

Health-evidence.ca
http://www.health-evidence.ca/
**This website sponsored by a group of Canadian health agencies, including the Canadian Institute for Health Information, provides an excellent search engine for health-related articles and reviews.

Health Council of Canada
http://www.healthcouncilcanada.ca/
Funded by the Government of Canada, the **Health Council of Canada fosters accountability and transparency by assessing progress in improving the quality, effectiveness, and sustainability of the health care system. Publications, videos, news, and events, as well as external links, are all posted on the site.

World Health Organization—Commission on Social Determinants of Health
http://www.who.int/social_determinants/en/
**The Commission on Social Determinants of Health (CSDH) supports countries and global health partners to address the social factors leading to ill health and inequities. This site has links to strategy documents, essays, and articles on health equity and social determinants of health, as well as summary reports from associated

collaborations or projects and people's stories about health inequities.

SexualityandU.ca
http://www.sexualityandu.com
**A comprehensive site about all aspects of sexuality over the life course administered by the Society of Obstetricians and Gynaecologists of Canada.

The Politics of Population Health
http://msl.stream.yorku.ca/mediasite/viewer/?peid=ac604170-9ccc-4268-a1af-9a9e04b28e1d
**A lecture by Dr Dennis Raphael, York University.

Health Disparities: From Genetics to Health Policy
http://video.google.com/videoplay?docid=-4129139685624192201&hl=en
A presentation by Dr Dennis Raphael on politics and health at the Centre for Health Disparities in Cleveland, Ohio.

CAGE(s) and the State

by Tammy Duerden Comeau and Julie McMullin

Introduction

In January 2003, André Le Corre, a retired medical lab technician, was in court presenting a $3 billion class-action suit against the Government of Canada for not informing him and 380,000 other seniors that they were eligible for the Guaranteed Income Supplement (GIS). The GIS is a federal social assistance program that tops up Old Age Security (OAS) benefits for seniors who earn less than $12,648 a year. This figure does not include the OAS benefits (approximately $5,000 a year in 2003), which is a point of confusion for some seniors. Mr Le Corre, who was 76 years old, had thought he was ineligible for the top-up because his pension income and OAS combined were greater than $12,648 a year. In fact, he had been eligible for the GIS benefits since 1994 but had never made a claim. Mr Le Corre's court case argues that Ottawa was negligent in not informing seniors who were eligible for benefits even though it could have used Revenue Canada data banks to identify these people. For Mr Le Corre, the GIS benefits would have made a big difference in the quality of his life, including 'the awful events that could have been prevented, the rent that could have been paid, the medications that could have been bought'. But for Mr Le Corre, the 'lawsuit is a matter of

principle. It's more about the sadness I feel for the poorer people' (Thuanh Ha 2003: A7).

This tiny glimpse into Mr Le Corre's life tells us a lot about the role the **state** plays in processes of distribution and in distributive outcomes of inequality for older adults. Without social assistance, Mr Le Corre's income would be less than $12,648 per year, well below official poverty lines. If he had claimed all the benefits for which he was eligible, the quality of his life would have been greatly enhanced. But in acknowledging the 'poorer people', Mr Le Corre recognizes that, while he is poor, there are many older Canadians who are worse off than he is. In fact, research has shown that 41 per cent of those eligible for the GIS have not applied, and in the oldest senior-age group, only 24 per cent of those eligible to receive a benefit of $2,000 or more applied (Poon 2005). Although significant gains have been made in eradicating poverty among older Canadians, 15 per cent of unattached Canadians aged 65 and older still live in poverty (National Council of Welfare 2007). Among seniors, the incidence of low income is greatest for senior women living alone (Turcotte and Schellenberg 2007). Hence, the ways in which gender relations shape the interrelated processes of production, reproduction, and distribution (see chapters 8 and 9) intersect with age relations in determining income inequality in later life. Of course, class, ethnicity, and race matter too. If Mr Le Corre were a member of the capitalist executive class, he would not likely have to worry about GIS. And yet his ethnicity and race put him in a position of privilege according to the Canadian state: recent immigrants to Canada are ineligible for OAS regardless of whether they become Canadian citizens.

Indeed, the state encompasses a vast range of institutions, policies, and programs that have a profound effect on the individuals living in a society. The workings of the state provide a strong example of the overlapping and intertwining nature of the processes of production, reproduction, and distribution. For instance, the Canadian state's influence on the processes of production and the labour market as discussed in chapter 9 are evident in the management of immigration policy, anti-strike legislation, pay-equity policies, maternity benefits, and unemployment insurance (see also Pupo 2001). The processes of reproduction and the work of caring discussed in chapter 8 are directly shaped and affected by maternity benefits, pensions, and immigration policy, particularly in the realm of paid reproductive work (Stasiulis and Bakan 1995, 2005). Governments dictate education and health policy, which influence the outcomes of health and education inequality discussed in chapters 10 and 11. Indeed, health and education policy have come under intense scrutiny in recent years as conservative policies have led to significant service cutbacks. All of these policies concern largely distributive processes, and the form in which wages and benefits are distributed in the family constitute another process through which inequality is manifested. While the state can act to ameliorate or mend unequal relations, and while agents have used the state for retribution, the state's actions are often ambiguous and contradictory (Armstrong and Connelly 1999). Armstrong and Connelly (1999) point out that the beneficiaries of state actions, such as women whose incomes are increased by pay equity, are often the most privileged in the first place and there is considerable difficulty in predicting the effects of even well-intentioned policies. Pupo (2001: 136) argues that the state's policy of treating men and women as the 'same' in divorce and child-custody legislation disadvantages women by discounting their care work in the family. The state's undervaluation of caregiving and nurturing puts women in a losing position even though the policy is ostensibly equitable.

According to Pupo (2001: 129), the state's main tasks are those of 'accumulation, legitimation, and coercion or social control', and these tasks are played out in the arenas of the economy, in the labour market, and among individuals and families. To carry out these tasks involves the establishment of a citizenship regime consisting of boundaries, rules, definitions, and geographic boarders (Dobrowolsky and Jenson 2004; Jenson and Papillon 2000: 246). Citizenship rights are defined, and avenues for obtaining access to these rights are made clear. A complex bureaucracy establishes the 'democratic rules of the game' and determines things such as acceptable ways in which to make claims. Nations are defined on the basis of historical claims and conceptualizations of nationality. Finally, states establish 'the geographical borders of the political community' as an exclusionary principle of citizenship (Jenson and Papillon 2000: 246).

One way to examine the reach of the state on groups and individuals is to look at the state's role in denoting who is deemed a **citizen** and what it is that citizens are entitled to in Canadian society. T.H. Marshall's concept of citizenship organizes the rights and responsibilities of citizens into three groups: **civil citizenship**, which includes basic human rights, such as the right to individual freedom and justice in the courts of law; **political citizenship**, which includes the franchise and the right to participate in the political process; and **social citizenship** (perhaps the broadest concept), which includes financial well-being, social heritage, and access to social services (T.H. Marshall 1950). Marshall's typology has been criticized for its generalization of the experience of white, European men to represent the process of citizenship in general (Walby 1997). In fact, Walby (1997) notes that the means by which white, European men achieved citizenship do not represent the experience of most other groups. However, in Walby's (1997: 168) analysis, there are 'degrees' of citizenry, and she argues that Marshall's conceptualization is a useful one for considering how portions of citizenship were meted out to different groups at different historical times. It is important to note that although the state has a substantial amount of power with which to structure and constrain the lives of its citizens, state institutions have also been successfully mobilized by agents for the purposes of social justice (Pupo 2001; Walby 2004). Individuals and groups can use state institutions (e.g., the legal system) and programs to their own ends (e.g., to seek redress or to monopolize resources).

In this chapter, 'social citizenship' will be a main point of discussion, because the state programs of unemployment insurance, parental benefits or maternity leave, social welfare, pensions, and old age security in many ways reproduce the existing inequalities and shore up long-standing advantages among the privileged. Although aid and assistance for the disadvantaged groups in Canadian society are desperately needed, the form that this aid has frequently taken has had mixed and often negative results. Furthermore, Canadian citizens are experiencing more and more infringements on their civil liberties with advances in surveillance technology and security measures (Brodie 1999; Crocker et al. 2007; Tator and Henry 2006).

This chapter will take a critical view of the role of the state, focusing on the state's role in social regulation and the social reproduction of the relations of class, gender, race, ethnicity, and age. The division of the chapter into separate sections on class, age, gender, and race and ethnicity is in some ways arbitrary and is done largely for the purposes of organization. The state's conceptualization of these social relations is integral to the way in which policies are conceived and developed and to the effects that they have on groups and individuals. Notions of who is counted as a citizen shape the penalties, constraints, and privileges meted out to Canadians.

Focusing on Class: Making Citizens, Making 'Class'

Poverty

The face of poverty and social class is deeply gendered, racialized, and age-based. Canadians living in poverty and low-income situations are more often women, particularly lone women raising children, who in 2004 had the highest poverty rate of any other group, at 35.6 per cent (CCSD 2007b. Women and men who have recently immigrated, particularly visible-minority immigrants, and Aboriginal men and women are also at increased risk of being poor and of having low incomes (CCSD 2007a; Kazemipur and Halli 2001; Palameta 2004). Aboriginal peoples in Canada have been described as a 'colonized' people, existing as a reserve labour army and kept dependent on the economic imperatives of the Canadian state (Frideres 1988; Frideres and Gadacz 2008). Immigration policies in Canada have historically favoured workers who could be more easily exploited, both by the manufactured vulnerability of their citizenship status and through overtly racist practices (Bolaria and Li 1988; Calliste 1996; Trumper and Wong 2007). Immigrants were allowed entry to Canada specifically to fill the need for cheap labour (e.g., Chinese workers were paid less than European workers in the construction of the Canadian Pacific Railway) and to toil at jobs that no one else wanted (for example, Caribbean black women were brought in to perform domestic labour) (Calliste 1996; Li

1988). Thus, because immigrants were desired largely for their labour, immigration practices constructed classes. Furthermore, strict limitations have often accompanied the entry of immigrants into the country (Calliste 1996). This is illustrated for Calliste (1996: 73) by the exclusion 'in July 1911, [of] eight Guadeloupean domestics when it was judged that they were likely to become a public charge because they were single parents. . . . The immigration officer surmised that they were likely to become pregnant again and would probably become a drain on the public purse.' Calliste (1996: 72) argues that these actions show the Canadian state's racialization of Caribbean women as 'immoral' because of the belief that they are 'likely to become single parents'. Assumptions about who was likely to be 'poor' and who would be supported in such a circumstance are evident in Canadian social assistance policy.

The Canadian state has a long history of policies designed to aid those who are poor, but the state's conceptualization of the 'deserving' poor has largely incorporated the image of the 'white, working-class, breadwinner' who is temporarily out of work (Scott 1996). The poor of Canadian society are not all viewed as entitled to the rights of economic well-being and social security. They are sorted and classified on the basis of their age, race and ethnicity, and gender in order to determine their measure of entitlement. Traditionally, the white, working-class breadwinner has been seen as the 'real' citizen, deserving of the guarantee of the rights of social citizenship. The conflation of the 'deserving worker-citizen' with the white, male, working-class worker engaged in paid work has long shaped policy making (Brodie and Bakker 2007; Evans 1997; Scott 1996).

Tracing the history of social assistance, Scott (1996) analyzes how the assistance for single mothers originated from the notion of entitlement owed to the 'worker', ostensibly the 'white, male, middle-aged, family supporter'. Thus, the 'deserving' mother-recipient of social citizenship

is fundamentally racialized as well, since 'racial' homogeneity in families (in particular the quest to reproduce a 'sanitized' white, northern citizen) was strongly encouraged (Mackey 1999; McLaren 1991; Valverde 1991). Consider the moral panics over the 'corruption' of young, white women by Chinese men (Valverde 1991), the exclusion of current and 'potential' Caribbean black mothers (Calliste 1996), and the effect that the Indian Act had on unions between Aboriginal people and white settlers (Aboriginal women who married a non-Indian were stripped of their Indian status) (Nelson 2002). The very possibility of existing in a family was itself also strongly controlled and racialized. For example, Chinese men who emigrated were not allowed to bring their families with them, and in this way the number of non-white families was limited (Das Gupta 1995; Li 1998).

Mother's Allowance (which evolved into Family Benefits) was introduced in 1920 and was only for First World War widows, who were eligible for support from the government because they were not to blame for their own widowhood (Scott 1996: 17). Evans (1997: 99) calls this the 'breadwinner/dependent model of the family'. In this case, the 'mother-citizen' was owed a stake in social citizenship; however, she had to adhere to the prevailing gender norms and strict behavioural guidelines (Scott 1996: 18; see also M. Little 1999). The gendering of social policy is noted by Scott (1996), who argues that women were not granted state support for their role as paid workers or even for their reproductive labour but only as a proxy for their relationship to a bona fide and entitled 'worker'. Scott (1996: 18) points to the 'man about the house' rule, which prohibits any woman living with a man from collecting government support. This prohibition is imbued with assumptions about men's presumed support of women. Though it is now called the 'spouse about the house' rule, heavy monitoring and policing of single women on welfare continues, with the assumption that a 'man' in the house means that he is contributing to finances (Mirchandani and Chan 2007). The family-class immigration status is yet another example of the state's construction of women as dependent on a male provider, for women are more likely than men to enter under this status, which effectively denies them the language training and social programs that are available to their 'independent'-class immigrant sponsor (Abu-Laban 1998; Ighodaro 2006). The notion of the 'deserving' recipient and the moral regulation and monitoring of those receiving state support illustrate the state's role in constructing gendered and racialized ideologies and in perpetuating class inequalities.

Poverty statistics in Canada show that lone-parent families headed by women are much more likely to be in poverty (35.6 per cent) than those headed by men (14.2 per cent), and these poverty rates have changed little since the year 2000 (CCSD 2007b P). The penalization of women for existing as single heads of families is evident in Kilkey and Bradshaw's international comparative analysis (1999) of mothers in lone- and two-parent families. The countries studied were the Nordic countries, France, Germany, Austria, the United States, the United Kingdom, Ireland,

the Netherlands, Australia, and Canada. In this comparison, Canada is grouped with the UK and Australia as a country where lone mothers have 'an above average rate of poverty whether in paid work or not' (Kilkey and Bradshaw 1999: 176). There are few incentives or legitimate opportunities for women in these circumstances to engage in paid work, and, the authors argue, in most cases the policies designed to support lone mothers do not make it possible to escape poverty, even if those women do join the labour force (Kilkey and Bradshaw 1999). For lone mothers on social assistance, there is little consideration for the difficulties of balancing work and child care (Gazso 2007; Lessa 2006; Stephensen and Emery 2003). Furthermore, in Ontario, the imperative to reduce government spending on social assistance means that for some lone mothers, working full-time leaves them 'worse-off' financially than lone mothers who work less than half and qualify for an Ontario Works supplement (Evans 2007). This paradox is evident in Box 12.1, where we see that leaving the welfare system is not synonymous with leaving poverty.

Single mothers such as Andrea Duffield (see Box 12.1) have simply joined the leagues of the working poor. In fact, many of the lone mothers

|||||||||||||||||||||||||||||||||||||||||||||||||||||||||||||||||||

Box 12.1 Having a Job, but Losing Ground; Report Shows Ontario Child Poverty Rate Still Rising; System Penalizes Working Poor

By Laurie Monsebraaten

When Andrea Duffield's youngest child started Grade 1 last fall, the single mother of three got a part-time job in the hope of pulling her family out of poverty.

But the extra income caused her subsidized rent to double. And after taxes and work-related

expenses, her Toronto family wasn't any further ahead.

Despite Ontario's growing economy and low unemployment rate, one in eight children (12.6 per cent) were living in poverty by 2005, a percentage that has been rising since 2001, says the

Ontario Campaign 2000 in its annual report to be released today.

That figure applies to after-tax incomes. In before-tax incomes, previously used as the yardstick, child poverty in 2005 was at 17.3 per cent. In 2001, the child poverty rate in Ontario was 10.3 per cent after taxes and 15.1 per cent before taxes.

The advocacy group is demanding that Ontario's upcoming anti-poverty strategy ensure that every adult working full-time full-year is able to live above the poverty line.

Duffield's predicament points to the need for continuing social support for people working in low-wage jobs.

'I don't know why they don't give low-income people a grace period before they raise [subsidized] rent,' Duffield said. 'We just need some time to get on our feet.'

Some 70 per cent of the province's poor children belong to families like hers, with at least one parent working, says Ontario Campaign 2000. More than 41 per cent have a parent working full-time, full year, the group says.

'A job is not a guaranteed pathway out of poverty,' says its report.

The report's 2005 findings define poor children as those living in families whose after-tax income is below Statistics Canada's low income cut-offs.

In 2005, the cut-off was $20,956 for a lone parent with one child living in a large city like Toronto. For a family of four, it was $32,556.

When she is not working, Duffield, 36, runs her family of four, which is not on welfare, on just $17,000 a year in child support and government child benefits.

While decrying poverty levels, Ontario Campaign 2000's new report says the province has taken some promising steps in the past year.

The minimum wage just went up to $8.75 an hour and will rise to $10.25 by 2011. Ontario low-income families will get a new child benefit worth up to $50 a month starting in July, increasing to $92 a month by 2011. And a Queen's Park poverty-reduction committee is expected to produce a legislative plan by the end of the year.

The advocacy group wants this anti-poverty strategy to help the children of single mothers, visible minorities, recent immigrants and aboriginals.

'These children are between 1.5 and almost three times more likely to be living in poverty,' the report says.

Ontario Campaign 2000 notes that Quebec has taken steps that reduced its after-tax child poverty rate by more than half to 9.6 per cent in 2005 from a peak of 22 per cent in 1997.

'This shows that it's achievable,' said the group's spokesperson Jacquie Maund.

Jan Vink, a principal in Flemington Park, an area teeming with immigrants, says Ontario has to do more to recognize the credentials of foreign-trained professionals who get stuck in menial jobs.

Source: Monsebraaten (2008).

in the UK, Australia, and Canada in Kilkey and Bradshaw's study (1999) were found to live in multigenerational households. Kilkey and Bradshaw (1999) suggest that the poverty rate (as measured by household income) may underestimate the extent of poverty and that those lone mothers who have paid jobs may be able to hold them only because of support from their families. Indeed, in 2003 nearly 40 per cent of Canadian families headed by employed single mothers lived in poverty (National Council of Welfare 2006). The lack of support from the state fuels the perpetuation of poverty for lone mothers and creates these women and their families as an 'underclass' in Canadian society.

Social Regulation: Class and the Law

Civil citizenship includes the right to justice and redress in a society's legal system. Class relations have an impact on the prosecution of crime and on who is considered a criminal. Some members of society, by virtue of their class, enjoy a certain amount of protection from criminalization and moral regulation. Visibility can make some populations more vulnerable, as in the case of young people living on the streets. Schissel (1997, 2006) contends that there is an unsubstantiated moral panic over youth delinquency and crime in Canada and that the law targets and processes youth differentially on the basis of their class, age, race or ethnicity, and gender. For example, Aboriginal youth constitute only 5 per cent of youth in Canada; however, they make up 20 per cent of admissions to secure custody (Brzozowski, Taylor-Butts, and Johnson 2006).

In fact, structural disadvantages are built into the fabric of the law itself. The state does not usually view harm inflicted by companies and corporations as 'crime'. Snider (1993) notes that crimes committed by corporations are not taken seriously by the state, despite the fact that the costs of these crimes in terms of environmental damage, financial loss, and loss of human life are often higher than those from 'street crime'. Indeed, even after Bill C-45, which was meant to make companies more liable under the Criminal Code for the damages inflicted by their action or inaction, corporations remain less accountable for crimes than do individuals in Canada (Bittle and Snider 2006). Bittle and Snider (2006: 490) conclude that 'there is little reason to believe this legislation will produce a crackdown on the most powerful economic actors, or seriously challenge companies to reduce workplace injuries and death in industries where fixing these conditions is complex and expensive. Bill C-45 will undoubtedly hold *some* businesses and executives criminally accountable, primarily the smallest and weakest.' **Corporate crime** includes a wide range of illegal activities that carry serious consequences for their victims. Consider the harm inflicted by inadequately tested drugs, such as thalidomide and DES (Peppin 1995).

According to Snider (1993: 1), in the early 1990s, every six hours a worker died on the job in Canada, and this statistic may be a significant underestimate. In fact, deaths in the workplace have risen dramatically. According to Sharpe and Hardt (2006), there are on average five fatalities each day in Canadian workplaces, meaning an increase of 45 per cent from 1993. Compared with 29 other countries, Canada ranks fifth in terms of workplace fatalities, and those most at risk are men; older workers; those working in industries like mining, logging, fishing and agriculture; and those holding occupations in trade and transport (Sharpe and Hardt 2006). The state's complicity in corporate crime may stem partly from the government's involvement with big business. Consider for example, the devastating environmental and health effects of steel production in Sydney, Nova Scotia, where government bureaucracies were intimately connected with the offending corporations (McMullan 2006; McMullan and Smith 1997).

Re-manufacturing Class: Workfare

Some observers suggest that the rights of Canadian citizens are in jeopardy (Fuller, Kershaw, and Pulkingham 2008; Mooers 1999). Mooers (1999: 288) argues that as with the idea of 'lean production' in the global workplace, there has been a shift in the notion of citizenship, such that social citizenship rights are being pared down and citizens are increasingly being required to 'earn' their right to social benefits. The requirement that Canadians perform labour for the right to economic survival can be seen as one example of the move to 'lean citizenship'. Similarly, Fuller Kershaw, and Pulkingham (2008: 157) state that there has been a move from 'rights-based concepts of citizenship to obligation-centred notions' where employment acts as the key signifier of 'active citizenship'. The obligation to contribute to society through paid employment is best illustrated through the ushering in of 'work-for-welfare' programs. **Workfare** has been described by some as a harking back to the era of the workhouses for the poor, who were required to 'pay' in one way or another for a minimal amount of aid (Shragge 1997). Indeed, this aid is truly minimal, as social assistance amounts continue to shrink and payments generally leave recipients living far below Statistic Canada's low income cut-off (Snyder 2006: 311). Shragge (1997: 26) notes that the Canadian governments' endorsement and development of workfare reflects the view that 'able-bodied individuals' who are collecting welfare do so simply because of their own lack of skills and lack of initiative. These recipients are now required to work or take training in order to receive government aid. The wider societal shifts in the labour market and the difficulty in finding work are discounted as explanations for receiving welfare. The assumption is that if workers are sufficiently qualified, they will be able to find a job that adequately supports themselves and, by extension, their family. Yet, in a study of the Ontario Works program in Toronto, those who left welfare for employment were found to be far worse off in all categories compared to the rest of the Canadian labour market (Lightman, Mitchell, and Herd 2005). For example, 30 per cent of welfare leavers were in non-permanent positions compared with 7 per cent of the labour force, and welfare leavers earned two-thirds (64 per cent) less than the adult labour force on average (Lightman, Mitchell, and Herd 2005: 71). In fact, Shragge (1997) argues that workfare is calculated more to use the unemployed and the vulnerable to perform work for less than a job would normally pay. Workfare is a 'coercive' method of government control over the most underprivileged in society (deRouche 2001: 329). Interestingly, although the significant decline in welfare caseloads in Ontario is commonly attributed to the Ontario Works workfare program, researchers have found that stricter eligibility requirements for collecting social assistance are

likely behind the decrease (Snyder 2006: 319). In either case, the right to social citizenship is being eroded in the face of demands that citizens must demonstrate that they deserve support.

In British Columbia, changes in eligibility requirements for welfare in 2002 and extensions in work and employment requirements have had devastating consequences (Klein and Pulkingham 2008). Indeed, in 2004 poverty rates for both individuals and families (at 14 per cent and 10 per cent respectively) were higher in British Columbia than in any other province and the rate of poverty for BC lone-parent families the highest by far, at 45.6 per cent (CCSD 2007b: 7). Klein and Pulkingham (2008) examined the impact of social assistance policies on 62 British Columbian longer-term welfare recipients over a span of two years (2004–6). They note that welfare is by no means 'generous' and document that during their study period, 'a single person considered employable received $510 per month —$325 for shelter and $185 (or about $6 per day) for all other needs, including food, clothing, transportation, telephone, etc.' (Klein and Pulkingham 2008: 2). For their participants, living on welfare was a matter of survival, and food, shelter, and basic necessities were difficult to obtain. The majority of their participants (77 per cent) frequented food banks and 46 per cent suffered from hunger in the past month (Klein and Pulkingham 2008).

Finding work and employment in these circumstances is clearly a great challenge, especially considering that at the start of the study 39 per cent of participants did not have a fixed address in the previous six months and half did not have a phone number (Klein and Pulkingham 2008). The investigators found that a key problem was the misclassification of many of their participants into the 'expected to work' category when physical, mental, and other health difficulties clearly made employment unobtainable. In fact, most were reclassified over the course of the study period, but Klein and Pulkingham (2008) argue that this took far too long and should have been evident much earlier to government officials. The expectation that valid societal contributions must take the form of work in productive processes, while ignoring reproductive labour and contributions in voluntary capacities, continues to penalize citizens in a number of ways (Fuller Kershaw, and Pulkingham 2008).

Workfare programs also illustrate inconsistency and contradictions inherent in state policies (Breitkreuz 2005; deRouche 2001; Evans 2007). For instance, despite the fact that historically some women have been able to obtain social assistance on the basis of their rights as mothers, the advent of 'workfare' programs has largely ignored gender and 'mother-status' (Evans 1997, 2007). In this case, the class status of individuals as 'welfare recipient' appears to take precedence. According to Breitkreuz (2005: 154),

> The most striking contradiction is that although some welfare states encourage middle-class women to be 'stay at home' moms and dependent on their husbands for financial sustenance, they simultaneously require low-income lone mothers to work for wages and pay someone else to care for their children. Thus, while 'stay at home' mothers with male breadwinners are saluted for their outstanding 'family values', poor women who wish to raise their children full-time are declared lazy and psychologically dependent on the state.

Similarly, in Alberta's social assistance program, single mothers are considered 'employable once the youngest child is six months old', and in the expansion of Ontario's workfare program, single mothers with children over the age of three are required to participate (Evans 1997: 100; Evans 2007). Therefore, Evans (1997: 100; 2007) argues, in the area of social assistance there has been a move to define 'mothers' as 'workers'

simultaneously with the increasing inaccessibility of child care. Indeed, the type of work that lone-mother welfare recipients most often obtain is inflexible, precarious, and unfriendly to the demands and requirements of raising a child (Breitkreuz 2005; Evans 2007). Training and education for those on welfare is minimal unless it seems likely to steer people as quickly as possible into work of any kind. Evans (2007: 35–6) points out that the motto 'any job is a good job' is made explicit in the Ontario Works policy guidelines, and education and training have been reduced and their access limited in recent years. For recipients of social assistance and employment insurance who are unskilled, workfare programs are unlikely to significantly improve their skills, or even their income for extended periods; however, with tightening requirements and workfare programs, the social assistance payments required of the province have been reduced, thus benefiting the state (deRouche 2001).

Agents in Action: Dissent and Co-optation

Although the preceding sections have emphasized the significant reach of the state into people's lives, this does not mean that individuals and groups in Canadian society do not exercise agency with regard to the state. Mooers (1999) uses Gramsci's idea of hegemony to discuss the co-optation of workers in the state's renewed emphasis on 'self-reliance' and 'active citizenship' (e.g., workfare). Certainly, these programs have had both widespread public support and strident opposition (as during the Days of Action), thus illustrating the contradictory and complex nature of hegemony (Mooers 1999). Mooers claims that the state's recruitment of public support and community input for government privatization projects have been tactics in the attempt to minimize opposition. Still, citizens have continued to mobilize against the state's welfare reforms and attempts to privatize various public enterprises (e.g., health care). Mr

Le Corre's decision to sue the federal government for not making people aware of their eligibility for GIS is another case in point.

Indeed, class actions against governments are quite common. In the last few years, gay- and lesbian-rights activists have challenged provincial and federal governments on various human-rights and family issues and gained significant ground. There has been somewhat less success for those contesting workfare programs. Louise Gosselin brought a class action against the Quebec government for its 'coercive' welfare policies. These policies substantially reduced payments to able-bodied welfare recipients under the age of 30 who do not participate in 'schooling, job training, or community work' (Seeman 2001). Gosselin contends that the welfare reforms are unconstitutional and that they violate basic citizenship rights. However, Neil Seeman, a journalist with the *Globe and Mail*, trivialized and condemned Gosselin's lawsuit, claiming that granting 'protected "rights"' . . . would spiral the country into debt . . . [and] would also reverse political priorities established by voters at the ballet box' (2001). Seeman's response and portrayal of Gosselin and workfare is an apt example of the hegemonic control of the state. Citizen protest and dissent exist, but they are often harshly challenged by those who support the ideologies of the ruling regime.

Focusing on Race: Making Citizens, Making 'Race'

The often oppressive nature of government policy and state action is evident in the history of policies concerning Aboriginal people in Canada. The outright denial of basic citizenship rights and the intricate and totalitarian declaration of the Indian Act (1876) have wreaked havoc on Aboriginal communities and crafted a perpetual cycle of poverty and dysfunction for many (R. Armstrong 1999; Dickason 2006; Frideres and Gadacz 2008). Political citizenship has been historically denied to Aboriginal groups by the Canadian government (Borrows 2001). The civil and social citizenship rights of Aboriginal peoples have also been strongly curtailed by the Indian Act and its legacy. If social citizenship includes the right to one's social heritage, than this entitlement has been severely compromised for Aboriginal Canadians. Heritage and social relations were ignored because Indian status was defined by the government on the basis of where one lived (e.g., on a reserve) and on the basis of band registration (Boyko 1995; D.G. Smith 1975). The Indian Act effectively denied people their social heritage, for Aboriginal women who married non-Indians were stripped of their Indian status, as were their children (Boyko 1995; Dickason 2006). These women were forced to leave the reserve and live apart from their families. This aspect of the policy illustrates that the Indian Act was both a racial and a gender project. Although Aboriginal women who married non-Indians were subsumed under their husband's status, this stipulation did not apply to Aboriginal men who married non-Indians. The policy is dehumanizing because it treats a person's identity and social heritage like a set of clothes that can be taken on and off (at will or by force).

This approach is also evident in the government's scheme of location tickets, by which Aboriginals were granted a plot of reserve land in exchange for their right to Indian status, as well as in the government's attempt to strip Aboriginal people of their culture and heritage through residential schools (Boyko 1995; Wotherspoon 2004).

Of course, these government acts and initiatives have been met with strong resistance on the part of Aboriginal peoples in Canada (Anderson 1992; Borrows 2001; Jenson and Papillon 2000). Aboriginal groups have made citizenship claims and have demanded that the Canadian government honour the historical land treaties and pacts (Borrows 2001; Dickason 2006). Jenson and Papillon (2000), who trace the citizenship claims and mobilization of the James Bay

Cree, argue that they have mounted challenges to the Canadian 'citizenship regime' in all of its four dimensions. These challenges will be discussed in more depth in the sections to follow.

Re-manufacturing 'Race'/Ethnicity: Immigration

Citizenship in Canada has long been a racial project (see chapter 4 for a discussion of racial and racist projects). Race affects who is allowed to enter Canada, what work people are allowed to perform, what 'class' of citizenship they are granted, and whether this citizenship can be revoked (Ighodaro 2006; Jakubowski 1997; Li 2003). The experience of Chinese Canadians is a poignant example of the extent to which citizenship rights can be denied and diluted. The history of immigration policies concerning Chinese immigrants also illustrates how policy is shaped by class-based and capitalistic imperatives policy, and the way in which gendering and racialization are built into these objectives. Bolaria and Li (1988: 106) contend that 'from the outset, the whole Chinese question in Canada was in essence a question of labour exploitation'. In the late nineteenth and early twentieth centuries, Chinese immigrants did the labour-intensive work that 'white' Canadians would not do, and they did so for a lesser wage. They worked on the railway, in salmon canneries, and, until they were barred from doing so, in mines (Bolaria and Li 1988; Li 1998). As soon as the exigencies of labour passed, citizenship infringements were imposed on Chinese immigrants. Head taxes were imposed as early as 1885, and by 1903 they were as high as $500 per person (Bolaria and Li 1988). The federal government required all Chinese in Canada to be registered and to have a certificate (Bolaria and Li 1988). The province of British Columbia barred the Chinese from voting in provincial and municipal elections, and they were legally excluded from numerous professions (including law, pharmacy, public works, and skilled jobs in

coal mines). The 'second-class' citizenship status of Chinese Canadians (both naturalized and immigrant) was upheld by the Supreme Court of Canada in 1903 despite the fact that the court conceded that the prohibitions enacted by the province 'were in truth devised to deprive the Chinese, naturalized or not, of the ordinary rights of the inhabitant of British Columbia' (Bolaria and Li 1988: 109).

The government's immigration policy significantly shaped social relations within Chinese communities, because women were effectively excluded from entering Canada for many years (Abu-Laban 1998; Li 1998). Although the vast majority of Chinese men who emigrated were married and had families, the head tax intentionally prevented most of them from bringing their families to Canada (Li 1998). Table 12.1 shows the impact of government immigration policies on the subsequent sex ratios of Chinese immigrants over the course of the twentieth century.

Chinese men were treated preeminently as 'last-resort' and expendable workers who were not entitled to the rights of white workers. Abu-Laban (1998: 17) notes that 'racialized immigrant minorities' were 'active[ly] discouraged from permanent settlement'. Chinese women were largely excluded from Canadian society, and those who were in Canada were also treated as 'second-class' citizens in the gendering of legislation. Like the Indian Act, the 1914 Naturalization Act made certain that a woman's status was that of her husband's; therefore, any Chinese woman with Canadian citizenship lost it if she married a man who was not a Canadian citizen (Li 1998). In the past quarter decade, racism against the Chinese in Canada has become more 'covert' (Zong 2007). Although China is now the country from which the majority of immigrants to Canada come (with 30,000–40,000 entering each year between 2000 and 2004), Chinese Canadian immigrants continue to face discrimination, encountering work opportunities that do not match their high skills and education (Zong

Table 12.1 Number and Sex Ratio of Chinese Immigrants Admitted to Canada,[a] and Major Immigration Legislation Affecting Chinese Immigration, 1906–1976

Period	Total # of Chinese Immigrants Admitted to Canada	Males per 100 Females	Major Immigration Legislation	Impact on Chinese Immigrants
1906–24[b]	43,470	3,578	Chinese Immigration Act, 1903	Head tax raised
1924–46[c]	7	–	Chinese Immigration Act, 1923	Exclusion of Chinese
1947–62[d]	21,877	98	Repeal of 1923 Act, 1947; Immigration Act, 1952	Repeal of exclusion, limited sponsored immigrants permitted
1963–67	18,716	72	Immigration Act, 1962	Independent and sponsored immigrants permitted
1968–76	91,490	98	Immigration Act, 1967	Universal point system applied

a Data Source: Annual Reports of the Department of the Interior (1906–17); Department of Immigration and Colonization (1918–36); Department of Mines and Resources(1936–49); Department of Citizenship and Immigration (1950–65); Department of Manpower and Immigration (1966–76). Figures from 1907–25 are based on reported nationality (China); 1926–8, racial origin (Chinese); 1929, nationality (China); 1930–1, racial origin (Chinese); 1932, nationality (China); 1933-49, racial origin (Chinese); 1950–1, nationality (China); 1952–4, racial origin (Chinese); 1956–61, ethnic origin (Chinese); 1962–6, country of last permanent residence (China, Hong Kong, Taiwan); 1967–71, country of former residence (China, Hong Kong, Taiwan); and 1972–6, country of last permanent residence (China, Hong Kong, Taiwan). Figures for 1905–55 are computed on fiscal year ending 31 March; for 1956–76, on calendar year ending 31 December.

b The Canada Yearbook, 1931 (Table 15, p. 184), provides somewhat different figures of Chinese immigration to Canada, which add up to 44,911 for the period of 1906–24. The sex ratio for this period is estimated from the sex distribution of the adult population, based on figures from the reports indicated in note a (approximate years). The figures for 1907 are based on a nine-month period.

c Six of the seven immigrants were male.

d Figures for the entire year of 1955 were not available, due to a change in reporting on calendar-year statistics from fiscal-year statistics in 1955.

Source: Abridged from Bolaria and Li (1988: 112). Reprinted with the permission of Garamond Press.

2007: 111). Overqualification, downward mobility, and devaluation of foreign qualifications are some of the consequences of institutionalized racism experienced by Chinese immigrants (Zong 2007). By undervaluing the education of highly skilled immigrants, skilled labour at 'cheaper' rates continues to be provided.

It has not only been men who have been targeted as 'cheap' labour through Canadian immigration policy. Domestic labour has a long history of being done by the most vulnerable members of any society (Glenn 1992). Immigrant women have historically been used to fill

the need for domestic labour and child care in Canada (Calliste 1996; Jakubowski 1997; Stasiulis and Bakan 2005). In the first half of the twentieth century, young, white, single women were targeted both for domestic labour and for 'nation-building' imperatives and were regarded as needed permanent propagators of a 'white, Canadian nation' (Abu-Laban 1998; Calliste 1996; Ng 1993). Significant restrictions were placed upon the entry of women from non-European countries (Bolaria and Li 1988; Calliste 1996). In the early twentieth century, Caribbean black women were recruited for Canadian domestic work only in the face of severe labour shortages, and their arrival was often opposed on racist perceptions of their 'unfitness' and 'undeservedness' for motherhood (Calliste 1996: 80). Unlike the view of white, European women as future 'mothers of the nation', black Caribbean women were wanted not for their biological reproductive capabilities but for their reproductive labour. The classification of minority women as 'workers' and not as 'mothers' has a long history, and the desire to separate migrant domestic workers from a 'motherhood' role continues to be evident in contemporary immigration policies (Glenn 1992; Stasiulis and Bakan 2005).

The current immigration policy concerning domestic labour, which was crafted in 1992, is called the **Live-In Caregiver Program** (Jakubowski 1997; Stasiulis and Bakan 1997). The overt discrimination in immigration policies has been replaced by more insidious forms of differentiation and preference. Jakubowski (1997) argues that the Live-In Caregiver Program has been 'deracialized' by removing specified 'race' preferences of caregivers in exchange for specified 'educational requirements' that are by and large available more readily in First World countries. In this way, applicants from First World countries can be given preferential treatment. Still, the majority of live-in domestic workers in Canada are women from Third World countries, and these workers are classified as temporary workers and are required to live in their employer's home for two years of a three-year period (Stasiulis and Bakan 2005). Their status as 'temporary residents' and their employment within a 'private' household leave them vulnerable to exploitation and abuse with little recourse (Stasiulis and Bakan 1997, 2005). Arat-Koc (1997: 431; 2006) notes the irony that immigrant women are effectively denied their right to 'motherhood' and femininity and have been classified as 'individual workers' similar to the male conceptualization of 'worker' and yet they are still excluded from citizenship.

According to Arat-Koc (1997: 432), there is a sharp difference between the nature of the domestic work expected and the classification of caregivers from the First World and the Third World. Domestic workers from Western Europe are conceptualized as 'deserving immigrants'. Arat-Koc argues that they are 'generally employed as 'nannies', expected to be involved only in childcare. . . . They are likely to get higher pay, better treatment, and recognition for their work' (1997: 432). In contrast, caregivers from the Philippines or the Caribbean are seen as 'undeserving immigrants', are required to do more for less, and are expected to be grateful for the 'opportunity' to do so (Arat-Koc 1997: 432). The poor working conditions and non-citizenship status of migrant domestic workers in Canada are considered justified on the basis of 'where they've come from'. Thus, a complex of intersection of social relations dictates the rights and privileges that people are thought to deserve. In this sense, the possession of a 'devalued social identity' is used as a justification for exclusion from basic citizenship rights and infringements.

Social Regulation: 'Race'/Ethnicity and the Law

Systemic discrimination in the Canadian justice system is evident in the disproportionate number of Aboriginal Canadians in the penal system, in the disproportionate targeting of racial minorities by police, and in the use of 'racial profiling' by government officials (Brzozowski, Taylor-Butts, and Johnson 2006; Tanovich 2006; Tator and Henry 2006). According to Tanovich (2006: 13),

racial profiling occurs when law enforcement or security officials, consciously or unconsciously, subject individuals at any location to heightened scrutiny based solely or in part on race, ethnicity, Aboriginality, place of origin, ancestry, or religion or on stereotypes associated with any of these factors rather than on objectively reasonable grounds to suspect that the individual is implicated in criminal activity.

Racial profiling sees 'race' first and then seeks out a crime (Tanovich 2006). Although the term *racial profiling* is relatively recent, the practice is not, and Smith (2006) compiles a large amount of data to show the extent to which racial minorities, and particularly African Canadians, have been and continue to be targeted by the law. He reports data from the *Toronto Star's* study of 480,000 incidents of criminal charges and ticketing offences showing that 34 per cent of African Canadians were charged with traffic violations, though they are only 8.1 per cent of Toronto's population—an overrepresentation of 4.2 times (C. Smith 2006: 90). Other data suggest that once in the system, African Canadians are treated more punitively (C. Smith 2006). Indeed, Perrault (2008) found that 14 per cent of visible minorities felt that they had experienced discrimination from the police or courts as compared to 8 per cent of non-visible minorities. As Maher Arar found out, citizenship is no guarantee of protection or fair treatment by the law. This Canadian citizen, IT worker, and father of two was detained on his way back from a family vacation and then sent to Syria, where he was tortured and held for a year before the efforts and lobbying of his wife resulted in his return (www.maherarar.ca). The Canadian government has now apologized and offered compensation, though this cannot undo the damage done. Arar continues to fight for justice (see Box 12.2).

In 2003/04, 18 per cent of those admitted to federal correctional services were Aboriginal, although Aboriginal peoples make up only 2.6 per cent of the population of Canada (Brzozowski, Taylor-Butts, and Johnson 2006: 12). Aboriginal peoples have been targeted, monitored, and regulated by the legal system as a potential disruptive force, and many miscarriages of justice have resulted (Boyko 1995; Smith

2006). Schissel (1997: 83) documented the significantly higher arrest rate for Aboriginal street youth than for youth from other backgrounds. He found that 77 per cent of Aboriginal street youth have been arrested in comparison to 44.2 per cent of non-Aboriginal street youth. He also notes that in Saskatchewan, 76 per cent of young offenders in custody are Aboriginal (Schissel 2006: 114). This treatment of Aboriginal youth may also lead to subsequently harsher sentences for any future offences, since they would now have a record and any prior offences would affect future sentences.

At the same time that Aboriginal peoples are targeted for surveillance, crimes against Aboriginal peoples have historically been treated lightly and many have gone unsolved (Amnesty International 2004; Boyko 1995). In fact, Aboriginal peoples in Canada are three times more likely to be victims of violent crime than non-Aboriginals, and for Aboriginal women this rate rises to three and a half times (Brzozowski, Taylor-Butts, and Johnson 2006). Canada's record on investigating and prosecuting crimes against Aboriginal women is abysmal and is the cause of international concern and outcry (Amnesty International 2004). Estimates suggest that as many as 500 Aboriginal women have gone missing in the past two decades in Canada and little has been done about it by officials (Amnesty International 2004; Monture 2007). Yet, as Monture (2007: 209) points out, 'the violent deaths of Aboriginal women in Canada are not a recent phenomenon and should not be viewed as an emerging problem'. There is a long history of violence against Aboriginal men and women in Canada that has been condoned and overlooked in white communities and white courtrooms (Monture 2007). Boyko (1995: 202) recounts the case of Helen Betty Osborne, a Cree teenager who was brutally raped and murdered in 1971 in The Pas, Manitoba. Betty Osborne's desire to become a teacher meant that she was required to move from the reserve to a school where upper grades were

Box 12.2 With Persistence, the Truth Will Come Out

By Maher Arar

On my way home to Canada from a family vacation in September of 2002, I was stopped and interrogated at John F. Kennedy Airport in New York. Within two weeks, against my will, the US government sent me to Syria, where I was tortured and detained for a year before being released back to Canada without any charge being filed against me.

Following a request by a US congressman shortly after my release, the inspector-general of the Homeland Security Department launched an investigation. Early this month, Richard Skinner released a much-anticipated report on the actions of US immigration officials surrounding the decision to send me to Syria.

Despite the limited scope of the investigation and the refusal by key decision-makers to be interviewed, the heavily redacted public version of the report points to the important fact that the decision to send me to Syria was made at the highest levels of President George W. Bush's administration. The report found that the decision to send me to Syria was made before, and without regard for, the Immigration and Naturalization Service's assessment that I would likely be tortured there.

Mr Skinner's report clearly establishes that what happened to me was a rendition in disguise. Mr Skinner found that on Sunday, Oct. 6, 2002, the government prepared the 'operations order' to remove me and sent flight clearances to Rome and Amman, so the United States could fly me on a private jet. These actions were taken before my six-hour interview with the INS concerning my fears of being tortured in Syria, before the INS concluded it was likely I would be tortured there and before the INS received supposed ambiguous 'assurances' that I would be protected.

In other words, my fate had already been decided—the 'immigration process' meant to safeguard me from torture was a sham.

So far, these high-level officials have evaded accountability and public scrutiny of their own wrongdoing by keeping me on their watch list, thereby attempting to keep the focus on me. The US government claims to rely on classified information to keep me on the watch list—information that New York Congressman Jerrold Nadler has seen and called 'nonsense', and that Canadian Public Safety Minister Stockwell Day has seen and confirmed that it does not justify keeping me on a watch list.

The Canadian government has already apologized and launched a full public inquiry. It is only my hope that the US government follows Ottawa's example and rights its wrongs by at least conducting an independent investigation examining the actions of all officials who shipped me off to Syria like a parcel without regard for my basic human rights, international law or the US Constitution.

I would like to commend the efforts of the US House of Representatives foreign affairs and judiciary subcommittees trying to get to the bottom of what happened to me. I appreciate their courage in standing up for justice and reminding Mr Bush's administration that America is a country of the rule of law. It is my hope that through their persistence and good work, the full truth will eventually come out.

Source: Arar (2008).

available and this meant a move to 'white' space in the town of The Pas (Monture 2007: 209). The white men who had raped and murdered her bragged about their crime and 'whispers around town indicated that everyone deemed to know who the four were' (Boyko 1995: 202).

In spite of this, the police did little to investigate and the crime went unpunished for nearly 16 years (Monture 2007). Still, Osborne's family did not give up, and eventually one of the four murderers was convicted. The Osborne case was specifically investigated in 1991 by a study examining the treatment of Aboriginal peoples in the Manitoba justice system, the conclusion being that Helen Betty Osborne was attacked and her case was allowed to languish because she was Aboriginal (Boyko 1995; Monture 2007). Clearly, the identity of the victim, as well as her attackers structured the response of the police and the justice system.

Agents in Action: Citizenship Claims

Aboriginal peoples have faced violence from the state through both its action and its inaction. After years of struggle, Aboriginal communities in Canada have gained compensation and an apology from the government for the creation and operation of residential schools (see Box 12.3). In Prime Minister Harper's statement, the intent of the residential schools and the devastating impact of their operation are laid bare. As part of the settlement, the Aboriginal Truth and Reconciliation Commission will work to compile a comprehensive record of the trauma inflicted by

Box 12.3 Prime Minister Stephen Harper's Statement of Apology

11 June 2008

Mr Speaker, I stand before you today to offer an apology to former students of Indian residential schools. The treatment of children in Indian residential schools is a sad chapter in our history.

In the 1870's, the federal government, partly in order to meet its obligation to educate aboriginal children, began to play a role in the development and administration of these schools.

Two primary objectives of the residential schools system were to remove and isolate children from the influence of their homes, families, traditions and cultures, and to assimilate them into the dominant culture.

These objectives were based on the assumption aboriginal cultures and spiritual beliefs were inferior and unequal.

Indeed, some sought, as it was infamously said, 'to kill the Indian in the child'.

Today, we recognize that this policy of assimilation was wrong, has caused great harm, and has no place in our country.

Most schools were operated as 'joint ventures' with Anglican, Catholic, Presbyterian or United churches.

The government of Canada built an educational system in which very young children were often forcibly removed from their homes, often taken far from their communities.

Many were inadequately fed, clothed and housed.

All were deprived of the care and nurturing of their parents, grandparents and communities.

First Nations, Inuit and Métis languages and cultural practices were prohibited in these schools.

Tragically, some of these children died while attending residential schools and others never returned home.

The government now recognizes that the consequences of the Indian residential schools policy were profoundly negative and that this policy has had a lasting and damaging impact on aboriginal culture, heritage and language.

While some former students have spoken positively about their experiences at residential schools, these stories are far overshadowed by tragic accounts of the emotional, physical and sexual abuse and neglect of helpless children, and their separation from powerless families and communities.

The legacy of Indian residential schools has contributed to social problems that continue to exist in many communities today. It has taken extraordinary courage for the thousands of survivors that have come forward to speak publicly about the abuse they suffered.

It is a testament to their resilience as individuals and to the strength of their cultures.

Regrettably, many former students are not with us today and died never having received a full apology from the government of Canada.

The government recognizes that the absence of an apology has been an impediment to healing and reconciliation.

Therefore, on behalf of the government of Canada and all Canadians, I stand before you, in this chamber so central to our life as a country, to apologize to aboriginal peoples for Canada's role in the Indian residential schools system.

To the approximately 80,000 living former students, and all family members and communities, the government of Canada now recognizes that it was wrong to forcibly remove children from their homes and we apologize for having done this.

We now recognize that it was wrong to separate children from rich and vibrant cultures and traditions, that it created a void in many lives and communities, and we apologize for having done this.

We now recognize that, in separating children from their families, we undermined the ability of many to adequately parent their own children and sowed the seeds for generations to follow, and we apologize for having done this.

We now recognize that, far too often, these institutions gave rise to abuse or neglect and were inadequately controlled, and we apologize for failing to protect you.

Not only did you suffer these abuses as children, but as you became parents, you were powerless to protect your own children from suffering the same experience, and for this we are sorry.

The burden of this experience has been on your shoulders for far too long.

The burden is properly ours as a government, and as a country.

There is no place in Canada for the attitudes that inspired the Indian residential schools system to ever again prevail.

You have been working on recovering from this experience for a long time and in a very real sense, we are now joining you on this journey.

The government of Canada sincerely apologizes and asks the forgiveness of the aboriginal peoples of this country for failing them so profoundly.

We are sorry.

In moving towards healing, reconciliation and resolution of the sad legacy of Indian residential schools, implementation of the Indian Residential Schools Settlement agreement began on September 19, 2007.

Years of work by survivors, communities, and aboriginal organizations culminated in an agreement that gives us a new beginning and an opportunity to move forward together in partnership.

A cornerstone of the settlement agreement is the Indian Residential Schools Truth and Reconciliation Commission.

This commission presents a unique opportunity to educate all Canadians on the Indian residential schools system.

It will be a positive step in forging a new relationship between aboriginal peoples and other Canadians, a relationship based on the knowledge of our shared history, a respect for each other and a desire to move forward together with a renewed understanding that strong families, strong communities and vibrant cultures and traditions will contribute to a stronger Canada for all of us.

Apology reaction: Putting the pain behind us

'Achievement of the impossible'

And then it was time for the aboriginal leaders gathered at the House of Commons to speak.

Initially, they were not going to speak in the House, but politicians decided to allow them at the last minute.

'This day testifies to nothing less than the achievement of the impossible,' Fontaine said.

'Never again will the House consider us the 'Indian problem' just for us being who we are,' he said. 'Finally we heard Canada say it was sorry.'

He acknowledged much more is to be done but that it was a 'new dawn'. It is now possible, he said, to end the 'racial nightmare' together.

Patrick Brazeau, of the Congress of Aboriginal Peoples, called it a historic day and a positive step forward and thanked Harper for doing something his predecessors had not. He said he was proud to be an aboriginal Canadian.

Mary Simon, president of Inuit Tapiriit Kanatami, the national Inuit organization, spoke in Inuktitut to show that the language and culture are still strong, she said.

Simon said that she dreamed of the day an apology would come and thought it might never happen, and that the pain and scars will still be there, but a new era has begun. Dignity, confidence and respect must be at the forefront of future efforts, she said.

Beverley Jacobs, president of Native Women's Association of Canada, told the House that residential schools took away the matriarchal system but it is coming back. She thanked the government for its apology.

'But in return, the Native Women's Association wants respect,' she said, getting a standing ovation in the House.

A day to remember

Hundreds gathered to watch the apology at the University of Winnipeg, including Kelly Houle, who listened closely as the prime minister spoke.

She didn't attend residential school, but her late mother did. Houle said she accepts the apology, but it does not erase painful memories.

'The full story of the residential school system's impact on our people has yet to be told,' said Grand Chief Edward John of the First Nations Summit, an umbrella group of BC First Nations.

'The responses to the apology are both individual and collective. It is extremely important that we respect the many survivors who, in their own discretion and time, will consider the prime minister's apology and determine how, in their own interest, each of them will deal with it. Collectively, we celebrate and stand on the dignity of who we are and celebrate our survival,' John said in a release issued by the First Nations Leadership Council, which includes a number of aboriginal groups in BC.

'Our first thoughts today are for our elders,' said Anishinabek Nation Grand Council Chief John Beaucage of Ontario. 'Many of them have suffered lifelong physical and emotional pain because of their residential school experiences.

'We are so proud that many Anishinabek lived long enough to hear Canada's apology to them. But the true test of Mr Harper's words will be his government's actions to help our children have a better future than their parents and grandparents.'

Each of the thousands who waited to hear the apology has her or his individual story.

Diane Louis, from the Okanagan Indian Band near Vernon, BC. spent five years at the residential school in Kamloops, BC, and most of her life recovering from what happened there. Louis said it started on the first day, when she was taken from her grandmother in a cattle truck.

She spent decades trying to relearn her language because she wasn't allowed to speak it.

Herman Alpine, who spent his childhood at the St. Eugene residential school near Cranbrook, BC, said the abuse started the day he arrived, when a priest yanked his long hair and cut it off, causing him to live in constant fear after that.

He was strapped after speaking his own language, and said he suffered sexual abuse at the hands of other students, abuse that was overlooked by the priest. In Nova Scotia, First Nations people retraced the steps to the site of a residential school in Shubenacadie, which 2,000 Mi'kmaq and Maliseet children from around Atlantic Canada were forced to attend until 1968.

In St. John's, they gathered at the Native Friendship Centre to watch Harper speak. Aboriginal Canadians also gathered in Iqaluit and Yellowknife.

In Winnipeg, the Assembly of Manitoba Chiefs hosted an event that featured performers who are children or grandchildren of residential school students. Outside of Edmonton at the River Cree Resort, people gathered to watch the apology at an event that featured an aboriginal comedian, singing and hoop dancing, as well as grief counsellors.

The residential schools were overseen by the Department of Indian Affairs and looked to force aboriginal children to learn English and adopt Christianity and Canadian customs as part of a government policy called 'aggressive assimilation'.

From as early as the 19th century to 1996, there were about 130 schools in Canada, in every territory and province except Newfoundland, Prince Edward Island and New Brunswick.

The Inuit in Labrador were represented by three members who flew to Ottawa to hear the apology in person at Parliament. They were in a unique situation, though, as a boarding school in North West River, in central Labrador, has not been recognized by Ottawa as a residential school because it was not operated by the Canadian government. And they were not formally invited to Ottawa for the apology.

'We're probably not feeling the same as the other people. The apology is not intended for us,' Nora Ford said in Happy Valley-Goose Bay on Tuesday, as she prepared to board the flight to Ottawa.

Source: CBC News, http://www.cbc.ca/canada/story/2008/06/11/pm-statement.html. Copyright cbc.ca.

residential schools in order to better understand their impact and to aid in the healing process.

The length of time Aboriginal people have had to wait for the government's apology and admission to the horror of Aboriginal schools and the theft of Aboriginal children from their families reveals a complicit public acceptance of racist and colonial policies. This apology at long last makes public that what the government did was wrong and validates Aboriginal communities' pain and need for justice. Indeed, Aboriginal communities have long sought out justice in regard to land claims and their right to citizenship (Dickason 2006).

The James Bay Cree have had success in the courts and in mobilizing and using **transnational action** through human-rights and environmental organizations to make citizenship claims. Jenson and Papillon (2000) document the success of the James Bay Cree in contesting the infringements on their territories and asserting their citizenship rights on the basis of 'nationhood' rather than as individual citizens. The Cree have fought the attempts of the Quebec

government to subsume them into questions of sovereignty through the Quebec referendum, arguing that they already exist as a sovereign nation (Jenson and Papillon 2000). Their first success came in 1971 when they opposed the attempts of the Quebec government to build an enormous hydroelectric project on the Cree's traditional hunting grounds. The James Bay Cree won their court challenge, which contended that they had title and rights to the land and the Quebec government was required to engage in negotiations. Jenson and Papillon (2000: 251) state that 'this was the first, and until very recently the only, comprehensive land claim settlement in Canada. . . . Beyond that, it was the first time in modern history that Canadian governments, in this case both federal and provincial, recognized that Canadian citizenship included collective rights for aboriginal peoples.' . The rarity of success in the courts for Aboriginal rights is a reason why Aboriginal groups' need to seek international support for the validity of their citizenship claims. The James Bay Cree have found widespread international support for their opposition to the Quebec government's plans for hydroelectric projects and have had considerable success in staving off encroachments and in defending their rights (Jenson and Papillon 2000).

A number of groups have made claims on the Canadian government to recognize their citizenship rights and to uphold the government's promise of democratic equality. Some of the descendants of Chinese immigrants who were forced to pay a head tax in order to enter Canada have taken legal action against the government for compensation. Box 12.4 outlines their long-awaited apology and compensation.

Focusing on Gender: Engendering Citizens

In Canada, women's access to the rights of citizenship have been (and continue to be) compromised by the state's adoption of the 'breadwinner' policy scheme with all of its racialized and gendered implications (Fuller Kershaw, and Pulkingham 2008; McDaniel 2002; Townson and Hayes 2007). Women who do not have access to **breadwinner wages**, either because their 'breadwinners' are low-income earners or because they themselves are unmarried or lesbians, are disadvantaged in this policy system. The state's ideal family type consists of a husband engaged in paid productive labour and a wife engaged in unpaid reproductive labour and dependent on the distribution of the 'family wage'. Again, it is important to note the ideology wrapped up in the package of the 'family' (Das Gupta 1995). Historically, the Canadian government's policies toward Aboriginal families, immigrant families, and visible-minority families (policies such as residential schools and 'family'-class immigration limitations and prohibitions) belie the valuation of the 'family' as specifically the white families who are Canadianized (Das Gupta 1995). Thus, the privileges of the breadwinner wage are largely limited to racial and ethnic majorities. Although the breadwinner formula is a

familiar one, it is not the only way in which to distribute the rights of social citizenship.

Sainsbury (1999: 78) compares three different gendered approaches to policy in democratic welfare states, as shown in Table 12.2. We can see in the table that caring work is given a monetary valuation from the state in the separate gender roles regime; however, women and men are explicitly divided and viewed as either productive or reproductive workers (Sainsbury 1999). The 'individual earner-carer' is a more equitable option, as women and men are viewed equally as potential earners and/or carers and carework is valued on par with 'productive' labour. In contrast, the characteristics of the typical 'male breadwinner policy regime' are considered to be predicated upon gender inequality and differential responsibilities (Sainsbury 1999: 78). Social citizenship and benefits in the form of income security are designed and distributed with the ideology of the patriarchal family in mind. In this schema, caring work in the household is unpaid, it is predominately performed by and expected of women, and these responsibilities penalize women in a citizenship regime that preferentially rewards paid work (particularly work that does not involve caring) (Evans 1997; FullerKershaw, and Pulkingham 2008; Sainsbury 1999).

Historically, the imperatives of the breadwinner policy have worked to exclude and limit the participation of women (especially married women) in the labour force (Pulkingham 1998; Townson and Hayes 2007). Pulkingham (1998) charts the evolution of unemployment insurance in Canada to illustrate the way in which social policy is gendered and the extent to which women were encouraged and expected to be dependent on a male breadwinner. From its beginnings in 1940, unemployment insurance was intended for the male breadwinner: married women could not receive direct compensation on the basis of their own work history (Pulkingham 1998). Instead, they were eligible for state support only through their status as a dependant of their

Box 12.4 MPs Hand Out Compensation for Chinese Head-Tax

The federal government has begun to redress the head tax once applied to Chinese immigrants, handing out the first of the $20,000 cheques to be issued as compensation for those who paid the tax.

Vancouver MP and International Trade Minister David Emerson, along with Canadian Heritage Minister Beverley Oda presented the cheques in Vancouver on Friday afternoon.

'In spite of obstacles you persevered and helped build a better, stronger Canada for all of us,' Oda said.

'And as the prime minister said in June, before we can move forward together as Canadians and achieve our full potential we believe we must first lay to rest the past wrong of the head tax.'

Oda said it's important to learn from the mistakes of the past, make amends, and 'begin to heal'.

Prime Minister Stephen Harper issued a formal apology to Chinese Canadians on June 22 in the House of Commons for the head tax that was charged between 1885 and 1923.

On Oct. 11, speaking to a group of Chinese immigrants, Harper said it is important that the payments come as soon as possible, while some of the immigrants who paid the tax to enter Canada are still alive.

In the speech, Harper praised the Chinese community's contribution to Canada, including helping build the CP Railway.

He called the tax a 'moral blemish on our country's soul' and said the Canada of today wouldn't be possible without their contribution.

'You are part of our family,' Harper said.

Chinese Canadians have pushed for an official apology for decades.

The head tax was brought in after Canada passed the Chinese Immigration Act in 1885—levying a tax for every Chinese immigrant entering the country.

The prime minister at the time, John A. Macdonald, had brought in Chinese immigrants to help build the cross-Canada railway.

Once it was completed, however, the government moved to discourage Chinese immigration amid fears they were taking jobs from Canadians.

The tax was set at $50 when it was first introduced in 1885, but it rose to $500 in 1903—then the equivalent of two years' wages.

The head tax was eventually replaced by the Exclusion Act which came into effect in 1923. The Act—which remained in place until 1947—effectively barred immigration from China.

Harper's official apology came as a relief to some, but for others it fell short of the mark.

Vancouver's Community Care and Advancement Association president Johnny Fong, thanked Harper for the apology.

'Your apology at the House of Commons this year has brought tremendous relief to so many in the community,' Fong told Harper.

The Association of Chinese Canadians for Equality, however, said Ottawa had been too slow to address the issue.

'He only addressed point-six per cent of the head tax families—less than one per cent—of the head tax families that have survivors,' the association's Sid Tan told The Canadian Press.

'What he has done is rewarded the government for dragging its feet for over 20 years. Shame on them for that.'

It is believed there are about 400 surviving head-tax payers or their widows from an estimated 81,000 immigrants who paid the tax.

Source: CTV News, 20 October 2006; www.ctv.ca.

Table 12.2 Three Gender Policy Regimes

Regime Attributes	Male Breadwinner	Separate Gender Roles	Individual Earner-Carer
Ideology	Strict division of labour Husband = earner Wife = carer	Strict division of labour Husband = earner Wife = carer	Shared tasks Father = earner-carer Mother = earner-carer
Entitlement	Unequal among spouses	Differentiated by gender role	Equal
Basis of entitlement	The principle of maintenance	Family responsibilities	Citizenship or residence
Recipient of benefits	Head of household Supplements for dependants	Men as family providers Women as caregivers	Individual
Taxation	Joint taxation Deductions for dependants	Joint taxation Deductions for dependants for both spouses	Separate taxation Equal tax relief
Employment and wage policies	Priority to men	Priority to men	Aimed at both sexes
Sphere of care	Primarily private	Primarily private	Strong state involvement
Caring work	Unpaid	Paid component to caregivers in the home	Paid component to caregivers in and outside the home

Source: Sainsbury (1999: 78). Reprinted by permission of Oxford University Press.

husband. In 1950, the impact of gendered ideologies on policy inequality becomes even more apparent, as a woman who married was rendered ineligible to claim unemployment insurance benefits for a period of two years following her marriage (Pulkingham 1998). This effectively barred '12,000 to 14,000 women each year' from collecting unemployment insurance until this stipulation was withdrawn in 1957 (Evans 1997: 102). In fact, in order to obtain unemployment insurance a woman was required to 'prove her attachment to the labour force' in a number of ways (Pulkingham 1998: 15). Women who refused to take low-paying jobs for which they were overqualified were also denied benefits, unlike men in similar circumstances (Pulkingham 1998). Thus, women's access to the 'first-track' citizenship benefits of unemployment insurance (as opposed to the 'second-track' benefits of social assistance) was made exceptionally difficult (Pulkingham 1998: 10). Here we see that 'claims made through social assistance on the basis of "citizen-mother" are accorded neither the degree

of legitimacy nor the level of benefits that accompanies "worker" claims through social insurance' (Evans 1997: 98).

Changes to Canada's unemployment insurance policy in 1996 meant to help women qualify for the program have in fact had the opposite effect, such that in 2004 only 32 per cent of unemployed women were eligible to get benefits compared with 40 per cent of men (Townson and Hayes 2007). Where eligibility once rested on the number of weeks worked, the new system required 420–700 hours (in most locales) in the 12 months prior in order to qualify for employment insurance (Townson and Hayes 2007). This requirement meant that many part-time workers (who are disproportionately women) were not eligible to qualify for benefits. Many women are therefore contributing to a program which they are unlikely to benefit from should the need arise (Townson and Hayes 2007).

Women are also disadvantaged in their access to social insurance on the basis of their paid productive and reproductive labour. Childbearing and caring responsibilities mean that women have more frequent departures and absences from the formal labour force than men do (Evans 1997, 2007; Townson and Hayes 2007). A parental leave policy was introduced in 1990 and extended in 2001, but the vast majority of claimants continue to be women, and in fact, the gender gap has increased in the usage of parental leave (Evans 2007). Further, a greater number of women in paid employment work in non-standard (e.g., part-time) employment than men (40 per cent vs 30 per cent) and their employment tends to be more precarious (Evans 2007; Townson and Hayes 2007). In addition, men on average work more hours and more paid overtime hours, both of which benefit them in Employment Insurance calculations (Townson and Hayes 2007). Even when women work full-time and year-round (as the majority of employed women do) and 'conform' to the 'male' worker formula, they have not received equal pay for their efforts, and this too affects the level of compensation they are eligible to receive (Pulkingham 1998; Statistics Canada 2006f).

As chapter 9 shows, there is considerable occupational segregation by sex, and the work that women have disproportionately performed has been devalued and paid less than the work done by men (Armstrong 1997). The job-evaluation schemes that determine levels of pay under Ontario's Pay Equity Act have tended to reinforce traditional gender ideologies of 'valued' work (Armstrong 1997; Busby 2006). For instance, 'garbage removal is considered more onerous than cleaning dirty diapers; police work more dangerous than dressing the wounds of patients with contagious diseases. . . . The stress created by working outdoors or in excessive heat is often counted, but the stress of working with dying patients or demanding children does not get counted' (Armstrong 1997: 261). Thus, the combination of domestic responsibilities, devalued work, and lower wages all work to make Employment

Insurance a predominately 'male' benefit (Evans 1997; Townson and Hayes 2007).

Social Regulation: Reproductive Rights

There are ironic contradictions in the state's regulation and control of aspects of women's lives. Historically, women's reproductive potential has been closely watched by the state, while in the areas of sexual assault and 'domestic' violence the state has been less willing to intervene on women's behalf (Walby 1997, 2004). For instance, women's sexuality and reproductive potential have been controlled in varying degrees by the state, from the outlawing of birth control until 1969 to the practice of sterilization for reproducers deemed 'unfit' (Findlay and Miller 2002; McLaren and McLaren 1997). While some women have been financially and ideologically supported for their reproductive potential (e.g., with baby bonuses and nationalistic rhetoric), other women have been penalized and degraded for it (Comacchio 1993; Valverde 1991). The right to have control over one's own body has not been a guaranteed right for women in general, especially for women of colour and working-class women (Egan and Gardner 1999). Greschner (1990, 1998) points to the case of Chantal Daigle in Quebec as an example of the extent to which fetal and paternal rights take precedence over a woman's right to autonomy. Daigle was forced to carry on with a pregnancy against her will by an abusive ex-boyfriend who obtained a court injunction to halt her attempt to end the pregnancy (Greschner 1990). Only in the Supreme Court was this injunction overturned. The discourse of fetal and paternal rights frequently emerge without an examination of the threats that they entail for women's personhood (M. Casper 1998; Greschner 1990, 1998; Martin and Coleman 1995).

In fact, there has been a renewed push for fetal rights that has the potential to further impinge upon women's rights (Sandstad 2008).

Bill C-484, The Unborn Victims of Crime Act, was brought forth as a private member's bill and passed a second reading in Parliament on 5 March 2008 (see http://www.parl.gc.ca/LEGIsINFO/index.asp?Language=E&query=5336&List=toc&Session=15). This bill intends to criminalize any act to 'injure, cause the death of or attempt to cause the death of a child before or during its birth while committing or attempting to commit an offense against the mother. Voluntary abortion or any act or omission by the mother are exempted in the legislation' (Canadian Federation for Sexual Health 2008). A number of social justice and women's rights groups have taken action to oppose the bill, stating that it provides no evidence that it will prevent violence against women and in fact, in the United States similar legislation has resulted in increased policing and regulation of pregnant women (Abortion Rights Coalition of Canada 2008). In its opposition statement, the Canadian Federation for Sexual Health (2008) states its concern that 'the bill's underlying intention is to create a separate legal status for a fetus . . . legal separation of individual rights is the premise on which woman's right to choose is built, and to dissolve this separation of rights strategically chips away at a women's right to an abortion'. Indeed, Greschner (1990) argues that the notion of 'fetal rights' represents a concerted effort to enforce traditional gender roles. The most disadvantaged women in society tend to be disproportionately targeted and prosecuted under these types of legislation. This tendency is illustrated in an American study of court-ordered Caesarean sections occurring in a teaching hospital where close to 90 per cent of the women involved were visible minorities, nearly half were unmarried, and all were welfare recipients (Martin and Coleman 1995).

Agents in Action: Violence against Women

As discussed in chapter 8, sexual assault is a weapon by which the relations of power and domination are reproduced and reinforced. McIntyre and Scott (2000) note that the act of sexual assault is strongly gendered, being predominately committed by men against women. While men are more likely to be physically assaulted, women are more likely to be sexually assaulted, and the number of sexual assaults is likely underestimated as they are the type of violent assault least likely to be reported to police (see Figure 12.1).

Some women are more vulnerable than others to the threat of violence. Aboriginal women report much higher rates of violence at the hands of their spouse, with 24 per cent experiencing spousal violence compared with 7 per cent of non-Aboriginal women (Statistics Canada 2006d: 64). Feminist groups and grassroots organizations have lobbied provincial and federal governments to take action against the violence in women's lives (Sheehy 2005; Ursel 1998). Sheehy (2005) outlines some of the difficulties inherent in Canadian laws covering violent domestic assault, one being the use of gender-neutral language and policies. For example, 'zero tolerance' policies whereby charges are laid for any domestic complaint have in some cases resulted in the criminalization of women who try to defend themselves from abuse (Sheehy 2005; Ursel 1998). Although some women may have been helped through zero-tolerance policies, their indiscriminate and inconsistent enforcement have had mixed results (Sheehy 2005).

Still, feminist action has had an impact on how the state deals with domestic violence (Ursel 1998). Ursel (1998) notes that policy changes in Manitoba resulted in the establishment of a specialized court for domestic cases. In 1990, the Family Violence Court (FVC) was instituted to handle all cases of spouse, child, and elder abuse (Ursel 1998). In the past, domestic violence cases were shuffled off to the least experienced prosecutors because they were regarded as 'a messy, low-profile case with a minimal chance of conviction' (Ursel 1998: 147). In the new system, these

Figure 12.1: Victimization by Violent Crime, Not Reported to Police, by Type of Offence, 2004, as Percentage of All Violent Crime

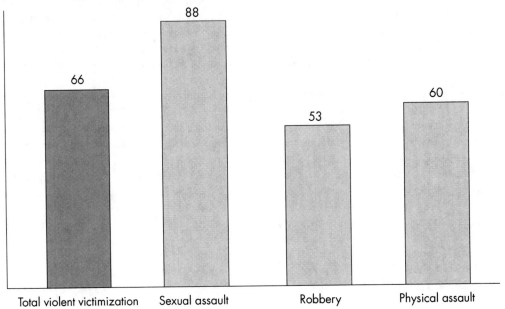

Source: Gannon and Mihorean (2006).

cases were redefined as requiring the legal experts who were adept at handling complex cases. The 'battered women's movement' has resulted in effective and more compassionate reforms in the legal system for victims of violence (Ursel 1998). Still, the problem is far from solved, and the serious consequences and wide reach of violence in Canada are apparent in Box 12.5.

Here we can see that although there has been government action, there are still not enough resources to meet the demands. On a one-day survey snapshot in 2006 of Canada's shelters for abused women, 306 women and 203 children could not be accommodated and had to leave (Taylor-Butts 2007). Indeed, on an average day as many as 200 women are turned away from shelters (Statistics Canada 2006d). Although the incidence of spousal assault against men has gained attention in recent years, it's important to note that the degree

and severity of assault for men and women differs significantly. For example, women were two and a half times as likely as men to report the most violent forms of assault such as choking or beating, and 44 per cent of women were physically injured from the assault compared to 19 per cent of men (Statistics Canada 2006d: 20, 33). Still, underreporting of spousal assault remains an issue, with only 36 per cent of woman spousal assault victims reporting to police in 2004 (and a mere 17 per cent of male spousal assault victims reporting) (Statistics Canada 2006d: 55). There has been a slight decline in five-year rates of spousal violence (from 8 per cent in 1999 to 7 per cent in 2004); however, spousal violence was the largest category of convictions for violent offences in non-specialized adult court between 1997/98 and 2001/02, and 90 per cent of offenders were men (Statistics Canada 2006d: 12)

Box 12.5 The Shocking Toll of Domestic Violence; Thousands of Women Feel Trapped

By Robert Remington

The attack was so brutal and violent that the force of Sarah being thrown against the wall shattered the drywall. She felt several of her ribs snap.

Her husband had whipped her around by her hair and thrown her into the wall like a sack of potatoes. He let go long enough for her to grab the phone. She dialled 911 but said nothing—the interlude in the attack was so brief she didn't have time. Instead, she tossed the phone aside where he wouldn't see it.

He then threw her against the dresser and began punching her in the head and body as she shielded their child, whom she managed to push under the bed. Her husband then lifted her by her neck.

As Sarah started to lose consciousness, she thought of the newscast she'd seen earlier that night and how she didn't want to be like the girl in Edmonton whose husband was just convicted of murder.

She was about to pass out when Sarah saw the lights of the police cruiser reflected in what was left of the window her husband had just put her head through. He let go.

'I remember hearing, "Calgary Police Service, open the door," and he stood over me and said: "What the [expletive] did you do?"' Loaded onto a stretcher, Sarah thought she was going to die. She had bruises, a dislocated jaw, broken teeth and broken ribs. The choking had caused the blood vessels in her eyes to burst.

A police officer looked down on her and said: 'You are one of so many.' It couldn't have been more sickeningly true.

'Of all the provinces, Alberta is the most dangerous place in Canada to be a woman,' says Jan Reimer, a former Edmonton mayor and provincial co-ordinator for the Alberta Council of Women's Shelters.

Alberta leads the nation in rates of stalking, domestic assaults and murder-suicide, and is third in domestic homicide. All 41 women's emergency shelters in the province are full. More than 27,000 women and children were turned away from Alberta shelters from April 2006 to March 2007, including 2,700 at one Calgary shelter alone.

Many of these women—more than six in 10—have no choice but to return home to the men who beat them and choke them and call them names and throw them down stairs and against walls because dinner isn't ready or the beds aren't made.

Often, the abuse intensifies when women are pregnant and at their most vulnerable. Sarah and Louise, the battered women interviewed for this story, were both pregnant when their partners first became physically abusive. The patterns of abuse they endured were nearly identical.

On the outside, both had what appeared to be perfect lives with beautiful houses, nice cars and beautiful children. Under the surface, it was a different story.

First came a forced isolation imposed by the men in their lives from friends and family, then financial dependency, then verbal abuse.

The physical abuse began slowly, with grabbing or shoving. In one case it was preceded by sexual abuse. Both were hospitalized, one of them multiple times, and both women came to fear for their lives. One still does.

Their names and some of their circumstances have been changed.

Often, I found myself nodding as they told their stories. Abusers are remarkably uncreative. Their actions are similar, predictable and cowardly. Invariably, repentant men make up with flowers and gifts, only to fall back into the same patterns of economic abuse, isolation, threats, intimidation and beatings. The stories that many battered women tell are nearly the same.

Louise discovered as much when she was handed a brochure on domestic violence at the YWCA's Sheriff King Home, a shelter in Inglewood with bulletproof windows. It was as if the generic handout were describing her situation.

'I was reading it and said, "You know my husband?"' It didn't start out this way for these women. In both cases, their relationships began like a fairy tale.

'He was my knight in shining armour, my best friend,' said Sarah. 'He was so charming and so wonderful, like out of a movie. It was nothing I had ever experienced before.' Hearing Sarah speak was like reading Chapter 5 of *The War on Women*, a new book by Brian Vallee. Chapter 5 is titled 'Tarnished Knights', and it opens thus: 'The knight in shining armour is an image that appears over and over in domestic violence research and first-person accounts of women who have been battered by their intimates. Therapists and shelter workers often hear the term used by victims describing the charming and considerate men they thought they were getting in the early stages of a relationship.' Vallee heard the term used by Ella Armour and Jane Hurshman in describing their relationships with Vernon Ince and Billy Stafford, the abusive men they murdered. Both of their cases are profiled in the book and they are remarkably similar.

Armour, known in Calgary's music scene simply as Miss Elly, was 19 and pregnant when she shot and killed Ince, her husband, in Nova Scotia in 1953. Hurshman shot Satfford, her abusive husband, as he drunkenly slept behind the steering wheel of his pickup truck near their home at Bangs Falls, NS. Both women were acquitted on self-defence.

Hurshman's story was chronicled by Vallee in *Life with Billy*, later a TV movie. *The War on Women* focuses mainly on Armour, a music promoter who moved to Calgary in 1987 and died in February 2006. The book refers to wife beaters as 'domestic terrorists' and compares domestic homicide numbers to police and soldiers killed in the line of duty between 2000 and 2006.

'In the same seven-year period when 4,588 US soldiers and police were killed by hostiles or by accident, more than 8,000 women—nearly twice as many—were shot, stabbed, strangled, or beaten to death by the intimate males in their lives. In Canada, compared to the 101 Canadian soldiers and police officers killed, more than 500 women—nearly five times as many—met the same fate,' Valee writes.

According to the book, the annual costs to Canadian taxpayers of the 'war on women' is estimated at $1.1 billion in direct medical costs. That rises to more than $4 billion a year when the costs of social services, lost productivity and the justice system are factored in.

'Shelters in Calgary are doing amazing work with minimal resources and they are saving lives,' says Reimer.

She says there are many other incalculable costs to domestic violence.

'Where do you think the bullies are coming from? The gangs? More than likely they are people who are exposed to family violence in the home.' The Calgary Police Service deals with more than 11,000 domestic violence-related calls every year. One in five battered women are abused during pregnancy.

One of those 11,000 was Louise, whose seven years of abuse followed the typical pattern of forced isolation, economic dependency, threats, intimidation and violence.

At first, 'He was very nice to me,' Sarah says of her knight in shining armour. 'The first time, he pushed me against the wall when I was pregnant. I thought, "Wow. Who is this person?" I almost stopped breathing.' She was not allowed to have her own bank account or associate with friends. He demanded a neat, tidy house, meals on the table, and sex every second day, which he kept track of on a calendar.

'It was hell. I didn't go out. I couldn't do anything. All I did was cook and clean. He was abusive to me sexually. I had no communication with my friends, no money.' He hit her with a rolled-up towel, threw food on her and, typical of abusers, always said he was sorry.

'Every time he did something, he'd say he didn't know what came over him. He bought me gifts, flowers.' His incessant name calling caused her to lose her self-esteem.

Then came the physical beatings. 'I became scared of him. I was terrified.' At one point, she stayed awake all night at her child's bedside in another room, afraid to sleep, going seven days without sleeping at night.

Then, one day, 'I had this bad feeling something bad is going to happen to me.' Her husband inflicted a beating that left her with a broken eardrum, then he threw her out in the snow, half naked.

In the hospital, it was a nurse who urged her to take action, saying: 'You are not going home. He'll kill you.' When police took her back home to gather her things, her husband had filled the house with flowers. This time, she didn't fall for it. She ended up at the YWCA's Sheriff King Home.

'If it wasn't for that, I would have never made it. That's how I survived. When I slept in the shelter, I was so happy to be free.' Today she runs her own business but still worries about her ex-husband, who has unsupervised access to their child.

Whenever she drives by the Sheriff King Home, she counts her blessings.

'It's like a light for freedom. I love to pass by it. It makes me feel good.' Sarah grew up with domestic violence.

'We left my dad more than 10 times. My earliest memory of domestic violence was before kindergarten.

'For me, calling the police was just normal. I didn't think anyone was any different. I thought people were nasty to each other and screamed and yelled and spanked each other and that was marriage.' In her own marriage, attacks by her husband left her hospitalized three times. The nurses asked if she was a victim of domestic violence, but she was in denial.

'In my mind I was screaming for help, but I said, "No, my marriage is fine." I said I had fallen down the stairs, anything. I didn't want to be that woman in that poster who is beaten and abused and has

no family and is homeless.' In one incident, she was trying to lock the door to keep her enraged husband outside. He burst open the door with such force that it knocked her down the stairs. She was six months' pregnant at the time.

'I remember lying at the bottom of the stairs saying, "He's going to kill me." But I never left. He said we were going to work it out. I knew something bigger was going to happen and, I know it sounds crazy, but I prayed for something big to happen because I wanted change, I needed change. I needed God to show me what to do because I didn't know what to do anymore. Every time he came home it got worse.' 'Something bigger' was being thrown by her hair into the wall with such force the drywall was damaged. At the hospital, a police officer told her: 'Your child will be an orphan if you go back because he will kill you.' The police officer's concern for Sarah's safety was real. Of the 28 murders recorded in Calgary so far this year, seven have been domestic homicides.

Sarah turned to Discovery House, opened in 1980 by the Calgary Family Support Society, now called the Discovery House Family Violence Prevention Society.

'I always say it takes a community to raise a child and an organization to heal a family and that's what Discovery did for our family,' Sarah says.

She also has high praise for the Calgary Police Service, which has a 12-member Domestic Conflict Unit, created in 1998, and a Child at Risk Response Team, made up of two-person teams, consisting of a police officer and a social worker.

'The police don't get enough credit. They saved my life.' Sarah refers to one officer in particular as 'my secret guardian angel'. 'Sometimes you need those angels.' But Discovery House, Sarah says, helped her break the cycle of domestic violence she was born into.

'The cycle can end and it does with my child and I. If there's one message I always say to people, it's that it can end. Just because that was your life doesn't mean it has to be your future. That's the biggest gift I was given. I'm going to be my child's role model. I'm a survivor. I'm not a victim. Being a battered woman did not define me. I'm a success. That's what defines me.

'I want to get a sign that says "freedom" because I didn't know how sweet freedom felt.'

Source: Remington (2007).

Focusing on Age: Citizenship over the Life Course

The examination of citizenship shows how the historical period and the socio-historical circumstances in which we live have a powerful impact on the structures of inequality (McDaniel 2001, 2004). Citizenship, in all its forms, has historically been denied to various groups on the basis of race, ethnicity, and gender. Consider that in the 1960s, employers in Canada had the legal right to fire women if they married or became pregnant (Sangster 1995). Individuals and groups have struggled and triumphed over inequality throughout history; however, in some ways we are fated to grapple with the socio-historical milieu into which we are born. Over time, this milieu has changed, especially in regard to citizenship in Canada.

Still, the expectation that women will perform most of the tasks involved in reproductive labour has remained fairly stable. As we have seen throughout this chapter, women's involvement in caring work over the life course puts them at a disadvantage in their ability to gain the rights of citizenship. And the life chances of women and men of different ethnic and racial groups and of different ages are shaped by the substantive birth cohort in which they were born. In this regard, McDaniel (2001, 2004) discusses 'gendered generations', pointing out, among other things that state benefits are influenced by the historical time in which one was born. These benefits must also be considered within the context of changes in gender relations, which have occurred over the last three generations.

McDaniel cautions, however, that we should not be overly optimistic about the opportunities for the youngest generation of women. Post-baby-boom women (born between 1965 and 1975), according to McDaniel (2001: 204), 'although benefitting from the legacies of previous generations of women in struggling for rights and job equity, are finding jobs difficult to find and family formation/dissolution economically challenging.'

Women's contributions to society go largely unrecognized and unrewarded. In spite of the devaluation and artificial separation of caring work in the home from the 'productive' realm, unpaid caring work is vital to the workings of the state (McDaniel 2002, 2004). McDaniel (2002: 136) argues that 'caring is central to welfare states, not because they are inherently caring (abundant evidence calls this into question), but because care (for the young, old, sick and infirm, and those who cannot work) leads to more productive, less discontented, workers and consumers for capitalist economies.' Indeed, McDaniel (2004: 37) states that one of many 'new normativities' or requirements of citizenship for women involves the increased downloading of care expected from the state, demonstrated in day surgeries and more intense forms of home care. As was outlined earlier, the weight of this imbalance in caring work intensity penalizes women through increased work absences, more departures from and entries into the labour force, and consequently, lower lifetime wages (Denton and Boos 2007; Gough 2001; B. Marshall 2000; Morissette and Ostrovsky 2006; Pyper 2006; Statistics Canada 2006f). For example, in 2004,

Figure 12.2: Seniors' Average Income, by Gender and Income Source, 2005

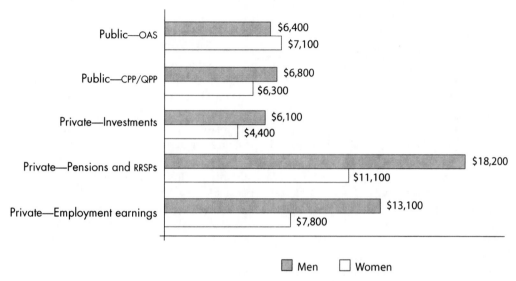

Source: Human Resources and Skills Development Canada calculations based on Statistics Canada data from the surveys of Consumer Finances and of Labour and Income Dynamics, CANSIM table 202-0407.

three-quarters of income-tax filers in the highest income category (the top 5 per cent) were men, even though men constituted less than 50 per cent of those who filed (Murphy, Roberts, and Wolfe 2007). Women make up the majority of minimum-wage workers, at slightly more than 60 per cent (Statistics Canada 2006e). The successive effects of wage inequality, marginalized work status, and interrupted or unstable work histories exact a specific toll for women in older age, though women's labour-force participation and pension contributions have been increasing (Gough 2001; Marshall and Ferrao 2007; Statistics Canada 2006f). Women aged 55–64 have seen a steady increase in their labour-force participation, from 32 per cent in 1976 to 53 per cent in 2007, and while same-aged men's labour-force participation remains higher (at 67 per cent in 2007), it has been more unstable, having declined overall from 76 per cent in 1976 (Marshall and Ferrao 2007: 6). Still, older

men (aged 55–64) earn substantially more than same-aged women, on average $300 more per week (Marshall and Ferrao 2007). Men have higher average retirement incomes from employment earnings and private pensions than women (see Figure 12.2).

All of the inequalities and discriminatory practices experienced in the labour force (e.g., the creation of 'reserve armies of labour' and the exclusion of groups through racism and sexism) have consequences for the class status of aging adults.

In the mid-twentieth century, the poverty of Canadian seniors sparked the enactment of a number of distributive policies designed to ameliorate this situation (Gaszo 2005; Myles 2000). The Canadian government instituted a network of financial coverage for elderly citizens, including Old Age Security, the Guaranteed Income Supplement, the Canada/Quebec Pension Plan, and incentives for retirement savings in the form of Registered Retirement Savings Plans (B. Marshall 2000). Although the financial coverage of the Canada/Quebec Pension Plan is dependent upon labour-force earnings, and although RRSPs require individual contributions, the other policies were intended to improve the situation of low-income seniors (B. Marshall 2000). All seniors receive Old Age Security (OAS) regardless of their employment history. In addition, there is the Guaranteed Income Supplement (GIS) and a Spouse's Allowance, which are intended to improve the financial situation of those seniors with low or no pre-retirement income (B. Marshall 2000). These policies have had success in alleviating extreme poverty among seniors (Myles 2000; Turcotte and Schellenberg 2007). For instance, 15.1 per cent of seniors were below the low-income cut-off before tax in 2003, compared to 34.1 per cent in 1980 (Myles 2000; Turcotte and Schellenberg 2007: 68). Poverty among unattached female seniors was also reduced over this period, dropping from 70 per cent in the lowest income quintile in 1980 to 42 per cent by 1995 (Myles 2000: 18). In 2004, 17 per cent of unattached women aged 65 and older were living in poverty—a dramatic reduction from 1980; and yet it is still high compared to the percentage of all Canadian families living in poverty (7.8 per cent) (CCSD 2007b). This and the fact that widows (in comparison to widowers) are highly vulnerable to experience significant income losses and low income in the years after their spouses' death suggest that 'safety nets' continue to be inadequate (Bernard and Li 2006). So too, does the fact that Aboriginal Canadians who live on reserves were not allowed to contribute to the Canada/Quebec Pension Plan until 1988 (Myles 2000). Thus, Canadians are differentially protected from the vulnerabilities of old age.

Older Canadians who have immigrated recently are also more vulnerable because they are ineligible for social security benefits (Morissette 2002). And evidence from Britain indicates that all ethnic minorities may have smaller pensions in later life. Ginn and Arber (2001), who document the extent of pension inequality in Britain by gender and ethnicity, find significant disadvantages for visible minorities in comparison to whites. After controlling for a number of other factors, they found that both minority men and women were significantly less likely to have private pensions (Ginn and Arber 2001). Discriminatory labour-market practices, shorter employment histories, and gendered ideologies are among the variables that disadvantage ethnic minority groups in the accumulation of private pensions (Ginn and Arber 2001). Hence, the likelihood of having a significant pension and financial stability in older age is not determined by chance. In Canada, 90 per cent of families with an after-tax income of $85,000 or more had RRSPs compared to 35 per cent of families with an income of $36,500 or less (Pyper 2008: 10). The experience of inequality throughout the life course casts a long shadow in old age.

Although secure and stable employment has long been denied to many groups, researchers have highlighted the lack of employment opportunities and citizenship participation for today's youth (Allahar and Côté 1994; Côté and Allahar 2006; Kapsalis, Morisette, and Picot 1999; Wanner 2001). Although this crisis may be somewhat overestimated, young men have seen some losses in their labour-market returns from educational investments (Wanner 2001). In general, today's youth are experiencing 'negative mobility compared to their parents and grandparents', and this means that the parents of these young people will encounter longer periods when they will be supporting their children financially (McDaniel 2002: 141; McDaniel 2004). For today's youth, pension prospects and life-course earnings appear to be less promising than for previous generations. The Canadian state's retreat from the tasks of caring has resulted in further 'intergenerational inequities' between women, as women responsible for children and elderly parents face additional burdens (McDaniel 2002: 141; McDaniel 2004). The intensification of private caring responsibilities means that youth and elderly people from the middle and upper classes will be protected and sheltered against the contingencies of market imperatives, while those from lower-income groups will be further disadvantaged (McDaniel 2002, 2004).

Social Regulation: Child Welfare Legislation

The state's intervention in the lives of its citizens starts in childhood (Ferguson 2007; Ursel 1990). Although the protection of children and young people would appear to be desirable, Ursel (1990) shows that the roots of the Canadian child welfare laws established in the late nineteenth and early twentieth centuries were paternalistic and punitive rather than supportive. The welfare agencies aimed strongly for the regulation of reproductive processes and were quick to remove children and make them wards of the state rather than work with parents to improve the family situation (Ursel 1990). Kline (1993, 2005) shows how this legacy continues to affect present-day child welfare practices. She examines how the ideology of motherhood, with its attendant racialized and bourgeois meanings, is applied in legal discourse to Aboriginal women who are then found to be 'lacking'. Kline (1993) argues that Aboriginal women have been construed by child welfare agencies as inadequate and uncooperative mothers who violate the dominant definitions of 'good' mothering. According to Kline (1993), the moralizing dictates of the good-mother ideology include an ethic of selflessness, whereby a mother is ready and able to provide her children with a stable and enriched environment. All of the expectations of 'good mothering' are judged without any consideration of the impact of the broader socio-structural factors of inequality (Kline 1993, 2005).

Kline (1993, 2005) points to several cases involving Aboriginal women and child welfare agencies to show that the courts individualize and personalize the societal inequalities stemming from colonization and racism that are present in the lives of Aboriginal women. For instance, Aboriginal women who were being abused have had their children taken from them with the rationale that the 'choices' these women made were unstable (Kline 1993). This is a classic case of blaming the victim and reducing social issues to individual problems. In this sense, the reduction of violent abuse to a 'lifestyle' carries strong elements of blame for the mothers involved (Kline 1993). The difficulties inherent in providing basic sustenance and adequate living conditions while living in poverty are subsequently ignored in assessments by the courts. In fact, Aboriginal women are much more likely to experience spousal violence, having a three and a half times greater risk than non-Aboriginal women in the same time period (Brzozowsky et al. 2006: 6). Investigators have noted that colonialism and government policies concerning Aboriginal groups have constructed a system in which Aboriginal women live disproportionately in poverty, with all of its disadvantages and hardships, and this leaves many Aboriginal women (like other poor women) much more vulnerable to state intervention and the potential dissolution of their families (Kline 1993; Waterfall 2006).

Agents in Action: Mandatory Retirement

The regulative force of the state stretches and intertwines through the life course and into the domains of reproduction, production, and distribution. At the end of the life course, the inequalities that have manifested themselves throughout these processes do not disappear, but rather crystallize and extend their reach. Privileged adults who have weathered little in the way of inequality or disadvantage are often introduced at this point to the experience of age discrimination in the processes of production.

The virtual exclusion of aging adults from the world of productive labour by the mechanism of mandatory retirement has been challenged and overturned in Canada (Ibbott, Kerr, and Beaujot 2006; Shellenbarger 2001). The right to remain active in the labour force and to re-enter the labour force have both been points of contention for the growing numbers of older workers. Box 12.6 outlines some of the changes underway.

Conclusion

The meanings of the term *citizen* have a significant effect on the development and delivery of policy, and these meanings are intimately structured by the social relations of class, gender, race, ethnicity, and age. Jenson (1997: 632) argues that there are a number of different citizenship 'identities', including the 'model citizen', the 'second-class citizen', and the 'non-citizen'. A 'model citizen' can expect to receive the full entitlements of citizenship, whereas those groups and individuals that are considered 'second-class' or 'non-citizens' are offered few, if any, of the benefits of citizenship. This chapter has shown that the fragility of citizenship is produced and reproduced through state policy and legislation that are shaped by the intersections of class, age, gender, ethnic, and race relations.

Box 12.6 Retiring Mandatory Retirement

Across much of Canada, mandatory retirement has been given the pink slip.

On Jan. 1, 2008, British Columbia became the latest province to enact legislation to amend its human rights code and end the practice. As of that date, workers in BC are no longer forced to quit when they turn 65.

When Attorney General Wally Oppal introduced the legislation, he said: 'Mandatory retirement is a policy of the past, not of the future.'

That was certainly the thinking in other provinces—such as Newfoundland and Labrador, Saskatchewan, and Ontario—when they moved in the past few years to eliminate mandatory retirement.

In fact, only one province or territory still generally allows employers to impose mandatory retirement, and that will end when new legislation comes into effect in Nova Scotia into July 2009.

But there are some limits elsewhere. Many provinces have provisions to allow mandatory retirement for jobs where physical ability is a must, such as firefighting and police work.

And in New Brunswick, the Human Rights Act prohibits mandatory retirement, but includes a provision allowing companies to enforce mandatory retirement under 'the terms or conditions of any . . . retirement or pension plan.'

On the other hand, if you want to retire at 65, nothing in the legislation will stop you from doing so.

Freedom 65? Not for all

Bankers love the concept of retirement, especially around the run-up to the February RRSP season.

Sure, many people don't like their jobs and want to retire if they can afford it. Just six per cent of workers continue to work full-time after age 65 and the average retirement age in Canada is 62.

Why should that six per cent, opponents of mandatory retirement ask, be forced out of their jobs merely because they have turned 65?

It has been shown that those with the most education tend to enjoy their work and are reluctant to be turfed out. And many people want to keep working for a variety of other reasons, including because they enjoy the office camaraderie, sense of purpose or routine.

Regional Breakdown of Retirement Rules

Province or Territory	Retirement Rules
Nunavut	No mandatory retirement age.
Northwest Territories	No mandatory retirement age.
Yukon	No mandatory retirement age.
British Columbia	Law to eliminate mandatory retirement took effect Jan. 1, 2008.
Alberta	No mandatory retirement age.
Saskatchewan	Law to eliminate mandatory retirement took effect November 2007.
Manitoba	No mandatory retirement age.
Ontario	Law to eliminate mandatory retirement took effect Dec. 12, 2006.
Quebec	No mandatory retirement age.
New Brunswick	No mandatory retirement, but companies allowed to enforce it under 'the terms or conditions of any . . . retirement or pension plan'.
Nova Scotia	There is mandatory retirement at age 65 if required by the employer. However, law to eliminate it takes effect July 1, 2009.
Prince Edward Island	No mandatory retirement age.
Newfoundland and Labrador	Law to eliminate mandatory retirement took effect May 26, 2007.

Sometimes it's a case of economic survival.

Geography comes into play. If public pensions total, say, $15,000—the amount can vary widely, depending on extra benefits—it makes considerable difference whether these pensioners live in Vancouver or Portage la Prairie, Man.

Compulsory retirement can also be especially hard on single women, who were (and often still are) paid significantly less than men and may have spent years out of the workforce to raise children.

So many haven't been able to put away as much money as men. And it gets worse down the line, as female life expectancy outpaces that of men by about five years.

Retiring earlier, living longer

In recent years, there has been a sea change in attitudes to public pensions and the very concept of retirement.

When the age of 70 was selected in the early 20th century as the age of eligibility for a government pension, life expectancy was about 60. Now, the population is aging—fast—but Canadians are allowed by government pensions to retire earlier, at 65.

The number of workers in Canada for every retired person is expected to fall to two in 2031, from five in the 1980s, as a wave of baby boomers retires from the workforce.

Increasingly, the worry is a shrinking workforce.

Because people live so much longer, and retire so much earlier, there will be increased pressure on public pensions. Demands to raise CPP contributions are expected in coming years.

Source: CBC News, 21 February 2008, http://www.cbc.ca/news/background/retirement/ mandatory_retirement.html. Copyright cbc.ca.

Regarding social welfare, for instance, there are clear distinctions between model citizens and second-class citizens or those who are deemed deserving or undeserving of social assistance. Consider the extremely high rates of poverty among lone mothers. Because welfare policies are often based on narrow ideas of 'productive' citizenship, the work that women do in the processes of reproduction are often unacknowledged in social welfare policy. This leads to state distributive processes that reproduce the gendered structures of inequality. In old age, when many adults are not allowed to work, pension schemes are established on the basis of a 'typical' labour-force career, or a secure and stable relationship with someone who has had such a career. Yet even if an Aboriginal Canadian has had a stable career, he or she will have a very small pension after retirement because of pre-existing biases in pension-contribution rules.

Hence, state distributive processes are not only gendered, but are also structured by age and race relations. And as the preceding sections of this chapter show, race, ethnicity, and class are implicated in state distributive processes as well. Indeed, views of morality and idealized traditional families still frame much of the political rhetoric around poverty; governments are committed to reducing child poverty, not poverty among single mothers, but of course those are part of the same thing.

To alleviate social inequality in Canada, state policy and legislation must evolve so that the complexities of inequality that result from coalescent CAGE(s) are its heart. This requires radical social change, and the process will be slow even if policy-makers have the best intentions. The value of 'neutral' social policy must be challenged if such change is to take place. It is to this issue that we turn in chapter 13.

||||||||||| Note ||||||||||||||||||||||||||||||||||||||||||||||||||||||||||||||||||||||||||||||

1.   Scott (1996).

||||||||||| Questions for Critical Thought ||||||||||||||||||||||||||||||||||||||||||||||||

1.   What do you see as the advantages and disadvantages of Sainsbury's (1999: 78)'three gender policy regimes'? What implications do these various regimes have for class, age, gender, ethnic, or race relations?

2.   How have immigration policies affected the processes of production, reproduction, and distribution in various families and communities? What type of compensation or redress, if any, should governments offer to individuals and groups that have been discriminated against and that have been denied citizenship rights in the past?

3.   How would you characterize the role of the state? Does the state primarily ameliorate or exacerbate societal inequities? Give examples to make your case.

4.   How have the social relations of class, age, race or ethnicity, and gender affected the achievement of citizenship rights in Canada? What rights do you think should be included in the notion of full citizenship? Explain why.

5.   How has the state's intervention and regulation of the processes of reproduction changed over time (e.g., reproductive rights, child welfare, and social welfare)? Do you support more intervention or less on the part of the state? What implications would this have for different groups in society?

||||||||||| **Glossary** ||||||||||||||||||||||||||||||||||||||||||||||||||||||||||||||||||||||||||||||||||||||||||

Breadwinner wages   The 'family-supporting' wages to which some men (especially white European men) were considered to be entitled during the twentieth century. State laws and support systems reinforced and sustained this gendered division of labour in the family, thereby reproducing an ideology of female economic dependence for some groups of women.

Citizen   Often considered a neutral term, *citizens* are members of nations or societies. Citizens are entitled to all the benefits of being a member of particular society (e.g., rights, political voice, social welfare); however, many individuals and groups within societies are denied the full rights of citizenship and are treated as second-class citizens (perhaps granted some rights but denied others; e.g., granted welfare benefits but not allowed to vote) (Jenson 1997). Those who are treated as 'non-citizens' are denied virtually all of the benefits of citizenship and are left extremely vulnerable to exploitation with little recourse.

Civil citizenship   T.H. Marshall's citizenship conceptualization of an individual's basic human rights. These include the right to sign a legal contract, the right to freedom of person and freedom of speech, and the right to seek redress in the courts for any violation of property or person.

Corporate crime   Illegal activities undertaken by businesses. In the course of procuring financial gain and minimizing economic losses, businesses (or rather the agents within them) have the potential to engage in numerous criminal acts (environmental contamination, health and safety violations, fraud, and so on).

Live-In Caregiver Program   An immigration policy that gives temporary work permits to women coming to fill the Canadian need for live-in caregivers (e.g., nannies). This policy aims to fill a demand for child care, while at the same time severely restricting the activities and the duration of stay for the women involved in the program.

Political citizenship   T.H. Marshall's conceptualization of an individual's right to political involvement in society. This guarantees a political voice for citizens in the form of voting and/or seeking political office.

Social citizenship   T.H. Marshall's conceptualization of an individual's right to full social inclusion in a society's wealth. Citizens should be guaranteed economic well-being, educational and health services, and participation or inclusion in the culture and heritage of their society.

State   A complex array of governing institutions in a society. The state includes national-security, parliamentary, judicial, and bureaucratic institutions, to name just a few. For this reason, the state itself cannot be said to act either consciously or uniformly; however, agents (both internal and external) can use the tools of the state to acquire, monopolize, or distribute resources and services and to maintain social order. This diversity of institutions means that dissent and conflict within and between institutions are a feature of democratic states. Clearly, some individuals and groups in a society are more vulnerable to punitive action on the part of state institutions, whereas individuals and groups with more power are better equipped to attempt to use the state to their advantage.

Transnational action   The mobilization of international agencies and non-governmental organizations (e.g., environmental or human-rights groups) to generate support for the protection of Aboriginal lands and land claims.

Workfare   A type of social assistance program that requires the recipients to take certain paid work or enroll in educational or training courses as a condition for receiving welfare benefits. Although some recipients, notably mothers of young children, have been exempt from this requirement, some of these exemptions are being revised or abolished.

‖‖‖‖‖‖ Recommended Reading ‖‖‖‖‖‖‖‖‖‖‖‖‖‖‖‖‖‖‖‖‖‖‖‖‖‖‖‖‖‖‖‖‖‖‖

Armstrong, Pat, and M. Patricia Connelly. 1999. *Feminism, Political Economy and the State: Contested Terrain*. Toronto: Canadian Scholar's Press. An anthology that looks at how welfare, health, and education policies have been shaped by feminist struggles, as well as examining how women's lives have been affected by the state. The countries examined include Canada and Latin American and European countries.

Hier, Sean P., and B. Singh Bolaria, eds. 2007. *Race and Racism in 21st Century Canada: Continuity, Complexity and Change*. Peterborough, ON: Broadview Press. An excellent volume of analyses on race and racism in Canada.

Pupo, Norene. 2001. 'The Role of the State in a Restructured Economy'. Chapter 4 in Dan Glenday and Ann Duffy, eds, *Canadian Society: Meeting the Challenges of the Twenty-First Century*. Toronto: Oxford University Press. In this book chapter, the author succinctly reviews theories of the state and explains the influence of the Canadian state in the economy, the labour market, and the lives of individuals and families.

Sainsbury, Diane, ed. 1999. *Gender and Welfare State Regimes*. New York: Oxford University Press. A valuable collection which provides international comparisons of welfare policies in a broad range of areas (including child care, taxation, the labour market, and employment equality) with an emphasis on gender issues.

Stasiulis, Daiva K., and Abigail B. Bakan. 2005. *Negotiating Citizenship: Migrant Women in Canada and the Global System*. Toronto: University of Toronto Press. The authors challenge predominant conceptualizations of 'citizenship', arguing that citizenship is a 'negotiated relationship' that is shaped by numerous societal axes of inequality. They illustrate this negotiation through the experience of foreign domestic workers in Canada.

Westhues, Anne, ed. 2006. *Canadian Social Policy: Issues and Perspectives*. 4th edn. Waterloo, ON: Wilfrid Laurier University Press. A comprehensive collection of analyses on contemporary Canadian social policies.

‖‖‖‖‖‖ Relevant Websites ‖‖

Canadian Council on Social Development
www.ccsd.ca
**A non-governmental, non-profit website that promotes social equity and equitable policies in Canada.

Citizen Voices
http://www.citizenvoices.gg.ca/
**Governor General Michaëlle Jean's website for Canadian youth features mentorship programs, blogs, forums, and opportunities to engage in discussion with Canada's governor general.

Native Women's Association of Canada
http://www.nwac-hq.org/en/index.html
**The Native Women's Association of Canada (NWAC) is an aggregate of thirteen Native women's organizations from across Canada. The organization aims to enhance, promote, and foster the social, economic, cultural, and political well-

being of First Nations and Métis women within First Nations, Métis, and Canadian societies.

Canadian Race Relations Foundation
www.crr.ca
**The Canadian Race Relations Foundation is committed to building a national framework for eliminating racism in Canadian society. It explores the causes and manifestations of racism, provides independent national leadership, and acts as a resource and facilitator in the pursuit of equity, fairness, and social justice.

Citizenship and Immigration Canada
http://www.cic.gc.ca/
**Citizenship and Immigration Canada provides information and services regarding issues relating to immigration, citizenship, and multiculturalism.

Conclusion: Equality, Politics, Platforms, and Policy Issues

The first chapters in this book discussed influential theoretical contributions to the study of class, gender, ethnicity, race, and age. After outlining the strengths and weaknesses of these theories, each of the chapters concluded with a working definition of the concept in question. These working definitions incorporated many elements of the theories previously assessed. Yet a crucial reason for formulating these concepts was to ensure that they would be compatible with one another in a conceptual framework that combined them all. Thus it was important to identify a nucleus around which class, age, gender, ethnicity, and race could be grouped. Three elements of this nucleus were identified: processes of production, processes of distribution, and processes of reproduction (see chapter 2 for definitions). These processes were chosen because they are essential for the survival of individuals and societies. Class, age, gender, ethnicity, and race are structured sets of social relations that organize the interrelated processes of production, distribution, and reproduction in Canada. Hence, class, age, gender, ethnicity, and race are characterized by power, oppression, opportunity hoarding, and exploitation.

Whereas chapters 2 to 5 discussed the structural dimensions of inequality, chapter 6 considered the idea that individuals are agents in the social construction of class, age, gender, ethnic, and race relations. Chapter 7 introduced a conceptual framework of social inequality that brought together many of the ideas discussed in the previous chapters into a cohesive whole. Besides organizing concepts that have traditionally been studied in research on social inequality, this framework contributes to our understanding of social inequality by explicitly considering social time, agency, and place.

Part II of this book examined various outcomes of inequality in five social domains. Chapters 8 and 9 considered outcomes of inequality that arise primarily through families and paid work, such as differences in the division of household labour, caregiving, violence, occupations, and income. Chapters 10 and 11 discussed inequalities in education and health, and chapter 12 examined the role the Canadian state plays in producing and reproducing various forms of inequality through its ideas of what constitutes citizenship. Each chapter considered examples or case studies that demonstrated the relevance of inequality in the social domain in question. These chapters also provided an overview of the Canadian literature on social inequality.

The purpose of Part II was twofold. In the first place, the chapters showed how outcomes of inequality in Canada are shaped by class, age, gender, and ethnicity, and race. In doing so, the chapters showed how certain groups of Canadians are disadvantaged in relation to others in various domains of social life. These chapters also identified issues that require further research. The ideas presented in the conceptual framework of the book were often captured most explicitly through the examples and case studies presented in the chapters. Although my goal was to organize the chapters in Part II with these ideas in mind, much of the available research is deficient in three important ways. First, very little of it has considered whether and how class, age, gender, and ethnicity and race work together simultaneously in creating systems of advantage and disadvantage. Second, and related to the first, there is a dearth of research on inequality that considers whether and how age and social time influence outcomes of inequality. Third, more research is needed into the strategies that agents use in conforming to or resisting the social-structural influences in their lives. Although a picture of inequality in Canada has evolved from the material presented, it remains incomplete.

Many aspects of social life need to change if inequality is to be eradicated in Canada. Widely held ideologies about gender, class, ethnicity, race, and age need to be challenged, and the processes through which the activities of production, distribution, and reproduction are organized need to change. Another avenue through which such changes may begin to take place is the reform of social policy. Although it would take another book to outline the specific policies needed to address all of the issues identified in this book, some general ideas about how such policies should evolve are worth considering. First and foremost, given what we know about how class, age, gender, ethnicity, and race work together in structuring inequality, it is useful to consider how policy makers might better integrate these structures of inequality into their programs. They will need to give up the idea that gender, class, age, ethnic, or racial 'neutrality' is desirable in social policy and,

instead, recognize that such neutrality actually reproduces systems of inequality.

The goal of 'neutral' social policy is to treat everyone the same way. Neutral social policy emerged in response to policies that explicitly treated certain groups of people unfairly. For example, in the early part of the twentieth century, laws and policies changed so that women were entitled to own property. Before that, women had to relinquish control of anything that was theirs—land, money, furniture, and so on—to their husbands when they married. The law became neutral so that both men and women were eligible to control their own possessions. Why then is neutral social policy that assumes formal equality problematic? Because 'strict adherence to the principle of formal equality in the absence of substantive equality leads to inequality; treating unalikes in the same way simply perpetuates differences' (Chunn 2000: 242). As an example, consider Canadian family law. Under the guise of equality, Canadian family law assumes that mothers and fathers are both able to contribute to the financial support of their children. Technically, of course, this is true. As a result, spousal support payment schemes are generally short-term and work on the assumption that an individual will and should be able to support themselves economically after a short time. The 'substantive' problem with such assumptions is that women are at a disadvantage in labour markets and are unlikely to be able to support themselves financially to the same extent as men (Chunn 2000). Clearly, such policy leads to the reproduction of inequality.

Equality means different things to different people. Consider, for instance, the version of equality that is presented by the Conservative Party of Canada. Equality is one of the basic political principles that guided the Canadian Alliance and the Progressive Conservative Party of Canada, the two parties that merged to form the Conservative Party of Canada in 2003. Indeed, 'a belief in the equality of all Canadians' is listed as the sixth founding principle of the Conservative Party of Canada. In Box 13.1 I compare the views of the Conservative Party of Canada, the Liberal Party of Canada, and the New Democratic Party of Canada on women, aboriginal peoples, and seniors in their policy and issue documents and in their 2006 election platforms. A comparison of the parties' 2008 election platforms is found in Box 13.2. Here we see differences among the parties in their views of equality. The Liberal Party identifies women, aboriginal peoples, and seniors as disadvantaged groups and outlines what

Box 13.1 Comparison of Conservative Party of Canada, Liberal Party of Canada, and New Democratic Party of Canada views on Women, Aboriginals, and Seniors

On Women
Conservative Party
Policy Declaration, 19 March 2005
(http://www.conservative.ca/media/20050319-POLICY%20DECLARATION.pdf)

- Recognizes that everyone should have equality of opportunity in the workplace, be judged on skills, merit, and qualifications and be free of discrimination.
- Recognizes that women are entitled to equal pay for work of equal value.
- Recognizes the value of the caregiver and hints at a child-care allowance (see below).

Federal Election Platform, 2006
(http://www.cbc.ca/canadavotes2006/leadersparties/pdf/conservative_platform 20060113.pdf)

- Makes no explicit statement about women.
- Promises a child-care allowance and the abolishment of the National Child Care Policy (adopted shortly after Prime Minister Stephen Harper was sworn in, February 2006).

Liberal Party
Federal Election Platform, 2006 (Securing Canada's Success, http://www.theglobe andmail.com/bnfiles/pics/2005election/lib platformoff.pdf, pp. 44–5)

Supports women as decision makers and entrepreneurs with:
- $25 million to help women expand their businesses and to seek new market opportunities outside Canada.
- Regional economic development agency services targeted to assist women entrepreneurs.

Would work to enhance women's health by:
- Ensuring that women aged 50–69 receive breast cancer screening every two years.
- Ensuring that women aged 18–69 receive cervical cancer screening every three years following two normal tests.

Supports women's equal right to respect, safety and health by:
- Recognizing what Canada owes its unpaid caregivers—mostly women—and giving them special tax benefits.
- Helping women strengthen their families.
- Funding the National Child Benefit—a comprehensive system of support for low-income families.

Press release, 8 June 2008 (http://www. liberal.ca/story_14039_e.aspx)

Promises to create a Commissioner of Gender Equality with authority to examine gender equality practices in all government departments.

New Democratic Party
Platform document (Getting Results for the People)

- Identifies equality for women as one of 10 key policy issues.
- Calls for the implementation of the Pay Equity Task Force's recommendations.
- Proposes expanding home care and caregivers' programs (to receive up to one year of Employment Insurance) and amending the Canada Pension Plan (to permit time spent caring for loved ones to count when determining benefit entitlements) to ease the burden of care for the elderly and other dependent relatives.
- Commits to making Canada safe for First Nations, Métis, and Inuit women.

Policy on Aboriginal Peoples

Conservative Party
Policy Declaration, 19 March 2005 (http://www.conservative.ca/EN/2692/)

- Recognizes obligation to improve living conditions of Aboriginal peoples with regard to economic opportunity, health, community safety, and education.
- Promotes self-government and legal and democratic authority by Aboriginal peoples over their own affairs.
- Promises accountability and transparency in the expenditure of public funds.
- Promises constitutional protection of all Canadians whether Aboriginal or non-Aboriginal.
- Supports educational choice in schooling for First Nations.

Federal Election Platform, 2006 (http://www.conservative.ca/EN/2590, p. 38)

- 'Support the development of individual property ownership on reserves, to encourage lending for private housing and businesses.'
- 'Let Aboriginal parents choose the schooling they want for their children, with funding following the students.'

- 'Replace the Indian Act (and related legislation) with a modern legislative framework that provides for the devolution of full legal and democratic responsibility to Aboriginal Canadians for their own affairs within the Constitution, including the Charter of Rights and Freedoms.'
- 'Pursue settlement of all outstanding "comprehensive claims" within a clear framework that balances the rights of Aboriginal claimants with those of Canada.'
- 'Implement all recommendations of the House of Commons Standing Committee on Aboriginal Affairs and Northern Development contained in its fourth report on residential school claims, to expedite the settlement of claims and save money.'
- 'Recognize the contributions of Aboriginal veterans and redress 60 years of inequity by implementing the resolution of the House of Commons to acknowledge the historic inequality of treatment and compensation for First Nations, Métis, and Inuit war veterans and to take action immediately to give real compensation to these veterans in a way that truly respects their service and sacrifice.'

Liberal Party of Canada
Federal Election Platform, 2006 (http://www.theglobeandmail.com/bnfiles/pics/2005election/libplatformoff.pdf, pp. 21–4)

- Encourages a culture of home ownership in Aboriginal communities.
- Proposes enhancing opportunities for education.
- Proposes expanding the skills of Aboriginal people and their governments to manage their land, infrastructure, and financing.
- Proposes building up a trained labour force to keep home-construction jobs in local communities.
- Promises to develop a regulatory regime for drinking water on reserve that will provide comparable water quality to that enjoyed by other Canadians.

- Supports improved access to the full range of public health services that non-Aboriginal Canadians currently enjoy.
- Promises recognition of historical grievances, including physical and sexual abuse at residential schools.
- Proposes enhancing Canada's Northern sovereignty and development.
- Promises to connect rural and remote communities to the world by bringing broadband Internet access to 250 more communities in the next 5 years.
- Supports enabling First Nations to assume jurisdiction and control of their oil and gas and related revenues.

New Democratic Party of Canada
(http://www.ndp.ca/page/4050)

- Lists Aboriginal peoples as one of 10 key policy issues.
- Promises to ensure that communities have infrastructure, housing, water, and other services equal to those enjoyed by other Canadians.
- Supports Aboriginal initiatives to improve health through better health care, wellness strategies, and community infrastructure.
- Promises to ensure speedy compensation for survivors of residential-school abuse.
- Ensures respect for the inherent right to self-governance and ensures responsible resolution of land claims.
- Supports developing community economies with people as the priority, through adequate infrastructure and access to capital for local economic development.
- Proposes creating approaches to justice that heal, including youth-focused crime prevention and systems of restorative justice that also support victims of crime.
- Emphasizes education and training, especially through programs encouraging employment in health, education, social services, sciences, commerce, engineering, and trades.

Policy on Seniors
Conservative Party
Policy Declaration, 19 March 2005 (http://www.conservative.ca/EN/2692/, p. 23)

- 'Commitment to ensuring quality of life, accessible health care, and the ability to stay in homes longer.'
- 'Eliminate mandatory retirement and promote choice in working or not past the age of 65 without the loss of federal retirement benefits.'
- 'Working persons aged 65 and over would no longer have to pay Employment Insurance as they are ineligible to collect it.'
- 'Increase support for home care through tax incentives for non-professional caregivers.'
- 'Tough stance on elder abuse.'
- 'Appoint a minister responsible for seniors.'
- 'Work to better identify seniors entitled to federal or provincial benefits.'

Federal Election Platform, 2006 (http://www.conservative.ca/EN/2590/, p. 32)

- 'Confirms its commitment to the Canada Pension Plan, (CPP) and Old Age Security, (OAS) as well as the Guaranteed Income Supplement (GIS) as fundamental guarantees of income security in retirement years.'
- 'Stop the Liberal attack on retirement savings and income trusts by not imposing any new taxes on them.'
- 'Protect the integrity of the CPP investment fund to stop politicians from raiding it to balance the budget or pay for other political projects.'
- 'Protect seniors from over-taxation by raising the pension income tax amount that is eligible for a federal tax credit from $1,000 to $2,000 per year in 2006, and to $2,500 in five years.'
- 'Appoint a Seniors Council comprised of seniors and representatives of seniors' organizations to advise the minister responsible for seniors on issues of national importance.'

Liberal Party

Federal Election Platform, 2006 (http:// www.theglobeandmail.com/bnfiles/pics/ 2005election/libplatformoff.pdf, pp. 18–19)

- Respects seniors' rights to dignity, independence, fairness, participation, and security.
- Would protect seniors' public pensions.
- Would support seniors and their families by increasing tax credits for caregivers, promoting active living, creating a plan to increase appropriate housing for seniors, allowing more seniors to access the equity in their homes, facilitating work past 65, and developing a new pharmaceutical strategy with the provinces.

New Democratic Party

Platform document, 2006 (http://archive. ndp.ca/page/4649)

- Identifies seniors as one of 10 key policy issues.
- Would work with the provinces to create 50,000 long-term care spaces over 5 years to provide dignity and comfort to seniors.
- Would work with the provinces to expand coverage of professional home care as another alternative to hospitalization, and would expand CPP/EI coverage to support those caring for senior family members at home.
- Promises to protect pensions by ending employer underfunding of pension plans, securing pensions when employers go bankrupt, launching pension insurance, and other measures.

Box 13.2 2008 Election Campaign Political Party Platforms

By Jay Makarenko

Conservative Party of Canada Platform

The Conservative Party's 2008 election platform was released in a policy document titled *The True North Strong and Free: Stephen Harper's Plan for Canadians* [http://www.conservative.ca/ media/20081007-Platform-e.pdf]. The Party's website also list eight key policy priorities on its website: sovereignty, leadership, the environment, health care, lower taxes, child care, tackling crime, and accountability. The website also provides a backgrounder on the Conservative government's February 2008 budget, which is titled *Responsible Leadership for Uncertain Times*. The following provides highlights of these various policy documents.

Economy: Central to the Conservative economic strategy is **tax reduction**. This includes previously announced tax reductions, such as the lowering of the Goods and Services Tax (GST) from seven to five percent, as well as reducing personal income and corporate taxes for individuals and businesses. New proposals include lowering taxes on diesel and aviation fuel by half and further reductions in corporate taxes for small and medium-sized business. Other economic policies include reducing the regulatory burden for small businesses and northern development; a new $75 million venture capital fund to **help businesses commercialize new technology developments; a $900 million** Strategic **Aerospace and Defence Initiative** and a $250 million

Automotive Innovation Fund to support these industrial sectors; a $1 billion **Community Development Trust** to support communities and workers in struggling industries; a commitment to reduce inter-provincial trade barriers by 2010; pursuing new trade agreements with emerging markets; as well as a reorganization of federal regional development strategies.

Environment: The Conservatives have committed to reducing Canada's greenhouse gases by 20 percent below 2006 levels by 2020, and cutting air pollution by 50 percent by 2015. There targets will be achieved through government laws imposed on industries, as well as national caps for industrial emissions commonly associated with smog and acid rain. Other environmental policies include promoting smarter energy use through the **ecoEnergy Initiative**; a **Chemical Management Plan** to regulate chemicals harmful to human health and the environment; $1.5 billion over seven years for the production of renewable fuels; a commitment to ensure that 90 percent of Canadian electricity needs are generated through non-emitting sources by 2020; and additional government funding to acquire and preserve ecologically sensitive lands.

Health care: The Conservative Party remains committed to Canada's system of public health care. Specific policies proposed or introduced by the Conservatives include Patient Wait Time Guarantee agreements with the provinces and territories; continued implementation of the 10-year $41.3 billion **Plan to Strengthen Health Care** (the plan was introduced by the previous Liberal government in 2004); establishing the Canadian **Partnership Against Cancer** to implement a national cancer strategy; increased funding for new training of doctors, nurses, and other health care professionals; increased investment in the **Canada Health Infoway** to develop electronic health records.

Social Justice: Conservative policies for social justice include a combination of targeted tax reductions, new spending programs, and new justice-related legislation. Specific policies include a **Canada Employment Credit and Tax Fairness Plan** to reduce taxes for working families and seniors; tax credits for public transit, kid's sports, textbooks, tools, and apprentices; increased support to the provinces and territories to create new child care spaces; increasing the **Senior Age Credit** amount by an additional $1,000; and allowing income splitting for caregivers of family members with disabilities. Also social policies include introducing stiffer punishments for serious crimes, including changes to Canada's youth offender laws and ending house arrest for some crimes; increased spending for police and security services to reduce crime.

Liberal Party of Canada Platform

The Liberal Party has outlined its 2008 election platform in a policy document entitled *Richer, Fairer, Greener: An Action Plan for the 21st Century* [www.llbc.leg.bc.ca/public/pubdocs/docs/446629/2008_liberal_action_plan.pdf]. Core planks of the platform include the economy, the environment, social justice, and foreign policy. Highlights of the document include:

Economy: A key component of the Liberal Party's economic policies is the encouragement of a green economy through the development of environmentally-friendly industries and jobs. The Liberals are also committed to reducing income and corporate tax rates and balanced federal budgets as means of spurring economic growth. The Liberals have also targeted infrastructure and education as critical to continued economic prosperity. Specific policies include a 10-year $70 billion plan to invest directly in Canada's infrastructure; increased support for university-based research; simplifying tax support for students; and reforms to student loan initiatives. The Liberals have also promised to create a $1 billion **Advanced Manufacturing Prosperity Fund** to assist manufacturing industries and workers facing economic difficulties.

For more information on the Liberal Party's economic policies:

- Liberal Party of Canada: Jobs Today, Jobs Tomorrow: A Liberal Plan for a More Prosperous Canada [http://www.scribd.com/doc/6308750/Liberal-Party-of-Canada-2008-English-Platform]

Environment: The Liberals have adopted the **Green Shift** as the core of their environmental policies. Central to the Green Shift is the reduction of greenhouse gas emissions by at least 20 percent below 1990 levels by 2020, 40 percent by 2035, and 60 to 80 percent by 2050. These goals will be achieved through a progressive carbon tax system, which place levies on carbon emissions. The Liberals are also committed to creating a national carbon trading system, enabling companies to trade emission credits in order to meet targets. Other Liberal environmental policies include a **Renewable Power Production Incentive** to encourage the development and use of non-carbon-emitting energy sources; providing incentives to Canadians for green home renovations; stiffer fuel efficiency standards for automobiles; the introduction of higher water and air quality standards to reduce pollution; a **Toxic Substance Reduction Strategy** to safe food products; and the development of a **National Ecosystem Stewardship Strategy** to protect Canadian wilderness, oceans, and endangered species.

For more information on the Liberal Party's environmental policies:

- Liberal Party of Canada: A Greener Canada (PDF)

Health Care: The Liberal Party has promised to maintain and improve Canada's public health care system. Specific policies include a **Doctors and Nurses Fund** to increase training capacity for new health care professionals; working with Aboriginal communities to close the gap in the health status of Aboriginal peoples; and the introduction of a drug plan to ensure Canadians have access to catastrophic drug coverage.

Social Justice: The Liberal Party is committed to a fairer Canada. Specific policies include the **30–50 Plan to Fight Poverty**, which is committed to reducing the number of people living below the poverty line by 30 percent and the number of children by 50 percent; an **Affordable Housing Plan**; pursing the long-term goal of a national high-quality, universal, community-based, early education and child care system; increasing the **Guaranteed Income Supplement** by $600 per year for low-income seniors; and creating a new relationship with Canada's First Nation, Inuit and Métis peoples, including re-instating the Kelowna Accord.

For more information on the Liberal Party's social justice policies:

- Liberal Party of Canada: A Fairer Canada (PDF)

New Democratic Party of Canada Platform

The New Democratic Party has released a document outlining is 2008 election platform. The document focuses on three key policy areas: the economy, health care renewal, and the environment. Highlights of the NDP's election platform include:

Economy: The NDP promises to promote Canadian jobs and make life more affordable for Canadian families. Specific policies include encouraging job creation and innovation in the new energy economy; improving the fairness of employment standards (including re-establishing the **National Minimum Wage**; reversing 'tax giveaways' to corporations; introducing and maintaining balanced budgets; protecting Canadians from 'price gouging' by businesses; implementing income stabilization programs for farmers; promoting long-term economic and environmental sustainability of marine and forestry resources; and re-investing in education, skills training and apprenticeships to help Canadians succeed in the economy.

For more information on the NDP's economic policies:

- New Democratic Party of Canada: Making Life More Affordable for Families—Creating Jobs [http://www.ndp.ca/platform/jobsandaffordability]

Health Care: Central to the NDP's renewal strategy for health care is a commitment to maintaining and improving the public health care system. Particular policies include training and hiring more doctors and nurses; improving home care; establishing a national prescription drug program; and promoting good health through physical fitness and amateur sport programs.

For more information on the NDP's health care policies:

- New Democratic Party of Canada: Hiring More Doctors and Nurses and Renewing Health Care [http://www.ndp.ca/platform/healthcare/]

Environment: The NDP promises to cut Canadian greenhouse gas emissions to 20 percent below 1990 levels by 2020, and 80 percent below 1990 levels by 2050. This will be accomplished through a combination of a '**cap and trade**' carbon pricing system, mandatory vehicle emission standards, and investing in renewable energy production and consumption. The NDP has also pledged to protect Canada's water resources by placing some restrictions on the export of bulk water, encouraging more efficient water consumption, and improving water quality through stronger regulations. The NDP has further pledged to: complete the **National Parks System**; ensure the integrity of parks and protected areas is not compromised by industrial activity or inappropriate development; improve endangered species protection; and establish an

Environment Commissioner as an independent Officer of Parliament to provide oversight on the government's environmental performance.

For more information on the NDP's environmental policies:

- New Democratic Party of Canada: A Plan for the Environment that Will Really Work [http://www.ndp.ca/platform/environment/]

Social justice: The NDP promises to: establish and fund a national child care and early learning program; end poverty in Canada by 2020; reform the Employment Insurance system to ensure fairness; implement a comprehensive and fully-funded affordable housing strategy; invest $5 billion over five years for First Nations, Métis, and Inuit peoples to improve health services, housing, water services, and local infrastructure; and improve fairness for women in the workplace through initiatives such as strengthening pay equity provisions in the **Canada Labour Code**.

For more information on the NDP's social justice policies:

- New Democratic Party of Canada: Making Life More Affordable for Families—Creating Jobs [http://www.ndp.ca/platform/jobsand affordability]
- New Democratic Party of Canada: Other Key Priorities for Canadians [http://www.ndp. ca/platform/otherpriorities]

Source: M akarenko (2008).

it has done or is trying to do in order to improve the quality of life for these groups. The NDP does the same but offers more broad reaching support for these disadvantaged groups. The Conservative Party of Canada on the other hand, does not mention women, and with respect to Aboriginal peoples and seniors, the implication is that their policies will treat these groups equally under Canadian law and encourage their individualism in ensuring their well-being. While this language may seem innocuous, the fact that groups are not treated equally under Canadian law and policy in the first place goes unacknowledged (see chapter 12). Furthermore, and as noted above, treating everyone as 'equal' under policy and law reinforces substantive inequality. Clearly, the Conservative Party of Canada's understanding of equality is different from that of the Liberal Party or NDP and from the ideas of equality that are adopted in this book.

The brief illustration of Conservative Party, Liberal Party, and NDP policies and electoral platforms in Boxes 13.1 and 13.2 shows three different understandings of equality. For the Conservative Party, equality reflects both the ontological view that all people are created equal and the idea of equal opportunity. It assumes that individuals, regardless of their class, age, gender, ethnicity, or race, are on a level playing field and that with similar levels of intelligence and ambition, they will have equal chances of success. The Liberal Party takes the idea of equality one step further. Along with an ontological view of equality, the Liberal Party promotes equality through social-policy attempts to make the playing field more level. Equal opportunities are not assumed, and social programs are established to help produce situations that treat groups equally. Such views of equality have led to equal-opportunity policies and legislation that have helped to open doors to paid work for women and members of ethnic- and visible minority groups in Canada and the United States.

Neither the Conservative Party's nor the Liberal Party's views of equality go far enough, however. For social policy to eradicate social inequality, it must rely on a definition of equality that also considers the outcomes of inequality discussed in this book (e.g., income, occupation, and health). In other words, social policy must be established with the goal of equality of outcomes in mind. The NDP policy statements come closest to this view of equality.

But still more is needed. To adequately lead to equality in outcomes, policy must simultaneously consider the intersecting structures of inequality and not simply consider one particular disadvantaged group at a time. An example of how such policy might be formulated is reproduced here in Box 13.3. On the basis of their research on gender inequality and poverty, Davies, McMullin, and Avison (2001) make policy recommendations that are informed by gender, class, and age. The guiding assumption in this work is that public policy must be situated within a life-course framework (see also V.W.

Box 13.3 Sensitizing Policies to Gender, Class, and Age

The introduction of the Canada Health and Social Transfer (CHST) in 1995 resulted in sweeping changes to the administration and funding of social programs across Canada. These changes jeopardized income security by providing provinces with greater autonomy over spending decisions (thereby reducing national standards for social assistance) and by limiting the availability of funds. The consequences of these changes affect women's economic circumstances in ways that are distinct from those of men. The analyses presented above examined the predictors of low income among women using both quantitative and qualitative data at the national and community level. In combination, our results suggest that in order to reduce low income among women, social policy changes are needed that target individuals at various points in the life cycle, beginning in childhood. The underlying goal of these policy changes should be to make it easier for women to acquire the education and job training that would ensure their economic independence *regardless of their marital and parental status*. In outlining the policy implications of our findings, we address the following questions:

- How can children's needs be better met to ensure greater opportunities to become economically independent adults?
- How can the frequency of unplanned teenage pregnancies be reduced? And how can we ensure that young mothers continue with their schooling and/or acquire life and job skills?

- What changes need to be implemented to social assistance programs to improve economic security and economic independence?
- What do our results reveal about the importance of maternity benefits and employment insurance for the economic security of low income women?
- What other changes should be made to social policies to enhance the economic security of women?

These questions reflect the life course perspective of the study and we address them below in turn.

5.2 Childhood

Although our quantitative results do not reveal a significant relationship between early adversities and low income in adulthood, other research does find that exposure to adversities in childhood and adolescence increases the likelihood of single parenthood. Given that economic disadvantages of single motherhood are widely documented both here and elsewhere, there is additional support for our qualitative findings that family background characteristics portend economic difficulties in adulthood. Specifically, our qualitative results suggest that parental absence is an adversity that makes it very difficult for children to acquire the social capital necessary to obtain life skills and human capital. Thus, within our community are children who, for example, witness and experience violence within their homes, and/or who have alcohol or drug dependent parents; in short, children whose parents for these or various other reasons are unwilling or unable to provide the time and effort necessary to build trusting relationships with their children.

Consequences for children include poor school performance, dropping out of school, running away from home, drug or alcohol dependency, and teenage pregnancy, each of which reduce educational attainment. And as our quantitative results underscore, lack of education increases the risk of low income. Thus, interventions that compensate for parental absence in childhood may significantly reduce economic insecurity in adulthood.

5.2.1 Recommendations

a. Increase the visibility of and access to organizations with a non-punitive mandate that will fill gaps left by parental absence (e.g., respite centres for families and/or Big Sisters, Big Brothers).
- the creation of family respite care centres that would also serve as a sounding board for families experiencing economic and social stress, and would provide a place where parents could temporarily leave children, and obtain information about other available resources within their community to deal with their particular circumstances
- organizations such as Big Sisters foster a mentoring relationship between adult and child, thereby providing important support that may be absent in her home

b. Incorporate education about family violence, sex education, birth control, drug and alcohol abuse within public and high school curriculums.
- educators must be trained to break down resistance to discussing these topics and to encourage open communication among students and teachers
- students must be made aware of agencies and community groups that can provide information and assistance to those who need it

c. Increase government funding to shelters and second stage housing for abused women and children and improve awareness of these options.
- Ensure that women and children who experience violence have a place to go and assistance to start a new life

Contrary to the common view of families as private refuges, economic and social conditions affect family relationships, and, in particular, the well-being of children. Investing in children has long-term implications for the health of a community. Thus, as we recommend above, it is important for government to support communities so that they can assume greater responsibility for the health of their children.

5.3 Young Adulthood

When faced with pregnancy (regardless of whether or not it is accompanied by marriage) the typical response of women is to leave school. While this is risky at any age, it is particularly consequential for young women because they have accumulated fewer years of schooling by the time of their pregnancy. Yet, pregnancy outside of marriage or a cohabiting union is rarely planned. Nonetheless, young girls grow up believing that marriage and motherhood should take precedence over education and careers. Social programs that dismantle the relationship among motherhood, education, and low income promise to improve women's economic security.

The Ontario government has clearly recognized the economic benefits that young mothers would accrue if they stayed in school. In March of this year, the Community and Social Services Minister revealed the details of a new mandatory program, Learning, Earning, and Parenting (LEAP), whose goal is to encourage teen mothers to stay in school. It falls under OntarioWorks and makes enrolment in school mandatory for mothers between the ages of 16 and 17 in order to receive welfare, and provides for transportation costs and offers child care subsidies. An additional requirement is participation in parenting workshops. The program also provides opportunities to develop employment skills and/or transitions to education beyond high school. The government should be commended for its efforts to improve the education of young mothers. Based on the results of our qualitative study, however, we recommend the following changes to this program, and propose an additional intervention that would increase accessibility of education to mothers generally.

5.3.1 Recommendations

1. Inject flexibility into the program by not tying eligibility for General Welfare Assistance to participation in LEAP.

Teen mothers will vary with respect to their readiness to combine schooling and parenting. There is evidence to suggest that teen mothers are selected into this status because of adverse family backgrounds. For those who had trouble managing school before they became pregnant, combining courses and a baby is unlikely to enhance human capital. Thus, LEAP delivery agents should be trained to evaluate the readiness of teen mothers to continue with their schooling, rather than enforce legislation that makes going to school a requirement of General Welfare Assistance.

2. Eliminate day care costs for all teen mothers rather than providing subsidies.
   • make more fully subsidized daycare spots available
   • provide additional funds to accommodate extra caregiving costs when children are sick, when schools are not operating etc. (i.e., professional development days, spring break)

Current LEAP childcare subsidies fall short of need and are problematic because any child care costs reduce the income available for food and shelter.

3. Provide on-site daycare facilities at all adult learning centres, colleges and universities
   • provide services to parents of infants as well as toddlers and preschool children

This will increase accessibility of education by reducing time, cost and stress of taking children first to daycare before going to school, and provide greater contact between children and parents during the day. We view the above recommendations as changes that would eventually be encompassed within a national childcare system.

5.4 Adulthood

5.4.1 Social Assistance

As others have noted and predicted our qualitative data confirm that changes to Ontario General Welfare Assistance since the introduction of the CHST have undermined the economic security of women. Two examples are the cuts to rates and the repeal of the three-year cohabitation rule. As a consequence of the 21.6 percent reduction in welfare rates, many women in our study report moving to less adequate housing, an increase in food bank use, as well as greater personal debt. For example, Carrie (#15) was a single mother with a 5 year old and a 3 year old when her cheque was reduced because of the cuts to General Welfare Assistance. As she explains,

When they took that $300 off me, it was just brutal, absolutely brutal. . . . I couldn't make ends meet. There was no way, I was not going to not have food in my kids mouths. So bills suffered a great deal. I got into financial trouble. I had bill collectors coming after me. I moved out of that apartment because I couldn't afford it. It was a cheap place anyway but I had to move out of there.

The intense stress involved in trying to manage on an inadequate income reduces mothers' real and perceived control over their lives, contributing to a state of helplessness rather than empowerment.

Another example of how changes to Ontario General Welfare Assistance jeopardize women's economic security is the decision to revoke the three-year cohabitation rule. On the one hand, marriage or cohabitation is an obvious pathway off of social assistance. On the other hand, marriage or cohabitation guarantee neither safety nor economic security. Understandably, many women have serious reservations about entering into a marital or cohabiting relationship again. Furthermore, equitable distribution of financial resources does not characterize all relationships. In describing a live-in relationship with a man during the period when the three-year cohabitation rule was in place, Martha (#35) says, 'The thing that made me mad . . . was that he got a really good job and he didn't give me rent. Because he figured he was on the road a lot that he didn't need to give me rent. And I kept asking for money.' The relationship did not last beyond three years and her social assistance was not compromised. Having a period where one can 'try out' relationships and still continue to receive assistance gives women more control over their ability to find a stable, equitable long-term relationship.

5.4.1.1 Recommendations

1. The Federal government should reinstate an open-ended federal–provincial cost-sharing arrangement like the Canada Assistance Plan and, in response, the Ontario government should revoke the changes it has made to General Welfare Assistance since 1995.

While this would be a start, our data underscore the importance of providing mothers on assistance with financial support that better reflects their expenses. Raising the standard of living for low income families would improve their health and well-being, reduce their stress, and therefore improve their ability to parent their children. In essence, governments need to recognize and value the work that mothers do; for example:

2. The Federal government should require that all low income families receive the Canada Child Tax Benefit and encourage provinces to allow those receiving social assistance benefits to keep the full amount.

3. The financial costs of post-secondary education should be reduced for mothers on social assistance by allowing them to receive student assistance in addition to their benefits.

This will ensure that the student loans cover only their educational costs and thus minimize their debt accumulation.

4. Childcare should be free to all parents receiving social assistance or those with comparable incomes.

This would enable women to better their lives by giving them the freedom to explore work and educational opportunities.

While decreasing financial constraints is critical, it must be accompanied by a social support system that recognizes and effectively confronts the disadvantages mothers face as they venture to improve their economic situation. Two problems with the current and previous social assistance systems is that first, they do not recognize the heterogeneity that exists among recipients, and mothers are no exception to this. Second, they do not understand that most women do not need incentives to be independent of assistance, they need opportunities. By emphasizing 'incentives' they grossly underestimate the barriers that exist between incentive and welfare independence and therefore maintain or even undermine the economic insecurity of women.

Many of the barriers facing mothers on social assistance are linked directly to their limited knowledge of available options and resources that would facilitate their entry into the labour force or educational system. Our qualitative results confirm previous research that finds 'information support . . . [to be] the type of support mothers are least likely to receive and with which they are least satisfied'. Limited knowledge of community supports and resources restrict women's ability to help themselves. For example, without up-to-date information, women who have been removed from the workforce for a significant period of time will be unaware of recent changes in the job search process; therefore, they will be less competitive in the job market. Additionally, women are often not aware of the opportunities for upgrading that are available to them. The ability of current social assistance case workers to help clients is limited because of their enormous caseloads and administrative duties. As such, they are unable to offer the individual support, disseminate information or provide the individualized assistance that would more effectively increase opportunities to become employment reliant.

5. Specialized workers are needed to give individualized help to women attempting to become self sufficient.

Communication among these workers, and then between workers and government officials, would convey information about programs that are not achieving their goals, would alert policy makers to program restrictions that limit accessibility and effectiveness, and would identify needs for other services that would enhance exit strategies and simultaneously improve economic security.

5.4.2 Employment Insurance and Maternity Benefits

It is revealing that only three of the women in this sample had ever received employment benefits, and in each instance receiving EI was followed by the receipt of social assistance. This reflects a national pattern whereby men are more likely than women to collect EI benefits, and points to the inapplicability and inaccessibility of EI for women. One of ways in which EI inadvertently excludes women is illustrated by a recent change to the policy that makes employees ineligible if they quit their jobs. This stipulation assumes that there is no valid reason for leaving one's employment. Yet, women in our sample described 'quitting' jobs because of sexual harassment and problems with childcare—situations that reflect broader disadvantages of women in society.

Further, EI is virtually inaccessible to low income mothers. As a monitoring report for Human Resources Development Canada finds, women are disproportionately represented in non-standard jobs and as such often do not accumulate enough hours to qualify for benefits. Further, because EI benefits only replace 55 percent of earnings, they do not offer enough assistance to support a family.

5.4.2.1 Recommendations

1. Consideration should be given to the reasons for quitting a job making allowances for exceptional circumstances.

2. Low income employees should receive 100 per cent of their earnings in employment benefits.

3. Lower the number of hours one has to work in a year to qualify for benefits.

4. Make allowances for repeat users who have family care responsibilities, thereby increasing the value of unpaid labour.

All of the preceding points regarding EI apply to maternity benefits as well because curiously, this program is tied to Employment insurance. Consequently, only those mothers who are strongly attached to the labour market (excluding self-employed women) qualify for benefits. In addition to the above recommendations we argue that:

5. Maternity benefits should be replaced by parental benefits and should be available to everyone, regardless of their labour force attachment. This would require disassociating maternity and paternity benefits from the EI system.

This would compensate women for the economic costs of child-bearing while encouraging a more equitable division of labour among couples. This would also reduce the barriers that prevent men from taking an employment leave to care for their infants, ultimately increasing gender equality and the value of unpaid work.

5.5 General Recommendations

In addition to the recommendations made above, we have also addressed divorce laws, and policies related to workplace flexibility that would further benefit women's economic security. The data from our study lead us to conclude that a concerted effort must be made on various fronts to make women economically independent. All of our suggested changes reflect this view. However, if we had to identify the change that is most necessary, it would be the implementation of a universal childcare system.

There has been a great deal of political rhetoric over the issue of providing stay-at-home mothers with tax relief. This is simply not an issue for low income mothers and such tax-relief would not have an impact on their lives. Further, this proposal is problematic for middle-class women because of the individual nature of the tax filing system. Tax credits would more directly benefit fathers because it is they who have the taxable earnings.

Regardless of social class, married mothers who are not economically independent are at risk for low income if their marriages end. Consequently, any policies aimed at implementing tax credits should be critically reviewed.

More important, in our view, is the necessity for a universal child care system. In addition to the child care system recommendations we have made earlier, we suggest the following:

1. After parental leave, quality child care should be available and affordable to all parents.
2. Transportation of children should be provided by child care centres.
3. Workplaces and educational institutions should receive incentives to implement on-site child care centres.
4. Recognize and support a diversity of child care arrangements to provide parents with as much choice and flexibility as possible concerning their children's needs.

In closing, Canadians should not underestimate the negative consequences of reducing social spending in favour of tax cuts. By undermining the economic security of women, these cuts put all families at risk of experiencing social, economic, mental and physical health hardships. The effects of these hardships on children are particularly worrisome because they will resonate throughout their lives, impairing their potential to be productive citizens of Canadian society.

Source: Davies, McMullin, and Avison (2001: 73–80)

Marshall and Mueller 2002) and must be developed in a way that does not penalize individuals for their responsibilities in processes of reproduction. Another assumption is that men and women should divide equally the work involved in production, reproduction, and distribution. The problem with the policies described in Box 13.3 is that it will be a long time before that is done in Canadian society (see chapter 8). Indeed, to achieve equality of outcomes, changes to social policy will not suffice. Rather, Canadians will need to challenge the ways in which the processes of production, distribution, and reproduction are organized and the dominant ideologies that shape such organization.

References

Abada, Teresa, Feng Hou, and Bali Ram. 2007. 'Racially Mixed Neighborhoods, Perceived Neighborhood Social Cohesion, and Adolescent Health in Canada'. *Social Science and Medicine* 65: 2004–17.

Abercrombie, Nicholas, Stephen Hill, and Bryan S. Turner. 2000. *The Penguin Dictionary of Sociology*. 4th edn. London: Penguin.

Abortion Rights Coalition of Canada. 2008. 'Oppose Bill C-484, "Unborn Victims of Crime Act"'. http://www.arcc-cdac.ca/c484.htm.

Abu-Laban, Yasmeen. 1998. 'Keeping 'Em Out: Gender, Race, and Class Biases in Canadian Immigration Policy'. Pp. 69–82 in Veronica Strong-Boag, Sherrill Grace, Avigail Eisenberg, and Joan Anderson, eds, *Painting the Maple: Essays on Race, Gender, and the Construction of Canada*. Vancouver: UBC Press.

Acker, Joan. 1988. 'Class, Gender and the Relations of Distribution'. *Signs* 13: 473–97.

———. 1989. 'The Problem with Patriarchy'. *Sociology* 23, 2: 235–40.

———. 2000. 'Rewriting Class, Race, and Gender: Problems in Feminist Rethinking'. Chapter 2 in Myra Marx Ferree, Judith Lorber, and Beth Hess, eds, *Revisioning Gender*. New York: Altamira Press.

———. 2006. *Class Questions, Feminist Answers*. Lanham, MD: Rowman & Littlefield.

Adair, Vivyan C. 2001. 'Branded with Infamy: Inscriptions of Poverty and Class in the United States'. *Signs* 27, 2: 451–71.

Adams, Ann, Christopher D. Buckingham, Anje Lindenmeyer, John B. McKinlay, Carol Link, Lisa Marceau, and Sara Arber. 2008. 'The Influence of Patient and Doctor Gender on Diagnosing Coronary Heart Disease'. *Sociology of Health and Illness* 30, 1: 1–18.

Adams, Tracy L. 2000. *A Dentist and a Gentleman: Gender and the Rise of Dentistry in Ontario*. Toronto: University of Toronto Press.

Adams, Tracy L., and Kevin McQuillan. 2000. 'New Jobs, New Workers? Organizations, Restructuring, and Management Hiring Decisions'. *Relations Industrielles/Industrial Relations* 55, 3: 391–412.

Adams, Tracy L., and Sandy Welsh. 2008. *The Organization and Experience of Work*. Toronto: Thomson Nelson.

Adler, Nancy E. 2006. 'When One's Main Effect Is Another's Error: Material vs Psychosocial Explanations of Health Disparities: A Commentary on Macleod et al., "Is Subjective Social Status a More Important Determinant of Health Than Objective Social Status? Evidence from a Prospective Observational Study of Scottish Men" (61(9), 2005, 1916–1929)'. *Social Science and Medicine* 63, 4: 846–50.

Adler, Nancy E., and David H. Rehkopf. 2008. 'U.S. Disparities in Health: Descriptions, Causes, and

Mechanisms'. *The Annual Review of Public Health* 29: 235–52.

Agrell, Siri. 2007. 'Unmarried and Unabashed'. *The Globe and Mail*, 13 September.

Aguiar, Luis M. 2001. 'Whiteness in White Academia'. Pp. 177–92 in Carl E. James and Adrienne Shadd, eds, *Talking about Identity: Encounters in Race, Ethnicity, and Language*. Toronto: Between the Lines.

Albanese, Patrizia. 2005. 'Ethnic Families'. Chapter 6 in Maureen Baker, ed., *Families: Changing Trends in Canada*. Toronto: McGraw-Hill Ryerson.

Albrecht, Don E. 2007. 'Income Inequality: The Implications of Economic Structure and Social Conditions'. *Sociological Spectrum* 27: 165–81.

Alcoba, Natalie. 2008. 'Making the Grade; Parents Going to Great Lengths to Buy Homes in Hot School Districts'. *National Post*, May 17.

Ali, Jennifer, and Edward Grabb. 1998. 'Ethnic Origin, Class Origin and Educational Attainment in Canada: Further Evidence on the Mosaic Thesis'. *Journal of Canadian Studies* 33, 1: 3–21.

Ali, Jennifer, Sarah McDermott, and Ronald G. Gravel. 2004. 'Recent Research on Immigrant Health from Statistics Canada's Population Surveys'. *Canadian Journal of Public Health* 95, 3: 19–13.

Allahar, Anton. 1995. *Sociology and the Periphery: Theories and Issues*. 2nd edn. Toronto: Garamond Press.

Allahar, Anton, and James E. Côté. 1994. *Generation on Hold: Coming of Age in the Late Twentieth Century*. Toronto: Stoddart.

———. 1998. *Richer and Poorer: Social Inequality in Canada*. Toronto: Lorimer.

Allard, Yvon E., Russell Wilkins, and Jean-Marie Berthelot. 2004. 'Premature Mortality in Health Regions with High Aboriginal Populations'. *Health Reports* 15, 1: 51–60. Statistics Canada Catalogue no. 82-003.

Amnesty International. 2004. *Stolen Sisters: Discrimination and Violence against Indigenous Women in Canada*. London: Amnesty International.

Anand, Sonia S., Salim Yusuf, Ruby Jacobs, A. Darlene Davis, Quilong Yi, Hertzel Gerstein, Patricia A. Montague, and Eva Lonn. 2001. 'Risk Factors, Atherosclerosis, and Cardiovascular Disease among Aboriginal People in Canada: The Study of Health Assessment and Risk Evaluation in Aboriginal Peoples (SHARE-AP)'. *The Lancet* 358: 1147–53.

Anderson, Alan. 1992. 'Policing Native People: Native Militancy and Canadian Militarianism'. Chapter 19 in Vic Satzewich, ed., *Deconstructing a Nation: Immigration, Multiculturalism and Racism in '90s Canada*. Halifax: Fernwood/Saskatoon: Social Research Unit, Department of Sociology, University of Saskatchewan.

Anderson, D.K., and D.G. Saunders. 2000. 'Leaving an Abusive Partner: An Empirical Review of Predictors, the Process of Leaving, and Psychological Well-Being'. *Trauma, Violence, and Abuse* 4, 2: 163–91.

Anderson, Norman B., and Cheryl A. Armstead. 1995. 'Toward Understanding the Association of Socioeconomic Status and Health: A New Challenge for the Biopsychosocial Approach'. *Psychosomatic Medicine* 57: 213–25.

Aneshensel, Carol S., and Clea A. Sucoff. 1996. 'The Neighborhood Context of Adolescent Mental Health'. *Journal of Health and Social Behavior* 37, 4: 293–310.

Anthias, Floya. 1992. 'Connecting "Race" and Ethnic Phenomena'. *Sociology* 26, 3: 421–38.

Aragones, N., M. Pollan, and P. Gustavsson. 2002. 'Stomach Cancer and Occupation in Sweden: 1971–89'. *Occupational and Environmental Medicine* 59, 5: 329–37.

Arar, Maher. 2008. 'With Persistence, the Truth Will Come Out'. *The Globe and Mail*, 17 June.

Arat-Koc, Sedef. 1995. 'The Politics of Family and Immigration in the Subordination of Domestic Workers in Canada'. In E.D. Nelson and B.W. Robinson, eds, *Gender in the 1990s: Images, Realities and Issues*. Toronto: Nelson.

———. 1997. 'Immigration Policies, Migrant Domestic Workers, and the Definition of Citizenship in Canada'. Pp. 224–36 in Veronica Strong-Boag and Anita Clair Fellman, eds, *Rethinking Canada: The Promise of Women's History*, 3rd edn. Toronto: Oxford University Press.

———. 2001. 'The Politics of Family and Immigration in the Subordination of Domestic Workers in Canada'. Chapter 23 in Bonnie J. Fox, ed., *Family Patterns, Gender Relations*. Toronto: Oxford University Press.

———. 2006. 'Whose Social Reproduction? Transnational Motherhood and Challenges to Feminist Political Economy'. Chapter 3 in K. Bezanson and M. Luxton, eds, *Social Reproduction: Feminist Political Economy Challenges Neo-Liberalism*. Montreal: McGill-Queen's University Press.

Arber, Sara, and Helen Cooper. 1999. 'Gender Differences in Health in Later Life: The New Paradox?' *Social Science and Medicine* 48, 1: 61–76.

Archer, Margaret. 1995. *Realist Social Theory: The Morphogenetic Approach*. Cambridge: Cambridge University Press.

———. 2000. *Being Human: The Problem of Agency*. Cambridge: Cambridge University Press.

———. 2007. Making Our Way through the World: Human Reflexivity and Social Mobility. Cambridge: Cambridge University Press.

Armstrong, Pat. 1997. 'The State and Pay Equity: Juggling Similarity and Difference, Meaning, and Structures'. Chapter 10 in Patricia M. Evans and Gerda R. Wekerle, eds, *Women and the Canadian Welfare State: Challenges and Change*. Toronto: University of Toronto Press.

Armstrong, Pat, and M. Patricia Connelly. 1999. 'Introduction: Feminism, Political Economy and the State: Contested Terrain'. Chapter 1 in Pat Armstrong and M. Patricia Connelly, eds, *Feminism, Political Economy and the State: Contested Terrain*. Toronto: Canadian Scholars' Press.

Armstrong, Robin. 1999. 'Mapping the Conditions of First Nations Communities'. *Canadian Social Trends*, no. 55: 14–18.

Aronson, Jane. 1992. 'Women's Sense of Responsibility for the Care of Old People: But Who Else Is Going to Do It?' *Gender and Society* 6: 8–29.

Aronson, Jane, Cindy Thornewell, and Karen Williams. 1995. 'Wife Assault in Old Age: Coming out of Obscurity'. *Canadian Journal on Aging* 14, suppl. 2: 72–88.

Asanin, Jennifer, and Kathi Wilson. 2008. '"I Spent Nine Years Looking for a Doctor": Exploring Access to Health Care among Immigrants in Mississauga, Ontario, Canada'. *Social Science and Medicine* 66: 1271–83.

Askam, Janet. 1995. 'The Married Lives of Older People'. Pp. 86–97 in Sara Arber and Jay Ginn, eds, *Connecting Gender and Ageing: A Sociological Approach*. Buckingham, UK: Open University Press.

Auger, Nathalie, Marie-France Raynault, Richard Lessard, and Robert Choiniere. 2004. 'Income and Health in Canada'. Chapter 3 in Dennis Raphael, ed., *Social Determinants of Health: Canadian Perspectives*, 2nd edn. Toronto: Canadian Scholars' Press.

Avison, William R., Jennifer Ali, and David Walters. 2007. 'Family Structure, Stress, and Psychological Distress: A Demonstration of the Impact of Differential Exposure'. *Journal of Health and Social Behavior* 48, 3: 301–17.

Avison, William R., and Lorraine Davies. 2005. 'Family Structure, Gender, and Health in the Context of the Life Course'. *Journals of Gerontology* 60B, spec. iss. 2: 113–16.

Avison, William R., and Ian H. Gotlib. 1994. 'Introduction and Overview'. Chapter 1 in William R. Avison and Ian H. Gotlib, eds, *Stress and Mental Health: Contemporary Issues and Prospects for the Future*. New York: Plenum Press.

Avison, William R., Terrance J. Wade, and Cathy F. Thorpe. 1996. 'Families' Experiences of Unemployment: Mental Health Consequences for Husbands and Wives'. Paper presented to the American Sociological Association, New York.

Bacigalupo, Mardy. 2003. 'How Did Your School Do? Overall Tests Results Show Improvement for City'. *The Londoner*, 30 January.

Bailis, Daniel S., Judith G. Chipperfield, and Tiffany R. Helgason. 2008. 'Collective Self-esteem and the Onset of Chronic Conditions and Reduced Activity in a Longitudinal Study of Aging'. *Social Science and Medicine* 66: 1818–27.

Baldus, Bernhard, and Meenaz Kassam. 1996. '"Make Me Truthful, Good and Mild": Values in

Nineteenth-Century Ontario Schoolbooks'. *Canadian Journal of Sociology* 21, 3: 327–57.

Baliunas, Dolly, Jayadeep Patra, Jürgen Rehm, Svetlana Popova, Murry Kaiserman, and Benjamin Taylor. 2007. 'Smoking-Attributable Mortality and Expected Years of Life Lost in Canada 2002: Conclusions for Prevention and Policy'. *Chronic Diseases in Canada* 27, 4: 154–62. Ottawa: Public Health Agency of Canada.

Ballantyne, Peri J. 1999. 'The Social Determinants of Health: A Contribution to the Analysis of Gender Differences in Health and Illness'. *Scandinavian Journal of Public Health* 27: 290–5.

Barndt, Deborah. 2002. 'Fruits of Injustice: Women in the Post-NAFTA Food System'. *Canadian Woman Studies* 21/22, 4/1: 82–8.

Barnes, Barry. 2000. Understanding Agency: Social Theory and Responsible Action. London: Sage.

Basran, Gurcharn S., and Li Zong. 1998. 'Devaluation of Foreign Credentials as Perceived by Visible Minority Professional Immigrants'. *Canadian Ethnic Studies* 30, 3: 6–23.

Beagan, Brenda L. 2000. 'Neutralizing Differences: Producing Neutral Doctors for (Almost) Neutral Patients'. *Social Science and Medicine* 51, 8: 1253–65.

Beaujot, Roderic. 2000. *Earning and Caring in Canadian Families*. Toronto: Broadview Press.

Beaujot, Roderic, and Robert Andersen. 2007. 'Time-Crunch: Impact of Time Spent in Paid and Unpaid Work, and Its Division'. *Canadian Journal of Sociology* 32, 3: 295–315.

Beaujot, Roderic, and Don Kerr. 2003. *Population Change in Canada*. Toronto: Oxford University Press.

Beaujot, Roderic, Kevin McQuillan, and Zenaida Ravanera. 2007. 'Population Change in Canada to 2017 and Beyond: The Challenges of Policy Adaptation'. *Horizons* 9, 4: 3–12.

Beck, Urlich. 1992. *Risk Society*. London: Sage.

———. 1999. *World Risk Society*. Cambridge: Polity Press.

———. 2000. *The Brave New World of Work*. Translated by Patrick Camiller. New York: Polity Press.

———, and Elizabeth Beck-Gernsheim. 2002. *Individualization*. London: Sage.

———, Wolfgang Bonss, and Christoph Lau. 2003. 'The Theory of Reflexive Modernization: Problematic, Hypotheses and Research Programme'. *Theory, Culture & Society* 20, 2: 1–33.

Bedard, Gabriel. 2000. 'Deconstructing Whiteness: Pedagogical Implications for Anti-racism Education'. Chapter 2 in George J. Sefa Dei and Agnes Calliste, eds, *Power, Knowledge, and Anti-racism Education: A Critical Reader*. Halifax: Fernwood.

Bell, Daniel. 1973. *The Coming of Post-industrial Society*. New York: Basic Books.

Bengtson, V.L., T.M. Parrott, and E.O. Burgess. 1994. 'The Third Generation of Theories in Social Gerontology'. Paper presented to the Annual Scientific Meeting of the Gerontological Society of America, 18–22 November, Atlanta.

Benoit, Cecilia, and Dena Carroll. 2001. 'Marginalized Voices from Vancouver's Downtown Eastside: Aboriginal Women Speak about Their Health Care Experiences'. Centres of Excellence for Women's Health, *Research Bulletin* 1, 2: 6–7.

Berger, Joseph, Anne Motte, and Andrew Parkin. 2007. *The Price of Knowledge: Access and Student Finance in Canada*. 3rd edn. Montreal: Canada Millennium Scholarship Foundation.

Berger, Peter L., and Thomas Luckmann. 1967. *The Social Construction of Reality*. New York: Doubleday.

Bernard, Paul, Rana Charafeddinea, Katherine L. Frohlich, Mark Daniela, Yan Kestensa, and Louise Potvin. 2007. 'Health Inequalities and Place: A Theoretical Conception of Neighbourhood'. *Social Science and Medicine* 65: 1839–62.

Bernard, Andre, and Chris Li. 2006. *Death of a Spouse: The Impact on Income for Senior Men and Women*. Analysis in Brief. Statistics Canada Catalogue no. 11-621-MIE200604. Ottawa: Statistics Canada.

Bernhard, Judith K., and Marlinda Freire. 1999. 'What Is My Child Learning at Elementary School? Culturally Contested Issues between Teachers and Latin American Families'. *Canadian Ethnic Studies* 31, 3: 72–94.

Betcherman, Gordon, and Norman Leckie. 1995. 'Age

Structure of Employment in Industries and Occupations'. Ottawa: Applied Research Branch, Human Resources Development Canada (R-96-7E).

Betts, Julian, Christopher Ferrall, and Ross Finnie (2007). The Role of University Characteristics in Determining Post-graduation Outcomes: Panel Evidence from Three Recent Canadian Cohorts. Analytical Studies Branch Research Paper Series. Statistics Canada Catalogue no. 11F0019MIE, no. 292. Ottawa: Minister of Industry.

Bittle, Steven, and Laureen Snider. 2006. 'From Manslaughter to Preventable Accident: Shaping Corporate Criminal Liability'. *Law & Policy* 28, 4: 470–96.

Black, S.M., and C.E. Hill. 1984. 'The Psychological Well-Being of Women in Their Middle Years'. *Psychology of Women Quarterly* 8: 282–91.

Blackwell, Judith. 1998. 'Making the Grade against the Odds: Women as University Undergraduates'. Pp. 60–71 in Jackie Stalker and Susan Prentice, eds, *Illusion of Inclusion: Women in Post-secondary Education*. Halifax: Fernwood.

Bloch, Gary. 2007. 'Poverty Takes Huge Toll on Health'. *The Toronto Star*, 10 September.

Bohatyretz, Sandra, and Garth Lipps. 1999. 'Diversity in the Classroom: Characteristics of Elementary Students Receiving Special Education'. *Education Quarterly Review* 6, 2: 7–19. Statistics Canada Catalogue no. 81-003.

Bolaria, B. Singh, and Peter Li. 1988. 'Capitalist Expansion and Immigrant Labour: Chinese in Canada'. Chapter 5 in B. Singh Bolaria and Peter S. Li, eds, *Racial Oppression in Canada*, 2nd edn. Toronto: Garamond Press.

Bonilla-Silva, Eduardo. 1997. 'Rethinking Racism: Toward a Structural Interpretation'. *American Sociological Review* 62: 465–80.

———. 1999. 'The Essential Social Fact of Race'. *American Sociological Review* 64: 899–906.

Boothby, Daniel, and Torben Drewes. 2006. 'Postsecondary Education in Canada: Returns to University, College and Trades Education'. *Canadian Public Policy / Analyse de Politiques* 32, 1: 1–21.

Borrows, John. 2001. 'Domesticating Doctrines:

Aboriginal Peoples after the Royal Commission'. *McGill Law Journal* 46: 615–61.

Bourdieu, Pierre. 1977. *Outline of a Theory of Practice*. Cambridge: Cambridge University Press.

———. 1998. *Practical Reason: On the Theory of Action*. Stanford, CA: Stanford University Press.

Bowlby, Jeffrey W., and Kathryn McMullen. 2002. *At a Crossroads: First Results for the 18 to 20-Year-Old Cohort of the Youth in Transition Survey*. Catalogue no. RH64-12/2002E. Ottawa: Human Resources and Development Canada.

———. 2005. 'Provincial Drop-out Rates: Trends and Consequences.' *Education Matters: Insights on Education, Learning and Training in Canada* 2, 4. Statistics Canada Catalogue no. 81-004-XIE.

Boyd, Chris, Jina Y. Zhang-Salomons, Patti A. Groome, and William J. Mackillop. 1999. 'Associations between Community Income and Cancer Survival in Ontario, Canada, and the United States'. *Journal of Clinical Oncology* 17, 7: 2244–55.

Boyko, John. 1995. Last Steps to Freedom: The Evolution of Canadian Racism. Winnipeg: Watson and Dwyer.

Bradshaw, James. 2008. 'Afrocentric Schools Not about Segregation, Advocates Argue'. *The Globe and Mail*, 8 February.

Braverman, Harry. 1974. Labor and Monopoly Capital: The Degradation of Work in the Twentieth Century. New York: Monthly Review Press.

Breitkreuz, Rhonda S. 2005. 'Engendering Citizenship? A Critical Feminist Analysis of Canadian Welfare-to-Work Policies and the Employment Experiences of Lone Mothers'. *Journal of Sociology and Social Welfare* 32, 2: 147–65.

Briggs, N.C, R.S. Levine, H.I. Hall, O. Cosby, E.A., Brann, and C.H. Hennekens. 2003. 'Occupational Risk Factors for Selected Cancers among African American and White Men in the United States'. *American Journal of Public Health* 93, 10: 1748–52.

Brodie, Janine. 1999. 'Neo-liberalism and the Rise of the Citizen as Consumer'. Chapter 2 in Dave Broad and Wayne Antony, eds, *Citizens or Consumers? Social Policy in a Market Society*. Halifax:

Fernwood.

Brodie, Janine, and Isabella Bakker. 2007. Canada's Social Policy Regime and Women: An Assessment of the Last Decade. Ottawa: Status of Women.

Bruno-Jofre, Rosa, and Dick Henley. 2000. 'Public Schooling in English Canada: Addressing Difference in the Context of Globalization'. *Canadian Ethnic Studies* 32, 1: 38–54.

Bryant, Toba. 2004. 'Housing and Health'. Pp. 217–32 in Dennis Raphael, ed., *Social Determinants of Health: Canadian Perspectives*. Toronto: Canadian Scholars' Press.

Brzozowski, Jodi-Anne, Andrea Taylor-Butts, and Sara Johnson. 2006. 'Victimization and Offending among the Aboriginal Population in Canada'. *Juristat* 26, 3: 14. Statistics Canada Catalogue no. 85-002-XIE.

Buckley, Neil J., Frank T. Denton, A. Leslie Robb, and Byron G. Spencer. 2006. 'Socio-economic Influences on the Health of Older Canadians: Estimates Based on Two Longitudinal Surveys'. *Canadian Public Policy* 32, 1: 59–83.

Burton, Clare. 1985. *Subordination: Feminism and Social Theory*. Sydney, Australia: Allen and Unwin.

Busby, Nicole. 2006. 'Affirmative Action in Women's Employment: Lessons from Canada'. *Journal of Law and Society* 33, 1: 42–58.

Bussiere, Patrick, Tamara Knighton, and Dianne Pennock. 2007. Measuring Up: Canadian Results of the OECD PISA Study, The Performance of Canada's Youth in Science, Reading and Mathematics: 2006 First Results for Canadians Aged 15. Statistics Canada Catalogue no. 81-590-XPE, no. 3. Ottawa: Minister of Industry.

Butlin, George. 2001. 'Bachelor's Graduates Who Pursue Further Postsecondary Education'. *Education Quarterly Review* 7, 2: 22–42. Statistics Canada Catalogue no. 81-003.

Butlin, George, and Jillian Oderkirk. 1997. 'Educational Attainment: A Key to Autonomy and Authority in the Workplace'. *Education Quarterly Review* 4, 1: 32–52. Statistics Canada Catalogue no. 81-003.

Cairney, John, and Robert Arnold. 1996. 'Social Class, Health and Aging: Socioeconomic Determinants of Self-Reported Morbidity among the Non-institutionalized Elderly in Canada'. *Canadian Journal of Public Health* 87, 3: 199–203.

Calasanti, Toni M. 1996. 'Incorporating Diversity: Meaning, Levels of Research, and Implications for Theory'. *The Gerontologist* 36: 147–56.

———. 2004. 'Feminist Gerontology and Old Men'. *Journals of Gerontology, Social Sciences* 59B, 6: S305–14.

———, and Kathleen E. Slevin. 2001. *Gender, Social Inequalities, and Aging*. Walnut Creek, CA: Altamira Press.

———. 2006. Age Matters: Realigning Feminist Thinking. New York: Routledge.

Calliste, Agnes. 1996. 'Race, Gender and Canadian Immigration Policy: Blacks from the Caribbean, 1900–1932'. Pp. 80–98 in Joy Parr and Mark Rosenfeld, eds, *Gender and History in Canada*. Toronto: Copp Clark.

———. 2001. 'Black Families in Canada: Exploring the Interconnections of Race, Class, and Gender'. Chapter 26 in Bonnie J. Fox, ed., *Family Patterns, Gender Relations*. Toronto: Oxford University Press.

Campaign 2000. 2007. *2007 Report Card on Child and Family Poverty in Canada*. Toronto: Family Service Association of Toronto. www.campaign2000.ca.

Canadian Council on Learning. 2007. Post-secondary Education in Canada: Strategies for Success: Report on Learning in Canada 2007. Ottawa: CCL.

———. 2008. 'High School Drop-out Rate.' Learning to Know CLI Indicator Fact Sheets. Ottawa: Canadian Council on Learning. www.ccl-cca.ca.

Canadian Council on Social Development. 2007a. *Age, Gender and Family: Urban Poverty in Canada, 2000*. Ottawa: Canadian Council on Social Development. http://www.ccsd.ca/pubs/2007/upp/age_gender_family.pdf.

———. 2007b. 'Economic Security Fact Sheet #2: Poverty'. Ottawa: Canadian Council on Social Development. http://www.ccsd.ca/factsheets/economic_security/poverty/index.htm, accessed January 2008.

Canadian Federation for Sexual Health. 2008. 'Bill C484 "Unborn Victims of Crime Act" Position Statement'. http://www.cfsh.ca/About_CFSH/Positions-Statements/C-484.html.

Canadian Institute for Health Information. 2004. *Improving the Health of Canadians*. Ottawa: Canadian Institute for Health Information.

———. 2006a. How Healthy Are Rural Canadians: An Assessment of Their Health Status and Health Determinants. Ottawa: Canadian Institute for Health Information.

———. 2006b. Improving the Health of Canadians: An Introduction to Health in Urban Places. Ottawa: Canadian Institute for Health Information.

———. 2007. Improving the Health of Canadians: Mental Health and Homelessness. Ottawa: Canadian Institute for Health Information.

———. 2008. *Health Indicators 2008*. Ottawa: Canadian Institute for Health Information.

Canadian Policy Research Networks. 2002. *Access to Postsecondary Education in Canada: Fact and Gaps*. Prepared by Sussex Circle Inc. Ottawa: Canadian Policy Research Networks. http://www.cprn.org/doc.cfm?doc=59&l=en.

Canadian Population Health Initiative. 2007. *Proceedings Report: Reducing Gaps in Health: Knowledge Synthesis, Translation and Exchange*. Ottawa: Canadian Institute for Health Information.

Cancian, Francesca M., and Stacey Oliker. 2000. *Caring and Gender*. Walnut Creek, CA: Altamira Press.

Carr, Paul R., and Thomas R. Klassen. 1996. 'The Role of Racial Minority Teachers in Anti-racist Education'. *Canadian Ethnic Studies* 28, 2: 126–38.

Carrier, Patricia Anne, and Lorraine Davies. 1999. 'The Importance of Power Relations for the Division of Household Labour'. *Canadian Journal of Sociology* 24, 1: 35–51.

Casper, Lynne M., Sara S. McLanahan, and Irwin Garfinkel. 1994. 'The Gender-Poverty Gap: What We Can Learn from Other Countries'. *American Sociological Review* 59: 594–605.

Casper, Monica J. 1998. *The Making of the Unborn Patient: A Social Anatomy of Fetal Surgery*. New Brunswick, NJ: Rutgers University Press.

Cassell, Philip, ed. 1993. *The Giddens Reader*. Stanford, CA: Stanford University Press.

CCL. See Canadian Council on Learning.

CCSD. See Canadian Council on Social Development.

Chae, David H., David T. Takeuchi, Elizabeth M. Barbeau, Gary G. Bennett, Jane Lindsey, and Nancy Krieger. 2008. 'Unfair Treatment, Racial/Ethnic Discrimination, Ethnic Identification, and Smoking among Asian Americans in the National Latino and Asian American Study'. *American Journal of Public Health* 98, 3: 485–92.

Chafetz, Janet Saltzman. 1990. Gender Equity: An Integrated Theory of Stability and Change. Newbury Park, NJ: Sage.

Charness, N., Dykstra, K., and Philips, C. 1995. *Luminance and Legibility in the Workplace*. Paper presented to the Canadian Aging Research Network 5th Annual Colloquium, Toronto.

Chen, Edith. 2004. 'Why Socioeconomic Status Affects the Health of Children: A Psychosocial Perspective'. *Current Directions in Psychological Science* 13, 3: 112–15.

Chen, Jiajian, and Feng Hou. 2002. 'Unmet Needs for Health Care'. *Health Reports* 13, 2: 23–33. Statistics Canada Catalogue no. 82-003.

Chen, Jiajian, Edward Ng, and Russell Wilkins. 1996. 'The Health of Canada's Immigrants in 1994–95'. *Health Reports* 7, 4: 33–45. Statistics Canada Catalogue no. 82-003.

Chen, Jiajian, Russell Wilkins, and Edward Ng. 1996. 'Health Expectancy by Immigrant Status, 1986 and 1991'. *Health Reports* 8, 3: 29–37. Statistics Canada Catalogue no. 82-003.

Chung, Lucy. 2006. 'Education and Earnings'. *Perspectives on Labour and Income*. Statistics Canada Catalogue no. 75-001-XIE.

Chunn, D.E. 2000. '"Politicizing the Personal": Feminism, Law, and Public Policy'. Pp. 225–59 in Nancy Mandell and Ann Duffy, eds, *Canadian Families: Diversity, Conflict and Change*, 2nd edn. Toronto: Harcourt, Brace.

Church, Elizabeth. 2000. 'Balancing Work and Family: Firms Still Struggling with How to Help

Workers Who Care for Others'. *The Globe and Mail*, 28 June.

CIHI. *See* Canadian Institute for Health Information.

Clark, Warren. 2000. '"Education" in 100 Years of . . .' *Canadian Social Trends* 58: 3–6. Statistics Canada Catalogue no. 11-008.

———. 2001. '100 Years of Education'. *Education Quarterly Review* 7, 3: 18–24. Statistics Canada Catalogue no. 81-003.

Clement, Wallace, and John Myles. 1994. *Relations of Ruling: Class and Gender in Postindustrial Societies*. Montreal: McGill-Queen's University Press.

Codjoe, Henry M. 2001. 'Fighting a "Public Enemy" of Black Academic Achievement: The Persistence of Racism and the Schooling Experiences of Black Students in Canada'. *Race, Ethnicity, and Education* 4: 343–75.

Collins, Patricia Hill. 1990. Black Feminist Thought: Knowledge, Consciousness, and the Politics of Empowerment. Boston: Unwin Hyman.

———. 2000. Black Feminist Thought: Knowledge, Consciousness, and the Politics of Empowerment. 2nd edn. New York: Routledge.

Coltrane, Scott. 2000. *Gender and Families*. Walnut Creek, CA: Altamira Press.

Comacchio, Cynthia. 1993. Nations Are Built of Babies: Saving Ontario's Mothers and Children, 1900–1940. Montreal: McGill-Queen's University Press.

Conley, James. 1999. 'Working-Class Formation in Twentieth-Century Canada'. Chapter 3 in James E. Curtis, Edward G. Grabb, and Neil L. Guppy, eds, *Social Inequality in Canada: Patterns, Problems, and Policies*. Scarborough, ON: Prentice Hall Allyn and Bacon Canada.

Connidis, Ingrid Arnet. 1982. 'Women and Retirement: The Effect of Multiple Careers on Retirement Adjustment'. *Canadian Journal on Aging* 1, 3/4: 17–27.

———. 2009. *Family Ties and Aging*. 2nd edn. Thousand Oaks, CA: Sage.

Connidis, Ingrid Arnet, and Julie Ann McMullin. 1994. 'Social Support in Older Age: Assessing the Impact of Marital and Parent Status'. *Canadian Journal on Aging* 13, 4: 510–27.

———. 2002. 'Sociological Ambivalence and Family Ties: A Critical Perspective'. *Journal of Marriage and Family* 64, 3: 558–67.

Conrad, Peter. 2007. The Medicalization of Society: On the Transformation of Human Conditions into Treatable Disorders. Baltimore, MD: Johns Hopkins University Press.

Cooke, M. 2005. 'Trajectories through Lone Motherhood, Social Assistance, and Work'. Paper presented to the annual meeting of the Canadian Anthropology and Sociology Association, 31 May–3 June, London, ON.

Cooper, Helen. 2002. 'Investigating Socio-economic Explanations for Gender and Ethnic Inequalities in Health'. *Social Science and Medicine* 54, 5: 693–706.

Côté, James E. 2000. Arrested Adulthood: The Changing Nature of Maturity and Identity. New York: New York University Press.

Côté, James E., and Anton L. Allahar. 1994. *Generation on Hold: Coming of Age in the Late Twentieth Century*. Toronto: Stoddart.

———. 2006. *Critical Youth Studies: A Canadian Focus*. Toronto: Pearson Prentice Hall.

Cott, Nancy F. 2001. 'Domesticity'. Chapter 9 in Bonnie J. Fox, ed., *Family Patterns, Gender Relations*. Toronto: Oxford University Press.

Courtenay, Will H. 2000. 'Constructions of Masculinity and Their Influence on Men's Well-Being: A Theory of Gender and Health'. *Social Science and Medicine* 50, 10: 1385–401.

CPRN. *See* Canadian Policy Research Networks.

Craig, Gerald. 1968. *Upper Canada: The Formative Years—1784–1841*. Toronto: McClelland and Stewart.

Crane, David. 2008. 'A Painful Time for Canada's Industrial Sector'. *The Toronto Star*, 17 February.

Creese, Gillian. 1996. 'Gendering Collective Bargaining: From Men's Rights to Women's Issues'. *Canadian Review of Sociology and Anthropology* 33, 4: 437–56.

———. 1999. Contracting Masculinity: Gender, Class, and Race in a White-Collar Union,

1944–1994. Toronto: Oxford University Press.

Crocker, D., A. Dobrowolsky, E. Keeble, C.C. Moncayo, and E. Tastsoglou. 2007. Security and Immigration, Changes and Challenges: Immigrant and Ethnic Communities in Atlantic Canada, Presumed Guilty? Ottawa: Status of Women.

Crompton, Susan. 2000. '"Health" in 100 Years of . . .' *Canadian Social Trends*, Winter: 12–17. Statistics Canada Catalogue no. 11-008.

Cruz, Grace T., Josefina N. Natividad, and Yashuiko Saito. 2007. 'Active Life Expectancy and Functional Health Transition among Filipino Older People'. *Canadian Studies in Population* 34, 1: 29–47.

Curtis, Bruce, D.W. Livingstone, and David Smaller. 1992. *Stacking the Deck: The Streaming of Working-Class Kids in Ontario Schools*. Toronto: Our Schools/ Our Selves Education Foundation.

Curtis, James E., Edward G. Grabb, and Neil L. Guppy, eds. 2003. *Social Inequality in Canada: Patterns, Problems, and Policies*. 4th edn. Scarborough, ON: Pearson Education Canada.

Curtis, Lori J., and William J. MacMinn. 2008. 'Health Care Utilization in Canada: Twenty-Five Years of Evidence'. *Canadian Public Policy* 34, 1: 65–87.

Curtis, Lori J., and Michael Pennock. 2006. 'Social Assistance, Lone Parents and Health: What Do We Know, Where Do We Go?' *Canadian Journal of Public Health* 97, suppl. 3: 4–10.

Curtis, Sarah, and Kim Lawson. 2000. 'Gender, Ethnicity and Self-Reported Health: The Case of African-Caribbean Populations in London'. *Social Science and Medicine* 50, 3: 365–85.

Dannefer, D. 1984. 'Adult Development and Social Theory: A Paradigmatic Reappraisal'. *American Sociological Review* 49: 100–16.

Dannefer, D., and R.R. Sell. 1988. 'Age Structure, the Life Course, and Aged Heterogeneity: Prospects for Research and Theory'. *Comprehensive Gerontology* B2: 1–10.

Das Gupta, Tania. 1995. 'Families of Native Peoples, Immigrants, and People of Colour'. Pp. 141–74 in Nancy Mandell and Ann Duffy, eds, *Canadian Families: Diversity, Conflict and Change*. Toronto:

Harcourt, Brace.

———. 1996. *Racism and Paid Work*. Toronto: Garamond Press.

———. 2000. 'Families of Native Peoples, Immigrants and People of Colour'. Pp. 215–30 in Barbara A. Crow and Lise Gotell, eds, *Open Boundaries: A Canadian Women's Studies Reader*. Toronto: Prentice-Hall.

———. 2002. 'Racism in Nursing'. Chapter 5 in Merle Jacobs, ed., *Is Anyone Listening? Women, Work, and Society*. Toronto: Women's Press.

Davies, Lorraine, Marilyn Ford-Gilboe, and Joanne Hammerton. 2009. 'Gender Inequality and Patterns of Abuse Post Leaving'. *Journal of Family Violence* 24, 1: 27–39.

Davies, Lorraine, and Donna D. McAlpine. 1998. 'Gendered Work and Family Relations: The Impact of Unemployment'. Paper presented to Restructuring Work and the Life Course: An International Symposium, Toronto, May.

Davies, Lorraine, Julie Ann McMullin, and William R. Avison. 2001. *Social Policy, Gender Inequality and Poverty*. Ottawa: Status of Women Canada.

Davies, Scott, and Neil Guppy. 1997. 'Fields of Study, College Selectivity, and Student Inequalities'. *Social Forces* 73, 4: 131–51.

———. 2006. The Schooled Society: An Introduction to the Sociology of Education. Don Mills, ON: Oxford University Press.

———, Clayton Mosher, and Bill O'Grady. 1996. 'Educating Women: Gender Inequalities among Canadian University Graduates'. *Canadian Review of Sociology and Anthropology* 33, 2: 127–43.

Davis, Kingsley, and Wilbert E. Moore. 1945. 'Some Principles of Stratification'. *American Sociological Review* 10: 242–9.

Dean, Kathryn. 1992. 'Double Burdens of Work: The Female Work and Health Paradox'. *Health Promotion International* 7, 1: 17–25.

Dei, George J. Sefa. 1993. 'The Challenges of Anti-racist Education in Canada'. *Canadian Ethnic Studies* 25, 2: 36–51.

———. 1996. Anti-racism Education: Theory and Practice. Halifax: Fernwood.

————. 2006. 'Black-Focused Schools: A Call for Revisioning'. *Education Canada* 46, 3: 27–31.

DeKeseredy, W.S., and M.D. Schwartz. 1998. *Women Abuse on Campus: Results from the Canadian National Survey*. Thousand Oaks, CA: Sage.

Dekkers, Midas. 2000. *The Way of All Flesh: A Celebration of Decay*. Translated by Sherry Marx-Macdonald. New York: Farrar, Straus, and Giroux.

Denton, F.T., Steven Prus, and Vivienne Walters. 2004. 'Gender Differences in Health: A Canadian Study of the Psychosocial, Behavioural and Structural Determinants of Health'. *Social Science and Medicine* 58: 2585–600.

Denton, Margaret, and Linda Boos. 2007. 'The Gender Wealth Gap: Structural and Material Constraints and Implications for Later Life'. *Journal of Women & Aging* 19, 3–4: 105–20.

deRouche, Constance P. 2001. 'Workfare's Cousin: Exploring a Labour-Force Enhancement Experiment in Cape Breton'. *Canadian Review of Sociology and Anthropology* 38, 3: 309–35.

DesMeules, Marie, Douglas Manuel, and Robert Cho. 2003. 'Mortality: Life and Health Expectancy of Canadian Women'. Chapter 8 in *Women's Health Surveillance Report: A Multidimensional Look at the Health of Canadian Women*. Ottawa: Canadian Institute for Health Information.

Dickason, Olive Patricia. 2006. *A Concise History of Canada's First Nations*. Toronto: Oxford University Press.

Dinnerstein, Myra, and Rose Weitz. 1998. 'Jane Fonda, Barbara Bush, and Other Aging Bodies: Femininity and the Limits of Resistance'. Chapter 14 in Rose Weitz, ed., *The Politics of Women's Bodies: Sexuality, Appearance, and Behavior*. New York: Oxford University Press.

Dobrowolsky, Alexandra, and Jane Jenson. 2004. 'Shifting Representations of Citizenship: Canadian Politics of "Women" and "Children"'. *Social Politics* 11, 2: 154–80.

Doucet, Andrea. 2006. *Do Men Mother? Fathering, Care, and Domestic Responsibility*. Toronto: University of Toronto Press.

Dowd, J.J. 1980. *Stratification among the Aged*.

Monterey, CA: Brooks/Cole.

————. 1987. 'The Reification of Age: Age Stratification and the Passing of the Autonomous Subject'. *Journal of Aging Studies* 1: 317–35.

Drolet, Marie. 2005. Participation in Post-secondary Education in Canada: Has the Role of Parental Income and Education Changed over the 1990s? Ottawa: Statistics Canada.

Dryburgh, H. 2000. 'Women and Computer Science: Alternative Routes to Computing Careers'. PhD dissertation, McMaster University.

Dua, Enakshi. 1999. 'Beyond Diversity: Exploring the Ways in Which the Discourse of Race Has Shaped the Institution of the Nuclear Family'. Chapter 10 in E. Dua and A. Robertson, eds, *Scratching the Surface: Canadian, Anti-Racist, Feminist Thought*. Toronto: Women's Press.

————. 2005. 'Beyond Diversity: Exploring the Ways in Which the Discourse of Race Has Shaped the Institution of the Nuclear Family.' In V. Zawilski and C. Levine-Rasky, eds, *Inequality in Canada: A Reader on the Intersections of Gender, Race, and Class*. Toronto: Oxford University Press.

Dunlop, Sheryl, Peter C. Coyte, and Warren McIsaac. 2000. 'Socio-economic Status and the Utilization of Physician's Services: Results from the Canadian National Population Health Survey'. *Social Science and Medicine* 51, 1: 123–33.

Dunn, James R., and Isabel Dyck. 2000. 'Social Determinants of Health in Canada's Immigrant Population: Results from the National Population Health Survey'. *Social Science and Medicine* 51, 11: 1573–93.

Duranceau, Richard, and Derek McCall. 2007. 'Setting the Stage: The Influence of Place on Health'. *Health Policy Research Bulletin* 14: 6–9.

Easterlin, R.A. 1987. *Birth and Fortune: The Impact of Numbers on Personal Welfare*, 2nd edn. Chicago: University of Chicago Press.

Edgell, Stephen. 1993. *Class: Key Ideas*. London: Routledge.

Egan, Carolyn, and Linda Gardner. 1999. 'Racism, Women's Health, and Reproductive Freedom'. Chapter 25 in E. Dua and A. Robertson, eds,

Scratching the Surface: Canadian, Anti-racist, Feminist Thought. Toronto: Women's Press.

Ehrenreich, Barbara, and John Ehrenreich. 1979. 'The Professional Managerial Class'. Pp. 5–45 in Pat Walker, ed., *Between Labor and Capital*. Boston: South End.

Eichler, Margrit. 1988. Families in Canada Today: Recent Changes and Their Policy Consequences. 2nd edn. Toronto: Gage.

Eichler, Margrit, and Patrizia Albanese. 2007. 'What Is Household Work? A Critique of Assumptions Underlying Empirical Studies of Housework and an Alternative Approach'. *Canadian Journal of Sociology/Cahiers canadiens de sociologie* 32, 2: 227–58.

Elder, Glenn H., Jr. 1974. *Children of the Great Depression: Social Change in Life Experience*. Chicago: University of Chicago Press.

———. 1985. Life Course Dynamics: Trajectories and Transitions, 1968–80. Ithaca, NY: Cornell University Press.

———. 1994. 'Time, Human Agency, and Social Change: Perspectives on the Life Course'. *Social Psychology Quarterly* 57: 4–15.

———. 1995. 'The Life Course Paradigm: Social Change and Individual Development'. Chapter 4 in Phyllis Moen, Glenn H. Elder, Jr, and Kurt Luscher, eds, *Examining Lives in Context: Perspectives on the Ecology of Human Development*. Washington, DC: American Psychological Association Press.

Elder, Glenn H., Jr, and Angela M. O'Rand. 1995. 'Adult Lives in a Changing Society'. Pp. 452–75 in Karen Cook, Gary Fine, and James S. House, eds, *Sociological Perspectives on Social Psychology*. New York: Allyn and Bacon.

Elder, G.H., Jr, and R.C. Rockwell. 1976. 'Marital Age in Life Patterns'. *Journal of Family History* 1: 34–53.

Ellwood, Wayne. 2001. *The No-Nonsense Guide to Globalization*. Toronto: New Internationalist Publications LTD / Between the Lines.

Elstad, Jon Ivar. 1995. 'Employment Status and Women's Health: Exploring the Dynamics'. *Acta Sociologica* 38: 231–49.

Erwin, Lorna, and Paula Maurutto. 1998. 'Beyond Access: Considering Gender Deficits in Science Education'. *Gender and Education* 10, 1: 51–69.

Essed, Philomena, 1991. Understanding Everyday Racism: An Interdisciplinary Theory. Newbury Park, CA: Sage.

Estes, C.L. 1979. *The Aging Enterprise*. San Francisco: Jossey-Bass.

———. 1991. 'The New Political Economy of Aging: Introduction and Critique'. Chapter 2 in M. Minkler and C. Estes, eds, *Critical Perspectives on Aging: The Political and Moral Economy of Growing Old*. Amityville, NY: Baywood.

———. 1999. 'The New Political Economy of Aging: Introduction and Critique'. Chapter 1 in M. Minkler and C. Estes, eds, *Critical Gerontology*. Amityville, NY: Baywood.

———, K.W. Linkins, and E.A. Binney. 1996. 'The Political Economy of Aging'. Chapter 18 in R.H. Binstock and L.K. George, eds, *Handbook of Aging and the Social Sciences*, 4th edn. San Diego, CA: Academic Press.

———, J.H. Swan, and L.E. Gerard. 1982. 'Dominant and Competing Paradigms in Gerontology: Towards a Political Economy of Ageing'. *Aging and Society* 12: 151–64.

Evans, Patricia M. 1997. 'Divided Citizenship? Gender, Income Security, and the Welfare State'. Chapter 4 in Patricia M. Evans and Gerda R. Wekerle, eds, *Women and the Canadian Welfare State: Challenges and Change*. Toronto: University of Toronto Press.

———. 2007. '(Not) Taking Account of Precarious Employment: Workfare Policies and Lone Mothers in Ontario and the UK'. *Social Policy & Administration* 41, 1: 29–49.

Fallo-Mitchell, L., and C.D. Ryff. 1982. 'Preferred Timing of Female Life Events: Cohort Differences'. *Research on Aging* 4: 249–67.

Farran, Sandy. 2006. 'The Average Student: SWF, 22, Some Debt, Seeks Degree, Job'. *Maclean's*, 26 June.

Ferguson, Lucinda. 2007. 'Uncertainty and Indecision in the Legal Regulation of Children: The Albertan

Experience'. *Canadian Journal of Family Law* 23, 2: 159–214.

Fillion, Kate. 2007. 'Housework Doesn't Pay: Leslie Bennet, Author of *The Feminine Mistake*, Talks to Kate Fillion about Women's Risks, Assets and Delusions'. *Maclean's*, 7 May.

Finch, Janet. 1989. *Family Obligations and Social Change*. Cambridge, UK: Basil Blackwell.

Fincham, S.M., A.M. Ugnat, G.B. Hill, N. Krieger, and Y. Mao. 2000. 'Is Occupation a Risk Factor for Thyroid Cancer?' *Journal of Occupational and Environmental Medicine* 42, 3: 318–22.

Findlay, Deborah A., and Leslie J. Miller. 2002. 'Through Medical Eyes: The Medicalization of Women's Bodies and Women's Lives'. Chapter 13 in B. Singh Bolaria and H. Dickinson, eds, *Health, Illness, and Health Care in Canada*. Toronto: Nelson.

Finnie, Ross. 2000. 'Holding Their Own: Employment and Earnings of Postsecondary Graduates'. *Education Quarterly Review* 7, 1: 21–37. Statistics Canada Catalogue no. 81-003.

————. 2002. 'Student Loans: Borrowing and Burden'. *Education Quarterly Review* 8, 4: 28–42. Statistics Canada Catalogue no. 81-003.

Finnie, Ross, Eric Lascelles, and Arthur Sweetman. 2005. *Who Goes? The Direct and Indirect Effects of Family Background on Access to Post-secondary Education*. Analytical Studies Branch Research Paper Series. Statistics Canada Catalogue no. 11F0019MIE2005237. Ottawa: Statistics Canada.

Firestone, Shulamith. 1971. *The Dialectic of Sex*. New York: Bantam Books.

Fleras, Augie, and Jean Leonard Elliott. 2007. Unequal Relations: An Introduction to Race, Ethnic, and Aboriginal Dynamics in Canada. Toronto: Pearson, Prentice Hall.

Foner, Anne. 1986. *Aging and Old Age: New Perspectives*. Englewood Cliffs, NJ: Prentice-Hall.

Foner, Anne, and Karen Schwab. 1981. *Aging and Retirement*. Monterey, CA: Brooks/Cole.

Fortner, Brian. 2007. 'Raise Kids Like a Man'. *Men's Health*, June.

Fox, Bonnie J. 1988. 'Conceptualizing "Patriarchy"'. *Canadian Review of Sociology and Anthropology* 25: 163–81.

————. 1989. 'The Feminist Challenge: A Reconsideration of Social Inequality and Economic Development'. Chapter 5 in R.J. Brym and B.J. Fox, eds, *From Culture to Power: The Sociology of English Canada*. Toronto: Oxford University Press.

————. 2001. 'The Formative Years: How Parenthood Creates Gender'. *Canadian Review of Sociology and Anthropology* 38, 4: 373–90.

————. 2009. When Couples Become Parents: The Creation of Gender in the Transition to Parenthood. Toronto: University of Toronto Press.

————, ed. 2001. *Family Patterns, Gender Relations*. 2nd edn. Toronto: Oxford University Press.

Fox, Bonnie, and Meg Luxton. 2001. 'Conceptualizing Family'. Chapter 3 in Bonnie Fox, ed., *Family Patterns, Gender Relations*, 2nd edn. Toronto: Oxford University Press.

Frenette, Marc. 2000. 'Overqualified? Recent Graduates and the Needs of Their Employers'. *Education Quarterly Review* 7, 1: 6–20. Statistics Canada Catalogue no. 81-003.

————. 2005. *The Impact of Tuition Fees on University Access: Evidence from a Large-Scale Price Deregulation in Professional Programs*. Analytical Studies Branch Research Paper Series. Statistics Canada Catalogue no. 11F0019, no. 263. Ottawa: Statistics Canada.

————. 2007. Why Are Youth from Lower-Income Families Less Likely to Attend University? Evidence from Academic Abilities, Parental Abilities, and Financial Constraints. Analytical Studies Branch Research Paper Series. Statistics Canada Catalogue no. 11F0019MIE2007295. Ottawa: Statistics Canada.

————, and Simon Coulombe. 2007. *Has Higher Education among Young Women Substantially Reduced the Gender Gap in Employment and Earnings?* Analytical Studies Branch Research Paper Series. Statistics Canada Catalogue no. 11F0019MIE2007301. Ottawa: Statistics Canada.

————, and Klarka Zeman. 2007. *Why Are Most*

University Students Women? Evidence Based on Academic Performance, Study Habits and Parental Influences. Analytical Studies Branch Research Paper Series. Statistics Canada Catalogue no. 11F0019MIE, no. 303. Ottawa: Statistics Canada.

Frideres, James S. 1988. 'Institutional Structures and Economic Deprivation: Native People in Canada'. Chapter 4 in B. Singh Bolaria and Peter S. Li, eds, *Racial Oppression in Canada*, 2nd edn. Toronto: Garamond Press.

Frideres, James S., and René R. Gadacz. 2008. *Aboriginal Peoples in Canada: Contemporary Conflicts.* 8th edn. Toronto: Pearson Education Canada.

Frohlich, Katherine L., and Louise Potvin. 2008. 'The Inequality Paradox: The Population Approach and Vulnerable Populations'. *American Journal of Public Health* 98, 2: 216–21.

Fry, Christine L. 1976. 'The Ages of Adulthood: A Question of Numbers'. *Journal of Gerontology* 3: 199–217.

———. 1980. 'Cultural Dimensions of Age: A Multidimensional Scaling Analysis'. Pp. 42–64 in C.L. Fry, ed., *Aging in Culture and Society: Comparative Viewpoints and Strategies.* New York: Praeger.

———. 1985. 'Culture, Behavior, and Aging in the Comparative in Perspective'. Pp. 216–44 in V.E. Birren and V.W. Schaie, eds, *Handbook on the Psychology of Aging.* New York: Van Nostrand Reinhold.

———. 1986. 'Emics and Age: Age Differentiation and Cognitive Anthropological Strategies'. Pp. 105–30 in C.L Fry and J. Keith, eds, *New Methods for Old Age Research.* South Hadley, MA: Bergin and Garvey.

Frye, Marilyn. 1983. *The Politics of Reality: Essays in Feminist Theory.* Freedom, CA: Crossing Press.

Fuller, Sylvia, Paul Kershaw, and Jane Pulkingham. 2008. 'Constructing "Active Citizenship": Single Mothers, Welfare, and the Logics of Voluntarism'. *Citizenship Studies* 12, 2: 157–76.

Galabuzi, Grace-Edward. 2004. 'Social Exclusion'. Pp. 235–52 in Dennis Raphael, ed., *Social Determinants of Health: Canadian Perspectives.* Toronto: Canadian Scholars' Press.

Gannon, M., and K. Mihorean. 2006. 'Criminal Victimization in Canada, 2004'. *Juristat* 25, 7. Statistics Canada Catalogue no. 5-002-XIE.

Gardiner-Barber, Pauline T. 2003. 'The "Culture of Making Do": Gender, Work, and Family in Cape Breton Working Class Life'. Chapter 14 in M. Lynn, ed., *Voices: Essays on Canadian Families*, 2nd edn. Scarborough, ON: Thomson Nelson.

Garriguet, Didier. 2006. Nutrition: Findings from the Canadian Community Health Survey, Overview of Canadian's Eating Habits 2004. Statistics Canada Catalogue no. 82-620-MIE. Ottawa: Minister of Industry.

Gaszo, Amber. 2005. 'The Poverty of Unattached Senior Women and the Canadian Retirement Income System: A Matter of Blame or Contradiction?' *Journal of Sociology and Social Welfare* 32, 2: 41–6.

———. 2007. 'Balancing Expectations for Employability and Family Responsibilities While on Social Assistance: Low-Income Mothers' Experiences in Three Canadian Provinces.' *Family Relations* 56: 454–66

Gazso-Windle, Amber, and Julie McMullin. 2003. 'Doing Domestic Labour: Strategising in a Gendered Domain'. *Canadian Journal of Sociology* 28, 3: 341–66.

Gee, Ellen. 2000a. 'Contemporary Diversities'. Chapter 3 in Nancy Mandell and Ann Duffy, eds, *Canadian Families: Diversity, Conflict, and Change*, 2nd edn. Toronto: Harcourt Brace.

———. 2000b. 'Population and Politics: Voodoo Demography, Population Ageing, and Social Policy'. Chapter 1 in Ellen Gee and G.M. Gutman, eds, *The Overselling of Population Aging: Apocalyptic Demography, Intergenerational Challenges, and Social Policy.* Toronto: Oxford University Press.

Geiger, H. Jack. 2001. 'Racial Stereotyping and Medicine: The Need for Cultural Competence'. *Canadian Medical Association Journal* 164, 12: 1699–704.

George, Linda K. 2007. 'Life Course Perspectives on Social Factors and Mental Illness'. Chapter 9 in William Avison, Jane McLeod, and Bernice

Pescosilido, eds, *Mental Health, Social Mirror*. New York: Springer.

Gerson, Judith M., and Kathy Peiss. 1985. 'Boundaries, Negotiation, Consciousness: Reconceptualizing Gender Relations'. *Social Problems* 32, 4: 317–31.

Gerstel, Judy. 2007. 'Mad? No, But They Deserve to Be; Post-menopausal Women Show Drop in Diseases after Giving Up HRT'. *The Toronto Star*, 4 September.

Giddens, Anthony. 1971. Capitalism and Modern Social Theory: An Analysis of the Writings of Marx, Durkheim, and Max Weber. Cambridge: Cambridge University Press.

———. 1979. Central Problems in Social Theory. London: Macmillan.

———. 1984. The Constitution of Society: Outline of the Theory of Structuration. Berkeley: University of California Press.

———. 1993. New Rules of Sociological Method: A Positive Critique of Interpretative Sociologies. 2nd edn. Stanford, CA: Stanford University Press.

———. 2002. Runaway World: How Globalisation Is Reshaping our Lives. London: Profile Books.

———, and Christopher Pierson. 1998. *Conversations with Anthony Giddens: Making Sense of Modernity*. Cambridge, UK: Polity Press.

Gillis, Kelly J., and John P. Hirdes. 1996. 'The Quality of Life Implications of Health Practices among Older Adults: Evidence from the 1991 Canadian General Social Survey'. *Canadian Journal on Aging* 15, 2: 299–314.

Gilmore, Jason. 2004. Health of Canadians Living in Census Metropolitan Areas. Ottawa: Minister of Industry.

Gilmour, Heather. 2007. 'Physically Active Canadians'. *Health Reports* 18, 3: 45–65. Statistics Canada Catalogue no. 82-003.

Gilmour, Heather, and Jungwee Park. 2006. 'Dependency, Chronic Conditions and Pain in Seniors'. *Health Reports* 16, suppl.: 21–32. Statistics Canada Catalogue no. 82-003-SPE.

Ginn, Jay, and Sara Arber. 2001. 'Pension Prospects of Minority Ethnic Groups: Inequalities by Gender and Ethnicity'. *British Journal of Sociology* 52, 3: 519–39.

Glazier, Richard H., Elizabeth M. Badley, Julie E. Gilbert, and Lorne Rothman. 2000. 'The Nature of Increased Hospital Use in Poor Neighbourhoods: Findings from a Canadian Inner City'. *Canadian Journal of Public Health* 91, 4: 268–73.

Glenn, Evelyn Nakano. 1992. 'From Servitude to Service Work: Historical Continuities in the Racial Division of Paid Reproductive Labour'. *Signs* 18, 1: 1–43.

———. 2000. 'The Social Construction and Institutionalization of Gender and Race: An Integrative Framework'. Chapter 1 in Myra Marx Feree, Judith Lorber, and Beth B. Hess, eds, *Revisioning Gender*. New York: Altamira Press.

Goffman, Erving. 1983. 'The Interaction Order'. *American Sociological Review* 48, Feb.: 1–17.

Goldthorpe, John. 2002. 'Globalisation and Social Class'. *Western European Politics* 25, July: 1–28.

Goodman, Marcene. 1996. 'Culture, Cohort, and Cosmetic Surgery'. *Journal of Women and Aging* 8, 2: 55–73.

Gore, Susan, Robert H. Aseltine Jr, and Elizabeth A. Schilling. 2007. 'Transition to Adulthood, Mental Health, and Inequality'. Chapter 10 in William Avison, Jane McLeod, and Bernice Pescosilido, eds, *Mental Health, Social Mirror*. New York: Springer.

Gorey, Kevin M., Eric J. Holowaty, Gordon Fehringer, Ethan Laukkanen, Nancy L. Richter, and Cynthia M. Meyer. 2000. 'An International Comparison of Cancer Survival: Relatively Poor Areas of Toronto, Ontario and Three US Metropolitan Areas'. *Journal of Public Health Medicine* 22, 3: 343–9.

Gough, Orla. 2001. 'The Impact of the Gender Pay Gap on Post-retirement Earnings'. *Critical Social Policy* 21, 3: 311–34.

Grabb, Edward. 2007. *Theories of Social Inequality*. 5th edn. Toronto: Thomson Nelson.

Graham, Jennifer. 2007. 'U.S. Border Set to Reopen to Older Canadian Cattle'. *The Globe and Mail*, 19 November.

Graham, Kathryn, Virginia Carver, and Pamela J. Brett.

1995. 'Alcohol and Drug Use by Older Women: Results of a National Survey'. *Canadian Journal on Aging* 14, 4: 769–91.

Gramsci, Antonio. 1971. *Selections from the Prison Notebooks*. Edited and translated by Quintin Hoare and Geoffrey Nowell Smith. New York: International.

Grant, Tavia. 2007. 'Immigrant Unemployment Most Acute in Quebec'. *The Globe and Mail*, 11 September.

Greaves, L., O. Hankivsky, and J. Kingston-Riechers. 1995. *Selected Estimates of the Costs of Violence against Women*. London, ON: Centre for Research on Violence Against Women and Children.

Green, Carla A., and Clyde R. Pope. 1999. 'Gender, Psychosocial Factors and the Use of Medical Services: A Longitudinal Analysis'. *Social Science and Medicine* 48, 10: 1363–72.

Grenon, Joanna, Greg Butler, and Randy Adams. 2007. 'Exploring the Intersection between the Built Environment and Health Behaviours'. *Health Policy Research Bulletin* 14: 29–32.

Greschner, Donna. 1990. 'Abortion and Democracy for Women: A Critique of Tremblay v. Daigle'. *McGill Law Journal* 35: 633–69.

———. 1998. 'Pregnant with Meaning: Discourse, Democracy, and the Daigle Decision'. Chapter 8 in Les Samuelson and Wayne Antony, eds, *Power and Resistance: Critical Thinking about Canadian Social Issues*, 2nd edn. Halifax: Fernwood.

Grimes, Michael, D. 1991. Class in Twentieth-Century American Sociology: An Analysis of Theories and Measurement Strategies. New York: Praeger.

Guillemard, A. 1982. 'Old Age, Retirement, and the Social Class Structure: Toward an Analysis of the Structural Dynamics of the Later Stage of Life'. Chapter 9 in T.K. Hareven and K. Adams, eds, *Aging and the Life Course Transition: An Interdisciplinary Perspective*. New York: Guildford Press.

———. 1983. 'The Making of Old Age Policy in France'. Pp. 75–99 in A.M. Guillemard, ed., *Old Age and the Welfare State*. Beverly Hills, CA: Sage.

Gunderson, Morley, Lee Jacobs, and François Vaillancourt. 2005. *The Information Technology (IT) Labour Market in Canada: Results from the National Survey of IT Occupations*. Prepared for the Software Human Resource Council (SHRC). Ottawa: Government of Canada, Sector Council Program.

Guppy, Neil, and Scott Davies. 1998. *Education in Canada: Recent Trends and Future Challenges*. Ottawa: Statistics Canada Catalogue no. 96-321.

Gupta, Shamali, and Nancy A. Ross. 2007. 'Under the Microscope: Health Disparities within Canadian Cities'. *Health Policy Research Bulletin* 14: 23–8.

Gyimah, Stephen Obeng, Jerry White, and Paul Maxim. 2003. 'Income and First Nations Elderly: Policies for a Better Future'. Chapter 4 in Jerry P. White, Paul Maxim, and Dan Beavon, eds, *Aboriginal Policy Research: Setting the Agenda for Change*. Toronto: Thompson Educational.

Habermas, Jürgen. 1984. The Theory of Communicative Action, vol. 1, Reason and the Rationalization of Society. Boston: Beacon Press.

———. 1987. The Theory of Communicative Action, vol. 2, Lifeworld and System: A Functionalist Critique. Cambridge, UK: Polity Press.

Hagestad, Gunhild. 1990. 'Social Perspectives on the Life Course'. Pp. 151–68 in R.H. Binstock and L.K. George, eds, *Handbook of Aging and the Social Sciences*, 3rd edn. Toronto: Harcourt Brace Jovanovich.

Hagestad, Gunhild, and Bernice Neugarten. 1985. 'Age and the Life Course'. Pp. 36–61 in E. Shanas and R. Binstock, eds, *Handbook of Aging and the Social Sciences*, 2nd edn. New York: Van Nostrand-Reinhold.

Hainsworth, Jeremy. 2006. 'Mail-Order Bride Industry Rife with Abuse, Study Says'. *The Globe and Mail*, 9 October.

Halli, Shiva S., and John P. Anchan. 2005. 'Structural and Behavioural Determinants of Immigrant and Non-immigrant Health Status: Results from the Canadian Community Health Survey'. *Journal of International Migration and Integration* 6, 1: 93–122.

Hampson, Sarah. 2007. 'The New Class Wars'. *The Globe and Mail*, 5 July.

Hango, Darcy, and Patrice de Broucker. 2007.

Education-to-Labour Market Pathways of Canadian Youth: Findings from the Youth in Transition Survey. Culture, Tourism and the Centre for Education Statistics Research Papers. Statistics Canada Catalogue no. 81-595-MIE2007054. Ottawa: Minister of Industry.

Hardy, Melissa, and Lawrence E. Hazelrigg. 1995. 'Gender, Race/Ethnicity, and Poverty in Later Life'. *Journal of Aging Studies* 9, 1: 43–63.

Hartmann, Heidi. 1981. 'The Unhappy Marriage of Marxism and Feminism: Towards a More Progressive Union'. Pp. 1–42 in L. Sargent, ed., *The Unhappy Marriage of Marxism and Feminism: A Debate on Class and Patriarchy.* London: Pluto Press.

Hatch, Stephani L., and Bruce P. Dohrenwend. 2007. 'Distribution of Traumatic and Other Stressful Life Events by Race/Ethnicity, Gender, SES and Age: A Review of the Research'. *American Journal of Community Psychology* 40: 313–32.

Health Canada. 2002. 'Income Inequality as a Determinant of Health'. Presentation summary, Social Determinants of Health Across the Life-Span Conference, Toronto, November. http://www.phac-aspc.gc.ca/phsp/phdd/overview_implications/02_income.htm.

———. 2006. Healthy Canadians: A Federal Report on Comparable Health Indicators 2006. Ottawa: Minister of Health Canada.

Health Disparities Task Group of the Federal/Provincial/Territorial Advisory Committee on Population Health and Health Security. 2005. *Reducing Health Disparities—Roles of the Health Sector: Discussion Paper.* Ottawa: Minister of Health.

Heinz, Walter. 2001. 'Work and the Life Course: A Cosmopolitan-Local Perspective'. Chapter 1 in V.W. Marshall, W.R. Heinz, H. Krueger, and A. Verma, eds, *Restructuring Work and the Life Course.* Toronto: University of Toronto Press.

Herd, Pamela, Brian Goesling, and James S. House. 2007. 'Socioeconomic Position and Health: The Differential Effects of Education versus Income on the Onset versus Progression of Health Problems'. *Journal of Health and Social Behavior* 48, 3: 223–39.

Hier, Sean P., and B. Singh Bolaria, eds. 2007. *Race and Racism in 21st Century Canada: Continuity, Complexity, and Change.* Peterborough, ON: Broadview Press.

House, James S. 2001. 'Understanding Social Factors and Inequalities in Health: 20th Century Progress and 21st Century Prospects'. *Journal of Health and Social Behavior* 43, 2: 125–42.

House, James S., James M. Lepkowski, Ann M. Kinney, Richard P. Mero, Ronald C. Kessler, and A. Regula Herzog. 1994. 'The Social Stratification of Aging and Health'. *Journal of Health and Social Behavior* 35, 3: 213–34.

Hughes, Karen D. 1999. *Gender and Self-Employment in Canada: Assessing Trends and Policy Implications.* CPRN Study no. W104. Changing Relationships Series. Ottawa: Renouf.

Huguet, Nathalie, Mark S. Kaplan, and David Feeny. 2008. 'Socioeconomic Status and Health-Related Quality of Life among Elderly People: Results from the Joint Canada/United States Survey of Health'. *Social Science and Medicine* 66, 4: 803–10.

Hum, Derek, and Wayne Simpson. 2007. 'Revisiting Equity and Labour: Immigration, Gender, Minority Status, and Income Differentials in Canada'. Pp. 89–110 in Sean P. Hier and B. Singh Bolaria, eds, *Race and Racism in 21st Century Canada: Continuity, Complexity, and Change.* Peterborough, ON: Broadview Press.

Humphries, Karin H., and Eddy van Doorslaer. 2000. 'Income-Related Health Inequality in Canada'. *Social Science and Medicine* 50, 5: 663–71.

Hunt, Kate. 2002. 'A Generation Apart? Gender-Related Experiences and Health in Women in Early and Late Mid-life'. *Social Science and Medicine* 54, 1: 663–76.

Hunt, Kate, and Ellen Annandale. 1999. 'Relocating Gender and Morbidity: Examining Men's and Women's Health in Contemporary Western Societies'. *Social Science and Medicine* 48: 1–5.

Hunter, Alfred A. 1981. *Class Tells: On Social Inequality in Canada.* Toronto: Butterworths.

Hurd Clarke, Laura. 2001. 'Older Women's Bodies and the Self: The Construction of Identity in Later

Life'. *The Canadian Review of Sociology and Anthropology* 38, 4: 441–64.

Hurd Clarke, Laura, Robin Repta, and Meridith Griffin. 2007. 'Non-surgical Cosmetic Procedures: Older Women's Perceptions and Experiences'. *Journal of Women and Aging* 19, 3/4: 69–87.

Ibbitson, John. 2007. 'Is Globalization Killing the American Middle Class?' *The Globe and Mail*, 17 October.

Ibbott, Peter, Don Kerr, and Roderic Beaujot. 2006. 'Probing the Future of Mandatory Retirement in Canada'. *Canadian Journal on Aging* 25, 2: 161–78.

Ighodaro, MacDonald E. 2006. Living the Experience: Migration, Exclusion, and Anti-racist Practice. Halifax: Fernwood.

Immen, Wallace, and James Rusk. 2002. 'Toronto's Tent City Sealed Off, Squatters Ejected'. *The Globe and Mail*, 25 September.

Industry Canada. 2009. 'Key Small Business Statistics—July 2008: How Many Businesses Are There in Canada?' Ottawa: Industry Canada. 23 July. http://www.ic.gc.ca/eic/site/sbrp-rppe.nsf/eng/rd02300.html.

Inhorn, Marcia C., and K. Lisa Whittle. 2001. 'Feminism Meets the "New" Epidemiologies: Toward an Appraisal of Antifeminist Biases in Epidemiological Research on Women's Health'. *Social Science and Medicine* 53, 5: 553–67.

Isajiw, Wsevolod W. 1999. Understanding Diversity: Ethnicity and Race in the Canadian Context. Toronto: Thompson Educational.

Jackson, Andrew. 2002. *Is Work Working for Workers of Colour?* Research paper no. 18. Ottawa: Canadian Labour Congress. http://canadianlabour.ca/en/Is_Work_Working_colour.

Jackson, Chris. 1996. 'Measuring and Valuing: Households' Unpaid Work'. *Canadian Social Trends*, Autumn: 25–9. Statistics Canada Catalogue no. 11-008.

Jackson, Pamela Braboy, and David R. Williams. 2006. 'The Intersection of Race, Gender and SES: Health Paradoxes'. Chapter 5 in Amy J. Schultz and Leith Mullings, eds, *Gender, Race, Class and Health: Intersectional Approaches*. San Francisco, CA: Jossey-Bass.

Jaine, Linda. 1993. *Residential Schools: The Stolen Years*. Saskatoon: University Extension Press.

Jakubowski, Lisa Marie. 1997. *Immigration and the Legalization of Racism*. Halifax: Fernwood.

Jenson, Jane. 1997. 'Fated to Live in Interesting Times: Canada's Changing Citizenship Regimes'. *Canadian Journal of Political Science* 30, 4: 627–44.

——— and Martin Papillon. 2000. 'Challenging the Citizenship Regime: The James Bay Cree and Transnational Action'. *Politics and Society* 28, 2: 245–64.

Jerrett, Michael, Michael Buzzelli, Richard T. Burnett, and Patrick F. DeLuca. 2005. 'Particulate Air Pollution, Social Confounders, and Mortality in Small Areas of an Industrial City'. *Social Science and Medicine* 60: 2845–63.

Johnson, Fred W., Paul J. Gruenewald, Andrew J. Treno, and Gail Armstrong Taff. 1998. 'Drinking over the Life Course within Gender and Ethnic Groups: A Hyperparametric Analysis'. *Journal of Studies on Alcohol* 59: 568–80.

Johnson, Holly. 1996. Dangerous Domains: Violence against Women in Canada. Toronto: Nelson.

Johnson, Holly, and Vincent Sacco. 1995. 'Researching Violence against Women: Statistics Canada's National Survey'. *Canadian Journal of Criminology* 37, 3: 281–304.

Johnson, Karen L., Donna Lero, and Jennifer Rooney. 2001. *Work-Life Compendium 2001: 150 Canadian Statistics on Work, Family, and Well-Being*. Guelph, ON: Centre for Families, Work, and Well-being / Human Resources Development Canada.

Jones, Vanessa E. 2007. 'Black and Not-So-Beautiful Stereotypes'. *The Globe and Mail*, 12 October. Originally published in the *New York Times*.

Julien, Ann-Marie, and Heidi Ertl. 1999. 'Children's School Experiences in the NLSCY, 1994–1995'. *Education Quarterly Review* 6, 2: 20–34. Statistics Canada Catalogue no. 81-003.

Kalbach, Madeline A., and Warren E. Kalbach, eds. 2000. *Perspectives on Ethnicity in Canada*. Toronto: Harcourt Canada.

Kamo, Y. 1988. 'Determinants of Household Division of Labour'. *Journal of Family Issues* 9: 177–200.

Kapsalis, Costa, René Morissette, and Garnett Picot. 1999. *The Returns to Education and the Increasing Wage Gap between Younger and Older Workers*. Statistics Canada Catalogue no. 11F0019MPE No. 131. Ottawa: Statistics Canada.

Karlsen, Saffron, and James Y. Nazroo. 2002. 'Relation between Racial Discrimination, Social Class, and Health among Ethnic Minority Groups'. *American Journal of Public Health* 92: 624–31.

Kazanjian, Arminée, Denise Morettin, and Robert Cho. 2003. 'Health Care Utilization by Canadian Women'. In *Women's Health Surveillance Report: A Multidimensional Look at the Health of Canadian Women*. Ottawa: Canadian Institute for Health Information.

Katz, Stephen. 1996. *Disciplining Old Age: The Formation of Gerontological Knowledge*. Charlottesville: University Press of Virginia.

Katz, Stephen, and Barbara Marshall. 2003. 'New Sex for Old: Lifestyle, Consumerism, and the Ethics of Aging Well'. *Journal of Aging Studies* 17, 1: 3–16.

Kawachi, Ichiro, and Bruce P. Kennedy. 1999. 'The Relationship of Income Inequality to Mortality'. Chapter 13 in Ichiro Kawachi, Bruce P. Kennedy, and Richard G. Wilkinson, eds, *The Society and Population Health Reader: Income Inequality and Health*. New York: New Press.

Kazemipur, Abdolmohammad, and Shiva S. Halli. 2001. 'The Changing Colour of Poverty in Canada'. *Canadian Sociological and Anthropological Review* 38, 2: 217–38.

Kelly, Karen. 2002. *Visible Minorities: A Diverse Population*. Statistics Canada Catalogue no. 1-008-XIE. Ottawa: Statistics Canada. http://statcan.ca/english/ads/11-008-XIE/ vismin.html, accessed December 2002.

Kilkey, Majella, and Jonathan Bradshaw. 1999. 'Lone Mothers, Economic Well-Being, and Policies'. Chapter 5 in Diane Sainsbury, ed., *Gender and Welfare State Regimes*. New York: Oxford University Press.

Kim, Daniel, Ichiro Kawachi, Stephen Vander Hoorn, and Majid Ezzati. 2008. 'Is Inequality at the Heart of It? Cross-country Associations of Income Inequality with Cardiovascular Diseases and Risk Factors'. *Social Science and Medicine* 66: 1719–32.

Klein, Seth, and Jane Pulkingham. 2008. *Living on Welfare in BC: Experiences of Longer-Term 'Expected to Work' Recipients*. Ottawa: Canadian Center for Policy Alternatives.

Kline, Marlee. 1993. 'Complicating the Ideology of Motherhood: Child Welfare Law and First Nation Women'. *Queen's Law Journal* 18: 310–19.

———. 2005. 'Complicating the Ideology of Motherhood: Child Welfare Law and First Nation Women'. Pp. 189–99 in B.A. Crow and L. Gotell, eds, *Open Boundaries: A Canadian Women's Studies Reader*, 2nd edn. Toronto: Pearson Prentice Hall.

Knight, Claudette. 1997. 'Black Parents Speak: Education in Mid-Nineteenth-Century Canada West'. *Ontario History* 89, 4: 269–84.

Knighton, Karen, and Sheba Mirza. 2002. 'Postsecondary Participation: The Effects of Parent Education and Income'. *Education Quarterly Review* 18, 3: 25–32. Statistics Canada Catalogue no. 81-003.

Knowles, Valerie. 1992. *Strangers at Our Gates: Canadian Immigration and Immigration Policy, 1540–1990*. Toronto: Dundurn Press.

Kobayashi, Karen M., Steven Prus, and Zhiqiu Lin. 2008. 'Ethnic Differences in Self-Rated and Functional Health: Does Immigrant Status Matter?' *Ethnicity and Health* 13, 2: 129–47.

Kohli, Martin. 1988. 'Ageing as a Challenge for Sociological Theory'. *Ageing and Society* 8: 367–94.

Kopec, Jacek A., Ivan Williams, Teresa To, and Peter C. Austin. 2001. 'Cross-cultural Comparisons of Health Status in Canada Using the Health Utilities Index'. *Ethnicity and Health* 6, 1: 41–50.

Kopun, Francine. 2007. 'The Canadian Family Is Slowly Being Reshaped: More Men Heading Up Single-Parent Households, Same-Sex and Common-Law Unions on Rise: Census'. *The Toronto Star*, 13 September.

Koretz, Gene. 2001. 'Why Married Men Earn More'. *Business Week*, 17 September.

Krahn, Harvey, J., and Graham S. Lowe. 1998. *Work,*

Industry, and Canadian Society. 3rd edn. Toronto: ITP Nelson.

Krahn, Harvey J., Graham S. Lowe, and Karen D. Hughes. 2007. *Work, Industry and Canadian Society*. 5th edn. Toronto: Thomson Nelson.

Krahn, Harvey, and Alison Taylor. 2007. 'Streaming in the 10th Grade in Four Canadian Provinces in 2000'. *Education Matters: Insights on Education, Learning and Training in Canada* 4, 2. Statistics Canada Catalogue no. 81-004-XIE. http://www.statcan.gc.ca/pub/81-004-x/2007002/9994-eng.htm.

Krieger, Nancy. 2003. 'Genders, Sexes and Health: What Are the Connections—and Why Does It Matter?' *International Journal of Epidemiology* 32: 652–7.

———. 2007. 'Why Epidemiologists Cannot Afford to Ignore Poverty'. *Epidemiology* 18, 6: 658–63.

———, Charles Quesenberry, Tiffany Peng, Pamela Horn-Ross, Susan Stewart, Susan Brown, Karen Swallen, Tessie Guillermo, Dong Suh, Luz Alvarez Martinez, and Felicia Ward. 1999. 'Social Class, Race/Ethnicity, and Incidence of Breast, Cervix, Colon, Lung, and Prostate Cancer among Asian, Black, Hispanic, and White Residents of the San Francisco Bay Area, 1988–92 (United States)'. *Cancer Causes and Control* 10: 525–37.

———, D.L. Rowley, A.A. Herman, B. Avery, and M.T. Phillips. 1993. 'Racism, Sexism, and Social Class: Implications for Studies of Health, Disease, and Well-Being'. *American Journal of Preventive Medicine* 9, 6: 82–122.

———, Kevin Smith, Deepa Naishadham, Cathy Hartman, and Elizabeth M. Barbeau. 2005. 'Experiences of Discrimination: Validity and Reliability of a Self-Report Measure for Population Health Research on Racism and Health'. *Social Science and Medicine* 61: 1576–96.

Krug, Etienne G., Linda L. Dahlberg, James A. Mercy, Anthony B. Zwi, and Rafel Lozano, eds. 2002. *World Report on Violence and Health*. Geneva: World Health Organization.

Langlois, Stephanie, and Peter Morrison. 2001. 'Suicide Deaths and Suicide Attempts'. *Health Reports* 13, 2: 9–21. Statistics Canada Catalogue no. 11-008.

Langton, Nancy, and Jeffrey Pfeffer. 1994. 'Paying the Professor: Sources of Salary Variation in Academic Labor Markets'. *American Sociological Review* 59: 236–56.

Lantz, Paula M., James S. House, Mero Richard P., and David R. Williams. 2005. 'Stress, Life Events, and Socio-economic Disparities in Health: Results from the Americans' Changing Lives Study'. *Journal of Health and Social Behaviour* 46: 274–88.

Lasch, Christopher. 1977. *Haven in a Heartless World: The Family Besieged*. New York: Basic Books.

Laslett, B., and J. Brenner. 1987. 'Gender and Social Reproduction: Historical Perspectives'. *Annual Review of Sociology* 15: 381–404.

Latham, Jim, and Tina Moffat. 2007. 'Determinants of Variation in Food Cost and Availability in Two Socioeconomically Contrasting Neighbourhoods of Hamilton, Ontario, Canada'. *Health and Place* 13: 273–87.

Laurence, Margaret. 1964. *The Stone Angel*. Toronto: McClelland and Stewart.

Layder, Derek. 1994. *Understanding Social Theory*. Thousand Oaks, CA: Sage.

Leach, Belinda, and Anthony Winson. 1995. 'Bringing "Globalization" Down to Earth: Restructuring and Labour in Rural Communities'. *Canadian Review of Sociology and Anthropology* 32: 341–64.

Leclere, Felicia B., Richard G. Rogers, and Kimberley D. Peters. 1997. 'Ethnicity and Mortality in the United States: Individual and Community Correlates'. *Social Forces* 76, 1: 169–98.

Lee, K., and P. Patel. 2003. 'Far from the Maddening Cows: The Global Dimensions of BSE and vCJD'. Chapter 4 in K. Lee, ed., *Health Impacts of Globalization: Towards Global Governance*. New York: Palgrave.

Lehmann, Wolfgang. 2007a. *Choosing to Labour? School–Work Transitions and Social Class*. Montreal: McGill-Queen's University Press.

———. 2007b. '"I Just Didn't Feel Like I Fit In": The Role of Habitus in University Dropout Decisions'. *Canadian Journal of Higher Education* 37, 2:

89–110.

Leisering, Lutz, and Leibfried, Stephan. 1999. *Time and Poverty in Western Welfare Studies*. Cambridge: Cambridge University Press.

Lemstra, Mark, Cory Neudorf, Carl D'arcy, Anton Kunst, Lynne M. Warren, and Norman R. Bennett. 2008. 'A Systematic Review of Depressed Mood and Anxiety by SES in Youth Aged 10–15 Years'. *Canadian Journal of Public Health* 99, 2: 125–9.

Lessa, Iara. 2006. 'Single Motherhood in the Canadian Landscape: Postcards from a Subject'. Pp. 291–308 in Anne Westhues, ed., *Canadian Social Policy: Issues and Perspectives*, 4th edn. Waterloo, ON: Wilfred Laurier University Press.

Li, Chris, Ginette Gervais, and Aurélie Duval. 2006. *The Dynamics of Overqualification: Canada's Underemployed University Graduates*. Statistics Canada Catalogue no. 11-621-MIE2006039. Ottawa: Statistics Canada.

Li, Peter S. 1988. *Ethnic Inequality in a Class Society*. Toronto: Wall and Thompson.

———. 1998. 'The Market Value and Social Value of Race'. Chapter 5 in Vic Satzewich, ed., *Racism and Social Inequality in Canada*. Toronto: Thompson Educational.

———. 2000. 'Earning Disparities between Immigrants and Native-Born Canadians'. *Canadian Review of Sociology and Anthropology* 37, 3: 289–311.

———. 2001a. 'Immigrants' Propensity to Self-Employment: Evidence from Canada'. *International Migration Review* 35, 4: 1106–28.

———. 2001b. 'The Market Worth of Immigrants' Educational Credentials'. *Canadian Public Policy* 27, 1: 23–38.

———. 2003. *Destination Canada: Immigration Debates and Issues*. Don Mills, ON: Oxford University Press.

———, and Chunhong Dong. 2007. 'Earnings of Chinese Immigrants in the Enclave and Mainstream Economy'. *Canadian Review of Sociology and Anthropology* 44, 1: 65–99.

Lian, Jason Z., and David Ralph Matthews. 1998. 'Does the Vertical Mosaic Still Exist? Ethnicity and Income in Canada, 1991'. *Canadian Review of Sociology and Anthropology* 35, 4: 461.

Lightman, Ernie, Andrew Mitchell, and Dean Herd. 2005. 'Workfare in Toronto: More of the Same?' *Journal of Sociology and Social Welfare* 32, 4: 65–75.

Link, Bruce G., Bruce P. Dohrenwend, and Andrew E. Skodol. 1986. 'Socio-economic Status and Schizophrenia: Noisome Occupational Characteristics as a Risk Factor'. *American Sociological Review* 51: 242–58.

Link, Bruce G., and Jo Phelan. 1995. 'Social Conditions as Fundamental Causes of Disease'. *Journal of Health and Social Behavior* 35: 80–94.

———. 2000. 'Evaluating the Fundamental Cause Explanation for Social Disparities in Health'. Chapter 3 in Chloe E. Bird, Peter Conrad, and Allen M. Fremont, eds, *Handbook of Medical Sociology*, 5th edn. Englewood Cliffs, NJ: Prentice-Hall.

Lipps, Garth, and Jeffrey Frank. 1997. 'The National Longitudinal Survey of Children and Youth, 1994–95: Initial Results from the School Component'. *Education Quarterly Review* 4, 2: 43–57. Statistics Canada Catalogue no. 81-003-XPB.

Little, Don. 1995. 'Earnings and Labour Force Status of 1990 Graduates'. *Education Quarterly Review* 2, 3: 10–20. Statistics Canada Catalogue no. 81-003.

Little, Margaret. 1999. 'The Blurring of Boundaries: Private and Public Welfare for Single Mothers in Ontario'. Chapter 6 in Pat Armstrong and M. Patricia Connelly, eds, *Feminism, Political Economy and the State: Contested Terrain*. Toronto: Canadian Scholars' Press.

Livingstone, David W. 2001. 'Public Education at the Crossroads: Confronting Underemployment in a Knowledge Society'. Chapter 5 in Dan Glenday and Ann Duffy, eds, *Canadian Society: Meeting the Challenges of the Twenty-First Century*. Toronto: Oxford University Press Canada.

Lobao, Linda M., Gregory Hooks, and Ann R. Tickamyer. 2007. *The Sociology of Spatial Inequality*. Albany: State University of New York Press.

Long, Cindy. 2007. 'Institutes at Odds over

Methodology: C.D. Howe Says Fraser Disregarded Socioeconomic Factors'. *Ottawa Citizen*, 1 March.

Looker, E. Diane, and Graham S. Lowe. 2001. *Postsecondary Access and Student Financial Aid in Canada: Current Knowledge and Research Gaps*. Ottawa: Canadian Policy Research Networks / Canadian Millennium Scholarship Foundation. http://www.millenniumscholarships.ca/images/Publications/cprn-bkgnd.pdf.

Lorber, Judith. 1994. *Paradoxes of Gender*. New Haven, CT: Yale University Press.

———. 2000. 'Believing Is Seeing: Biology as Ideology'. Chapter 1 in Maxime Baca Zinn, Pierrette Hondagneu-Sotelo, and Michael A. Messner, eds, *Through the Prism of Difference*, 2nd edn. Needham Heights, MA: Allyn and Bacon.

———. 2006. 'Shifting Paradigms and Challenging Categories.' *Social Problems* 53, 4: 448–53.

Lorde, Audre. 1982. *Zami: A New Spelling of My Name*. Freedom, CA: Crossing Press.

Loveman, Mara. 1999. 'Is "Race" Essential?' *American Sociological Review* 64: 891–8.

Lowe, Graham S. 2000. *The Quality of Work: A People-Centred Agenda*. Toronto: Oxford University Press.

Lukes, Steven. 1974. *Power: A Radical View*. London: MacMillan.

Lundberg, Olle. 1997. 'Childhood Conditions, Sense of Coherence, Social Class and Adult Ill Health: Exploring Their Theoretical and Empirical Relations'. *Social Science and Medicine* 44, 6: 821–31.

Luxton, Meg. 1980. *More Than a Labour of Love: Three Generations of Women's Work in the Home*. Toronto: Women's Press.

Luxton, Meg, and June Corman. 2001. *Getting By in Hard Times: Gendered Labour at Home and on the Job*. Toronto: University of Toronto Press.

Lynch, J.W., G.A. Kaplan, and J.T. Salonen. 1997. 'Why Do Poor People Behave Poorly? Variation in Adult Health Behaviours and Psychosocial Characteristics by Stages of the Socio-economic Lifecourse'. *Social Science and Medicine* 44, 6: 809–19.

Lynn, Marion, ed. 2003. *Voices: Essays on Canadian Families*. 2nd edn. Scarborough, ON: Nelson.

McAll, Christopher. 1990. *Class, Ethnicity and Social Inequality*. Montreal: McGill-Queen's University Press.

MacBride-King, Judith, and Kimberley Bachmann. 1999. *Is Work-Life Balance Still an Issue for Canadians and Their Employers? You Bet It Is*. Ottawa: Conference Board of Canada.

McCourt, Frank. 1996. *Angela's Ashes: A Memoir*. New York: Touchstone.

McDaniel, Susan A. 2001. 'Born at the Right Time? Gendered Generations and Webs of Entitlement and Responsibility'. *Canadian Journal of Sociology* 26, 2: 193–214.

———. 2002. 'Women's Changing Relations to the State and Citizenship: Caring and Intergenerational Relations in Globalizing Western Democracies'. *Canadian Review of Sociology and Anthropology* 39, 2: 125–50.

———. 2004. 'Generationing Gender: Justice and the Division of Welfare'. *Journal of Aging Studies* 18, 1: 27–44.

———. 2005. 'The Family Lives of the Middle-Aged and Elderly in Canada'. Chapter 9 in M. Baker, ed., *Families: Changing Trends in Canada*. Toronto: McGraw-Hill Ryerson.

McDonald, L., J. Hornick, G. Robertson, and J. Wallace. 1991. *Elder Abuse and Neglect in Canada*. Toronto: Butterworths.

McDonald, L., and B. Wigdor. 1995. 'Taking Stock: Elder Abuse Research in Canada'. *Canadian Journal on Aging* 14, suppl. 2: 1–6.

McDonough, Peggy, and Vivienne Walters. 2001. 'Gender and Health: Reassessing Patterns and Explanations'. *Social Science and Medicine* 52, 4: 547–59.

McDonough, Peggy, David R. Williams, James S. House, and Greg J. Duncan. 1999. 'Gender and the Socioeconomic Gradient in Mortality'. *Journal of Health and Social Behavior* 40, 1: 17–31.

McGregor, Gaile. 2001. *A Fact Sheet on the Economics of Aging in Canada*. London, ON: Terraconnaissance.

Macintyre, Sally, Graeme Ford, and Kate Hunt. 1999. 'Do Women 'Over-report' Morbidity? Men's and

Women's Responses to Structured Prompting on a Standard Question on Long Standing Illness'. *Social Science and Medicine* 48, 1: 89–98.

McIntyre, Sheila, and Jennifer Scott. 2000. 'Submissions to the Committee on Justice and Legal Affairs Review of Bill C-46'. Pp. 348–56 in Barbara A. Crow and Lise Gotell, eds, *Open Boundaries: A Canadian Women's Studies Reader*. Toronto: Prentice-Hall.

Mackey, Eva. 1999. The House of Difference: Cultural Politics and National Identity in Canada. London: Routledge.

McKinlay, John B. 1996. 'Some Contributions from the Social System to Gender Inequalities in Heart Disease'. *Journal of Health and Social Behavior* 37, 1: 1–26.

McLaren, Angus. 1991. *Our Own Master Race: Eugenics in Canada, 1885–1945*. Toronto: McClelland & Stewart.

———, and Arlene Tigar McLaren. 1997. The Bedroom and the State: The Changing Practices and Politics of Contraception and Abortion in Canada, 1880–1997, 2nd edn. Toronto: Oxford University Press.

McLeod, Jane D., and Kathryn J. Lively. 2007. 'Social Psychology and Stress Research'. Chapter 12 in William Avison, Jane McLeod, and Bernice Pescosilido, eds, *Mental Health, Social Mirror*. New York: Springer.

McLeod, Jane D., and Michael J. Shanahan. 1996. 'Trajectories of Poverty and Children's Mental Health'. *Journal of Health and Social Behavior* 37, 3: 207–20.

McMahon, Martha. 1995. Engendering Motherhood: Identity and Self-Transformation in Women's Lives. New York: Guilford Press.

MacMillan, Harriet L., Christine A. Walsh, Ellen Jamieson, Maria Y-Y. Wong, Emily J. Faries, Harvey McCue, Angus B. MacMillan, David (Dan) R. Offord, and the Technical Advisory Committee of the Chiefs of Ontario. 2003. 'The Health of Ontario First Nations People: Results from the Ontario First Nations Regional Health Survey'. *Canadian Journal of Public Health* 94, 3: 168–72.

McMullan, John L. 2006. 'News, Truth and the Recognition of Corporate Crime'. *Canadian Journal of Criminology and Criminal Justice* 48, 6: 905–39.

———, and Stephen Smith. 1997. 'Toxic Steel: State-Corporate Crime and the Contamination of the Environment'. Chapter 3 in John McMullan, David Perrier, Stephen Smith, and Peter Swan, eds, *Crimes, Laws and Communities*. Halifax: Fernwood.

McMullen, Kathryn. 2004. 'The Gap in Achievement between Boys and Girls'. *Education Matters: Insights on Education, Learning and Training in Canada* 1, 4. Statistics Canada Catalogue no. 81-004-XIE.

———. 2005. 'Aboriginal Peoples in Canada's Urban Area: Narrowing the Education Gap'. *Education Matters: Insights on Education, Learning and Training in Canada* 2, 3. Statistics Canada Catalogue no. 81-004-XIE.

McMullin, Julie Ann. 1995. 'Theorizing Age and Gender Relations'. Chapter 3 in Sara Arber and Jay Ginn, eds, *Connecting Gender and Ageing: A Sociological Approach*. Buckingham, UK: Open University Press.

———. 1996. 'Connecting Age, Gender, Class, and Ethnicity: A Case Study of the Garment Industry in Montreal'. PhD dissertation, University of Toronto.

———. 2000. 'Diversity and the State of Sociological Aging Theory'. *The Gerontologist* 40: 517–30.

———. 2002. 'Negotiating Mothering and Caring in an Inflexible Paid Work Environment: A Case Study of Older Garment Workers'. *Hallym International Journal on Aging* 4, 2: 141–60.

———, and Peri Ballantyne. 1995. 'Employment Characteristics and Income: Assessing Gender and Age Group Effects for Canadians Aged 45 Years and Over'. *Canadian Journal of Sociology* 20, 4: 529–55.

———, and Ellie Berger. 2006. 'Gendered Ageism/Age(ed) Sexism: The Case of Unemployed Older Workers'. Chapter 9 in Toni Calasanti and Kate Slevin, eds, *Age Matters: Realigning Feminist Thinking*. New York: Routledge.

———, and John Cairney. 2004. 'Self-Esteem and the

Intersection of Age, Class, and Gender'. *Journal of Aging Studies* 18: 75–90.

———, and Victor W. Marshall. 1999. 'Structure and Agency in the Retirement Process: A Case Study of Montreal Garment Workers'. Chapter 11 in C.D. Ryff and V.W. Marshall, eds, *The Self and Society in Aging Processes*. New York: Springer.

———. 2001. 'Ageism, Age Relations and Garment Industry Work in Montreal'. *The Gerontologist* 41: 111–22.

———, and Kim M. Shuey. 2006. 'Ageing, Disability and Workplace Accommodations'. *Aging & Society* 26: 831–47.

Mahalik, James R., Shaun M. Burns, and Matthew Syzdek. 2007. 'Masculinity and Perceived Normative Health Behaviors as Predictors of Men's Health Behaviors'. *Social Science and Medicine* 64: 2201–9.

Maher, Timothy. 1998. 'Environmental Oppression: Who Is Targeted for Toxic Exposure?' *Journal of Black Studies* 28, 3: 357–67.

Makarenko, Jay. 2008. '2008 Election Campaign Political Party Platforms'. *Mapleleafweb*, 3 October. http://www.mapleleafweb.com/features/2008-election-campaign-political-party-platforms.

Malat, Jennifer R., Michelle van Ryn, and David Purcell. 2006. 'Race, Socioeconomic Status, and the Perceived Importance of Positive Self-Presentation in Health Care'. *Social Science and Medicine* 62: 2479–88.

Mandell, Nancy, and Ann Duffy. 2005. 'Explaining Family Lives'. Chapter 1 in Nancy Mandell and Ann Duffy, eds, *Canadian Families: Race, Class, Gender, and Sexuality*, 3rd edn. Toronto: Thomson Nelson.

Mannheim, Karl. [1928] 1952. 'The Problem of Generations'. Part 7 in Karl Mannheim, *Essays on the Sociology of Knowledge*, edited by P. Kecskemeti. London: Routledge and Kegan Paul.

Mao, Yang, Jinfu Hu, Anne-Marie Ugnat, Robert Semenciw, and Shirley Fincham. 2001. 'Socioeconomic Status and Lung Cancer Risk in Canada'. *International Journal of Epidemiology* 30: 809–17.

Mao, Y., J. Hu, A.M. Ugnat, and K. White. 2000. 'Non-Hodgkin's Lymphoma and Occupational Exposure to Chemicals in Canada'. *Annals of Oncology* 11, suppl. 1: 69–73.

Margolis, Maxine, 2001. 'Putting Mothers on the Pedestal'. Chapter 10 in Bonnie J. Fox, ed., *Family Patterns, Gender Relations*. Toronto: Oxford University Press.

Marmot, M.G. 2005. 'Social Determinants of Health Inequalities'. *The Lancet* 365: 1099–104.

———. 2006. 'Status Syndrome: A Challenge to Medicine'. *JAMA* 295, 11: 1304–7.

———. 2007. 'Achieving Health Equity: From Root Causes to Fair Outcomes'. *The Lancet* 370: 1153–63.

Marshall, Barbara L. 2000. *Configuring Gender: Explorations in Theory and Politics*. Peterborough, ON: Broadview Press.

Marshall, Barbara L., and Stephen Katz. 2002. 'Forever Functional: Sexual Fitness and the Ageing Male Body'. *Body and Society* 8: 4: 3–70.

Marshall, Katherine. 1993a. 'Dual Earners: Who's Responsible for Housework?' *Canadian Social Trends* 31: 11–14.

———. 1993b. 'Employed Parents and the Division of Housework'. *Perspectives on Labour and Income* 5, 3: 23–30.

———. 2000. 'Incomes of Younger Retired Women: The Past 30 Years'. *Perspectives on Labour and Income* 12, 4: 9–17. Statistics Canada Catalogue no. 75-001-XPE.

———. 2006. 'Converging Gender Roles'. *Perspectives on Labour and Income* 7, 7. Statistics Canada Catalogue no. 75-001-XIE.

Marshall, Katherine, and Vincent Ferrao. 2007. 'Participation of Older Workers'. *Perpectives*, August. Statistics Canada Catalogue no. 75-001-XE.

Marshall, T.H. 1950. *Citizenship and Social Class*. Cambridge: Cambridge University Press.

Marshall, Victor W. 1983. 'Generations, Age Groups, and Cohorts: Conceptual Distinctions'. *Canadian Journal on Aging* 2: 51–61.

———. 1995. 'The Micro-Macro Link in the Sociology of Aging'. Pp. 337–71 in C. Hummel and

C. Lalive D'Epinay, eds, *Images of Aging in Western Societies*. Proceedings of the 2nd Images of Aging conference. Geneva: Centre for Interdisciplinary Gerontology, University of Geneva.

Marshall, Victor W., Walter Heinz, Helga Krueger, and Anil Verma, eds. 2001. *Restructuring Work and the Life Course*. Toronto: University of Toronto Press.

Marshall, Victor W., Fay Lomax Cook, and Joanne Gard Marshall. 1993. 'Conflict over Intergenerational Equity: Rhetoric and Reality in a Comparative Context'. Pp. 119–40 in Vern L. Bengtson and W.A. Achenbaum, eds, *The Changing Contract across Generations*. New York: Aldine de Gruyter.

Marshall, Victor W., and Margaret Mueller. 2002. *Rethinking Social Policy for an Aging Workforce and Society: Insights from the Life Course Perspective*. Ottawa: Canadian Policy Research Networks. Document no. 11849.

Marshall, Victor W., and J. Tindale. 1978. 'Notes for a Radical Gerontology'. *International Journal of Aging and Human Development* 9: 163–75.

Martin, Sheilah, and Murray Coleman. 1995. 'Judicial Intervention in Pregnancy'. *McGill Law Journal* 40: 947–91.

Martin, Steven P., and John Robinson. 2007. 'The Income Digital Divide: Trends and Predictions for Levels of Internet Use'. *Social Problems* 54: 1–22.

Martin-Matthews, Anne. 2000. 'Intergenerational Caregiving: How Apocalyptic and Dominant Demographies Form the Questions and Shape the Answers'. Pp. 80–79 in Ellen M. Gee and Glori M. Guttman, eds, *The Overselling of Population Aging: Apocalyptic Demography, Intergenerational Challenges, and Social Policy*. Don Mills, ON: Oxford University Press.

Marx, Karl. [1852] 1963. *The 18th Brumaire of Louis Bonaparte*. New York: International Publishers.

———.[1848] 1983. 'The Communist Manifesto'. In *The Portable Karl Marx*. New York: Penguin.

———. [1893–94] 1956. 'Capital, Vol. III'. Pp. 178–9 in Karl Marx, *Selected Writings in Sociology and Social Philosophy*, translated by T.B. Bottomore, edited by T.B. Bottomore and Maximilien Rubel. New York: McGraw-Hill.

———. 1969. *Selected Works*. Vol. I. Moscow: Progress Publishers.

Marx, Karl, and Friedrich Engels. [1848] 1970. *The Communist Manifesto*. New York: Washington Square Press.

Mata, Fernando. 1997. Intergenerational Transmission of Education and Socio-economic Status: A Look at Immigrants, Visible Minorities and Aboriginals. Income and Labour Dynamics Working Paper Series. Statistics Canada Catalogue no. 97-077-5F0002M. Ottawa: Statistics Canada.

Matheson, Flora I., Rahim Moineddin, and Richard H. Glazier. 2008. 'The Weight of Place: A Multilevel Analysis of Gender, Neighborhood Material Deprivation, and Body Mass Index among Canadian Adults'. *Social Science and Medicine* 66, 3: 675–90.

Matthews, Sharon, Orly Manor, and Chris Power. 1999. 'Social Inequalities in Health: Are There Gender Differences?' *Social Science and Medicine* 48, 1: 49–60.

Maxwell, Judith. 2008. 'Bridging the Access Gap: It Starts with First-Generation Students'. *The Globe and Mail*, 19 May.

May, Martha. 1993. 'Bread before Roses: American Workingmen, Labour Unions and the Family Wage'. Chapter 11 in Bonnie J. Fox, ed., *Family Patterns, Gender Relations*. Toronto: Oxford University Press.

Mayer, L.U., and W. Muller. 1986. 'The State and the Structure of the Life Course'. Chapter 10 in A.B. Sorensen, F.E. Weinert, and L.R. Sherrod, eds, *Human Development and the Life Course: Multidisciplinary Perspectives*. Hillsdale, NJ: Lawrence Erlbaum Associates.

Menaghan, Elizabeth G. 1990. 'Social Stress and Individual Distress'. *Research in Community and Mental Health* 6: 107–41.

Menec, Verena H., Lisa Lix, and Leonard MacWilliam. 2005. 'Trends in the Status of Older Manitobans, 1985 to 1999'. *Canadian Journal on Aging* 24, suppl.: 5–14.

Menendez, Maria, Joan Benach, Carles Muntaner, Marcelo Amable, and Patricia O'Campo. 2007.

'Is Precarious Employment More Damaging to Women's Health Than Men's?' *Social Science and Medicine* 64: 776–81.

Messing, Karen. 1997. 'Women's Occupational Health: A Critical Review and Discussion of Current Issues'. *Women and Health* 25, 4: 39–68.

———. 1998. One-Eyed Science: Occupational Health and Women Workers. Philadelphia: Temple University Press.

Metcalfe, Chris, George Davey Smith, Jonathan A. C. Sterne, Pauline Heslop, John Macleod, and Carole L. Hart. 2005. 'Cause-Specific Hospital Admission and Mortality among Working Men: Association with Socioeconomic Circumstances in Childhood and Adult Life, and the Mediating Role of Daily Stress'. *European Journal of Public Health* 15, 3: 238–44.

Middlesex-London Health Unit. 2000. *Final Report of the Task Force on the Health Effects of Women Abuse*. London, ON: Middlesex-London Health Unit.

Miech, Richard Allen, and Michael J. Shanahan. 2000. 'Socioeconomic Status and Depression over the Life Course'. *Journal of Health and Social Behavior* 41, 2: 162–76.

Miles, Robert. 1989. *Racism*. London: Routledge.

Miles, Robert, and Rudy Torres. 2000. 'Does Race Matter? Transatlantic Perspectives on Racism after "Race Relations"'. Chapter 2 in Madeline A. Kalbach and Warren E. Kalbach, eds, *Perspectives on Ethnicity in Canada*. Toronto: Harcourt Canada.

Millar, Wayne. 1992. 'Place of Birth and Ethnic Status: Factors Associated with Smoking Prevalence among Canadians'. *Health Reports* 4, 1: 7–24. Statistics Canada Catalogue no. 82-003.

Millett, Kate. 1969. *Sexual Politics*. New York: Avon Books.

Mirchandani, Kiran, and Wendy Chan. 2007. *Criminalizing Race, Criminalizing Poverty: Welfare Fraud Enforcement in Canada*. Halifax: Fernwood.

Mitchell, B. 2000. 'The Refilled "Nest": Debunking the Myth of Families in Crisis'. Pp. 80–99 in E.M. Gee and G.M. Guttman, eds, *The Overselling of Population Aging: Apocalyptic Demography,*

Intergenerational Challenges, and Social Policy. Don Mills, ON: Oxford University Press,.

Mitchell, B., and E.M. Gee. 1996. 'Boomerang Kids and Midlife Parental Marital Satisfaction'. *Family Relations* 45: 442–8.

Mitchinson, Wendy. 1991. The Nature of Their Bodies: Women and Their Doctors in Victorian Canada. Toronto: University of Toronto Press.

Mittelstaedt, Martin. 2007. 'Sarnia's Emissions Affecting Health, Study Says'. *The Globe and Mail*, 4 October.

Monsebraaten, Laurie. 2008. 'Having a Job, but Losing Ground; Report Shows Ontario Child Poverty Rate Still Rising; System Penalizes Working Poor'. *The Toronto Star*, 2 April.

Monture, Patricia A. 2007. 'Racing and Erasing: Law and Gender in White Settler Societies'. Pp. 197–216 in Sean P. Hier and B. Singh Bolaria, eds, *Race and Racism in 21st Century Canada: Continuity, Complexity, and Change*. Peterborough, ON: Broadview Press.

Mooers, Colin. 1999. 'Can We Still Resist? Globalization, Citizenship Rights and Class Formation'. Chapter 20 in Dave Broad and Wayne Antony, eds, *Citizens or Consumers? Social Policy in a Market Society*. Halifax: Fernwood.

Morgan, D.H.J. 1985. *The Family, Politics, and Social Theory*. London: Routledge and Kegan Paul.

Morgan, Kathryn Pauly. 1998. 'Women and the Knife: Cosmetic Surgery and the Colonization of Women's Bodies'. Chapter 11 in Rose Weitz, ed., *The Politics of Women's Bodies: Sexuality, Appearance, and Behavior*. New York: Oxford University Press.

Morissette, René. 2002. 'Pensions: Immigrants and Visible Minorities'. *Perspectives on Labour and Income* 3, 6: 5–11. Statistics Canada Catalogue no. 75-001-XIE.

Morissette, René, and Yuri Ostrovsky. 2006. 'Earnings Instability'. *Perspectives on Labour and Income* 18, 4: 5–16. Statistics Canada Catalogue no. 75-001-XIE.

Morris, Margaret E., and Anthea Symonds. 2004. '"We've Been Trained to Put Up with It": Real Women and the Menopause'. *Critical Public Health*

14, 3: 311–23.

Morris, Martina, Annette D. Bernhardt, and Mark S. Handcock. 1994. 'Economic Inequality: New Methods for New Trends'. *American Sociological Review* 59, 2: 205–19.

Mullings, Leith, and Amy J. Schultz. 2006. 'Intersectionality and Health: An Introduction'. Chapter 1 in Amy J. Schultz and Leith Mullings, eds, *Gender, Race, Class and Health: Intersectional Approaches*. San Francisco, CA: Jossey-Bass.

Muntaner, Carles, Carme Borrell, and Haejoo Chung. 2007. 'Class Relations, Economic Inequality and Mental Health: Why Social Class Matters to the Sociology of Mental Health'. Chapter 6 in William Avison, Jane McLeod, and Bernice Pescosilido, eds, *Mental Health, Social Mirror*. New York: Springer.

Muntaner, C., W.W. Eaton, C. Diala, R.C. Kessler, and P.D. Sorlie. 1998. 'Social Class, Assets, Organizational Control and the Prevalence of Common Groups of Common Groups of Psychiatric Disorders'. *Social Science and Medicine* 47, 12: 2043–53.

Murdock, George. 1949. *Social Structure*. New York: MacMillan.

Murphy, Brian, Paul Roberts, and Michael Wolfe. 2007. 'High-Income Canadians'. *Perspectives on Labour and Income* 19, 4: 5–17. Statistics Canada Catalogue no. 75-001-XIE.

Mustard, Cameron A., Shelley Derkson, Jean-Marie Berthelot, Michael Wolfson, and Leslie L. Roos. 1997. 'Age-Specific Education and Income Gradients in Morbidity and Mortality in a Canadian Province'. *Social Science and Medicine* 45, 3: 383–97.

Myers, Karen, and Patrice de Broucker. 2006. *Too Many Left Behind: Canada's Adult Education and Training System*. Research Report 34, Work Network. Ottawa: Canadian Policy Research Networks. www.cprn.org/documents/43977_en.pdf.

Myles, John F. 1980. 'The Aged, the State, and the Structure of Inequality'. Pp. 317–42 in J. Harp and J. Hofley, eds, *Structural Inequality in Canada*. Toronto: Prentice Hall.

———. 1981. 'Income Inequality and Status Maintenance'. *Research on Aging* 3: 123–41.

———. 1984. The Political Economy of Public Pensions. Boston: Little Brown.

———. 1989. Old Age in the Welfare State: The Political Economy of Public Pensions. Rev. edn. Lawrence: University Press of Kansas.

———. 1995. 'The Market's Revenge: Old Age Security and Social Rights'. Wilson Abernathy Distinguished Lecture, University of Toronto, April.

———. 2000. *The Maturation of Canada's Retirement Income System: Income Levels, Income Inequality and Low-Income among the Elderly*. Statistics Canada Catalogue no. 11F0019MPE, no. 147. Ottawa: Statistics Canada / Tallahassee: Florida State University.

———, and Debra Street. 1995. 'Should the Economic Life Course Be Redesigned? Old Age Security in a Time of Transition'. *Canadian Journal on Aging* 14: 335–59.

Nabalamba, Alice, and Wayne J. Millar. 2007. 'Going to the Doctor'. *Health Reports* 18, 1: 23–35. Statistics Canada Catalogue no. 82-003.

Nakhaie, M. Reza. 1995. 'Ownership and Management Positions of Canadian Ethnic Groups in 1973 and 1989'. *Canadian Journal of Sociology* 20, 2: 167–92.

———. 1997. 'Vertical Mosaic among the Elites: The New Imagery Revisited'. *Canadian Review of Sociology and Anthropology* 34, 1: 1–24.

———. 2006. 'A Comparison of the Earnings of the Canadian Native-Born and Immigrants, 2001'. *Canadian Ethnic Studies* 38, 2: 19–46.

———, and James Curtis. 1998. 'Effects of Class Positions of Parents on Educational Attainment of Daughters and Sons'. *Canadian Review of Sociology and Anthropology* 35, 4: 483–515.

National Council of Welfare. 2000. *Poverty Profile: A Report*. Ottawa: Minister of Public Works and Government Services Canada.

———. 2006a. 'Persistence of Poverty'. http://www.ncwcnbes.net/en/research/povertstats/related-factsheets.html.

———. 2006b. *Poverty Profile 2002–2003*. Ottawa:

Minister of Public Works and Government Services.

———. 2007. *Poverty Statistics 2004*. Ottawa: Minister of Public Works and Government Services.

———. 2008. 'Factsheet 1: Statistics Canada's Before-Tax Low Income Cutoffs (1992 Base) for 2006'. http://www.ncwcnbes.net/documents/researchpublications/OtherFactSheets/PovertyLines/2006ENG.pdf.

Nelson, Jay. 2002. '"A Strange Revolution in the Manners of the Country": Aboriginal-Settler Intermarriage in Nineteenth-Century British Columbia'. Chapter 1 in John McLaren, Robert Menzies, and Dorothy E. Chunn, eds, *Regulating Lives: Historical Essays on the State, Society, the Individual and the Law*. Vancouver: UBC Press.

Neugarten, B.L. 1970. 'The Old and the Young in Modern Societies'. *American Behavioral Scientist* 4: 13–24.

Neugarten, B.L., and G.O. Hagestad. 1976. 'Age and the Life Course'. In R.H. Binstock and E. Shanas, eds, *Handbook of Aging and the Social Sciences*. New York: Van Nostrand Reinhold.

Neugarten, B.L., J.W. Moore, and J.C. Lowe. 1965. 'Age Norms, Age Constraints, and Adult Socialization'. *American Journal of Sociology* 70: 710–17.

Newbold, Bruce. 1998. 'Problems in Search of Solutions: Health and Canadian Aboriginals'. *Journal of Community Health* 23, 1: 59–73.

———. 2005. 'Health Status and Health Care of Immigrants in Canada: A Longitudinal Analysis'. *Journal of Health Services Research & Policy* 10, 2: 77–83.

Ng, Edward, Russell Wilkins, François Gendron, and Jean-Marie Berthelot. 2005. 'Dynamics of Immigrants' Health in Canada: Evidence from the National Population Health Survey'. *Healthy Today, Healthy Tomorrow? Findings from the National Population Health Survey* 1, 2: 1–11. Statistics Canada Catalogue no. 82-618. Ottawa: Statistics Canada.

Ng, Roxanna. 1993. 'Racism, Sexism and Nation-Building in Canada'. Pp. 50–9 in Cameron McCarthy and Warren Crichlow, eds, *Race, Identity and Representation in Education*. New York:

Routledge.

———. 2002. 'Freedom for Whom? Globalization and Trade from the Standpoint of Garment Workers'. *Canadian Women's Studies* 4: 74–81.

Nicholas, Andrea Bear. 2001. 'Canada's Colonial Mission: The Great White Bird'. Chapter 1 in K.P. Binda, ed., with Sharilyn Calliou, *Aboriginal Education in Canada: A Study in Decolonization*. Mississauga, ON: Canadian Educators' Press.

Nicholson, Linda. 1994. 'Interpreting Gender'. *Signs* 20, 1: 79–105.

Noh, Samuel, Morton Beiser, Violet Kaspar, Feng Hou, and Joanna Rummens. 1999. 'Perceived Racial Discrimination, Depression, and Coping: A Study of Southeast Asian Refugees in Canada'. *Journal of Health and Social Behavior* 40, 3: 193–207.

Noh, Samuel, Violet Kaspar, and K.A.S. Wickrama. 2007. 'Overt and Subtle Racial Discrimination and Mental Health: Preliminary Findings for Korean Immigrants'. *American Journal of Public Health* 97, 7: 1269–74.

O'Brien, Mary. 1981. *The Politics of Reproduction*. Boston: Routledge and Kegan Paul.

Offe, C., and V. Ronge. 1982. 'Thesis on the Theory of the State'. Pp. 249–56 in A. Giddens and D. Held, eds, *Classes, Power and Conflict*. Berkeley: University of California Press.

Offman, Alia, and Peggy J. Kleinplatz. 2004. 'Does PMDD Belong in the DSM? Challenging the Medicalization of Women's Bodies'. *Canadian Journal of Human Sexuality* 13, 1: 17–27.

Oliver, Lisa N., and Michael V. Hayes. 2008. 'Effects of Neighbourhood Income on Reported Body Mass Index: An Eight-Year Longitudinal Study of Canadian Children'. *BMC Public Health* 8: 16.

O'Loughlin, Jennifer. 1999. 'Understanding the Role of Ethnicity in Chronic Disease: A Challenge for the New Millennium'. *Canadian Medical Association Journal* 161, 2: 152–5.

Omi, Michael, and Howard Winant. 1994. *Racial Formation in the United States from the 1960s to the 1990s*. 2nd edn. New York: Routledge.

O'Neill, Katherine. 2008. 'Graphic List of Abuse to Settle Claims: Complex System of Determining

Payment Seen as Necessary to Manage Huge Numbers of Complaints by Former Residential-School Students'. *The Globe and Mail*, 25 February.

Ontario Health Quality Council. 2008. *Qmonitor: 2008 Report on Ontario's Health System*. Toronto: Ontario Health Quality Council.

O'Rand, Angela. 1996a. 'The Cumulative Stratification of the Life Course'. Pp. 188–207 in R.H. Binstock and L.K. George, eds, *Handbook of Aging and the Social Sciences*, 4th edn. New York: Academic Press.

———. 1996b. 'The Precious and the Precocious: Understanding Cumulative Disadvantage and Cumulative Advantage over the Life Course'. *The Gerontologist* 36: 230–8.

———, and Jennifer Hamil-Luker. 2005. 'Processes of Cumulative Adversity: Childhood Disadvantage and Increased Risk of Heart Attack across the Life Course'. *Journals of Gerontology* 60B, spec. iss. 2: 117–24.

Osberg, Lars. 1992. 'Canada's Economic Performance: Inequality, Poverty, and Growth'. Pp. 39–52 in Robert Allen and Gideon Rosenbluth, eds, *False Promises: The Failure of Conservative Economics*. Vancouver: New Star Books.

Osborne, Ken. 2000. 'Public Schooling and Citizenship Education in Canada'. *Canadian Ethnic Studies* 32, 1: 8–37.

Oxman-Martinez, Jacqueline, Shelly N. Abdool, and Margot Loiselle-Leonard. 2000. 'Immigration, Women and Health in Canada'. *Canadian Journal of Public Health* 91, 5: 394–5.

Pakulski, Jan, and Malcolm Waters. 1996. *The Death of Class*. London: Sage.

Palameta, Boris. 2004. 'Low Income among Immigrants and Visible Minorities'. *Perspectives on Labour and Income* 5, 4. Statistics Canada Catalogue no. 75-001-XIE.

Palameta, Boris, and Xuelin Zhang. 2006. 'Does It Pay to Go Back to School?' *Perspectives on Labour and Income* 7, 3: 5–11. Statistics Canada Catalogue no. 75-001-XIE.

Palaniappan, U., L. Starkey Jacobs, J. O'Loughlin, and K. Gray-Donald. 2001. 'Fruit and Vegetable Consumption Is Lower and Saturated Fat Intake Is Higher among Canadians Reporting Smoking'. *Journal of Nutrition* 131, 7: 1952–8.

Pampel, Fred C. 1998. *Aging, Social Inequality, and Public Policy*. Thousand Oaks, CA: Pine Forge Press.

Parker, Marti G., and Mats Thorslund. 2007. 'Health Trends in the Elderly Population: Getting Better and Getting Worse'. *The Gerontologist* 47, 2: 50–8.

Parkin, Frank. 1979. *Marxism and Class Theory: A Bourgeois Critique*. London: Tavistock.

Parsons, Talcott. 1929. 'Capitalism in Recent German Literature: Sombart and Weber—Concluded'. *Journal of Political Economy* 37: 31–51.

———. 1942. 'Age and Sex in the Social Structure of the United States'. *American Sociological Review* 7: 604–16.

———. 1949. *The Structure of Social Action: A Study in Social Theory with Reference to a Group of Recent European Writers*. Glencoe, IL: Free Press.

———. 1951. *The Social System*. Glencoe, IL: Free Press.

Passuth, P.M., and V.L. Bengtson. 1988. 'Sociological Theories of Aging: Current Perspectives and Future Directions'. Pp. 335–55 in J.E. Birren and V.L. Bengtson, eds, *Emergent Theories of Aging*. New York: Springer.

Patten, Scott, and Heather Juby. 2008. *A Profile of Clinical Depression in Canada*. Research Data Centre Network, Research Synthesis Series no. 1. Calgary: Department of Community Health Science and Psychiatry, Faculty of Medicine, University of Calgary. http://hdl.handle.net/1880/46327.

Pavalko, Eliza K., and Shari Woodbury. 2000. 'Social Roles as Process: Caregiving Careers and Women's Health'. *Journal of Health and Social Behavior* 41, 1: 91–105.

Pearce, Tralee. 2007. 'Adolescence Is Obsolete'. *The Globe and Mail*, 25 August.

Pearlin, Leonard I., Scott Schieman, Elena M. Fazio, and Stephen C. Meersman. 2005. 'Stress, Health, and the Life Course: Some Conceptual Perspectives'. *Journal of Health and Social Behavior* 46, 2:

205–19.

Peek, M. Kristen, and Raymond T. Coward. 2000. 'Antecedents of Disability for Older Adults with Multiple Chronic Health Conditions'. *Research on Aging* 22, 4: 422–44.

Peppin, Patricia. 1995. 'Feminism, Law, and the Pharmaceutical Industry'. Chapter 5 in Frank Pearce and Laureen Snider, eds, *Corporate Crime: Contemporary Debates*. Toronto: University of Toronto Press.

Perkel, Colin. 2000. 'Ontario's Black Guards Want Probe into Workplace Racism'. *The Globe and Mail*, 7 April.

Perreault, Samuel. 2008. *Visible Minorities and Victimization 2004*. Canadian Centre for Justice Statistics Profile Series. Statistics Canada Catalogue no. 85F0033MIE, no. 15. Ottawa: Statistics Canada.

Pheasant, Valerie Bedassigae. 2001. 'My Mother Used to Dance'. Pp. 38–43 in Carl E. James and Adrienne Shadd, *Talking about Identity: Encounters in Race, Ethnicity, and Language*. Toronto: Between the Lines.

Phelan, Jo. C., and Bruce G. Link. 2005. 'Controlling Disease and Creating Disparities: A Fundamental Cause Perspective'. *Journals of Gerontology* 60B, spec. iss. 2: 27–33.

Phelan, Jo C., Bruce G.Link, Ana Diez-Roux, Ichiro Kawachi, and Bruce Levin. 2004. '"Fundamental Causes" of Social Inequalities in Mortality: A Test of the Theory'. *Journal of Health and Social Behavior* 45, 3: 265–85.

Phillips, L.R. 1986. 'Theoretical Explanations of Elder Abuse: Competing Hypotheses and Unresolved Issues'. Pp. 197–217 in K.A. Pillemer and R.S. Wold, eds, *Elder Abuse: Conflict in the Family*. Dover, MA: Auburn House.

Phillips, Paul, and Erin Phillips. 2000. *Women and Work: Inequality in the Canadian Labour Market*. Toronto: James Lorimer.

Phillipson, C. 1982. *Capitalism and the Construction of Old Age*. London: Macmillan.

Pichora, E.C., and J.I. Payne. 2007. 'Trends and Characteristics of Compensated Occupational Cancer in Ontario, Canada, 1937–2003'. *American Journal of Industrial Medicine* 50, 12: 980–91.

Picot, Garnett, Feng Hou, and Simon Coulombe. 2008. 'Poverty Dynamics among Recent Immigrants to Canada'. *International Migration Review* 42, 2: 393–424.

Picot, Garnett, and John Myles. 1995. *Social Transfers, Changing Family Structure, and Low Income among Children*. Statistics Canada Catalogue no. 11F0019MPE, no. 82. Ottawa: Statistics Canada.

Pinto, Laura. 2006. 'The Streaming of Working Class and Minority Students in Ontario'. *Our Schools, Our Selves* 15, 2: 79.

Plager, Laurie, and Edward Chen. 1999. 'Student Debt from 1990–91 to 1995–96: An Analysis of Canada Student Loans Data'. *Education Quarterly Review* 5, 4: 10–35. Statistics Canada Catalogue no. 81-003.

Podnieks, Elizabeth. 1992. 'National Survey on Abuse of the Elderly in Canada'. *Journal of Elder Abuse and Neglect* 4: 5–58.

Pollan, M., and P. Gustavsson. 1999. 'High-Risk Occupations for Breast Cancer in the Swedish Female Working Population'. *American Journal of Public Health* 89, 6: 875–81.

Pomerleau, Joceline, Linda L. Pederson, Truls Ostbye, Mark Speechley, and Kathy N. Speechley. 1997. 'Health Behaviours and Socio-economic Status in Ontario, Canada'. *European Journal of Epidemiology* 13: 613–22.

Poon, Preston. 2005. 'Who's Missing Out on the GIS?' *Perspectives on Labour and Income* 6, 10. Statistics Canada Catalogue no. 75-001-XIE.

Popenoe, David. 1993. 'American Family Decline, 1960–1990: A Review and Appraisal'. *Journal of Marriage and the Family* 55: 527–55.

———. 2005. *War over the Family*. New Brunswick, NJ: Transaction Publishers.

Porter, John. 1965. *The Vertical Mosaic: An Analysis of Social Class and Power in Canada*. Toronto: University of Toronto Press.

Poulantzas, Nicos. 1975. *Classes in Contemporary Capitalism*. London: New Left Books.

Power, Elaine M. 2005. 'Determinants of Healthy Eating among Low Income Canadians'. *Canadian*

Journal of Public Health 96, S3: 37–42.

Premji, Stéphanie, Frédéric Bertrand, Audrey Smargiassi, and Mark Daniel. 2007. 'Socio-economic Correlates of Municipal-Level Pollution Emissions on Montreal'. *Canadian Journal of Public Health* 98, 2: 138–42.

Prus, Steven G. 2007. 'Age, SES, and Health: A Population Level Analysis of Health Inequalities over the Lifecourse'. *Sociology of Health & Illness* 29, 2: 275–96.

Prus, Steven G., and Ellen Gee. 2003. 'Gender Differences in the Influence of Economic, Lifestyle, and Psychosocial Factors on Later Life Health'. *Canadian Journal of Public Health* 94, 4: 306–9.

Public Health Agency of Canada. 2006. *The Human Face of Mental Health and Mental Illness in Canada*. Ottawa: Public Health Agency of Canada.

———. 2008. *Healthy Settings for Young People in Canada*. Catalogue no. HP35-6/2007E-PDF. Ottawa: Minister of Health Canada.

Pulkingham, Jane. 1998. 'Remaking the Social Divisions of Welfare: Gender, "Dependency", and UI Reform'. *Studies in Political Economy* 56, Summer: 7–48.

Pupo, Norene. 2001. 'The Role of the State in a Restructured Economy'. Chapter 4 in Dan Glenday and Ann Duffy, eds, *Canadian Society: Meeting the Challenges of the Twenty-First Century*. Toronto: Oxford University Press.

Pyper, Wendy. 2006. 'Aging, Health, and Work'. *Perspectives on Labour and Income* 18, 1: 5–15. Statistics Canada Catalogue no. 75-001-XIE.

———. 2008. 'RRSP Investments'. *Perspectives on Labour and Income* 9, 2: 5–11. Statistics Canada Catalogue no. 75-001-XIE.

Quan, Hude, Andrew Fong, Carolyn De Coster, Jianli Wang, Richard Musto, Tom W. Noseworthy, and William A. Ghali. 2006. 'Variation in Health Services Utilization among Ethnic Populations'. *Canadian Medical Association Journal* 174, 6: 787–91.

Quan, Hude, Fu-Lin Wang, Donald Schopflocher, and Carolyn De Coster. 2007. 'Mortality, Cause of Death and Life Expectancy of Chinese Canadians in Alberta'. *Canadian Journal of Public Health* 98,

6: 500–5.

Ralston, Helen. 1996. *The Lived Experience of South Asian Immigrant Women in Atlantic Canada: The Interconnections of Race, Class, and Gender*. New York: Edwin Mellen Press.

Ranson, Gillian. 2003. 'Beyond Gender Differences: A Canadian Study of Women's and Men's Careers in Engineering'. *Gender, Work, and Organization* 10, 1: 22–41.

———. 2005. 'Paid and Upaid Work: How Do Families Divide Their Labour?' Chapter 5 in M. Baker, ed., *Families: Changing Trends in Canada*. Toronto: McGraw-Hill Ryerson.

———. forthcoming. *Against the Grain*. Toronto: University of Toronto Press.

Raphael, Dennis. 2006. 'Social Determinants of Health: An Overview of Concepts and Issues'. Chapter 5 in Dennis Raphael, Toba Bryant and Marcia Rioux, eds, *Staying Alive: Critical Perspectives on Health, Illness, and Health Care*. Toronto: Canadian Scholars' Press.

———. 2007. *Poverty and Policy in Canada: Implications for Health and Quality of Life*. Toronto: Canadian Scholars' Press.

Raphael, Dennis, ed. 2004. *Social Determinants of Health: Canadian Perspectives*. Toronto: Canadian Scholars' Press.

Rapoport, B., and C. Le Bourdais. 2006. 'Parental Time, Work Schedules, and Changing Gender Roles'. Chapter 4 in K. McQuillan and Z.R. Ravanera, eds, *Canada's Changing Families: Implications for Individuals and Society*. Toronto: University of Toronto Press.

Ray, Raka. 2006. 'Is the Revolution Missing or Are We Looking in the Wrong Places?' *Social Problems* 53, 4: 459–65.

Reiter, Ester. 1996. *Making Fast Food: From the Frying Pan into the Fire*. Montreal: McGill-Queen's University Press.

Reitz, Jeffrey G. 2007. 'Immigrant Employment Success in Canada, Part I: Individual and Contextual Causes'. *Journal of International Migration and Integration* 8, 1: 11–36.

Reitz, Jeffrey G., and Rupa Banerjee. 2007. *Racial*

Inequality, Social Cohesion and Policy Issues in Canada. Montreal: Institute for Research on Public Policy. www.irpp.org.

Remington, Robert. 2007. 'The Shocking Toll of Domestic Violence; Thousands of Women Feel Trapped'. *Calgary Herald*, 2 December.

Reynolds, L.T. 1992. 'A Retrospective on "Race": The Career of a Concept'. *Sociological Focus* 25, 1: 1–14.

Rich, Adrienne. 1980. 'Compulsory Heterosexuality and Lesbian Existence'. *Signs* 5: 631–60.

Richardson, K., P.R. Band, G. Astrakianakis, and N.D. Le. (2007). 'Male Bladder Cancer Risk and Occupational Exposure According to a Job-Exposure Matrix: A Case-Control Study in British Columbia, Canada'. *Scandanavian Journal of Work and Environmental Health* 33, 6: 454–64.

Rieker, Patricia P., and Chloe E. Bird. 2000. 'Sociological Explanations of Gender Differences in Mental and Physical Health'. Chapter 7 in Chloe E. Bird, Peter Conrad, and Allen M. Fremont, eds, *Handbook of Medical Sociology*, 5th edn. Englewood Cliffs, NJ: Prentice Hall.

———. 2005. 'Rethinking Gender Differences in Health: Why We Need to Integrate Social and Biological Perspectives'. *Journals of Gerontology* 60B, spec. iss. 2: 40–7.

Riley, Matilda White. 1971. 'Social Gerontology and the Age Stratification of Society'. *The Gerontologist* 11: 79–87.

———. 1985. 'Age Strata in Social Systems'. Pp. 369–411 in R.H. Binstock and E. Shanas, eds, *Handbook of Aging and the Social Sciences*. New York: Van Nostrand Reinhold.

———. 1988. 'On the Significance of Age in Sociology'. Pp. 24–45 in M.W. Riley with B.J. Huber and B.B. Hess, *Social Structures and Human Lives*. Newbury Park, CA: Sage.

———. 1994. 'Aging and Society: Past, Present and Future'. *The Gerontologist* 34: 436–46.

Riley, Matilda White, Anne Foner, and Joan Waring. 1988. 'Sociology of Age'. Pp. 243–90 in N.J. Smelser, ed., *Handbook of Sociology*. Newbury Park, CA: Sage,.

Riley, Matilda White, Marilyn Johnson, and Anne Foner. 1972. *Aging and Society*, vol. 3, *A Sociology of Age Stratification*. New York: Russell Sage Foundation.

Riley, Matilda White, and John W. Riley, Jr. 1994a. 'Age Integration and the Lives of Older People'. *The Gerontologist* 34: 110–15.

———. 1994b. 'Structural Lag: Past and Future'. Chapter 1 in M.W. Riley, R.L. Kahn, and A. Foner, eds, *Age and Structural Lag: Society's Failure to Provide Meaningful Opportunities in Work, Family, and Leisure*. New York: John Wiley.

Rinehart, James W. 2006. *The Tyranny of Work: Alienation and the Labour Process*. 5th edn. Toronto: Harcourt Brace.

Risman, Barbara J. 1998. *Gender Vertigo: American Families in Transition*. New Haven, CT: Yale University Press.

Robertson, Ann. 1998. 'Shifting Discourses on Health in Canada: From Health Promotion to Population Health'. *Health Promotion International* 13, 2: 155–66.

Rodgers, Karen. 1994. 'Wife Assault in Canada'. *Canadian Social Trends*, Autumn: 2–8. Ottawa: Statistics Canada.

Roos, Leslie L., Jennifer Magoon, Sumit Gupta, Dan Chateau, and Paul J. Veugelers. 2004. 'Socioeconomic Determinants of Mortality in Two Canadian Provinces: Multilevel Modelling and Neighborhood Context'. *Social Science & Medicine* 59, 76: 1435–47.

Roos, Noralou P., and Cameron A. Mustard. 1997. 'Variation in Health and Health Care Use by Socioeconomic Status in Winnipeg, Canada: Does the System Work Well? Yes and No'. *Milbank Quarterly* 75, 1: 89–111.

Rose, Kathryn M., April P. Carson, Diane Catellier, Ana Diez Roux, Carles Muntaner, Herman A. Tyroler, and Sharon B. Wyatt. 2004. 'Women's Employment Status and Mortality: The Atherosclerosis Risk in Communities Study'. *Journal of Women's Health* 13, 10: 1108–18.

Rosenberg, T., and S. Martel. 1998. 'Cancer Trends from 1972–1991 for Registered Indians Living on Manitoba Reserves'. *International Journal of Circumpolar Health* 57, suppl. 1: 391–8.

Rosenthal, C.J., S.H. Matthews, and V.W. Marshall. 1989. 'Is Parent Care Normative? The Experiences of a Sample of Middle-Aged Women'. *Research on Aging* 11, 2: 244–60.

Ross, David P., Katherine J. Scott, and Peter J. Smith. 2000. *The Canadian Fact Book on Poverty*. Ottawa: Canadian Council on Social Development.

Ross, David P., E. Richard Shillington, and Clarence Lochhead. 1994. *The Canadian Fact Book on Poverty*. Ottawa: Canadian Council on Social Development.

Ross, Nancy. 2004. *What Have We Learned Studying Income Inequality and Population Health?* Ottawa: Canadian Institute for Health Information.

Rotermann, Michele. 2006. 'Seniors' Health Care Use'. *Health Reports* 16, suppl.: 33–46. Statistics Canada Catalogue no. 82-003-SPE.

Rowntree, J., and Rowntree, M. 1968. 'The Political Economy of Youth'. *Our Generation* 6, 1–2: 155–90.

Rubenson, Kjell, Richard Desjardins, and Ee-Seul Yoon. 2007. *Adult Learning in Canada: A Comparative Perspective: Results from the Adult Literacy and Life Skills Surve'*. Statistics Canada Catalogue no. 89-552, no. 17. Ottawa: Minister of Industry.

Ryder, N. 1965. 'The Cohort as a Concept in the Study of Social Change'. *American Sociological Review* 30: 834–61.

Sabourin, Sharon. 2003. 'My Story—A Narrative: Refusing Mediocrity: Barriers to Higher Education for Sole Support Parents'. Unpublished manuscript.

Safaei, Jalil. 2007. 'Income and Health Inequality across Canadian Provinces'. *Health and Place* 13: 629–38.

Sainsbury, Diane. 1999. 'Gender and Social-Democratic Welfare States'. Chapter 3 in Diane Sainsbury, ed., *Gender and Welfare State Regimes*. New York: Oxford University Press.

Sales, Arnaud, Rejean Drolet, and Isabelle Bonneau. 2001. 'Academic Paths, Ageing, and the Living Conditions of Students in the Late 20th Century'.

Canadian Review of Sociology and Anthropology 38, 2: 167–88.

Samuel, John, and Kogalur Basavarajappa.2006. 'The Visible Minority Population in Canada: A Review of Numbers, Growth and Labour Force Issues'. *Canadian Studies in Population* 33, 2: 241–69

Sandstad, Nora Christie. 2008. 'Pregnant Women and the Fourteenth Amendment: A Feminist Examination of the Trend to Eliminate Women's Rights during Pregnancy'. *Law & Equality* 26, 1: 171–202.

Sangster, Joan. 1995. 'Doing Two Jobs: The Wage-Earning Mother, 1945–70'. Pp. 98–134 in Joy Parr, ed., *A Diversity of Women: Ontario, 1945–1980*. Toronto: University of Toronto Press,.

Satzewich, Vic. 1998. 'Race, Racism and Racialization: Contested Concepts'. Chapter 1 in Vic Satzewich, ed., *Racism and Social Inequality in Canada*. Toronto: Thompson Educational.

Schick, Carol. 2001. 'Keeping the Ivory Tower White: Discourse of Racial Domination'. Pp. 99–119 in S.H. Razack, ed., *Race, Space and the Law: Unmapping a White Settler Society*. Toronto: Between the Lines.

Schissel, Bernard. 1997. *Blaming Children: Youth Crime, Moral Panics and the Politics of Hate*. Halifax: Fernwood.

———. 2006. *Still Blaming Children: Youth Conduct and the Politics of Child Hating*. Black Point, NS: Fernwood.

———, and Terry Wotherspoon. 2003. *The Legacy of School for Aboriginal People: Education, Oppression and Emancipation*. Don Mills, ON: Oxford University Press.

Scott, Katherine. 1996. 'The Dilemma of Liberal Citizenship: Women and Social Assistance Reform in the 1990s'. *Studies in Political Economy* 50, Summer: 7–36.

Seeman, Neil. 2001. 'A Right to Welfare Is a Loss of Democracy'. *The Globe and Mail*, 31 October.

Sewell, William H.J., Jr. 1992. 'A Theory of Structure: Duality, Agency, and Transformation'. *American Journal of Sociology* 98: 1–29.

———. 2005. *Logics of History: Social Theory and*

Social Transformation. Chicago: University of Chicago Press.

Shaienks, Danielle, and Tomasz Gluszynski. 2007. *Participation in Postsecondary Education: Graduates, Continuers and Drop Outs, Results from YITS Cycle 4*. Culture, Tourism and the Centre for Education Statistics Research Papers. Statistics Canada Catalogue no. 81-595-MIE2007059. Ottawa: Statistics Canada.

Sharpe, Andrew, and Jill Hardt. 2006. *Five Deaths a Day: Workplace Fatalities in Canada, 1993–2005*. CSLS Research Paper 2006-04. Ottawa: Centre for the Study of Living Standards.

Sheehy, Elizabeth A. 2005. 'Legal Responses to Violence against Women in Canada'. Pp. 256–65 in B.A. Crow and L. Gotell, eds, *Open Boundaries: A Canadian Women's Studies Reader*, 2nd edn. Toronto: Pearson Prentice Hall.

Shellenbarger, Sue. 2001. 'Anger over Age Discrimination Grows as Baby Boomers Hit 55'. *The Globe and Mail*, 4 June.

Shields, Margot. 2004. 'Stress, Health and the Benefit of Social Support'. *Health Reports* 15, 1: 9–38. Statistics Canada Catalogue no. 82-003.

Shields, Margot, and Laurent Martel. 2006. 'Healthy Living among Seniors'. *Health Reports* 16, suppl.: 7–20. Statistics Canada Catalogue no. 82-003.

Shields, Margot, and Stéphane Tremblay. 2002. 'The Health of Canada's Communities'. *Health Reports* 13, suppl.: 1–24. Statistics Canada Catalogue no. 82-003.

Shim, Janet K. 2002. 'Understanding the Routinised Inclusion of Race, Socioeconomic Status and Sex in Epidemiology: The Utility of Concepts from Technoscience Studies'. *Sociology of Health and Illness* 24, 2: 129–50.

Shragge, Eric. 1997. 'Workfare: An Overview'. Chapter 1 in Eric Shragge, ed., *Workfare: Ideology for a New Underclass*. Toronto: Garamond Press.

Shuey, Kim M., and Andrea E. Willson. 2008. 'Cumulative Disadvantage and Black-White Disparities in Life-Course Health Trajectories'. *Research on Aging* 30, 2: 200–25.

Simmons, Alan B., and Dwaine E. Plaza. 1998.

'Breaking through the Glass Ceiling: The Pursuit of University Training among African-Caribbean Migrants and Their Children in Toronto'. *Canadian Ethnic Studies* 30, 3: 99–120.

Simon, Robin. 2000. 'The Importance of Culture in Sociological Theory and Research on Stress and Mental Health: A Missing Link?' Chapter 5 in Chloe E. Bird, Peter Conrad, and Allen M. Fremont, eds, *Handbook of Medical Sociology*, 5th edn. Englewood Cliffs, NJ: Prentice-Hall.

———. 2007. 'Contributions of the Sociology of Mental Health for Understanding the Social Antecedents, Social Regulation, and Social Distribution of Emotion'. Chapter 11 in William Avison, Jane McLeod, and Bernice Pescosilido, eds, *Mental Health, Social Mirror*. New York: Springer.

Singh, Sheldon M., Lawrence F.Paszat, Cindy Li, Jingsong He, Chris Vinden, and Linda Rabeneck. 2004. 'Association of Socioeconomic Status and Receipt of Colorectal Cancer Investigations: A Population-Based Retrospective Cohort Study'. *Canadian Medical Association Journal* 171, 5: 461–5.

Smith, Charles C. 2006. 'Racial Profiling in Canada, the United States, and the United Kingdom'. Chapter 3 in Frances Henry and Carol Tator, eds, *Racial Profiling in Canada: Challenging the Myth of 'A Few Bad Apples'*. Toronto: University of Toronto Press.

Smith, Derek G. 1975. *Canadian Indians and the Law: Selected Documents, 1663–1972*. Toronto: McClelland & Stewart.

Smith, Dorothy E. 1987. *The Everyday World as Problematic: A Feminist Sociology*. Toronto: University of Toronto Press.

Snider, Laureen. 1993. *Bad Business: Corporate Crime in Canada*. Toronto: Nelson Canada.

Snyder, Linda. 2006. 'Workfare: Ten Years of Pickin' on the Poor'. Pp. 309–30 in Anne Westhues, ed., *Canadian Social Policy: Issues and Perspectives*, 4th edn. Waterloo, ON: Wilfrid Laurier University Press.

Sokal, Laura, Herb Katz, Matthew Adkins, Tannis Grills, Crystal Stewart, Greg Priddle, Anastasia

Sych-Yereniuk, and Lori Chochinov-Harder. 2005. 'Factors Affecting Inner-City Boys' Reading: Are Male Teachers the Answer?' *Canadian Journal of Urban Research* 14, 1: 107–30.

Spitzer, Denise L. 2005. 'Engendering Health Disparities'. *Canadian Journal of Public Health* 96, suppl. 2: S78–96.

Stackhouse, John. 2001. 'Canada's Apartheid, Part 2, Crystal's Choice: The Best of Both Worlds'. *The Globe and Mail*, 5 November.

Stasiulis, Davia. 1999. 'Feminist Intersectional Theorizing'. Chapter 12 in Peter Li, ed., *Race and Ethnic Relations in Canada*, 2nd edn. Toronto: Oxford University Press.

Stasiulis, Davia, and Abigail B. Bakan. 1995. 'Making the Match: Domestic Placement Agencies and the Racialization of Women's Household Work'. *Signs* 20, 2: 303–35.

———. 1997. 'Negotiating Citizenship: The Case of Foreign Domestic Workers in Canada'. *Feminist Review* 57, 1: 112–39.

———. 2005. *Negotiating Citizenship: Migrant Women in Canada and the Global System*. Toronto: University of Toronto Press.

Statistics Canada. 2001a. *Annual Demographic Statistics*. Statistics Canada Catalogue no. 91-213XPB. Ottawa: Minister of Industry.

———. 2001b. 'Death-Shifting Trends'. *Health Reports* 12, 3: 41–6. Statistics Canada Catalogue no. 82-003.

———. 2001c. *Family Violence in Canada: A Statistical Profile, 2001*. Statistics Canada Catalogue no. 85-224. Ottawa: Minister of Industry.

———. 2001d. 'Health Care/Self-Care'. *Health Reports* 12, 3: 33–40. Statistics Canada Catalogue no. 82-003.

———. 2001e. 'The Health Divide: How the Sexes Differ'. *The Daily*, 26 April. Ottawa: Statistics Canada.

———. 2001f. *A Report on Adult Education and Training in Canada: Learning a Living*. Statistics Canada Catalogue no. 81-586-XPE. Ottawa: Minister of Industry.

———. 2001g. *Spousal Violence after Marital Separation*. Statistics Canada Catalogue no. 85-002-XIE. Ottawa: Minister of Industry.

———. 2001h. 'Stress and Well-Being'. *Health Reports* 12, 3: 21–32. Statistics Canada Catalogue no. 82-003.

———. 2001i. 'Taking Risks/Taking Care'. *Health Reports* 12, 3: 11–20. Statistics Canada Catalogue no. 82-003.

———. 2002a. CANSIM II, Table 282-0008. www.statcan.ca.

———. 2002b. *Family Violence in Canada: A Statistical Profile, 2002*. Statistics Canada Catalogue no. 85-224. Ottawa: Minister of Industry.

———. 200a. *Ethnic Diversity Survey 2002*. Ottawa: Statistics Canada.

———. 2003b. *Women and Men in Canada: A Statistical Glance*. Ottawa: Statitics Canada. http://dsp-psd.pwgsc.gc.ca/Collection/SW21-50-2003E.pdf.

———. 2004a. *Health Indicators*, no. 1. Statistics Canada Catalogue no. 82-221-XIE.

———. 2004b. 'Long-Term Unemployment'. *The Daily*, 21 April. Ottawa: Statistics Canada.

———. 2005a. 'Family Violence in Canada: A Statistical Profile'. *The Daily*, 14 July. Ottawa: Statistics Canada.

———. 2005b. *Family Violence in Canada: A Statistical Profile*. Statistics Canada Catalogue no. 85-224-XIE. Ottawa: Statistics Canada.

———. 2005c. *Income in Canada*. Statistics Canada Catalogue no. 75-202-XIE. Ottawa: Minister of Industry.

———. 2005d. *Survey of Earned Doctorates*. Statistics Canada Catalogue no. 81-595-MIE2005032. Ottawa: Statistics Canada.

———. 2006a. *The Canadian Labour Market at a Glance, 2005*. Ottawa: Statistics Canada, Labour Statistics Division.

———. 2006b. 'Health-Adjusted Life Expectancy, at Birth and at Age 65, by Sex and Income Group, Canada and Provinces, Occasional (years)'. CANSIM Table 102-0121. Ottawa: Statistics Canada.

———. 2006c. *Health Indicators*, no. 1. Statistics Canada Catalogue no. 82-221-XIE. Ottawa: Statistics Canada.

———. 2006d. *Measuring Violence against Women: Statistical Trends 2006*. Statistics Canada Catalogue no. 85-570-XIE. Ottawa: Statistics Canada.

———.2006e. 'Minimum Wage'. *Perspectives on Labour and Income* 7, 9: 12–17. Statistics Canada Catalogue no. 75-001-XIE.

———. 2006f. *Women in Canada: A Gender-Based Statistical Report*. Statistics Canada Catalogue no. 89-503-XIE. Ottawa: Statistics Canada.

———. 2007a. 'Deaths, by Selected Grouped Causes, Age Group and Sex, Canada, Provinces and Territories, Annual'. CANSIM Table 102-0551. Ottawa: Minister of Industry.

———. 2007b. 'Deaths, by Selected Grouped Causes and Sex, Canada, Provinces and Territories, Annual'. CANSIM Table 102-0552. Ottawa: Minister of Industry.

———. 2007c. *Family Violence in Canada: A Statistical Profile, 2007*. Statistics Canada Catalogue no. 85-224-XIE. Ottawa: Minister of Industry.

———. 2007d. *Mortality, Summary List of Causes 2004*. Statistics Canada Catalogue no. 84F0209XIE. Ottawa: Minster of Industry.

———. 2007e. *Navigating Family Transitions: Evidence from the General Social Survey, 2006*. Statistics Canada Catalogue no. 89-625-XIE, no. 2. Ottawa: Statistics Canada.

———. 2007f. *Participation and Activity Limitation Survey 2006: Analytical Report*. Statistics Canada Catalogue no. 89-628-XIE, no. 002.Ottawa: Minister of Industry.

———. 2008a. *Aboriginal Peoples in Canada in 2006: Inuit, Métis and First Nations, 2006 Census*. Statistics Canada Catalogue no. 97-558-XIE. Ottawa: Statistics Canada.

———. 2008b. *Deaths 2005*. Statistics Canada Catalogue no. 84F0211X. Ottawa: Minister of Industry.

———. 2008c. *Educational Portrait of Canada, 2006 Census*. Statistics Canada Catalogue no. 97-560-X. Ottawa: Minister of Industry.

———. 2008d. *Labour Force Survey, Monthly Statistics*. Tables 282-0087 and 282-0089. Ottawa: Statistics Canada. http://www40.statcan.ca/l01/cst01/labor66a.htm.

———. 2008e. *Labour Force Characteristics by Age and Sex*. CANSIM Table 282-002. Ottawa: Statistics Canada. http://www40.statcan.ca/l01/cst01/labor20b.htm.

———. 2008f. *2006 Census of Population*. Statistics Canada Catalogue no. 97-562-XCB2006017. Ottawa: Statistics Canada. http://www12.statcan.ca/english/census06/data/topics/Print.cfm.

Statistics Canada and the Canadian Institute for Health Information. 2008. *Health Indicators 2008*. Ottawa: Canadian Institute for Health Information.

Street, Debra, and Ingrid Connidis. 2001. 'Creeping Selectivity in Canadian Women's Pensions'. Pp. 158–78 in Jay Ginn, Debra Street, and Sara Arber, eds, *Women, Work and Pensions*. Buckingham, UK: Open University Press.

Stephensen, Marylee, and Ruth Emery. 2003. *Living beyond the Edge: The Impact of Trends in Non-standard Work on Single/Lone-Parent Mothers*. Ottawa: Status of Women.

Tanovich, David M. 2006. *The Colour of Justice: Policing Race in Canada*. Toronto: Irwin Law 2006.

Tator, Carol, and Frances Henry. 2006. *Racial Profiling in Canada: Challenging the Myth of 'A Few Bad Apples'*. Toronto: University of Toronto Press.

Taylor, Alison, and Harvey Krahn. 2005. 'Aiming High: Educational Aspirations of Visible Minority Immigrant Youth'. *Canadian Social Trends* 79, Winter. Statistics Canada Catalogue no. 11-008.

Taylor-Butts, Andrea. 2007. 'Canada's Shelters for Abused Women, 2005/2006'. *Juristat* 27, 4. Statistics Canada Catalogue no. 85.

Thiessen, Victor, and Christy Nickerson. 1999. *Canadian Gender Trends in Education and Work*. Catalogue no. MP32-30/00-4E. Ottawa: Applied Research Branch, Strategic Policy, Human Resources Development Canada (T-00-4E).

Thomas, E.M. 2006. *Readiness to Learn at School among Five-Year-Old Children in Canada*. Children and Youth Research Paper Series. Statistics Canada Catalogue no. 89-599-MIE2006004. Ottawa: Statistics Canada.

Thompson, E.P. 1963. *The Making of the English*

Working Class. New York: Vintage.

Thuanh Ha, Tu. 2003. 'Senior Seeks to Sue Ottawa over Unpaid Supplement'. *The Globe and Mail*, 31 January.

Tickamyer, Ann R. 2000. 'Space Matters! Spatial Inequality in Future Sociology'. *Contemporary Sociology* 29: 805–13.

Tilly, Charles. 1998. *Durable Inequality*. Berkeley: University of California Press.

Tindale, J., and V.W. Marshall. 1980. 'A Generational-Conflict Perspective for Gerontology'. Pp. 43–50 in V.W. Marshall, ed., *Aging in Canada: Social Perspectives*. Toronto: Fitzhenry and Whiteside.

Tjaden, P., and N. Thoennes. 2000. *Extent, Nature and Consequences of Intimate Partner Violence: Findings from the National Violence against Women Survey*. Ottawa: National Institute of Justice and the Centre for Disease Control Prevention.

Tjepkema, Michael. 2002. 'The Health of the Off-Reserve Aboriginal Population'. *Health Reports* 13, suppl.: 1–16. Statistics Canada Catalogue no. 82-003.

———. 2004. 'Alcohol and Illicit Drug Dependence'. *Health Reports* 15, suppl.: 9–19. Statistics Canada Catalogue no. 82-003.

———. 2005. 'Non-fatal Injuries among Aboriginal Canadians'. *Health Reports* 16, 2: 9–22. Statistics Canada Catalogue no. 82-003.

Tomiak, Monica, Jane F. Gentleman, and Maurice Jette. 1997. 'Health and Gender Differences between Middle and Senior Managers in the Canadian Public Service'. *Social Science and Medicine* 45, 10: 1589–96.

Tomic, Patricia, and Ricardo Trumper. 1992. 'Canada and the Streaming of Immigrants: A Personal Account of the Chilean Case.' Chapter 7 in Vic Satzewich, ed., *Deconstructing a Nation: Immigration, Multiculturalism and Racism in '90s Canada*. Halifax, NS: Fernwood Publishing and Social Research Unit, Department of Sociology, University of Saskatchewan.

Townsend, P. 1981. 'The Structured Dependency of the Elderly: A Creation of Social Policy in the Twentieth Century'. *Ageing and Society* 1: 5–28.

Townson, Monica, and Kevin Hayes. 2007. *Women and the Employment Insurance Program: The Gender Impact of Current Rules on Eligibility and Earnings Replacement*. Ottawa: Status of Women Canada.

Tran, Kelly. 2004. 'Visible Minorities in the Labour Force: 20 Years of Change'. *Canadian Social Trends* 73, Summer: 7–11. Statistics Canada Catalogue no. 11-008.

Trovato, Frank. 2001. 'Aboriginal Mortality in Canada, the United States and New Zealand'. *Journal of Biosocial Science* 33: 67–86.

Trovato, Frank, and N.M. Lalu. 1995. 'The Narrowing Sex Differential in Mortality in Canada since 1971'. *Canadian Studies in Population* 22, 2: 145–67.

———. 2007. 'From Divergence to Convergence: The Sex Differential in Life Expectancy in Canada, 1971–2000'. *Canadian Review of Sociology and Anthropology* 44, 1: 101–22.

Trumper, Ricardo, and Lloyd L. Wong. 2007. 'Canada's Guest Workers: Racialized, Gendered and Flexible'. Pp. 151–74 in Sean P. Hier and B. Singh Bolaria, eds, *Race and Racism in 21st Century Canada: Continuity, Complexity, and Change*. Peterborough, ON: Broadview Press.

Tumin, Melvin. 1953. 'Some Principles of Stratification: A Critical Analysis'. *American Sociological Review* 18: 387–93.

Turcotte, Martin, and Grant Schellenberg. 2007. *A Portrait of Seniors in Canada, 2006*. Statistics Canada Catalogue no. 89-519-XIE. Ottawa: Minister of Industry.

Turner, Heather A., and R. Jay Turner. 2005. 'Understanding Variations in Exposure to Social Stress'. *Health: An Interdisciplinary Journal for the Social Study of Health, Illness & Medicine* 9, 2: 209–40.

Turner, Jonathan H. 1988. *A Theory of Social Interaction*. Stanford, CA: Stanford University Press.

Turner, Jonathan H., and Leonard Beeghley. 1981. *The Emergence of Sociological Theory*. Homewood, IL: Dorsey Press.

Turner, R. Jay, and William R. Avison. 2003. 'Status Variations in Stress Exposure: Implications for the Interpretation of Research on Race, Socioeconomic Status, and Gender'. *Journal of Health and Social*

Behavior 44, 4: 488–505.

Turner, R. Jay, and Donald A. Lloyd. 1999. 'The Stress Process and the Social Distribution of Depression'. *Journal of Health and Social Behavior* 40, 4: 374–404.

Ujimoto, Victor K. 1994. 'Aging, Ethnicity and Health'. Pp. 220–43 in B.S. Bolaria and H.D. Dickinson, eds, *Health, Illness and Health Care in Canada*, 2nd edn. Toronto: Harcourt Brace.

Urmetzer, Peter, and Neil Guppy. 2004. 'Changing Income Inequality in Canada'. Chapter 5 in James E. Curtis, Edward G. Grabb, and Neil L. Guppy, eds, *Social Inequality in Canada: Patterns, Problems, and Policies*. 2nd edn. Scarborough, ON: Prentice Hall Allyn and Bacon.

Ursel, Jane. 1990. 'The State and the Maintenance of Patriarchy: A Case Study of Family, Labour, and Welfare Legislation in Canada'. Pp. 108–45 in Arlene Tigar McLaren, ed., *Gender and Society: Creating a Canadian Women's Sociology*. Toronto: Copp Clark Pitman.

———. 1998. 'Eliminating Violence against Women: Reform or Co-optation in State Institutions?' Chapter 7 in Les Samuelson and Wayne Antony, eds, *Power and Resistance: Critical Thinking about Canadian Social Issues*, 2nd edn. Halifax: Fernwood.

Valverde, Mariana. 1991. *The Age of Light, Soap, and Water: Moral Reform in English Canada, 1885–1925*. Toronto: McClelland & Stewart.

van Doorslaer, Eddy, Cristina Masseria, and Xander Koolman. 2006. 'Inequalities in Access to Medical Care by Income in Developed Countries'. *Canadian Medical Association Journal* 174, 2: 177–83.

Van Praet, Nicolas. 2008. 'Manufacturing Slump Deepens: Auto Sector May Merely Be Canary in Mine to Troubled Economy in Ontario'. *National Post*, 16 February.

van Ryn, Michelle, and Jane Burke. 2000. 'The Effect of Patient Race and Socio-economic Status on Physicians' Perceptions of Patients'. *Social Science and Medicine* 50, 6: 813–28.

van Ryn, Michelle, Diana Burgess, Jennifer Maiat, Jennifer, and Joan Griffin. 2006. 'Physicians'

Perceptions of Patients' Social and Behavioral Characteristics and Race Disparities in Treatment Recommendations for Men with Coronary Artery Disease'. *American Journal of Public Health* 96, 2: 351–7.

Verbrugge, Lois M. 1989. 'The Twain Meet: Empirical Explanations of Sex Differences in Health and Mortality'. *Journal of Health and Social Behavior* 30, 3: 282–304.

Vertinsky, Patricia. 1998. '"Run, Jane, Run": Central Tensions in the Current Debate about Enhancing Women's Health through Exercise'. *Women and Health* 27, 4: 81–115.

Vinograd, Julia. 1997. *Dead People Laughing*. Berkeley, CA: Zeitgeist.

Vosko, Leah F. 2007. 'Gendered Labour Market Insecurities: Manifestations of Precarious Employment in Different Locations'. Chapter 3 in Vivian Shalla and Wallace Clement, eds, *Work in Tumultuous Times: Critical Perspectives*. Montreal: McGill-Queen's University Press.

Wadsworth, M.E.J. 1997. 'Health Inequalities in the Life Course Perspective'. *Social Science and Medicine* 44, 6: 859–69.

Walby, Sylvia. 1989. 'Theorizing Patriarchy'. *Sociology* 23: 213–34.

———. 1990. *Theorizing Patriarchy*. Oxford: Basil Blackwell.

———. 1997. *Gender Transformations*. London: Routledge.

———. 2004. 'The European Union and Gender Equality: Emergent Varieties of Gender Regime'. *Social Politics* 11, 1: 4–29.

Walker, Alan. 1981. 'Towards a Political Economy of Old Age'. *Ageing and Society* 1: 74–94.

Walters, Vivienne. 1993. 'Stress, Anxiety and Depression: Women's Accounts of Their Health Problems'. *Social Science and Medicine* 36, 4: 393–402.

———. 2003. 'The Social Context of Women's Health'. Chapter 1 in *Women's Health Surveillance Report: A Multidimensional Look at the Health of Canadian Women*. Ottawa: Canadian Institute for Health Information.

Walters, Vivienne, Rhonda Lenton, Susan French,

John Eyles, Janet Mayr, and Bruce Newbold. 1996. 'Paid Work, Unpaid Work and Social Support: A Study of the Health of Women and Men Nurses'. *Social Science and Medicine* 43, 11: 1627–36.

Walters, Vivenne, Peggy McDonough, and Lisa Strohschein. 2002. 'The Influence of Work, Household Structure, and Social, Personal and Material Resources on Gender Differences in Health: An Analysis of the 1994 Canadian National Population Health Survey'. *Social Science and Medicine* 54, 5: 677–92.

Wanner, Richard A. 1999. 'Expansion and Ascription: Trends in Educational Opportunity in Canada, 1920–1994'. *Canadian Review of Sociology and Anthropology* 36, 3: 409–42.

Waterfall, Barbara. 2006. 'Native Peoples and Child Welfare Practices: Implicating Social Work Education'. Pp. 223–44 in Anne Westhues, ed., *Canadian Social Policy: Issues and Perspectives*, 4th edn. Waterloo, ON: Wilfrid Laurier University Press.

Weber, Max. [1922] 1978. *Economy and Society: An Outline of Interpretive Sociology*. Vol. 1. Edited by Guenther Roth and Claus Wittich. Berkeley: University of California Press.

Welsh, Sandy. 1999. 'Gender and Sexual Harassment'. *Annual Review of Sociology* 25: 169–90.

Welsh, Sandy, Jacquie Carr, Barbara MacQuarrie, and Audrey Huntley 2006. '"I'm Not Thinking of It as Sexual Harassment": Understanding Harassment across Race and Citizenship'. *Gender and Society* 20, 1: 87–107.

Wente, Margaret. 2006. 'Cancer Care at the Grocer's'. *The Globe and Mail*, 16 November.

West, Candace, and Don Zimmerman. 1987. 'Doing Gender'. *Gender and Society* 1: 125–51.

Westhues, Anne, ed. 2006. *Canadian Social Policy: Issues and Perspectives*. 4th edn. Waterloo, ON: Wilfrid Laurier University Press.

Wheeler, Mark. 2007. 'Being Strategic with Our Interventions'. *Health Policy Research Bulletin* 14: 3–5.

Whitbeck, Les B., Dan R. Hoyt, Barbara J. McMorris, Xiaojin Chen, and Jerry D. Stubben. 2001. 'Perceived Discrimination and Early Substance Abuse among American Indian Children'. *Journal*

of Health and Social Behavior 42, 4: 405–24.

Wight, Richard G., Amanda L. Botticello, and Carol S. Aneshensel. 2006. 'Socioeconomic Context, Social Support, and Adolescent Mental Health: A Multilevel Investigation'. *Journal of Youth and Adolescence* 35, 1: 115–26.

Wight, Richard G., Janet R. Cummings, Dana Miller-Martinez, Arun S. Karlamangla, Teresa E. Seeman, and Carol S. Aneshensel. 2008. 'A Multilevel Analysis of Urban Neighborhood Socioeconomic Disadvantage and Health in Late Life'. *Social Science and Medicine* 66, 4: 862–72.

Wilkins, Kathryn. 2006. 'Predictors of Death in Seniors'. *Health Reports* 16, suppl.: 57–67. Statistics Canada Catalogue no. 82-003.

Wilkins, Russell, Jean-Marie Berthelot, and Edward Ng. 2002. 'Trends in Mortality by Neighbourhood Income in Urban Canada from 1971 to 1996'. *Health Reports* 13, suppl.: 1–27. Statistics Canada Catalogue no. 82-003.

Wilkins, Russell, Sharanjit Uppal, Philippe Finès, Sacha Senécal, Éric Guimond, and Rene Dion. 2008. 'Life Expectancy in the Inuit-Inhabited Areas of Canada, 1989 to 2003'. *Health Reports* 19, 1: 1–14. Statistics Canada Catalogue no. 82-003.

Wilkinson, Richard G., and Kate E. Pickett. 2006. 'Income Inequality and Population Health: A Review and Explanation of the Evidence'. *Social Science and Medicine* 62: 1768–84.

———. 2007. 'The Problems of Relative Deprivation: Why Some Societies do Better Than Others'. *Social Science and Medicine* 65: 1965–78.

Williams, Cara. 2002. 'Time or Money? How High and Low Income Canadians Spend Their Time'. *Canadian Social Trends*, Summer: 7–11.

———. 2006. 'Disability in the Workplace'. *Perspectives on Labour and Income* 7, 2. Statistics Canada Catalogue no. 75-001-XIE.

Williams, Christine L. 1992. 'The Glass Escalator: Hidden Advantages for Men in the "Female" Professions'. *Social Problems* 39, 3: 253–67.

———. 1995. *Still a Man's World: Men Who Do 'Women's Work'*. Berkeley: University of California

Press.

Williams, David R. 2005. 'The Health of U.S. Racial and Ethnic Populations'. *Journals of Gerontology* 60B, spec. iss. 2: 53–62.

Williams, David R., and Chiquita Collins. 2004. 'Reparations: A Viable Strategy to Address the Enigma of African American Health'. *American Behavioral Scientist* 47, 7: 977–1000.

Willis, Paul. 1977. *Learning to Labour.* Farnborough, UK: Saxon House.

Willson, Andrea E., Kim M. Shuey, and Glen H. Elder. 2007. 'Cumulative Advantage Processes as Mechanisms of Inequality in Life Course Health'. *American Journal of Sociology* 112, 6: 1886–924.

Winson, Anthony, and Belinda Leach. 2002. *Contingent Work, Disrupted Lives: Labour and Community in the New Rural Economy.* Toronto: University of Toronto Press.

Wolfson, Michael, Geoff Rowe, Jane F. Gentleman, and Monica Tomiak. 1993. 'Career Earnings and Death: A Longitudinal Analysis of Older Canadian Men'. *Journal of Gerontology* 48, 4: S167–79.

Wollstonecraft, Mary. 1792. *A Vindication of the Rights of Woman: With Strictures on Political and Moral Subjects.* London.

World Health Organization. 2002. Preamble to the Constitution of the World Health Organization. http://www.who. int/about/definition/en, accessed September 2002.

———. 2007. *Third Milestones of a Global Campaign for Violence Prevention Report.* Geneva: World Health Organization. http://www.who.int/violence_injury prevention/violence/en/, accessed February 2008.

Worts, D. 2005. '"It Just Doesn't Feel Like You're Obviously In": Housing Policy, Family Privacy, and the Reproduction of Social Inequality'. *Canadian Review of Sociology and Anthropology* 42, 4: 445–65.

Wotherspoon, Terry. 2004. *The Sociology of Education in Canada: Critical Perspectives.* 2nd edn. Don Mills, ON: Oxford University Press.

Wright, E.O. 1985. *Classes.* London: Verso.

———. 1997. *Class Counts: Comparative Studies in Class Analysis.* Cambridge: Cambridge University Press.

———. 1999. 'Foundations of Class Analysis: A Marxist Perspective'. Paper presented to the annual meeting of the American Sociological Association, Chicago.

Wu, Zheng, Samuel Noh, Violet Kaspar, and Christoph M. Schimmele. 2003. 'Race, Ethnicity, and Depression in Canadian Society'. *Journal of Health and Social Behavior* 44, 3: 426–41.

Wu, Zheng, Margaret J. Penning, and Christoph M. Schimmele. 2005. 'Immigrant Status and Unmet Health Care Needs'. *Canadian Journal of Public Health* 96, 5: 369–73.

Yezierska, Anzia. 1979. 'A Window Full of Sky'. In Anzia Yezierska, *The Open Cage.* New York: Persea Books.

Young, Iris. 1981. 'Beyond the Unhappy Marriage: A Critique of the Dual Systems Theory'. Pp. 43–69 in Lydia Sargent, ed., *The Unhappy Marriage of Marxism and Feminism: A Debate on Class and Patriarchy.* London: Pluto Press.

Zeitlin, I.M. 1990. *Ideology and the Development of Sociological Theory.* 4th edn. Englewood Cliffs, NJ: Prentice Hall.

Zeman, Klarka. 2007. 'A First Look at Provincial Differences in Educational Pathways from High School to College and University'. *Education Matters: Insights on Education, Learning and Training in Canada* 4, 2. Statistics Canada Catalogue no. 81-004-XIE. http://www.statcan.gc.ca/pub/81-004-x/2007002/9989-eng.htm.

Zhang, Xuelin, and Boris Palameta. 2006. *Participation in Adult Schooling and Its Earnings Impact in Canada.* Analytical Studies Branch Research Paper Series. Statistics Canada Catalogue no. 11F0019MIE, no. 276. Ottawa: Statistics Canada.

Zong, Li. 2007. 'Recent Mainland Chinese Immigrants and Covert Racism in Canada'. Pp. 111–30 in Sean P. Hier and B. Singh Bolaria, eds, *Race and Racism in 21st Century Canada: Continuity, Complexity, and Change.* Peterborough, ON: Broadview Press.

Index